By the Same Author

Patterns in History
Leicester: Inter-Varsity Press, 1979

The Nonconformist Conscience
Chapel and Politics, 1870–1914
London: Allen & Unwin, 1982

The Baptists in Scotland
A History
(Editor)
Glasgow: Baptist Union of Scotland, 1988

Victorian Nonconformity
Bangor, Gwynedd: Headstart History, 1992

William Ewart Gladstone
Faith and Politics in Victorian Britain
Grand Rapids, Michigan: William B. Eerdmans, 1993

Evangelicalism
Comparative Studies of Popular Protestantism in North America,
the British Isles and Beyond, 1700–1990
(Co-editor)
New York: Oxford University Press, 1994

EVANGELICALISM
IN MODERN BRITAIN

A HISTORY
FROM THE 1730s TO THE 1980s

D. W. Bebbington
Department of History, University of Stirling

London and New York

First published in 1989 by
Unwin Hyman Ltd

Reprinted 1993, 1995 by
Routledge
11 New Fetter Lane, London EC4P 4EE
29 West 35th Street, New York, NY 10001

© 1989 D. W. Bebbington

Set in 10 on 12 Bembo
Printed in Great Britain at the University Press, Cambridge

British Library Cataloguing in Publication Data
Bebbington, D. W. (David W.)
Evangelicalism in modern Britain.
1. Great Britain. Christian Church Evangelicalism, 1730–1987
I. Title
274.1′08

Library of Congress Cataloguing in Publication Data
Bebbington, D. W. (David William), 1949–
Evangelicalism in modern Britain: a history from the 1730s to the 1980s /
D. W. Bebbington.
p. cm.
Bibliography: p.
Includes index.
1. Evangelicalism—Great Britain—History. 2. Great Britain—
Church history. I. Title
BR1642.G7B43 1988   88–14572
274.1′08   dc19

ISBN 0-415-10464-5

Contents

Preface

The Evangelicals of Britain have been neglected. A few themes have been selected for attention by historians – such as John Wesley and the rise of Methodism, William Wilberforce and the struggle against slavery, Lord Shaftesbury and the campaigns for social reform – but many aspects of the movement remain in obscurity. Light has been shed by studies of particular organisations and denominations, but the development of Evangelicalism as a whole has been examined very little. That is surprising, because it has been a major tradition within the Christian churches. In the mid-nineteenth century it set the tone of British society. In the 1970s both archbishops of the Church of England were drawn from it. And from the 1790s onwards the missionaries it despatched did much to mould the Christian faith in many other parts of the world. The neglect of the Evangelicals is undeserved.

This book attempts to fill a gap by providing an overall survey of the movement. It therefore has a twofold task. One dimension is to consider the influence of Evangelicals on society. More research has been done on this aspect of the movement in the eighteenth and nineteenth centuries than on any other. The dependence of this study on earlier work will be very apparent here. More attention, however, is paid to how Evangelicalism itself has changed. Religion, as Edward Gibbon once remarked with tongue in cheek, has never existed in the pure form in which it descended from heaven. It has always been affected by its surroundings at the same time as influencing those surroundings. Studies of churches founded by missionaries have been well aware of this principle. Discussion of British Evangelicalism has been much less alert to the effects of its host culture. So the second main dimension of the book is an exploration of the ways in which Evangelical religion has been moulded by its environment.

The movement has been self-consciously distinctive and unitary. It has consisted of all those strands in Protestantism that have not been either too high in churchmanship or too broad in theology to qualify for acceptance. It has spanned the gulf between the Established Church and Nonconformity in England and Wales and has bound together bodies north and south of the Scottish border. It has nourished close links with co-religionists abroad, especially in the English-speaking world. Although this study considers influences from overseas, and particularly from America, it concentrates on developments within Britain. Even Ireland, united constitutionally with Britain for much of the period, is left out. But it does try to take account of the remarkable sectarian mosaic that existed alongside the larger churches.

Although much material has been drawn from biographies and other monographs, research has paid particular attention to some of the immense number of periodicals generated by Evangelicalism. The secondary literature is surveyed incidentally in the notes to the chapters, and so no separate booklist has been included. It should also be noted that research has been greatly facilitated over the years by participant observation. Services of worship can reveal a great deal about Christian traditions.

Many debts have been incurred. The draft has been read in whole or in part by Dr Clyde Binfield, Dr Ken Brown, Professor Roy Campbell, the Rev. Professor Colin Gunton, Dr David Hempton, Dr Iain Hutchison, Dr Neil Keeble, Mr John McIntosh, Professor Mark Noll, Dr Brian Stanley and Dr John Walsh. I am extremely grateful for their comments, but none of them bears responsibility for the text. A pilot essay was read by Dr Sheridan Gilley, Dr Richard Holt, Dr David Lyon, Professor Arthur Pollard, Professor Andrew Walls, Professor R. K. Webb, Dr Haddon Willmer and Dr David Wright. I much appreciated their observations. Members of my family have greatly helped the process of writing: my mother, Mrs Vera Bebbington, my mother-in-law, Mrs Margaret Lacey, and especially my wife Eileen, who supplied constant encouragement. My daughter Anne also helped by urging me to 'cut the chapters'.

I have been grateful for access to material in the possession of the Billy Graham Evangelistic Association, the London City Mission and Church Society (to which I was guided by Dr Brenda Hough). Most of the research was done in the British Library, Cambridge University Library, the John Rylands University Library of Manchester, the National Library of Scotland and Stirling University Library. I appreciate the help given by their staff, and especially assistance, following earlier guidance, from Miss Alison Peacock of the Methodist Church Archives at the John Rylands. Several friends have generously provided accommodation during research trips, and I want to express particular gratitude to Fitzwilliam College, Cambridge, for its warm hospitality.

The project was originally stimulated by an invitation to give the Trustees' Lectures at Union Theological College, Belfast, in 1980, and the Laing Lecture at London Bible College in 1982. Discussion with students in my course at the University of Stirling on Church, State and Society in Nineteenth-Century Britain helped to crystallise some of the points, and I am particularly indebted to one of them, Mr Colin Rogerson, for a remark (which he may have forgotten) that illuminated a crucial area. Conversation with several friends – particularly the Rev. Dr Richard Kidd – has been stimulating. Theological Students' Fellowships at other Scottish universities forced me to explore several aspects of the subject by inviting me to speak on them. The University of Stirling granted a sabbatical semester for the basic research in 1983, and I am grateful for financial support to the British Academy, the Carnegie Trust for the Universities of Scotland and the Whitley Lectureship. Miss Margaret Hendry, assisted by Mrs Margaret Dickson, has word-processed the text with immense care and skill. The Rev. James Taylor, Minister of Stirling Baptist Church, has helped the writing of the book by being a distinguished exemplar of the tradition it discusses. To him the book is dedicated.

David Bebbington
Stirling, February 1988

Note to 1993 printing

A few minor alterations have been made. None of them, however, affects the substance of the book.

David Bebbington
Stirling, May 1993

[1]

Preaching the Gospel:
The Nature of Evangelical Religion

. . . woe is unto me, if I preach not the gospel! (1 Cor. 9:16)

Evangelical religion is a popular Protestant movement that has existed in
Britain since the 1730s. It is not to be equated with any single Christian
denomination, for it influenced the existing churches during the eighteenth
century and generated many more in subsequent years. It has found
expression in a variety of institutional forms, a wine that has been poured
into many bottles. Historians regularly apply the term 'evangelical' to the
churches arising from the Reformation in the sixteenth and seventeenth
centuries.[1] The usage of the period justifies them. Sir Thomas More in
1531 referred to advocates of the Reformation as 'Evaungelicalles'.[2] Yet
the normal meaning of the word, as late as the eighteenth century, was
'of the gospel' in a non-partisan sense. Isaac Watts, for example, writes
of an 'Evangelical Turn of Thought' in 1723.[3] There was a reluctance,
most marked in Scotland, to apply the word to a particular group, since
by implication those outside the group would be branded as not 'of the
gospel'.[4] Other terms were used, especially by critics. In 1789 Joseph
Milner wrote of 'Evangelical religion, or what is often called Calvinism
or Methodism'.[5] Steadily, however, the word 'Evangelical' supplanted
the others as the standard description of the doctrines or ministers of the
revival movement, whether inside or outside the Church of England.[6] In
1793 *The Evangelical Magazine* was founded to cater for members of any
denomination dedicated to spreading the gospel. That is the sense in which
the word is employed here. Although 'evangelical', with a lower-case
initial, is occasionally used to mean 'of the gospel', the term 'Evangelical',
with a capital letter, is applied to any aspect of the movement beginning in
the 1730s.[7] There was much continuity with earlier Protestant traditions,
but, as Chapter 2 contends, Evangelicalism was a new phenomenon of the
eighteenth century.

Who was an Evangelical? Sometimes adherents of the movement were
in doubt themselves. 'I know what constituted an Evangelical in former

times', wrote Lord Shaftesbury in his later life; 'I have no clear notion what constitutes one now.'[8] Part of the problem was that, as Shaftesbury implies, Evangelicalism changed greatly over time. To analyse and explain the changes is the main purpose of this book. Yet there are common features that have lasted from the first half of the eighteenth century to the second half of the twentieth. It is this continuing set of characteristics that reveals the existence of an Evangelical tradition. They need to be examined, for no other criterion for defining Evangelicalism is satisfactory. An alternative way would be to appeal to contemporary opinion about who was included within the movement. That approach, however, risks being ensnared in the narrow perspective of a particular period. For polemical purposes the right of others to call themselves Evangelicals has often been denied, particularly in the twentieth century. The danger is that the historian may be drawn into the battles of the past. It is therefore preferable to identify adherents of the movement by certain hallmarks. Evangelicals were those who displayed all the common features that have persisted over time.

Evangelical apologists sometimes explained their distinctiveness by laying claim to particular emphases. The Evangelical clergy differed from others, according to Henry Venn (later Clerical Secretary of the Church Missionary Society) in 1835, 'not so much in their systematic statement of doctrines, as in the relative importance which they assign to the particular parts of the Christian System, and in the vital operation of Christian Doctrines upon the heart and conduct'.[9] Likewise Bishop Ryle of Liverpool asserted that it was not the substance of certain doctrines but the prominent position assigned to only a few of them that marked out Evangelical Churchmen from others.[10] By that criterion, Ryle was able to distinguish his position from that of the great number of late nineteenth-century High Churchmen whose message was similar to his own, whose zeal was equal to his own and who preached as much for conversions.[11] They elevated certain doctrines surrounding the church and the sacraments to a standard of importance that he believed to be untenable. The tone of Evangelicalism permeated nearly the whole of later Victorian religion outside the Roman Catholic Church, and yet the Evangelical tradition remained distinct. It gave exclusive pride of place to a small number of leading principles.

EVANGELICAL CHARACTERISTICS

The main characteristics emerge clearly. The High Churchman G.W.E. Russell remembered that the Evangelicals of his childhood in the mid-nineteenth century divided humanity into two categories: 'a converted character' differed totally from all others. Russell had also been taught to be active in charity, to read the Bible and to maintain 'the doctrine of the Cross'.[12] There are the four qualities that have been the special marks of

Evangelical religion: *conversionism*, the belief that lives need to be changed; *activism*, the expression of the gospel in effort; *biblicism*, a particular regard for the Bible; and what may be called *crucicentrism*, a stress on the sacrifice of Christ on the cross. Together they form a quadrilateral of priorities that is the basis of Evangelicalism.

In the early days of the revival there was normally a stress in Evangelical apologetic on the first and the last. John Wesley was willing to describe two doctrines as fundamental: justification, the forgiving of our sins through the atoning death of Christ; and the new birth, the renewing of our fallen human nature at the time of conversion.[13] Similarly a group at Cambridge received the 'three capital and distinguishing doctrines of the Methodists, viz. Original Sin, Justification by Faith and the New Birth'.[14] Original sin, the condition from which we are rescued by the other two, was also on Joseph Milner's checklist of four doctrines absolutely necessary to salvation: the 'divine light, inspiration, or illumination' of conversion; original sin; justification by faith in the merits of Christ by which 'the great transaction of the Cross is appropriated'; and spiritual renovation, the consequent working out of duty from the motive of gratitude.[15] This final factor implies activism, but in the eighteenth century Evangelicals rarely spelt out its importance in doctrinal terms. They nevertheless threw themselves into vigorous attempts to spread the faith. Likewise they did not normally put the Bible among the most important features of their religion. The Bible, after all, was professedly held in high esteem by all Protestants. Yet they were notably devoted in their searching of the scriptures. The centrality of the Bible could still be taken as read in the mid-nineteenth century, even when activism was mentioned explicitly. 'An Evangelical believer', according to William Marsh in 1850, 'is a man who believes in the fall and its consequences, in the recovery and its fruits, in the personal application of the recovery by the power of the Spirit of God, and then the Christian will aim, desire, endeavour, by example, by exertion, by influence, and by prayer to promote the great salvation of which he himself is a happy partaker . . . '[16] Thus the earlier phase of Evangelical history concurred with the late Puritan divine Matthew Henry in dwelling on three Rs: ruin, redemption and regeneration.[17] In practice, however, from its commencement the movement showed immense energy and a steady devotion to the Bible also.

Later generations, while still displaying the four main characteristics, tended to present them rather differently. The first leading principle of Evangelical religion, according to Bishop Ryle, is 'the absolute supremacy it assigns to Holy Scripture'. There followed, as other leading principles, the doctrines of human sinfulness, the work of Christ in salvation, the inward work of the Holy Spirit in regeneration and his outward work in sanctification. The primacy of scripture was directed against those who exalted the authority of either church or reason.[18] Other late nineteenth-century writers adopted a similar defensive posture, particularly against High Church doctrine on the priesthood and the sacraments. Edward Garbett claimed in 1875 that the three cardinal Evangelical principles are the direct contact of the individual soul with God the Father, the freedom and sovereignty of the Holy Ghost and the sole High Priesthood of God the Son. His intent is to repudiate High Church teaching about the role of the priest in mediating the grace of God to the people.[19] Likewise the ministers of the London Baptist Association set about defining Evangelicalism negatively. 'In our view', they announced in 1888, 'the word "evangelical" has been adopted by those who have held the Deity of our Lord, in opposition to Socinianism; the substitutionary death of the cross, in opposition to Sacramentarianism; the simplicity of the communion of the Lord's Supper, in opposition to the doctrine of the Real Presence. It certainly has also further references . . . in opposition to those who deny the infallibility of Scripture on the one hand, and who assert another probation for the impenitent dead on the other.'[20] One eye is constantly being cast over the shoulder at the ritualists and the rationalists. Instead of the joy of new discovery that pervades eighteenth-century lists of distinctives, there is a resolve to resist an incoming tide of error.

Twentieth-century formulations again put the stress elsewhere. In asking 'What is an Evangelical?', in 1944, Max Warren, General Secretary of the Church Missionary Society, gave priority to evangelism over everything else, even worship. The need for conversion, trusting the Holy Spirit to sustain the believer's new life and the priesthood of all believers were his other three cardinal principles. Thus activism now comes first, with the centrality of the cross and the study of the Bible, though both are mentioned, relegated to a lower place in the scheme of things.[21] Warren, however, was not among the more conservative Evangelicals, whose strength was to grow later in the century. Conservatives usually attributed most importance to the authority of the Bible. Once that was granted, they believed, all other features would be assured. Thus John Stott, in asking Warren's question, 'What is an Evangelical?', in 1977, replied that two convictions cannot be surrendered. First, he claimed, 'We evangelicals are Bible people'. It followed, secondly, that Evangelicals possessed a gospel to proclaim. The cross, conversion and effort for its spread were all placed under that comprehensive heading.[22] Similarly J. I. Packer put the supremacy of scripture first in a list of six Evangelical fundamentals in 1979. To the familiar categories of the work of Christ, the necessity of conversion and the priority of evangelism he added the lordship of the Holy Spirit (in deference to charismatics) and the importance of fellowship (in deference to Catholics).[23] Variations there have certainly been in statements by Evangelicals about what they regard as basic. There is nevertheless a common core that has remained remarkably constant down the centuries. Conversionism, activism, biblicism and crucicentrism form the defining attributes of Evangelical religion. Each characteristic can usefully be examined in turn.

CONVERSIONISM

The call to conversion has been the content of the gospel. Preachers urged their hearers to turn away from their sins in repentance and to Christ in faith. G. W. McCree, 'a London Baptist minister of the mid-nineteenth century, was typical in holding 'that conversion was far above, and of greater importance than, any denominational differences of whatever kind'.[24] A vivid account of conversion, pinpointed by Matthew Arnold as a classic, is given in the autobiography of Sampson Staniforth, then a soldier on active service and later one of the Wesley's early preachers:

> As soon as I was alone, I kneeled down, and determined not to rise, but to continue crying and wrestling with God, till He had mercy on me. How long I was in that agony I cannot tell; but as I looked up to heaven I saw the clouds open exceeding bright, and I saw Jesus hanging on the cross. At the same moment these words were applied to my heart, 'Thy sins are forgiven thee'. My chains fell off; my heart was free. All guilt was gone, and my soul was filled with unutterable peace.[25]

Staniforth's narrative is a classic not only because of its patent sincerity but also because of its inclusion of agony, guilt and immense relief. The great crisis of life could stir deep emotion. The experience was often ardently sought, for others as well as for oneself. Prayer requests for conversion appeared in the Evangelical press: 'For a gentleman on the road to destruction, who fancies he is saved. – For an unconverted brother who is addicted to excessive drinking – . . . For my late foreign governess, an avowed Unitarian'.[26] Conversions were the goal of personal effort, the collective aim of churches, the theme of Evangelical literature. They could seem a panacea. 'Conversions not only bring prosperity to the Church', declared the Wesleyan Samuel Chadwick at about the start of the twentieth century; 'they solve the social problem.'[27] A converted character would work hard, save money and assist his neighbour. The line between those who had undergone the experience and those who had not was the sharpest in the world. It marked the boundary between a Christian and a pagan.

Preaching the gospel was the chief method of winning converts. Robert Bickersteth, Bishop of Ripon from 1857 to 1884, held that 'no sermon was worthy of the name which did not contain the message of the Gospel, urging the sinner to be reconciled to God'.[28] There was a danger, Evangelical preachers believed, of offering only comfort from the pulpit. Hearers needed to be aroused to concern for their spiritual welfare. If the delights of heaven were described, so were the terrors of hell. Jonathan Edwards, the American theologian who stands at the headwaters of Evangelicalism, believed in insisting on the reality of hell; Joseph Milner, an erudite early Anglican Evangelical, would preach sermons on topics like 'The sudden destruction of obdurate offenders'; and a Methodist preacher assured a backslider 'that the devil would soon toss [him] about in the flames of hell with a pitchfork'.[29] Normally, however, there was more circumspection. The minister, according to an article of 1852 'On the method of preaching the doctrine of eternal death', should remember 'that he is sent to be a preacher of the Gospel of the grace of God, and not to be a preacher of death and ruin'.[30] Fear was not neglected as a motive for conversion, but more emphasis was generally laid on the forgiving love of God. It was essential, however, that the preacher himself should be converted. How could he speak of what he had not known? Some ministers underwent conversion experiences when already in the ministry. Thomas Chalmers, the Evangelical leader in the early nineteenth-century Church of Scotland, was among them.[31] One clergyman was even converted by his own sermon. Preaching on the Pharisees in his Cornish parish, William Haslam realised that he was no better than they, but then felt light and joy coming into his soul. The cry went up, 'The parson is converted!'[32] The experience turned him into an Evangelical.

Conversion was bound up with major theological convictions. At that point, Evangelicals believed, a person is justified by faith. Because human beings are estranged from God by their sinfulness, there is nothing they can do by themselves to win salvation. All human actions, even good works, are tainted by sin, and so there is no possibility of gaining merit in the sight of God. Hence salvation has to be received, not achieved. Jesus Christ has to be trusted as Saviour. Acceptance by God, as Luther had insisted, comes through faith, not works. Justification by faith, as we have seen, was one of the distinguishing doctrines of Evangelicalism in the eighteenth century. Critics declared it to be subversive of all morality. To the typical mind of the period it seemed to destroy the obligation to observe the divine law. If salvation was available without good works, the door was opened for any form of profligacy. Gratitude, replied the Evangelicals, was the strongest motive for moral behaviour. Henry Venn, the Evangelical Vicar of Huddersfield, declared that 'faith is not understood, much less possessed, if it produce not more holiness, than could possibly be any other way attained'.[33] Consequently it was dwelt on. To the growing son of an Evangelical Anglican home in the mid-nineteenth century it seemed that the clergy taught nothing else but justification by faith.[34] Although the doctrine was sometimes watered down in the later nineteenth century,[35] it was championed so vigorously by Evangelicals in the Church of England in the 1980s that it became a central topic of theological dialogue with the Roman Catholic Church.[36] Justification by faith embodied much that was most precious to them.

Assurance was another doctrine closely connected with conversion. Once a person has received salvation as a gift of God, he may be assured, according to Evangelicals, that he possesses it. Not only is he a Christian; he knows he is a Christian. John Wesley laid great emphasis on this teaching. 'I never yet knew', he told an enquirer in 1740, 'one soul thus saved, without what you call "the faith of assurance": I mean a sure confidence, that by the merits of Christ he was reconciled to the favour of God.'[37] The idea was not distinctive to Wesley and his followers, for those affected by Evangelicalism in the Calvinist tradition were equally attached to it. Assurance had been an important theme of pre-Evangelical Protestant spirituality, but the experience had never been regarded as the standard possession of all believers. The novelty of Evangelical religion, as Chapter 2 will show, lay precisely in claiming that assurance normally accompanies conversion. Other Christians, especially those of more Catholic traditions, found the expectation of assurance among Evangelicals eccentric, presumptuous or even pathological.[38] Yet it remained characteristic of them. Max Warren defended the doctrine in 1944 as 'the here and now certainty that "I am 'in Grace' because I have been converted"'.[39] The confidence of Evangelicals had its roots in the inward persuasion that God was on their side.

Since conversion was the one gateway to vital Christianity, parents looked anxiously for signs of it in their growing children. The Scots Evangelical mother of W. E. Gladstone, the future Prime Minister, wrote in a letter when he was about ten years old that she believed her son to be 'truly converted to God'.[40] Conversion was most common among teenagers, but the average age at the experience seems to have fallen during the nineteenth century. In the first half of the century, a higher proportion of conversions took place in adulthood. Later on, as churches drew more on Christian homes, the stage of decisive commitment tended to occur earlier. The mean age at conversion among future Methodist ministers in the period 1780–1840 was 16.9 years; the mean age in the period 1841–1900 was 15.8 years.[41] Home background clearly remained an influential factor in the 1960s. An Evangelical Alliance survey of about 5,000 Christians established that one in six had been converted before the age of twelve and three in four before the age of twenty.[42] Conversion was statistically less likely the older a person was.[43] Among the exceptions, conviction usually went deep. Sir Wilfrid Lawson, a Cumberland baronet, for example, underwent a decisive experience while suffering from a dangerous illness in middle age. Though retaining the sporting interests of his class, he became a generous patron of local religious services, temperance work and the whole Evangelical Union denomination.[44] For the adult there could be a drastic reappraisal of life's priorities.

'Conversion is a great and glorious work of God's power', wrote Jonathan Edwards, 'at once changing the heart, and infusing life into the dead soul . . . But as to fixing on the *precise time* when they put forth the very first act of grace, there is a great deal of difference in different persons; in some it seems to be very discernible when the very time was; but others are more at a loss.'[45] The question of timing was perplexing to subsequent generations. Could conversion sometimes be gradual rather than sudden? Anglican Evangelicals, commonly more educated, sober and respectable than their brethren in other denominations, never had qualms about accepting the validity of gradual conversions. Charles Simeon, their leading spokesman in the early nineteenth century, was emphatic: 'we require nothing *sudden*'.[46] Likewise William Jay of Bath, an Independent minister with a fashionable congregation, could testify to no 'distinct and unique experience'.[47] Methodists, on the other hand, usually looked for a datable crisis, though equally they expected it to be preceded by a long period of 'awakening'.[48] Revivalists in the mid-nineteenth century stressed the change of a particular moment. Thus, Reginald Radcliffe sought to impress on Sunday School teachers in 1860 that 'conversion is an instantaneous work'.[49] James Caughey, a vigorous American revivalist in Methodism, asserted that 'the work of conversion is so momentous, that no man can pass through it, and not know it'.[50] There was nevertheless an undoubted drift towards the standard Anglican position as the nineteenth century wore on. Alexander Raleigh, a distinguished Independent preacher between the 1840s and the 1870s, made a conscious change of heart central in his earlier sermons, but later accepted that conversion could be gradual and unconscious.[51] By 1905 only the Baptist contributors to an interdenominational symposium on *The Child and Religion* expected a crisis of personal religious decision.[52] Conservative and sectarian Evangelicals often continued to think in these terms, but gradualism was stronger among the more open-minded. Differences of emphasis remained unresolved in the twentieth century.

Another issue revolved round the means of conversion. The orthodox teaching was that true conversion is the work of the Holy Spirit.[53] Challenges to trust Christ were thought legitimate human means for bringing about conversions, but the Spirit was still held to be responsible. In the nineteenth century, however, some of the more enthusiastic Evangelicals, eager to maximise conversions, began to teach that the crucial factor is a person's *will* to be saved. Carefully planned methods, such as meetings designed for anxious enquirers, could encourage the desire to believe. In *Lectures on Revivals of Religion* (1835), Charles Finney, the leading American exponent of this line of thinking, presented revivalism as a science, a powerful technique for securing mass conversions. It was an immensely popular work, selling 80,000 copies by 1850 and making a great impact in Britain, not least because it was adapted for the British market by removing, for example, strictures on drinking tea. Finney came close to denying the need for the intervention of the Holy Spirit. Some did draw that inference. J. H. Hinton, later a leading Baptist minister, wrote in 1830 that 'a sinner has power to repent without the Spirit'. He subsequently declared that he had been misunderstood, explaining that he did believe that the Spirit acts in conversion overall. But others did not retract. Nine students at Glasgow Congregational Theological Academy were expelled in 1844 for 'self-conversionism'. They went on to form part of the new Evangelical Union, a largely Scottish denomination committed to revivalism.[54] Eagerness for converts had the effect of modifying the theology of a section of Evangelicalism. The same motive operated later in the century on the mind of R. F. Horton, an eminent Congregationalist who reached the identical conclusion that a person may exercise his will in order to be converted.[55] Such thinkers were trying to reduce the mysterious element in conversion for the sake of making the experience more widely known.

The most celebrated issue raised by conversion was its relation to baptism. This was the substance of what probably qualified as the chief theological controversy of the early and mid-nineteenth century. The problem was one of reconciling the conviction of Evangelicals that conversion is the time when a person becomes a Christian with two statements in the Book of Common Prayer of the Church of England. According to the order for baptism, an infant is declared regenerate at the end of the ceremony; and according to the catechism, baptism is the occasion of our new birth. Evangelicals who were also Anglicans had a tangled knot to untie. Furthermore, Anglicans of other schools were able to claim that Evangelicals were disloyal to the formularies of their church. The best known incident, remembered as what provoked Henry Manning's secession to Rome, was the Gorham case of 1847–51. Bishop Philpotts of Exeter, a punctilious High Churchman, refused to institute George Gorham, an Evangelical clergyman, to a living in Devon because he did not accept the Prayer Book teaching that baptism is the time when a person is born again. On appeal to the Judicial Committee of the Privy Council, Gorham's right to reject the doctrine of baptismal regeneration was upheld.[56] But this affair was only the tip of an iceberg. Controversy had begun as early as 1812, when Richard Mant, a traditional High Churchman, had criticised Evangelicals for rejecting the Prayer Book doctrine of baptismal regeneration.[57] Evangelicals made a variety of replies. The order of infant baptism, some held, expresses a charitable hope about the future regeneration of the child; or, according to others, the service is designed for believers who could pray with confidence for the salvation of the child.[58] Others again felt that they had to embrace a doctrine of baptismal regeneration, going on to redefine regeneration to mean not 'becoming a Christian', but something less decisive. This was the course taken, for instance, by J. B. Sumner, later Archbishop of Canterbury.[59] It is a shaky answer, a sign that Evangelicals found this apparent discrepancy between their doctrine and their liturgy embarrassing.

It is not surprising that the question was aired repeatedly. In Scotland, for example, a leading Episcopalian and later Primus, James Walker, insisted in 1825 that baptismal regeneration was the teaching of his church.[60] His arguments were met by a number of Evangelical clergy, and a spirited pamphlet war ensued. In England, C. H. Spurgeon, the great Baptist preacher of the Metropolitan Tabernacle, censured the Evangelical Anglican clergy in a sermon of 1864 for failing to repudiate the principle of baptismal regeneration. A storm of indignation burst about him.[61] A Prayer Book Revision Society, guided by Lord Ebury from 1859 to 1889, wished to remove 'everything which can be held to imply that Regeneration by the Holy Spirit is *inseparably connected with the Rite*'.[62] But the anomaly remained to trouble twentieth-century Evangelical Anglicans. In 1965 *The Church of England Newspaper* asked its largely Evangelical readership whether the church should cease baptising infants altogether. Of the clergy, 289 replied no, but 47 replied yes. Of the laity, 455 said no, but a remarkable 268 said yes.[63] Clearly a high proportion of the respondents were worried about what infant baptism was supposed to signify. The problem was perennial because the idea that infants are regenerate through baptism does appear in the Book of Common Prayer, whereas Evangelicals have believed that only through conversion does a person become a Christian. The recurring difficulties on this subject are a corollary of the centrality of conversion in Evangelical religion.

ACTIVISM

A second leading characteristic of Evangelicals has been their activism. It flows from the first, as Jonathan Edwards remarked. 'Persons', he wrote, 'after their own conversion, have commonly expressed an exceeding great desire for the conversion of others. Some have thought that they should be willing to die for the conversion of any soul . . . '[64] Henry Venn, by his own computation, was instrumental in the conversion of some 900 people during three years at Huddersfield.[65] A Methodist missioner of the later nineteenth century claimed to have seen nearly 90,000 led to Christ at his meetings.[66] Wesley's early preachers threw themselves into efforts to spread the gospel. A typical one attended class and band meetings, visited the sick and preached five or six times a week; another, when stationed at York in 1760, rode a circuit of 300 miles every six weeks, visiting some sixty societies; a third frequently managed no more than eight hours of sleep a week.[67] Preaching services at 5 a.m. were common.[68] Sunday could be immensely demanding, as the resolutions of a Methodist and his wife in 1774 reveal: 'We will attend the preaching at five o'clock in the morning; at eight, go to the prayer meeting; at ten, to the public worship at the Foundery; hear Mr. Perry at Cripplegate, at two; be at the preaching at the Foundery, at five; meet with the general society, at six; meet in the united bands at seven, and again be at the prayer meeting at eight; and then come home, to read and pray by ourselves'.[69] The dedication of laypeople that was so marked a feature of Methodism was imitated in the Church of England. Paid full-time and voluntary part-time workers became general in Evangelical parishes. There was a similar development in the Church of Scotland, where Thomas Chalmers appointed deacons for parochial visitation.[70] 'The Evangelical saint of to-day', declared the Congregationalist R. W. Dale in 1879, 'is not a man who spends his nights and days in fasting and prayer, but a man who is a zealous Sunday-school teacher, holds mission services among the poor, and attends innumerable committee meetings. "Work" has taken its place side by side with prayer . . . '[71]

The result was a transformation in the role of a minister of religion. The English parish clergyman of the later eighteenth century was very like a member of the gentry in how he spent his time. Duty consisted almost exclusively in taking services.[72] For the Evangelical, however, pastoral work was laborious. 'To acquaint ourselves', ran a clerical manual of 1830, 'with the various wants of our people; to win their affections; to give a seasonable warning, encouragement, instruction, or consolation; to identify ourselves with their spiritual interests, in the temper of Christian sympathy, and under a sense of Ministerial obligation; to do this with the constancy, seriousness, and fervid energy which the matter requires, is indeed a work of industry, patience, and self-denial.'[73] In the 1840s Spencer Thornton, Rector of Wendover, each week delivered seven evening lectures, gave two afternoon readings and conducted four Bible classes; he also held five monthly and three quarterly meetings.[74] At a higher level, Bishop C. R. Sumner of Winchester wrote more than 3,500 business letters in his last year of office and Bishop Bickersteth of Ripon excited surprise by choosing to preach three times each Sunday on his arrival in the diocese.[75] At the 1851 census of religion, whereas Anglican churches overall provided an average of 2.06 services a Sunday, a sample of churches belonging to the Evangelical Simeon Trust provided 2.52. An unsympathetic commentator was forced to conclude in 1860 that 'the evangelical clergy as a body are indefatigable in ministerial duties'.[76]

The Methodists were equally exemplary. Wesley was a typhoon of energy, preaching more than 40,000 sermons and issuing more than 400 publications.[77] John Fletcher of Madeley, a clergyman who was Wesley's designated successor, was described by his wife as 'always on the stretch for God'.[78] Adam Clarke gave up tea and coffee on Wesley's advice in 1782, and consequently saved several whole years of time over the rest of his life for devotion to Christian scholarship. 'For a short time after he left off the use of those *exotics*', according to his biographer, 'he took in the evenings, a cup of *milk and water*, or a cup of *weak infusion of camomile*; but as he found that he gained no time by this means, and the gaining of time was his great object, he gave that totally up . . . '[79] Time was scarce. A working week of between 90 and 100 hours was expected of men in the nineteenth-century Wesleyan ministry.[80] It is hardly surprising that the connexion maintained a 'Worn-Out Ministers' Fund'. An identical shift to a new dynamism is apparent in the life of the Scot, Thomas Chalmers. In his early ministry he was not an Evangelical. After the satisfactory discharge of his duties, Chalmers commented at the time, 'a minister may enjoy five days in the week of uninterrupted leisure'. After his conversion, by contrast, Chalmers was reputed to have visited 11,000 homes in his Glasgow parish during a single year.[81] Evangelicalism brought about a striking change of attitude.

There were other effects of the imperative to be up and doing. Learning, for example, could be regarded as a dispensable luxury. At the beginning of the nineteenth century Independent ministers were trained not in theology or Greek, but simply in preaching. It would have been 'highly improper', according to a contributor to their magazine, 'to spend, in literary acquisitions, the time and talents which were so imperiously demanded in the harvest field'.[82] The same factor could inhibit scholarship even at the universities. It was said of James Scholefield, Regius Professor of Greek at Cambridge from 1825, that 'had his other numerous and important duties allowed sufficient leisure, his Editions of the ancients would doubtless have exhibited more of original research'.[83] As it was, the quest for souls generally drove Evangelicals out from centres of learning to the parishes and to the foreign mission field. The missionary movement of the nineteenth and twentieth centuries was the fruit of the Evangelical Revival. That is not to claim sole credit for the Evangelicals. On the contrary, Roman Catholic missions had for long put Protestants to shame. Yet a direct result of the revival was the creation of new missionary societies, beginning with that of the Baptists in 1792, that did so much to make the Christian faith a worldwide religion.[84] The dedication of the Cambridge Seven, a set of promising young graduates who entered the China Inland Mission in 1885, was a celebrated case of Evangelical zeal.[85] But activism often spilled over beyond simple gospel work. 'Toil, toil, toil', wrote Lord Shaftesbury in his diary for April 1850, 'nor should I lament, could I say fruit, fruit, fruit.'[86] Shaftesbury's efforts in such causes as public health provided a further outlet for Evangelical energy. Wilberforce's campaign against the slave trade and Nonconformist political crusades around 1900 are but the most famous instances of attempts to enforce the ethics of the gospel. A host of voluntary societies embodied the philanthropic urge. Hannah More, the Evangelical authoress of the turn of the nineteenth century, summed up succinctly the prevailing Evangelical attitude. 'Action is the life of virtue', she wrote, 'and the world is the theatre of action.'[87]

BIBLICISM

The third main feature of the Evangelicals, their devotion to the Bible, has been the result of their belief that all spiritual truth is to be found in its pages. The Bible alone, John Wesley contended, was the source of his doctrine of salvation. 'Let me be *homo unius libri* [a man of one book]', he declared in the preface to his collected sermons of 1746.[88] His brother Charles was so immersed in scripture that in one of his hymns, 'Lord, and is Thine anger gone', twenty-six biblical allusions are crowded into sixty-four lines.[89] Opponents of an early Methodist preacher, he reported, 'said I made my Bible my god!'[90] Another declared that after his conversion the Bible 'seemed an entirely new book'.[91] This frequent experience among

Evangelicals led to charges by eighteenth-century opponents that they were subjecting the Bible to arbitrary interpretation under the alleged illumination of the Holy Spirit. The opponents, often maintaining a doughty tradition of Anglican apologetic, claimed to be the more scriptural party in appealing to the bare text.[92] Yet Evangelicals were certain they understood the Bible clearly. Hence the nineteenth-century Scottish revivalist Brownlow North 'spent hours every day in hard and prayerful study of its pages'.[93] A contemporary evangelist, Henry Moorhouse, was similarly devoted. 'He would not suffer anything, not even a sheet of paper, to be laid upon his Bible. There alone, apart, it must lie, unique, matchless, wonderful, the very mind and presence of the infinite and eternal God.'[94] Evangelicals revered the Bible.

Respect for the Bible did not necessarily lead them into far-fetched views. The passage from the first book of Corinthians about a rock following Israel through the wilderness came up for discussion at a conversation party for Cambridge undergraduates led by Charles Simeon. Did the rock really move? 'Oh yes, of course', replied Simeon, 'with a hop, skip and a jump!'[95] Here was no wooden literalness. It is true that doctrinal preoccupations often encouraged an instinct for turning to the New Testament letters in preference to the gospels.[96] Yet Evangelicals did not normally concentrate on obscurities. For the end of the nineteenth century, when the age of the questionnaire was just dawning, we possess a detailed breakdown of texts taken by preachers in a variety of Evangelical pulpits on a Sunday in March 1896. The survey came about because, intriguingly, the journal *Tit-Bits*, on receiving a complaint from a reader about the length of sermons, launched a competition to find the longest – it was, it turned out, a sermon preached at a Primitive Methodist chapel lasting one hour eighteen minutes. *The British Weekly*, an interdenominational paper, repeated the survey and also investigated texts. Three-quarters were drawn from the New Testament. John's gospel was the most popular source, followed closely by the first letter of John and then by the other three gospels. In the Old Testament, most texts came from Psalms, Genesis and Isaiah. None was taken from Philemon, 2 or 3 John, Lamentations, Obadiah, Micah, Nahum, Habakkuk or Zephaniah. The single verse that inspired most sermons was Galatians 2.20 about being crucified with Christ.[97] Certainly there is no evidence here of the deliberate searching out of obscure texts.

There was agreement among Evangelicals of all generations that the Bible is inspired by God. When it came to determining the implications of inspiration, however, there were notable divergences. Henry Venn of Huddersfield referred incidentally in 1763 to 'the infallible word of God' and the Countess of Huntingdon's Connexion confessed its belief in 1783 in 'the infallible truth' of the scriptures.[98] 'The Bible is altogether TRUE', wrote Edward Bickersteth in his extremely popular *A Scripture Help* (1816). 'It is truth without any mixture of error.'[99] Yet in the period up to that date there was no attempt to elaborate any theory of infallibility or inerrancy.

On the contrary, there was remarkable fluidity in ideas about the effects of inspiration on the text. The overriding aim of early Evangelicals was to bring home the message of the Bible and to encourage its devotional use rather than to develop a doctrine of scripture. A body of Evangelical opinion, however, began to insist from the 1820s onwards on inerrancy, verbal inspiration and the need for literal interpretation of the Bible.[100] In reaction against the publication of *Essays and Reviews* (1860), a Broad Church manifesto for studying the Bible in the manner of any other book, the newer dogmatic school of thought became more vocal.[101] 'To us', wrote the Baptist C. H. Spurgeon, 'the plenary verbal inspiration of the Holy Scripture is a fact and not a hypothesis.'[102] From the chair of the Congregational Union in 1894, by contrast, G. S. Barrett repudiated the 'crude and mechanical theory of verbal inspiration'.[103] Attitudes to the Bible drew apart until, in the wake of the First World War, the Evangelical world divided into conservatives and liberals primarily on that issue. The importance attributed by Evangelicals to the Bible eventually led to something approaching schism in their ranks.

CRUCICENTRISM

The doctrine of the cross, fourthly, has been the focus of the gospel. The Evangelical movement, in the words of Gladstone, 'aimed at bringing back, and by an aggressive movement, the Cross, and all that the Cross essentially implies'.[104] Nothing in the Christian system, according to John Wesley, 'is of greater consequence than the doctrine of Atonement. It is properly the distinguishing point between Deism and Christianity.'[105] The reconciliation of humanity to God, that is to say, achieved by Christ on the cross is why the Christian religion speaks of God as the author of salvation. 'I am saved', wrote an early Methodist preacher, 'through faith in the blood of the Lamb.'[106] There is a cloud of witnesses on the theme. An eighteenth-century Scottish theologian, John Maclaurin, like many subsequent Evangelicals, preached on 'Glorying in the cross of Christ'.[107] 'The death of Christ', according to the clerical manual of 1830, 'in this scriptural and comprehensive view, includes the whole Christian system.'[108] Representative twentieth-century Evangelicals in the Church of England said much the same.[109] Theologians elaborated the point: R. W. Dale, with telling reasonableness in 1875; James Denney, with scrupulous clarity in 1902; John Stott, with contemporary awareness in 1986; and, greatest of all, P. T. Forsyth in a series of vibrant treatises in the early twentieth century.[110] Critics deplored what they saw as an obsession. The Quaker statesman John Bright, having heard G. B. Bubier, a Congregational divine, is said to have murmured to himself, 'The atonement, always the atonement! Have they nothing else to say?'[111] Even those who professed a liberal version of Evangelical belief in the twentieth century like the Methodist W. R. Maltby felt compelled to lay great stress on the cross.[112] 'If men are Evangelical Christians at all', declared the Congregationalist Alexander Raleigh in 1879, 'they can say without a shadow of insincerity, "God forbid we should glory, save in the cross of our Lord Jesus Christ . . . "'[113]

Looking back on an interwar childhood in the Brethren, Anne Arnott recalled trying on Christmas Day to escape in imagination to Bethlehem from the ministry which, as always, centred on the crucifixion.[114] The atonement eclipsed even the incarnation among Evangelicals. In 1891 Charles Gore, a rising young Anglo-Catholic, inaugurated a central tradition in Anglican thought by arguing in the Bampton Lectures for the incarnation as the heart of Christian theology.[115] The warning issued to Methodists in the following year is instructive:

> We rejoice in the prominence which is being given to the doctrine of the Incarnation, with all its solemn lessons and inspirations. But we must be careful lest the Cross passes into the background, from which it is the glory of our fathers to have drawn it. Give to the *death* of Christ its true place in your own experience and in your Christian work – as a witness to the real and profound evil of sin, as an overwhelming manifestation of Divine love, as the ground of acceptance with God, as a pattern of sacrifice to disturb us when life is too easy, to inspire and console us when life is hard, and as the only effectual appeal to the general heart of men, and, above all, as the Atonement for our sins.[116]

To make any theme other than the cross the fulcrum of a theological system was to take a step away from Evangelicalism. The Congregationalist James Baldwin Brown, to the dismay of many co-religionists, had already followed the Broad Churchman F. D. Maurice along that path, and by 1897 a Methodist, J. Scott Lidgett, was doing the same.[117] Christopher Chavasse was still urging caution on Anglican Evangelicals about this trend of thought in 1939. 'Let us', he told them, 'keep close to Scripture, and allow the Atonement to explain the Incarnation – Christ was born in order to die . . . '[118] Michael Ramsey, Archbishop of Canterbury, showed he knew his Evangelicals when, in addressing their Keele Congress in 1967, he urged them to recognise that other Anglicans also upheld, in different ways, the 'supreme assertion that in the Cross of Christ alone is our salvation'.[119]

The standard view of Evangelicals was that Christ died as a substitute for sinful mankind. Human beings, they held, were so rebellious against God that a just penalty would have been death. Yet, as Thomas Scott the commentator discovered to his delight, 'Christ indeed bore the sins of all who should ever believe, in all their guilt, condemnation, and deserved punishment, in his own body on the tree'.[120] Belief in a substitutionary atonement originally distinguished Evangelicals from even the strictest divines of other schools. William Law, an outstanding devotional writer drawn on by Scott, among many others, explicitly repudiated the idea that Christ suffered in our stead.[121] Probably the greatest sermon by Robert Hall, Baptist minister in Cambridge at the opening of the nineteenth century and the ablest preacher of his day, was a defence of the doctrine of substitutionary atonement.[122] Its argument was still being repeated, with due acknowledgement of Hall, in a statement of Evangelical principles by the Anglican W. R. Fremantle in 1875.[123] By the 1870s, however, the fear was expressed that substitution was being discarded, and even the leading Wesleyan theologian W. B. Pope was equivocal on the subject.[124] The humanitarian tone of public opinion was veering against this understanding of the death of Christ. George Bernard Shaw voiced the newer attitude in characteristically searing fashion. 'I detest the doctrine of the Atonement', he once wrote, 'holding that ladies and gentlemen cannot as such possibly allow anyone else to expiate their sins by suffering a cruel death.'[125] In the early years of the twentieth century the teaching was fading from the Methodist pulpit.[126] It survived nevertheless in conservative Evangelical circles, enshrined, for instance, in the statement of faith of the Inter-Varsity Fellowship of Christian Unions. Jesus Christ was there described as dying not only as our representative but also as our substitute.[127] Belief that Christ died in our stead was not uniform in the Evangelical tradition, but it was normal.

The implications of the cross for life were also important for Evangelicals. There was a bond between the atonement and the quest for sanctification. 'All treatises', wrote Henry Venn, '. . . written to promote holiness of life, must be deplorably defective, unless the cross of Christ be laid as the foundation . . . '[128] The motive for spiritual growth was gratitude for Calvary. Preoccupation with the cross led to some exaggerated forms of spirituality. Mrs Penn-Lewis, an early twentieth-century holiness advocate, for example, went about teaching that there must be a decisive experience for the believer of crucifixion of the self.[129] But it was also common for preachers to dwell, as did the Congregationalist David Thomas in the 1840s, on the 'relation of the Atonement to practical righteousness'.[130] By 1908 this line of thought had generated in the mind of the Wesleyan J. E. Rattenbury a sanction for socialism. The gospel declares that human beings are to be considered not for their station, rank or riches but for their potential as sons of God. Consequently, he contended, 'the theology of the cross . . . is well fitted to be the soul of the Collectivist movement'.[131] Richard Heath, an extreme proponent of the social gospel, went further. The vicarious suffering of Christ was for him a symptom of the never-ceasing fact of human solidarity in adversity. God was suffering with his creatures.[132] Attention to the cross could lead in diverse directions.

The *theologia crucis* gave rise to debate. For whom did Christ die? For the elect only, as Calvinist believers in particular redemption affirmed? Or for all, as Arminian advocates of general redemption insisted? The Evangelical ranks were riven in the eighteenth century by controversy between Methodists, who were Arminians, and most others, who were

Calvinists. By the beginning of the nineteenth century, however, this debate was dying down. Most Evangelicals were content to adopt a 'moderate Calvinism' that in terms of practical pulpit instruction differed only slightly from the Methodist version of Arminianism. Leading Anglican Evangelicals expressed the view in 1800 that redemption is both general and particular. Arminians were right to stress human responsibility to repent and Calvinists right to stress the need for divine grace.[133] 'I frankly confess', wrote William Wilberforce, 'that I myself am no Calvinist, though I am not either an anti-Calvinist.'[134] Discussion of the scope of the atonement became moribund. It was dismissed as mysterious, impractical, a subject ill suited to bringing about conversions. Hence denominations that had maintained a separate existence because of the issue eventually came together. In England the gap between General and Particular Baptists that went back to the early seventeenth century steadily narrowed during the nineteenth, and in 1891 the two bodies formally fused. In Scotland, the Congregational Union, professedly Calvinist, and the Evangelical Union, revivalist and Arminian in style, united in 1897. What Evangelicals agreed on seemed of infinitely greater importance than their disagreements, and their pre-eminent ground of agreement was the cruciality of the cross.

THE BACKGROUND

Evangelical religion displaying these four characteristics burst on western Christendom at an epoch when the fundamental division between Catholics and Protestants had become firmly established over two centuries. Although in 1770 there were some 80,000 Roman Catholics in England,[135] the state in Britain was Protestant. The crown was restricted to Protestants, and so were a number of other offices of state. The Church of England, the Established Church of England and Wales, had retained its bishops at the Reformation but emerged from the seventeenth century as an unequivocally Protestant body. Its establishment meant that the Church of England was intertwined with the state. The monarch was the supreme head of the church. Theoretically, all his subjects in England and Wales belonged to it. The bishops of the Church of England sat of right in the House of Lords. Parliament exercised as much authority in spiritual matters as in temporal affairs. With the decay of church courts, ecclesiastical cases increasingly came before the secular courts. More than half the patrons of livings who appointed parish clergymen were laypeople. For advancement in a clerical career the patronage of some member of the social elite was essential. Clergymen were expected to display the manners of the gentry, among whom they were educated at Oxford and Cambridge. Their pulpit ministry was partly designed to teach the lower orders their place in the order of things. Conscientious men there were in the Church of England, notably at episcopal level, but there was little effective check on clerical negligence. The church played a salient role in everyday life, but at the expense of imbibing a strong dose of secularity.[136]

Protestant Dissent, though possessing roots in the sixteenth century and perhaps earlier, was primarily indebted to the strength of the Puritan movement in the seventeenth century. In the 1650s, under Cromwell, the Puritans had enjoyed a brief spell of official favour, but with the Restoration of Charles II in 1660 their period in the sun came to an abrupt end. Some 2,000 ministers who refused to accept the Book of Common Prayer of 1662 in its entirety were expelled from the Church of England. Despite persecution, the Dissenting congregations survived to enter an era of toleration following the Glorious Revolution of 1688. Dissenters were allowed to practise their religion unmolested, but, with hardly any of the gentry in their ranks, were reduced to a marginal role in society. Most of them retained the Calvinist theology in the Reformed tradition of their Puritan forebears, though there were some General Baptists who held Arminian views and the more numerous Quakers professed a belief in an 'inner light'. This credal difference, together with distinctive clothes, language and even calendar, set the Quakers apart from their Dissenting brethren. The mainstream consisted of the 'three denominations'. Presbyterians, who numbered many merchants in their ranks, formed the section of Dissent that was to be least influenced by Evangelicalism. Adopting increasingly broad theological views as the eighteenth century advanced, many of them reached a Unitarian position by its end. Independents, also known as Congregationalists, believed in the independence from all external authority of the local congregation. Like the less numerous Particular Baptists, who were identical apart from holding that baptism should be by immersion and for believers only, the Independents generally remained orthodox during the eighteenth century. These bodies were to be swept along by the Evangelical Revival.[137]

In Scotland there was an entirely different situation. The seventeenth-century kirk had wavered between Episcopalianism and Presbyterianism, contriving to blend them both after the Restoration. With the Glorious Revolution, however, the Church of Scotland became definitely Presbyterian. Bishops were at last repudiated. Episcopalian congregations, which were numerous in the north-east, began a life outside the Established Church. The whole population of Scotland belonged in theory to the Church of Scotland, and in practice an effective form of social discipline was maintained in many parishes against notorious sins. There was a continuing appreciation of Puritan classics and every minister had to profess at his ordination an acceptance of the Reformed theology of the Westminster Confession. The more rigid adherents of traditional ways and doctrine, however, began to detect a relaxation of standards. Several were particularly dismayed that, following the Union of Scotland with England in 1707, lay patronage had been restored to the Church of Scotland. Discontent on this issue induced Ebenezer Erskine, one of the ministers of Stirling, to lead a secession from the church in 1733. Presbyterian Dissent became a feature of Scottish church life, and small Independent and Baptist groups followed soon after. The Puritan legacy in the eighteenth century was greater in Scotland than in England.[138]

The changing role of Evangelical religion in modern Britain forms the theme of the following pages. There is a pattern of overlapping chapters. Chapter 2 examines the nature of the movement in the first century of its existence up to about 1830. It enquires why the movement began and discovers the answer in the cultural mood impinging on the Protestant tradition. Contrary to the common view, Evangelicalism was allied with the Enlightenment. Chapter 3 deals with a change of direction in Evangelicalism that occurred in the 1820s and 1830s, tracing the shift of emphasis once more to its cultural roots – this time in Romanticism – and examining some of the consequences down to about 1860. In Chapter 4 there is a study of the impact of Evangelical religion on British society as a whole during the nineteenth century, when its influence was at its peak. Chapter 5 analyses a movement in late nineteenth-century spirituality that again helped to reorient the movement. Chapter 6 deals with the effects of earlier factors in dividing Evangelicals into conservative and liberal camps during the interwar years. The transforming effect of twentieth-century cultural trends on Evangelicalism is the subject of Chapter 7. Chapter 8 tries to pick up the threads by analysing developments since the Second World War and Chapter 9 reaches some general conclusions. It becomes clear that Evangelical religion in Britain, despite the four constant elements discussed in this chapter, has altered enormously over time in response to the changing assumptions of Western civilisation.

[2]

Knowledge of the Lord:
The Early Evangelical Movement

---

*And they shall teach no more every man his neighbour, and every man his brother,
saying, know the LORD: for they shall all know me, from the least of them unto
the greatest of them, saith the LORD. (Jer. 31:34)*

The decade beginning in 1734 witnessed in the English-speaking world
a more important development than any other, before or after, in the
history of Protestant Christianity: the emergence of the movement that
became Evangelicalism. Priority in the British Isles must go to Wales. A
young schoolmaster living near Brecon, Howel Harris, came to faith during
the spring of 1735.[1] A few weeks later Daniel Rowland, curate at Llangeitho
in Carmarthenshire, underwent a similar experience of forgiveness. Soon
both began travelling round South Wales, gathering large audiences and
preaching the arresting message that salvation could be known now.[2] England followed. George Whitefield, converted as an Oxford undergraduate
in the spring of 1735, stirred both Bristol and London by his oratory two
years later, exhorting his hearers to seek the new birth.[3] Charles Wesley,
who at Oxford had been Whitefield's mentor in his religious quest, did not
reach assurance of faith for himself until 1738. In the same week, on 24 May,
his brother John felt his heart 'strangely warmed' as he trusted 'in Christ,
Christ alone for salvation'. Prompted by Whitefield, John Wesley began his
career of open-air preaching at Bristol in the following year.[4] Whitefield
roused parts of Scotland in 1741, and in the next year there broke out at
Cambuslang near Glasgow a revival in which men and women anxiously
looked for pardon.[5] Already there had been a comparable phenomenon in
the colony of Massachusetts. In 1734–5, exactly when Harris and Rowland
were wrestling with their conviction of sin in Wales, Jonathan Edwards
was involved in a revival in the town of Northampton, where he was
minister. His published analysis of the revival had impressed Wesley between
his experience of trusting Christ and the inauguration of his travelling
ministry and was well known to the Scottish ministers most involved at
Cambuslang.[6] The movement in America, which Whitefield fanned into a

larger flame, is usually styled 'The Great Awakening'. But it was part and parcel of 'The Eighteenth-Century Revival',[7] a quickening of the spiritual tempo in Britain and beyond.

The quickening seemed desperately needed. The Dissenters, the immediate inheritors of the Puritan legacy in England, were at a low ebb. In the 1730s there was a proliferation of writings on 'the decay of the Dissenting interest'. Philip Doddridge, writing in 1740, believed that the decline was concentrated chiefly in the west and south of England,[8] but there it was acute. In the same year the Western Association of the Particular Baptists urged four fast days to repent of spiritual declension.[9] Fewer new Independent and Baptist places of worship were registered in the 1730s than in any other decade when the system of registration was in force.[10] Evangelicalism, however, transformed the situation. Later in the century, when the revival movement impinged significantly on the Old Dissent, numbers of Independents and Baptists rose steadily. It has been estimated that in 1750 there were about 15,000 Independent and 10,000 Particular Baptist church members. By 1800 the respective figures had risen to 35,000 and 24,000.[11] Although there was marked population growth in the period, this rate of church growth outstripped it. The number of churches in the Particular Baptist Western and Midland Associations approximately doubled between 1780 and 1820. Furthermore, the overall increase in membership per church doubled over the period. And the most spectacular change among Calvinistic Dissenters was a great rise in the number of those who attended regularly as 'hearers' without becoming members. One church, at Gold Hill in Buckinghamshire, was said in 1818 to have five hearers for every member.[12] So the Dissenters touched by the revival enjoyed far more success afterwards than before.

The Methodists made even greater progress. Their membership increased from 22,410 in 1767, the first year when it was recorded, to 88,334 in 1800 and 232,074 in 1830.[13] Round the core of loyal members Methodist 'hearers' formed a large penumbra. In the Church of England, by contrast, the number of communicants seems to have decreased during the eighteenth century. It continued falling relative to population until the 1830s.[14] Evangelicalism had made much less impact on the Established Church than among Dissenters. In the Church of Scotland, whose Evangelical strength was greater than that of the Church of England, communicant levels probably kept pace with population during the eighteenth century. But it was Presbyterian Dissent, much of it fired with evangelistic fervour, that grew most in Scotland. By 1835, only a century after the first secession, it enjoyed the allegiance of nearly a third of Edinburgh churchgoers.[15] It is clear that the appearance of Evangelicalism was the signal for a major advance by Protestant Christianity in the ensuing century.

The motor of expansion was the message of justification by faith. Lost sinners must trust Christ for salvation. In the classic compendium of Evangelical faith and practice, *The Complete Duty of Man* (1763), Henry

Venn, Vicar of Huddersfield, defines saving faith as 'a dependence upon
Christ for righteousness and strength, as having paid to the justice of
God full satisfaction for his broken law, and obtained acceptance for all
believers in his name, to the reward of eternal life'.[16] Christ had done
all that was needed to achieve salvation. It remained only for men and
women to accept forgiveness at his hands. Faith was therefore seen as the
gift of grace. It was 'simply to hang upon Him'.[17] To insist on faith as the
way of approaching God was to reject certain popular alternatives. Venn
condemns three. Our ground of hope, he explains, cannot be works, that
is, the performance of good deeds, for even the best actions have flaws and
so are unacceptable as an offering to a God of absolute holiness. Sincerity
is equally inadequate. God expects perfect obedience (which only Christ
could perform), not our good intentions. Nor will a mixture of faith and
works help us. If we rely partly on our good deeds, the grand difficulty
of their being tainted by sin remains.[18] 'Attempts to complete what grace
begins', according to Venn's Baptist friend Abraham Booth, 'betray our
pride and offend the Lord, but cannot promote our spiritual interest'.[19]
Thus ordinary Methodists would go about urging that mere morality was
of no avail in justification, for faith alone did everything.[20] They would
swap texts with broader-minded Bible students. 'Whenever I read in St.
Paul's Epistles on justification by faith alone', recalled James Lackington,
then an apprentice shoemaker, 'my good mistress would read in the Epistle
of St. James, such passages as suggest a man is not justified by faith alone,
but by faith and works . . . '[21] It was a telling riposte, but scholarly
Evangelicals were able to point out that while Paul writes of the condition
of justification, James is discussing the nature of genuine faith.[22] If faith is
real, it will automatically produce good works. Holiness is the fruit of faith.
This explains the apparently paradoxical position of Wesley: 'we are justified
by faith alone', he wrote, 'and yet by such a faith as is not alone . . . '[23]
Faith is the only means by which we are made right with God; but faith,
as soon as it exists, creates an impulse towards living a better life. Views
differed about whether or not it was essential to understand the notion of
justification by faith. Joseph Milner, a clergyman near Hull and the leading
Evangelical historian, held the doctrine absolutely necessary to salvation.[24]
Wesley, with his customary latitude in matters of opinion, supposed that
those ignorant of the belief, or even hostile to it, might be saved.[25] But
Evangelicals were united in holding that the reality of faith – as opposed
to belief about it – is the sole condition of acceptance by God.

The bearers of the message did not always find a ready welcome. To
be told that sincerity in the performance of the religious duties of one's
station did not command the blessing of God was startling, if not insulting.
To be assured that good works were as filthy rags seemed subversive
of all morality. To hear faith lauded to the skies aroused suspicions of
fanaticism, the 'enthusiasm' that the eighteenth century shunned because
its seventeenth-century version had killed a king. Polite society was

alarmed. It is true that Frederick, Prince of Wales, was so impressed that he was rumoured to be intending to use his powers as monarch to make Whitefield a bishop.[26] But Frederick was on bad terms with his father, George II, and in any case predeceased him in 1751. Evangelical penetration of high society, with the notable exceptions of the Countess of Huntingdon and the Earl of Dartmouth, was deferred until the aftermath of the French Revolution, when a high religious profile began to have welcome anti-revolutionary connotations. So the Evangelical movement laboured under severe disadvantages. Undergraduates were expelled from Oxford for Methodist practices in 1768;[27] young men suspected of Evangelical views were denied ordination in certain dioceses of the Church of England;[28] and unwelcome ministers of more sober outlook were imposed on parishes with Evangelical preferences in the Church of Scotland.[29]

There is a vivid fictional portrayal of resistance to Evangelicalism in George Eliot's tale, 'Janet's repentance'. Mr Tryan, a new Evangelical curate, arrives at a chapel-of-ease on the outskirts of the parish of Milby. His proposal to deliver Sunday evening lectures in the parish church of the town itself on the grounds that the resident clergyman does not preach the gospel arouses the ire of the town lawyer. A petition is organised to oppose the application to lecture. Tryan, according to the lawyer, preaches against good works. 'Tell a man he is not to be saved by his works', the lawyer declaims, 'and you open the floodgates of all immorality. You see it in all these canting innovators; they're all bad ones by the sly; smooth-faced, drawling, hypocritical fellows . . . '[30] When the lecture is eventually established, Tryan has to run the gauntlet of 'groans, howls, hisses, and hee-haws' on the way to church. Stories circulate about the minister and his hearers. Tradespeople among them are warned that they will lose good customers. 'Mr Budd harangued his workmen, and threatened them with dismissal if they or their families were known to attend the evening lecture; and Mr Tomlinson, on discovering that his foreman was a rank Tryanite, blustered to a great extent, and would have cashiered that valuable functionary on the spot, if such a retributive procedure had not been inconvenient.'[31] The storm subsides precisely because convenience triumphs. This narrative is set in the 1820s. At an earlier date resistance was commonly both fiercer and more sustained. Wesley endured mobbing when he first preached in Staffordshire in the 1740s.[32] His followers were violently assaulted. Christopher Hopper was the victim of 'invectives and lies, dirt, rotten eggs, brickbats, stones and cudgels'; Peter Jaco 'was struck so violently with a brick on the breast that the blood gushed out through my mouth, nose, and ears'; John Nelson's wife was beaten by a crowd of women 'so cruelly that they killed the child in her womb, and she went home and miscarried directly'.[33] Opposition was sometimes led by members of the elite and had a measure of local co-ordination. A clergyman fearful for his congregation or his standing might egg on a crowd to violence. Or else popular resistance might possess its own dynamic. It was rightly perceived that Evangelicalism threatened to divide community life. Customary ways were under attack and the mob retaliated in the only way available to the plebeian population of the eighteenth century.[34]

Evangelicals created their own community life. Methodism was famous – or notorious – for it. The weekly class meeting for the exchange of spiritual experience was the essence of Wesley's system for building up those who had been awakened by preaching. The pattern began almost accidentally at Bristol in 1742. A building debt had to be extinguished. Consequently the 'society', the body of all Methodists in the city, was broken down into short lists, to each of which was assigned a collector of weekly contributions. The collectors soon developed a pastoral role, and Wesley directed that members on each list should gather to seek their guidance.[35] To possess a quarterly ticket as a class member was the defining quality of a Methodist; to be noted as having 'ceased to meet' in class was to be no longer a Methodist. By 1783 in Bristol there were fifty-seven classes, each including from nine to eighteen members. The allocation to classes was on a purely geographical basis.[36] In addition to classes, however, early Methodism possessed other tight-knit groups. Only those professing justification were admitted to the bands, which also met weekly, and which were divided according to sex and marital status. This arrangement permitted greater intimacy. 'In the classes', it was recalled, 'they only confessed in general terms, that they have been tempted by the world, the flesh, and the devil. But in the bands they confessed the particular sins which they had been tempted to commit, or had actually committed.'[37] Those Methodists judged to be near or in the state of entire sanctification, at least in the larger societies, assembled in select bands. There were sometimes also penitents' meetings for backsliding band-members.[38] The plethora of preaching meetings, watch-nights, covenant services at new year and love-feasts, that is larger gatherings for the relating of testimonies while buns and water were handed round – all these bound Methodists strongly together in a hostile environment. 'Such was our love to each other', according to John Haime, the promoter of a Methodist society in the army, 'that even the sight of each other filled our hearts with divine consolation.'[39] Visits to the sick and dying brought genuine sympathy; substantial interest-free loans were available, at least in London, from a common fund; and Methodists looked after the businesses of sick brothers.[40]

Although the organisational structure was unique to Methodism, the spirit was characteristic of Evangelicalism as a whole. Jonathan Edwards knew the value of religious conversation as an antidote to spiritual melancholia.[41] The Yorkshire and Lancashire Particular Baptist Association, perhaps inspired by the Methodist example, urged in 1764 an increase of 'private meetings for mutual conference on the things of God'.[42] Samuel Walker, the Evangelical curate of Truro, organised societies for converts using material drawn from the Book of Common Prayer, less tightly controlled groups for religious conversation and a Parsons' Club, the prototype for many subsequent societies of Evangelical clergy, from about 1750.[43] Societies for prayer were promoted in and about Glasgow during the 1740s by John Maclaurin, minister of the North West Church there, and others.[44] Meetings for prayer became the hallmark of congregations touched by the revival. There was a natural tendency for Evangelicals to meet for religious purposes. The resulting fellowship was no ethereal thing but a strongly cemented form of social solidarity.

Who composed the Evangelical communities? The Methodist membership list for Bristol in 1783, which includes occupations, may be taken as an example. Of 790 names, only 99 are unidentified. The largest occupational group is the servants, of whom there are 55 of each sex. In addition, 26 women are concerned with laundry work, 24 with dressmaking – and so in many cases are probably more specialised servants. Shoemakers and members of related trades, together with their wives, form a group of 80 names. Apart from 29 gentlemen and gentlewomen and 25 classified as old, poor or almswomen, no other group contains as many as 20 names. There are only 13 labourers.[45] The list is fairly representative of evidence from elsewhere. The large number of servants, for example, is repeated in a sample of the converts in the Cambuslang revival of 1742, although not, apparently, among Evangelical Nonconformists in England.[46] More uniformly, a high proportion of shoemakers is found in Evangelical communities of the eighteenth and early nineteenth centuries. The most consistent finding has been that the artisan section of society, embracing shoemakers but also including a variety of tradesmen such as carpenters and coopers, was heavily over-represented in Evangelical ranks. Such skilled men and their families formed as high as 66 per cent of a Relief Church in Glasgow between 1822 and 1832.[47] A thorough trawl of evidence has shown that this social group was more than twice as numerous in eighteenth-century Methodism, at 47 per cent, as in society at large.[48] Unskilled men were few, at least among committed members of Evangelical bodies. There may well have been more of them among the 'hearers', the regular attenders who had not actually joined. Although artisans could be impoverished in bad times for their trade, Evangelicalism was rarely the religion of the poorest and outcast. Nor was it the religion of the prosperous and successful in the eighteenth century. The gentry may sometimes have been marginally over-represented in Methodism,[49] as the Bristol statistics illustrate, but the impact of the Evangelicalism of the Church of England on the elite was only just beginning when Hannah More and William Wilberforce composed their appeals to the great in the 1780s and 1790s.[50]

Women were numerous in the movement. 'I have heard Mr. Wesley remark', reported a rather jaundiced ex-Methodist, 'that more women are converted than men; and I believe that by far the greatest part of his people are females; and not a few of them sour, disappointed old maids . . . '[51] A measure of confirmation is provided by the discoveries that about 55 per cent of a sample of East Cheshire Methodists in the later eighteenth century were women and that nearly half of them were unmarried.[52] Religion may have provided psychological reassurance, even emotional outlet, for this section of the population. In any case, women were consistently found in larger numbers than men. Both Cambuslang converts in 1742 and Bristol Methodists in 1783 included two women for every man.[53] Nor were they necessarily kept in the background. Outside the formal setting of public worship, and even occasionally in it, women found opportunities for self-expression. In the proliferating cottage meetings of early Evangelicalism it was often women who took the lead in prayer and praise, counsel and exhortation.[54] In 1803 Wesleyans effectively prohibited female preaching for the sake of propriety, but the custom was restored by the Primitives. The Bible Christians of south-western England, too, put what they called 'female brethren' on the preaching plan.[55] In the upper echelons of society Hannah More, blue-stocking and Evangelical ideologue, played a no less significant role.[56] In an age when avenues for women into any sphere outside the home were being closed, Christian zeal brought them into prominence.

The places where Evangelicalism struck deepest root were usually of certain particular kinds. Where artisans were most numerous, vital religion was most likely to do well. Therefore, areas springing into life with proto-industrial employment for the skilled worker, townships like Paddiford Common in 'Janet's Repentance' with weaving and mining as the chief occupations, were ideal territory.[57] Methodism and Calvinistic Dissent as well as the Evangelical Anglicanism that George Eliot depicts thrived there. Growing industrial areas, including the big cities, were deliberately targeted by Wesley and his contemporaries, for there dwelt the most concentrated populations. In the countryside, patterns of settlement were highly significant determinants of Evangelical strength. Scattered dwellings of recent erection in large parishes or on parish boundaries, together with market towns, proved more receptive to the gospel than ancient nucleated villages of small size.[58] It was partly that in areas of scattered settlement the parish church was often far distant, so that when travelling preachers arrived they offered a monopoly of religious provision, whereas tight-knit communities usually clustered round the parish church. Only on the rare occasions when a clergyman of the Church of England held Evangelical convictions was this an advantage. Similarly in Scotland Evangelicals gained most ground in the vast parishes of the Highlands as well as in the new industrial regions.[59] Landownership also played a part. In so-called close parishes, where land was held by one or at most three proprietors, penetration by Evangelicalism was rare. Land for erecting a chapel was far more likely to be available in open parishes where landownership was fragmented.[60] Many of the determinants boil down to the issue of social control. Wherever authority could be exerted from above to encourage conformity to established ways, the innovations of popular religion would be resisted. Squire or parson, or both together, could publicise their distaste for enthusiasm. The mob would be conscious of their support – albeit normally tacit – for throwing the Methodist preacher in the duckpond.[61] Conversely, where the expectations of squire and parson could be ignored with impunity, gospel preaching would be sustained. In particular, artisans who prided themselves on avoiding dependence on the landed order for their daily bread would assert their self-reliance by giving the new message a hearing – and perhaps more. Evangelism was most effective where deference was weakest, whether in town or countryside. It is no accident that Yorkshire and Cornwall, with their large parishes and numerous artisans, were the fields of the greatest Methodist harvests.[62]

VARIETIES OF EVANGELICALISM

Despite its self-conscious unity, the Evangelical movement comprised several distinct strands. The Methodists were set apart from other groupings by both doctrine and discipline. They asserted a strong doctrine of assurance that will call for detailed scrutiny; and they believed in Christian perfection, which again deserves fuller attention.[63] The essence of their distinct doctrinal position, however, was Arminianism. Christ, they claimed, made salvation available to all who believed, and not just to the limited number of the elect. Such a rejection of Calvinism was not quite unique among Evangelicals, for a few of the clergy unconnected with Wesley shared Arminian beliefs.[64] So did the New Connexion of General Baptists, founded by an ex-Methodist, Dan Taylor, in 1770.[65] But Methodism was the chief bulwark of Arminianism. Charles Wesley filled many a hymn with anti-Calvinist polemic: 'The invitation is to all'; 'For all, for all, my Saviour died!'; 'Thy sovereign grace to all extends'.[66] His brother John called the connexional journal *The Arminian Magazine*. The first issue carried an article on Jacobus Arminius, the early seventeenth-century Dutch divine who drastically modified Reformed theology.[67] Yet John Wesley did not adhere closely to the structure of Arminius's thought. Nor was his theological system similar to the arid scheme of those rational Dissenters who treated Arminianism as a staging post to Unitarianism. Theirs, as Dr Nuttall has pointed out, was an Arminianism of the head; Wesley's was a version of the heart.[68] It was a dynamic message, a proclamation that the love of God is vast and free. No fatalism cast a shadow over the experience God wishes all to enjoy. Any man or woman can receive saving faith.

Wesley could not tolerate several aspects of the Calvinist scheme of salvation. It is true that he sometimes minimised the distance between his own and the Reformed position. 'I think on justification', he wrote to John Newton in 1765, 'just as . . . Mr. Calvin does.'[69] But Wesley rejected outright belief in predestination, the doctrine that some human beings are foreordained to salvation by God's decree. It was alien to his upbringing, for both parents stoutly denied it.[70] It was equally far removed from the ethical cast of his thought. If some are chosen and others are not, so that human beings cannot affect their destiny, the sanction for morality disappears. This was what Wesley meant by claiming that the teaching led to antinomianism. So he deplored the defection of a Cornish clergyman who had 'fallen into the Pit of the Decrees'.[71] A related objection was to the Calvinist doctrine of imputed righteousness. Reformed theologians held that God treats sinners as righteous by the legal fiction that Christ's merits are theirs. Wesley again held that this principle undercut the biblical summons to holy living. According to Calvinists, believers may commit sins and yet still be accepted by God for Christ's sake. According to Wesley, a person ceases to be a Christian as soon as he performs a sinful act. Calvinism was lulling people into a baseless sense of their security. Furthermore, Reformed theologians taught that any true believer would remain one until death – the doctrine of the perseverance of the saints. God would guarantee their ultimate salvation. Again, Wesley viewed such teaching as licence for immorality.[72]

Although he repudiated it, Wesley pursued no vendetta against Calvinism. Men holding Reformed views were admitted to his annual conference, and during the 1760s Wesley employed without examination a preacher, Thomas Taylor, who read little but Calvinist authors and leaned to imputed righteousness and final perseverance.[73] There was more eagerness for battle on the other side. The publication of the minutes of the 1770 Methodist Conference, referring to good works as a 'condition' of salvation, provoked an outcry by Calvinists such as Rowland Hill and Augustus Toplady. Wesley seemed to be rejecting no less a doctrine than justification by faith. In reality he did not. Good works, according to Wesley, were not the way to justification, but they were essential to final salvation. So the 'Calvinistic Controversy' of the 1770s that drove Methodism further apart from other Evangelicals was based in part on a misunderstanding.[74] There was, nevertheless, substantial theological disagreement between Wesley and the Reformed tradition. Evangelical Arminianism was a distinct body of thought.

Methodism was also differentiated from other strands of the Evangelical movement by its discipline. Wesley professed to be a loyal son of the Church of England, constantly resisting calls for separation.[75] Yet Methodism was an elaborate religious organisation that had no dependence, except for the sacraments, on existing ecclesiastical structures. Wesley personally supervised the whole massive machine. All the preachers were his 'helpers'; membership lists were revised by his decision, against which there was no appeal. Some suggested that 'the love of power seems to have been the main spring of all his actions'.[76] By and large, however, his authority was willingly accepted. The problems arose with his death in 1791. How was the machine to operate without Wesley's guiding hand? Some preachers, led by Alexander Kilham and inspired in part by the egalitarianism of the French Revolution, pressed for greater local autonomy and more lay power. They were routed, however, and forced to leave the Wesleyan body to set up the Methodist New Connexion in 1797.[77] By the 1810s another autocracy had been established. Less openly than Wesley but only slightly less firmly, Jabez Bunting shaped the policies of Wesleyan Methodism until the middle of the nineteenth century. It was Bunting who ensured, especially during the turbulent years following the Napoleonic Wars, that radicals were summarily cashiered from the movement.[78] Theoretically, the Wesleyan connexion was ruled after its founder's death by the so-called 'Legal Hundred' of travelling preachers who in law formed the conference. The hundred were those named by Wesley in 1784 and, as they died, their successors. In practice, far more of the travelling preachers participated. Conference was supreme in its decisions and on occasion it could overrule even Bunting; but the powers of conference were limited by its being in session for only three weeks or less each summer. It was conference that allocated preachers to circuits, the parts of the country where they were to itinerate, raising up and sustaining the societies. By 1791 there were 87 circuits in Britain, each with from one to three travelling preachers, who were normally changed each year.[79] Although under Wesley most of them were untrained laymen, the travelling preachers gradually evolved into the Methodist ministry. The title 'Reverend' was officially adopted in 1818.[80] Far more of the meetings, however, were conducted by local preachers. With class leaders and band leaders, stewards in charge of society funds and trustees in charge of society buildings, they formed a formidable army of lay workers. Methodism provided a host of opportunities for laymen to assume prominent public roles. If they lacked power, they possessed responsibility.

Methodism also arose in several Calvinistic forms. George Whitefield's preaching gave rise to societies that, like him, adhered to Reformed teaching. He established in the capital the Moorfields Tabernacle in 1741 and the Tottenham Court Chapel in 1756.[81] By 1747 there were 31 Whitefieldian societies and 27 preaching stations.[82] Selina, Countess of Huntingdon, converted in 1739, was sufficiently free of family duties by 1760 to devote herself largely to organising evangelism. She appointed gospel clergymen as her chaplains, directing them as firmly as Wesley treated his assistants, and erected chapels for their eloquence in fashionable resorts such as Brighton (1760), Bath (1765) and Tunbridge Wells (1765). In 1768 she created at Trevecca, under the superintendence of Howel Harris, a college to train candidates for the ministry, and in 1777 a chapel at Spa Fields, London, which soon attracted a wealthy congregation.[83] By her death in 1791 there were between 55 and 80 congregations supplied with preachers trained at Trevecca.[84] She had already, in 1782, reluctantly seceded from the Church of England, but she failed to make adequate provision for the government of the new denomination. Only seven chapels, as her personal property, were transferred to the continuing Countess of Huntingdon's Connexion.[85] Whitefield's connexion disintegrated even more catastrophically. He had begun as moderator of a Calvinistic Methodist 'association' in 1743, the year before Wesley held the first meeting of his equivalent conference.[86] With Whitefield frequently absent in America, however, his place was taken by John Cennick, but in 1745 he departed to the Moravians. His successor, Howel Harris, also withdrew in 1749, and central direction of the movement stopped. Because the Whitefieldian societies (if Moorfields is representative) permitted congregational decision-making, it was easy for them to develop into Independent churches.[87] Preachers were similarly attracted over the narrow dividing-line. In 1748, for instance, one Herbert Jenkins 'went off to the Independents'.[88] In 1764 the Moorfields Tabernacle and Tottenham Court Chapels were themselves registered as Independent.[89] Although a Gloucestershire Calvinistic Methodist Association was still functioning in 1784,[90] the connexion virtually dissolved following Whitefield's death in 1770. Only in Wales did Calvinistic Methodism become a permanent force. Howel Harris resumed his organisational work in 1763, but, making no headway with a plan for a 'General Union' embracing Wesleyans and Moravians, concentrated his efforts in the principality.[91] His legacy was a body which in the nineteenth century, as the Welsh Calvinistic Methodist Connexion, became the strongest single denomination in Wales.

Another strand consisted of Evangelicals in the Church of England, its ordained clergy and their associates. Few were Methodist converts or even touched by Calvinistic Methodism. Rather they normally discovered their vital faith by painful steps in seclusion. Thomas Scott, curate at Ravenstone and Weston Underwood in Buckinghamshire and subsequently the eighteenth-century Evangelicals' greatest commentator on the Bible, has left a classic account of such a spiritual pilgrimage during the 1770s, *The Force of Truth* (1779). Entering the ministry for the sake of preferment, he began with virtually Socinian views, holding Christ to be nothing but a man proclaiming enlightened doctrines. Struck by the conscientious pastoral care of the Evangelical, John Newton, his near neighbour, he was convinced by Bishop Burnet's book on the same subject that he must be more attentive to his duties. A reading of Samuel Clarke, the early eighteenth-century champion of a more liberal doctrine of the Trinity, paradoxically drew him back from Socinianism towards orthodoxy. William Law persuaded him to give far more time to devotion; Hooker attracted him to Reformed divines; from them he learned justification by faith. Strangely, as he puts it, 'my faith was now fixed upon a crucified Saviour (though I dishonoured his person, and denied his Deity)'.[92] Other reading eventually brought him to profess Calvinism. Scott, as he insists, changed his sentiments 'very gradually' and not because of the teaching of Evangelicals.[93] A similar process took place in many parts of the land. At St Gennys in Cornwall in 1733 or 1734, George Thomson was awakened by dreams of judgement and gained confidence of salvation through Romans, Chapter 3.[94] At Wintringham in

Lincolnshire, Thomas Adam, though corresponding with the Evangelical Thomas Hartley, was influenced during a perplexing decade chiefly by the mystical writings of Law before he reached settled convictions in 1748.[95] In London around 1750, 'like most others', according to his biographer, William Romaine probably 'grew clearer by degrees, through the word, prayer, and experience'.[96] By such means the number of Evangelical clergy increased. In 1769 Wesley knew of between fifty and sixty who preached salvation by faith. He wrote to them all inviting co-operation, but received only three replies. In a phrase long remembered, he dismissed them as 'a rope of sand'.[97] Although they were later to consolidate in clerical societies, in the early years of the revival the Evangelical clergy were few and scattered.

Respect for church order varied among them. Samuel Walker of Truro was at one pole of opinion, persuading others 'to keep close to the discipline of mother Church'.[98] He believed in 'regularity', that is, confining his work to the parish he served. Others, like John Berridge, of Everton, Cambridgeshire, felt bound to itinerate outside the parish – to 'go round the neighbourhood, preaching in the fields, wherever a door is opened, three or four days in every week'.[99] William Grimshaw, at Haworth in the West Riding, even acted as one of Wesley's stated 'helpers'.[100] There was a broad range of different degrees of 'irregularity', which ensured that the boundary between loyal Churchmen and their more flexible brethren was blurred. Thomas Haweis, finding the parish of Aldwincle, Northamptonshire, too small a sphere for his labours, put himself at the service of the Countess of Huntingdon from 1774.[101] The trend of opinion, however, was in the opposite direction. As Evangelical clergy became more numerous, the need for itinerancy seemed to lessen; and as criticism of Evangelicals mounted, it became valuable to be able to stress loyalty to the forms of the Church of England. Accordingly, Henry Venn, who at Huddersfield up to 1771 co-operated with the Wesleyans in field preaching, later became aware of what his son called 'the evils of schism' and dissuaded others from irregularity.[102] The views of Charles Simeon, Vicar of Holy Trinity, Cambridge, from 1783 to 1836 and mentor to generations of Evangelical ordinands, were decisive for the future course of the movement. 'A Preacher has enough to do in his own parish', he roundly declared.[103]

Concentration on a parochial ministry could be highly effective. At Aldwincle, for example, Haweis found no households maintaining family prayers, but by never leaving a house without praying soon ensured that family devotions became the rule.[104] The grand difficulty of the Evangelicals in the Church of England, however, was in sustaining an awakened congregation when the gospel minister left the parish. The next clergyman was unlikely to be an Evangelical. The flock might then disperse. More likely, it would go over to Independency, securing its own building and its own preacher of the gospel. This happened after Venn's departure from Huddersfield (with his sanction), and even in Truro after the death of

Walker, the arch-defender of parish loyalty.[105] The problem was a result of the patronage system that entrusted the choice of a clergyman to laypeople who were rarely sympathetic to the cause of the gospel. Hence many early Evangelical clergy were to be found in places of worship outside the normal patronage system: in proprietary chapels erected, especially in London, by converted notables; in daughter chapels where the appointment was in the hands of an Evangelical minister; and in lectureships, often survivals from Puritan days, where the choice was by some form of election. But it was Simeon who dealt most effectively with the problem of continuity. In order to achieve a sucession of Evangelical clergy in strategic parishes such as Cheltenham, he created, in 1817, a trust to purchase rights of patronage.[106] It expanded and was also imitated by other trusts. In this, as in many other ways, Simeon gave an assured place to what was becoming an Evangelical party in the Church of England.

The impact of Evangelicalism on orthodox Dissent in England and Wales did not become general until the last years of the eighteenth century. The delay is partly explained by factors that inhibited the effectiveness of Dissenters in mission. It was prudent for those outside the Established Church to posses licences for their places of worship, and licences would hardly be granted for the type of field preaching adopted so powerfully by Methodists, whether Arminian or Calvinistic. Dissenters in any case suffered from the reputation of being peculiar people, a disadvantage not shared by those operating at least nominally under the auspices of the Church of England. And Dissenting congregations, by and large, were isolated and introspective.[107] Non-involvement in the revival was a matter of deliberate choice. People proud of their traditions did not wish to associate with those who at best neglected the niceties of doctrine and discipline and often actually veered into what seemed to be theological laxity. The foibles and wild ways of the new evangelists startled and repelled.[108] Worst of all, the revival was divisive. Thomas Morgan, Independent minister at Morley, Yorkshire, lamented in 1765 the 'unhappy *Divisions* almost in all the Congregations in the Kingdom chiefly occasion'd by *Methodistical Delusions*'.[109]

Yet even in the early days inhibitions about the new movement were overcome by some. Risdon Darracott, Independent minister at Wellington, Somerset, was in close touch with Evangelical clergymen including Samuel Walker and Henry Venn.[110] Darracott's tutor, Philip Doddridge, co-operated fully with Whitefield.[111] Doddridge's pivotal role in turning orthodox Dissenters into friends of the revival was subsequently played by Thomas Gibbons, Independent minister at Haberdashers' Hall, London, and tutor at Mile End Academy.[112] Men converted through the Calvinistic Methodists soon swelled the ranks of Dissent. The Saviour, according to Whitefield, 'has inclined many converted unto him thro' his Grace by us, to join with the Dissenting Congregations . . . '[113] Baptists profited as well as the Independents. Henry Philips, converted through Howel Harris and later

Baptist minister at Salisbury, was preaching at Tiverton with 'freedom and affection' on the universality of the gospel invitation in 1765.[114] Robert Robinson and John Fawcett, two of the most influential Baptist ministers of the later eighteenth century, were both converted under Whitefield.[115] Furthermore, whole congregations sometimes joined the Dissenters, perhaps on the termination of an Evangelical ministry at a parish church or when a Wesleyan preacher turned Calvinist.[116] The New Connexion of General Baptists, which remained Arminian in theology and made marked headway in the East Midlands, was also the fruit of the revival. Its core churches, based on Barton-in-the-Beans, Leicestershire, arose from the evangelism of a servant of the Countess of Huntingdon. Its creation as a separate denomination, by fission from the older General Baptist Churches that in general had moved to a more liberal theology, was the work in 1770 of Dan Taylor, an ex-Wesleyan preacher who shared Wesley's genius for co-ordination.[117] Dissent gained a new vitality from the infusion of Evangelicalism.

Scotland was home to several strands of the movement. In the Established Church a substantial section of the ministry – how large we do not know – held Evangelical views. The leaders of this body of men, John Maclaurin, John Erskine and John Gillies among them, were highly respected in the Kirk. Maclaurin, an able Highlander in a Glasgow charge, corresponded with Jonathan Edwards and others in New England and so learned early of the revivals there. He urged concerted prayer to stir up similar awakenings in Scotland and rejoiced in the events at Cambuslang in 1742.[118] Erskine, who acknowledged his debt to sermons by Maclaurin, became minister of New Greyfriars Church, Edinburgh. During a long career he gave publicity to Cambuslang, defended Whitefield and edited some of Edwards's posthumous works.[119] Gillies, Maclaurin's son-in-law and a close friend of Erskine, became Whitefield's first biographer.[120] Such men identified wholly with the Evangelical cause. In the second half of the eighteenth century they became embroiled in party warfare in the Church of Scotland. The problem was fundamentally the same one that confronted their brethren in the Church of England: how was continuity of godly ministry to be obtained when parish ministers were appointed by patronage? Their solution was to join others in urging that congregations, or at least their leading lights, the elders and heritors, should have a right of veto over presentees to charges. The so-called Moderate party, insisting on the letter of church law, resisted resolutely and successfully.[121] Consequently non-Evangelical ministers were imposed on unwilling congregations. Quite frequently from 1761 onwards a congregation would respond by deserting the parish church to form a 'Relief Church'. So was born a wholly Evangelical body, Presbyterian in polity but outside the Established Church, that earned the nickname the 'Scots Methodists'.[122] They existed alongside the congregations of the Secession that in 1733 had also split off from the Church of Scotland on the patronage issue. It was the Secession

Church that originally invited Whitefield to Scotland in 1741, and, despite disillusionment when he would not embrace their distinctive principles, many of the more open-minded in the Secession remained Evangelical in thought and practice.[123] By the end of the century Presbyterian Dissent was a powerful force in Scotland, especially in urban Scotland. At Jedburgh, admittedly an extreme case, in the 1790s, more than 70 per cent of the adult population were Dissenters.[124] Despite the weakness of Methodism north of the border, Evangelical religion had put down deep roots there.

CONTINUITY WITH THE PAST

The multi-faceted movement that was the Evangelical Revival was to touch the lives of millions. But was it nothing new? Was it simply a massive expansion of pre-existent patterns of faith and practice, a popularisation of received forms of religion? With meticulous scholarship, Dr Geoffrey Nuttall has demonstrated that there was a large measure of continuity between elements of the Reformed tradition embodied in Dissent and the revival. He singles out a common eagerness for unity in Christian work, a consequent impatience with divisive doctrinal tests and a stress on personal experience in devotion to Christ. He discerns a tradition that runs from Richard Baxter in the mid-seventeenth century through Philip Doddridge in the early eighteenth to Evangelicals such as the Baptist, Andrew Fuller.[125] Baxter and Doddridge certainly fit his specification. So does Whitefield, whose division of opinion with the Secession in Scotland was the result of the overriding importance he attached to catholicity, comprehensiveness and heart work. Whitefield was aware of the affinity. He assured Doddridge that a recently published sermon of his 'contains the very life of preaching, I mean sweet invitations to close with CHRIST'. 'I do not wonder', he added, 'that you are dubbed a Methodist on account of it.'[126] Dr Nuttall can point to the assistance rendered to Whitefield by Thomas Cole, the Dissenting minister in the evangelist's home city of Gloucester, who was already in pastoral charge long before Whitefield's conversion.[127] He also draws attention to the experimental devotion of individual Dissenters, both laymen and ministers, especially in the west of England, in the early eighteenth century. 'These', he writes, 'were Evangelicals before the Revival . . . '[128] The thesis of continuity from the pre-revival period can be supported by evidence drawn from the Baptists, from Scotland and from Wales. Bristol Baptist Academy was producing a stream of ministers with vital spirituality, evangelistic concerns and a catholic outlook under the three principals who served from 1720 to 1791, Bernard Foskett, Hugh Evans and Caleb Evans.[129] In Scotland, John Maclaurin and his circle, those who welcomed the Cambuslang Revival in the 1740s, were already resisting liberal theological trends in the name of heart religion during the protracted Simson case of the 1720s.[130] And, for Wales, recent scholarship has stressed the circulation of literature, the Dissenting preaching and the gospel themes of both that anticipated the emergence of the revival in the 1730s.[131] It is clear that in many respects Evangelical religion prolonged existing lines of development.

Even Methodism, the new growth on Evangelical soil, had roots in Puritan tradition. Wesley's mother, Susanna, herself the daughter of one of the ejected divines of 1662, esteemed Baxter highly.[132] Although her son John was deliberately guarded from Dissenting literature when young, Susanna lived with him in the crucial years 1739–42 when his position was crystallising after the experience of 24 May 1738. Baxter, especially in his *Aphorisms of Justification*, became Wesley's mentor. Baxter's moderate version of Puritanism appealed almost as much to him as to Doddridge.[133] The fifty-volume *Christian Library* published by Wesley for his followers contains far more literature of a Puritan stamp than of any other ecclesiastical genre.[134] A Methodist convert so devoted to books that he saved money for their purchase by living on bread and tea assembled a collection overwhelmingly Puritan.[135] John Bunyan's *Pilgrim's Progress* and Joseph Alleine's *Alarm to the Unconverted* were particularly prized by the early preachers.[136] A clergyman trying to dissuade a parishioner from attending Methodist meetings had no doubt of the identification: 'he showed him several old Puritanical books, which treated on the new birth, &c., and told him, "It is a false religion, because it is an old religion!".'[137] The call for conversion, embracing an expectation of a period of conviction of sin preceding the crisis of the new birth, was reminiscent of seventeenth-century Reformed divinity. So was the constant appeal to scripture and what a visiting Swede noticed as Wesley's message of 'a crucified Saviour and faith in his merits'.[138] Three characteristic marks of Evangelicalism, conversionism, biblicism and crucicentrism, had been as much a part of Puritanism as they were of Methodism. It has been argued that the affinities go beyond such theological areas to include aspects of liturgy, pastoralia, family piety and ethics.[139] Although features of Methodism in these areas also had an ancestry elsewhere, it is true that Wesley originally met the practice of extempore prayer among Scots in America who were maintaining earlier Reformed practice; that the Methodist covenant service owed a great deal to the individual covenants beloved of Puritan authors; that class meetings resembled the fellowship groups fostered by the godly of the seventeenth century; that Wesley's pattern of family prayer was drawn from the Nonconformist Philip Henry; and that Wesley's rigorism, for all its High Church ascetic flavour, had parallels in Puritan moral teaching.[140] Methodists inherited a substantial legacy from the Puritans.

DISCONTINUITY WITH THE REFORMED TRADITION

The Evangelical Revival nevertheless does represent a break with the past. Apart from the emergence of new denominations, perhaps the most marked discontinuity was in the Church of England. The doctrine of justification by faith had well-nigh disappeared. Calvinism was at a discount after the Restoration. 'Puritan' had become a term of abuse. Professor Rupp has suggested that there must be a thread linking the Reformed tradition of the seventeenth century with the Evangelicals of the eighteenth.[141] Yet there is scant evidence for so inherently likely a hypothesis. The last Calvinist bishop, Hall of Bristol, died in 1710.[142] Among the clergy, it was said in the 1730s that some had abandoned the Reformation teachings of their youth. Richard Seagrave, an unbeneficed clergyman, was a lonely voice in the 1730s calling for allegiance to the doctrines of the Thirty-Nine Articles. He had no identifiable influence in bringing the early Evangelicals to their mature position.[143] Thomas Allen of Kettering (1714–55) was exceptional in retaining a Puritan stance and then being classified (by Simeon, for instance) as an Evangelical.[144] James Hervey, Rector of Weston Favell, Northamptonshire, the most popular *littérateur* among the first generation of Evangelical clergy, was aware of likeminded men in an earlier age. 'Is it Puritanical?' he asked. 'Be not ashamed of the name.'[145] But, as was usual, his faith had come independently – in his case through Oxford Methodism. Other Evangelicals, like James Bean at the beginning of the nineteenth century, were eager to repudiate all connection with the Puritans, who were so widely seen as virulent critics of the constitution of the Church of England. The Reformation he honoured, but not its dyspeptic successors.[146] Occasionally, there are traces of the persistence of Puritan faith and experience without benefit of clergy. For example, an early Methodist preacher came on a serious young man at Newark. 'It was evident that the Lord had graciously visited his soul, though he had never heard a gospel sermon in his life, and had solely the Bible, the Common Prayer-Book, and Milton's *Paradise Lost* to read.'[147] Pockets of lay piety were no doubt sustained in obscurity and nourished by old books. It remains true, however, that the men of eminence were now in their graves. The tide of Reformed teaching that continued to flow in the Church of Scotland and in English Dissent was at an ebb in the Church of England.

There were three significant symptoms of discontinuity. One was the stimulus given to the revival by the alternative High Church tradition of the *Ecclesia Anglicana*. The ideal of 'primitive Christianity', stripped of the decadent accretions of later centuries, had been popularised by William Cave, Vicar of Islington, in 1673. Five years later, under the guidance of Anthony Horneck, a German who had become preacher at the Savoy, there was created the first 'religious society'. Appealing chiefly to young men, the religious societies soon became the vehicle for spreading 'primitive Christianity' throughout the land. Members bound themselves to self-examination, directed prayer, monthly communion, fasting and the quest for holiness. Society meetings, normally weekly, were tightly controlled by clergymen, excluded controversy over theology and church government and were designed overall to ensure that the members should (as the model rules put it) 'keep close to the Church of England'. By 1714, 27 per cent of London places of worship in the Established Church received support from some religious society.[148] It was a body of this type that Wesley gathered round himself at Oxford from 1729 onwards. Attracting the nickname 'The Holy Club', it was designed to nurture the religious attainments of young men through guided reading, spiritual exercises and good works. Prison visiting, attendance on the sick and help for the poor formed part of the traditional discipline of the religious societies.[149]

The decoding of the diaries of Wesley and Benjamin Ingham, one of his associates, is revealing a more complex organisation in this Oxford Methodism than had previously been supposed. Wesley's care group spawned several sub-groups, which in turn created a number of other groups. The programme of pursuing the Christian ideal not according to any system of theology but by imitating the lives of Christlike people was evidently enjoying something of a vogue among successive cohorts of undergraduates.[150] Self-examination was taken to an extreme. Members were encouraged to test themselves hourly on various aspects of devotion and record their ratings on a scale from one (low) to nine.[151] Wesley carried forward the ascetic temper of the Holy Club into the mature Methodism of the revival. His followers were exhorted to pursue a regimen in exactly the manner of Horneck with a dedication to precise self-scrutiny, works of charity and attendance on the means of grace.[152] Methodists were to be found observing Lent and it was a standard practice to fast before watch-night services.[153] Furthermore, the existing religious societies of the Church of England formed a reservoir of zealots in earnest for their souls that the early evangelists could tap. Some societies went over virtually en bloc to the Methodists or the Moravians. Half the Moravian members in London in 1742 were believed to have come from the religious societies.[154] The revival owed an enormous debt to the methods and the personnel of this set of institutions.

There was also a debt to the teaching of the High Church tradition. The pursuit of holiness, Wesley's grand aim, was grounded in a number of esteemed devotional writers both ancient and modern. Foremost among them was Jeremy Taylor, once chaplain to Archbishop Laud and Charles I and, after the Restoration, a bishop in Ireland. His treatise on *Holy Living and Dying* (1650–1) made an immediate impact on Wesley in 1725 at the age of twenty-two. 'Instantly', he recalls, 'I resolved to dedicate *all my life* to God, *all* my thoughts, and words, and actions, being thoroughly convinced, there was no medium . . . '[155] Taylor urged a Laudian form of devotion, at once strict and sacramental. Wesley in his later Evangelical years adopted a rule of life based on Taylor's recommendations.[156] A year after discovering Jeremy Taylor he came on Thomas à Kempis's *Imitation of Christ*, the classic of fifteenth-century piety. Although he felt à Kempis exaggerates the need for renunciation, the *Imitation* illuminated for him what he called 'the religion of the heart'.[157] In the next couple of years two works

by Wesley's contemporary William Law, his *On Christian Perfection* (1726)
and *A Serious Call to a Devout and Holy Life* (1728), convinced Wesley
more than ever (as he put it) of 'the absolute impossibility of being *half
a Christian*'.[158] It was Taylor, à Kempis and Law who laid the foundation
for the rigorism of the Holy Club.

Another strand of influence over Wesley, derived partly from Roman
Catholic authors and in some tension with the teaching on obedience to
constituted authority found in Taylor and Law, was the mystical element
in the Christian inheritance. Wesley's mother Susanna valued the *Pugna
Spiritualis* of Lorenzo Scupoli, an Italian work, and *The Life of God in
the Soul of Man* (1677) by Henry Scougal of Aberdeen almost as highly as
Baxter.[159] Growing up in this atmosphere, Wesley was naturally attracted
to John Norris, the last of the Cambridge Platonists, who had contrived to
blend intellectual analysis with mystical apprehension. He read fifteen works
by Norris in the period 1725–35, more than the number from any other
author.[160] A range of continental mystics was known and absorbed by
Wesley. The most enduring mark was made by Jean Baptiste de Saint-Jure's
Holy Life of Monsieur de Renty, a seventeenth-century French aristocrat of
mystical temperament who became Wesley's most admired model of a
Christian.[161] After 1736 Wesley turned away from mysticism itself as too
passive, introspective and anti-institutional, but it continued to exercise a
lifelong fascination over his brother Charles.[162] Certain eighteenth-century
Evangelicals were drawn back towards the mystical, especially the forms
propagated by Law in his later years, for the Evangelical and the mystic
shared a common attachment to experiencing the divine.[163]

The patristic and liturgical preoccupations of High Church scholarship had
less in common with the revival, yet they too played a part in preparing its
way. Wesley imbibed a fascination for eastern Orthodoxy that reinvigorated
his ideal of perfection at the fountainhead of monastic spirituality; and his
zeal for the early centuries of the church eventually drove him back to
the Bible as a uniquely authoritative account of primitive Christianity.[164]
Many an individual Evangelical, especially among the clergy, had passed
through a High Church phase of some type. It had served, they would later
have said, as a schoolmaster to bring them to Christ.

A second symptom of discontinuity was the assimilation of influences
from continental Protestantism. The decisive impulse to the brothers
Wesley came from Luther: Charles was reading his commentary on
Galatians and John was listening to his preface to the letter to the
Romans when they first came to vital faith.[165] Yet neither subsequently
rated Luther very highly, so that Lutherans of their own day came to be
more important than the reformer. The experience of the Protestants in
the central European regions where the Counter-Reformation had gained
the upper hand was part of the context in which revival was born. There
were anxieties about the future of the Protestant cause that encouraged
a willingness to experiment with novel religious methods. In Silesia in

particular, Protestants retained few places of public worship and so were forced back on informal techniques of open-air preaching and domestic meetings to sustain the faith. Again, in 1731, the Protestants of Salzburg were expelled by Austrian troops and had to seek refuge elsewhere. Charity sermons were preached on their behalf in London, and John Wesley sailed in 1737 alongside a vessel carrying a party of them to Georgia.[166] Their ministers, whom Wesley consulted about their convictions, were trained at Halle, which was the centre of the Lutheran movement that most affected Evangelical origins: Pietism. Philip Spener had written in 1675 the manifesto of the movement, *Pia Desideria*, urging the need for repentance, the new birth, putting faith into practice and close fellowship among true believers.[167] His disciple August Francke created at Halle a range of institutions for embodying and propagating Spener's vision. Chief among them was the orphan house, then the biggest building in Europe, with a medical dispensary attached. It was to inspire both Wesley and Whitefield to erect their own orphan houses and Howel Harris to establish a community as a centre of Christian influence at Trevecca. Francke printed Bibles and spiritual reading in huge quantities for dissemination in Germany and far beyond to the south and east, and at Halle there were trained ministers to carry the gospel even further.[168] Under the patronage of the King of Denmark, a mission was launched to India in 1705. Griffith Jones, the creator of the Welsh circulating schools, and his patron Sir John Philipps, an influential member of the Society for Promoting Christian Knowledge, were admirers of Francke who tried to imitate the missionary impetus of Halle in their native Wales. These two, clergyman and layman, were the closest approximation to Evangelicals in the Church of England before the revival. Francke's writings were to take their place in the spiritual biographies of Whitefield and both Wesleys.[169] Pietism had already achieved in Lutheranism a great deal of what these men were to undertake in the English-speaking world.

Even more decisive for the emergence of Evangelicalism were the Moravians. Beginning as the followers of Jan Hus in Bohemia in the early fifteenth century, this body, officially the *Unitas Fratrum* or Unity of the Brethren, had become accepted as Protestants after the Reformation. Their popular nickname was the result of their prominence in Moravia until they were harried into exile and decline by the advancing Counter-Reformation. A party of refugees settled in 1722 at Herrnhut in Saxony on the estate of Count Nicholas von Zinzendorf, a man who had been touched by Pietism but now identified wholly with the Moravians. Under Zinzendorf's guidance they were reorganised in 1727 as the Renewed Unity of the Brethren and became a dynamic missionary force.[170] Zinzendorf spread the message that true religion must be a matter of experience, not of speculation. Each for himself must accept the forgiveness made available by the Lamb of God sacrificed for sins. The cross, faith, forgiveness and assurance were the keynotes. Intense devotion, especially to the crucified Christ, was the result.[171]

Wesley encountered the Brethren on his missionary trip to Georgia. One of their number, Peter Böhler, was his chief guide in the months following his return in 1738 that led to his own experience of forgiveness. For more than two years Wesley was actually a member of a predominantly Moravian fellowship in Fetter Lane. Even after his withdrawal there were many comings and goings between the early Methodists and the Moravians, who developed their own itinerant missionary work in England and Wales. There were negotiations for reunion as late as 1785–6.[172] The initial obstacle to combined work was the common Moravian teaching on 'stillness', a denigration of prayer, Bible-reading, church attendance, receiving the sacrament and good works, in order 'wholly to rely on the blood and wounds of the Lamb'.[173] It was an exaggeration of Luther's insistence on faith alone as the instrument of salvation. There were other peculiarities caused by the German ethos and language of the movement, as when it was recorded that the unmarried sisters held 'a Heathen Love-Feast' – that is, a tea to encourage support for missions to the heathen.[174] Yet the Moravians had a special appeal for those seeking 'primitive Christianity': a threefold pattern of ministry, bishops, priests and deacons, whose orders were recognised by the Archbishop of Canterbury in 1737; a firm discipline, a warm fellowship and an apostolic zeal for missions; and, from 1746 at Fulneck in Yorkshire, and soon elsewhere, the community life of Herrnhut imitated in England.[175] Apart from a crucial element of their teaching whose importance will be discussed shortly, the Moravians transmitted a substantial legacy to the revival, especially in its Methodist variety. Their practice of an *ecclesiola in ecclesia* (a tight-knit religious fellowship within a broader church), their organisation in bands and their hymn-singing were taken over by Wesley – although each was blended with the inheritance of the religious societies. Perhaps the watch-night services and conference of Methodism were imitated from the Moravians; this is certainly true of the love-feast and the use of the lot for discerning the will of God, though the latter practice was discontinued by Wesley after the early 1740s.[176] Evangelicalism learned much from the Moravians.

The third of the striking symptoms of discontinuity was a new emphasis on mission. In the sixteenth and seventeenth centuries it was rare to find a Protestant divine commending the spread of the gospel beyond the bounds of Christendom. Richard Baxter was most unusual among the Puritans in expressing an eagerness for the conversion of the nations.[177] There were efforts during the Commonwealth to propagate the faith in 'the dark corners of the land', which effectively meant Wales, the north and the south-west, and subsequently certain Independents and Baptists engaged in itinerant evangelism in their areas.[178] But the evangelistic work of John Eliot among the Iroquois Indians of Massachusetts became celebrated precisely because it was exceptional. Protestant missionary effort was pitiably weak by comparison with the Roman Catholic record.[179] The Great Commission at the end of Matthew's gospel, 'Go ye therefore, and teach all nations', was given no expository comment in the Geneva Bible that was widely used among English-speaking Protestants of the seventeenth century.[180] The text, it was supposed, applied only to the early church. Cotton Mather, a leading Puritan of the New World writing early in the eighteenth century, regretted the scandal 'of so little having been done by the churches of the Reformation to spread the faith.[181]

The activism that, as we have seen, was an enduring hallmark of the Evangelical movement stood in stark contrast. It was still believed, by Jonathan Edwards for instance, that God exercises his sovereignty in men's salvation by bestowing the means of grace on one people but not on another.[182] Now, however, it was increasingly held that human beings could be the appointed agents of bringing the gospel to unevangelised nations. We know, wrote Edwards, 'that it is God's manner to make use of means in carrying on his work in the world . . . '[183] 'Means' was the key word signifying the whole apparatus of human agency. Like Edwards, the Baptist Abraham Booth argued in 1768 that such means were entirely legitimate in the furtherance of the purposes of God.[184] His co-religionist William Carey put the case more strongly in 1792 in a work entitled *An Enquiry into the Obligation of Christians to Use Means for the Conversion of the Heathen.* Means were now held to be obligatory, for, as Carey contended, the Great Commission is still binding on believers.[185] The new breed of Evangelicals practised what they preached. Edwards supported his friend David Brainerd in a mission to the Indians and at the end of his life undertook the same work himself.[186] Carey established the Baptist Missionary Society, the first foreign mission to spring from the revival, and by 1793 was pioneering its operations in India.[187] Mission was now held to be essential to Christianity.

The activism was at first most apparent among the Methodists. A Moravian devotee of stillness reported to Zinzendorf in 1740 that Wesley was 'resolved to *do* all things himself . . . I will let our Saviour govern this whirlwind'.[188] Wesley's preachers felt a similar gusting impetus from their conversions. 'Now the same spirit that witnessed my adoption', according to one of them, 'cried in me, night and day, "Spend and be spent for God!"'[189] The dynamic was soon equally evident among those Evangelicals who felt in conscience bound to stick to their parish work. Apart from taking Sunday services, Walker of Truro conducted prayers on Wednesdays and Fridays together with burials and baptisms, visited the sick, directed his converts, spent every evening from Monday to Friday speaking either publicly or privately and occupied Saturday in preparing Sunday's sermon.[190] Such men were far from the normal image of an easy-going eighteenth-century parson with plenty of time for diverting recreations and ample dinners. As the evangelistic impulse came to dominate orthodox Dissent in the last two decades of the eighteenth century it gave rise to a transformation of its organisation. Independents and Baptists began to imitate the Methodist itinerancy. In most English counties *ad hoc* societies or county unions were created to evangelise the villages.[191] In Scotland the Relief Church led the way and the brothers Haldane, Robert and James, with Christopher Anderson and others, followed in despatching travelling preachers to the Highlands.[192] Schemes for foreign missions were likewise in the air. Wesley, after all, had travelled to Georgia with the aim of evangelising the Indians even before his decisive experience of 1738. Yet in later life he discouraged missions to the heathen by Methodist preachers on the grounds that there were more immediate prospects of success at home. Consequently, no Wesleyan Missionary Society was set up until 1813. The Countess of Huntingdon toyed with the idea of a mission, again to the Indians of Georgia, and there was a plan for sending men from the Church of England to Bengal.[193] But it was Carey, fired by Captain Cook's account of the peoples of the South Seas, who first brought a mission to birth. His example roused others. In 1795 the London Missionary Society, undenominational at first but increasingly an Independent body, was set up with the South Seas as its chief target; in 1796, although the General Assembly of the Church of Scotland rejected an Evangelical overture for the foundation of a missionary society, interdenominational missionary bodies were founded in Edinburgh, Glasgow and elsewhere; and in 1799 the Church Missionary Society was established to spread the gospel on lines acceptable to the Church of England.[194] Overseas missions were to remain a permanent expression of the energy that characterised the Evangelical movement.

THE DOCTRINE OF ASSURANCE

The three symptoms of discontinuity in the Anglo-Saxon tradition of conservative Protestantism should not be seen in isolation from each other. They are bound together by an underlying factor, a shift in the received doctrine of assurance with all that it entailed. Those who pursued the High Church quest for holiness with single-minded devotion frequently felt a nagging doubt. For all their self-discipline, were they to be numbered among those finally saved? Their efforts gave them no certainty; sometimes their failures heightened their anxiety. So the novel assurance they discovered in Evangelicalism was greeted with relief. Again, continental Protestantism exercised its most decisive influence on the origins of Evangelicalism not in the sphere of practice but in that of doctrine. The Moravians taught that assurance is of the essence of faith. By embracing this principle for a while and approximating to it throughout his life, Wesley was one of those responsible for disseminating a newly enhanced doctrine of assurance.[195] And the dynamism of the Evangelical movement was possible only because its adherents were assured in their faith. Without assurance, the priority for the individual in earnest about salvation had to be its acquisition; with it, the essential task was the propagation of the good news that others, too, could know the joy of sins forgiven. All this is not to claim that assurance appeared for the first time in the Evangelical Revival. On the contrary, as Professor Rupp has pointed out, the doctrine was rooted 'deep within the Puritan tradition'.[196] There was as much desire for confident knowledge of one's own salvation in the seventeenth century as in the eighteenth. But if there was a common preoccupation with assurance, the content of the doctrine was transformed. Whereas the Puritans had held that assurance is rare, late and the fruit of struggle in the experience of believers, the Evangelicals believed it to be general, normally given at conversion and the result of simple acceptance of the gift of God. The consequence of the altered form of the doctrine was a metamorphosis in the nature of popular Protestantism. There was a change in patterns of piety, affecting devotional and practical life in all its departments. The shift, in fact, was responsible for creating in Evangelicalism a new movement and not merely a variation on themes heard since the Reformation. For that reason it demands close scrutiny.

Calvinists had faced a problem. They believed in predestination in a strong sense. God is sovereign in determining who should be saved. A favourite text, Romans 8:30, teaches that 'whom he did predestinate, them he also called: and whom he called, them he also justified: and whom he justified, them he also glorified'. God's purpose in predestination would certainly be fulfilled. Nobody chosen, called and justified by God could fall away so as not to share in heavenly glory. Yet it frequently happened that men and women professing to have become true Christians deserted the faith. Experience seemed to suggest that justification was no guarantee that believers would persevere to the end. The parable of the sower apparently supports this view by declaring that some 'receive the word with joy' but 'in time of temptation fall away' (Luke 8:13). A solution to the dilemma was found by the Elizabethan Puritan divine William Perkins in the doctrine of temporary faith. It was possible, he held, for a person numbered among the non-elect, those not chosen for salvation, to possess faith for a time but then for it to pass away.[197] Consequently, there was a doubt hanging over the faith of any individual. He could not be confident that he was elect and would therefore be saved. Ordinary Elizabethan Puritans experienced few difficulties in this area, for in the sixteenth century the notion of temporary faith held by Perkins had not yet been popularised.[198] But Perkins and a host of seventeenth-century divines in his wake insisted on its implications. A person, they urged, must question whether or not his faith is permanent. Already, in the sixteenth century, it had been mooted among Calvinists that saving faith does not necessarily include assurance.[199] Now it was taught that the lack of assurance is in some ways an advantage. The ignorance of the believer about his future destiny would drive him to scrutinise himself for signs of grace. He was told that he should 'rest not satisfied without a persuasion from the Spirit of Adoption that God is your Father'.[200] But self-examination was protracted. 'These things', wrote the Scot William

Guthrie in his immensely popular *The Christian's Great Interest* (1659), 'will keep a man in work all his days'.[201] Confidence in one's own salvation was the rare blessing of a mature faith. 'No Christian', wrote Perkins, 'attaineth to this full assurance at the first, but in some continuance of time, after that for a long space he hath kept a good conscience before God, and before men . . . '[202] Many might not reach the experience until after death.[203] The developed Puritan view of the subject is formalised in the Westminster Confession. Certainty of being in a state of grace is attainable in this life. But there is a major reservation. 'This infallible assurance doth not so belong to the essence of faith, but that a true believer may wait long, and conflict with many difficulties before he be partaker of it.'[204]

The difficulties were expected to be substantial, for the Christian life was conceived as a constant struggle. The conflict was partly with temptation. The believer must flee from sin. But equally there was an obsession with doubt. Perhaps the inclination to sin was itself a sign that God's grace had not yet been planted in the heart. The numerous Puritan works of casuistry were designed to deal with precisely this fear. Thomas Brooks's *Precious Remedies against Satan's Devices* (1669) enumerated among the diabolical methods for keeping souls in 'a sad, doubting, questioning, and uncomfortable condition' the suggestion that 'their graces are not true, but counterfeit . . . faith, is but fancy'. The remedy was rigorous self-examination. Brooks offers a checklist of ten particulars for distinguishing between sanctifying and temporary grace.[205] Perhaps it is no surprise that scrutiny according to so thorough a catalogue merely served to intensify the terrors about the fate of his soul felt by William Grimshaw in 1739, shortly before his conversion to an Evangelical faith.[206] Yet Puritans were convinced that this introspective technique was the kernel of the spiritual life. They appealed to the scriptural injunction to 'give diligence to make your calling and election sure' (2 Peter 1:10). High on the lists of the signs of grace – of which Baxter alone supplies at least four[207] – was the evidence of works. The Reformation had decried all reliance on works as a means of meriting salvation, but increasingly works were valued as an indication of the reality of divine grace.[208] To do good was a sign of sanctification, the Spirit's fruit in the life of the true believer. It was this concern with works that, according to the sociological pioneer Max Weber, drove Protestants to 'worldly asceticism', the disciplined lives in the secular world that gave rise to capitalism.[209] Certainly the attention paid to works generated an imperative to godliness. The individual was called upon to validate his faith by his works; but, finding his works to be imperfect, he was driven back to reliance on God. The quest for assurance, together with its non-attainment, created 'the internal spiritual dynamic of puritan religion'.[210] The style of piety persisted into the eighteenth century wherever Puritan divines continued in esteem. In 1716 John Willison, Minister of the South Church, Dundee, urged self-examination on intending communicants. 'I pity those poor trembling, and doubting souls, who cannot attain to any light or clearness about their condition', he declares. 'To such I would say, that you ought to wait on God, and hold on in the way of duty to your lives' end, and whatever discouragements you may meet with therein, God in his own time will let you know that your labour is not in vain.'[211] A persistent phase of gloom was a sign of true religion. Assurance was by no means the norm.

The doctrine among Evangelicals was far more robust. 'I *knew* that I was His child', wrote Howel Harris, the emphasis being his own.[212] 'My God! I know, I feel thee mine', echoed Charles Wesley.[213] His brother John, with characteristic thoroughness, set off to Germany shortly after his experience of 24 May 1738 to investigate the authentic Moravian view of the matter at its source in Herrnhut. His mentor Böhler had taught that a man cannot have peace with God without knowing that he has it. Wesley discovered at Herrnhut that, although certain Moravian leaders concurred with Böhler, others, including Zinzendorf and Michael Linner, the oldest church member, held that assurance may come long after justification. More usually, however, according to Linner, forgiveness and a full assurance of forgiveness come 'in one and the same moment'.[214] So Wesley returned from his visit believing that assurance is not intrinsic to faith but a distinct gift;[215] and yet that assurance is the normal possession of the believer. This position he maintained for life, though sometimes stressing the one side and sometimes the other.[216] Thus the first Methodist Conference of 1744 announced that no man can be justified and not know it; yet the Conference of 1745 admitted that there may be cases where a sense of God's pardoning love is not a condition of his favour.[217] We preach assurance, explained Wesley in old age, 'as a common privilege of the children of God; but we do not enforce it, under the pain of damnation, denounced on all who enjoy it not.'[218] Other Evangelicals likewise taught that assurance is the 'common privilege of the children of God', though the Calvinists, believing in the perseverance of the saints, necessarily held that the Christian is sure not only of his present state of grace but also of his future share in glory. The sermons of Romaine and Hervey seemed to suggest there is no true faith without assurance, and Grimshaw actually held this opinion.[219] Walker of Truro thought there was a risk in this direction of identifying faith with feeling, and preferred to rest assurance on the objective work of Christ.[220] The intermediate view that prevailed in the Church of England was that of Venn. Faith, he taught, must not be based on inward feeling only. Yet real faith produces a clear and permanent sense of dependence on Christ. 'No one can possess it', he contends, 'without being conscious he does so . . . '[221] Later Evangelicals in the Church of England admitted that the comforts of religion may sometimes be withdrawn, either by God or by Satan.[222] But the eclipse would be temporary and an awareness of the favour of God would return. 'It is not reasonable . . . to suppose a man to have the Spirit of God', according to Joseph Milner, a leading Evangelical author, 'if he have no evidence of it.'[223] Assurance, in the teaching of the fathers of the

Evangelical movement, is the normal experience of the believer from the time of his conversion onwards.

Ordinary Christians touched by the revival enjoyed a new style of piety. Converts seeing the glory of Christian truths, according to Jonathan Edwards, could no more doubt them than doubt the existence of a blazing sun in a clear sky.[224] There was no need for a plunge into anxious discouragement, Abraham Booth declared, for the Christian has as much warrant to believe as the hungry to feed. Accordingly, for Booth, wrestling was no longer with fears but with sins alone.[225] It is a dangerous error, asserted an early Methodist preacher, to suppose that a man may be accepted by God and yet be unaware of it. 'To be a real member of Christ's Church is to feel Christ in us.'[226] Doubt over one's standing with God could arise only when the sense of pardon was not incontestably clear.[227] For the most part it was banished from Christian experience. There was still self-examination with a view to discovering the marks of a real change made by the Spirit of God.[228] Now, however, the process was, as it were, non-recurrent: it was expected that the verdict would be favourable. If ever there appeared gloom or fear that an individual had no part in Christ, he would be able 'to prove his [sic] self a believer, by proving his whole dependence for salvation is on Christ alone'.[229] The difference from traditional teaching was unmistakable. A Methodist preacher exhorted a Dissenter not to rest till he was sure that Christ had died for him. 'I hate to hear people talk of being assured of any such thing', was the retort.[230] Another Methodist, Thomas Payne, had believed. 'But', he recounts, 'I had a Calvinian library, which I often read. And hence I imbibed that miserable notion, that it was absolutely necessary every believer should come down from the mount. Hence I was persuaded that . . . I must doubt of my justification, which those wretched casuists lay down as one mark of sincerity. For want of knowing better, I listened to these, till I lost the witness of the Spirit.'[231] The age of such Puritan casuists was passing.

There was an important consequence of their supersession by new teaching. In the devotional life there was bubbling confidence. 'O! with what joy', declared Whitefield, '– joy unspeakable – even joy that was full of and big with glory, was my soul filled, when . . . a full assurance of faith broke in upon my disconsolate soul!'[232] The radiant spirit was most apparent in adversity. During the battle of Fontenoy in 1745 wounded Methodist troops rejoiced to be going to Jesus; a preacher with both his legs taken off by a cannon ball was laid across a cannon to die, but as long as he could speak was praising God; another who suffered injuries to both arms announced that he was as happy as he could be out of paradise and survived to report to Wesley that it was 'one of the sweetest days I ever enjoyed'.[233] Such striking exuberance was rooted in a settled inclination to be happy. Sins were certainly forgiven; there could be delight in fellowship with Jesus. There were, of course, exceptions among Evangelicals. The hymn-writer William Cowper suffered from inveterate melancholy.[234] But in his case the disposition was a result of anxieties that sometimes took him over the boundary of insanity. In general, Evangelicals turned from a spirituality that expected bouts of despondency to a calmer, sunnier devotional life.

The turning point between the two attitudes to assurance can be located precisely. It occurred in the work of Jonathan Edwards at Northampton, Massachusetts, during the revival of 1734–5. As he was at pains to stress, there was no novelty in the content of his teaching. His sermons consisted of 'the common plain Protestant doctrine of the Reformation'.[235] Nor was the phenomenon of revival new. There had been five similar harvests of souls at Northampton under his father-in-law and predecessor as minister, Solomon Stoddard, and another four or five under his own father at East Windsor.[236] What was fresh was the pastoral guidance Edwards offered to converts. Those who claimed to have undergone a decisive spiritual experience were interviewed by the minister. If he was satisfied that they had truly been converted, he assured them that they were real Christians. Received Puritan practice would have been to encourage them to wrestle through their own doubts and fears over a protracted period. Consequently, Edwards was sharply criticised for his departure from customary ways. He had two justifications. Guidance was essential to avoid the sheer distress that some would otherwise unnecessarily suffer; and the confident avowals of conversion that resulted from his practice stimulated an awakening of spiritual concern in others.[237] Edwards recounts the effect on those who had previously doubted if they were among the elect:

> Grace in many persons, through this ignorance of their state, and their looking on themselves still as the objects of God's displeasure, has been like the trees in winter, or like seed in the spring suppressed under a hard clod of earth. Many in such cases have laboured to their utmost to divert their minds from the pleasing and joyful views they have had, and to suppress those consolations and gracious affections that arose thereupon. And when it has once come into their minds to inquire, whether or not this was true grace, they have been much afraid lest they should be deceived with common illuminations and flashes of affection, and *eternally* undone with a false hope. But when they have been better instructed, and so brought to allow of *hope*, this has awakened the gracious disposition of their hearts into life and vigour as the warm beams of the sun in spring have quickened the seeds and productions of the earth.[238]

The better instruction Edwards subsequently systematised in his book *The Distinguishing Marks of a Work of the Spirit of God* (1741). He sets out a checklist of signs that conversion had been valid. Through it others in the Reformed tradition learned how to hearten new believers rather than throw them back into painful introspection. Edwards created an Evangelical framework for interpreting Christian experience.

How could he be so bold? It was because he was far more confident than his Puritan forefathers of the powers of human knowledge. A person, he held, can receive a firm understanding of spiritual things through a 'new sense' which is as real as sight or smell. Unbelievers might languish in ignorance of God, but at conversion the Holy Spirit originates 'a new inward perception or sensation of their minds'.[239] Assured knowledge of God is therefore possible. This was the capacity he encouraged among those touched by revival. Edwards's attention to epistemology, the theory of knowledge, was typical of his age. The emerging Enlightenment was generating an imperative to enquire into the nature of things. The philosophically inclined were reflecting in particular on how human beings acquire knowledge. John Locke was primarily responsible. In his *Essay concerning Human Understanding* (1690) he denies that the mind possesses innate ideas. Nobody, he teaches, is born with automatic knowledge, even of morality of God. All we know comes through the five senses from the external world. Experience is the source of all understanding.[240] Traditionalists were scandalised that the powers of the mind were held to be so circumscribed. Others felt they could not dispute Locke's premisses. But, while accepting his axiom that knowledge comes from experience, they set about explaining what human beings do know in terms that modified Locke's analysis. Thus, for instance, Francis Hutcheson taught that human beings possess a moral sense for discerning right and wrong.[241] Edwards's 'new sense' is analogous to Hutcheson's moral sense. Responding to the Lockean spirit of the age, he was postulating a capacity for religious knowledge acceptable to philosophers of his era.

The determining influence of Locke over Edwards has in the past been exaggerated.[242] He absorbed a variety of other recent authors including the Platonist Henry More, the scientist Isaac Newton and the French philosopher Nicolas Malebranche. Edwards's teaching in moral philosophy, logic and metaphysics differs from Locke's.[243] Yet it remains true that the debt to Locke in certain specific fields was substantial.[244] And there is a palpably Enlightenment tone about Edwards's form of expression. Although he is prepared to describe the soul's awareness of God in traditional theological language as a spiritual infusion or in phraseology derived from the Platonic tradition as illumination, he is generally eager to translate the older idiom into up-to-date terminology.[245] The new sense, he says, is 'what some metaphysicians call a new simple idea'.[246] Because philosophical discourse in his day was shaped so largely by Locke, Edwards inevitably speaks as his disciple. For Locke, knowledge derived from the senses is certain. Edwards was simply extending the range of senses available to a human being when he put the capacity to embrace the gospel in that category. Once seen in that light, knowledge of God is also indubitable. It is something not to be brooded over in solitude but to be joyously affirmed. Edwards derived his confidence about salvation from the atmosphere of the English Enlightenment.

The case of Wesley is similar. The issue of whether we can be certain of being in a state of salvation was raised for him by Jeremy Taylor in 1725. He found temporary solace in the belief that 'our sincere endeavours' guarantee us present acceptance by God.[247] Preoccupation with the question increased in the 1730s. Sincerity, good works and the contempt of the world[248] remained the rather sandy foundation for his hope of salvation. Responsible as he was for instruction in aspects of philosophy and diligent as he was in his reading, Wesley necessarily formulated his concern for assurance in intellectual terms. How is God known? A variety of sources was available. His favourite John Norris, for example, offered a theory of knowledge drawn from a blending of Platonic and Cartesian sources.[249] But Wesley, like Edwards, was affected by Locke. He read the philosopher in 1725 and gave the *Essay concerning Human Understanding* more extensive study in 1727 and 1732.[250] He later appealed explicitly to Locke's authority, propagated his writings and, while disagreeing on points like his low valuation of logic, concurred in the thrust of his argument about the processes of gaining knowledge.[251] Certainly Wesley agreed with Locke in rejecting innate ideas. Infants brought up without religious instruction, he contended, would have no more knowledge of God than the beasts of the field.[252] Understanding is the fruit of experience.

Probably the largest debt in the field of epistemology was owed by Wesley to Peter Browne, Bishop of Cork and Ross, whose work *The Procedure, Extent, and Limits of Human Understanding* (1728) Wesley abridged during three months in 1730 and followed closely in his own philosophical compendium in later life. Browne transposed Locke's *Essay* into a theological key. He also rejected Locke's doctrine that ideas may come from reflection, that is, the operation of the human mind on itself. The sole source of ideas is direct sensation of the external world. It followed, according to Browne, that knowledge of God, who as spirit is not part of the material external world, could only be indirect, the result of reasoning about experience.[253] The early influence of Browne upon Wesley was twofold. On the one hand, he was encouraged to adopt as his enduring point of view the appeal to experience shared by Browne with Locke. On the other, the tendency of Browne's teaching was to distrust any claims to immediate experience of God. But that was a position in which Wesley could not bear to abide. He craved assurance. 'I want that faith', he wrote in his journal early in 1738, 'which none can have without knowing that he hath it.'[254] He was driven towards seeking direct experience of God.

It was the Moravians who taught him that it is possible. One of them in Georgia enquired whether Wesley had the witness within.[255] Peter Böhler insisted that to know God he must lay aside 'that philosophy', no doubt Wesley's supposition, buttressed by Browne, that claims to direct contact with God are a symptom of enthusiasm – the eighteenth-century term for fanaticism.[256] Experience showed Wesley in 1738 that the pardon of God may be felt. It confirmed the conviction drawn from empiricist writers that knowledge is a matter of sensation. He characteristically describes faith in almost identical terms to Edwards. It is 'a supernatural inward sense, or sight'.[257] Faith in the spiritual world is what sight is in the natural. 'It is necessary', he writes, 'that you have the *hearing* ear, and the *seeing* eye, emphatically so called; that you have a new class of senses opened in your soul . . . '[258] Like other Enlightenment thinkers, Wesley teaches that the only valid source of knowledge is what is experienced by the senses, but he adds, as it were, a sixth sense. He agrees with Hutcheson, for instance, that there must be a moral sense for human beings to have awareness of right and wrong; but he diverges from Hutcheson in claiming that it is not natural to man. It is imparted as a supernatural gift of God.[259] The basis of Wesley's doctrine was still Browne's epistemology. Although he now held that direct knowledge of God is possible, it comes, as Browne claimed, through sensation alone: this he termed the 'Direct Witness'. Confirmation of the knowledge can be derived from reasoning about experience, the evaluation of the marks of a true believer: this he called the 'Witness of Our Own Spirit'. The two witnesses agree, but the first, because it is the work of the Spirit of God, is incontrovertible. Wesley was charged by critics with holding 'perceptible inspiration', the belief that the Spirit communicates his will infallibly to an individual. Although Wesley rebutted the charge by pointing to the need to evaluate the evidences of grace, it remains true that he propagated a strong view of the certainty instilled in the believer by the Spirit.[260] It often seemed the greatest novelty about Methodism. At Leeds, uproar was caused by a convert claiming to know that his sins were forgiven.[261] When Charles Wesley preached that 'we might know our sins forgiven in this life, yea, this very moment', an early Methodist recalled, 'it seemed to me new doctrine, and I could not believe it at all'.[262] The Methodist teaching about assurance was new because it was part and parcel of the rising Enlightenment. It was a consequence of Wesley's application of an empiricist philosophy to religious experience.

THE INFLUENCE OF THE ENLIGHTENMENT

To recognise the alignment of Edwards, Wesley and the revival with the Enlightenment has not been customary. The whole movement of eighteenth-century thought has been depicted as irreligious in tendency. Voltaire's assault on revealed and organised religion has been taken to be typical.[263] The trends within the Enlightenment, on this view, necessarily acted as a solvent of Christian orthodoxy. Reason was banishing superstition. The new prestige of science associated with the name of Isaac Newton inspired the ambition to investigate all aspects of the world with the aim of dispassionately establishing truth. As wisdom spread from the enlightened elite, it was believed, tyranny in church and state would be put down and humanity would progress towards a happier future. It is generally acknowledged that the temper of the age affected religion in Britain. Deists put themselves beyond the bounds of the churches by rejecting the very notion of revealed religion. Their slogan was the title of one of the chief works produced by this school of thought, *Christianity not Mysterious* (1695) by John Toland.[264] Within the Church of England the Latitudinarians attempted to meet the Deists on their own ground of reason. The clergyman cast by many in the role of Locke's successor as England's leading philosopher, Samuel Clarke, gained a Cambridge DD by arguing that 'no article of the Christian faith is opposed to right reason'.[265] Clarke's *Scripture Doctrine of the Trinity* (1712), though not endorsing unorthodoxy, contended that received Trinitarian doctrine had no explicit biblical sanction either. He persuaded many that Trinitarianism was a matter of abstruse metaphysics alien to the spirit of primitive Christianity.[266] John Simson, professor of divinity at Glasgow, taking his signal from Clarke, adopted a similarly liberal – though biblicist – position in theology.[267] Later in the century the Church of Scotland was to produce a crop of distinguished scholars who stood in the vanguard of the Scottish Enlightenment.[268] The intellectual leaders of English Dissent, nourished in their academies, were similarly swayed by the secular learning of the day. Unrestrained by subscription to articles or a confession of faith, they moved less equivocally towards the Socinian heresy that denies the divinity of Christ. Joseph Priestley, chemist as well as theologian, was perhaps the most eminent of these 'rational Dissenters'.[269] The effect of the Enlightenment on the churches was undoubtedly to liberalise thought. The Evangelicals, by contrast, were wedded to orthodoxy. It is hardly surprising that they should be supposed to have been exempt from the influence of the Enlightenment.

The revival, furthermore, has often been treated as a reaction against the tide of rationalism.[270] Certainly, Evangelicals treated reliance on reason as a grand cause of spiritual deadness. The gospel, according to the Baptist Abraham Booth, is 'contrary to every scheme of salvation which human reason suggests'.[271] Evangelicals in Scotland dismissed those influenced by Hutcheson as 'paganized' divines.[272] Learning could appear a dangerous snare. To one early Methodist the study of Latin and other scholarly languages was firmly set down as an alternative to Christian devotedness.[273] To another, the pursuit of education seemed the high road to heresy. 'I hoped my acquaintance with authors on most subjects might be of some use to me', he reflected; 'but I was greatly mistaken . . . If I attempted any such thing, I was instantly filled with my old deistical ideas again.'[274] Accordingly some seemed to turn from reason to emotion. One Methodist became 'the weeping prophet', another 'the *damnation preacher*'.[275] Conversion, according to an ex-Methodist, could be a matter of psychological self-indulgence. 'At last', he recalled, 'by singing and repeating enthusiastic amorous hymns, and ignorantly applying particular texts of scripture, I got my imagination to the proper pitch, and thus I was born again in an instant . . .'[276] Wesley himself appeared to encourage this withdrawal from the world of the intellect to the dispositions of the heart. In the preface to his *Sermons* of 1746 he famously remarked, 'I design plain truth for plain people'. He therefore avoided, he continued, philosophical speculations, intricate reasonings, show of learning, difficult words, technical terms and an educated manner of speaking.[277] Wesley can plausibly be represented as no more than a popular propagandist – or, if anything more, then as a 'believer in dreams, visions, immediate revelations, miraculous cures, witchcraft, and many other ridiculous absurdities, as appears from many passages of his Journal, to the great disgrace of his abilities and learning . . . '[278] This contemporary estimate has often been echoed subsequently. It is easy to depict Wesley the pedlar of quack medical cures such as marigold flowers for the plague[279] as credulous, uncritical, a champion of the ancients against the moderns. Voltaire seemed to him a 'consummate coxcomb'.[280] Wesley, together with the whole revival movement, can appear to be devoted to resisting the Enlightenment's march of mind.

This was not, however, Wesley's own estimate of the matter. 'It is a fundamental principle with us', he claimed, 'that to renounce reason is to renounce religion, that religion and reason go hand in hand, and that all irrational religion is false religion.'[281] On 11 June 1738, less than a month after the turning point of his life, he preached before the University of Oxford on 'Salvation by Faith'. There was no ranting or hectoring, but instead logical order, careful argument and a nearly total absence of exhortation.[282] Increasingly, Wesley is being recognised as an Enlightenment thinker in his own right.[283] The sceptical Enlightenment of the continent he certainly rejected, but the whole cast of his mind was moulded by the new intellectual currents of his time. Supremely he was an empiricist. He drew out the implications of his position in many fields alongside the area of epistemology that has already been examined. His beliefs in religious tolerance, freewill and anti-slavery have rightly been identified as Enlightenment affinities.[284] So was his antipathy to 'enthusiasm'. He spelt out his attitude in a letter to Thomas Maxfield, an early preacher who eventually led a secession from Methodism that laid extravagant claims to special revelations. 'I dislike something that has the appearance of *enthusiasm*', wrote Wesley: 'overvaluing *feelings* and inward *impressions*: mistaking the mere work of *imagination* for the voice of the Spirit: expecting the end without the means, and undervaluing *reason*, *knowledge* and *wisdom* in general.'[285] Likewise Wesley's loyal followers could appeal to 'rational, scriptural evidence'; favour a rational religion that deprecated visions and revelations; incur censure from Moravians for being 'so full of law and reason'; and accord the highest praise to a society by calling its members 'sincere, peaceable, humble, and rational Christians'.[286]

Other Evangelicals spoke in similar vein. Joseph Milner defended Adam of Winteringham as a teacher of divinity properly called rational; Walker of Truro advised his young converts to take a course in logic.[287]

The Independent Thomas Gibbons published verse entitled, 'A Religious, the only Reasonable Life; or Reason and Religion the Same'; the Baptist Abraham Booth condemned Socinianism as 'unphilosophical'.[288] Preachers on the Evangelical fringe could lapse into rationalist heresies that drifted towards Unitarianism.[289] Seceders from Wesley's connexion in north-east Lancashire actually formed a Methodist Unitarian movement.[290] Among the great majority who retained their orthodoxy, Evangelical religion was rarely chosen as an escape-route from the fearful illumination of modern thought. Only in upper social circles did a number of people, swayed by Latitudinarianism or Deism, begin to doubt the evidences of Christianity before embracing the gospel.[291] Rather, Evangelicalism was accepted along with many characteristic traits of the Enlightenment. Its emergence was itself an expression of the age of reason.

To recognise the early phase of Evangelicalism as an adaptation of the Protestant tradition through contact with the Enlightenment helps explain its timing, a problem that has baffled many commentators. Why should the revival have begun in the 1730s? The great French historian Elie Halévy offered the fullest proposed answer in 1906. The fusion of traditional Protestant piety with High Church loyalties, the achievement of the Wesleys, was possible, according to Halévy, because of the continental influence that led to their conversion and the Welsh example that stimulated field preaching. But an essential third condition explaining the warm reception given to the message was an industrial crisis in 1739 creating popular unrest that was directed into religious channels.[292] The problem with this hypothesis (apart from doubts about the extent of the alleged 1739 crisis) is that the economic conditions of the industrialising parts of England where distress prevailed were totally different from those in the backwoods of New England; and yet there, too, sustained revivalism broke out.

It is far more convincing to hold the high cultural environment to be the essential novel ingredient. Between 1727 and 1760 Locke's *Essay* appeared in nine separate English editions and four collected editions. Although it would be an error to identify the English Enlightenment with the philosophical influence of John Locke alone, these figures form one index of the rising ascendancy of a new idiom in the intellectual world. Before this period, Locke had been championed only by forward spirits like Joseph Addison in 1711;[293] from about 1730 an empiricism owing a great debt to Newton as well as Locke became the prevailing philosophical temper. In the 1730s both George Berkeley, with his *Theory of Vision* (1733), and David Hume, with his *Treatise of Human Nature* (1739), were pressing empiricist thinking towards more drastic conclusions. Classicism had made corresponding progress in the arts. Alexander Pope's *Essay on Criticism* of 1711 had been a radical summons to rigorous observance of classical literary models. By the 1730s his *Essay on Man* (1733–4), conforming to the ideals he had announced two decades before, enjoyed a great vogue.

The Enlightenment approach, whether in matter or manner, was becoming more general, at least among the educated. The Lockean mode in political theory may have been less prominent during the eighteenth century than was once supposed,[294] but in philosophy, and especially in epistemology, a fresh era was opening. It is hardly surprising that men immersed in the learning of the age such as Edwards and Wesley should recast Protestant thought in the new style and set about persuading others to do the same. The timing of their remoulding of the doctrine of assurance according to empiricist canons has to be understood as a result of the spread of a new cultural mood.

This analysis is confirmed by the attitude of those in the Reformed tradition who most welcomed the revival. They too were men of the Enlightenment. Although he held reservations about Whitefield, the Independent divine Isaac Watts was eager to promote a renewal of religious vitality. In 1737 he arranged the first publication of Edwards's *Narrative* of the revival in his parish; he had already begun corresponding with Walker of Truro following the clergyman's conversion.[295] Watts held Locke to be 'the ingenious Director of modern Philosophy' and many truths of his *Essay* to be 'worthy of Letters of Gold'.[296] Although he rejected Locke's opinion that matter may think and even his repudiation of innate ideas, Watts followed his method in its essentials.[297] The notion of relying on a 'clear and distinct idea', for example, is drawn direct from Locke.[298] He was persuaded by Locke to embrace universal religious toleration.[299] Watts shares the characteristic ideals of the *avant-garde* of his day: moderation, a concern for utility and an admiration for the classical in art. The obscure he could not abide, whether in philosophy or literature. His achievement in the modification of the Psalms for public worship he succinctly described as 'dark expressions enlightened'.[300] Likewise his friend Philip Doddridge made constant appeal to Locke in his lectures to students for the Dissenting ministry.[301] Doddridge was opposed to subscription to any creed for the sake of free enquiry; he used English rather than Latin as the medium of instruction for the sake of clarity.[302] The great seventeenth-century Puritan divines John Goodwin and John Owen he dismissed with the comment that he was not very fond of 'such mysterious men'.[303] Doddridge can appear a conundrum for having both favoured the revival and trained ministers who carried freedom of thought to new lengths. The conundrum is resolved, however, when it is recognised that Doddridge was as much an Enlightenment thinker as a Calvinist theologian. The 'enlightened' tone of his teaching could lead students either towards unorthodoxy or towards gospel preaching – for both were rooted in the Enlightenment. Men training for the ministry in contemporary Edinburgh, where Locke's *Essay* appeared in the curriculum in the 1730s, could similarly emerge either as Moderate literati or as Evangelical leaders like John Erskine and John Witherspoon.[304] When the Enlightenment impinged on Calvinism, the result was not necessarily a doctrinal downgrade. From the 1730s onwards it could generate the new light of the gospel.

RESISTANCE TO ENLIGHTENMENT

Since the adoption of revivalism was bound up with a whole new cultural mood, it is no wonder that it encountered deep-rooted resistance in the Reformed tradition. In America, as is well known, opponents of Whitefield in Presbyterianism denounced the new-fangled ways so vehemently that a schism occurred. The Old Side wished to reject candidates for the ministry infected by Whitefield's indiscriminate zeal or his neglect of traditional points of church order and, significantly, accused the New Side of holding over-rigid views of assurance.[305] Similar happenings in Scotland have been less noticed. The Seceders who had left the Established Church over patronage in the 1730s welcomed Whitefield to Scotland in 1741. But they were not content with hearing plain preaching of the gospel. They wished, as Whitefield complained, 'to set me right about the matter of church government and the solemn league and covenant'. The evangelist would not turn rigid Presbyterian or confine himself to Secession pulpits. He was 'determined to go out into the highways and hedges'.[306] The Seceders rated ecclesiastical punctilio above gospel outreach in the manner of the seventeenth century. Their ethos, even in the later eighteenth century, was that of the Puritans. They maintained terminological exactitude in doctrine, intense self-scrutiny in devotion. Conscious of their own imperfections and depravities, they frequently fell into doubts about their salvation. 'Hence they were often sorrowful, when they might have been glad . . . '[307] Yet there were signs of change. Some of their ministers began to pay less attention to approved patterns of piety from the past and turned to their own independent researches. New light, as it was actually called, was dawning. Both branches of the Secession, the Anti-Burghers and the Burghers, split as a result of the New Light controversies of the 1790s. The occasion for debate was whether ministers were still bound to hold, following the Westminster Confession, that the secular ruler had power over the church and that the solemn league and covenant taken by Scots in the seventeenth century was still binding. But the underlying issue was whether they should embrace Enlightenment attitudes. Knowledge, held the progressives, advances over time. Consciences should not be tied to earlier statements of faith. The Westminster Confession might err. They claimed that 'no human composition . . . can be supposed to contain a full and comprehensive view of divine truth; so . . . we are not precluded from embracing . . . any further light which may afterward arise from the word of God . . . '[308] They were rejecting, like Doddridge, the principle of subscription. The ranks of the 'New Lichts' swelled in the early nineteenth century, for they were active in evangelism. But a dwindling minority of Seceders continued in the traditional ways, faithful to their archaic testimony as the 'Auld Lichts', long into the nineteenth century.

The introspective piety of pre-Evangelical days lingered on elsewhere. Its strongest bastion was the Highlands of Scotland. On their fringe, at Rhu in Dumbartonshire, McLeod Campbell discovered this apparently joyless form of religion in the 1820s.[309] It was to survive into the late twentieth century in the Gaelic-speaking territory of the north-western coastline and the Western Isles. In the mid-nineteenth century, its heartland was still Ross-shire. Lowlanders criticised Highland religion for its expectation of a fictitiously high standard of spiritual experience. 'The Christian Highlander, they say, is employed in determining whether he is a true servant of Christ or not, when he should be proving that he is so by being "up and doing".'[310] Conversely, the Highlander was astonished at the ease with which the Lowlander adopted the language of assurance: 'he thinks the confidence with which his brother speaks cannot always be in his heart, and if it is not there, he cannot, he thinks, be right in using words which express it'.[311] Highland religion seemed marked by gloom and an extraordinary inhibition about receiving communion until the believer attained the rare confidence that he was a child of God.

Among the Calvinist Dissenters south of the border the old ways tended to pass away more rapidly. In 1814 a traditionalist was lamenting their loss of 'peculiarity of character' through 'laxity of principle, and indiscriminate zeal which distinguished the Methodists'.[312] Yet there was resistance among them to itinerancy as an unwarranted instance of being 'up and doing'.[313] In Wales 'the strange fire' of Evangelical preaching was held at bay by Baptists until late in the eighteenth century.[314] And in East Anglia tensions in the Norfolk and Suffolk Baptist Association culminated in schism in 1830.[315] The issues were closely related to those in America which in the 1820s spread an anti-mission movement among Baptists.[316] The evangelistic imperative was felt to be less important than testimony to the truth. For Baptists this meant an insistence on believer's baptism as a condition of communion. William Gadsby, minister at Manchester from 1805 to 1844, provided a rallying-point for those who adhered to this principle, the Strict Baptists.[317] As the nineteenth century wore on, this minority of Calvinistic Baptists emerged as a separate denomination. Their piety remained modelled on pre-Enlightenment patterns. The title of the biography of their minister at Trowbridge who died in 1857 is eloquent of an earlier world: *Mercies of a Covenant God, being an Account of Some of the Lord's Dealings in Providence and Grace with John Warburton*. It is replete with accounts of soul-searching anxieties. 'Where is your good hope now, that you have talked about? . . . O how I sank down into the very pit of despair, and could only whisper, "Let not the pit shut her mouth upon me".'[318] Frowning on decadent times, the Strict Baptists maintain their witness down to the present, chiefly in the rural nooks of the south-east.[319] In the 1970s their publications were on sale in the

Free Presbyterian book-room in Inverness. Although the Strict Baptists were touched by later Evangelical influences, the core of the religion they shared with the most traditional of Highland Christians was still the Puritan divinity of the seventeenth century.

ENLIGHTENMENT ASSUMPTIONS

The Evangelical movement, however, was permeated by Enlightenment influences. Its leaders would casually refer to the opinion of Locke as settling an issue or to his *Essay* as providing the best account of the human mind.[320] The empiricist method learned by the eighteenth century from Locke became equally habitual. Thomas Scott appealed to the joint authority of 'the Scriptures and universal experience and observation'; Henry Venn put together experience and scripture, in that order.[321] Edwards rejected all views built upon 'what our reason would lead us to suppose without, or before experience'.[322] This was to adopt the inductive method of science. Isaac Newton had shown the eighteenth century the power of scientific investigation to discover truth. Why should its methods not be applied elsewhere? Hypotheses should be put to the test of the facts. Moving from the particular to the general, the investigator could establish general laws. Thus Wesley was reluctantly forced to admit that errors about the Trinity could accompany real piety when he came across an instance of it because, he declared, 'I cannot argue against matter of fact'.[323] Consequently, there was in the eighteenth century and long into the nineteenth no hint of a clash between Evangelical religion and science. 'We can make no progress in any science', wrote Venn, 'till we understand its first principles. In religion it is the same, that science, in which we all are most deeply interested.'[324] Admittedly a few Evangelicals in the Church of England were attracted by Hutchinsonianism, a system of belief rejecting Newton's views on the ground that the Bible contains a complete system of natural philosophy. T. T. Biddulph of Bristol held this position, as did William Romaine in his earlier years. But it is significant that Romaine was weaned from Hutchinsonianism as his Evangelical convictions deepened and Walker of Truro tried to guard Oxford undergraduates against imbibing the system.[325] Far more common was a warm appreciation of Newton, such as that of Joseph Milner.[326] It is the context of a fascination with science that explains much of Wesley's apparent credulity. He actually published a book on electricity, a field then on the borders of knowledge, as a curative agency.[327] It was impossible to distinguish in advance between promising and unpromising areas for exploration, but investigation, he held, is essential. Experiments, he urged, were the foundation of success in medicine.[328] In the light of these assumptions, it is not surprising that Evangelicals frequently spoke of true Christianity as 'experimental religion'. It must be tried by experience. Wesley called his 1780 hymn book 'a little body of experimental and practical divinity'.[329] Edwards summed up the attitudes of his co-religionists. 'As that is called experimental philosophy', he wrote, 'which brings opinions and notions to the test of fact; so is that properly called experimental religion, which brings religious affections and intentions, to the like test.'[330] Evangelicals held Newtonian method in high esteem.

A number of consequences flowed from this position. Early Evangelicals, like their educated contemporaries, had an anti-metaphysical bent. In the past, it was generally held, philosophers, especially of the scholastic camp, had spent their time spinning cobwebs of discourse that obscured reality. Now investigation of the facts made antiquated theories superfluous. Thus John Witherspoon, the organiser of the Evangelical party in the Church of Scotland who crossed the Atlantic to become Principal of Princeton, found there that teaching was 'tinctured with the dry and unedifying forms of the schools . . . He introduced into their philosophy all the most liberal and modern improvements of Europe'.[331] Venn, by concentration on observation and scripture, avoided 'all abstract reasoning about the nature of the soul'.[332] Josiah Conder, a learned and highly orthodox Congregationalist of the early nineteenth century, preferred plain scripture language to what he called the 'vain philosophy' of the Westminster Assembly's catechism, by which he meant Puritan technical terms like 'effectual calling'.[333] 'Keep off metaphysical ground', declared Richard Cecil, probably the leading thinker among Evangelicals in the Church of England at the turn of the nineteenth century.[334] Aversion to imposing theoretical structures on scripture probably grew over time, culminating in Simeon's dictum, 'Be Bible Christians, not system Christians'.[335] Systems were not only distant from the facts; they were also bound to generate differences of opinion. Enlightenment Evangelicals were eager to avoid disputation. Biddulph steered clear of 'controverted points of doctrine'.[336] One of two grand criticisms made by Wesley against the Puritans was that 'they drag in controversy on every occasion, nay, without any occasion or pretence at all'.[337] His desire for peace was echoed by an early follower. 'I have always been averse to disputing', wrote John Mason. 'I remember how much I suffered thereby in the beginning of my turning to God. And I believe it would be happy if all the children of God would strive to agree as far as possible . . .'[338] Methodism, it has been pointed out, was remarkably free in its earlier years from internal doctrinal controversy.[339] It was a symptom of a principled preference for harmony over exact theological definition.

The devotion to science, experiment and investigation nevertheless did not lead to a rejection of all philosophy. On the contrary, it generated its own philosophical stance. Like their contemporaries, Evangelicals saw a law-governed universe around them. Order had been established by the Creator. The natural world furnished material for praise. Thus once at the seaside William Wilberforce broke out into exuberant delight that God, far from erecting a granite wall to prevent incursions by the sea, appointed its bounds by means of mere grains of sand.[340] Natural theology was important. There were abundant evidences in the world of God's design. The chief role of reason, according to the Evangelical leaders as much as their orthodox contemporaries, was to weigh up the evidences in the way popularised by William Paley.[341] Reason must conclude in favour of the existence of a God who could reveal his will. This was no mere hope: James Lackington, a bookseller who deserted Methodism for freethinking, was restored to his faith by a battery of books on the evidences.[342] In the early nineteenth century the task of welding this scientific apologetic into the body of Christian theology was triumphantly achieved by Thomas Chalmers.[343]

Chalmers built on a class of writing increasingly regarded as the foundation of Evangelical thinking, the works of the Scottish common-sense school of philosophers. The founder of the school, Thomas Reid, argued in his *Inquiry into the Human Mind* (1764) that human beings perceive not ideas, as Locke had supposed, but the real world direct. This realism, or common-sense view, allowed that certain basic axioms of thought are grasped intuitively.[344] It enabled Evangelicals to express in a fresh way their belief in the accessibility of God. Defenders of the validity of conversions at Cambuslang anticipated an aspect of Reid in asserting the trustworthiness of the senses.[345] In fact, John Witherspoon, the organiser of Scottish Evangelicals before his departure to Princeton, claimed to have done battle for the philosophy of common sense for a decade before Reid published his treatise.[346] Certainly Witherspoon expounded the views of Reid and his circle, 'some late writers', once he reached America: 'there are certain first principles, or dictates of common sense, which are either simple perceptions, or seen with intuitive evidence. These are the foundation of all reasoning, and without them to reason is a word without a meaning. They can no more be proved than you can prove an axiom in mathematical science . . . '[347] Like Reid, Witherspoon uses this premiss as a ground for repudiating unwelcome elements in the thought of Locke and Hume. He regards Locke's objections to innate ideas as 'wholly frivolous': human beings do possess, for example, a moral sense. Again, Hume had contended that, since all we know is in the form of ideas, there can be no guarantee that our ideas correspond to reality. His scepticism extended to questioning the very existence of causation. Witherspoon insists on the contrary that the condition of all understanding of the world is the belief that everything must have a cause.[348] The conviction that the pattern of cause and effect, the scientist's natural assumption, underlies all phenomena was to pervade Evangelical thinking long into the nineteenth century and, in many quarters, beyond that.[349] The academic citadel of such an approach was Scotland, but, as common-sense philosophy spread through the propagandism of Dugald Stewart and the Edinburgh reviewers, it increasingly became the standard supposition of the educated Englishman as well.[350] Evangelicals were integrating their faith with the rising philosophy of the later Enlightenment. They were in harmony with the spirit of the age.

OPTIMISM

Likewise Evangelicals reflected the later Enlightenment in their optimistic temper. The eighteenth century, and especially its second half, characteristically believed that humanity enjoyed great potential for improvement. It was the later eighteenth century that witnessed the emergence of the idea of progress, the conviction that human beings are steadily becoming wiser and therefore better.[351] The Arminianism of the Methodists can be seen as an equivalent 'optimism of grace', a theology that does not limit the possibility of Christian renewal to the narrow company of the elect.[352] There was also greater hope about the human condition among the Reformed who learned from Edwards to trust their quickened religious affections. One of Edwards's American disciples calculated that the proportion of the lost to the saved would eventually be in the ratio of 1 to 17,456 1/3.[353] All Evangelicals were animated in their outreach by the expectation that salvation was widely available.

They were also convinced that God wished human beings to be happy. 'Holiness is happiness' has been seen as the fundamental principle of Wesley's theology.[354] Many of his followers behaved as though it were. 'I was still happy', wrote one; 'but found a strong desire to be more holy that I might be more happy.'[355] But identification of happiness as the grand goal of humanity, a typical theme of more liberal moralists such as Hutcheson, was shared by Calvinists as well as Methodists. Maclaurin wrote a 'Philosophical Inquiry into the Nature of Happiness'; Venn contended that the children of God 'know more pleasure than any people on earth'; Wilberforce described happiness as the end of civil society.[356] Yet Methodists went further in embracing the perfectibility of man. Wesley disagreed with those enlightened thinkers who supposed that all human beings might attain perfection. For Wesley, only the regenerate possess the essential qualification. Experience taught him, however, as he explains in his *Plain Account of Christian Perfection* (1766), that believers may progress to a state in which they are free from all known sin. No aspect of Methodist teaching gave more openings for ridicule. There was much glee when a 'perfect' sister was detected stealing coal from a 'sanctified' brother.[357] Wesley sorrowfully noted such cases, concluding that the state could readily be lost, but he nevertheless insisted on its reality.[358] He criticised the Puritans for holding so low and imperfect a view of sanctification.[359] In this area, Calvinist Evangelicals remained loyal to their Puritan forefathers. Their arguments could nevertheless be cast in a new form. Walker of Truro, for instance, laid down that perfect holiness is necessary for perfect happiness; the perfect can be a work of God alone; it cannot be expected in this life; there can be progress only in the perfecting of the believer.[360] Even in rejecting Wesley's teaching, Walker commended progress towards the goal of happiness. As much as the Utilitarian school, Evangelicals elevated happiness into the primary place among human objectives. In seeing vital Christianity as the way to achieve it, they were differing from the Utilitarians about means, not ends.

The basis for optimism was the doctrine of providence. God, Evangelicals believed, is in active control of the world. Confidence in his government formed a larger part of their creed than might be supposed. For Biddulph, providence was pre-eminent among doctrines.[361] John Newton's hymns are full of the theme. 'There is no such thing as accident', he declared.[362] A distinction was normally drawn between general providence, the overall superintendence of the earth by its Creator, and particular providences, direct divine interventions in the course of events. Particular providences were of two kinds, displaying either the judgement or the mercy of God. In the first category were put such incidents as when the town clerk of Wincanton, after reading the Riot Act to disperse the hearers of a Methodist preacher, immediately started to bleed copiously from the nostrils, became a lunatic and soon afterwards died.[363] Judgement was expected on nations as well as individuals if they persisted in corporate sins like tolerating the slave trade.[364] Likewise mercies could be individual or national. Thomas Scott believed that God 'always steps in just at the crisis . . . I never prayed for money but I got it'.[365] One Methodist was brought to conviction of sin by deliverance from an overturning wagon; another saw divine mercy in a narrow escape from the fall of a building; another, in being preserved from the collapse of a roof in a Cornish tin mine.[366] The Eclectic Society of London ministers spent a meeting in 1801 cataloguing 'the signal interpositions of providence in favour of Britain during the late war'. The death of the Czar of Russia shortly after he had turned from opposing to supporting France was cited as one of many wonderful examples.[367]

If particular providences were sometimes dwelt on at the Eclectic, however, there was also a tendency to caution. In accordance with the canons of scientific investigation, alleged instances of special divine interference contrary to the course of nature should be treated with 'the most rigid suspicion'. The providential government was normally maintained by 'second causes', that is, through the regular course of events.[368] The very order of the Newtonian universe, in history as well as nature, glorified its divine architect. 'God has so assigned to things their general tendencies', according to Wilberforce, 'and established such an order of causes and effects, as . . . loudly proclaim the principles of his moral government . . . '[369] If Evangelicals were sometimes more forward than their contemporaries in detecting the hand of God in particular events, their general attitude to providence was close to that taught by central eighteenth-century thinkers such as Joseph Butler and Edmund Burke.[370] All alike saw the historical process as subject to the divine sovereignty. That was why all alike could look with confidence to the future.

Optimism was expressed in doctrinal form through belief in a millennium. In the eighteenth century millenarianism was no fanatical aberration of the social outcast but a common preoccupation of the intellectual. Expectation of a future state of unblemished happiness on earth was widely held by philosophically inclined theologians of the time.[371] Many Evangelicals shared the belief. It appeared to be founded on the statement in Revelation, chapter 20, that Satan would be bound for a thousand years. It drew extra support from passages predicting a future outpouring of the Spirit in the latter days. The particular version of the belief held in the Enlightenment era was uniformly postmillennial: the second coming of Christ, that is to say, would not take place until after the millennium. There would therefore be no sharp break from preceding history. Rather, the millennium would be the result of gradual improvement – a belief that shaded into the idea of progress. Evangelicals identified the future epoch as a time of peace and glory for the church that would follow on persistent mission.

They could draw on earlier Reformed writers who cherished a similar hope.[372] The outbreak of revival, however, quickened expectations of the imminent approach of the latter days. Erskine expressed such anticipations in his work on Cambuslang, *The Signs of the Times Consider'd* (1742).[373] More famously Edwards announced the same, but added, in a work of 1743, the speculation that the millennium would come to birth in America. 'The new world', he wrote, 'is probably now discovered, that the new and most glorious state of God's church on earth might commence there . . . '[374] Perhaps more congenial to British readers was his subsequent argument, in *An Humble Attempt* (1747), that unfulfilled prophecy is an incentive to prayer.[375] This work, influential in Britain after its republication in 1784, did much to foster millennial expectations. Its editor, the Baptist John Sutcliff, nevertheless expressed the hope that if a reader held different views of prophecy he would not withhold prayer for revival.[376] Doddridge had rejected the very notion of a millennium; Erskine's biographer excused him for his apocalyptic guesswork on the score of youth; and Conder, writing in 1838, treated millenarianism as an aberration.[377] It is clear that the Evangelical world was far from unanimous on the matter. Yet William Carey, explicitly appealing to Edwards, held that no fulfilment of prophecy would intervene before the conversion of the heathen that would usher in the millennium.[378] Similar expectations surrounded the foundation of the London Missionary Society.[379] John Venn, son of Henry, told the Eclectic Society that a future period of peace and glory for the church is clearly predicted in scripture. Scott and Cecil concurred.[380] A Scottish Secession Presbytery minuted in 1787 its anticipation of 'the iminent [*sic*] glory of the latter days'.[381] Thomas Chalmers wrote of 'that universal reign of truth and of righteousness which is coming'.[382] The postmillennial theory was evidently widespread. Evangelicals shared high hopes for the future with their contemporaries.

MODERATE CALVINISM

The substance of Reformed doctrine was also remodelled under Enlightenment influence. Apart from Methodists, General Baptists and a few avowedly Arminian clergy, some of the other Evangelical Anglicans, especially by the start of the nineteenth century, were beginning to disclaim Calvinist tenets.[383] The remainder of the Evangelical world, however, was professedly Calvinist. Yet there was also a certain reserve in their allegiance. Edwards was content to be called a Calvinist, 'for distinction's sake: though I utterly disclaim a dependence on Calvin'.[384] The influential Baptist Andrew Fuller similarly declared, 'I do not believe every thing that Calvin taught, nor any thing because he taught it'.[385] John Erskine was Calvinistic in doctrine, but his version, according to his biographer, was 'not the vulgar Calvinism, which exhausts itself on intricate and mysterious dogmas'.[386] In 1808 an Evangelical clergyman claimed to have heard only one sermon on predestination in twenty years.[387] 'Calvinism', according to John Newton, 'should be, in our general religious instructions, like a lump of sugar in a cup of tea; all should taste of it, but it should not be met with in a separate form.'[388] This diffuse doctrinal system was sometimes labelled 'moderate Calvinism'.[389] In its refusal to subordinate free inquiry to the authority of one man, in its repudiation of mysterious dogma, in its very moderation, it was a typical product of the eighteenth century.

This was supremely true of its moralistic tone. Because Evangelicals preached salvation by faith, they could on occasion be heard teaching that obedience to the divine law is humanly impossible or dismissing misrepresentations of Christianity as a 'mere system of ethics'.[390] A small number like Romaine so exalted faith that they seemed to depreciate law. Romaine was said to have made many antinomians – that is, to have propagated the view that the believer is not bound by the moral law.[391] This was the central charge thrown in the face of Evangelicals as a whole by their critics. They were condemned for subverting morality, at least at the theoretical level. But it was a judgement wide of the mark in nearly every case. With the possible exception of Romaine and a few others, Evangelicals urged only that obedience to the law will not avail for salvation unless preceded by faith. 'Christ the lawgiver', declares Venn, 'will always speak in vain, without Christ the Saviour is first known.'[392] Venn's *Complete Duty of Man* insists that faith is essential if the law is to be obeyed. Equally, however, it teaches that the law does apply to the believer.[393] Hence Evangelicals concentrated on ethical themes. Venn dwells on family duties. Of Erskine's published sermons it was noted that sound morality occupied by far the greatest part.[394] All true faith, according to a central plank of Scott's teaching, 'must and will prove itself by its fruits'.[395] The summons to holiness was constantly heard in the Evangelical pulpit. A preoccupation with moral instruction was quite as characteristic of Evangelicals as of other theological parties of the period.

Evangelical Calvinism was also moderate in that it rejected stronger views of God's control of human destiny. Evangelicals were not fatalists. Human beings, they emphatically taught, are responsible agents. Edwards supplied the intellectual tools for their approach in his treatise on *Freedom of the Will* (1754). He distinguishes between the natural necessity of human actions, which he rejects, and their moral necessity, which he commends. He means that human beings are not compelled by God to behave contrary to their wills. Rather, the freedom they possess to follow their wills is compatible with their actions being determined by preceding conditions. Free acts are not forced, though they are caused. This was to contend that human beings are part of an ordered universe, but to hold that they are nevertheless responsible for what they do.[396] Edwards was reinterpreting the sovereignty of God as an expression of the law of cause and effect. He was echoed in England by Scott, according to whom divine sovereignty is 'in perfect consistency with . . . free agency and accountableness'.[397] Hence human beings, not God, are responsible for their own damnation. Scott laid down, in the words of his biographer, 'that none fail of being saved . . . except by their own fault'.[398] Evangelicals generally repudiated the traditional Calvinist doctrine of reprobation, that God had destined certain souls to hell. Instead human beings were considered guilty of causing their own perdition by failing to respond to the gospel.[399]

A cardinal principle of the Evangelical scheme was 'duty faith'. 'It is the duty of men to believe', declared William Goode at the Eclectic.[400] Debate between Calvinists touched by enlightened thought and those who clung to older forms often revolved round whether believing in Christ can be considered a moral obligation. It was the so-called 'modern question'. The controversy first arose among Northamptonshire Independents in the late 1730s. It drew in John Gill, the Baptist systematic theologian, on the side of the traditionalists, while Doddridge supported the promoters of 'modern' thought.[401] Strict Baptists continued to repudiate duty faith in the following century.[402] The issue proved the dividing line between Evangelicals and unreconstructed Calvinists partly because it was highly practical. If believing was an obligation, preachers could press it on whole congregations. If it was not, they could merely describe it in the hope that God would rouse certain predetermined hearers to faith. Those on the modern side had a rationale for urgent evangelism, the so-called invitation system.[403] The logic of Evangelical activism was founded on the doctrine of duty faith. It was most systematically expounded by Andrew Fuller, the Baptist theologian who put his convictions into practice by becoming the first secretary of the Baptist Missionary Society. Fuller's *The Gospel Worthy of All Acceptation* (1785) is the classic statement of eighteenth-century Evangelical Calvinism. But the inspiration for Fuller's thinking can be traced back to Edwards, and especially his formulation of the distinction between moral and natural necessity.[404] Edward Williams, the Independents' equivalent of Fuller, owed the same debt to Edwards; Milner refers to Edwards's 'masterly treatise on Free-will'; and in Scotland Chalmers declared, 'My Theology is that of Jonathan Edwards'.[405] There can be no doubt that Edwards was the chief architect of the theological structures erected by Evangelicals in the Reformed tradition. That was sufficient to ensure that they were built on Enlightenment foundations.

PRAGMATISM

The spirit of the age – flexible, tolerant, utilitarian – affected Evangelicals as much in practice as in thought. Field preaching, an activity that lay near the heart of the revival, was an embodiment of the pragmatic temper. If people would not come to church, they must be won for Christ in the open air. Wesley was content to flout parish boundaries for the sake of souls. His justification was the effectiveness of open-air preaching in attracting large numbers, inducing conviction of sin and bringing about conversions.[406] His utilitarian approach to religious practice helps explain why Wesley quotes Proverbs and Ecclesiastes more than any other biblical books.[407] The same temper informed other Evangelicals. Typical was Charles Simeon's attitude to church buildings. Having acquired the living of Cheltenham in 1817, he set about planning a new church. It must be severely functional, like a Methodist chapel rather than a traditional parish church. In the style of Bentham's Panopticon, it was to be cheap and there were to be no obstacles to clear vision such as pillars. Supremely it was designed for preaching. Old churches, he wrote, were not built to preach in; 'and after the experience we have had of them it is folly & madness to raise for preaching any further edifices after their model'.[408]

Likewise the priorities of the gospel dictated the deployment of manpower. Although the most rigid of Evangelical churchmen remonstrated with Wesley on the matter,[409] the existence of Methodism depended on the use of preachers who were laymen. Their employment in church work became a hallmark of Evangelicals in the Church of England, so that their creation in 1836, the Church Pastoral Aid Society, was intended (to the disgust of High Churchmen) to support lay parish workers as much as additional parish clergy.[410] In the Church of Scotland, Chalmers's ministry was notable for the revival of the lay office of deacon;[411] and in English Dissent laymen were sent out in large numbers as preachers, either voluntary or salaried.[412] Justification for female preaching was expressed in terms of gospel pragmatism. 'If persons who exercise in the ministry are of good report', wrote the Primitive Methodist leader Hugh Bourne with particular reference to women, 'and the Lord owns their labours by turning sinners to righteousness, we do not think it our duty to endeavour to hinder them . . . '[413] It was an argument from success characteristic of Evangelicals in their Enlightenment era.

The relegation of principle relative to pragmatism was evident in church order. Methodism, as some of its nineteenth-century defenders delighted to insist, was totally flexible on this subject.[414] Wesley and his adjutants initially had 'no plan at all'.[415] He approved of bishops, but could see no reason for restricting certain powers to their office and so was prepared, in 1784, to ordain presbyters for America himself.[416] The Plan of Pacification of 1795 that settled connexional practice after Wesley's death was an avowed compromise between contesting parties.[417] Above all, Methodists did not have to be Christians. Admission as full class members was open to all who sought the forgiveness of sins and not just to those already converted. Thus a preacher could report 38 new members of a group of classes at the same time as 23 additions 'to the church of the living God'.[418] There was no correspondence between joining the Methodist organisation and entering the true church. The organisation was merely an environment suitable for gaining converts.

A similar utilitarian spirit modified ecclesiastical order among Dissenters, whose *raison d'être* had originally been the creation of church structures of pristine purity. The New Connexion of General Baptists could not contemplate merger with the Old partly because the traditionalists insisted on the imposition of hands at baptism and the obligation of abstaining from blood.[419] For the Evangelicals of the New Connexion these were matters of no importance. Particular Baptists shifted towards opening the Lord's Table to those not baptised as believers when Evangelicalism moderated their views.[420] Likewise, in the ecclesiastical strife of Scotland over patronage in the later eighteenth century, the Evangelicals of the Popular party, unlike their Moderate opponents, thought little of the letter of church law.[421] In England churchmen were prepared to co-operate with Dissenters. 'In this day of darkness and licentiousness', according to Walker of Truro, 'it becomes all the friends of the Gospel to bear with one another; and while they differ in opinion and denomination, to unite together in heart and endeavour for the support of the common cause.'[422] Although it has recently been pointed out that modern denominations were themselves the fruit of the revival, essentially agencies to promote evangelism,[423] it is nevertheless true that what Whitefield called a *'catholic spirit'*[424] was generated among Evangelicals. This was perhaps most true in the late 1790s when home mission was at its most vigorous. The interdenominational temper led to the establishment of a variety of organisations for joint endeavour, including the London Missionary Society, which drew supporters from many denominations in the early years, and the British and Foreign Bible Society, an enduring monument to the possibilities of co-operation.[425] Such bodies exemplified an abandonment of exclusive denominationalism, a certain practical empiricism.

LITERATURE

The Enlightenment mood affected the taste of Evangelicals. It is a mistake to suppose that they shunned literature. Theatrical performances they did deplore as tending to demoralise, but many of them enjoyed reading selected dramatic works in the privacy of their own homes. Fiction, a recent art form, was sometimes suspect, although Wesley abridged a novel for publication. Almost the whole Evangelical world read poetry.[426] Even among Dissenters there was an elite devoted to literature. The Pattisson family of Witham in Essex eagerly discussed the latest publications in the years round 1800.[427] After ordination to the ministry of the Church of Scotland in 1742, according to his biographer, John Gillies's 'fondness for literary amusements still continued'.[428] Taste was formed by the classics. Gillies could quote appositely (and 'sometimes with pleasantry and humour') from Horace and Virgil; Horace was likewise Wesley's favourite.[429] The Baptist divine Robert Hall declared 'that we should gain nothing by neglecting the unrivalled productions of genius left us by the ancients, but a deterioration of taste . . . '[430] Hence classical canons of literary decorum prevailed. '"What is it", asked Wesley, "that constitutes *a good style?*" Perspicuity and purity, propriety, strength, and easiness, joined together.'[431] Wesley commended Swift, with his ability to wield language like a rapier, as a model for imitation.[432] Swift's favourite genre, satire, was indulged in by Evangelicals, for were there not classical precedents? The most telling published assault on the Moderates in the Church of Scotland, John Witherspoon's *Ecclesiastical Characteristics* (1753), was no reasoned argument, but rather an unrestrained ridiculing of their legalistic zeal for church discipline.[433] Charles Wesley incorporated satirical sallies against Calvinism in many of his hymns.[434] It was all entirely in accordance with the temper of an age that regarded ridicule as the test of truth. Protestantism had passed through a Baroque phase but had emerged, in its Evangelical form, in the Augustan atmosphere of the Enlightenment.

There is a host of other symptoms. The prolix scholarship of the earlier era was no longer congenial. Although John Wesley prepared for the press his father's discursive *Studies in the Book of Job* (1735), he later commented that it 'certainly contains immense Learning, but of a kind which I do not admire'.[435] The number of headings in Independent sermons plummeted from the twenties or thirties to two or three.[436] Erotic themes, common in the religious verse of the Metaphysical school and still present in Watts, were eliminated by Charles Wesley and censured by his brother.[437] The Evangelicals were deeply imbued with the classicism of Pope. Thus, when their Unitarian friend Crabb Robinson tried to interest the Pattissons of Witham in Kant and Wordsworth, they resolutely adhered to a preference for Locke and Pope.[438] Reading as much as thinking was conditioned by the Enlightenment.

The Augustan tone is evident in the greatest literary achievement of the revival, the hymnody of Charles Wesley. Because his hymns express feeling in common vocabulary, they have sometimes been classified as anticipations of the Romantic era. The content and the manner, however, both bear testimony to their being characteristic expressions of Augustanism.[439] The themes are often the standard ones of the classical lyric poet. There is, for example, material on melancholy and pastoral retirement.[440] Because content is primarily dictated by Christian purpose, however, the manner is where the spirit of the age is most obvious. Classical metrical forms are drawn from near contemporaries. Dryden, Pope and Prior are the models for diction, and Cowley, the pioneer of classical correctness in verse, is admired.[441] While also esteeming poets of more traditional idiom such as Milton and Young, Charles Wesley is therefore a disciple of the *avant-garde* of the literary Enlightenment in its displacement of the Baroque. Emotion is present, but always carefully controlled, as in his meditations on the passion of Christ. The hymns are didactic, for their aim is to transmit doctrine to their singers. Yet this quality is as much a feature of the age as a consequence of their purpose. The language is clear, precise and succinct. Latin-derived words are strategically placed to embody a depth of meaning in a short space. In one line profundity can be mingled with paradox: 'Impassive He suffers, immortal He dies'.[442] John Wesley supplied the most apt comment on his brother's verse in his preface to the 1780 *Collection of Hymns* for Methodist use: 'Here are (allow me to say) both the purity, the strength, and the elegance of the English language – and at the same time the utmost simplicity and plainness, suited to every capacity'.[443] It was a fair statement of the Augustan ideal.

Hymns were part of a vast educational campaign undertaken by the Wesleys. As much as the circle around *The Edinburgh Review*, they aimed for the diffusion of useful knowledge. 'Reading Christians', according to John Wesley, 'will be knowing Christians.'[444] He designed *The Christian Library* (1749–55) in fifty volumes to convey practical divinity to his followers. It consisted of a range of spiritual classics, many of them abridged by the editor. In conformity with his canons of taste, Wesley believed in brevity: 'if Angels were to write books', he remarked, 'we should have very few Folios'.[445] Conciseness would increase circulation. His preachers dutifully absorbed the series, and in the 1820s there still existed sufficient demand to call for the reprint of one of the volumes every two months.[446] From 1778 Wesley issued the monthly *Arminian Magazine* to encourage the reading habit. By his death its monthly circulation was about 7,000.[447] One Methodist father presented each of his children with a copy of the magazine bound in calf.[448] Wesley tried to maintain a tight control over ideas circulating in the connexion. No preacher, on pain of expulsion, was to go into print without his approval, or, after 1781, without his correction.[449] 'There are thousands in this society', wrote a critic in 1795, 'who will never read anything besides the Bible, and books published by Mr Wesley.'[450] All preachers were to carry a stock of his writings to sell or give away; they must spend at least five hours a day in study; they were to ride with a slack rein so that, in imitation of Wesley himself, they could read on horseback; and when staying in a household above an hour, they should take out a book to read as a good example.[451] Wesley expected high standards of his men. In 1764 he read through the first edition of his work on philosophy with the London preachers.[452] Through the efforts of the preachers, through class meetings and reading circles, learning spread among the rank and file of his followers. Because they wasted little time but regularly heard sermons, poor Methodists, it was said, possessed far more knowledge than the poor in general.[453]

What was systematically organised in Methodism was pursued ad hoc in other branches of Evangelicalism. Yet a zest for understanding the faith, often nourished on libraries in church or chapel, did much to foster self-improvement. Dissenting colleges modelled on Trevecca multiplied, and their products, though rarely distinguished academically, at least imbibed a respect for knowledge.[454] From 1783 the Sunday School movement expanded rapidly, bringing basic instruction to thousands.[455] Tracts were distributed in huge quantities. From 1799 there existed the Religious Tract Society for their production.[456] In 1841 alone the Methodist Book Room sold 1,326,049 of them.[457] Evangelical religion was a force dedicated to the advance of education. The imperative of spreading Bible knowledge demanded it. But the fulfilment of religious duty was entirely in harmony with the goal of eighteenth-century progressive thinkers: the enlightenment of the masses.

HUMANITARIANISM

The Evangelical education enterprise has often been seen as a masked attempt at social control. The bulk of the population, growing in numbers and entering a phase of rapid social change induced by industrialisation, had to be kept in its place. Evangelical teaching was a suitable tool. Especially in the wake of the French Revolution, submission to the existing order was given a divine sanction.[458] A variant of the argument is the thesis of Ford K. Brown that Evangelicals with Wilberforce at their head were concerned to seize control of church and state in order to seek power through enforcing their own values on the nation at large.[459] It is true that the 'reformation of manners' was an Evangelical preoccupation. Wilberforce and his circle secured in 1787 a royal proclamation against crime and public immorality and formed a Proclamation Society to prod backward magistrates into enforcing it.[460] But this was not primarily designed to enhance the power of the rulers. Significantly, the measure came before the French Revolution had broken out. It was an expression of Evangelical hostility to sin coupled with a pragmatic preparedness to employ state power, as much as private exhortation or pulpit admonition, to do battle with it. Wilberforce's friend Hannah More composed a series of tracts in the 1790s that were intended to repress revolutionary tendencies and were circulated at government expense. *Village Politics* (1792), the first in the series, presents the homely counsel of Jack Anvil, the village blacksmith, to live contentedly in a well-ordered England under the wise dispensations of providence. But if Hannah More insisted on the duties of the poor, she had already written on the obligations of their superiors. In *Thoughts on the Importance of the Manners of the Great* (1788) she had castigated the gentry for neglect of their paternalist role.[461] Like many others in the eighteenth century, Evangelicals put the emphasis in social teaching on reciprocal duties, not exclusively on passive acceptance of their lot by the worse off.

Traditionalist they were, by and large, but Evangelicals believed in a conscientious performance of traditional responsibilities. With the growth of their influence in the following century, a much higher proportion of the gentry resided on their estates in order to take a personal interest in their tenants. It has been suggested that Evangelicalism is a cause and greater residence the effect.[462] Likewise ministers of religion were roused to greater zeal in the performance of their duties. Although in Scotland the custom of visiting the flock had been generally maintained, in England, as the clergy rose in income and social status during the eighteenth century, mixing with their inferiors became less expected of them. The hunting, shooting and fishing parson was a common type. It was the Evangelical movement that prompted the clergy to greater diligence, especially in cottage visiting.[463] Stirring the elite in church and state to care for the poor may have had the effect of reinforcing the social order, but its primary purpose was to ensure that the privileged took a humane interest in the welfare, secular and spiritual, of those committed to their charge.

Philanthropy was actively promoted by Evangelicals from the beginning of the movement. Wesley's generosity was legendary. He would scatter coins to beggars, he waded through snow in old age to raise money for the relief of the poor and he died worth virtually nothing because his considerable income from publications was given away.[464] Evangelicalism as a whole taught that good works are a fundamental element of Christian duty.[465] There was continuity between traditional teaching on concern for the poor, as expressed for instance in the religious societies of the Church of England, and the charitable work of Evangelicals. What the revival added was its characteristic zeal. There was a proliferation of local schemes for doing good. Wesley encouraged his followers to visit the sick, going in pairs.[466] The Calvinistic Methodist London Tabernacle ran a workshop for a while and later an employment exchange.[467] Perhaps most strikingly, there were the orphan houses. Halle provided the model. Both Whitefield and Wesley lavished their care on similar institutions, in Georgia and Newcastle respectively. Whitefield expended enormous energy on planning, organising, supporting and defending his orphanage. 'I called it Bethesda', he wrote, 'that is, the House of Mercy; for I hope many acts of mercy will be shewn there . . . '[468] The Evangelical impulse was to give rise to an empire of philanthropy in the nineteenth century,[469] but already before the eighteenth was over almsgiving was becoming systematically organised. Methodism gave rise to a number of Strangers' Friend Societies. The first existed in London by 1784. 'A few poor men', according to Wesley, '. . . agreed to pay each a penny a week in order to relieve strangers who had no habitation – no clothes – no food – no friends. They met once a week, and assigned to each his share of the work for the ensuing week; to discover proper objects (who, indeed, were easily found); and to relieve them according to their several necessities.'[470] Such charitable work can hardly be attributed to the Enlightenment. It was the spontaneous expression of a Christian movement. Yet it was entirely in harmony with the spirit of an age that set benevolence among its highest values.

On the other hand, the greatest example of Evangelical humanitarianism, the anti-slavery campaign, was undoubtedly the fruit of the Enlightenment. Anti-slavery was not intrinsic to Evangelicalism: some of the stoutest defenders of slavery in the American South were preachers of the gospel.[471] It was the tide of opinion running against slavery among the philosophical luminaries of the eighteenth century that prepared the way for British abolition of the slave trade in 1807 and the extinction of the institution in British dominions under an act of 1833. Benevolence, happiness and liberty, three leading principles of the time, all created a presumption in favour of abolition. Unless they had been thoroughly imbued with these values themselves, Evangelicals would not have taken up the cause. As it was, however, Wilberforce and the Clapham Sect, overwhelmingly though not exclusively Evangelicals of the Church of England, dedicated themselves to the elimination of what, with other progressive thinkers, they condemned out of hand. What Evangelicals brought to the campaign was not a fresh theoretical perspective but the dedication that compelled them to act.[472]

The ending of the slave trade did not come about (as was once held) because it had ceased to be profitable to Britain. Evangelicals were by no means pawns in the hands of economic interests.[473] There is nevertheless a tendency in contemporary historiography to play down the Evangelical contribution to anti-slavery. It is true that other groups took important parts. The Quakers, only beginning to be touched by Evangelical religion, supplied money, manpower and ideas, moving into action before the Evangelicals.[474] There was popular radical participation in anti-slavery from the 1790s onwards.[475] The slaves, by their frequent rebellions that created problems of colonial administration, helped free themselves.[476] Yet Evangelicals were central to the whole enterprise. Wilberforce contributed able leadership, his college friendship with Pitt, the Prime Minister, proving a huge advantage to the cause; information was assiduously collected by Thomas Clarkson and the James Stephens, father and son; missionaries fostered sympathy for the oppressed blacks; and in 1831–3 there was a mighty upsurge of Evangelical public opinion in favour of ending slavery.[477] A number equivalent to ninety-five per cent of the connexion's membership signed Wesleyan anti-slavery parliamentary petitions in those years.[478] It has been suggested that mass abolitionism was created not by Evangelicalism but by the vision of artisans whose ambience was also favourable to Evangelical Nonconformity. Yet contemporaries were in no doubt that arguments based on biblical principle did most to rouse anti-slavery feeling.[479] Although favourable parliamentary circumstances must also be taken into account – the Talents administration of 1806–7 was more sympathetic to abolition than its Pittite predecessor and the extension of the franchise in 1832 sounded the death-knell of slavery – it remains true that the main impetus against both trade and institution came from the religious public. Evangelicalism cannot be given all the credit for the humanitarian victory over slavery, but it must be accorded a large share.

POLITICS

Although anti-slavery swept a large proportion of the Evangelical public into exerting pressure on government, in general its leaders discouraged involvement in the political sphere. Here was an area of sharp contrast with their Puritan forebears, who for the most part saw the achievement of a holy commonwealth as one of their grand aims. Partisan endeavour now seemed a diversion from the one essential task of preaching the gospel. 'Politics', declared Thomas Jones of Creaton, a leading Evangelical clergyman, 'are Satan's most tempting and alluring baits.'[480] It is sinful, according to John Witherspoon in Scotland in 1758, for a minister 'to desire or claim the direction of such matters as fall within the province of the civil magistrate'.[481] Even Dissenters, who operated largely as a united political phalanx in the interest of civil and religious liberty, began to have doubts about the wisdom of pressing their cause. It is true that in the early 1790s Robert Hall was defending the freedom of the press and his fellow-Baptist William Winterbotham was imprisoned for preaching sermons allegedly sympathetic to the French Revolution.[482] Political activity in the wartime years that followed, however, was minimal. The Baptist Western Association, for instance, did little more than announce its opposition to military training on the sabbath.[483] Hall became so indifferent to political concerns that he scarcely ever read a newspaper.[484] Fuller was typical of the Evangelical sector of Dissent in deprecating strife between Whigs and Tories: 'it is not for the wise and the good to enlist themselves under their respective standards, or to believe half what they say'.[485] Wesley's legacy to his followers was a 'no politics' rule that forbade the agitation of controverted questions within the connexion.[486] It is clear that Wesleyan voters took no common line. At Bristol in 1784, for instance, they divided in approximately the same proportions as the electors at large.[487]

What vital Christianity entailed, according to many Evangelicals, was a blend of quietism and loyalism. 'I meddle not with the disputes of party', wrote John Newton, 'nor concern myself about any political maxims, but such as are laid down in scripture.'[488] He was no doubt thinking chiefly, as did Wesley, about commands to respect those in authority and pay taxes.[489] Wesley lamented popular participation in politics, discouraged sympathy for the Americans in the 1770s and helped ensure that after his death official Methodism steered a steady patriotic course.[490] Wilberforce eulogised 'the unrivalled excellence' of the British constitution.[491] Alongside his friends with reforming objectives in the Clapham Sect, there was a much larger bloc of Evangelical MPs from 1784 onwards with unqualified Tory views.[492] Likewise, after the French Revolution the Evangelical clergy were overwhelmingly Tory.[493] Most enfranchised Dissenters continued to prefer the Whigs. Nevertheless, attachment to the existing political order was the most prominent feature of attitudes to public affairs among all sections of Evangelical opinion down to the end of the French Wars.

There were, however, two areas apart from anti-slavery in which sections of the Evangelical world were more liberal. One was the American Revolution. Dissenters and the Popular party in the Church of Scotland generally backed the American cause. Caleb Evans of the Baptist College at Bristol rebutted Wesley's attack on the colonists as a revival of 'the good old Jacobite doctrine of hereditary, indefensible, divine right and of passive obedience and non-resistance'.[494] Most Baptist ministers in the provinces and all but two of them in London were believed to have taken the American side.[495] Scottish Evangelicals similarly upheld the colonists' case. John Erskine warned against conflict with the colonies as early as 1769 and in 1776 called for a compromise settlement.[496] John Witherspoon, the Scottish Evangelical who had become Principal of Princeton, so far forgot his earlier objections to ministers dabbling in politics as to be the only one to sign the Declaration of Independence.[497] The bonds between Presbyterians on the two sides of the Atlantic helped foster the sympathy for American resistance to George III. So did a dislike for oppression and a fear that true religion was under threat in North America from Catholics and Episcopalians.

Similar motives induced many Evangelicals to adopt another liberal stance in the era of toleration. It was to be expected that Dissenters such as Hall would approve of the principle of religious liberty.[498] But so did others. Thomas Scott wrote of 'the vast obligation' owed to Locke for his *Letters Concerning Toleration*.[499] Adam Clarke, admittedly the most Whiggish of Methodist leaders, broadened the principle into an Arminian constitutional axiom. 'Of all forms of government', he commented, 'that which provides the greatest portion of civil liberty to the subject, must be most pleasing to God, because most like his own.'[500] Wesley himself favoured religious tolerance. He opposed the removal of Catholic disabilities, it is true, but on the ground that the Roman Catholic Church was itself theoretically committed to persecution. He was not prepared to tolerate intolerance. Otherwise he was the foe of bigotry, the champion of entire liberty of conscience.[501]

Scottish Evangelicals, though convinced in the same way as Wesley that concessions to Catholics were too much of a gamble,[502] shared a favourable disposition towards religious toleration. It was part of that broad, humane, pragmatic outlook that characterised their attitudes in so many spheres.

THE RISE OF EVANGELICALISM

The Evangelical Revival represents a sharp discontinuity in the Protestant tradition. It was formed by a cultural shift in the English-speaking world, the transition from the Baroque era to the Enlightenment. In most spheres of taste and fancy a new phase opened early in the eighteenth century. The philosophy of Locke was the greatest motor of change, but literature and art, all forms of human expression, were affected. The prose of Addison and the verse of Pope marked a breakthrough to severe classicism from the greater exuberance of the previous age. The Third Earl of Shaftesbury censured Wren, an architect recently venerated, for having failed to follow classical or Italian models and so ruining the skyline of the City of London with buildings tainted by the Gothic.[503] Religion could not go unscathed by such a revolution in taste. It is a commonplace that much Protestant thought followed a path of religious liberalism that led through Latitudinarianism and Socinianism towards a Unitarian destination, though sometimes stopping far short of that goal. What has rarely been perceived is that other strands of Protestantism, despite being tenaciously orthodox, were equally affected by the Enlightenment atmosphere. The legacy of the Puritans, in both faith and practice, was modified by the temper of the new era without losing its grasp of central Christian tenets. The old introspective piety, with its casuistry and reflex syllogisms, and the old polemical divinity, with its metaphysical distinctions and ecclesiastical preoccupations, faded away before the preaching of a simple gospel. A rearguard action was fought by men like Adam Gib, the theologian of the Anti-Burgher Seceders in Scotland, who suffered from gloomy spiritual apprehensions, split his denomination on a fine point of principle and published in his seventy-third year a rambling theological work entitled *Sacred Contemplations in Three Parts* (1786).[504] But the future lay with those who heard or read Whitefield, Harris, Edwards or Wesley. The fulcrum of change was the doctrine of assurance. Those who knew their sins forgiven were freed from debilitating anxieties for Christian mission. Typical was Abigail Hutchinson, a young girl whose experience of conversion Edwards related. 'She felt a strong inclination immediately to go forth to warn sinners', according to Edwards; 'and proposed it the next day to her brother to assist her in going from house to house . . . '[505] The activism of the Evangelical movement sprang from its strong teaching on assurance. That, in turn, was a product of the confidence of the new age about the validity of experience. The Evangelical version of Protestantism was created by the Enlightenment.

[3]

A Troubling of the Water: Developments in the Early Nineteenth Century

---

. . . an angel went down at a certain season into the pool, and troubled the water. (John 5:4)

In the years around 1830 there was a change of direction in Evangelicalism. Not all sections of the Evangelical community were equally affected, but those that took the new path entered a phase in which many of their previous assumptions were superseded. It was not that their most fundamental convictions altered. Evangelicals continued to preach for conversions, to engage in ceaseless activity, to respect the Bible and to dwell on the theme of the cross. But fresh attitudes became characteristic of the movement – towards the church and the world, towards public issues and even towards the purposes of God. A different mood was abroad. It was partly because a new generation was coming to the fore. The old leaders were going to their reward: Robert Hall, Adam Clarke, William Wilberforce, Hannah More, Rowland Hill and Charles Simeon all died between 1831 and 1836.[1] Their successors had risen within an Evangelicalism whose place in the world was assured. They were much less inclined towards a careful pragmatism that would recommend the movement to suspicious onlookers. Rather they expected their views to be given a hearing. They were more confident, more outspoken, more assertive. But the altered tone of much of the Evangelical world was far more than a matter of changing personnel. New influences and fresh circumstances directed currents of opinion into different channels. The shift of mood has often been detected but little analysed. Ford K. Brown notices the change, but his explanation hardly goes beyond the break between the generations.[2] Ian Bradley censures 'a new obscurantism and fanaticism' without diagnosing it further.[3] Alec Vidler, like many others, treats the shift as partly a reaction against the Oxford Movement.[4] In fact, however, the process was well under way before the Oxford Movement

began; and the new Evangelical mood shared a great deal in common
with the Oxford Movement. The fresh trends have recently been valuably
summarised,[5] but they call for more detailed examination. Evangelicalism,
it becomes clear, was far from a static creed.

THE STRATEGY OF MISSION

One of the reasons for the emergence of new views was doubt about
existing methods of spreading the gospel. Organisations like the Bible
Society might be at work, but were they proving sufficiently effective?
Churchgoing was not improving significantly, if at all. During the decade
1811–21 population growth was extremely rapid. In those ten years, in
fact, demographic expansion was at its highest rate in British history.
Although Dissent was spreading, attendance at the parish churches was
falling relative to population, especially in the developing urban areas.[6]
Attention was drawn to the gulf yawning between the Church of England
and the labouring masses by Richard Yates, chaplain to the Chelsea Hospital,
with two works on the need for church extension published in 1815 and
1817. The public disorder provoked by economic troubles in the wake of
the Napoleonic Wars induced politicians to take note. Church building
was seen as the antidote to revolution, and so in 1818 parliament voted
£1 million for new churches.[7] In this context Evangelicals were acutely
conscious of the challenge to their strategy of mission. The people had not
yet been won for Christ. Thomas Chalmers, serving as a parish minister in
Glasgow from 1815, recommended fresh methods of re-Christianising the
urban poor in a series of quarterly papers on the *Christian and Civic Economy
of Large Towns* (1819–23). His technique concentrated on administering poor
relief only through the churches.[8] Some of his proposals were to be widely
heeded in subsequent decades.

Others were driven to believe that the sole remedy lay in an appeal
for divine assistance. In 1821, James Haldane Stewart, a respected London
Evangelical clergyman, issued a call to prayer for a special effusion of
the Holy Spirit. The societies designed to advance the kingdom of Christ,
he argued, had managed to achieve much less than they desired. That
showed 'the inadequacy of means, even of divine appointment, without a
peculiar divine agency accompanying these means'.[9] Stewart's summons,
although in no sense hostile to the religious societies, was the first public
questioning of their potential from within the Evangelical camp. Later in
the decade, stimulated by news of awakenings in America, there was
much prayer for revival.[10] Cries for supernatural aid began to seem
preferable to the plodding methods of the societies. Foreign missions
seemed no more effective than those working at home. The sharpest
challenge to the existing approach came in a sermon preached before the
London Missionary Society in 1824. Edward Irving, a celebrated young

Scottish minister in London, urged that missionaries, like the earliest apostles, should be sent forth 'destitute of all visible sustenance, and of all human support'.[11] They should be compelled to rely on God alone. Why should they need the bureaucratic organisation of a missionary society to back them? Spurning the hospitality of the LMS, Irving created a great stir by denouncing its system of operation. The circle of radicals that gathered round Irving went on to develop a coherent critique of religious societies in general as embodiments of worldly expediency. Pressure from Irving's party induced a number of organisations to symbolise the fact that they were more than business enterprises by opening their meetings with prayer. The Jews' Society first adopted the practice in 1828.[12] There was a powerful onslaught on existing patterns of mission.

THE REVIVAL OF CALVINISM

A second factor that contributed to altering the face of Evangelicalism in this period was renewed interest in Calvinism. In part this movement derived from contacts with Geneva. With the reopening of the continent to British travellers after the defeat of Napoleon, visitors were attracted to the city of Calvin. There, a revival was springing up from roots in Moravian piety. Robert Haldane, a Scottish Evangelical who had launched extensive home missionary work in his native land, turned his attention to Europe in 1816. He settled in Geneva, delivering regular lectures on the letter to the Romans with the intention of re-establishing Calvin's leading doctrines. The depth of conviction and the obvious vitality of the Genevan revival helped create in Britain an idealised vision of the meaning of Calvinism. It was less specific doctrines than 'a way of thinking and a quality of life' that inspired certain British Evangelicals.[13] The man most affected by Geneva was Henry Drummond, a banker who was to become closely associated with Irving. Drummond followed Haldane as spiritual mentor to the Evangelical community in Geneva and, when the state church looked askance on their new-found opinions, encouraged certain ministers to secede. In 1819 Drummond created a Continental Society to employ some of those who withdrew as itinerant missionaries, particularly in France.[14] These roving figures became the exemplars of the new style of missionary envisaged by Irving in his LMS sermon – men relying on providence for their support, spreading gospel light in a dark land. The separation of the Genevan Evangelicals from the state church prepared Drummond and ultimately others to contemplate the same step. And 'Calvinism' became the label for the ideal of a primitive, apostolic Christianity. 'I saw also in the history of the church', declared a speaker invented by Drummond as a vehicle for his own views, 'that in proportion as she became Arminian she relapsed into the world, and that in proportion as she became Calvinistic she came up out of the world.'[15] As in the early years of Elizabeth I, the example of Geneva stirred up reformers of the church in Britain to push ahead with their task.

Native traditions exercised a similar influence. A handful of champions of Calvinism survived from the controversies of the 1770s to sway the minds of the next generation but one. Chief among them was Robert Hawker, a redoubtable clergyman who had laboured at Plymouth since 1778.[16] Another high Calvinist, but in this case an eccentric Dissenter, was William Huntington, an ex-coalheaver who delighted to place the letters 'S.S.' after his name to indicate that he was a 'Sinner Saved'.[17] These were the men alluded to by Simeon in 1815 when he lamented, 'Five pious young men are running into Huntingdon's [sic] and Dr. Hawker's principles, and are leaving the Church'.[18] Simeon was referring to the so-called 'Western Schism'. A number of clergymen in the West Country, led by George Baring, seceded from the Church of England on reaching the conclusion that its principles were incompatible with their Calvinist views. One of them, James Harington Evans, was provided in 1818 with a London chapel by the munificence of Drummond, who no doubt saw this as a parallel enterprise to his efforts in Geneva. Evans had come to see, he wrote, that 'salvation is not of debt but of grace'.[19] Like Hawker, he held that since flawed human works can form no test of the reality of acceptance with God, faith is its sole evidence. Faith was exalted at the expense of works. Dismayed by teaching that he knew would open Evangelicals to censure and alarmed by its disruptive consequences, Simeon preached a sermon in Dublin condemning the Calvinist system as 'unfair and unscriptural'.[20] But the trend of the times was away from the views of men of the older generation like Simeon. In 1811 it was guessed that there were not as many as ten full-blooded Calvinists in the ministry of the Church of England.[21] By the late 1820s, however, Calvinism was the religious vogue among the young at Oxford. Their pulpit idol was Henry Bulteel, Curate of St Ebbe's from 1826, who had been influenced by Hawker.[22] He was in touch with Irving, who was calling his own convictions 'Calvinistical' and teaching that God's sovereignty is so absolute that he was responsible for the fall of man.[23] Simeon's repudiation of human systems was on the decline; there was a growing yearning after the primitive convictions of the Reformation divines.

EDWARD IRVING

Already it has emerged that the central figure in the ferment of the period was Edward Irving. His personal charisma played a remarkable part in changing the direction of Evangelicalism, even if his tragic career ended in an early death. In 1822 at the age of twenty-nine he arrived as minister of the Church of Scotland congregation in Hatton Garden, London. His capacity for self-dramatisation was enhanced by a striking physical presence – an athletic figure standing six feet two inches, with a strong, rich bass voice.

In his later years the hair, in the manner of an artistic genius, was parted right and left so as to hang down on his shoulders 'in affected disorder'.[24] During 1823 his eloquence attracted the cream of fashionable society, so that on one Sunday no fewer than thirty-five carriages bearing aristocratic coronets were counted outside his church. Fame changed to notoriety in 1824 with his sermon before the London Missionary Society denouncing its own missionary methods. Irving's reputation for erratic ways increased when, two years later, in *Babylon and Infidelity Foredoomed of God*, he announced his adoption of distinctive prophetic beliefs. Christ would soon return, he went on to declare, in glory and majesty. Suspicious eyes were turned in Irving's direction. Soon he was teaching that Christ at the incarnation assumed not human nature *per se* but fallen human nature. He continued to assert the sinlessness of Christ (the result of the power of the Holy Spirit), but charges were laid against him which culminated, in 1833, in his deposition from the ministry of the Church of Scotland for heresy on this question. Already the most controversial phase of his life had begun. In 1830 speaking in tongues was heard in two parishes in the west of Scotland, often identified as the first modern instance of the Pentecostal gift. Irving accepted the cases as genuine, and in the following year strange tongues were heard in his own congregation. The scandalised trustees excluded Irving from his own church, and so he established the so-called Catholic Apostolic Church, purveying a strange blend of adventism, tongues, elaborate liturgy and punctilio over ecclesiastical order. Its mentor, though remaining the 'angel' (minister) of a London congregation, lost control over the course of events when a prophet debarred him from appointment as an apostle.[25] Irving fell ill and died in Glasgow in December 1834 when still only forty-two.

What is the explanation of Irving's quixotic career? He was eager to present the full orbit of Christian doctrine in a fresh guise. 'We feel', he wrote in his first work, 'that questions touching the truths of revelation have been too long treated in a logical or scholastic method, which doth address itself to I know not what fraction of the mind; and not finding this used in Scripture, or successful in practice, we are disposed to try another method, and appeal our cause to every sympathy of the soul which it doth naturally bear upon.'[26] He intended to appeal to the heart. There was therefore a need to rouse his hearers by vigorous declamation on vivid themes. In the years of Walter Scott's greatest vogue, it helped if Irving's subject-matter could be tinctured by the atmosphere of an age gone by. 'He affected the Miltonic or Old-English Puritan style', recalled his friend Thomas Carlyle.[27] Anything venerable warranted his respect; anything modern was suspected of degeneracy. The ideal in oratory was not the recent notion of Augustan economy but rhetorical extravagance. The sermon before the LMS was so long that he had to pause twice during its delivery for a hymn to be sung.[28] Contemporary German thought held attractions. Although he disliked the infidelity of Schiller and Goethe, Irving encouraged Carlyle in his study of Schiller and would allude as a matter of course to Goethe's *Faust*.[29] It was Germany, he held, 'where alone any powerful poetry exists'.[30] Nevertheless he was eager to discover any sign that Wordsworth was appreciated.[31] Irving was being swept along by the spirit of the age in its reaction against the manner of the Enlightenment. Bentham, the toast of recent 'enlightened' opinion, was dismissed as 'the apostle of expediency', perhaps the most limited philosopher of the day.[32] Like the young John Stuart Mill in the same decade, Irving was freeing himself from the ascendancy of the Utilitarian mode of thinking; but his liberation was more complete than that of Mill. In short, Irving was a Romantic. He owed his celebrity to a capacity for blending Evangelical religion with the latest intellectual fashions.

THE INFLUENCE OF ROMANTICISM

The chief agent of Irving's liberation was S. T. Coleridge. Again like Mill, Irving discovered in Coleridge a new world of thought and feeling. The ripening friendship of the two men from 1823 to 1826, when, despite continuing mutual esteem, they diverged on account of Irving's prophetic studies, can be traced in Coleridge's correspondence. Coleridge adjudged Irving 'the greatest *Orator*, I ever heard'.[33] For his part, Irving counted Coleridge (as he declared to a surprised religious world) 'more profitable to my faith in orthodox doctrine, to my spiritual understanding of the Word of God . . . than any or all of the men with whom I have entertained friendship and conversation . . . '[34] When taken by Irving to meet Coleridge, a bewildered Thomas Chalmers discovered that there was 'a secret and to me as yet unintelligible communion of spirit betwixt them, on the ground of a certain German mysticism and transcendental lake-poetry which I am not yet up to'.[35] From this intimacy Irving derived a Coleridgean reverence for the ideal. The poet also confirmed in the preacher a developing contempt for the expediency of the age that was to be the germ of much subsequent Evangelical socio-political thought.[36] But most of all, as the Scotsman avowed, Coleridge taught him a 'right conception of the Christian Church'. By 1825 Irving was laying great stress on proper ecclesiastical order and appealing to a typical Coleridgean rationale. 'The twofold nature of man, body and spirit', he asserted, 'maketh it necessary that every thing by which he is to be moved should have an outward form.' Thus 'the visible Church is the sensible form of the heavenly communion'.[37] The substance of his exalted ecclesiology was Coleridgean. Deep draughts of the teaching of Coleridge fortified Irving to lead the adaptation of Evangelicalism into the Romantic idiom of the day.

Romanticism was well fitted to be a vehicle for religious thought. The term is used here not in the narrow sense of the literary generation that was fading by the 1820s but in the much broader sense of the whole mood that was inaugurated by that generation and lasted throughout the nineteenth century and beyond. This was the movement of taste that stressed, against the mechanism and classicism of the Enlightenment, the place of feeling and intuition in human perception, the importance of nature and history for human experience. Goethe embodied the Romantic spirit in Germany, where the initial impact of the movement was strongest, while Wordsworth, Coleridge, Keats, Shelley and Byron represented its various expressions in English verse. Its quintessence was what has been called 'natural supernaturalism', the ability to discern spiritual significance in the everyday world.[38] Awe before the numinous in nature is the hallmark of Wordsworth's poetry, and a revelling in the strange, the uncanny and the mysterious runs like a thread through Romantic art and literature. There was immense potential affinity for religion. Broad and High Churchmanship in Britain were both deeply affected during the nineteenth century,[39] but the Evangelical tradition was no less touched by the new cultural style. This is not to argue that there was an intrinsic bond between the Romantic and the Evangelical. It has frequently been held that such a connection did in fact subsist. 'Now Evangelical Christianity', writes Dr Kitson Clark, 'seems to satisfy all the categories of romanticism, except the love of fancy dress.' The leading Romantic characteristics, as expounded by Dr Kitson Clark, were the importance of emotion and imagination, with a consequent emphasis on moments of intense experience, a profounder appreciation of the values of the past and a spirit of escape and revolt from present conditions.[40] All these, however, far from being part and parcel of the Evangelical Revival, were novelties in the years around 1830. Reason, not emotion, had been the lodestar of the Evangelicals; many of them looked to the millennium of the future, not to the past, for their ideal of a Christian society; and far from wishing to flee from existing conditions, they used normal contemporary methods, whether in business, politics or religion, to accomplish their aims. So the outburst of imaginative energy represented by Irving constituted a revolt against the conventions of the Evangelical world. There was a new appreciation of the dramatic, the extraordinary and the otherworldly element in religion. That is the key to the thought of Edward Irving. His mind bore the impress of a heightened supernaturalism.

MILLENARIANISM

A distinguishing feature of Irving and his circle was the advent hope. Many Evangelicals, as the previous chapter has illustrated, were expecting the millennium to be attained through the preaching of the gospel. Only after this period of prosperity for the church would Christ come again.[41] But an alternative millenarian view had frequently been held in Christian history. Christ would return, according to this alternative version, before the commencement of the millennium. The second advent, far from being deferred to the distant future beyond the triumph of Christ's earthly church, was to be expected imminently. This form of prophetic interpretation is usually called *pre*millennialism (since Christ is to come *before* the millennium) to distinguish it from the *post*millennial view (according to which Christ is to be expected *after* the millennium). Premillennialism was taken up by Irving's new school of Evangelicals. They believed, as their prophetic journal *The Morning Watch* put it in 1830, 'that our Lord Jesus Christ will return to this earth in person before the Millennium'.[42] J. F. C. Harrison has recently attributed this premillennial view to the largely self-educated, characterising postmillennialism, by contrast, as a more intellectually sophisticated belief. Yet, as Professor Harrison himself admits, the distinction cannot be drawn rigidly along these lines. The premillennialists numbered the highly literate and extremely sophisticated Irving in their ranks. The postmillennialists had no monopoly on respectability or scholarship.[43] The distinction was not so much one of educational attainment as of period. Whereas in the first three decades after the French Revolution it was normal among students of prophecy to expect a steady spread of Christian truth, from the 1820s onwards there was a growth of the premillennial advent hope.

The seminal influence in drawing the attention of the Evangelical world to this alternative approach to prophecy was James Hatley Frere, with his work *A Combined View of the Prophecies of Daniel, Esdras, and St. John* (1815). William Cuninghame, a Scottish Presbyterian, had published a premillennial work two years earlier, and was to continue propagating his views in the 1830s,[44] but Frere enjoyed the prestige of predicting, shortly before Waterloo, the downfall of Napoleon. The second coming, he argued, would take place at the start of a phase in the millennium that would occur in 1822–3. In Frere, however, the second coming is treated merely as a metaphor – 'some extraordinary manifestation of the power of Christ'.[45] It is to be a spiritual, not a literal, event. Irving, who imbibed his opinions from Frere, agreed in a publication of 1826 that the advent is imminent, but not literal.[46] In the same year, however, Irving fell to translating from Spanish a strange work by a Chilean Jesuit masquerading as a converted Jew ('Ben-Ezra') entitled *The Coming of Messiah in Glory and Majesty*. It drove its translator to the conclusion that Christ would certainly return in person.[47] The publication of this book in 1827 marked the decisive re-emergence of the premillennialist tradition.

A receptive audience for 'Ben-Ezra' had been created by the growing desire for the conversion of the Jews. Organised missionary work concentrating on the Jews alone was a novelty of the early nineteenth century. The London Society for Promoting Christianity among the Jews was established in 1809 as an interdenominational body and in 1815 was reconstituted as an Anglican organisation.[48] Its prime mover, Lewis Way, was inspired by the prophecies of the return of the Jewish people to their own land and, noticing the connection drawn in the Bible between this event and the last things, came to believe in the nearness of Christ's coming again. Between 1820 and 1822, under the pseudonym 'Basilicus', Way ventured a series of speculations on the future prospects of the Jews in the society's journal *The Jewish Expositor*. Christ, he claimed in the course of the letters, would soon return in person.[49] Four years later the majority of the committee believed the doctrine of the imminent second coming.[50] Most crucially, Way's views had spread to Henry Drummond, who became a Vice-President of the Jews' Society in 1823. It was Drummond, 'abundant in speculations as well as money',[51] who set about exploring prophetic views in depth. He assembled twenty or so people, including Way and Irving, at his country estate in Surrey, Albury Park, for eight days during Advent 1826. It was the first of an annual series of prophetic conferences at Albury that lasted until 1830.[52] If the return of the Messiah is to be associated with the restoration of the Jews, they concluded, the millennium can be located only after the second coming. Conversation ranged over a variety of other topics – the dignity of the church, the iniquities of the religious societies, the political implications of these doctrines – but two of the six major points of agreement at the 1829 conference still concerned the Jews: the Christian dispensation, like the Jewish, would be terminated suddenly in judgements; and the Jews would be restored to their land during the judgements.[53] The gloomy expectations of the Albury participants grew out of their more sanguine hopes for the Jews.

THE ADVENT HOPE

The significance of the emerging premillennial position lay less in its expectation of a coming millennium than in its confidence in the imminent return of Christ. There was little, if any, dwelling on the status reversal of the millennium, whereby the great of the earth would be subject to the authority of the humblest believer. In that respect, the radical eschatology of the nineteenth century differed from what was typical of most millenarian movements.[54] It was, in fact, more concerned with the coming achievement of Christ than with any state of earthly beatitude, more adventist than millenarian. The kernel was what Irving called Christ's 'own personal appearance in flaming fire'. The return, it was often stressed, would be a literal coming. The reason is that previously belief in a visible return by Christ in the flesh had been no part of accepted doctrine. Many Protestants, Irving observed, 'start when you say that Christ will appear again in personal and bodily presence upon the earth'.[55] Like Frere when he wrote *A Combined View*, the most respected Evangelicals did not believe it. Thomas Scott declared in 1802 that in the future there would be 'no visible appearance of Christ'; and in 1830 Charles Simeon assured a correspondent that it was a matter with which he had not the slightest concern.[56] Certain early advocates of a premillennial eschatology spelt out the novelty of their belief in the return of Christ in the flesh.[57] Other writers like Haldane Stewart can be detected hesitating on the brink of deciding in favour of a personal advent.[58] The doctrine long continued to be rejected by the Evangelical mainstream. In a prize essay on missionary work selected by a panel of adjudicators drawn from five denominations in 1842, John Harris, President of Cheshunt College, contended that the coming of Christ would be 'in strange providences, and at critical junctures'.[59] Although he explicitly set aside discussion of whether the coming would be personal, he evidently did not believe it. In the 1840s, in fact, premillennialists sometimes claimed that expectation of a personal advent was confined to their ranks.[60] They were mistaken, but their case was plausible. The belief that Christ would come again in person was an innovation in the Evangelical world of the 1820s.

It was part of the Romantic inflow into Evangelicalism. Christ the coming king could readily be pictured by poetic imaginations fascinated by the strange, the awesome and the supernatural. 'To such minds', a critic of premillennialism argued, 'any other view of the subject is perfectly bald and repulsive, while theirs is encircled with the glory that excelleth. To them it carries the force of intuitive perception; they *feel* – they *know* it to be true.' The advent hope was far more than a bare doctrine. Because the content of the expectation was Jesus Christ himself, the hope became an object of devotion. 'Souls that burn with love for Christ' were 'ready to embrace it almost immediately *con amore*'.[61] To Lord Shaftesbury, for instance, it was something to 'delight in', 'a moving principle in my life'. His close friend Alexander Haldane, according to Shaftesbury himself, 'intensely loved' Christ, 'and ever talked with a holy relish and a full desire for the Second Advent'.[62] There was nothing anomalous, according to the new way of looking at the world, in expecting a divine figure to appear suddenly in the midst of the affairs of the nations. To minds nurtured on earlier ideas of cause, effect, order and gradualness, however, there was little appeal: 'whatever Scripture intimations regarding the future destinies of the Church and of the world involve events out of the usual range of human occurrences, or exceeding the anticipations of enlightened Christian sagacity, are almost instinctively overlooked or softened down'.[63] So the expectation of Christ's personal return attracted younger men in tune with the rising temper of the age, who were prepared to break with part of the legacy of the Enlightenment. But it was left to one member of the younger generation to incorporate the advent hope into an Enlightenment framework. David Brown, once Irving's assistant minister in London and eventually Principal of the Aberdeen Free Church College, published the most popular nineteenth-century restatement of the postmillennial scheme, *Christ's Second Coming: Will it be Premillennial?* (1846). Brown was a man of 'a poetical nature' who wrote verse in his youth, carried about with him a copy of Keble's *Christian Year* and had once been a premillennialist himself.[64] His book was persuasive precisely because, unlike earlier postmillennial advocates, his Romantic temperament led him to commend the personal return.[65] Brown constitutes an exception to the normal rule of the association of this doctrine with the premillennial position. But he well illustrates the cultural affinities of the reviving belief in the second coming as a personal event. Adventism was a symptom of Romanticism.

VARIETIES OF PREMILLENNIALISM

As prophetic interpretation settled into established grooves during the 1830s and 1840s, two schools of thought emerged. The dominant school was that normally called 'historicist', although at the time, because of its origins in Reformation polemic, its advocates usually preferred to style it 'the Protestant view'.[66] With this approach the book of Revelation and the prophecies of Daniel were to be interpreted as narratives that could be decoded by pairing symbols such as vials of wrath with remarkable historical events. The basic premiss was that prophetic references to days should be understood as years. There was great scope for debate about the proper starting point for calculation, but most commentators pointed to 1866–8 as the likely date for the second coming. A chart in *Horae Apocalypticae* (1844), a four-volume work of scholarly prophetic studies published by E. B. Elliott, a Fellow of Trinity College, Cambridge, clearly depicts the beginning of the millennium at a point two-thirds of the way through the nineteenth century.[67] After 1868 commentators nevertheless took the need for recalculation in their stride.[68] Although one of the best known exponents of historicist premillennialism was a Presbyterian, John Cumming, a self-professed populariser of the work of Elliott,[69] this form of the advent hope became most entrenched in the Church of England. It was propagated through the twice-yearly meetings of the Prophecy Investigation Society, begun in November 1842 at St George's, Bloomsbury.[70] H. M. Villiers, the Rector of St George's, promoted an annual series of published lectures that spread the message far and wide.[71] By 1854 the new prophetic convictions were sufficiently common to provoke a systematic rebuttal in the Bampton Lectures by Samuel Waldegrave, himself an Evangelical and shortly to become Bishop of Carlisle.[72] In the following year it was thought that probably a majority of the Evangelical clergy favoured premillennial views.[73] The great majority had embraced a version of prophetic interpretation that drove them to scan their newspapers for indications of 'the signs of the times'. Historicist premillennialism, as we shall see, was to encourage specific attitudes to the public affairs of the day.

The second school of thought, by contrast, fostered withdrawal from public concerns into an esoteric world of speculation about supernatural events still to come. This, the futurist school, held that the book of Revelation depicts not the course of history but the great happenings of the future. In 1826 there appeared a book arguing strongly for a futurist interpretation of Revelation in order to undermine all millenarian

notions. The unintended effect of this work by S. R. Maitland, the future
historian, was to inspire an alternative tradition of millennial thought.[74]
At Albury, Maitland's theory that Revelation was yet to be fulfilled
was already being canvassed, and by 1843 half a dozen other writers
had taken the field in favour of the same principle.[75] Irving's Catholic
Apostolic Church embraced a moderate type of futurism, teaching that
many of the events predicted in Revelation were still to come.[76] But the
most significant figure to adopt a form of futurist premillennialism was
J. N. Darby, the fertile mind behind another adventist sect, the Brethren.
Darby was an Irish ex-clergyman, originally trained as a lawyer, who in
the late 1820s and early 1830s was a leading participant in a series of
conferences held in imitation of Albury under the sponsorship of Lady
Powerscourt near Dublin. He steadily elaborated the view that the predictions of Revelation would be fulfilled after believers had been caught up to
meet Christ in the air, the so-called 'rapture'. No events in prophecy were
to precede the rapture. In particular, the period of judgements on
Christendom expected by other premillennialists, the 'great tribulation',
would take place only after the true church had been mysteriously translated to the skies. The second coming, on this view, was divided into two
parts: the secret coming of Christ *for* his saints at the rapture; and the public
coming *with* his saints to reign over the earth after the tribulation. Darby's
teaching is often termed 'dispensationalism' because it sharply distinguishes
between different dispensations, or periods of divine dealings with mankind.[77] Although never the unanimous view among Brethren, dispensationalism spread beyond their ranks and gradually became the most popular
version of futurism. In the nineteenth century it remained a minority view
among premillennialists, but this intense form of apocalyptic expectation
was to achieve much greater salience in the twentieth.

THE INSPIRATION OF SCRIPTURE

In addition to the advent hope, the radical Evangelicals of the 1820s
bequeathed another enduring legacy to their successors, a more exalted
estimate of scripture. In the earliest years of the nineteenth century
Evangelicals shared the standard attitude of contemporary theologians to the
Bible. Henry Martyn, the distinguished Cambridge scholar who abandoned
his academic career to travel as a missionary to the East, was at one
point closely questioned by a high-ranking official in Persia. Believing in
the verbal inspiration of the Koran, the Persian enquired whether Martyn
considered the New Testament to be the word spoken by God. 'The sense
from God', Martyn replied, 'but the expression from the different writers
of it.'[78] Martyn did not believe in verbal inspiration. Simeon, Martyn's
mentor, while sometimes using language suggesting a strong view of inspiration, could also maintain that scripture contains 'inexactnesses in reference

to philosophical and scientific matters'.[79] Similarly, Daniel Wilson, Vicar of Islington and subsequently Bishop of Calcutta, supposed that the Bible had been preserved only from 'every kind and degree of error relating to religion';[80] and T. H. Horne, the author of a four-volume *Introduction to the Critical Study and Knowledge of the Holy Scriptures* (1818), freely admitted that there are discrepancies in the text of scripture.[81] The chief court of appeal on the question of inspiration and its effects was Philip Doddridge.[82] Even the high Calvinist Robert Hawker treated the opinion of Doddridge on this subject as decisive.[83] Doddridge distinguished between different modes of inspiration, so that some passages were held to afford greater insight than others into the divine mind. It was Doddridge's view that predominated in the discussion of inspiration in 1800 by the Eclectic Society, the body consisting of London Evangelical leaders. Richard Cecil declared that 'there is some danger in considering *all* Scripture as *equally* inspired'. Although Henry Foster ('a plain and deeply pious man') propounded a theory of verbal inspiration, John Davies argued that the ideas, and not the words, of scripture are inspired.[84] Here were sober, experimentally minded men concerned to investigate the nature of the scriptures.

Such views began to be challenged by a much more robust attitude. It originated with Robert Haldane, the Scottish Evangelical who in 1816 found vital religion at a low ebb in Geneva. The Bible was neglected there, he soon concluded, because of misty Romantic notions to the effect that scripture is inspired in the same sense in which poetry is inspired. In reaction, Haldane contended for a much higher view of biblical inspiration. Parts of the Bible could not be accepted or rejected according to the judgement of human reason, he argued, for the whole, containing 'things evidently mysterious', was to be revered as divine teaching. This was to counter one Romantic attitude with another – the assertion that men should 'receive with adoring faith and love what they could not comprehend'.[85] Haldane had elaborated his case in *The Evidence and Authority of Divine Revelation*, first published in the same year. The scriptures, he taught, make 'a claim of infallibility and of perfection' for their own inspiration. The Doddridgean view of different degrees of inspiration was dismissed as sophistry.[86]

Haldane's ideas might have made little impression but for the Apocrypha controversy that embroiled the British and Foreign Bible Society in the 1820s. For many years the society had been sponsoring versions containing the Apocrypha for use on the continent, where its inclusion was normal among Catholics and Protestants alike. Haldane protested that this policy was an adulteration of the pure word of God. Uninspired material was being mingled with inspired scripture. The secretaries of the society, supported by Simeon and others who held the traditional lower views of inspiration, were reluctant to abandon a means of increasing the acceptability of the Bible. It was a clash of principle against expediency. Although by 1826 the society had gone a long way towards meeting the demand for change (even agreeing to remove existing Bibles containing the Apocrypha from stock), the Edinburgh and Glasgow auxiliaries remained dissatisfied and withdrew.[87] The fundamental issue, the nature of inspiration, was raised explicitly when, in 1826, John Pye Smith, tutor at the Independent Homerton College, referred favourably to a preface inserted in Bibles furnished by the British and Foreign. The preface, by a French theologian, Dr Haffner, treated inspiration in the way that had so disgusted Haldane in Geneva: Ezekiel, for instance, was said to have possessed 'a very lively imagination'.[88] Pye Smith pointed out that there was nothing explicitly erroneous about Haffner's opinions and added a statement of his own views on inspiration, which closely resembled those of Doddridge. Haldane arranged for an impoverished Baptist pastor in Ulster, a man of strong dogmatic views, Dr Alexander Carson, to assault Pye Smith's position. Haldane himself threw in a treatise *On the Inspiration of Scripture* in 1828. Although the extremely able Pye Smith had the best of the arguments, the effect was to publicise the views of Haldane.[89] A new and stronger understanding of inspiration had been broached.

BIBLICAL LITERALISM

One of the chief reasons for the spread of the new attitude was its association with premillennialism. Haldane did not toy with prophetic speculation, but many of those who fought the Apocrypha battle at his side were among those whose concern for the Jews blossomed into expectation of the advent. There was a tight logical connection between high hopes for the Jews and a new estimate of scripture. Those who looked for indications in the Bible that God's chosen people would be gathered into his fold were inclined to take Old Testament prophecies literally.[90] By contrast, Evangelical commentators had customarily argued that the prophecies of the Old Testament should be read spiritually, not literally: they should be applied to the Christian church. The beginning of the innovatory interpretation can be located precisely. In a pamphlet called *The Latter Rain* (1821) Lewis Way, the sponsor of the Jews' Society, urged special prayer for the children of Israel on the ground that Old Testament prophecies had a '*primary* and *literal* reference to the Jews'.[91] The literal interpretation of scripture became a battle-cry of the radical Evangelicals of Albury. One anonymous student of prophecy was soon to assert that the highway of Isaiah and the chariots of Ezekiel were to be construed literally as having reference to 'railroads and railway conveyance by locomotive carriages'.[92] Literalism did not imply restraining the imagination. It is not surprising that, in the opinion of a contributor to *The Eclectic Review*, 'the most dangerous feature of Millenarian theology, is the erroneous method of Biblical interpretation . . . '[93] Innovations in the fields of prophecy and the understanding of scripture went hand in hand.

Different views of what literalism implied jostled each other during the 1830s and 1840s. Horatius Bonar, the chief Scottish premillennial champion, conceded that, 'No one maintains that *all* Scripture is literal, or that *all* is figurative'.[94] Historicists found it hard to be thoroughgoing advocates of literal interpretation. There was too great a gulf between the detail of biblical images and their alleged historical fulfilment to make any such claim plausible. Futurists did not suffer from this handicap. Consequently, they shouted louder for literalism – and, among the futurists, the dispensationalists shouted loudest of all. J. N. Darby was contending as early as 1829 that prophecy relating to the Jews would be fulfilled literally.[95] As his thought developed during the 1830s, this principle of interpretation became the lynchpin of his system. Because Darby's opinions were most wedded to literalism, his distinctive scheme enjoyed the advantage of taking what seemed the most rigorist view of scripture. Conversely, the preference for the literal over the figurative approach to biblical exposition drew growing popular support from the advance of millenarianism.[96] The rising prestige of biblical literalism in turn reinforced the stronger convictions about scripture propounded by Haldane and his circle.

TOWARDS FUNDAMENTALISM

The classic text setting out the new and more exalted doctrine of scripture was Louis Gaussen's *Theopneustia* (1841). Gaussen was a professor of theology at Geneva whose high doctrine of inspiration was originally derived from Haldane.[97] His book was directed against Schleiermacher and others who denied miraculous inspiration in whole or in part, but also against English authors influenced by Doddridge, such as Pye Smith. The English theologians, he points out, admitted the existence of unique divine in-breathing (the 'theopneustia' of the title) in the Bible, but not to the same degree in all parts.[98] Gaussen, by contrast, asserts the plenary inspiration of the whole Bible. The word 'plenary' was subsequently adopted by many advocates of his case, but its use was not confined to the new school. Followers of Doddridge employed it freely.[99] The distinctiveness of Gaussen's position can be characterised more accurately by two other terms – verbal inspiration and inerrancy. Verbal inspiration is professed in a section of his book directed to meeting what he calls an 'evasion', the belief that the ideas rather than the words of the Bible are inspired. He also offers a precise statement of inerrancy. 'Theopneustia' he defines as 'that inexplicable power which the Divine Spirit, aforetime, exercised upon the authors of Holy Scripture, to guide them even to the words which they have employed, and to preserve them from all error, as well as from any omission.'[100] He did not support any theory of divine dictation, as critics both at the time and subsequently have alleged.[101] On the subject of inspiration, he remarks in the book, 'Scripture never presents to us either its mode or its measure, as an object of study'.[102] It seems clear that he would have agreed with Haldane that full inspiration did not imply that 'the ordinary exercise of the faculties of the writers was counteracted or suspended'.[103] The verbal inspirationists, that is to say, believed in the possibility of simultaneous divine and human agency. If God gave the words, there is no implication that the human mind did not also give them. So Gaussen provided, for the first time, a carefully argued defence of the inerrancy of the Bible.

His effort was part of the intensified supernaturalism of the times. Gaussen was jealous for the divine honour. 'Is the Bible from God?' he demanded in the preface. 'Or, is it true (as has been affirmed) that it contains sentences purely human, inaccurate narratives, vulgar conceits, defective arguments . . . ?' The approach of Doddridge, and most contemporary British Evangelicals, was degrading to the miraculous documents provided by God. 'According to their view', he wrote, 'inspiration . . . would be unequal, often imperfect, accompanied with harmless errors, and meted out according to the nature of the passages, in very different measure, of which they constitute themselves more or less the judges.'[104] Such theologians were guilty of pitting their own reason against God's revelation. Gaussen's target is essentially the inductive method, the critical sifting of evidence to discover the nature of inspiration in any particular book. By this means, observing 'the Baconian rules of inductive reasoning', Pye Smith had concluded that the Song of Songs and Esther should probably be rejected from the canon.[105] So unpalatable a conclusion confirmed the diagnosis in the circles of Gaussen and Haldane that there was a flaw in the method. They therefore adopted what has justly been styled a deductive approach to the doctrine of inspiration. Beginning with the axiom that God in his perfect wisdom had inspired the writing of the Bible, they went on to deduce its qualities and then tried to match the results of empirical examination of the text with their *a priori* assumptions.[106]

It was too much for many who had been schooled to the Enlightenment values of free inquiry. Pye Smith's views did not change, although he knew Gaussen's book; his fellow-Congregationalist John Harris, lecturing as principal on 'The Inspiration of the Scriptures' at the opening of New College, London, in 1851, pointed out that 'the sacred writers nowhere claim for themselves immediate and universal verbal inspiration'; and two years later T. R. Birks, then a trusted leader of the Evangelical clergy, explicitly rejected dogmatic inerrancy on the ground that we should engage in inquiry into the mode of inspiration.[107] But the deductive method soon won converts. William Steadman at Bradford Baptist Academy abandoned Doddridge's system in favour of Haldane's, and Thomas Chalmers at Edinburgh used Haldane and even Carson as class-books on inspiration.[108] James Bannerman, who later wrote a treatise on *Inspiration* (1865), and Alexander Black, a colleague at New College, Edinburgh, both held by 1850 the new view that the whole Bible is 'fully and verbally inspired'.[109] There was a clear division of Evangelical opinion. With the backing of *The Record*,[110] inerrantism made progress among the Anglican clergy.

Nevertheless, at a representative clerical meeting in 1861 a majority still favoured the traditional view that there might be biblical inaccuracies on non-religious topics.[111] If Fundamentalism as a theological phenomenon is defined as belief in the inerrancy of scripture, Fundamentalism had not prevailed among Evangelicals by this date. The common supposition of historians that Evangelicals of the mid-nineteenth century and before held, as a deduction from the doctrine of inspiration, that the Bible must necessarily contain no error is quite mistaken. This conviction was a novelty, a Romantic innovation. In the middle years of the century there was no more than a rising tide of Fundamentalist opinion.

SUPERNATURAL INTERVENTION

The most vivid instance of the increasing supernaturalism that marked the Evangelical world of the 1820s and 1830s was the appearance of speaking in tongues. The traditional view was that such miraculous signs had been withdrawn from the church after its early years. At Albury it was suggested that they ended solely because faith had grown cold.[112] It followed that, as faith was rekindled, the gifts might be restored. A. J. Scott, Irving's assistant minister, reached this conclusion and, on holiday on the Clyde in 1830, opened his mind to Mary Campbell of Roseneath. It was she who, a few months later, first spoke in tongues. News of the manifestations in Scotland led to intense expectancy in London, where the earliest instance occurred in April 1831. By October Irving was permitting the exercise of tongues inspired by the Spirit in public worship. 'An awful stillness prevailed for about five minutes', wrote a critical visitor. 'Suddenly an appalling shriek seemed to rend the roof, which was repeated with heart-chilling effect. I grasped involuntarily the bookdesk before me; and then, suddenly, a torrent of unintelligible words, for about five minutes, followed by – "When will ye repent? Why will ye not repent?"'[113] Prophecies in English and miraculous healings were also known. In one year forty-six spiritual cures were reported among the Irvingites of England alone. These unfamiliar proto-Pentecostal happenings soon became confined to Irving's Catholic Apostolic Church, which, despite erecting some magnificent places of worship, never became a power in the land. Its numbers in the United Kingdom were estimated in 1878 to be under six thousand.[114] But for a while – probably significantly, in the years during and immediately after the great cholera outbreak of 1831–2 – the revival of spiritual gifts in the church was a subject of widespread attention among Evangelicals. It was an extreme sign of the new craving for the divine to break into the world.

A complementary tendency was the downgrading of natural theology. Evangelicals, as we have seen, had previously delighted in the scientific arguments that defended the faith on the basis of the Newtonian cosmology.[115] Now the radicals began to feel that their theology had been too strongly marked by natural philosophy. They had left little or no room for divine intervention in the present or future. Prejudice, confessed the respected G. T. Noel, had previously prevented him from accepting the possibility of miraculous intercourse between heaven and earth in a millennial state.[116] The prejudice was identified and condemned at Albury as a habitual looking at second causes rather than at first. 'Nothing can be so opposed to the disposition of faith', ran the first conference report, 'as that which is only to be convinced by external evidences. It is, in fact, saying that we will not believe God unless He can bring a voucher for the truth of what He says.'[117] The demolition of the structure of natural theology would leave the way clear for the bare trust in divine revelation characteristically urged by Irving and his friends. But to those who continued to see 'the mechanical philosophy' as the main buttress of Christian truth it was highly alarming. They remained convinced, as the Congregational theologian John Harris put it, that 'the moral department of the Divine government is conducted on a plan equally with the natural or the physical; that in the world of mind, as well as of matter, certain causes produce certain effects'.[118] It was a clash between those who inherited the eighteenth-century beliefs in order, design and gradualness and those who, in the iconoclastic spirit of the nineteenth century, wished to substitute the free, the dynamic and the cataclysmic. The older school was to retain its hegemony at least until the debates stirred up by Darwinism from the 1860s onwards.[119] But from as early as the 1820s a new force was in the field.

DOCTRINAL REFORMULATION

The same novel influences were affecting central doctrines. One of the most significant developments was a reaction against Calvinism in favour of the belief that the atonement was general in its scope. A landmark was the publication, in 1828, of *The Unconditional Freeness of the Gospel* by Thomas Erskine, a Scottish Episcopal layman whose Romantic sensibility was nourished by a love for works of art.[120] 'The Gospel', he writes, 'reveals to us the existence of a fund of divine love containing in it a propitiation for all sins, and this fund is general to the whole race . . .'[121] His views received a warmer welcome than might have been expected: Henry Drummond approved the book, and even Chalmers, though dissenting from its main conclusion, 'went cordially with its leading principles'.[122] Most crucially, a Church of Scotland minister in the west of Scotland, John McLeod Campbell, concurred wholeheartedly. McLeod Campbell, who in 1856 was to publish a treatise on general redemption entitled *The Nature of the Atonement*, was deposed from the ministry of the Church of Scotland in 1831 for departing from Reformed orthodoxy. It was McLeod Campbell who, in 1828, persuaded Irving of the truth of these views.[123] It seems strange at first sight that Irving, who gloried in what he called

Calvinism, should adopt this anti-Calvinist kernel of an alternative scheme of theology. The apparent contradiction is resolved when it is recognised that Irving perceived an inadequate doctrine of redemption as the root problem of contemporary Evangelical thought.[124] If God is sovereign, he held, then his redeeming power must be totally effective and therefore encompass the whole of humanity. The conviction of Erskine, McLeod Campbell and Irving that Christ died for all rested on a sense of the absoluteness of divine authority. It was newly held that humanity enjoys a solidarity – a typical theme of nineteenth-century thought – because it is subject as a whole to Christ. Such themes were to be propagated by A. J. Scott, once Irving's assistant and later the first Principal of Owen's College, Manchester, and by F. D. Maurice, the leading Broad Church theologian of the mid-nineteenth century, who professed a deep debt to Erskine and Irving.[125] If it was formally condemned at the time, the broader view of the atonement adumbrated by Erskine was to enjoy increasing favour among Evangelicals and non-Evangelicals alike as the century advanced.

Another doctrinal field marked by innovation in the 1820s was Christology. Irving propounded the belief that at the incarnation Christ assumed not just humanity but sinful humanity. 'The point at issue is simply this', he explained: 'whether Christ's flesh had the grace of sinlessness and incorruption from its proper nature, or from the indwelling of the Holy Ghost. I say the latter.'[126] It was for his book arguing this case, *The Orthodox and Catholic Doctrine of our Lord's Human Nature* (1830), that Irving was excluded from the ministry of the Church of Scotland. The condemnation rested on the received doctrine of the union of the two natures of Christ in one person. If God and man were united, Irving's claim amounted to the assertion that a person who was God was capable of sin – a conclusion of definite unorthodoxy. Irving, however, insisted that he was speaking not of Christ as a person but of the humanity he assumed.[127] It is clear that Irving was not wishing to deviate from the mainstream of Christian teaching. He wished to contend that Christ was subject to all the influences of his day without in some sense being guarded by the coat-of-mail of intrinsic sinlessness. The incarnation was utterly real. This aligned Irving with tendencies gaining momentum in the early nineteenth century making for greater emphasis on the doctrine of the incarnation that, once again, came to fruition in the thought of Maurice. It was a distinctly Romantic trend.[128] To claim that the Holy Spirit was responsible for preserving Christ's sinlessness was to exalt the work of the third person of the Trinity, just as Irving did in explaining the manifestations in his congregation. He was contending once more for a higher estimate of divine involvement in the contemporary world. Underlying the Christology was his central preoccupation with the irruption of the supernatural into the human sphere.

For the discernment of the supernatural, faith was essential. One of the most enduring legacies of the ferment surrounding Irving was the idea that faith must be magnified if God is to be served aright. This, according to

Irving, is to be the governing principle of Christian mission. 'It was Faith they had to plant', he declared of the earliest apostles in his LMS sermon of 1824; 'therefore he made his missionaries men of Faith, that they might plant Faith, and Faith alone.' Faith entailed reliance on God for material as well as spiritual needs. Today's missionaries should therefore imitate the apostles in going out 'destitute of all visible sustenance, and of all human help'.[129] Similar convictions were maturing in other minds. A. N. Groves, an Exeter dentist, both preached and practised entire dependence on God in missionary service.[130] His brother-in-law, George Müller, established an orphanage at Bristol in 1835 on the same principles. Whenever money was exhausted, 'prayer and faith were again resorted to'. Part of Müller's inspiration derived from the example of August Francke,[131] but part was drawn from the atmosphere of radical devotion to God that Müller discovered in the circles around Groves that were developing into the Brethren movement. Müller's principle of living by faith was taken up later in the century by J. Hudson Taylor, another adherent of Brethren, and made the basis of his China Inland Mission in 1865. The CIM differed from previous missionary societies in possessing no structure of home support. Its backing came simply from those committed to praying for its agents in the field, who were thrown into dependence on God for their needs.[132] Hudson Taylor vividly illustrated an extreme version of this attitude to mission when, at a time when shipwreck seemed imminent on his first voyage to China in 1853, he gave away his life belt to assure himself that his trust was in God alone.[133] 'Living by faith' was to become the practice of an increasing proportion of full-time workers in the Evangelical world in later years. The origins of the policy can be traced back to the new desire to rely wholly on God that marked the juncture around 1830. If faith was strong, the reality of God's involvement in his world would be evident in the care he exercised over his servants.

HIGH CHURCHMANSHIP

A further feature of the new mood around 1830 was a stronger sense of churchmanship. It came to rapid fruition in the Albury circle, which hoped that a corporate awareness, 'a catholic, and universal spirit', would rescue Evangelicals from individualism. Churchmanship had suffered: 'we have almost forgotten that there is a church at all; . . . Christ, and the believer; that is all.'[134] Irving set out to retrieve the situation. He even claimed to doubt whether those who failed to give 'due reverence' to the church would reach the heaven that it symbolised.[135] But Irving and his immediate friends were not alone in publicising a higher view of the church. A. S. Thelwall, a young clerical graduate of Trinity College, Cambridge, was publishing similar ideas in his sermons.[136] It was also the burden of Henry Budd, the clerical secretary of the Prayer Book and Homily Society.

'Our Church is a glorious Church', he wrote in 1827, 'if it had but a soul.'[137] A sense of corporate solidarity had come into vogue. Coleridge, as we have seen, was a primary source. The whole movement of opinion was Romantic in inspiration.

The new school was also coming to fresh conclusions as a result of examining ecclesiastical tradition with more care. Irving derived something of his corporate sense from the seventeenth-century Scottish heritage of a covenanted nation.[138] Budd identified with 'the design of our Reformers', many of whose works he was responsible for reissuing.[139] There were appeals to the Thirty-Nine Articles and to the formularies.[140] This was part and parcel of the growing historical awareness of the age. Irving was glad the Church of England retained 'Baptismal and communion services, comminations, fastings, and festivals, ordinations, and all the other revered forms of the Latin Church'. They constituted a monument to past glories: 'like the ancient armour of our fathers, they mock their puny children'.[141] There was value as well in the church year, 'the various anniversaries which were instituted by the first Christians, in commemoration of different important events'.[142] By 1828 Drummond had reached the striking conclusion 'that the Popish practice of praying from a liturgy . . . *without preaching*, is nearer being a proper ceremonial for God's house, than making it a *mere preaching house* without prayer, as it is generally considered now'.[143] The whole trend culminated in the elaborate liturgy of the Catholic Apostolic Church, which moved ahead of all but the most advanced ritualists in the Church of England by introducing reservation of the consecrated elements in 1850, altar lights and incense in 1852, the mixed chalice in 1854 and holy water in 1868.[144] In this case High Churchmanship could hardly be higher.

There was a corresponding rise in the value attached to the sacraments. Drummond affirmed in 1828 that Catholic estimates of baptism and the Lord's Supper were nearer the truth than the idea that these sacraments 'are mere signs, as held by all the Dissenters, and by most of the Church of England Evangelicals'.[145] Drawing on such writers as Hugh of St Victor, a copy of whose medieval treatise on the sacraments he gave to Coleridge in 1829,[146] Irving adopted the same position. A sacrament, he held, is a 'sign containing the grace signified'. He scolded the church for its neglect of the Lord's Supper, which revealed, he contended, its unholy state.[147] Other Evangelicals were just beginning to adopt a loftier view of the sacrament. W. A. Shirley, who was eventually to become a bishop, commenced a Church Communion Society at about the same time.[148] The Brethren from their beginnings believed that the Christian community was constituted by its meeting to 'break bread' every week.[149] There was a growing appreciation of the holy communion in certain Evangelical circles.

In general, however, more attention was paid to baptism by the radicals. 'I know', wrote Irving, 'that amongst no class of the Church doth so much darkness and indifference exist upon the subject of baptism, as amongst the Evangelical, amongst whom I have hardly found one who hath even an idea of what is meant by this most excellent service of the Church.'[150] His *Homilies on the Sacraments* of 1828, in fact concerned entirely with baptism, were designed to make good the deficiency. Baptism, he teaches, 'involves a real ingrafting into Christ'.[151] It may well be that he adopted so strong a view partly because of emotional stress following the death of two infant children. Certainly he derived comfort from the doctrine in his affliction.[152] But it became a foundation stone of Irving's ecclesiology, 'the boundary of separation between the creature regenerate, and the creature unregenerate'.[153] Irving did not stand alone in magnifying the effects of baptism. Henry Budd, from the ranks of the Church of England, composed a thorough study of *Infant Baptism* (1827). Budd argues that infant baptism highlights the principle that God graciously fulfils his promises and therefore exalts the need for faith. 'We may then hope', he writes, 'that as faith pleads and acts on the PROMISE, God will bless his own mode of ameliorating the human character, and that our population shall not be a community of mere natural men, but a Communion of the Saints of God.'[154] Budd gained the approval of Shirley, of Drummond and, in some measure, of Maurice.[155] It was a time when, it has been suggested, belief in the innocence of childhood generated sentiment that could readily be transferred to the baptismal service.[156] Something of this kind was occurring among advanced Evangelicals.

Such developments, though highly reminiscent of the Tractarians, were proceeding before the Tractarian movement began at Oxford in 1833. The radical Evangelicals held in the 1820s views that sound characteristic of Newman, Pusey, Keble and their circle in the following decade. 'The communion of saints and the holy catholic church', recorded Drummond in 1827, 'are grown to be dead letters in the creed; their meaning is understood, their comfort felt, no more.'[157] Irving was using the phrase 'the idea of the Christian church' as early as 1825.[158] At Albury in 1827 the mark of unity in the church was valued so highly that attenders believed they had a duty to prove the Roman Catholic Church to be apostate in order to clear themselves of the sin of schism.[159] There was an associated high doctrine of the ministry. Irving was prepared to use the word 'priesthood' in 1828 when lamenting the growing disrespect for it.[160] 'The interference of laymen in ecclesiastical affairs is arrived at a fearful height', wrote Drummond (paradoxically a layman himself) in the same year.[161] He was glad to appeal to the Fathers.[162] The first Albury report concludes with a quotation from Keble, whose *Christian Year* is described as 'exquisite poetry'.[163] It becomes apparent that the radical Evangelicals were not just similar to the Tractarians but were actually an earlier phase of the same movement that in the 1830s proliferated into many strands – including Brethren and the Catholic Apostolic Church as well as Tractarianism.

Newman is a bond between the earlier phase and the Oxford Movement proper. During the 1820s, already a Fellow of Oriel, Newman was an Evangelical. He dabbled in prophecy, and as late as 1829 was elected co-secretary of the CMS auxiliary at Oxford.[164] He came to accept, like Irving, the doctrine of baptismal regeneration, and in 1826 noted in his diary that 'Pusey accused me the other day of becoming more High Church'.[165] Increasingly, Newman diverged from the extremists at Oxford around Bulteel, but he fully shared their heightened supernaturalism. Late in 1833 he published five letters in *The Record* urging Evangelicals to support the Oxford Movement.[166] The hope that they might rally to the cause was no chimera, for the influences affecting Newman were also playing on them. Similarly, the sons of William Wilberforce, with Henry Manning, found the transition from Evangelicalism to a much higher churchmanship a natural evolution.[167] Later, when the battle lines were drawn between Evangelical and Anglo-Catholic, the affinity was forgotten, but at the time it was substantial. Suspicion of the Tractarians soon arose among Evangelicals, and in 1838 it hardened into hostility on the publication of Hurrell Froude's *Remains* with its repudiation of Protestantism.[168] Admissions of links between the two sides became guarded. Budd's *Infant Baptism*, according to his biographer in 1855, 'gave the first hints of several reforms in the Church, which the Tractarians have caught up, and distorted'.[169] But when, in the second half of the century, the first wave of alarm at Tractarian innovation passed, many Evangelicals, as will appear, were prepared to alter their thinking, and especially their practice, in a more churchly direction.[170] They were returning to a tendency already marked in the Evangelical ferment of the later 1820s.

CHURCH AND DISSENT

Not all the changes that marked the period round 1830 can be attributed primarily to the changing cultural context. The diverging paths taken by Anglicans and Dissenters is an instance where other circumstances were more decisive. The increasingly secure position of Evangelicals in the Church of England was a factor distancing them from Dissent. There was a growing commitment to the Church of England as an institution. Edward Bickersteth, for instance, encouraged Evangelical churchpeople to make a point of attending the ministry of their parochial clergymen, in his *Christian Hearer* of 1826.[171] There were fewer scruples about the liturgy, and younger men were beginning to regard it as close to perfection. J. E. Gordon, an earnest Evangelical who entered parliament in 1831, was to praise its order of service as sublimely devotional.[172] It is not surprising that Gordon and many of his contemporaries displayed a higher regard for the establishment principle than had been customary among their predecessors.[173] The relations between church and state, furthermore, were brought to public attention by the so-called 'constitutional revolution' of 1828–32. With the national legislature no longer expressly Protestant and the church notoriously riddled with abuses, ecclesiastical reform seemed likely to come next after parliamentary reform. Lord Henley, an Evangelical, put forward his own proposals for church reform in 1832,[174] but, especially when the Whig government set out to restructure the Church of Ireland in the following year, the more wary began to fear the spectre of disestablishment.

The intellectual atmosphere, though undoubtedly secondary, did play its part in encouraging Evangelicals to a stouter defence of the Church of England as established. The radical Evangelicals were beginning to think, like Coleridge in *Church and State* (1830), about the complementarity of church and nation. 'It is the duty of the State to establish the Christian religion', declares an Albury conference report.[175] The rationale was that, just as the church represents Christ's priestly office, so the state represents his kingly office. In Parliament during 1831–2 Spencer Perceval, the son of the assassinated Prime Minister and later an apostle of the Catholic Apostolic Church, rose several times, Bible in hand, to summon the nation to greater dependence on God.[176] In 1834, R. B. Seeley, an Evangelical publisher, issued a set of *Essays on the Church* in which he contends, in anticipation of Gladstone's book on *The State in its Relations with the Church* (1838), that the corporate personality of the state makes it competent to honour God by establishing the church.[177] Already William Dealtry had published *The Importance of the Established Church* (1832) and James Scholefield *An Argument for a Church Establishment* (1833). *The Record* gave its loud support to the establishmentarian position; groups of Evangelicals founded a Christian Influence Society and an Established Church Society in 1832 and 1834 respectively.[178] Under the auspices of the Christian Influence Society, in 1838 Thomas Chalmers delivered the most popular defence of the establishment of the decade to crowded audiences in London.[179] There was a marked trend of Evangelical opinion in the Established Churches in favour of active support for the union of church and state.

Naturally, the same trend was not apparent in the Dissenting churches. The repeal of the Test and Corporation Acts in 1828 was the result of their pressure. Dissenters had proved themselves to be loyal subjects of the crown for nearly a century and a half. Why, they asked, should they continue to be defined as unworthy of holding office in town corporations? Although in practice the legislation was virtually a dead letter, Dissenters felt that it made them the victims of social discrimination. So they successfully demanded that government should remove one of the leading stigmas of Dissent.[180] With the reform of Parliament enfranchising many Dissenters four years later, there was bound to be pressure for an end to their other grievances. In the winter of 1833–4 there was a remarkable upsurge of Dissenting feeling that adopted the disestablishment cry.[181] Permanent damage was done to relations between Evangelicals in church and chapel. It was long recalled (when his qualifications of the statement were forgotten) that Thomas Binney, a leading Congregationalist, had declared that the Established Church destroyed more souls than it saved.[182] Political battles over church rates and other questions of religious equality multiplied during the 1830s and 1840s. Co-operation in evangelism, as in the foundation of the interdenominational London City Mission in 1835, and in public work, as in the Evangelical Alliance from 1845, was fraught with bickering.[183] *The Christian Observer*, representing moderate Anglican Evangelicalism, claimed in 1843, a little disingenuously, not to have changed its former sympathetic attitude to Dissenters. Yet the Dissenters were showing a less kind spirit towards the Evangelicals of the Established Church than earlier in the century.[184] From the 1830s onwards, despite rapprochements from time to time, the gulf between church and chapel generally yawned much wider than before.

A DEFENSIVE POSTURE

Within the Church of England there developed a sense of being a bastion under assault. Like continental conservatives or Newman, Anglican Evangelicals identified the hostile force as Liberalism. They shared Newman's diagnosis of its primary assertion: 'No religious tenet is important, unless reason shows it to be so.'[185] Liberalism was any philosophy of life not built on divine revelation. Its adherents were called the 'Infidel, or indifferent party of our politicians . . . who separate the Policy of the state from the Supremacy of religion'.[186] The grand crime of the Dissenters was entering a coalition with such men and worshipping 'their idol liberalism'.[187] There were serious secular implications. Liberalism attacked primogeniture, the basis of landed property, and so threatened the social order with the 'evils of democracy'.[188] It insinuated that 'the people, and not God, are the source of legitimate power'.[189] The true foundation of political authority was, on the contrary, that kings hold power delegated by Christ. And political economy, fostered by Liberalism, denied the paternalist responsibility of Christian governments to care for the poor and oppressed.[190] So the effect of Liberalism was socially and politically disastrous. 'Liberalism', according to a report of Albury, 'is a system of unbindings, of setting free from all ties'.[191] Its anarchic individualism betokened revolution in the pattern of things ordained by God. Hence it was at all costs to be opposed. It is no wonder that exponents of such views turned towards whatever promised to resist the advances of Liberalism. During the 1830s most Evangelicals in the Church of England severed any previous links they might have had with Whiggery. *The Christian Observer* never supported the Whigs after 1834. Remaining Evangelical Whigs, in fact, became suspect.[192] Peelite Conservatism seemed a bulwark of true religion.

Infidelity, the apparent premise of Liberalism, seemed to be on the increase. The grand sin of these days, according to an Albury report, was 'scepticism, infidelity, the deification of the intellect of man, reasoning pride, disbelief in the Word of God'.[193] The tide of unbelief had swept in since the French Revolution; Voltaire, Rousseau, Diderot, Condorcet and other free-thinking writers were selling well in France; Tom Paine was influencing even the Reformed religion in Britain.[194] There had been an outburst of infidel propaganda during the Queen Caroline affair of 1820–1, some of it blasphemous and much of it scurrilous, that must have troubled Evangelicals.[195] Increasingly they lumped together what others naturally contrasted – the highly respectable Utilitarian body of social thought stemming from the Enlightenment and the popular printed material that poured scorn on the existing order in church and state. The former, whose advance was celebrated in the 1820s as 'the march of mind', was as much an expression of irreligion as the latter. Satan was manipulating both to ensure that people would accept nothing on the bare testimony of God's word, but only with reasons. 'This is the natural and inevitable consequence', it was said, 'of all education which is not founded upon the doctrines of Christianity . . . '[196] Hence the radical Evangelicals were vocal opponents of the creation in 1828 of London University, the institution that became University College, London. Nobody denounced this 'godless institution in Gower Street' where there was to be no religious instruction more vigorously than did Irving and Drummond. 'The Bible', wrote Drummond, 'does prescribe the mode in which youth shall be trained, namely, in the nurture and admonition of the Lord; and a system founded on the intentional neglect of, and disobedience to, that command, is an infidel system, or rather a system of premeditated and obstinate rebellion against God.'[197] The need to preserve the religious element in education became a standard characteristic of Evangelicals in the Established Church.

A corollary of this stance was that, even before the rupture between church and chapel, the circle around Irving and Drummond became fiercely hostile to co-operation with Unitarians. Evangelical Dissenters had retained their traditional links with the English Presbyterians who had adopted lower, more rationalist, 'Socinian' views of the person of Christ. William Smith, the leading Dissenting MP, shared these views and yet was a close colleague of Wilberforce and his parliamentary friends.[198] The new Evangelical school, however, regarded Unitarians with distaste as a species of infidel within the professing church. Socinianism, for Irving, was a form of apostasy.[199] Joint activities with Unitarians must therefore cease. In 1830–1 an attempt was made, with followers of Irving and Haldane in the van, to purge the Bible Society of its Socinian supporters.[200] In 1836 the orthodox Dissenters similarly determined to end their alliance with Unitarians, who were forced to withdraw from the representative General Body of Protestant Dissenting Ministers.[201] Orthodoxy was coming to be seen as a condition of co-operation.

ANTI-CATHOLICISM

The other grand threat to Evangelical values came from Roman Catholicism. Although its numbers had grown during the eighteenth century, the Catholic Church in Britain remained in the 1820s a docile, unassertive body, eager to demonstrate the qualification of its members for the parliamentary franchise.[202] Evangelicals shared the common British aversion to popery as a compendium of all that was alien to national life, whether religious, political or moral. They inherited the Reformation identification of the papacy as Antichrist, the seventeenth-century fears that linked popery with continental autocracy and the popular suspicions that hovered round celibacy and the confessional. They added their own specific sense of the spiritual deprivation of Catholics. Yet the unobtrusiveness of the Catholic population and the predisposition to toleration of the early Evangelicals meant that virulent anti-popery was remarkably rare in the first three decades of the century. It was, after all, supposed that popery was a spent force, already tottering (since the French Revolution) to its ultimate fall, and so it seemed no threat.

Developments in the 1820s, however, began to point towards a more wholehearted anti-Catholicism. In Ireland Protestant–Catholic controversy took on a sharper edge following the provocative primary charge by William Magee, Anglican Archbishop of Dublin, in 1822.[203] Methodists were arousing Catholic resentment in Ireland by their evangelism and fuelling the growth of anti–Catholic feeling among their English co-religionists.[204] And in Britain the intense public discussion of the 1820s over whether or not to concede political rights to Catholics stirred up the ashes of ancient disputes.[205] Dissenters were divided among themselves on the question of Catholic emancipation, the more educated seeing the analogy with their own case against civil discrimination on grounds of religion, the rank and file a prey to traditional suspicions.[206] A similar fissure ran through the ranks of Evangelical Anglicans, though there were sophisticated figures such as Sir Robert Inglis and William Marsh who were devotedly opposed to the Catholic claims.[207] Irving was at first neutral, but later decided that a concession to Catholics would infringe his ideal of a state professing the true religion.[208] It was in his circle that the strongest anti-Catholic attitudes sprang up. In 1827, a Reformation Society for anti-Catholic propaganda was set up, with J. E. Gordon as secretary.[209] The church of Rome might be apostate, but its power to deceive had not disappeared. Catholicism was once more seen as a deadly foe.

The strongest stimulus to anti-Catholicism was the influx of Catholic Irish. Even before the famine of the mid-1840s brought a vast torrent from Ireland, the trickle of immigrants had swelled into a substantial flow. By the 1820s the pressures of over-population and cheaper rates for the passage to England stimulated a large-scale exodus. By 1851 half a million Irish-born had settled in England and Wales.[210] Apart from traditional disdain for the Irish, anti-Catholicism was fostered by fears of their revolutionary tendencies and a stereotype of poverty and laziness, barbarism and ignorance, which came close to the reality of immigrant existence in the urban 'rookeries'.[211] When these attitudes were mingled with inherited anxieties and enhanced by Evangelical fervour, the result was a heady and distasteful brew.[212]

It was most potent in the Anglican circles where premillennialism had taken hold. In the historicist scheme, there was no doubt that Antichrist was Rome. Thus the chief practical application of E. B. Elliott's massive four-volume work on the interpretation of Revelation was a warning that we should not 'seek nationally to identify ourselves with the Papal antichristian religion' or to 'abandon our distinctive Protestant character'.[213] But others untouched by the new prophetic movement also succumbed to a virulent anti-popery. Hugh Miller, editor of the newspaper of the Free Church of Scotland and a literary figure of some standing, was alarmed by the hordes of impoverished Irishmen crowding into the Edinburgh slums. 'We must employ betimes more missionaries and Bibles soon', he wrote, 'or we shall soon have to employ soldiers and cannon.'[214] The most politicised version of anti-Catholicism was the Protestant Association, founded in 1835 by J. E. Gordon. Its greatest strength was in Lancashire, where popular apprehensions about immigration were most intense, since Liverpool was the chief port of entry from Ireland. Hugh McNeile, once Drummond's vicar at Albury and now in Liverpool, set up in 1839 a Protestant Operative Society linked with the Association.[215] McNeile treated the Protestant cause as the defence of his country, argued explicitly for 'Nationalism in Religion' and declared that 'we cannot allow our spirituality as Christians entirely to supersede our patriotism as Britons'.[216] Inevitably, the Protestant Association and the strongest of the other anti-Catholics were firmly aligned with the Conservatives. Therefore the apparent betrayal of the Protestant cause by Peel in 1845, when he increased the government grant to the Catholic seminary at Maynooth, was an immense shock.[217] It provoked an upsurge of angry protest in the whole Evangelical community that was to be surpassed only once in the subsequent history of anti-Catholic opinion – the *levée en masse* in 1850–1 against the so-called papal aggression, when Pius IX restored the hierarchy of the Catholic Church in England and Wales.[218] By the middle of the century hatred of the papacy and all its works had been powerfully reinforced in the Evangelical mentality.

AN OUTLOOK OF PESSIMISM

The assaults by infidels and papists on the truth of God and, for an increasing number, the onslaught by Dissenters on the establishment, made the prospects for Christianity seem dark. Expectations that the gospel would usher in a superior world order were dismissed by the new school as a sinister deception. 'Fye, oh, fye upon it!' exclaimed Irving, 'ye Christians have fathered upon the scriptures the optimism of the German and French infidels!'[219] Dreams of human improvement without decisive divine intervention were chimerical. The Brethren produced the most extreme version of the new pessimism with their assertions that the whole professing church, Protestant as well as Catholic, had lapsed into apostasy so that security lay in 'gathering to the name alone', that is, in withdrawing from existing ecclesiastical organisations to worship Christ in seclusion and simplicity.[220] Fears for the future were aggravated when the bastion of the Church of England turned out to be harbouring a fifth column. When, in the late 1830s, the Tractarians were perceived as crypto-Romanists, alarm scaled new heights. A typical comment was that Tractarians were 'working to poison' the education of the national church at its source in Oxford.[221] Prophecy added its seal by announcing the last days. Symptoms were all around. The prophetic writer J. W. Brooks censured 'the depraved taste of the age', citing '*Nicholas Nickleby*, abounding with the lowest vulgarity' as a good example.[222] The world seemed degenerate.

Resistance to the upsurge of gloom came from those who rejected premillennialism. Samuel Waldegrave still held in 1854 that the Old Testament predicted the blessings of gospel days.[223] John Harris, representing the predominant school of opinion among Dissenters, argued that hopes for the spread of the gospel must be sustained for the sake of encouraging support for foreign missions.[224] But the newer and darker view, propagated especially by *The Record*, was making headway. At some distance, *The Christian Observer* followed in its tracks. By 1844 this journal that had once been renowned for its humanitarianism was expressing doubts about the potential for reform. Social improvement through legislation and popular institutions was limited by the fallen state of man. Education might do something, but only regeneration could supply the remedy. In the field of social reform, 'men begin with expecting too much; and conclude with hoping for nothing'.[225] Francis Close, Vicar of Cheltenham and a leading exponent of the new attitudes, voiced the political implications of pessimism. 'In my humble opinion', he declared, 'the Bible is conservative, the Prayer Book conservative, the Liturgy conservative, the Church conservative, and it is impossible for a minister to open his mouth without being conservative.'[226] Evangelicals in the Church of England were turning into embattled defenders of the existing order.

The chief explanation for the transformation of Evangelicalism in the years around 1830 is the spread of Romanticism. Much must be attributed to the alarming political events of the times. The constitutional revolution in particular precipitated a revision of Evangelical attitudes. The changing religious situation, encompassing the immigration of the Catholic Irish, the rise of the Oxford Movement and the growing strength of Evangelicalism itself, played an essential part. But Evangelicals were most affected by the new cultural mood that in the 1820s spread beyond the small literary caste to a wider public. Before any of the shock-waves of repeal, emancipation and reform, a new world-view for Evangelicals had been fashioned by the radical coterie of Albury. Despite the retreat of Irving and Drummond to the private world of the Catholic Apostolic Church, they had already injected most of their attitudes into the mainstream of Evangelical life. An intensified sense of the supernatural spread in many forms and in many ways, revolutionising the inherited outlook.

Those who responded to the new ideas tended to be the young, and so they lived long to propagate their views. They were also drawn primarily from the social elite. The students of prophecy, it was noted as late as 1864, 'are not mere ignorant enthusiasts, but belong in considerable numbers to the respectable and educated classes of society'.[227] The Catholic Apostolic Church, embodying the full range of the new views, included in its ranks the seventh Duke of Northumberland, a viscount and four baronets; it was also disproportionately supported by lawyers, ex-clergymen, bankers, businessmen and physicians.[228] Likewise the well-to-do, including several peers, were attracted into the Brethren.[229] Because the new opinions had greater appeal for the upper and professional classes, they were much more widespread in the Church of England than outside. Dissenters were acting on the very Liberalism that Anglicans deplored, and so remaining loyal to the Enlightenment heritage. In the long run the new opinions of the years around 1830, and especially the prophetic and biblical convictions, were to reach a broader audience, percolating down eventually to the lower-class sectarian fringe. But in the middle third of the nineteenth century it was a section of the educated world that embraced the innovations. That is precisely because it was educated: it was more familiar with fresh ideas and more willing to accept them. The leaders of Evangelical opinion were swayed by the fashionable Romantic assumptions of their day. The gospel was being remoulded by the spirit of the age.

[4]

The Growth of the Word:
Evangelicals and Society
in the Nineteenth Century

But the word of God grew and multiplied. (Acts 12:24)

'Miss Drusilla Fawley was of her date, Evangelical.'[1] So Thomas Hardy
describes the elderly aunt of the protagonist in his last novel, *Jude the
Obscure*. While acidly implying that Evangelicalism, for all its claims to
represent eternal truth, is entirely transient, Hardy incidentally points us to
the period of Evangelical ascendancy in Britain. His novel, after publication
in parts, appeared complete in 1895: the prime of Miss Drusilla Fawley must
have been thirty to forty years before, that is, in the 1850s and 1860s. The
cult of duty, self-discipline and high seriousness was at its peak in those
decades. In 1850 the Lord Lieutenant of a Midland shire remembered a time
when only two landed gentlemen in the county had held family prayers,
but by that year only two did not.[2] When fast days were carefully observed
during the Crimean War, there was satisfaction at the 'improved religious
tone' of the age.[3] And sabbatarian opinion, a useful gauge of Evangelical
social influence, reached its apogee in the campaigns of the 1850s to ensure
the Sunday closure of the Crystal Palace and British Museum.[4] Evangelical
attitudes were characteristic of the times as never before or since. The
earliest favourable appreciation of Victorian civilisation, swimming against
the tide of previous hostility to all things Victorian, G. M. Young's *Portrait
of an Age*, fully recognised this broad ascendancy: 'Evangelicalism had
imposed on society, even on classes which were indifferent to its religious
basis and unaffected by its economic appeal, its code of Sabbath observance,
responsibility, and philanthropy; of discipline in the home, regularity in
affairs; it had created a most effective technique of agitation, of private
persuasion and social persecution.'[5] Such 'Victorian values' should perhaps
more accurately be styled 'high Victorian values', the social norms of the
years immediately following the middle of the nineteenth century. Their
dominance was primarily the fruit of Evangelical religion.

Not all mid-Victorians welcomed this development. To some more venturesome spirits the yoke of high Victorian values was irksome. A person, lamented J. S. Mill, 'who can be accused either of doing "what nobody does", or of not doing "what everybody does", is the subject of as much depreciatory remark as if he or she had committed some grave moral delinquency'.[6] Mill's *Essay on Liberty*, from which this quotation is taken, was an eloquent protest by the most distinguished English philosopher of his century against the forces making for conformity. It is the classic text of nineteenth-century Liberalism. But its shafts are directed less against the oppressive authority of the state than against what Mill calls 'the despotism of custom'. Completed in 1857 and published in 1859, the book is a condemnation of social pressures, and only secondarily of state interference. Mill was objecting to the power of opinion to wear down creative individuality to a uniform level of mediocrity. Although he never uses the word, Evangelicalism is his chief target. He criticises what he calls the theory of Calvinism, which is held, he suggests, by many who do not consider themselves Calvinists. According to Mill's caricature of the theory, human beings have but to submit to the divine will. All must bow to the same purposes, and so all must behave alike. The 'stricter Calvinists and Methodists . . . these intrusively pious members of society', in their passion for the improvement of morals, may well attempt the prohibition of popular amusements. Already they have launched three efforts to abridge personal liberty. There has been formed a United Kingdom Alliance to obtain the prohibition of the sale of liquor; there are outbreaks of sabbatarianism; and there is open hostility to Mormons.[7] All three of Mill's instances can be laid at the door of Evangelicals and their associates. Mill's powerful onslaught illustrates the extent to which popular Protestantism was (as it saw the matter) trying to be its brother's keeper. It is testimony to the mid-Victorian social influence of Evangelicalism.

Within the Church of England, as Gladstone pointed out in 1879, the Evangelical movement never became dominant, yet 'it did by infusion profoundly alter the general tone and tendency of the preaching of the clergy; not, however, at the close of the last or the beginning of the present century, but after the Tractarian movement had begun, and, indeed, mainly when it had reached that forward stage . . . of Ritualism'.[8] If the initiative had passed to the Oxford Movement and its offspring, the greatest influence of the Evangelicals as an Anglican party came in the period just after the middle of the century. The number of Evangelical clergy had been estimated in 1803 at five hundred.[9] In 1823 there had been 1,600 clerical subscribers to the Church Missionary Society.[10] By 1853 the Evangelical clergy were judged to embrace 6,500, that is, well over a third of the whole number.[11] The pace of change had increased in the 1830s and 1840s as a higher proportion of ordinands was drawn from the Evangelical camp. More young men were offering themselves for ministry, so that the balance of allegiance within the profession altered the more rapidly. By 1854 a majority of clergy had been ordained in the previous twenty years.[12] The younger men, even if outside the party boundary of Evangelicalism, had grown up in a world more favourable to vital religion, and its idiom, as Gladstone suggested, affected their preaching in particular.

The rising Evangelical tide was also evident in the episcopate. The first Evangelical bishop, Henry Ryder, was appointed to Gloucester in 1815 (and to Lichfield in 1824). The second and third, the brothers C. R. and J. B. Sumner, were elevated to Llandaff in 1826 (Winchester in 1827) and to Chester in 1828 respectively. Several clergy of Evangelical sympathies, if not firm party men, were consecrated during the 1830s.[13] In 1846 and 1848 W. A. Shirley and John Graham became Bishops of Sodor and Man and of Chester.[14] Between 1856 and 1860 six more Evangelicals were added to the bench: H. M. Villiers went to Carlisle (and later Durham), Charles Baring to Gloucester, Robert Bickersteth to Ripon, J. T. Pelham to Norwich, J. C. Wigram to Rochester and Samuel Waldegrave to Carlisle. This flurry of appointments owed more, it was said, to Shaftesbury's influence with Palmerston than to the candidates' merits. But that was unfair: Palmerston, like Shaftesbury, was looking for conscientious pastoral bishops and, not surprisingly, found suitable men among the enlarged ranks of the Evangelicals.[15] By this time, furthermore, there was an Evangelical Archbishop of Canterbury in J. B. Sumner (1848–62), who, if no striking personality, was as hard-working as his colleagues. The Evangelical school, dominant in the churches of Scotland and the chapels of England and Wales, had come into its own even in the Church of England.

THE 1851 RELIGIOUS CENSUS

It so happens that the Evangelical ascendancy coincided with the only official census of religion ever taken in Britain. It was calculated at the time that, of the population of England and Wales over the age of ten that could have attended, 54 per cent chose to be in church on census Sunday. A more recent recalculation has suggested that a minimum of 35 per cent of the total population attended church, or 47 per cent of the total population over the age of ten.[16] We can safely conclude that about half the available adult population went to church. Contemporaries were dismayed that attendance figures turned out to be so low, and historians have tended to echo them. In particular, they have drawn attention to the disparity between rural and urban churchgoing. The index of attendance (total attendances as a percentage of the population) was 71.4 for rural areas and small towns; but for large towns with a population of more than 10,000 it was 49.7. All eight London boroughs and Birmingham, Manchester, Liverpool, Leeds, Sheffield and Bradford recorded an index of attendance below 49.7. The figure for Preston was as low as 25.5. The cities of Victorian England seemed to be weak spots for the churches.[17] In the relatively static countryside they might have retained their hold on the population, but in the growing urban centres they appeared to be failing in their mission. Population growth, industrialisation and urbanisation had transformed the face of much of the country, and the churches had not adjusted to altered circumstances.

There is good reason, however, to call in question so pessimistic a verdict on the impact of the churches. For only half the available population to be churchgoers might trouble those mid-Victorians who assumed the whole nation should conform to religious worship. Yet that figure compares favourably with the statistics of the late twentieth century. In 1979 adult church attendance as a proportion of the adult population of England was 11 per cent.[18] By that yardstick mid-nineteenth-century congregations were flourishing. Furthermore, scattered evidence from the eighteenth century suggests that attendance was often low in a period long before the census. In thirty Oxfordshire parishes between 1738 and 1811 the number of communicants formed less than 5 per cent of the population. Likewise, communicant levels were poor in late eighteenth-century Cheshire.[19] Such findings are congruent with the torpor that commonly gripped the Georgian Church of England. Consequently, it is certain that the churches were facing no novel problem in the levels of abstention from worship in 1851.

On the contrary, the rates of attendance in that year represented a significant improvement on the pattern prevailing in the previous century. The churches had managed to recruit more effectively despite the immense growth in population of the early nineteenth century, despite industrialisation and urbanisation. Their success can confidently be attributed primarily to the hunger for souls of Evangelicalism. In the case of Methodism the process of growth can be documented from the careful membership statistics kept by the connexions. In 1801 Methodists formed 1.5 per cent of the adult English population; in 1851, 4.4 per cent.[20] Similarly, Congregationalists in England grew from an estimated 35,000 in 1800 to 165,000 in 1851 while population merely doubled.[21] In Scotland, the proportion of churchgoers in 1851 at congregations of the Free and United Presbyterian Churches, both wholly Evangelical bodies, was 51 per cent, and at the much more mixed Church of Scotland it was 32 per cent.[22] It can also be shown from the 1851 census that the Evangelicals of the Church of England had achieved more than their contemporaries of the same communion. Returns for a sample of Evangelical parishes belonging to the Simeon Trust have been compared with those for a sample of equivalent nearby parishes of unknown churchmanship. The index of attendance for the Simeon Trust parishes turned out to be 44, whereas for the equivalent parishes it was only 25.[23] Evidently Evangelical Anglicans shared fully in the large-scale recruitment of the early nineteenth century. Massive church growth underlay the Evangelical social influence of the mid-century.

If the 1851 religious census reveals overall success by the churches in winning men and women to Christian practice, it also shows great geographical variation in their support. A broad regional contrast existed between the south-east, where the Church of England was generally stronger, and the north-west, where it was weaker. The contrast reflected the division of England and Wales into a lowland arable zone, where greater prosperity had created smaller parishes and richer endowments centuries before, and an upland pastoral zone, where larger, less sought-after parishes had received less intensive pastoral care. The Old Dissent was most powerful in its historic heartland, a swathe of territory embracing East Anglia, the South Midlands and the West Country, together with Wales. The strength of Methodism lay primarily in the upland zone of the north and west where the Church of England had been least efficient. Local diversity was immense, having a great deal to do with how effective squire and parson could be in excluding Nonconformity from the parish.[24] Consequently rural churchgoing varied between an index of attendance of 104.6 in Bedfordshire (a result of frequent multiple attendances) and one of 37.3 in Cumberland. It is entirely mistaken to suppose that there was anything like monolithic religious conformity in the countryside.

The level and denominational balance of churchgoing in large towns resembled, though usually at a lower level, the pattern of the surrounding countryside. Migrants to the towns were preponderantly drawn from the adjacent villages and brought their religious preferences with them.[25] Urban churchgoing also tended to be lower where the town was larger and its economy more industrialised. The three large towns possessing an index of attendance above the rural average of 71.4, Bath, Colchester and Exeter, were centres of administration, commerce and leisure rather than of industry. There can be no doubt about where the greatest strength of Evangelicalism lay. The Methodists, far more numerous than the other Nonconformist bodies, gathered throngs of worshippers in several of the northern counties. In Stoke-on-Trent they actually attracted more attendances than all the other denominations put together. In Yorkshire they did almost as well, achieving a percentage share of attendances of 47.3 in the East Riding, 45.4 in the North Riding and 42.3 in the West Riding.[26] It is possible to assess the strength of Evangelicalism within the Church of England according to the percentage of congregations in a county supporting the Church Missionary Society. By far the highest figures relate to Yorkshire: 42.5 for the East Riding, 40.2 for the North Riding and 39.7 for the West Riding. The adjacent counties of Durham (27.2), Derbyshire (26.0) and Lancashire (25.3) come next on the list.[27] It is plain that the combined forces of Methodism and Evangelical Anglicanism had become firmly entrenched in the north of England, with Yorkshire as a huge bastion. There were many remote rural nooks in the county, but equally it contained several of the most important industrial cities. The gospel did not lack appeal in an urban, industrial environment.

SOCIAL CLASS

In addition, the religious census lays bare a correlation between churchgoing and social class. Large towns with a similar class structure possessed similar rates of churchgoing. Again, more detailed analysis of the returns has shown that where middle-class inhabitants were numerous, church attendance was higher. Conversely, in the poorer parishes, attendance was lower.[28] It seems that this pattern was general. Only in Liverpool, where some Catholic Irish showed conspicuous loyalty to their church, did predominantly working-class parishes record higher attendances than predominantly middle-class parishes.[29] The growth of class-specific suburbs in the later nineteenth century accentuated the tendency. By 1902 in London there was a close correspondence between levels of churchgoing and the position of a suburb in the social hierarchy. Thus, in Ealing, near the top of the social scale, 47 per cent of the population was in church, while in Fulham, near the bottom, only 12 per cent.[30] Where the social mix was more varied, the parish church might draw in different grades – though not necessarily to the same service. But this principle did not apply to Nonconformists. 'Class position amongst the Nonconformists goes very much by congregations', concluded an observer in 1902, 'the worshippers sorting themselves in this way much more than do those who attend parish churches.'[31] Throughout the century church attendance was most common at the highest social levels. The ability of the churches to attract those possessing wealth and power, it has been justly observed, was a significant achievement, a sign of the importance of religion in society.[32]

A consequence, however, was that some denominations were almost entirely middle-class in composition. Although this was truest of the non-Evangelical Unitarians and the only partly Evangelical Quakers, it was also commonly the case among Congregationalists. Their denomination, according to the same observer of London in 1902, was 'more than any other the Church of the middle classes, its membership being practically confined within the limits of the upper and lower sections of those included under that comprehensive title'.[33] During the second half of the century the middle-class proportion of the worshipping community increased, not least because of the growth in size of the lower middle classes in society at large. Between 1851 and 1911 the proportion of occupied males over 15 in clerical and similar posts increased from 2.5 per cent to 7.1 per cent.[34] Children from churchgoing families in the working classes, often giving promise of steadiness and reliability, thronged into this emerging sector. In 1902, even in predominantly working-class Bethnal Green, 34.6 per cent of worshippers in Congregational chapels and 24.0 per cent of those in their Baptist equivalents were clerical workers.[35] Nor were the Primitive Methodists, with their proletarian image, exempt. At Ashton-under-Lyne, between 1850 and 1870, 4 per cent of their worshippers were lower middle-class; for the period between 1890 and 1910 the proportion had risen to 21 per cent.[36] The process of embourgeoisement reinforced over time the tendency of the churches to be more successful further up the social scale.

This feature of churchgoing was so marked that it is sometimes suggested that the working classes abstained from Christian worship altogether. A pioneer historian of the subject has written of 'the general widespread alienation of the artisan classes from the churches'.[37] It is easy, especially on the hypothesis of urbanisation being intrinsically unfavourable to churchgoing, to reach too blanket a conclusion. In reality, the figures for the 1851 census show that there must have been extensive working-class attendance. Too many people went to church for religious practice to have been confined to the middle classes, which accounted for less than a quarter of the population. A majority of the working people did not attend, but a significant proportion did. More detailed research has shown that skilled workers, the artisans proper, were far more likely to enter a place of worship than unskilled labourers. In the early nineteenth century it was the skilled who were overwhelmingly attracted to Evangelical Nonconformity. Whereas artisans constituted some 23 per cent of society at large, they composed 59 per cent of Evangelical Nonconformist congregations.[38] The Secession churches of Glasgow made a parallel appeal to the skilled men of the city.[39] The great number of tiny contributions to the CMS suggests that Evangelicalism in the Church of England drew heavily on the same constituency.[40] Artisans were commonly to be found in church.

Unskilled workers, usually the majority and in some areas the great majority of the working classes, were drawn into places of worship in much smaller numbers. The case of the Primitive Methodists, normally supposed to have provided a religion for the poor, is instructive. It is true that in some areas they did penetrate the unskilled working classes. In part of Lincolnshire, for instance, 51 per cent of identified Primitive lay preachers in the mid-nineteenth century were agricultural labourers.[41] Generally, however, Primitive Methodist chapels catered for the skilled much more than for the unskilled. In a national sample of Primitive congregations in the first third of the century 16 per cent were labourers and another 12 per cent were miners, most of them unskilled; but 48 per cent were artisans.[42] An exhaustive study has shown that, although between 80 per cent and 100 per cent of nineteenth-century Primitive Methodists were manual workers, they were much more likely to be semi-skilled or craftsmen than labourers.[43] There was, of course, a natural tendency for converted characters to gain skills, find regular employment and so rise out of the lowest ranks of society. Evangelical religion, as many commented at the time, was itself an avenue of upward social mobility. Yet this process meant that the gospel abstracted individuals from their original setting rather than mingling with the lifestyle of the poor. So it can be concluded that although Evangelicalism enjoyed substantial working-class support it never secured the allegiance of the masses of the labouring population.

NON-CHURCHGOING

Why was there widespread alienation among the lower working classes from the churches? A primary factor was sheer poverty. Even at the end of the century, by which time the working-class standard of living had risen significantly, the family income could often be too low to buy the essentials of existence such as shoes and clothes. To appear at church was to court the contempt of neighbours for not being able to dress the family adequately. Nor could many families afford pennies for the offering.[44] And one of the chief deterrents was the pew rent system. Most nineteenth-century places of worship, apart from older parish churches, were financed at least in part by hiring out particular pews to those who would pay for them. Grades of comfort dictated price differentials. Consequently, variations in social status were imported into church. Cheap or free seating was normally made available for the poor, but often in inconvenient corners behind pillars. A working-class newcomer would be assigned what an Evangelical clergyman condemned in 1859 as 'a pauper's post outside the well-cushioned pew'.[45] Despite a chorus of criticism from many quarters, the system persisted in places long into the twentieth century. It was symptomatic of the barriers to church attendance erected by what a leading Congregational minister called 'the English caste system'.[46]

Unskilled workers outside Methodism, with its plethora of official posts, rarely found themselves involved in church administration or exercising church discipline. Conversely, discipline, as enforced by Nonconformists and all Scottish Presbyterians, tended to bear more heavily on the poorer section of the working classes whose offences were normally more public.[47] This factor should not be exaggerated, for discipline was exercised over even the eminent and prosperous: the affairs of Sir Morton Peto, a bankrupt building and railway contractor, were fully investigated and partly censured in 1867 by the Baptist church he had founded.[48] Furthermore, vigilance in exercising discipline declined in all churches during the last third of the century, so that by its end the practice could hardly be a grievance.[49] Although working-class resentment of failure by the churches to criticise the class system existed, it seems not to have been a major reason for absence from worship until the end of the century. Only then did wholesale condemnation of the churches for ignorance of industrial questions and contempt for the working people affect more than a small proportion of the population.[50] Class consciousness had by that time reached new heights. Yet a certain ecclesiastical insensitivity to proletarian self-respect had previously caused a diffuse but powerful indignation among the working classes. 'Let the poor learn', Bishop Robert Bickersteth declared in 1860, 'that there is a sympathy felt for them amongst the classes which, in social rank, are above them.'[51] Although the intention was kindly, a tone so patently *de haut en bas* was noticed and, by some, resented. The result was a reinforcement of traditional anticlericalism, 'antagonism . . . to the parson as a paid teacher of religion'.[52] Dislike for lazy clergy, incomprehensible worship and overbearing class assumptions could combine with the expense of involvement to deter many of the poor from churchgoing.

Perhaps the most widespread explanation within Evangelical churches for working-class non-attendance in the late nineteenth century was what the Congregational minister already quoted called 'the drink habit'.[53] Alcohol clouded the spiritual faculties, and its purchase (it was commonly held) was responsible for the poverty that kept people outside the church doors. Simplistic as this analysis undoubtedly was, it held a measure of truth. The consumption of alcohol probably mounted steadily until 1876 and, although it fell thereafter, it remained at high levels.[54] Alcohol was available from a vast array of outlets. In 1854 in Merthyr Tydfil there were 506 licensed drinking places, that is, one for every 93 of the population, and the town was not exceptional.[55] The public house, as it had done down the centuries, formed the chief alternative centre of community life to the church. 'Pub-going' was the only social activity to attract more people than churchgoing. So it represented a different use of leisure time that constantly posed a threat to the churches.

From the years around 1870 onwards, furthermore, there was a great expansion in organised leisure activities that rivalled the churches in drawing power. Traditional recreations had probably suffered less in the early industrial period than has been supposed, but now, with increasing middle-class patronage, they were turned into disciplined, rule-governed games that harnessed extensive popular enthusiasm. The general adoption of the Saturday half-holiday permitted a great expansion of football and cricket clubs in the 1870s. The churches, sensitive to the popular mood, realised the need to provide recreational facilities. At Bolton a third of the cricket clubs and a quarter of the football clubs had a religious connection; and in Birmingham at least a fifth of the cricket clubs and a quarter of the football clubs.[56] Although such agencies retained the allegiance of some young men, their creation was evidence of a recognition by churches of their potential power to draw away. Like the contemporary working men's clubs and music halls, they supplied communal enjoyments that an earlier generation might have found through religious outlets.

The counter-attraction of organised atheism was much less potent. Committed secularists numbered no more than about twenty thousand at any time in Victorian Britain, with the National Secular Society in 1880, near its peak, claiming only six thousand members.[57] Agnosticism was as yet merely a fashion of the intelligentsia. It may well be, however, that a stronger influence on the lower working classes was a folk religion heavily indebted to paganism. The survival of rural witchcraft is vividly illustrated in the novels of Hardy, but there is also a growing body of evidence suggesting widespread popular belief in esoteric remedies for misfortune, the sacredness of nature and the importance of ritual observances at turning points in personal life and the annual cycle. Such notions were not confined to the countryside. City churches, as in Lambeth, were thronged with working-class attenders at harvest festival and on New Year's Eve, the two occasions when church services regularly marked events in nature rather than in Christian story.[58] A deep-rooted though residual nature religion could only hamper the evangelism of the churches. But when all the obstacles to churchgoing have been reviewed, there remains a fundamental explanation for the alienation from the churches. As a recent historian has put it, the otherworldly preoccupations of the churches were too distant from the needs of day-to-day living.[59] Evangelicals were making a similar point when they contended that the heart of man is not naturally sympathetic to the truth of God. In view of this inevitable gulf, the wonder of the nineteenth-century Evangelical record is not its shortcomings but its degree of success.

REVIVALISM

Church growth was partly a steady, sustained process and partly a matter of short, sharp increases. The bursts of revival were most marked in Methodism, but also affected other denominations in some parts of Britain. In Wales, for example, there was a rhythm of booms and slumps in recruitment, with good periods in 1807–9, 1815–20, 1828–30, 1839–43 and 1849.[60] Such variations invite interpretation in terms of factors external to the life of the churches. The trade cycle, itself a sequence of booms and slumps, is an obvious explanatory candidate. There is evidence that economic adversity sometimes coincided with falls in Nonconformist recruitment rates.[61] Inability to make financial contributions may well have enhanced inhibitions about chapel-going at such times. On the other hand, during the cotton famine of the 1860s that blighted Lancashire's industrial heartland with depression, its Wesleyan circuits achieved remarkable results. The average recruitment rate for the whole connexion was 2.6 per cent, but for ten cotton towns it was 15.1 per cent.[62] At times, acute hardship could encourage resort to supernatural aid. No consistent correlation between economic and religious cycles emerges.

Discussion of an alternative hypothesis explaining patterns of church growth has emerged from E. P. Thompson's contention that popular religion was a form of stunted radicalism. Periods of religious revival, he argues, followed socio-political excitements.[63] Supporting evidence comes from the aftermath of the so-called Captain Swing riots, outbreaks of rural incendiarism in 1830–2. Primitive Methodist expansion was immediate and striking in the affected areas.[64] In other cases, however, political agitation and evangelism were rival activities (as in the north of England following the French wars) or else Evangelical religion dampened the potential for radical politics (as in Cornwall in the Chartist years).[65] The commonest relationship, it has been suggested, was that religious and political ferment were simultaneous. When religious and political issues became interwoven, churches could be mobilised for vigorous evangelism and political assertion at the same time.[66] The clearest instance is a late one, the upsurge of Nonconformist membership in 1902–6, when the chapels were roused to political indignation against the Conservative Education Act of 1902.[67] Other alleged instances, however, turn out to be invalid: there was no such thing as 'a massive popular disestablishment campaign' in 1875–6 to explain the high Nonconformist recruitment rate of those years.[68] So it appears that political stimuli could bring church growth either at the time or in their wake, but that there was no necessary connection.

Death has been proposed as another precipitant of large-scale recruitment. 'Terrible accidents and fearful deaths', it was said of South Wales, '[are] not uncommon in these iron and coal districts . . . [H]ence funeral sermons are frequent, and are often attended with good moral and religious effect.'[69] The most obvious spur to revival of the nineteenth century was the cholera epidemic of 1832 that killed thousands. The twelve months up to March 1833 saw the largest membership increase ever recorded in Wesleyan history, and other denominations also reaped a harvest.[70] In the most popular Evangelical tract, Legh Richmond's *The Dairyman's Daughter*, the heroine dies of consumption; and diaries regularly turn to spiritual issues on the death of friends and relations. The fall of the death rate in the later nineteenth century and its greater fall in the twentieth century must have been disadvantageous for recruitment. If it seems clear that the pattern of church growth was not controlled by external determinants, it seems equally clear that crises – whether economic, political or, most insistent of all, the crisis of death – could provide a favourable context for the propagation of the faith.[71]

A revival could be a form of spontaneous combustion. Typical was an outbreak at Burslem reported by a Wesleyan preacher in 1832:

> Two colliers had been playing at cards all the night, and were . . . cursing and swearing in a dreadful manner; when as they thought lightnings began to dart upon them with a strong smell of brimston[e] . . . They began to cry for mercy. The neighbourhood was all alarmed . . . For several days and nights, nearly the whole population of the place which is considerable, were engaged in incessant prayer . . .[72]

Such currents of feeling could readily overflow the official channels dug by denominational functionaries and, for that reason, the Wesleyan authorities often looked askance on the more exuberant displays. In particular, they discountenanced the camp meeting, a technique of American frontier religion at which open-air preaching and prayer would go on deep into the night. The Wesleyan condemnation of a camp meeting held in 1807 on Mow Cop, a hill overlooking Stoke-on-Trent, led to the emergence in the Potteries of a new connexion, the Primitive Methodists, committed to revivalism.[73] The early years of the Primitives were marked by loud cries of emotion, exorcisms of the devil and vivid dreams. Women saw visions in which was revealed a sort of celestial pecking order of the leading revivalists of the day, with individuals moving up or down the league table: 'the head of the Church', it was recorded in 1811, 'now stands as follows: James Crawford 1, Lorenzo Dow 2, Mary Dunnel 3 . . . '[74] Strange new ways were part and parcel of the uninhibited expression of a spontaneous revival.

As the century wore on, however, spontaneity gradually gave way to arranged revivals. A landmark was the appearance in 1839 of Charles Finney's *Lectures on Revivals of Religion*, originally published in America in 1835, with its argument that conversions could be encouraged by the adoption of certain techniques – such as the isolated 'anxious seat' for the troubled sinner in search of salvation. Although the book was a major stimulus in 1839–43 to traditional, uncontrived revivals in Wales, it heralded a new age of revival planning.[75] In Scotland a wave of revivalism beginning at Kilsyth in 1839 led to enthusiasm for Finney's methods among young men, the expulsion of candidates for the ministry from the Congregational theological academy for 'self-conversionism' and the creation in 1843 of a new denomination, the Evangelical Union, designed to foment revivals. An American evangelist, James Caughey, toured British Methodism in the 1840s, relying on well-tried techniques to obtain converts.[76] It was but a short step to the end-of-century trumpeter-revivalist with his carefully contrived performance depicted by Arnold Bennett in *Anna of the Five Towns*.[77] By 1860, when revival broke out at Hopeman on the Moray Firth, the local newspaper felt bound to state that 'no attempts were made to "get up" this movement'.[78] There was a gradual transition during the century from folksy outbursts of anguished guilt to professionally planned occasions for much more conventional 'decisions for Christ'.

This distinction is the key to understanding what happened to British Evangelicalism in 1859–60. It has been argued by Edwin Orr, himself a distinguished evangelist, that in those years there began a nationwide and sustained revival, 'the second Evangelical awakening in Britain'. He adduces evidence from all over the country of revival activities in those years.[79] What he does not attempt, however, is to discriminate between spontaneous popular revival, deeply rooted in the community, and meetings carefully designed to promote the work of the gospel. His case faithfully reflects his chief source, *The Revival* magazine, set up by R. C. Morgan in 1859 to foster the cause. Morgan deliberately created the impression that a single phenomenon, revival, was already aflame throughout Britain. He was eager to extend the traditional variety to untouched areas.

In reality, however, its range was severely limited. The movement began in America in 1857–8, breaking out in Ulster early in 1859. It made a powerful impact, bringing about mass conversions and physical prostrations of a kind that would have been familiar to Wesley or the early Primitives. It was greatly hoped that revival, perhaps without the prostrations, would reach Britain. Parts of Scotland were affected. Scarcely a town or village between Aberdeen and Inverness, it was said early in 1860, had not been visited by the Spirit.[80] At Portessie in Banffshire for nearly three days and nights there was continuous praying, singing and exhortation of neighbours. 'Labour is totally suspended', it was reported. 'Even the cooking of victuals is much neglected . . . '[81] Revival was general in the Isle of Lewis, and at Greenock in Renfrewshire a thousand, chiefly working people, were said to have been converted in less than six months.[82] It is significant that the centre of revival meetings in Greenock was the Seamen's Chapel, for repeatedly fishermen were chiefly involved. At Portassie the five hundred engaged in religious exercises were 'purely seafaring' and at neighbouring Buckie crews came to shore already converted.[83] Fishing communities were tightly knit, often isolated and well aware of the high risk of death at sea. They were particularly likely to retain corporate expectations of turning to God. In Wales, too, there were similar outbreaks, beginning in remote Cardiganshire.[84] In England, however, instances were rare. One researcher has discovered only three.[85] There were more, but almost entirely in Cornwall and north Devon, where, again, fishermen were concentrated.[86] Community revivals in Britain, it is clear, were virtually confined to the periphery and were most likely within a single occupational group.

The hope that such movements would spread, on the other hand, was an inducement to redouble organised efforts for the spread of the gospel. *The Revival* was itself a novel technique, a magazine devoted to spreading information about the movement. Open-air preaching, already being adopted by Evangelical clergy in the 1850s, became common again. Iron mission halls were erected. Laymen entered careers as full-time popular evangelists, whether gentlemen like Brownlow North or working-class characters like Richard Weaver, 'the converted collier'. Even female ministry, justified as an exceptional measure for exceptional times, became common, just as it had done among the early Primitives.[87] The Methodist spirit of pragmatic, aggressive evangelism was spreading beyond the bounds of Methodism. A new ethos, negligent of denominational forms, emerged. The Brethren sect created much of the network responsible for the new temper and drew in many of the converts.[88] All the Evangelical denominations nevertheless felt the new winds, and the way was prepared for the arrival of the enormously influential undenominational evangelists Moody and Sankey in the 1870s.[89] It is therefore quite just to see 1859–60 as the threshold of a fresh phase in organised evangelism; but events of those years show that revival of the spontaneous variety was becoming marginal in Britain.

METHODS OF EVANGELISM

Most of the nineteenth-century impact of Evangelicalism, however, was achieved not through revivals but through regular methods of mission.

Ordinary Sunday services were fundamental. At the evening service, normally the second or third of the day, the pattern of worship and the style of preaching were adapted to the supreme task of implanting the gospel in the hearers, who by that hour would include domestic servants and (in the countryside) agricultural labourers. In the less inhibited denominations, evening service would be followed by a prayer meeting or after-meeting where a significant proportion of conversions would take place. Beyond Sunday gatherings, however, there was a battery of other activities designed to convince or sustain converts. Weekly prayer meetings, often on a Friday or Saturday evening, were intended primarily to seek God's blessing on the Sunday services. Two or three individuals might be asked by the minister to lead the prayer, or else free prayer might be permitted, the minister closing the proceedings.[90] A midweek preaching service, or else in the Church of England a meeting for communicants, would supplement the instruction given on Sunday. Cottage meetings, often in remoter parts of the district, would provide opportunities for guidance to smaller groups. Bible classes were held for special sections of the congregation: female servants, mothers from the working classes, working men, ladies, young men, candidates for confirmation or church membership and children.[91] Other gatherings such as monthly sewing meetings for the poor could subserve spiritual purposes. 'Associations of the promising young females of the higher or middle rank in our parishes are very desirable.'[92] Ideally each social group was catered for.

Perhaps most important, Evangelicals did not wait for people to come to their places of worship; Evangelicals went to the people. House-to-house visitation began on a significant scale with the formation of the Strangers' Friend Society in London in the 1780s,[93] but it received an immense fillip from the publication of the first volume of Thomas Chalmers's *Christian and Civic Economy of Large Towns* in 1821. Chalmers described the system of lay visitation he had set in motion in the inner-city parish of St John's, Glasgow, and soon he was widely imitated.[94] In 1825 London Nonconformists established the Christian Instruction Society. By 1832 it had assembled about 1,150 members who paid a Christian visit once a fortnight to nearly 32,000 families.[95] Its success made it a model for further similar efforts. Voluntary visitors, most of them women, would call on perhaps twenty families at frequent intervals, always delivering tracts, encouraging attendance at worship and reporting cases of need to the minister. There were risks of petty officiousness: district visitors were warned 'never to indulge in culinary curiosity and peep in the pot'.[96] Yet the technique ensured that there was a point of contact between the church and non-attenders. It was supplemented from 1857 by Mrs Ranyard's Bible women, full-time paid visitors of a lower social class.[97] With a multitude of organisations, subordinate clergy and district visitors to co-ordinate, the incumbent of a large urban parish could have charge of a huge administrative machinery. As Rector of St George's, Southwark,

William Cadman assembled nearly 200 voluntary parish workers in 1850.[98] Sustained evangelistic activity on such a scale could hardly fail to make inroads on religious indifference.

Local effort was supported by a large and heterogeneous machinery of organisations. Official structures could help. A sympathetic bishop such as C. R. Sumner of Winchester could back the exhortations to mission of his pastoral charges with bodies like the diocesan Church Building Society, founded in 1837.[99] The London Diocesan Home Mission, set up by A. C. Tait, provided special preachers of varied churchmanship, yet was valued by many Evangelicals.[100] Among Nonconformists, the Congregational and Baptist Home Missionary Societies placed evangelists in neglected areas or decayed causes.[101] The Baptists also operated a national Building Fund and a Metropolitan Chapel Building Fund that contributed greatly to their enduring strength in the capital.[102] The Methodists led the way in the central allocation of funds and were followed in Scotland by the Free Church, which defied prophets of financial disaster for the new denomination with its rapidly created and generously supported Sustentation Fund for ministers.[103] In the second half of the century the Congregational and Baptist Unions, though serving independent congregations, developed a central apparatus for augmenting stipends.[104] Foreign missionary societies stimulated evangelism at home not by financial backing but by providing an object lesson. Interest in foreign missions, it was cogently argued, 'stimulates, encourages, directs Christian life by calling attention to the example of converts from heathenism'.[105]

Much of the home missionary work was designed to grapple with the growing nineteenth-century problem of neglected inner-city areas where the non-churchgoing masses increasingly congregated. The difficulties of Manchester incumbents were becoming greater year by year, it was reported in 1858, because the more respectable parishioners were moving to the outskirts.[106] Similarly, the Minister of Shoreditch Baptist Tabernacle in East London recalled that his church possessed its share of the well-to-do until the mid-1890s, but then, because it was continually feeding suburban congregations, found it difficult to maintain its work on the offerings of the poor.[107] The Church Pastoral Aid Society, launched in 1836, came to the relief of Evangelical clergy by supporting extra staff in needy parishes. Though incurring High Church frowns for financing non-clerical workers and operating beyond episcopal control, the society expanded so that in 1858 it paid for 378 curates and 162 lay agents.[108] Its work was supplemented by the Scripture Readers' Association, begun in 1844 and consolidated as an Anglican body in 1849, supporting men who neither preached nor distributed literature.[109] Lay agents were also provided by the interdenominational city missions of which the largest and most successful was the London City Mission, founded in 1835. The LCM financed evangelists who were normally attached to particular congregations, but who sometimes ministered to particular ethnic groups like the Welsh or particular industrial occupations like the dockers. After half a century its staff reached 460. A slightly higher social group, consisting of shop assistants and their peers, was the special target of the Young Men's Christian Association, founded in London in 1844 and soon possessing branches in most cities.[110] A broad range of other bodies, similar but smaller, often local or specialised, existed to help with evangelism: the Evangelization Society (1864), the Christian Colportage Association (1874) and the Missions to Seamen (1856) are but three examples.[111] Behind them all stood the munificence of men such as Samuel Morley, a millionaire hosiery manufacturer who was a broad-minded Congregationalist. 'The distribution of his money', according to his biographer, 'was . . . the main business of his life.'[112] Christian mission benefited hugely from the organisations that brought to it some of the fruits of British economic prosperity.

PHILANTHROPY

The poor who were not attracted to church by the gospel were sometimes drawn in by charity. 'Neither Jesus nor his apostles', according to *The Christian* in 1880, 'ever separated the physical from the spiritual well-being of men. He and they fed and healed the bodies of the people, and the sympathy thus manifested won their attention, and enabled them to impart food and healing to their souls.'[113] The gospel and humanitarianism, even in this rather pietistic journal, were seen not as rivals but as complementary. Because God had created the body as well as the soul, argued the prince of philanthropists, Lord Shaftesbury, each body must be 'cared for according to the end for which it was formed – fitness for His service'.[114] Although the career of Shaftesbury was never forgotten, it is remarkable that the charitable theory and practice of the mass of nineteenth-century Evangelicals were to be minimised by many later commentators.[115] Probably the chief explanation is that Evangelicals of the nineteenth century have been tainted by the repudiation of Christian social obligation that marked certain of their successors in the following century.[116] In the nineteenth century, however, even if private philanthropy was common in all religious bodies and beyond, Evangelicals led the way. Among charitable organisations of the second half of the century, for instance, it has been estimated that three-quarters were Evangelical in character and control.[117] The prison reform work of Elizabeth Fry, a Quaker of Evangelical inclination, early in the century became celebrated precisely because it was held up as an inspiration to subsequent generations.[118] Dr Barnardo of the Brethren earned equivalent fame in caring for orphans later in the century.[119] The sick in body and mind, the blind, the deaf, the infirm, the elderly, vagrants, navvies, soldiers, prostitutes, and above all the poor received attention according to their particular needs. Evangelical activism carried over into social concern as an end in itself.

There was, however, a diffidence among many Evangelicals about certain aspects of relief work. Not all the needy deserved help; if at all possible, the poor should help themselves; and public assistance was to be rejected out of hand. This cluster of tenets flowed from the general acceptance, at least by the upper and middle classes, of the teachings of political economy. The great masters in the tradition of Adam Smith held that no disincentive to hard work could be permitted in a well-ordered society. Lesser figures such as Samuel Smiles in the mid-nineteenth century sang the praises of self-help. Christians of all traditions assimilated these opinions to a greater or lesser extent.[120] The result was a tight circumscription of the bounds of charity that sometimes has a harsh ring. Chalmers insisted that in no circumstances, high unemployment included, should the able-bodied poor have a right to relief. Poverty, following Malthus, he held to be the great spur to industry. Financial assistance for the destitute, furthermore, must never be the result of compulsory exactions. The poor should rely on the generosity of the better-off.[121] A leading exponent of similar, though marginally less rigid, views in the Church of England was J. B. Sumner, subsequently the first Evangelical Archbishop of Canterbury. Charity, he contended, should consist of private benevolence. Only in very rare instances where social evils were so deeply seated as to frustrate private action, should the state intervene.[122]

A leading Evangelical clergyman who later became a Dissenter, Baptist Noel, reveals the ambiguity that was the result. He urged the Christian duty of relieving those in need, but he also warned that the charitably disposed might turn the poor into greedy mendicants. Requests for money must be rejected because the worth of applicants could not be ascertained. 'It is painful', he admitted, 'to turn away from the request of those who *may* be suffering from extreme want . . . '[123] It became accepted wisdom that the poor should not be helped unless they were known to be 'deserving' and then only in kind, not in cash. 'Indiscriminate almsgiving is a great curse', declared John Clifford, a Baptist who was later to modify his views, 'Government relief is mostly lifting a man up by dropping him into a deeper abyss.'[124] Ideas shaped by political economy probably made greater progress among Evangelicals outside the Established Churches, for within them there were countervailing traditions of parochial responsibility for the poor. The most influential Evangelical clerical handbook nevertheless recommended giving only partial relief, leaving to the poor a stimulus to their own exertions.[125] The regiment of seven clergy and eleven scripture readers or city missionaries operating during the 1850s in the Evangelical parish of St Giles, Bloomsbury, was enjoined to concentrate on spiritual objects and so give no charity.[126] Resentment spread among the poor when they were spurned. The Evangelical record in the philanthropic field was not an unqualified asset for evangelism.

Yet there is no doubt that social concern did bring some of the less advantaged within the sphere of Christian influence. The philanthropic machinery of an individual congregation could be huge, especially as the century advanced. Kensington Congregational Church already possessed by the early 1820s, apart from schools and evangelistic agencies, a Benevolent Society run by ladies for visiting, instructing and relieving the sick poor; a Blanket Society, making free distributions in winter; an Infants' Friendly Society, through which ladies provided clothes and food for poor mothers and their children during their confinement; and collections in severe winters for the poor of the area.[127] A well equipped urban parish church at mid-century was expected to have a District Visiting Society, whose members could issue tickets for obtaining relief in kind from local tradesmen; a Provident Fund, collecting sums of not more than sixpence weekly, adding interest and returning coals or clothing in June or December; soup distribution at a penny a quart in winter; Maternal Charity tin boxes containing a Bible, Prayer Book, oatmeal, sugar, soap and sometimes linen for pregnant mothers; and (rather less popular) a Lending Library.[128] At Reading in the 1890s the various churches and chapels provided similar but even more numerous agencies: a Poor Fund in most chapels, Ladies' Visiting Associations, perhaps with paid sick visitors, Sunshine Funds attached to most Christian Endeavour groups, Dorcas Societies encouraging sewing for the poor, Soup Kitchens, Mothers' Meetings on behalf of the poor, Provident Clubs, Coal and Clothing Clubs, Loan Blanket Societies, Infants' Friends Societies, Penny Banks, maternity groups and much else. [129] All this battery of assistance amounted to far more than a minor palliative. Apart from the heartily disliked Poor Law, the churches were the most obvious source of help in a society which, until shortly before the First World War, lacked a state welfare system.

Local ecclesiastical provision was supplemented by the various societies that sprang up to channel funds from generous to the needy. Organisations like the Indigent Blind Visitation Society and the Destitute Children's Dinner Society proliferated. In the first half of the nineteenth century, it has been calculated, new philanthropic bodies were founded at an average rate of six a year.[130] With their annual gatherings entrenched among the May Meetings of the Exeter Hall, they held an honoured place in the Evangelical world. It was easy to satirise their blend of earnestness, business sense and bureaucratic officiousness. The annual meeting of the fictitious Society for the Distribution of Moral Pocket Handkerchiefs (Secretary: Soapy Bareface, Esq. Committee members: the Rev. Augustus Cant and the Rev. Nasal Whine) was gleefully chronicled by a High Church journal in 1860. The society's purpose was purchasing handkerchiefs, printing moral maxims on both sides and selling them to the poor. The annual accounts recorded committee expenses of £640, not entirely balanced by receipts from the sale of handkerchiefs: 3s. 4 1/2d.[131] Self-importance, incompetence and fraud were by no means absent from these bodies, but they did make inroads on the mass of deprivation, redistributing some of the country's wealth to those in most need. Whether locally or nationally organised, voluntary philanthropic societies were a monument to the activist temper of Evangelical religion.

EDUCATION

The traditional assumption that education fell within the province of the churches was reinforced among Evangelicals by an awareness of its moral value. Although it was no substitute for the gospel, it could subserve the gospel. 'Man', wrote John Venn in 1804, '. . . cannot by education be made a real Christian; but by education he may be freed from prejudices and delivered from the dominion of dispositions highly favourable to temptation and sin.'[132] Even more important, literacy was a precondition for reading the Bible. Reading skills had long been fostered primarily for that purpose throughout Protestant northern Europe, often by informal methods outside schools. By the mid-eighteenth century some 60 per cent of men in England and 65 per cent in Scotland were literate according to the gauge of the ability to sign their names, together with some 40 per cent of women in England and 15 per cent in Scotland.[133] Reading ability, however, was probably more widespread than ability to sign one's name. Certainly converts in the Cambuslang revival of 1742 for whom evidence survives could all read, male and female alike.[134] Around the year 1800 signing ability decreased in certain regions, often the most industrialised,[135] and so there was an extra reason for organised Christian effort to promote literacy.

Once reading skills had been achieved, they were used to promote understanding of the faith. The accepted method was catechising. Children and young people were required to learn their catechism (that of the Church of England or the Westminster Assembly), or else some equivalent, and were examined on their prowess, often in the afternoon service. Catechising, however, was steadily supplanted during the first half of the century by a combination of Sunday and day schooling,[136] though it was to survive long into the twentieth century in the Scottish Highlands. Sunday Schools had occasionally existed in earlier years, but it was in the 1780s that they became fashionable. Originally they were agencies for mass schooling largely independent of particular congregations, and their immense appeal was grounded on their free teaching of reading. Writing skills were sometimes taught as well, though stricter sabbatarians looked askance on the practice. Increasingly, Sunday Schools were attached to particular places of worship, the curriculum became more exclusively religious and general education was left to the better-trained day-school teachers.[137] In 1859 a typical Anglican Sunday School would meet twice, perhaps from 9.15 to 10.15 and from 3.00 to 4.30. In the morning the lesson would be the repetition of a hymn and text; in the afternoon, when attendance was normally higher, it would consist of the recitation of a collect, a New

Testament passage and an oral examination of the whole school by the superintendent.[138] The attenders were chiefly working–class, the teachers, at least in the first half of the century, often being the epitome of working-class respectability. Although children, especially the boys, rarely remained after the day–school leaving age of about 11, so that the Sunday School was inefficient as a direct recruiting agency, the proportion of the population reached was remarkably high. Of those aged 15 and above at twelve Manchester cotton mills in 1852, 90 per cent had at some time been to Sunday School.[139] And the legacy was lasting. According to a 1957 Gallup Survey of adults, 73 per cent had once attended Sunday School regularly.[140] The Sunday School established a point of contact with the working-class population at large that could sometimes be enlarged by subsequent evangelism.

Other branches of education also formed a bridge between the churches and the working people. Employers of strong Christian conviction some-times provided a school for their own workers, as, for instance, did J. J. Colman, the Nonconformist mustard manufacturer of Norwich.[141] Night schools for adult workers on the pattern of Mechanics' Institutes but run by the churches drew significant numbers: in the heavily industrial diocese of Ripon there were 8,131 such attenders in 1870.[142] The Ragged Schools for the children of the streets, whose Union was founded under Shaftesbury's presidency in 1844, gave a rudimentary training to some of the most destitute.[143] More important in terms of the proportion of the population influenced were the elementary schools. At mid–century, the religious bodies sponsored schools providing for 1,049,000 out of the overall total of 2,109,000 pupils in day schools. Pride of place among the organisations promoting public education along Christian lines went to the National Society of the Church of England. In 1851, when other Anglican schools contained 336,000 pupils, National Schools educated 465,000. Launched in 1811 to propagate the schemes of Andrew Bell for cheap popular training in basic skills through monitors (senior pupils who passed on their lessons to the younger ones), the society relied entirely on local initiative. Evangelicals played a disproportionate part in the early years, but in 1853, dismayed by High Church leanings in its policy, a body of Evangelicals left to form a separate Church Education Society. Although it continued to function for many years, the new society never flourished, and Evangelical influence in the central counsels of the National Society was shattered.[144]

A parallel organisation was the British and Foreign School Society, founded in 1814 to support educational plans already begun by Joseph Lancaster, a Quaker. British Schools also initially adopted the monitorial system, but differed from National Schools in giving undenominational rather than distinctively Anglican instruction. Often attached to Non-conformist places of worship, British Schools nevertheless enjoyed the support of some Churchmen.[145] In 1851 they trained 123,000 pupils. The Congregationalists with 47,000 pupils and the Wesleyans with 37,000 also made valiant educational efforts,[146] but it was clear by the 1860s that voluntary schemes were failing to keep pace with population growth. The 1870 Education Act was the remedy, providing for rate-supported schools under local boards wherever there was a gap in voluntary facilities. Board Schools, like those set up under the equivalent 1872 act consolidating the various Presbyterian schools in Scotland, did not exclude religious training, but concentrated on Bible teaching. There was less Christian content in the curriculum than in the first half of the century, when religious topics were introduced on every page of readers used in National Schools, but the Board Schools at the end of the century still exerted a diffuse influence in the direction of biblical religion on the whole of the rising generation.[147] In rural Church schools the clergy would still regularly appear, sometimes to teach the first half-hour's lesson every day.[148] The nature of public elementary education, even as it gradually came under state inspection and control, helps explain the continuing esteem for Christianity in the non-churchgoing population.

SOCIAL PRESSURES

Attendance at a place of worship was a public act open to scrutiny by social superiors. In the countryside an awesome power was potentially wielded by many landlords. Those not seen in church on Sunday, whether farmers or labourers, could face the displeasure of the squire and, ultimately, eviction. This power was ambiguous in its effects on Evangelical religion. On the one hand, where the incumbent clergyman was himself an Evangelical, the landlord's expectations could help create larger congregations under the sound of the gospel. Only when squire and parson fell out would parish discord be likely to weaken religious practice.[149] On the other hand, the hostility of landlords, who overwhelmingly adhered to the Established Churches, could imperil Evangelical Nonconformity. When the Ecclesiastical Commissioners acquired a Lincolnshire parish in 1862, the four chief tenants were evicted as Methodists.[150] In England Lord Salisbury's refusal to sell land for the Wesleyans to build a chapel at Hatfield was but one instance of a serious obstacle that in Scotland the Free Church also encountered in its early years.[151] Decisive opposition of this kind by landlords, however, was relatively rare. More common was traditional deference by country folk to the wishes of the gentry, a factor that tended to strengthen whatever churchmanship was on offer in the parish. Although deference was reinforced by 'attentions' like Christmas coal and summer treats, the extent of rural paternalism has probably been exaggerated in the past. Only 17 per cent of a sample of National Schools was found to have a landlord patron, and clergymen were usually left to their own efforts to raise money for church building.[152] Landlords frequently preferred their own pleasures to supervising the people of their parishes.

Yet if rural pressures making for social and therefore religious conformity have often been overstated, the equivalent urban pressures have sometimes been understated. The nineteenth-century city was no more a place of freedom from a sense of social obligation than a scene of constant industrial oppression. Employers in later Victorian Lancashire, it has been shown, fostered a community spirit of devoted loyalty among their workforce. Deference was willingly given.[153] In this setting, the social leaders were divided approximately equally between Church and Dissent.[154] Neighbourhoods took their religious tone from the leading local industrialist. Churchgoing offered prospects of employment or promotion. Thus, at Monkwearmouth it was known to be an asset when applying for work in the shipyards to be a member of the local Wesleyan Hall, for its leading spirit had built up the shipbuilding industry.[155] Some captains of industry, such as Sir Titus Salt at Saltaire or Lord Leverhulme at Port Sunlight, prided themselves on exerting no compulsion over their workers to attend the churches they had erected. But in both cases the silent example of the social leader ensured that his own Congregational church was packed.[156] On a smaller scale, an apprentice might be expected to attend the place of worship of his master. Thus the son of a Baptist deacon was temporarily compelled to conform to the Established Church when apprenticed to a Monmouthshire chemist in the 1850s.[157] And domestic servants were often denied independent religious choice. A Durham brewer and colliery owner, for instance, insisted that his servants, including the Methodists, should attend the Church of England.[158] Although such pressure might take employees away from a gospel ministry, its effect was equally commonly to strengthen the Evangelical cause.

Influence could be exerted more subtly but hardly less effectively by social peers. The wish for acceptance and esteem from one's fellows – in a word, respectability – was a powerful force in nineteenth-century Britain, closely bound up with Christian practice. Respectability, it was remarked in 1854, was to be found among the 'religious public'.[159] It was the kernel of high Victorian values – what Edward Baines, the Congregationalist newspaper proprietor of Leeds, itemised as education, religion, virtue, industry, sobriety and frugality.[160] Respectability remained the lodestar in the 1890s of Charles Pooter, the archetypal City clerk with social pretensions portrayed only a little larger than life in the classic satire by George and Weedon Grossmith. For Pooter, two peaks of beatitude were acting as a sidesman in the parish church and holding a conversation after morning service with the curate.[161]

Respectability, however, was no mere preoccupation of the greater and lesser bourgeoisie. It was an element in the artisan culture, an outward expression of economic and intellectual independence that permeated the working-class movements of the times.[162] It encouraged the adoption of personal conviction and, frequently in consequence, alignment with some branch of organised religion. To join a Dissenting church, it has been suggested, was to acquire a badge of social standing, not least because the congruence of daily practice with Christian profession was made the subject of inquiry.[163] Avoidance of drunkenness, gambling, debt and sabbath-breaking were the hallmarks of a disciplined life. Careful observance of such prohibitions inevitably permitted higher standards of clothing, better quality furniture and, for some, more commodious homes.[164] Upward social mobility was the reward of prudence. Working people of London who joined a church at the end of the century, it was noted, 'become almost indistinguishable from the class with which they then mix' and so there was a change 'not so much *of* as *out of* the class to which they have belonged'.[165] This was the goal of many, the fruit of perseverance in a policy of self-help. The Congregationalist Thomas Binney published a book for young men entitled *Is it Possible to make the Best of Both Worlds?* and gave a resoundingly affirmative answer. He set out his leading contentions in a logical train: 'the Evangelical form of Christian ideas, – best produces that religious faith, – which most efficiently sustains those virtues, – which, by way of natural consequence, secure those things, – which contribute to the satisfaction and embellishment of life'.[166] Many were swayed by such reasonings. Evangelicalism seemed to offer a passport to advancement in life.

ATTRACTIONS OF CHURCHGOING

The churches had other benefits to offer. Rites of passage were particularly important. Human societies in general create ceremonies to mark the great turning points of life – birth, marriage and death. In nineteenth-century Britain the churches held a virtual monopoly in this field. Infant baptisms were performed, especially in the Established Churches, even for children of families that had no previous church connection. In England and Wales between 1753 and 1836 no marriage was legally valid (Quakers and Jews apart) unless solemnised by the Church of England. Civil marriage was available from 1836, but, in 1851, 84.9 per cent of marriages were still conducted by the Church of England.[167] And although burial according to other rites in private grounds was legitimate, the Established Church possessed the sole right of interment in parish graveyards down to 1880. Custom, respectability and a popular association of church ceremonies with good luck ensured that each of these services was a regular part of the experience of all sections of the community.[168] A sense of church connection was created that an astute clergyman or district visitor could build on.

Furthermore, the churches could offer a great deal by way of fellowship to those who ventured within their doors. The dislocations created by demographic, industrial and urban development meant that the churches provided friendship and security at a time when traditional landmarks were being removed. The regular round of tea meetings, so characteristic of the chapels and so despised by Matthew Arnold, fulfilled an important need. Even in the countryside, compensation for increasing social distance stemming from agricultural prosperity could be discovered in the Methodist chapel.[169] Methodism, in fact, delighted in supplying a happy family atmosphere.[170] The Congregationalists, though more dignified in their ways, also created a community life for their members. Their very foundation principle of congregational independency demanded it.[171] And the strength of communal ties surrounding a Baptist chapel can be illustrated by a Sunday School reunion service at Bacup that attracted well over two thousand people.[172] Nonconformity fostered the spirit of fellowship much more consciously and much more effectively than most Anglican churches. Steadily, however, the clergy came to realise the importance of social activities, and by 1890 one Evangelical was recommending a village library with a club-room containing games, especially bagatelle, a temperance society and Band of Hope, a coffee or cocoa room, a recreation ground, a school treat, harvest home, choir supper, a parochial or communicants' tea – but *not* entertainments or any concession that would further 'the present mania for theatricals'.[173] A similar penumbra of facilities was created round congregations in Lowland Scotland.[174] Clearly the auxiliary side of church life was popular. The churches were catering for a substantial demand.

Women were undoubtedly attracted in greater numbers than men. Non-conformist membership statistics usually reveal disproportionate female strength. Between 58 and 68 per cent of nineteenth-century Cumbrian Congregationalists in different churches were women.[175] Nevertheless the proportions among churchgoers were normally much nearer equality in Nonconformity than in the Church of England. At York in 1901 there were 49 men for every 51 women in the chapels, but only 35 men for every 65 women in the parish churches.[176] In the borough of Lambeth at morning service in 1902 there were 1.2 adult women for every adult man among Nonconformists compared with 1.7 among the Anglicans, and in the evening 1.6 women per man compared with 2.0. The disparity was not, as some complained at the time, because Anglo-Catholics preyed on weak women with their parade of aesthetic delights and ecclesiastical millinery. In Lambeth, Evangelical parish churches on average attracted a higher proportion of women than those celebrating a more elaborate liturgy. The differential seems to have been more related to class than to theology. In places of worship that catered for working people, whereas men were numerous in morning congregations they were strikingly few in the evening.[177] This was partly because female domestic servants were generally released only in the evening, and partly because many mothers and housewives were effectively prevented by domestic responsibilities from attending in the morning.

Whatever the explanation, working-class women seem to have been more inclined to religious involvement than their menfolk. Religion was often regarded as part of the mythical world of childhood and so appropriate for women, the guardians of the young. Men, after all, had their own foci of sociability in the public houses and sport. Churches provided virtually the only equivalent for women. At a time when respectability (often reinforced by Evangelical arguments) closely circumscribed the role of women,[178] church work was one of their few outlets. Although Sunday School teachers were overwhelmingly male in the early nineteenth century, they were chiefly female by its end.[179] Philanthropy was a major channel for women's energies. Missionary support work, the YWCA, Christian Endeavour and the Student Volunteer Movement all springing from Evangelical soil, contributed to what one writer called the 'Epiphany of Women'.[180] Women could even occupy official positions – as deaconesses in the Church of England from 1862, as preachers among the Quakers, the Primitive Methodists and the Bible Christians and as officers in the Salvation Army.[181] It has been persuasively argued that Evangelical religion, despite its emphasis on the domestic role of women, was more important than feminism in enlarging their sphere during the nineteenth century.[182] In the churches women of all classes found much to satisfy their aspirations.

A STYLE OF LIVING

When, for all these reasons, Evangelicalism made its vast impact on British society, the strongest influence was felt in the home. Ronald Knox, the Roman Catholic son of an Evangelical bishop, recalled being brought up at the very end of the nineteenth century in an old-fashioned form of Protestant piety. Apart from its devotion to scripture, it was marked by 'a careful observance of Sunday; framed texts, family prayers, and something indefinably patriarchal about the ordering of the household'.[183] Prayers presided over by the paterfamilias erected the framework, morning and evening, within which life was lived. Henry Thornton of the Clapham Sect compiled one of the volumes most widely used on these occasions.[184] It was against such a hothouse atmosphere that those who discarded their Evangelical upbringing rebelled. Samuel Butler and Edmund Gosse, who wrote two celebrated accounts of rebellion, found it all too constricting. The problems of Butler and Gosse, however, seem to have derived more from their parents' personal idiosyncrasies than from anything intrinsic to Evangelicalism.[185] A pile of testimony can be put in the opposite scale. The most influential Evangelical handbooks on childcare, those written by Louisa Hoare, a sister of Elizabeth Fry, were full of sanity, warmth and affection. And she practised what she preached. One of her sons recalled the scripture readings at 7.15 each morning. 'Nothing can efface the lovely impression made on those occasions. There she used to be by a bright fire in her little room, in her snow-white dressing-gown . . . '[186] Evangelical homes were often happy homes.

The Evangelicals nevertheless attracted a disproportionate volume of contemporary criticism. Aristocrats might disdain their intensity, as when

Lady Palmerston, Shaftesbury's mother-in-law, 'spoke scornfully of every-
one and everything which bordered in the least on serious views'.[187]
Working-class radicals might hold that 'all Christians are sad bigots;
Churchmen are among the worst, and Evangelicals are worst of all'.[188]
Writers singled out hypocrisy for censure, whether through Dickens's
shallow caricature of Chadband in *Bleak House* or George Eliot's devastating
portrayal of Bulstrode in *Middlemarch*.[189] Such criticisms are inevitable, it
has been pointed out by Professor Best, against those setting high standards
of conduct; certain aspects of regularity of life were commercial virtues
predating Evangelicalism; and the maintenance of a respectable public
front was as general among High Churchmen or non-churchmen. Only in
the unnecessary use of religious jargon, according to Professor Best, does
the censure stick.[190] Even ministers at the time felt the same. Dr David
Thomas, Congregational minister at Stockwell, inspired in 1880 the writing
of a protracted satire of the Evangelical sub-culture, *The World of Cant*.
'Mr. Crayford', runs a typical passage, 'talked continually to Lorraine of
the "light" that his wife enjoyed, and begged him in the most unctuous
terms to accept her faith and to be "converted".'[191] Language once densely
loaded with spiritual experience could be debased by over-use. Evangelicals
were not immune to the risk of all tight-knit groups of generating their
own argot that was well-nigh impenetrable to outsiders.

Criticism was also directed at Evangelicals as killjoys. There was no antagonism, according to Wilberforce, between religion and any amusement that
was *really* innocent. 'The question, however, of its innocence', he went on,
'must not be tried by the loose maxims of worldly morality, but by the spirit
of the injunctions of the word of God . . . '[192] Behaviour not itself sinful
could be dangerous if it diverted a believer from faithful religious practice,
led him into bad company or gave any appearance of evil. Deciding what fell
into any of these categories was no easy task. It is not surprising either that
Evangelicals tended to shelter behind blanket prohibitions that avoided the
need for careful evaluation in doubtful cases, or that the list of taboos varied
over time. Evangelicals in the Church of England seem to have become more
rigid during the early nineteenth century. Henry Venn, the secretary of the
CMS at mid-century, excluded all but one novel from his house, whereas his
father, John Venn of Clapham, had devoured Scott's novels avidly.[193]
Among those influenced by premillennialism, it was axiomatic that there
should be no trifling with the vain things of a world about to perish.

Other Anglicans, and Nonconformists generally, tended to broaden in
their views in the later part of the century. Thus, when the theatre was
condemned by members of the Eclectic Society in 1800, they were reflecting
the unanimous opinion of the Evangelical community. The profaneness
on stage, the low moral reputation of actresses and the specious appeal to
the senses were the worst offences of the drama.[194] At mid-century it was
still held that 'to sanction the representation of sin, is surely equivalent to
mocking at it'.[195] When a United Presbyterian minister startled Edinburgh

in 1883 by claiming that the drama could in principle be 'an educative force', he nevertheless conceded that its present unreformed state had prevented him from setting foot in a theatre.[196] But in 1894 the Chairman of the Congregational Union denied that it was wrong to see a play.[197] Resistance to the theatre was beginning to crumble.

A change of mind about musical performances took place more rapidly. The 1805 Wesleyan Conference prohibited recitatives and solos, but even at the start of the century it was recognised that music, as the handmaid of worship, had a certain value.[198] In the 1840s a young Congregational minister declined to attend a concert in deference to the convictions of others, but later in his career he felt no qualms of conscience on the point.[199] By the end of the century the chapels of Wales and the north had begun their tradition of regular choir festivals. Only rarely were there relics of resistance, as when in 1898 an 'ultra-Baptist' on a school board near Llandovery objected on principle to school concerts.[200]

To novels there was probably always more opposition in theory than in practice. The elite of Congregationalism gossiped to each other about their latest reading in the 1810s even though John Angell James, minister at Birmingham until 1859, 'could not endure fiction'.[201] *The Christian Observer* was urging resistance to novel-reading (fiction made light of sin, wasted time and had worldly associations) at a time when Sir Walter Scott was making inroads into pious households.[202] Attitudes broadened over time. The first Congregational novelist was probably Sarah Stickney, with her *Pictures of Private Life* (1833); by 1876 a Methodist novel was published and fiction was being serialised in *The Wesleyan Methodist Magazine*.[203] At the end of the century, a whole fictional genre, the so-called Scottish 'Kailyard School', existed to convey a Christian message, and the most popular novelist was Silas K. Hocking, a Methodist.[204] Like the concert, though unlike the theatre, the novel was Christianised.

Recreation was even more of a moral minefield than the arts. Contamination by associating with the unconverted was a greater risk. Although dinner parties were least suspect because restrained by the conventions of the home, they had their dangers – drowsiness after wine, splendid displays of plate and so on. The friend of a correspondent of *The Christian Observer* consequently abandoned 'the dinner system' as a violation of the moral law, 'pure Antinomianism'.[205] Balls could stir preachers to a frenzy of denunciation. Charles Clayton, Vicar of Holy Trinity, Cambridge, declaimed against the university Bachelors' Ball of 1857, contending that a murderer had once been prompted to his reckless crime by the sight of six clergymen at a ball.[206] Clerical standards of behaviour were fixed particularly high. J. C. Wigram, the Evangelical Bishop of Rochester, attracted some ridicule when, apart from censuring their beards and whiskers, he reprimanded his clergy for attending cricket clubs and archery meetings.[207] Henry Venn gave up cricket on his ordination in 1820, and football played by candidates for the Wesleyan ministry at Didsbury College attracted censure in the

early 1860s.[208] Marbles might be less fraught with danger: the venerable
Methodist Adam Clarke enjoyed playing – and winning – the game.[209]
Yet a boy in a Calvinistic Methodist home in Merthyr Tydfil in the 1820s
could have qualms:

> One of his schoolfellows remembers how wistfully he stood, on one occasion,
> watching the other boys as they played at marbles, a game which had much
> fascination for him, but in which, being perhaps at that time a Church member,
> or about to become such, he did not feel at liberty to indulge . . .[210]

A similar sensitive conscience fashioned the Evangelicals into opponents
of many forms of popular recreation. At Derby, pressure by Evangelicals
led to the abandonment of the races in 1835 and the suppression (by the
use of troops) of football in the streets in 1845 and the succeeding years;
at Cheltenham, Francis Close led a campaign directed impartially against
the theatre, undesirable literature, any breach of the sabbath and the local
races; at Bolton, the clergy sustained demands for the withdrawal of a
licence for a 'singing saloon'.[211] Such efforts were repeated all over Britain.
'Evangelicalism', George Eliot observes of the early nineteenth century,
'had cast a certain suspicion as of plague-infection over the few amusements
which survived in the provinces.'[212] It was not simply a middle-class
affair, as the unyielding Primitive Methodist hostility to popular sport in
the Potteries illustrates.[213] Nor was it merely an expression of the killjoy
spirit, for a strong element in the movement was opposition to cruelty,
whether to animals (as in cock-fighting) or to human beings (as in prize
fighting).[214] The essence of the campaigns was the belief that various
forms of popular recreation were occasions of sin. By the last thirty years
of the century, however, Evangelicals were to the fore in the general
shift in favour of providing organised leisure facilities for the working
people. Suspicion of amusements melted away as they came to be seen as
valuable adjuncts of church life.[215] It was another instance of a sphere
that early nineteenth-century Evangelicals had seen as worldly coming to
be recognised as having potential in the mission of the church.

PRESSURE FOR REFORM

The approach of Evangelicals to politics was also marked by a parade of
conscience. Some supposed political activity to be so corrupt as to exclude
Christians from participating. 'Thinks it wicked to vote', ran a note on an
elector in a mid-century Norwich canvassing book, ' – Leaves politics to
the world.'[216] Quietism of this order, though it persisted in some quarters
such as the Brethren movement, was a declining force among Evangelicals
as the century advanced. Increasingly, Evangelicals were drawn into mass
crusades against social evils. Only governments or local authorities held

sufficient power to remedy the moral blots on national life. By the 1832 Reform Act and the 1835 Municipal Corporations Act a large section of the Evangelical public was given a share in determining who held the power. Accordingly, beginning with the campaign for the emancipation of colonial slaves in 1832–3,[217] there were regular forays into public life.

There was a remarkable measure of consistency in the features of reform movements mounted by Evangelicals. It sprang primarily from their possessing a common target for attack: sin. George Stephen, the chief anti-slavery lecturer in the years 1830–3, found that he could best rouse the religious public against colonial slavery by branding it as 'criminal before God'.[218] Again and again in the rhetoric of subsequent crusades the object of attack was wickedness. This fundamental feature of the political campaigns should cause no surprise, for Evangelicals were, by definition, opposed to sin. As soon as they became convinced that they were responsible as citizens for a state of affairs that necessarily entailed sin, they considered themselves bound to act. Because the target was outright evil, the crusades cannot properly be labelled 'humanitarian', the traditional term used by historians to describe Evangelical socio-political attitudes.[219] It is true that the leaders often wished to eliminate suffering: Shaftesbury, with his strong sense of aristocratic responsibility for the poor, is a good example. It is also true, as in the case of anti-slavery, that the mass campaigns frequently had the effect of reducing suffering. That, however, was not their *raison d'être*. The Evangelical public was aware of the cruelties perpetrated by slaveholders long before the sudden upsurge of demands for the termination of slavery. Inhumanity in itself did not prod their consciences. Evangelicals did not display a blanket humanitarianism in politics. Rather, they mounted periodic campaigns against particular evils.

Three broad classes of wickedness stirred them into political action. The first is what may be called obstacles to the gospel. Anything that prevented human beings from hearing the gospel was a threat to their salvation that must be hateful to God. Slavery became the target of Evangelical assault in the early 1830s because it began to be seen, for the first time, as an absolute barrier to missionary progress in the Caribbean. Slaveowners suspected missionaries of having fomented the Jamaica slave rebellion of 1831 and determined to harry them from the island. Evangelicals concluded, in the words of John Dyer, secretary of the BMS, that 'either Christianity or slavery must fall'.[220] The 'Ten Hours' movement that campaigned to restrict the working day in the mills of the West Riding had a similar inspiration. Parson Bull of Byerley, an Evangelical, perceived that because the hands had too much work to attend religious meetings, the factory system must be subject to parliamentary regulation. It had become an obstacle to the gospel.[221]

A second class of evils attacked by Evangelicals consisted of what they saw as substitutes for the gospel. Alternative systems of belief, religious or secular, were condemned as affronts to the God who had revealed his truth in the Bible. Most threatening because most powerful was the Roman Catholic Church. Many of them did not scruple to label Catholic worship 'idolatry'.[222] The anti-Maynooth outburst of 1845 expressed the anxiety of Evangelicals that they, as taxpayers, would be promoting the soul-destroying errors of popery.[223] Likewise paganism, though normally less alarming, was an alternative to Christianity in the mission field. The British government was therefore successfully pressed to end official concessions to forms of Hindu worship in India.[224] Conflict about education was similarly fuelled by fears of forces hostile to Christianity in state schools. On the one hand, Anglican Evangelicals were anxious lest the Bible should be excluded from schools. 'I believe it were better almost for man that [education] were crushed', declared Hugh Stowell, 'than it were given unless it were christianised.'[225] On the other hand, Nonconformists were fearful of religious teaching with an Anglo-Catholic flavour, what they saw as indoctrination in sacerdotalism, as well as state support for the errors of Catholicism itself. 'Rome on the rates' was the war-cry of their opposition to the 1902 Education Act.[226] Doctrines alien to scriptural religion seemed to be preying on young minds, and their public endorsement made Evangelicals responsible for them.

Sins – in the most usual sense of the word – formed the third class of targets for Evangelical crusades. This is the category of infringements of the gospel code for living. Sexual wrongdoing came high on the list. In the 1870s even Christians who normally steered clear of politics – including undenominational evangelists and the Wesleyan authorities – were roused to agitate for the ending of health inspection of prostitutes under the Contagious Diseases Acts on the ground that it implied public sanction for sexual immorality.[227] Worries about sexual misbehaviour often turn out to underlie what at first sight were entirely different concerns. In 1842 there was an outcry by the religious public against conditions in the mining industry that enabled Shaftesbury to promote a bill prohibiting the employment of women and children underground. The cause of the high feeling, rather than being simple outrage at the inhuman treatment of the weak, was shock at the discovery, from an illustration in a Royal Commission report, that male and female children were being lowered to work together half-naked.[228] In the 1880s a chorus of voices, predominantly Evangelical, protested against overcrowded housing conditions in London. The explanation is that the Christian public had just been made aware that families living in single rooms were prone to incest.[229]

Next to sexual lapses as an object of attack was drunkenness. Although total abstinence became much more widespread among Nonconformists than among Anglicans, restriction of licensing hours and regulation of drink outlets were shared aims in national and local campaigns of the late nineteenth century. Associated with Hurdsfield Parish Church, near Macclesfield, the Evangelical vicar organised a Band of Hope for children, a Temperance Society for adults, a Teetotal Club with skittle alley and a Coffee Tavern.[230] From such agencies committed to 'moral suasion' of the population sprang hosts of dedicated workers eager to support any political measure tending towards prohibition.[231] Then there was a series of campaigns against cases of sabbath-breaking. So central was this issue to the Evangelical mind that when Henry Martyn undertook his missionary venture to India and Persia he set himself two objectives. He was intending to teach, together with the gospel of Christ, the observance of the sabbath.[232] In the mid-nineteenth century Sunday trains ran at their peril, proposals for the Sunday opening of the Crystal Palace met a wall of resistance and Shaftesbury secured, if only briefly, a cessation of Post Office work on the sabbath.[233] The dynamic of the Evangelical approach to politics was hostility to sin.

One consequence was that Evangelicals were committed to a negative policy of reform. Their proposals were regularly for the elimination of what was wrong, not for the achievement of some alternative goal. Their campaigns were often explicitly 'anti', as in the anti-slavery and the anti-Contagious Diseases Acts movements. Other pressure groups might advocate an innovation (like the six points of the Charter) or represent an interest (like the Trades Union Council), but Evangelical reform movements were designed to condemn features of existing policy. 'It was not his business', announced Arthur Guttery, the leading Primitive Methodist campaigner of the turn of the century, 'to propose schemes of redress or to suggest legislative measures. That was the duty of Statesmen and Cabinets. It was his business to denounce abuses and wrongs and shams . . . '[234] The campaigns were essentially protest movements. Their negative stance could in some cases be their strength: it is frequently easier for governments to abandon an old policy than to commence a new one. Slavery was abolished and the Contagious Diseases Acts were repealed. And even when the chief objective was not reached, the existence of mobilised Evangelical opinion sometimes prevented authorities from taking further steps in undesired directions. Repeatedly governments deferred proposals for a Catholic university in Ireland for fear of the reaction.[235] Governments had no desire to stir up a hornets' nest.

The policy of protest dictated a method of agitation. If the authorities were to be impressed by the strength of the movement, protest must be outspoken and widespread. Paid lecturers ('agitators') or voluntary speakers would address a series of public meetings up and down the country in an attempt to whip up a maximum pitch of outrage. William Knibb, a returned Jamaica missionary, carried round from gathering to gathering in 1832 a spiked iron collar to brandish in illustration of the punishment meted out to the slaves.[236] The grand 'indignation meetings', frequently the settings for the launching of petitions to Parliament or the approval of letters to MPs, constituted a spectacular form of entertainment. Furious denunciation of sin commonly degenerated into distasteful personal censure. This was (among other things) a poor political tactic, as Hugh Price Hughes, an embodiment of the late nineteenth-century 'Nonconformist Conscience', discovered when he tried to enlist the support of Lord Rosebery, the Liberal leader, for one cause after castigating him for backwardness in another. Rosebery refused because of Hughes's previous lack of charity.[237] Clamour could be counter-productive.

Another handicap was the stern moral absolutism of the crusades. Their demands were immutable, sacrosanct, certainly not open to negotiation. They were marked by an intransigence that is well illustrated by the policy of the United Kingdom Alliance, the chief prohibitionist pressure group. When a government offered legislation to restrict the consumption of alcohol that fell short of the Alliance's goal, the organisations condemned the proposals outright.[238] Half a loaf was often refused. While continuing to demand a whole loaf, Evangelicals commonly found themselves with no bread. Again, the same absolutism showed itself over the timing of reform. Change, Evangelicals regularly argued, must come urgently. Hence orators of the 1830s called for the *immediate* termination of slavery.[239] Sin, once identified, must not be tolerated. Policy, technique and style were all determined by the fundamental characteristic of mass Evangelical politics as a crusade against wrong.

The sharpest fissure that divided Evangelicals one from another during the nineteenth century and on into the twentieth was largely political. Church and chapel were at odds with each other on the establishment issue. Nonconformists felt branded as inferior by the alliance of the Church of England with the state. In the earlier days of the disestablishment movement they were roused because they saw the cause as another struggle for right against wrong on the pattern of the anti-slavery campaign. The union of church and state was condemned because it encouraged idle, unconverted men to enter the ministry of the Church of England for the sake of financial security and a certain social standing. Soon the development of the Oxford Movement raised the additional spectre of Romanising clergy within the Established Church. Furthermore, state aid for religion implied that the gospel could not bring in converts by itself – which seemed nothing less than an insult to the power of Christ.[240] So the disestablishment movement, organised from 1844 as the Anti-State Church Association and from 1853 as the Liberation Society, assumed the features of an Evangelical crusade.

In the same period the defence of the church as established was increasingly seen as a duty of Evangelical Anglicans. By 1856 a Committee of Laymen of Protestant inclinations was operating at Westminster to resist Nonconformist claims, and from 1859 the Church Institution, later the Church Defence Institution, existed to counteract the work of the Liberation Society.[241] The issue of the establishment principle was kept to the fore by the agitation of a variety of grievances by Nonconformists. They were compelled to pay any local rates that were levied for the upkeep of parish churches until 1868, excluded from degrees at Oxford and Cambridge until changes in the 1850s and 1871, and prevented from using their own forms of service in parish graveyards until 1880. Broader experience of social discrimination also helped to consolidate the traditional support of Nonconformists for the Liberal Party.[242] Celebrations in 1862 of the bicentenary of the Great Ejection and the controversy over Irish disestablishment during the 1868 election campaign drove church and chapel further apart.[243] In most parts of England, and even more fiercely in Wales, elections up to the First World War were commonly referendums on the relative strength of the Church of England and Nonconformity.[244] In Scotland too the disestablishment issue between 1874 and 1895 deeply divided the United Presbyterian and Free Churches on the one hand from the established Church of Scotland on the other.[245] Within the Free Church and the Church of Scotland there were significant minorities of Conservatives and Liberals respectively,[246] but in England and Wales polarisation was more complete. A handful of Evangelical Churchmen, including J. C. Miller and Robert Bickersteth, were Liberals,[247] and a small group of prosperous Conservatives existed among the Wesleyans and Presbyterians, strengthened after 1886 by opponents of Home Rule.[248] But the basic pattern was one in which political and denominational allegiance went hand in hand. Rivalry may have spurred the two sides to outdo each other in church growth. In general, however, the energy diverted into political feuding must have weakened the religious impact of Evangelicalism on society.

INTELLECTUAL ACHIEVEMENT

It is commonly supposed that there was little or no Evangelical scholarship. Newman in his *Apologia* remarked that the Evangelical party 'at no time has been conspicuous, as a party, for talent or learning'.[249] John Foster, a Baptist minister who retired to literary seclusion, penned an essay 'On some of the causes by which Evangelical religion has been rendered less acceptable to persons of cultivated taste' (1805), depicting and deploring the gulf between learning and gospel truth.[250] Contemporary opinion was certainly not wholly mistaken. It was a basic premiss of Evangelicalism that, in the last resort, scholarship must be counted as nothing when compared with the one thing needful. 'Without this knowledge of our want of Christ', an early Yorkshire Evangelical had declared, 'all human learning, all other knowledge whatever, is no better than florid nonsense and polite foolishness.'[251] The acquisition of human wisdom would not bring a person to heaven. On the other hand, it might so inflate his pride as to turn him aside from the heavenly path. It might even (especially if derived from Germany) be subversive of Christian truth.

The time of the believer, furthermore, had other calls upon it. Practical work so occupied Shaftesbury, who had gained a first-class degree, that he 'lost the art' of reading.[252] A zealous clergyman in particular, as an

Evangelical reminded a clerical audience in 1838, had more immediate duties: 'the Christian minister who can, in the present day, spend much time in the fields of literature and science, must either be ignorant of the dangers by which the flock is threatened, or heedless of the responsibilities by which he himself is bound.'[253] Many young Evangelicals fresh from achieving university laurels followed the example of Henry Martyn (senior wrangler at Cambridge in 1801) in devoting themselves to missionary work. Of forty-two Cambridge men enrolled by the CMS in the period 1841–61, twenty-eight had taken honours and nine had been wranglers (the equivalent of the first class in mathematics). R. B. Batty (second wrangler in 1852, Fellow of Emmanuel from 1853) took service with the CMS in 1860, only to die at Amritsar the following year.[254] Likewise F. W. Kellett (Fellow of Sidney Sussex, an able historian) abandoned the prospect of academic honours in England to join the Wesleyan Missionary Society in India.[255] Their distinction came not through scholarship but through service. Again, the Evangelical party could boast a fine array of colonial bishops, men such as Charles Perry, Bishop of Melbourne (1847–76), W. S. Smith, Bishop then first Archbishop of Sydney (1890–1909), and Robert Machray, Bishop then first Archbishop of Rupert's Land (1865–1904). But the fostering of the churches in the growing colonies was achieved at the expense of diverting such figures from the field of learning. Perry had been summoned to Trinity College, Cambridge, to assist Whewell, the Master, in his teaching; Smith had been a Fellow of Trinity as well as President of the Union; Machray had been Dean of Sidney Sussex.[256] The characteristic activism of Evangelicals made them chafe at the bit of reclusive scholarship.

Yet within Evangelicalism there was a leaven conducive to intellectual endeavour. The doctrinal preoccupations incumbent on a believer stimulated an early, sometimes precocious, capacity for abstract thought. The imperative to Bible study similarly accustomed him to reading. The role of Protestantism in encouraging popular literacy over the centuries has already been noted,[257] but it is important to insist that it could give rise to an intense bookishness. A rural Aberdeenshire minister of the Free Church possessing slender means was capable of purchasing, in a single and far from exceptional year, 518 volumes and 12 pamphlets and of reading 58 books in their entirety, with much of several others and 17 pamphlets.[258] It was impossible for a child reared in such an environment to avoid a taste for learning. Mill Hill, the Nonconformist boarding school, under the headship of Dr Weymouth, himself a translator of the New Testament, from 1869 to 1886, had twenty-three former pupils gain first-class degrees.[259] Even before Oxford and Cambridge opened their master's degrees to Dissenters in 1871, some Evangelical Nonconformists were entering Cambridge (as they were permitted to do) and carrying off academic honours including the senior wranglership.[260] Higher education was a preoccupation of many Evangelicals.

The University of Cambridge, or parts of it, became something of an Evangelical citadel. Trinity maintained a strong Evangelical presence from Simeon's day onwards. St John's was a particular resort of impoverished young men of ill breeding – called 'Sims' after Simeon – eking out their pittance in order to qualify for the ministry.[261] Other colleges served successively as havens for the sons of Evangelical parents, and consequently were bursting at the seams – Magdalene, Queens', Caius and Corpus Christi.[262] Simeon at Holy Trinity was assisted by eight wranglers, including James Scholefield, subsequently Regius Professor of Greek. The first three Jacksonian Professors of Natural and Experimental Philosophy (1783–1836) were Evangelicals: Isaac Milner, Francis Wollaston and William Farish.[263] There were distinguished men of the same party in the second half of the century including Edwin Guest, President of the Society of Antiquaries, chief founder of the Philological Society and Master of Caius (1852–80); and G. G. Stokes, Lucasian Professor of Mathematics (1849–1903), Master of Pembroke (1902–3), MP for the University and President of the Royal Society.[264]

Oxford, though much less fertile ground for Evangelicals, could boast a few men such as John Conington, Corpus Professor of Latin Literature (1854–69), who underwent a striking conversion from infidelity, and Sir Monier Monier-Williams, Boden Professor of Sanskrit (1860–87), who opened his home to undergraduates on Sunday evenings.[265] At London the first Professor of Divinity at King's College (from 1846) was Alexander McCaul, an Evangelical clergyman who had served the Jews' Society and had been offered the bishopric of Jerusalem; and the first Professor of History at University College (1834–43) was Robert Vaughan, afterwards Principal of the Lancashire Independent College.[266] The Scottish universities and theological colleges were replete with men of Evangelical conviction, of whom Robertson Smith, later Professor of Arabic at Cambridge (from 1889), is merely the best known.[267] There were Dissenters of high intellectual calibre outside the universities such as Robert Hall or John Pye Smith, and learned clergymen pursuing their studies in parish work such as Josiah Allport, of St James's, Ashted, near Birmingham, who translated the works of Bishop Davenant.[268] Ability, the spirit of inquiry and high attainments in the arts and sciences were by no means foreign to the Evangelical temper.

What was achieved in theology? The standard view, expressed equally by the German authority Otto Pfleiderer in 1890 and the most recent historian of nineteenth-century doctrine, Bernard Reardon, is that the Evangelical contribution was tiny. Only Thomas Erskine and McLeod Campbell among theologians drawn from any Evangelical tradition qualify for more than a sentence from Pfleiderer, and Reardon's survey follows broadly similar lines.[269] It was said at the time that there was a lack of Evangelicals qualified by their learning for the episcopal bench. Yet J. B. Sumner, who became Archbishop of Canterbury in 1848, had published *A Treatise on the Records of the Creation* (1816) which (before Chalmers's synthesis) reconciled the new learning of Malthus and the political economists with the teaching of scripture.[270] Both Charles Baring and Samuel Waldegrave held Oxford double firsts, and Waldegrave had delivered the Bampton Lectures in 1854.[271] So academic ability was by no means entirely absent from the Evangelical episcopate.

On the publication of *Essays and Reviews*, a correspondent of *The Record* suggested a counterblast from the Evangelical party. It is instructive to examine the names of established scholars that sprang to his mind as potential contributors.[272] Some, though advanced in years, had once made their mark. T. H. Horne had written the standard work on biblical criticism, Alexander McCaul had composed the most esteemed apologetic directed towards Jews, and Christopher Benson, the first Hulsean Lecturer at Cambridge in 1820, had published *A Chronology of Our Saviour's Life* in the previous year.[273] Joseph Baylee issued a privately printed work on the principles of scriptural interpretation, and J. B. Marsden, a student of Puritanism, had published a more general *History of Christian Churches* (1856).[274] T. R. Birks, who had been second wrangler in 1834, wrote *The Bible and Modern Thought* (1861), a single-handed riposte to *Essays and Reviews*, and later a series of solid works on ethics following his election to the Knightbridge Chair of Moral Philosophy at Cambridge in 1872.[275] William Goode, Dean of Ripon, though specialising in controversial theology, was undoubtedly a thinker of the first rank. His great assault on the Tractarians, *The Divine Rule of Faith and Practice* (1842), was argued, as an obituarist remarked, with 'logical justness'.[276] The final Evangelical notable, E. A. Litton, had shared the Oriel Senior Common Room with Newman in the 1830s and so was well qualified for his major work, *The Church of Christ* (1851), again a repudiation of Tractarian teaching.[277] Judged by the yardstick of this list of potential defenders of the faith, Evangelicals could justly claim to muster considerable intellectual power.

If the net is cast wider, the verdict is confirmed. Another Evangelical Anglican, Edward Garbett, delivered, as the Boyle Lectures for 1861, a lucid defence of Christianity as a body of revealed truth. As Bampton Lecturer for 1867 he took a similar theme, though admittedly making little impact on Oxford.[278] Robert Payne Smith, Regius Professor of Divinity at Oxford (1865–70) and Dean of Canterbury (1870–95), was an erudite Syriac scholar who worked on a thesaurus of the language for the last thirty-one years of his life.[279] Equally learned was Nathaniel Dimock, whose field was historical theology. His work on *The Doctrine of the Sacraments* (1871) was a particularly telling statement of an Evangelical position.[280] In Scotland there was much able scholarship. Patrick Fairbairn, Principal of the Free Church College, Glasgow, is a representative figure. Although his chief work was on the apparently pietistic theme of *The Typology of Scripture* (1845–7), it gave him an international reputation. He also ventured into the contested field of the interpretation of prophecy (1856) and wrote illuminatingly on the still vexed subject of biblical hermeneutics (1858). His academic reputation ensured him a place among those who translated the Revised Version of the Old Testament.[281]

There were many other unreconstructed Evangelicals in the Presbyterian north – men such as James Orr and James Denney.[282] One of the Scots whose theology was reconstructed on a Hegelian basis, and therefore hovers on the edge of the Evangelical category, was A. M. Fairbairn, who eventually became the founding Principal of Mansfield College, Oxford.[283] And the Evangelical world embraced two other Congregationalists of great distinction. The *oeuvre* of R. W. Dale, minister at Carr's Lane, Birmingham (1853–95), contains some slight pieces, but his work on *The Atonement* (1875) was a masterly restatement that was widely adopted for use in Anglican seminaries.[284] P. T. Forsyth, eventually Principal of Hackney College (1901–21), passed through a phase in which Evangelical formulations were irksome to another in which they formed the raw material for a series of passionately felt works on central theological topics – Christology, authority, theodicy and so on. Drawing on German sources far more than his contemporaries, Forsyth was a patently original thinker.[285] Originality, it must be admitted, was not the forte of most Evangelical theologians, who from the 1830s normally saw their task as essentially defensive. Yet Evangelicalism did generate academic theology. Its adherents did not spurn the task of reflecting on their faith.

THE DECAY OF EVANGELICAL ASCENDANCY

The prominence of Evangelicals in society shortly after the middle of the nineteenth century was never again to be repeated. Already by 1864 Shaftesbury was lamenting that the Protestant feeling of the nation was not what it was,[286] but the contraction of Evangelical influence was more marked from the 1870s. It was the era of the so-called 'Victorian crisis of faith' when young men began to discern insuperable objections to Christian belief. The proportion of graduates proceeding to ordination, and especially of first-class men, registered a sharp down-turn.[287] At Cambridge the characteristic attitude of the new academic vanguard to religion was 'indifference'.[288] An index of the changing national mood was its literature. In 1870 most new books were on religion, with fiction in fifth place; in 1886 most new books were fiction, with religion behind it in second place.[289] The belief was spreading that the greatest need of humanity was not rescue from its futile ways through salvation, but effort that would apply knowledge for the betterment of the world. The resulting stance has been labelled 'meliorism', the belief that, if only skills were exerted, the human race would make rapid progress. This widely diffused offspring of Enlightenment optimism seemed to fit the experience of industrial growth in the mid-Victorian years. It was systematised in a number of theories of which Herbert Spencer's so-called 'Social Darwinism' was the most popular.[290] A range of alternative worldviews to the Christian faith became available. At the same period several explicit assaults on Christianity were published. W. E. H. Lecky, for instance, depicted the steady advance of rationalism in European history as a dimension of human progress. Certain natural scientists of a polemical bent – T. H. Huxley and John Tyndall were prominent – did their best to show that science and religion were inveterate foes.[291]

The challenge of Darwin was part of the ferment. It is easy to mistake the consequences of the appearance of *The Origin of Species* in 1859. It did not give rise to immediate and sustained debate over the veracity of the early chapters of Genesis. The issue rarely resolved itself into a question of 'evolution or the Bible' until the following century. Rather, Darwin subverted what had seemed the most assured argument for Christian belief, the contention that the adaptation of particular species for their mode of life was evidence of a beneficent Creator. 'The old argument of design in nature, as given by Paley', wrote Darwin himself, 'which formerly seemed to me so conclusive, fails, now that the law of natural selection has been discovered.'[292] Animals and plants appeared to care for themselves. The divine hypothesis seemed redundant. To many Evangelical leaders trained up in Paley's apologetic, acceptance of evolution entailed rejecting a Guiding Intelligence. 'Then the universe will exhibit to us', wrote T. R. Birks, 'nothing but a Proteus without reason or intelligence, going through a series of endless changes, without conscious design, or any intelligible end or purpose in those changes.'[293] Other Evangelicals, however, willingly embraced the idea of evolution. Henry Drummond, a professor at the Glasgow Free Church College, even turned evolution into a vehicle for evangelism.[294] There was certainly no serious alarm among the occupants of the pews, but Darwinism did contribute to the shift in the fulcrum of educated opinion away from Christian belief. At least among the intellectual aristocracy, Evangelicalism was giving way to 'honest doubt'.

More widespread in their effects were changes in social circumstances. The second half of the nineteenth century was marked by an acceleration in the improvement of the standard of living. Between 1860 and 1900 there was an increase of some 60 per cent in the real wages of the average urban worker.[295] The quality and variety of food, longevity and health conditions all changed significantly for the better. With higher disposable income, the working population was able to turn to new activities outside the churches, ranging from cycling to the music hall. The provision of state education after 1870 meant that the churches rapidly lost their ascendancy in popular education. The new Board Schools might spread a general body of Bible teachings, but parents were less inclined to feel a need for churches as civilising agencies for their children. The creation of public welfare facilities had a comparable result. Libraries, baths and open spaces were provided by local authorities in the decades before the First

World War. Liberal legislation after 1906 made more elaborate provision, especially old age pensions and health insurance, that effectively superseded equivalent services previously offered by the churches. District visiting fell into decay.[296]

Paternalism was likewise becoming a thing of the past. With enlargement of company size, the end of family control and the appointment of anonymous managers, especially from the 1890s onwards, the solidarity of employer and workforce crumbled. No longer were employees at particular factories looked for at particular places of worship.[297] The other side of the coin was an upsurge of working-class consciousness. Better times fostered demands for higher wages, and in a series of waves – the early 1870s, 1888–92 and 1910–14 – working people increasingly banded together in trade unions to press their claims. Versions of socialism began to take root and the seeds of the Labour Party were sown.[298] The visionary idealism of the Independent Labour Party was far from anti-religious – indeed, it was an amalgam of the religious and the political – but the churches often seemed an irrelevance. 'I claim for Socialism', wrote Keir Hardie, the chairman of the ILP, 'that it is the embodiment of Christianity in our industrial system.'[299] All too often, according to a swelling chorus of working-class opinion, the churches ignored the appalling conditions of the poor along with 'the evils of competitive middle-class society'.[300] In these circumstances churchgoing was steadily eroded. By 1902 in London only 19 per cent of the population attended worship.[301] Some of the consequences will call for examination in Chapter 6, but it is clear that the churches were swimming against the social tide.

THEOLOGICAL CHANGE

At the same time the message of some of the churches was becoming less sharply defined. Despite the innovations of Irving's circle, the bulk of Evangelicals at mid-century retained their confidence in the Enlightenment appeal to evidences, scientific method and an orderly universe governed by cause and effect. At the beginning of 1863 *The Record* announced that 'the good sense of LOCKE, the analogies of BUTLER, and the "Common Sense" of REID, will preserve us from the vagaries of Prussian or German Rationalists . . . '[302] It was devotion to 'the inductive principles of the philosophy of Bacon and Newton' that buttressed T. R. Birks against Darwin.[303] The leaders of Evangelical Anglicanism were staunchly resistant to newer intellectual fashions. *The Record* saw Dr John Campbell, Minister of Whitefield's Tabernacle until 1866, as standing for the same traditional orthodoxies in Nonconformity.[304] Henry Rogers, author of *The Eclipse of Faith* (1852) and President of Lancashire Independent College from 1857 to 1864, was probably a more effective apologist in the traditional mould.[305] It was common, however, to draw a contrast: '*conservation* is the object of Evangelical Episcopalians, *progress* of Evangelical Dissenters'.[306] The inherited aversion of Nonconformists to creeds imposed by law predisposed them to look for fresh ways of stating Christian truth. The methods of science enjoyed particular prestige. And the idea of progress, so much in the air, became a normal assumption, especially among the better educated Congregationalists. Accordingly their organ, *The British Quarterly Review*, wished to adhere to orthodox truth and yet 'to encourage free and reverent enquiry'.[307] Investigation was seen as the motor of the advance of knowledge.

Devotion to this principle, itself an Enlightenment tenet, was, paradoxically, a corrosive of the Enlightenment version of Evangelicalism that prevailed among Nonconformists. At first it was held that research would not alter the framework of belief. Joseph Angus, Principal of Regent's Park Baptist College, taught in the 1860s that theology is an inductive science, with the texts of scripture as its facts and the rules of Francis Bacon as its method. Progress is possible, not through the appearance of new truth, but through better understanding of the old.[308] But by 1873, starting from the same premiss of the importance of inductive method in theology, it was being argued by a Nonconformist that no doctrines could be regarded as permanent. Any credal statement is an obstacle in the path to truth.[309] The implication was that, as Alexander Raleigh, a leading Congregational divine, put it in 1879, 'religious people have left the principle of authority, and have begun free inquiry, and the use of private judgment, and the practice of complete toleration'.[310] Fixed doctrines seemed outmoded. Starting with the same Enlightenment legacy as Evangelical Anglicans, several leaders in Congregationalism dwelt on its imperative to seek new knowledge, and so moved far along the path towards theological liberalism.

A second solvent of received theological opinion was Romanticism. Its influence was felt not only on particular doctrines, as the last chapter has shown, but also in due course on the whole temper of theology. German theology, the neology that Shaftesbury branded 'Christianity without Christ',[311] was one source. At the Congregational Spring Hill College, Birmingham, for example, D. W. Simon, who had spent ten years in Germany, dropped the traditional study of Christian evidences from the curriculum.[312] Another source was the English school of poetry. The feeling of one Congregational minister for Wordsworth 'amounted almost to a passion'.[313] Browning, himself brought up in Congregationalism, exercised an even stronger fascination.[314] Broad Churchmen, of whom F. D. Maurice and Charles Kingsley were chief, mediated the same influences. Some Evangelical Churchmen were affected, but, partly because of their inclination to free enquiry, Nonconformists imbibed Maurice more readily.[315] The blurring of the edges of doctrine, a characteristic symptom of the sub-Romantic influences, caused more than one stir in Congregationalism. In 1856 a collection of hymns entitled *The Rivulet* was condemned by John Campbell and other conservatives for its doctrinal vagueness. In 1877 a conference at Leicester of the most advanced ministers, men holding that religious communion depended on spiritual sympathy rather than theological agreement, provoked further alarm.[316] James Baldwin Brown, who defended the liberal stance in both these clashes, was the Congregationalist who did most to popularise Maurice in his denomination.[317]

Members of the new school, it was said in 1879, apart from treating all spheres of life as sacred, were distinguished 'by the milder views they take of the character of God; by the disuse of terror as an instrument of persuasion; by a timid denial of miracles; or, short of denial (which is a strong step), by keeping judicious silence about them . . . '[318] The Fatherhood of God was a typical theme, eternal punishment a typical omission. No specific doctrinal change was more marked than the decline of hell. Humble Methodist preachers might continue to excel in the 1870s at 'holding them over the pit', but even eminent Evangelicals in the Established Church, Birks and Samuel Garratt among them, departed from belief in everlasting retribution for the lost.[319] Edward White had led the way among the Congregationalists by arguing in *Life in Christ* (1846) that immortality is conditional on faith in Christ. The finally impenitent, on this view, face extinction, not punishment. Baldwin Brown went as far as the belief that all will ultimately be saved.[320] No consensus emerged within Congregationalism, let alone in the wider Evangelical community, but there can be no doubt that, under the sway of the sentiment of the age, opinion had been transformed.[321] A 'Christian humanitarianism' had come to dominate at least one denomination, the Congregationalists,[322] and sections of other bodies were not far behind. Something of the incisiveness of Evangelical theology had been lost.

The drift of opinion was sharply challenged in the Down Grade Controversy of 1887–8. C. H. Spurgeon, the pastor of the Baptist Metropolitan Tabernacle and by far the most popular preacher of the day, condemned the tendency to theological vapidity. In 1876 he had been dismayed to hear of a Congregational minister who did not preach the gospel. Modern culture, intellectual preaching and aesthetic taste, he claimed, were obscuring the truth.[323] He warned the Baptist Union in 1881 that some sermons were leaving out the atonement – 'and, if you leave out the atonement, what Christianity have you got to preach?'[324] Spurgeon's growing despondency about current trends culminated in 1887. He gave his backing to a series of anonymous articles appearing in his widely circulated church magazine under the heading 'The Down Grade'. Gaining little support, he withdrew from the Baptist Union, stigmatising such bodies that bound together the unorthodox with the orthodox as 'Confederacies in Evil'. His refusal to name individuals as guilty of error, as a result, probably, of earlier undertakings, aroused great resentment and few Baptist ministers followed him into isolation.[325]

Spurgeon was resisting the currents of thought that were running over from Congregationalism into Baptist territory. Theological investigations that might remould doctrine did not attract him. 'Rest assured', he wrote, 'that there is nothing new in theology except that which is false; and the facts of theology are today what they were eighteen hundred years ago.'[326] Hence he approved having creeds. In his scrapbook Spurgeon underlined two offending sentences in a sermon by J. G. Greenhough: 'Our preaching of hell wins none but the base and cowardly . . . Hopes are much larger than creeds.'[327] Another young minister whose utterances alarmed him, W. E. Blomfield, had been censured for appealing to non-Evangelical authorities like Maurice and Kingsley.[328] Spurgeon's protest against emerging liberal tendencies may not have carried many with him at the time, but the enduring esteem in which he was held in the whole Evangelical world ensured a wider hearing for conservative opinion in subsequent generations. He was widely applauded by Evangelical Anglicans, and his influence remained particularly powerful among the Baptists through men trained for the ministry at his college. The Down Grade Controversy helped prepare the way for sharper divisions among Evangelicals in the following century.

THE IMPACT OF HIGH CHURCHMANSHIP

The influence of the Evangelicals on society also suffered because of their displacement within the Church of England by men of higher churchmanship. Between 1865 and 1900 only six outright Evangelicals became bishops,[329] but moderate High Churchmen, heirs of Pusey's sober devotion to the forms of the Church of England, crowded on to the bench. Evangelicals themselves were more troubled by the 'advanced High Churchmen', the ritualists who indulged their Romantic taste by imitating the more elaborate features of medieval or contemporary Catholic practice. In the 1840s ritualism meant little more than intoning prayers, lighting candles on the communion table and preaching in a surplice. But bolder spirits steadily raised the level of display, adding full vestments, choral music and even incense, together with wafer or unleavened bread and a mixed chalice containing water as well as wine. To symbolise their status as priests, the clergy adopted the eastward position at communion, standing with their backs to the people so as to face the God who was believed to enter the elements. They began to hear confessions and declare absolution.[330]

Ritualism touched a raw nerve in Evangelicalism. Rome was within the gates. Acts like the elevation of the bread and wine for adoration seemed, in the full sense of the word, 'idolatrous'.[331] A service at St Alban's, Holborn, according to Shaftesbury, was outwardly 'the worship of Jupiter or Juno'.[332] Here was an outstanding target for a crusade. Ritual prosecutions in the ecclesiastical courts began in 1853 with an unsuccessful attempt to remove a high altar, its cross, candlesticks, coloured cloths and credence table from St Paul's, Knightsbridge. Protests against vestments at St George's-in-the-East in 1859–60 degenerated into brawls.[333] From 1865 there was an Evangelical organisation, the Church Association, designed to conduct legal cases against ritualists, and from 1874, under the Public Worship Regulation Act, there was a clear mode of procedure. Prosecution, however, failed to stem the advancing tide of ritual practices. Many blamed the bishops, who were permitted under the act to forbid the commencement of a case. When, in consequence, the wrath of the Church Association was turned in 1888 against the bishop observing the most advanced form of liturgy, the saintly Edward King of Lincoln, the result was an ignominious failure that convinced most respectable Evangelicals of the futility of legal action.[334] Only the Protestant Truth Society, founded in 1890 by John Kensit, sustained a continuing campaign, often taking direct action to disrupt obnoxious services. At All Saints, East Clevedon, the ritualist vicar issued brass knuckle-dusters so that members of his congregation could resist the Kensitites.[335]

It should not be supposed that the Church Association, let alone the Protestant Truth Society, enjoyed the support of all Anglican Evangelicals. Although J. C. Ryle, their leading figure, was a Vice-President of the Association until his elevation to the see of Liverpool in 1880,[336] many others agreed with Samuel Garratt, writing in the following year, that 'if there is one thing which, more than another, has injured the estimation in which Evangelical truth is regarded, by thoughtful and religious men, it is these prosecutions'. Yet the Evangelical body in the Church of England was so preoccupied with the ritualist menace that it neglected what Garratt called 'its old crusade against public evils'.[337] It was left largely to Nonconformists in these years to pursue campaigns on social questions. Anti-ritualism was an alternative form of an agitation against perceived evil. The energy poured into it was diverted away from other channels.

On the other hand, a higher churchmanship proved attractive to many Evangelicals. Their clergy, as Samuel Butler illustrates in *The Way of all Flesh*, discarded the old-fashioned gown and bands in the pulpit and introduced choral music into the service.[338] 'Churches now deemed decidedly Evangelical', it was remarked in 1883, 'would, thirty years ago, have been regarded as High Church.'[339] There are several reasons. For one thing, Evangelicals had never been uniformly Low Church in practice. Daniel Wilson introduced 8 a.m. communion, often thought a uniquely High Church practice, in 1824.[340] John Bickersteth, who always had salt fish on his table on Fridays, introduced a new organ, a choral service and the *Te Deum* after evening prayer soon after going to Sapcote, Leicestershire, in 1837.[341] There was therefore no entrenched bar to a higher liturgical pattern. For another, loyalty to the Book of Common Prayer could induce a punctilious observance of the rubrics. Thus from 1859 William Cadman obeyed the directive to daily prayer and weekly communion.[342] Again, Evangelicals participating in the life of the same church as High Churchmen could hardly avoid being affected by their attitudes. Clergy in particular necessarily rubbed shoulders from time to time. High Churchmen shared a similar spiritual discipline, often an identical religious vocabulary. There were men in the late nineteenth century such as G. H. Wilkinson who professed 'Evangelical-Catholic' principles, and by 1869 they were promoting a form of Anglo-Catholic revivalism.[343] Such High Churchmen were acceptable in certain Evangelical pulpits. Holding that the two parties had been moving together in belief ever since the Gorham Judgement, Edward Garbett announced in 1871 his conviction that they should actually combine.[344] Evangelicals had neglected the doctrine of the church 'as a visible organised society', he held, and the *Tracts for the Times* had done some good.[345] Copying High Church practice where it seemed to involve no sacrifice of principle was the result.

More elaborate services, furthermore, were partly a matter of following public taste. With all their poetic associations, flowers came back into use at funerals in the later nineteenth century. High Churchmen also used them to decorate their churches.[346] Evangelicals resisted for a while, the more conservative among them for a long while. In 1880, floral decorations lavished on altars, together with flower services, flower festivals and sepulchral flowers, were still being condemned as having a 'Pagan purpose'.[347] But most Evangelicals eventually succumbed. Again, they tried for a while to withstand the introduction of anthems, musical services and robed choirs. Bishop Waldegrave sternly insisted in 1868 that a service he was to attend should be 'of the simplest character – hymns or psalms (metrical) and chanting of the canticles – but no monotones, the rest of the service, both reading and responding, unmusical . . . '[348] It was in vain, however, and many Evangelicals gradually fell into line. By the early 1880s William Cadman at Holy Trinity, Marylebone, had extended the music to the responses and psalms and the choir was surpliced. He was ready to advance 'with the tastes of the times'.[349] It is clear that this is the fundamental explanation of the process, for similar developments were beginning to take place among the Presbyterians of Scotland and the Nonconformists of England. The pioneer of worship reform in Scotland, Dr Robert Lee, was at the broad end of the range of theological opinion, but through the Church Service Society, founded in 1865, Evangelicals were affected.[350] Chanting was begun at Union Chapel, Islington, in 1856 or 1857, F. B. Meyer was observing communion weekly before the end of the century and by 1906 one Congregational minister was even wearing a surplice.[351] So even where there was no heritage of liturgical worship, no Prayer Book and no Oxford Movement, the form and setting of the service were swayed by the Romantic temper of the age.

Change entailed friction. In Nonconformity there was some difference of opinion about architectural styles. Dissenting Gothic made swift strides in the later nineteenth century, especially in the suburbs.[352] Spurgeon, by contrast, erected his Metropolitan Tabernacle in the Grecian style of architecture. That, he believed, was the appropriate setting for the exposition of a New Testament written in Greek. He castigated congregations that put 'hobgoblins and monsters on the outside of their preaching houses'.[353] The loudest uproar in Methodism was about organs. The installation of an organ at Brunswick Chapel, Leeds, in the 1820s to meet the taste of a middle-class congregation actually precipitated the creation of a separate denomination, the Protestant Methodists.[354] Resistance to organs was also substantial in Scotland until the 1860s.[355]

In the Church of England, however, the great division of opinion among Evangelicals was over the surplice. Wearing the surplice to preach represented a preparedness to conform to the prevailing mode in the church. Evangelicals in the early nineteenth century ordinarily followed the customary procedure of discarding the surplice on entering the pulpit in order to preach in a black gown. Preaching in a surplice, however, was laid down in the Book of Common Prayer, and from the 1840s disciples of the Oxford Movement began to uphold the practice as a sign of submission to the authority of the church. The issue could generate enormous feeling, for it was a very visible shift in the 'popish' direction. When the High Church Bishop Philpotts directed the clergy of his diocese to adopt the surplice for preaching in 1844 there was serious rioting in Exeter.[356] Opposition was not merely a matter of vulgar prejudice. In 1867 Bishop Waldegrave was still describing wearing the surplice in the pulpit as 'in many cases but the first of a series of Romeward movements'.[357] The gown became the public badge of the Evangelical school. In 1871, however, the decision of the Judicial Committee of the Privy Council in the Purchas case was that the surplice must be worn in all ministrations. Evangelicals faced a dilemma. They wished to uphold the law in order to restrain ritualism; and yet the law commanded preaching in the surplice. A hardier soul like Garratt might persist in wearing the gown to the end of his parochial ministry,[358] but others wavered. In 1887 the surplice was introduced at Holy Trinity, Cambridge.[359] As in other respects, the trend was towards accommodation with the dominant practice of the Church of England. But the process divided the Evangelical party. When Ryle preached in a surplice while on holiday without his gown in 1876, he was much censured.[360] The tensions resulting from the growing preference for the decorous and the aesthetic in worship helped to blunt the impact of Evangelicalism as the century wore on. They also, once more, prefigured the division of the following century.

THE EVANGELICAL CENTURY

The hundred years or so before the First World War nevertheless deserve to be called the Evangelical century. In that period the activism of the movement enabled it to permeate British society. Righteousness, as Evangelicals might have put it, abounded in the land. Major inroads were made on the existing mass of religious indifference. Less impact was made on the lower working classes than on higher social groups, but it is quite mistaken to hold that the working classes as a whole were largely untouched by the gospel. Manners and politics were transformed; even intellectual life was affected far more than is normally admitted. If hypocrisy is the tribute vice pays to virtue, then the undoubted existence of hypocrisy is a sign of the Evangelical achievement in setting new standards of behaviour. Historians have sometimes been misled into minimising the role of popular Protestantism by the very omnipresence of an Evangelical atmosphere. The gospel conditioned unspoken assumptions. Historians have also been deceived by contemporary comments lamenting the scarcity of godliness. Shaftesbury's writings are full of them. Apart from Shaftesbury's dyspeptic temperament, the phenomenon can be explained by the scale of Evangelical ambitions. Nothing short of a nation united in the fear of the Lord was their aim. If achievements were great, expectations were always greater. Outsiders like Mill are the safer witnesses. So are those who broke away from the constraints of a pious home. The mind of Leslie Stephen, for instance, is inexplicable without analysis of his Evangelical inheritance.[361] Earnestness remained when Christianity faded.

The enduring power of the same legacy is evident in the group that gathered round Leslie Stephen's daughter, Virginia Woolf. The creed of Bloomsbury was a new revelation, a substitute for the gospel, but very similar to old-time religion in some of its characteristics. 'We are the mysterious priests of a new and amazing civilisation', wrote Lytton Strachey to Virginia's future husband, Leonard Woolf. 'We have abolished religion, we have founded ethics, we have established philosophy, we have sown our strange illumination in every province of thought, we have conquered art, we have liberated love.'[362] Strachey knew what their new set of values had to replace. His pungent polemic *Eminent Victorians* represents, according to his biographer, an 'onslaught upon the evangelicalism that was the defining characteristic of Victorian culture'.[363] Bloomsbury's attack was launched when Evangelicalism was well past its zenith. Social change, shifts within theology and alterations in the pattern of worship were already sapping the foundations of its ascendancy. Like British overseas trade or British power abroad in the same period, it stood so high relative to its rivals at mid-century that the only way was down. The initiative passed to other hands. But, at least for a while, Evangelicals had remoulded British society in their own image.

[5]

Holiness unto the Lord: Keswick and its Context in the Later Nineteenth Century

In that day shall there be upon the bells of the horses,
HOLINESS UNTO THE LORD. (Zech. 14:20)

From the 1870s onwards Evangelicalism was deeply influenced by a new movement. Advocates of holiness teaching urged that Christians should aim for a second decisive experience beyond conversion. Afterwards they would live on a more elevated plane. No longer would they feel themselves ensnared by wrongdoing, for they would have victory over sin. They would possess holiness, enjoying 'the higher life'. Initiates spoke 'a new spiritual language'.[1] They shared the belief that holiness comes by faith. Effort, conflict, endeavour were rejected as the path of sanctification. 'There is a mighty struggle going on in the Church of God between two doctrines', declared one advocate of the new views in 1874. 'Which will you have – sanctification by works or sanctification by faith?'[2] The sound Reformation principle, they could point out, was that salvation is the gift of God to the person who trusts him. They were simply pressing the principle further by contending that progress in the Christian life as well as its commencement can be had for the asking. God is as willing to give holiness as he is to confer salvation. The apostles of the new teaching were Robert and Hannah Pearsall Smith, an American couple who addressed gatherings 'for the promotion of scriptural holiness' at Oxford in 1874 and Brighton in 1875. In 1875 also there was held the first of the conventions at Keswick, in the Lake District, that were to become the focal point of the new spirituality. The message was taken up by many other bodies, including the Salvation Army, but the Keswick idiom became dominant. It shaped the prevailing pattern of Evangelical piety for much of the twentieth century.

The new style of devotion laid stress on 'the rest of faith'. With spiritual struggle over, trust brought calm to the soul. This attitude was clearly of a piece with the conviction of those who ran organisations or missions on

the faith principle. As much as George Müller of the orphanage or Hudson
Taylor of the China Inland Mission, the advocates of holiness by faith
appealed to the trustworthiness of God. Just as human means must be
laid aside in Christian mission, so human effort must be abandoned in the
Christian life. Defence against temptation would be granted by a God who
ensured a supply of funds. Hudson Taylor fitted naturally into the new world
of holiness by faith, testifying that he had enjoyed the experience before it
was widely proclaimed.[3] Furthermore, the new doctrine, with its strong
dimension of supernaturalism, had a ready affinity for premillennialism.
Those who believed in the imminence of the second advent, the decisive
divine entry into history, were attracted by the idea that the power of
God could already break into human lives. And when Christ returned,
he would surely expect his people to be pure. Advent teaching was
heard on its platform from the very first Keswick Convention, achieving
greater prominence in the 1880s.[4] The consonance of the new teaching
about sanctification with the faith mission principle and premillennialism
betrays its origins. The holiness movement was another expression of the
permeation of Evangelicalism by Romantic thought. The sensibility of the
age (as it will appear) lay behind the new spiritual language.

The movement was partly a response to the circumstances outlined at the
end of the previous chapter. By the early 1870s Evangelicalism was on the
ebb. The rise in the standard of living was allowing the working classes to
turn away from the churches for their leisure activities. Vital religion seemed
threatened at the same time by the twin foes of rationalism and ritualism.
When confronted with the choice of swimming with the tide or resisting
it, some Evangelicals wished to escape from the dilemma. Accommodation
to social trends by providing sport or entertainment for the masses was to
erode the distinction between the church and the world. Watering down
belief to make it acceptable to the contemporary mind was worse. Yet
blank resistance to the social and intellectual currents of the times in the
manner of Spurgeon seemed just as unacceptable. It stirred up controversy
without achieving anything concrete. What was to be done? 'I came here',
announced a clergyman at the Oxford holiness conference, 'because I felt
a great want in my ministry. Crowds came and went, and yet with small
result. I could not believe that all was right, and I came to see what was
the secret of the spiritual power which some of my brethren possess.'[5]
A more intense form of piety offered a fresh dynamic. A spirituality
that harmonised with the thought of the age promised to reinvigorate
evangelism. 'Above all', a historian of late antiquity has concluded, 'the
holy man is a man of power.'[6] Rising above circumstance, he can control
his destiny. Repeatedly, holiness advocates emphasised the availability of
power. The attenders of the Oxford conference, it was said, had discovered
'a secret of power in service'.[7] The holiness movement offered what many
late nineteenth-century Evangelicals wanted: a means of coping with the
challenges of their era.

THE METHODIST HOLINESS TRADITION

The way was prepared for the assimilation of the fresh thinking by a wide range of background factors. There was, in the first place, the tradition in Methodism that Christian perfection is attainable on earth. John Wesley had taught that there is a second stage beyond justification in the Christian life when a believer 'experiences a total death to sin, and an entire renewal in the love, and image of God, so as to rejoice evermore, to pray without ceasing, and in everything give thanks'.[8] No Christian, Wesley held, commits sinful acts, but the perfect Christian is also freed from evil thoughts or tempers. He still makes mistakes for which Christ's atoning work is necessary, but involuntary mistakes of this kind are not properly sins. The only type of action that can reasonably be classified as a sin Wesley calls (in a phrase much quoted in later holiness debates) 'a voluntary transgression of a known law'.[9] So restricted a definition made it plausible for a number of the early Methodists, though not Wesley himself, to claim the state of Christian perfection or, as they usually preferred to call it, 'perfect love'. It was held to be gained instantaneously, although progress in holiness normally preceded and followed it; and it was received, Wesley insisted, by faith.[10] Here were many of the materials out of which the late nineteenth-century holiness movement was to forge its teachings. Before the 1870s, however, at least in Britain, these doctrines were almost entirely restricted to Methodism. After Wesley's death some of the preachers prized them as the sacred deposit of the connexion. Perfection, Disney Alexander pointed out at Halifax in 1800, is a divine command. 'If God gives us laws', he contended with a strict Enlightenment logic that Wesley had used in the same way, 'he gives us likewise an ability to keep them . . . '[11] But the tradition fell into decay. The more respectable in the connexion turned to a watered-down version of the tradition rendered by William Arthur in *The Tongue of Fire* (1856). In elegant phraseology the author, a Secretary of the Wesleyan Methodist Missionary Society, urged his readers to pray for a richer experience of the Holy Spirit. He tones down, however, the idea of a 'second blessing'. 'The difference between receiving the Spirit and being filled with the Spirit', he writes, 'is a difference not of kind, but of degree.'[12] This was to empty Wesleyan entire sanctification of its distinctiveness: indeed, one of Arthur's motives appears to have been to enhance the standing of the Wesleyans in the eyes of other denominations. Arthur's book gained considerable popularity and assisted in the natural process whereby the sharp outlines of Wesley's teachings were forgotten. By the 1860s the idea that there is a decisive second stage in Christian sanctification was at a low ebb among the generality of Wesleyans.

Yet in these years the legacy of Wesley's ideas continued to have an effect on Methodism. His *Plain Account of Christian Perfection*, a lucid apologetic work, encouraged some to seek the blessing.[13] The writings of John Fletcher of Madeley, Wesley's coadjutor and a claimant to the experience, were

another source.[14] The lives of earlier Methodist preachers were similarly
influential.[15] All these literary influences surrounded those growing up in
the denomination in their most impressionable years. Candidates for the
ministry were questioned as a matter of course on Christian perfection,
and Wesley's sermons, including expositions of the subject, functioned as
the subordinate standard of belief in the connexion.[16] Wesleyan theologians
remained formally committed to their founder's doctrine. Agar Beet, who
was to be appointed a tutor at Richmond College in 1885, published a book
asserting instantaneous and entire sanctification by faith in 1880 despite
remaining outside the reviving holiness movement; and W. B. Pope, the
author of the magisterial *Compendium of Christian Theology* (1875), taught
the possibility of the 'extinction of sin'.[17] Here and there entire sanctification
retained zealous advocates. James Carr was still preaching it at Wesley
Chapel, Nottingham, in the mid-1850s so that the young men fell to earnest
discussion of the topic and some in the congregation, including the father
of the founder of Boot's the Chemists, entered the experience.[18] A few
well-placed men claimed 'full salvation'. Benjamin Hellier, classical tutor at
Richmond between 1857 and 1868 and subsequently at Headingley College,
was both an exponent and seemed an embodiment of the teaching.[19]
Benjamin Gregory, who long before had startled those examining him
as a candidate for the ministry by professing the experience, continued
to testify to it as a connexional editor.[20] And Alexander McAulay, who
was to become President of Conference in 1876 and Secretary of the Home
Missions Department from then until 1885, was prepared to speak of his
'entire surrender to Christ' and, as though to substantiate it, was marked
by a certain 'apartness'.[21] Such men were eager to welcome any sign of a
revitalisation of the decaying tradition.

The thirst for holiness was resuscitated in Methodism by a small
group of relatively obscure younger ministers. J. Clapham Greaves,
W. G. Pascoe, I. E. Page and John Brash were drawn together in 1870 by a
common experience of 'perfect love'. In 1871 they held several meetings
to promote scriptural holiness in New Street Chapel, York, and during
Conference that year there were informal discussions on the theme.[22]
These were followed in 1872 by the first of an annual series of public
meetings at Conference sponsored by Cuthbert Bainbridge, a wealthy
Newcastle warehouse-owner. Bainbridge also provided the money to
launch, in January 1872, *The King's Highway*, a substantial monthly
periodical. The journal established a healthy circulation, secured more
than seventy Wesleyan contributors in its first twelve years and was to
last, under the care of Page and Brash, for twenty-eight years. It had
some impact on other Methodist denominations, whose representatives
were admitted to a share in its management.[23] Its influence extended
even beyond Methodism. 'I have just got two copies of *The King's
Highway*', reported a hyper-enthusiastic Baptist minister in 1872, 'and
am eating them'.[24] By 1874 it was possible for the promoters to hold a

conference devoted to holiness alone. Gathering at Wakefield, it attracted about fifty ministers and laymen.[25] By this point, however, a great deal of the eagerness to learn about the ways of holiness clearly derived from the stir made by the Pearsall Smiths, whose Oxford conference had just taken place. Robert Pearsall Smith, while still in America, had explained to the editor of *The King's Highway* that they had to be so careful not to confuse non-Methodists when talking of the experience 'that we may sometimes *seem* as though we did not mean the same thing practically as our dear Methodist brethren'. Nevertheless, he wanted to insist, their differences were no more than verbal.[26] In reviewing Pearsall Smith's new periodical, *The Christian's Pathway of Power*, soon to become the official organ of Keswick, the Methodist contributor agreed: 'THE CHRISTIAN'S PATH-WAY and THE KING'S HIGHWAY are different names for the same divine road to heaven – the old way of holiness.'[27] Consequently, it is not surprising that the new wind blowing from America gave fresh impetus to the holiness movement in Methodism. But it is equally clear that the reinvigoration of the Methodist inheritance was under way before the American breeze was felt. The wider holiness revival of the 1870s drew strength from the native tradition of British Methodism.

QUAKER SPIRITUALITY

Another indigenous influence was exerted by the Society of Friends. The Society, standing apart even from the Dissenting mainstream in the eighteenth century, had cherished its own highly distinctive spirituality, drawing heavily on earlier mystical and hermetic strands in European thought. The central notion in the early nineteenth century remained 'the light within', the guiding principle, to be distinguished from reason or conscience, that is given to each human being. Salvation depended on response to its illumination. As the Evangelical Revival remoulded Quaker life, however, doubts began to arise about the received spirituality. Could it be squared with belief in salvation through the atoning death of Christ as taught in the Bible? In 1835 Isaac Crewdson, a Manchester Evangelical Quaker, issued *A Beacon to the Society of Friends* to declare that it could not. He entirely repudiated 'the inward light', arguing that it was a barrier to the understanding of scriptural truth.[28] Although Crewdson left the Society in the following year, it became plain in the controversy surrounding the *Beacon* that the new generation of Quaker leaders was in fundamental sympathy with him.[29] J. J. Gurney, a Norwich banker and probably the chief figure in the Society in the 1830s and 1840s, found it hard to fit the idea of 'universal light' into his Evangelical way of thinking.[30] Evangelicalism became dominant in the Society, so that, for instance, from the 1870s Sunday evening home mission meetings, with hymn singing and an evangelistic address, were introduced alongside the traditional

Sunday morning meetings for worship, with their silence punctuated by contributions made under a sense of compulsion by the Holy Spirit.[31] Sharing in interdenominational work through agencies such as the Bible Society and the British and Foreign School Society, the Quakers had become accepted as part of the Evangelical world.

The older style of spirituality nevertheless lived on among Friends, an undercurrent or perhaps a backwater of Quietism. God, held the traditionalists, is to be discovered through passive acceptance of the influences he brings to play on the soul, through nature, humanity and interior reflection. They looked for their inspiration to the writings of the early Friends, and particularly those of George Fox, the founder of the Society, and Robert Barclay, the author of *An Apology for the True Christian Divinity* (1676). There they found extensive teaching about the development of the spiritual life. 'For looking down at sin, and corruption, and distraction, you are swallowed up in it', wrote Fox; 'but looking at the light which discovers them, you will see over them. That will give victory; and you will find grace and strength: and there is the first step of peace.'[32] The message of victory over sin bringing peace was to be the keynote of the Keswick Convention. Likewise, Barclay expounded the doctrine of Christian perfection. It is possible, he contended, 'to be free from actual sinning and transgressing of the *law of God*, in that respect *perfect*: yet doth this *perfection* still admit of a growth; and there remaineth always in some part a possibility of sinning . . . '[33] Both principle and qualifications would have found favour with the editors of *The King's Highway*. Such texts continued to mould nineteenth-century Quietists.

Much of the Quaker phraseology was to be taken up by the holiness movement. The 'baptism of the Holy Ghost', 'full surrender' and 'rest' were terms bandied around in holiness circles after 1870, but had long been in frequent use among Friends. There was often, however, some difference in meaning. Whereas the later movement used 'the baptism of/with the Holy Ghost' and 'full surrender' as descriptions of the moment of entire sanctification (or even of a subsequent experience), the Quaker practice was to apply them to a person's initial conversion. Similarly, 'rest' appears in an official Quaker statement of 1862 as a term describing the life of any true believer, not as a depiction of the state of someone who has received a second blessing.[34] For Quakers there was no decisive second stage in Christian experience, but it was certainly expected that believers would enjoy the condition of holiness. The whole Society, Hannah Pearsall Smith was to conclude, formed a sort of holiness organisation.[35] Evangelicals among the Friends, far from repudiating the call to advance in the spiritual life, were eager to endorse it. Their only wariness was that spiritual experience should be, as a Pastoral Epistle of the Yearly Meeting put it in 1883, 'grounded upon genuine conversion'.[36] With that assured, Evangelicals in the Society accepted much of the Quietist legacy of holiness teaching. They saw great value not only in Quaker texts but also in sources esteemed among Quietists like those by Fénelon and Mme Guyon – works that were to have a vogue in the holiness movement.[37] The assimilation of Quietist influences by Evangelicals within the Society of Friends was one of the ways in which alien ideas were sanitised, as it were, before reception by the broader Evangelical community.

Many of the Quaker influences were transmitted through the Pearsall Smiths. Hannah was brought up among Friends falling under the jurisdiction of the Philadelphia Yearly Meeting, which sustained distinctive Quaker customs and the Quietist spirituality with more natural vigour than in England. Despite a complicated subsequent history of religious exploration, Hannah was very much the Quaker on her arrival in Britain. Apart from retaining distinctive dress, she used 'thee' in correspondence, even to her husband, and insisted on receiving the approval of English Friends before undertaking public ministry.[38] Robert professed to be undenominational, but, as his critics noted, he too betrayed his Quaker background. The undogmatic call to holiness of living ('We did not come to Oxford . . . to discuss doctrines') bore the hallmark of Quakerism. So did the occasional unguarded idiom ('upon my light and guidance') and, most of all, the pivotal points in his teaching like 'the Rest of Faith'. The Quaker practice of meditation in stillness came over with the Pearsall Smiths. The Oxford conference included regular times of silence, 'an exercise which, as the congregations became more and more accustomed to it, proved increasingly acceptable'.[39] Quakers were naturally drawn to the ministry of the American visitors. During the communion service at the Brighton conference, about a hundred held their own 'spiritual observance' at the local meeting house; other less strict Friends were willing to participate in the communion.[40] One of the Quakers present was Robert Wilson, a gentleman from Broughton Grange, near Cockermouth in Cumberland. Together with T. D. Harford-Battersby, Vicar of St John's, Keswick, Wilson went on to organise the Keswick Convention. Although he took no part in public teaching, he chose the conference motto, 'All one in Christ Jesus', and set much of the tone.[41] Quaker spirituality was one of the foundations of the holiness movement.

BRETHREN TEACHING

A third Christian body, the Brethren, shared in the creation of the new ethos. Several strands in Brethren teaching contributed. There was the insistence on the 'heavenly calling' of the church. If true believers were about to be snatched away to meet the Lord in the air, the great task of the church was to prepare for that event. Holiness was one of the requirements taught in scripture for those who lived in the shadow of the second coming.[42] There was also the idea that underlay the whole movement of 'gathering to the Lord only'. Existing churches were condemned as organisations of human contrivance whose systems of government were a hindrance to the work of God. True assemblies, by contrast, were gathered by the Holy Ghost to Jesus as the only centre.[43] Brethren assemblies were therefore marked by a certain apartness that tended to encourage a desire for holiness by withdrawal. Furthermore, the main line of Brethren teaching on sanctification could readily lead on to a Keswick stance. Sanctification, according to the chief Brethren authorities, takes place in principle at conversion. What follows in the Christian life is merely the working out in experience of the reality already given. Hence, when seen from the point of view of the standing of the believer, sanctification is not progressive, but the immediate result of faith.[44] Both the immediacy and the stress on faith were to be characteristic of the holiness movement, especially in its earlier phases. The difference, however, is that whereas Brethren placed the crucial stage of sanctification at conversion, Keswick put it at a subsequent stage of 'full surrender'. Keswick teaching did enter Brethren circles, but it never became their orthodoxy. On the contrary, as late as 1919 the Brethren standpoint expressed in their most respected journal was that the second decisive experience taught at Keswick was illusory. 'When we hear of believers making a full surrender', ran the reply to a reader's question on consecration, ' . . . it generally means that they have by the Spirit been taught their sanctification through the blood . . . '[45] That is to say, they merely perceive that they have been wholly sanctified beforehand, at conversion. The difference between the dominant Brethren doctrine and the notions of the holiness movement was substantial. Yet the affinities were real. Already in the 1860s among Brethren the idea of instant and entire sanctification by faith was abroad.

Some were prepared to claim a distinctive spiritual experience. During the Oxford conference on scriptural holiness in 1874, one of the Brethren from George Müller's Bethesda Chapel, Bristol, rose at a communion service 'to say that he had lived in unbroken unclouded communion with Jesus for very many years'.[46] Others were ready to preach it. John Hambleton, 'the converted actor', one of the most popular Brethren evangelists of the 1860s, was propagating what has been identified as Keswick teaching in 1861.[47] In fact, it must have been the rather different holiness teaching of the Brethren, but holiness teaching it was. Consequently it is not surprising that critics should have seen Robert Pearsall Smith as having been 'led astray by Plymouth Brethren and other ill-instructed Christians'.[48] Pearsall Smith repudiated the charge, pointing out that 'the Plymouth Brethren or Exclusives' (he must have meant the Exclusives alone) had met his views with decided opposition.[49] Yet the Brethren of Philadelphia had been a significant influence on the developing thought of his wife. Although they were responsible chiefly for insisting on the importance of firm doctrinal convictions, they also asserted the centrality of faith as the way of justification – and, no doubt, in view of standard Brethren views, of sanctification.[50] So there was an element, albeit a small one, of Brethren teaching behind the Pearsall Smiths' doctrine of holiness by faith. Far more important, however, was the wider Brethren role in fostering expectations of higher attainments in practical holiness. In the wake of the 1859–60 revival they were expanding in numbers and seemed to be the *avant-garde* of keen Evangelicalism.[51] Consequently, they were heeded when they spoke about what one of their leading teachers called 'the blessed possibility of living in such unbroken communion with God . . . as that the flesh or the old man may not appear'.[52] Brethren influence helped cultivate the belief that entire consecration is possible.

THE MILDMAY CIRCLE

The Church of England, which was to be far more affected by Keswick ideas than the other denominations, had also anticipated aspects of the new wave of holiness convictions. Since 1856 there had been held, first at Barnet and then at Mildmay Park in north London, an annual (except in 1857) conference for Christian workers. William Pennefather summoned the conference while incumbent of Christ Church, Barnet, and transferred it to Mildmay Park when he moved to St Jude's there in 1864. Pennefather combined devotional intensity with remarkable energy: he also pioneered a number of other enterprises including an orphanage and the work of deaconesses in the Church of England. The conferences drew large numbers – some 1,000 by 1869[53] – to hear addresses from the leading evangelists of the day. Personal holiness was one of the central themes from the first; others, receiving varying degrees of emphasis from year to year, were foreign missions, home missions and the Lord's coming. The conferences were open to all who were in sympathy with these concerns. They were, in fact, assertively undenominational, designed as expressions of 'the great principle, often slighted, sometimes positively disowned by the Church of Christ, that her union in Christ, the living, glorified Head of all His members, is a *spiritual* union'.[54] Although the chief constituency always consisted of revivalist-inclined Evangelical Anglicans, likeminded groups were also represented. Outside influences spread into the Church of England at Barnet and Mildmay. Pennefather himself, who wrote of 'my love for Friends', drew a number of Quakers into the conference. Brethren also joined in.[55] And a third influence, usually repudiated by Evangelicals, probably left its trace on the conferences. William Haslam, Rector of Curzon Chapel, Mayfair, a regular speaker at Mildmay and an early promoter of the other holiness meetings, had once been caught up in the Tractarian movement, with its yearnings for holiness, until his dramatic conversion.[56] The High Church devotion to the holy life persisted in him. Mildmay introduced a section of the Evangelical party in the Church of England to higher spiritual aspirations than were normally entertained in the middle years of the century.

The tone of the Barnet and Mildmay conferences was set by Pennefather, who chose the speakers, and by his flock, who arranged hospitality. At Barnet, Pennefather wrote to a friend, 'the Church is very separate from the world'. He would rebuke worldly conformity from the pulpit. 'It was at a time when very small bonnets were in fashion', recalled a member of the congregation. 'Pausing and looking round the church, he said, with all the energy he could command, "Where is the shamefacedness of our daughters?"' But for all his attention to details of dress, Pennefather, unlike the Keswick school of the future, taught no particular path of consecration. The distinctive note in his instruction was the stress on the work of the Holy Spirit. The Saviour had promised to send the Comforter. 'Are we not then to look for the power of the Holy Ghost?'[57] Quite characteristically he opened the 1868 Mildmay Conference with an exhortation to seek the Holy Spirit.[58] All this was well calculated to stir up expectations that the holiness movement was later to satisfy. Furthermore, although Pennefather said nothing about a second blessing as such, his guidance could lead enquirers towards a decisive stage in Christian experience beyond conversion. One lady learned from him about what she called 'a second step of my Christian life . . . entire *consecration* to Christ'.[59] This was but a short distance from fully-blown holiness teaching. Nevertheless, Mildmay, which continued meeting into the twentieth century, long after Pennefather's death in 1873, never capitulated wholly to the characteristic message of the post-Pearsall Smith era. It permitted speakers on its platform who expounded holiness by faith, but, under the chairmanship of Stevenson Blackwood, it also invited speakers opposed to the new teaching – Grattan Guinness at a special conference in 1874 and Horatius Bonar at the regular one in 1875.[60] It never achieved the singleness of purpose of the Keswick Convention, and, though its attendance rose to 3,000,[61] it was destined to have a lesser sway than Keswick. But its role as a precursor was crucial. It injected a more intense form of piety into the bloodstream of Evangelical Anglicanism.

Mildmay quickened the zeal for holiness in the circle that was to sponsor the Pearsall Smiths. William Haslam gave Pearsall Smith his first public speaking opportunity in Britain in 1873; T. B. Smithies, the Primitive Methodist editor of *The British Workman*, was a Mildmay speaker who ran breakfast meetings for Nonconformists to hear Pearsall Smith; Stevenson Blackwood, later chairman of Mildmay, had been converted under Pennefather and proposed the Oxford conference of 1874; Alfred Christopher, Rector of St Aldate's, Oxford, and a close friend of Pennefather's, organised the Oxford conference; T. D. Harford-Battersby, who called together the early meetings of the Keswick Convention, had been a host to Pennefather in 1868; Admiral E. G. Fishbourne, a gentleman-evangelist and Pennefather's 'valued friend and constant coun-sellor', became Pearsall Smith's lieutenant in his work during 1875.[62] The Mildmay circle provided the core of personnel for the new movement of the 1870s. The chief institutional framework of the new phase also derived from this source. Barnet and Mildmay pioneered annual convention-going. Even before the advent of the Pearsall Smiths, imitations sprang up. By 1869 it was already being noted that certain villages had their annual gatherings.[63] But the chief conferences on the Mildmay pattern were at Perth and Clifton, both founded in 1863. The Perth conferences laid a foundation for the acceptance of convention-going in Scotland.[64] It was easy for Admiral Fishbourne to bring the views of Pearsall Smith to the Clifton platform in 1874.[65] From 1873 onwards, holiness conventions mushroomed – at Dover and Bath, Gloucester (moving to Salisbury) and Bristol, Aberdeen and Birmingham.[66] The distinctive message of holiness by faith usually rubbed shoulders with more traditional Mildmay views on sanctification. Keswick, unusual in insisting on holiness by faith alone, was but a drop in a mighty flood. The network of conventions was essential to the dissemination of the new ideas. They looked to Pennefather's conference as their model.

THE REVIVALIST BACKGROUND

The Christian workers drawn to Mildmay were usually part of the revivalist world. The heightened spiritual atmosphere of 1859–60 left a legacy of urgent evangelistic concern that prepared the way for the holiness movement. The work of laymen in preaching the gospel created a precedent for the ministry of the unordained Robert Pearsall Smith. Without the toleration of female preaching that emerged in the 1860s the role of Robert's wife Hannah would have been unthinkable.[67] The playing down of denominational allegiance, what one revivalist called 'the spirit of loving union of the present day',[68] led on to the undenominational temper of Keswick. The newspaper of popular evangelism, *The Revival*, carried articles by the Pearsall Smiths on holiness from 1867 onwards.[69] Its editor, R. C. Morgan, travelled in 1869 to America, attending one of the meetings of the burgeoning holiness movement there.[70] He republished a variety of works on 'the higher Christian life'.[71] From 1873 to 1875 all the events featuring the Pearsall Smiths were faithfully related in the newspaper, now called *The Christian*. The world of the revivalists provided a natural constituency for the assimilation of sanctification by faith. Their ideas also cleared a path for the new teaching. Their theological stance increasingly approximated in practice to Arminianism. The constant text of Henry Moorhouse, a leading revivalist, was John 3:16 and his message was summarised in the chorus 'Whosoever will may come'.[72] Calvinists remained Calvinists, but their version was no longer so high. William Pennefather, for instance, unconsciously influenced another clergyman, Clarmont Skrine, to modify his views on election. 'I found he was as strongly attached as I was to the doctrines of grace', wrote Skrine, 'but was not led to make them, as I believe I had done, a barrier to the free proclamation of Christ's gospel to the poor sinner.'[73] Calvinists were less prepared to look askance at Arminians. 'If a Methodist has begun work in a court', declared Reginald Radcliffe, 'and a Calvinist comes to the same place, let him ask for a blessing on his brother, and go on to the next court . . .'[74] There was less of a doctrinal barrier to co-operation. Consequently, too, Calvinists of the revivalist stamp had fewer inhibitions about embracing teaching that rejected traditional Reformed convictions on sanctification. The lower version of Calvinism in vogue among them was a more elastic worldview.

At the same time there was a shift of emphasis among revivalists away from theology towards ethics. Basic doctrine alone was important for evangelism. 'But if good is to be done', declared Baptist Noel in 1861, 'we must be holy ourselves.'[75] Manner of life impinged directly on the effectiveness of witness. With the burning low of revival fires that warmed the early 1860s, there was a widespread longing in the following years to recover the earlier intensity of religious experience. 'My heart has often been stirred with desires for holiness', R. C. Morgan confided to his diary in 1868, 'but the pressure of earthly cares seems to choke the Word, and it becomes unfruitful. Lord, cleanse me!'[76] The Pearsall Smiths spoke to this mood. They seemed to offer a short cut to a state of moral elation that would guarantee evangelistic success. 'Let us notice God's own way of revival', observed Pearsall Smith at Oxford. 'It did not commence with effort . . . but with cleansing.'[77] The ethical note of revivalism gave the message of sanctification by faith an immediate appeal. Likewise the very language of the revivalists pointed forward to a fulfilment in the holiness movement. They spoke freely of being 'filled with the Holy Spirit', usually of times when Christians were aware of converting power in their midst, but also of the state of believers who had made moral growth.[78] During the Evangelical Alliance week of prayer in 1860 there were petitions for 'our own entire sanctification' and 'an entire consecration of ourselves to God'.[79] The technical terms that would be employed in the new teaching of the 1870s were already in use during the revival period. In many ways the quickened tempo of revivalist religion in the 1860s was a precondition for the new frame of mind of the following decade.

Another expression of revivalism that favoured the reception of holiness teaching was the evangelistic work of the Americans Dwight L. Moody and his singing colleague, Ira D. Sankey. Moody and Sankey carried a simple gospel message round the British Isles between June 1873 and August 1875. Moody, who had spoken at Mildmay in 1872, was invited to Britain by William Pennefather and by Cuthbert Bainbridge, but both died before he arrived. Without official sponsors, campaigns in York, Sunderland and Jarrow turned out rather unspectacular affairs. In Newcastle, however, there was a breakthrough in attendances, conversions and popularity; success was far greater in Edinburgh; and the climax came with a stay in Glasgow from February to April 1874 that was to have enduring consequences for the life of the city. After an Irish interlude, Moody and Sankey returned to visit English cities, reaching London for a campaign from March to July 1874.[80] Moody's preaching has been adjudged 'Calvinist if anything'.[81] The Sunderland Wesleyan ministers withheld support because he seemed Calvinistic, while champions of Reformation orthodoxy in the Church of England rallied to his defence.[82] Moody preached the same brand of homely divinity, spiritual yet practical, that Pennefather had commended – entirely consonant with Calvinism, but erecting no barriers to free offers of the gospel. His anecdotal style, like the paraphernalia of inquiry rooms and all-day meetings, seemed excitingly unconventional. Even his sermon on the solemn theme of 'The Blood' was punctuated by illustrative stories in everyday speech: 'You go to a railway station, and you buy a ticket . . . There is a story told of the great Napoleon . . . A good many years ago, when the Californian gold-fever broke out . . . '[83] He cultivated the commercial image that came naturally to one who had originally been a shoe salesman. Sankey's singing drew in the crowds. Harmonium, solos, singalong choruses that stuck in the memory – all were new.[84] Evangelistic success gave the pair and their methods enormous prestige. Moody and Sankey encouraged an openness to novel techniques for wielding spiritual power.

According to Robert Pearsall Smith early in 1874, Moody was now preaching entire sanctification as definitely as the forgiveness of sins.[85] Pearsall Smith's over-eager temperament was leading him astray, for at no point did Moody endorse distinctive holiness teaching, let alone proclaim it. He stood close to it in his tendency to asceticism, which usually emerged not in his preaching but in his answers to questions at Christian conventions. 'A true Christian had no taste and desire for the world and its amusements', he declared at one of these; 'he was crucified to it, and it to him.'[86] But his conviction of the need for separation from the world was merely received Evangelical opinion, not a belief that carried him into the holiness camp. Again, he had enjoyed an experience in 1871 not unlike a second conversion, 'the *conscious* incoming to his Soul of a presence and power of His Spirit such as he had never known before'.[87] Thereafter he emphasised the importance of seeking such an 'enduement with power', publishing while in Britain a study called *Power from on High*.[88] Although this way of describing a second (or subsequent) blessing was common in holiness circles, it did not necessarily set its users within them. Moody could be found deprecating obsession with the higher Christian life, rebuking those who held (with extreme holiness teachers) that they had passed beyond a life of moral struggle and (in his farewell address at Liverpool) advising young converts that they would not lose their sinful natures until the end of their earthly pilgrimage.[89] In later years, although he welcomed Keswick teachers to America and spoke from the Keswick platform in 1892, he was to deny teaching entire sanctification as such.[90] It is clear that, though touched by currents of opinion similar to those that created the holiness movement, at no stage – least of all when in Britain – did he identify with it. Nor, however, did he condemn it; and he went out of his way to send a telegram to the Brighton convention of 1875 expressing the hope that great results would follow.[91] In such circumstances it was easy to suppose that the two pairs of visiting Americans were carrying the same – or at least complementary – teaching. Hence critics of the Pearsall Smiths, such as J. C. Ryle and Dean Close, were at pains to distinguish one pair from the other.[92] There can be no doubt that they were fighting an uphill battle. The Moody and Sankey campaigns greatly assisted the arrival of holiness teaching in Britain by making it generally believed for the first time among Evangelicals that sound innovations could come from America.

THE AMERICAN INFLUENCE

Stronger than any one of the native influences, and probably stronger than all of them put together, was what one Methodist holiness leader called 'the great wave from America'.[93] Its origins in the United States went back to the 1830s, when the Methodist doctrine of sanctification suddenly achieved unprecedented respectability. At Oberlin College, Ohio, Charles Finney, the leading revivalist of his day, and the principal, Asa Mahan, both claimed to pass through the crisis of sanctification in 1836. A furious controversy broke out as the various defenders of Calvinist orthodoxy vied with each other in condemning 'Oberlin heresy'. The advance of holiness teaching beyond the bounds of Methodism profited from the enormous publicity given by its opponents. It became one of the widespread features of mid-century American Protestantism.[94] Finney's *Views on Sanctification* (1840) achieved less circulation in Britain than his prestige as a revivalist might lead one to expect, but Mahan's *Scripture Doctrine of Christian Perfection* (1844) exercised more influence, chiefly (it seems) among Methodists.[95] The breakthrough into the non-Methodist world came with W. E. Boardman's work, *The Higher Christian Life* (1858). It was republished in London at a propitious time, when revival excitement was at its height in 1860, and it achieved considerable success in commending full salvation to the Reformed tradition.[96] Boardman brought his message to Mildmay in 1869, and, with Mahan, helped propagate holiness views in Britain during 1873–5.[97] Perhaps the most significant American before the Pearsall Smiths, however, was Phoebe Palmer, who taught 'a shorter way' to holiness. Christ, according to Mrs Palmer, is the altar that immediately cleanses anyone touching it in simple faith. Her writings and a protracted visit in 1859–64 rooted her message in British Methodism.[98] There were also to be echoes of her 'altar theology' in the teachings of the Pearsall Smiths.[99] Most important, she recruited to the holiness cause William and Catherine Booth, still a minister and his wife in the Methodist New Connexion but later the creators of the Salvation Army. Sanctification understood in Mrs

Palmer's fashion was duly embodied in the Army's doctrinal standards. In the early phase following its emergence in the 1870s, the Salvation Army was a vigorous holiness organisation, concerned to carry 'the fire of the Holy Ghost' into all its work.[100] Its message reflected the American influence on Britain.

The shock of the Civil War, supplemented by the centenary of American Methodism in 1866, drove Methodists in the United States to examine their basic convictions. Many of them saw in scriptural holiness, as interpreted by nineteenth-century commentators like Mrs Palmer, their *raison d'être*. John S. Inskip, a senior minister in New York City, received sanctification in 1864 and three years later launched a series of annual holiness camp meetings. Such outdoor gatherings, usually lasting several days, had long been a feature of frontier Methodism, but Inskip and his friends ran them near cities and gave holiness teaching only. It was the beginning of a vast expansion of the holiness movement that was to transform American religion.[101] The stir in America, Methodist-dominated but not wholly Methodist, played its part in rousing British Methodists to greater zeal in the cause of holiness.[102] The camp meetings provided a model for the British holiness gatherings. The Oxford meetings, the Americans were told, 'more nearly approach one of your National Camp Meetings than anything we have hitherto seen in England'.[103] The climate dictated the fundamental difference that British gatherings should be held indoors, but the camp meeting style stamped its mark on Keswick. Most important, however, was the effect of the holiness upsurge on the Pearsall Smiths. Hannah trusted for sanctification at a small-town Methodist meeting, Robert at a camp meeting in 1867. 'Suddenly', recalled his wife, 'from head to foot he had been shaken with what seemed like a magnetic thrill of heavenly delight, and floods of glory seemed to pour through him, soul and body, with the inward assurance that this was the longed-for Baptism of the Holy Spirit.'[104] The ideas that the Pearsall Smiths set out in the articles they transmitted to Britain and that were crystallised supremely in Hannah's *Holiness through Faith* (1870) and *The Christian's Secret of a Happy Life* (1875) were essentially those of the camp meetings in America. The British holiness movement depended for its very existence on the contribution of the United States.

THE CULTURAL CONTEXT

The movement has been seen as a religious equivalent of the secular cult of self-improvement.[105] Its classic embodiment was in *Self-Help* (1859) by Samuel Smiles. 'The highest object of life we take to be, to form a manly character', he declares, 'and to work out the best development possible, of body and spirit – of mind, conscience, heart, and soul.' Individuals, from whatever class they might originate, could rise to higher degrees of respectability and independence. To draw a parallel between self-help and holiness tendencies, however, would be mistaken. The summons of Samuel Smiles was to persevering effort. 'The battle of life', he writes, ' . . . must necessarily be fought uphill; and to win it without a struggle were perhaps to win it without honour.'[106] The holiness movement, in total contrast, encouraged its adherents to turn aside from struggle as a futile assertion of the self in order to discover the rest of faith. The secret of the way of holiness, according to an early exponent, was 'simply in ceasing from all efforts of our own, and trusting Jesus'.[107] Again, self-improvement normally entailed the provident laying aside of small sums of money on a regular basis over many years. The prospect of reward had to be deferred to the distant future. Holiness teachers, on the other hand, spoke of a crisis followed directly by the gratifications of the higher life. D. B. Hankin, Vicar of Christ Church, Ware, and one of the leading Anglican exponents of the holiness message in the 1870s, urged his hearers at the Oxford conference to 'an immediate and complete surrender of self-will and unbelief'.[108] The holiness movement represents a break with the spirit of self-help, not its expression in the religious sphere. The critics of 'Pearsall Smithism', in fact, had far more in common with the ethos of self-improvement. Bishop Perry of Melbourne, addressing the 1875 Islington Clerical Meeting after Hankin, explained his difference from the preceding speaker. 'He believed that the Christian life was one of progress, advance, step after step onwards; but Mr Hankin seemed to speak of something into which a believer might pass, as by a jump, all at once.'[109] Perry's belief seems an echo of Samuel Smiles. 'Great results', asserts Smiles, 'cannot be achieved at once; and we must be satisfied to advance in life as we walk, step by step.'[110] There is an evident affinity between the traditional Evangelical doctrine of sanctification and the contemporary spirit of self-help. The explanation is not far to seek. The primary intellectual source of the notions about effort, improvement and the goal of independence was the Enlightenment.[111] These notions constituted a variant, forged by the experience of industrialisation, of the idea of progress. Likewise the opponents of Pearsall Smith were defending an Enlightenment inheritance: the belief that sanctification is slow, steady, progressive.[112] Gradualism was the ideology of the social consensus of the high Victorian years, and it was this bastion that Pearsall Smith assaulted.

The kinship of the holiness movement was not with the legacy of the Enlightenment, but with the reaction against it that was gathering force at the time. Convictions were starting to be remoulded in many fields. In law, social theory and political economy there were shifts towards forms of developmental and organic thought, in response, largely, to the defects of the Utilitarian school. There was a new sense of historical relativism abroad. Patterns of evolutionary thinking, often crudely summarised as 'Social Darwinism', were coming into play.[113] There was 'a counterrevolution of values' stemming from dissatisfaction with simplistic notions of progress. Enterprise, technology and economic growth were seen as false idols whose veneration had led to the sacrifice of the aesthetic and the humane.

Industrial success had been purchased at too great a price. A point of view that in the first half of the century had been associated with a few names of brilliant but erratic genius – Carlyle and Pugin among them – became the orthodoxy of the educated. The mood is evident in Ruskin, Dickens's later novels, Mill's works of the 1850s and 1860s and, perhaps as obviously as anywhere, in Matthew Arnold.[114] 'The idea of perfection as an *inward* condition of mind and spirit', he argues in *Culture and Anarchy*, 'is at variance with the mechanical and material civilization in esteem with us . . . '[115] The holiness movement in America has rightly been diagnosed as an expression of the same cultural tendencies that generated the sentimentalised moralism of the New England Unitarian elite known as Transcendentalism. Emerson, its foremost exponent, taught the idea of 'communion with the oversoul', a milk-and-water version of the orthodox notion of fellowship with God described in language reminiscent of Mrs Palmer on entire sanctification.[116] Transcendentalism was the core of American Romanticism. All the currents of thought germane to the holiness movement – the relativism of social theory, the aestheticism of Matthew Arnold and the Transcendentalism of Emerson – were Romantic in form and substance. It is not surprising that holiness teaching bears the hallmark of Romanticism.

A ROMANTIC MOVEMENT

This is evident, first of all, in its atmosphere and associations. Critics over the years made great play with the charge that the holiness movement was all gush and no sinew. Pearsall Smith's strength, commented *The Record* disparagingly in 1875, lay in the 'emotional and sentimental'; a Scottish opponent in 1892 condemned its 'dreamy sentimental piety which only befits the cloister'; and the spirituality of Bishop Moule of Durham, the Keswick figure to rise highest in the ecclesiastical world, was said to be marked by 'a flavour of the sorry, syrupy stuff the world calls "pietism"'.[117] Many of the *habitués* of Keswick delighted in poetry. C. A. Fox, Pennefather's last curate, the most gifted orator of the Keswick platform, a devotee of Wordsworth and himself a poet with a special love for waterfalls, conferred on verse a high theological function. 'I believe the poetry of the spiritual', he wrote to another Keswick speaker, 'is one of the most purifying and elevating forces God has given us to lift us to Himself and out of self.'[118] When Wordsworth's poem *The Excursion* had been published in 1814, the Dissenting poet James Montgomery had contemptuously dismissed its portrayal of 'the study of nature as a sanctifying process',[119] but now Wordsworth was appreciated for this very quality. 'It was his interpretation of nature as a revelation of God', observed the biographer of J. B. Figgis, another leading Keswick figure, 'that inspired him to pen several verses of poetry.'[120] The great Mecca of the movement, Keswick,

could not have been better placed to blend all the attractions of mountains
and lakes, remoteness and grandeur, artistic associations and memories of
Lake Poets. The setting was essential to the experience. 'The lovely face
of nature's panorama in this valley', ran a report of the 1895 convention,
'if gazed upon with eyes sanctified by thankfulness to God for the gift
and the vision to appreciate its charms, must ever have a chastening and
purifying effect. The consecrated Christian of all men has a right to enjoy
these outer garments of creation that speak so eloquently of God's power,
and wish to make all things of the soul beautiful as well as new.'[121] It was as
though Wordsworthian pantheism had become an additional article of the
Evangelical creed. All was of a piece with the contemporary idealisation
of the countryside in Thomas Hardy's early novels or Norman Shaw's 'Old
English' architecture.[122] The educated public was turning to Romantic
sensibilities as an escape-route from the urban, industrial present, and the
holiness movement was part of the process.

Many of the *leitmotifs* normally found in Romantic thought were present
in holiness teaching. There was, for instance, a stress on the power of
the individual will, the force that according to many a Romantic such
as Carlyle rules the world. Pearsall Smith was unusually explicit on
this point, disagreeing with Jonathan Edwards's Enlightenment analysis
of human psychology. 'President Edwards' teaching of the affections
governing the will I believe to be untrue', he explained. 'The will governs
the affections.'[123] A believer, according to Evan Hopkins, the chief mentor
of Keswick, is placed in a state of perfect holiness 'by a decisive act of
will'.[124] From the centrality assigned to the will, there followed a limited
doctrine of sin. Only willed disobedience is sin. What Pearsall Smith calls
'an undesigned sin of ignorance' is not properly sin. That type of error
cannot be escaped. Hence we, no more than the apostles, can claim 'an
absolute holiness'.[125] This restriction of sin to particular known instances
(a point on which he agreed with Wesley) enabled Pearsall Smith to rebut
the charge of teaching sinless perfection. 'Faith's victory over *known* sin', he
wrote, 'is not "Perfectionism".'[126] But there were other implications. The
human capacity to commit sins is on this view conditioned by the extent
of the individual's knowledge. Pearsall Smith offered the illustration of a
newly converted heathen who may be observing the standards of morality
to which he is accustomed and so, at one and the same time, be living in
full communion with God and yet following practices that he will abandon
through further knowledge of God's will.[127] The consequence is that there
can be no objective morality. The standard for behaviour varies according
to circumstances. Prebendary H. W. Webb-Peploe, one of the central circle of
Keswick, declared that the rule for the man of God is 'the measure of light
he had received'.[128] Such ethical relativism sounds strange on the lips of
men professing new attainments in the paths of holiness, but in its context
it is entirely comprehensible. Just as social theorists were concluding that
the values of human groups vary according to their historical experience,

so Evangelical teachers were reaching the position that duty depends on knowledge. Both views bear the stamp of the historical relativism associated with Romanticism that had come to dominate Germany and was spreading slowly into the Anglo-Saxon world.[129] The holiness movement was part of the most far-reaching cultural shift of the century.

OVERCOMING THE CALVINIST CRITIQUE

The contrast between the new holiness teaching and traditional views was probably most marked on the issue of whether sanctification is sudden or gradual. The distinctive note of the new school, as we have seen, was that it is sudden. They had come together, announced Pearsall Smith on the first day of the Oxford conference, 'to bring you to a *crisis* of faith'.[130] Such teaching was a world away from Hannah More's measured exhortation to sanctification from early in the century. 'Let us be solicitous that no day pass without some augmentation of our holiness', she writes, 'some added height to our aspirations, some wider expansion in the compass of our virtues. Let us strive every day for some superiority to the preceding day, something that shall distinctly mark the passing scene with progress.'[131] Such steady plodding was the received Evangelical view, hallowed by a long tradition of Reformed exposition. Hence it was the immediatism of holiness doctrine that drew the strongest fire. G. T. Fox, Vicar of St Nicholas, Durham, fulminated against instant sanctification in *Perfectionism* (1873); Horatius Bonar denounced it in *The Rent Veil* (1875). God is glorified, he argued in a subsequent letter, 'not in the instantaneous perfection of his redeemed, but in their gradual deliverance from imperfection'.[132] The whole idea of immediate sanctification seemed alien to minds nurtured on a belief in the orderly operation of a mechanistic universe: 'the notion of full consecration *per saltum*', wrote another Presbyterian critic in 1892, 'is inconsistent with the natural law of gradual development, which is the prevailing method in all the various departments of Divine activity. It were as reasonable that an acorn should all at once become a majestic oak . . . '[133] In the face of the barrage from Calvinist opponents, there was an increasing tendency to play down the crisis dimension until 'a manual of Keswick teaching' published in 1906 included scarcely a mention of the immediacy of receiving sanctification.[134] Outside Keswick circles there was less need to mollify critics, and in the Methodist and sectarian dimensions of the holiness movement the insistence on a moment of consecration retained its hold. Thomas Cook, for instance, the chief holiness preacher among the Methodists at the turn of the century, pressed believers to accept full salvation '*now*'.[135] The explanation of the initial popularity of sudden sanctification is an increasing acceptance that dramatic moments form a part of normal experience. That is simply another way of saying that the holiness movement appealed to spreading Romantic sensibilities.

Another battleground was the nature of Christian experience. Traditionally it was seen as a constant struggle against sin. One of the strongest selling points of the new teaching, by contrast, was its promise of rest for the weary. Christ has won our sanctification for us; our response is to accept it by faith; then we shall enjoy a calm repose. The catchphrase 'the Rest of Faith', though dating back to the Wesleys,[136] became a slogan of the holiness movement. It was part and parcel of the characteristic Romantic urge to escape – to flee the everyday world of strife in order to discover the secret of harmony. In literature the motif might find expression in fresh versions of the legend of the Holy Grail (discovered, significantly, by the pure). On the lips of Pearsall Smith it meant the continuing experience of the consecrated believer.[137] The champions of traditional Calvinism would have none of this. Bishop Perry repeatedly warned an Islington Clerical Meeting against the present-day danger of ignoring the fact that the life of the believer is 'a continual conflict'.[138] J. C. Ryle hammered away at the same theme by letter, pamphlet and, eventually, the treatise on *Holiness* (1877).[139] The theological issue, according to the traditionalists, was also a practical one. It was a favourite gibe that belief in the cessation of wrestling against sin was a sure path to the neglect of moral duties.[140] Rumours about the downfall of Robert Pearsall Smith seemed to vindicate the charge. During the Brighton Convention the apostle of purity allowed himself to whisper indiscretions to a young woman in his hotel bedroom. Although the matter was hushed up, his sponsors immediately packed him off to America.[141] Alarm spread again in 1884–6 about instruction given by two young men, Messrs Pigott and Oliphant, to the Cambridge Inter-Collegiate Christian Union during an outburst of holiness enthusiasm. Pigott eventually joined the notorious Agepomonites, who practised something approaching free love in a remote Somerset community, and was venerated there as Messiah.[142] The criticism that it encouraged antinomianism troubled the holiness school. The life of faith, its defenders increasingly conceded, is a matter of conflict, but whereas before full surrender defeat is a likelihood, afterwards victory is virtually assured. Moment-by-moment trust in Christ, it was explained, is the way to triumph over temptation. 'Victory' became probably the best known Keswick catchword. So the need for a measure of effort was introduced into the teaching of the holiness movement. Yet 'resting and rejoicing' remained the normative experience commended to the believer.[143] Even though the new school gradually came to accommodate the convictions of the old, the original debate between the two represented a fundamental clash of cultural styles.

Traditional Calvinists, especially in the Church of England, were equally critical of what they called the anti-doctrinal cast of holiness teaching. J. C. Ryle delivered a crisp paper to the 1878 Islington Meeting on 'The Importance of the Clear Enunciation of Dogma in dispensing the Word, with reference to Instability among Modern Christians'. The Pearsall Smiths, he contended, had disparaged theology.[144] The indictment was entirely just:

'We did not come to Oxford to set each other right', Pearsall Smith had declared, 'or to discuss doctrines . . . '[145] The difference between Moody and the Oxford conference, according to Ryle, was the difference between sunshine and fog.[146] The tradition stemming from the conference was markedly less concerned with didactic theology than Ryle and his school. 'The essence of Christianity seems to lie', wrote A. T. Pierson, a leading Keswick speaker, in 1900, 'not so much in doctrine, even historical, as in the surrender of the will . . . '[147] The Keswick stress on experience made dogmatic formulae remote and, to some, otiose. At the annual Broadlands conference, which began in 1873 and ran in parallel with Keswick until 1888, there was no dogmatism, but 'a gracious freedom that was like the air of open fields'.[148] Evan Hopkins, who did more to shape Keswick teaching than any other man, was drawn to Broadlands in Hampshire year after year.[149] There was no identity, but there was an affinity, between Broadlands and Keswick. William Cowper-Temple, the host at Broadlands, was seen as a Broad Churchman,[150] and other figures round and about the holiness movement were marked by a similar breadth of outlook. Hannah Pearsall Smith was a known universalist; Boardman and John Brash, an editor of *The King's Highway*, had both once been pantheists; Brash was an admirer of F. D. Maurice; and Harford-Battersby, not originally a professed Evangelical, had been chosen to go as curate to Keswick by a predecessor described as 'the Maurice of the north' who was 'dreamy, mystical, fond of German speculations'.[151] There is a danger, wrote Harford-Battersby himself, of 'leaving out too much the mystical element, if I may so call it, in our teaching and keeping to the hard, dry lines of scientific theology'.[152] Pearsall Smith spoke favourably of Roman Catholic mystics and published a selection of hymns by F. W. Faber, the Catholic convert and polemicist.[153] Pearsall Smith's eulogy of Faber, remarked Horatius Bonar, 'had introduced the whole of his idolatrous volumes into Protestant families, and . . . they lie side by side with Perfectionist works in London drawing-rooms. There must be some affinity between these hymns and Mr Smith's teaching . . . '[154] There was indeed, but it was not between Pearsall Smith and Faber's Catholicism. Rather it was between Pearsall Smith and Faber's tone, what Smith calls in the preface his 'sweet breathings'.[155] Any expression of Romantic devotion to God secured his approval. In a similar way the holiness school was drawn towards any version of intense piety, whether liberal or mystical. It is no wonder that many touched by Keswick were to move on in the years around the First World War towards a liberal form of Evangelicalism.[156]

REMODELLING THE METHODIST TRADITION

Perhaps what most troubled Calvinist critics of the holiness movement was that it might be nothing but Methodism renewed. They suspected that the holiness teachers would follow Wesley on the question of eternal security. Once a real Christian, stated the Reformed tradition, always a Christian. But Wesley had argued that someone performing a known sinful action forthwith ceases to be a Christian. Salvation can be lost.[157] At the Brighton conference, when a Methodist minister told people that if they were in a certain condition it was time to ask if they were Christians at all, a Calvinist jumped up to correct him by claiming that their Christian standing might be right even if they were in that condition. Care was taken to guard the movement against similar infringements of Reformed orthodoxy at Keswick.[158] The divergence in this area between the new holiness teaching and the Methodist tradition becomes apparent in their different interpretations of Romans 7. Here the apostle Paul laments his inability to do right. Whereas Calvinists never had difficulty in seeing this as a description of the lifelong struggle of the believer, Methodists argued that it must refer to Paul's sinful condition before his conversion. Pearsall Smith and the Keswick school adopted a third view. Paul recounts his own experience as a believer, according to Harford-Battersby, 'but not as one using and applying the all–conquering might of Christ, but rather as he is in himself, apart from Christ'.[159] The condition described is that of someone who has received justification but not sanctification. In reviewing these three positions, the Methodist learned journal concluded that its own stance was as different from the new holiness interpretation as it was from the old Calvinist opinion.[160] Although, as we have seen, the holiness movement was heavily indebted to Methodism, in no sense did it simply resuscitate the connexion's established opinions. John Brash had imbibed his holiness convictions from traditional Methodist sources, but later had been swept into the stream of the new movement. At Southampton a Methodist who stuck to the older presentation told him bluntly that he was 'very modern', meaning that he was not sufficiently definite. Looking back on his own early teaching, Brash found it 'very mechanical'. After prolonged exposure to Keswick, his view of sanctification became much more organic: 'the one central thought to me is living union with the living Saviour'.[161] The shift was therefore from the specific to the indefinite, from the mechanical to the organic – terms standardly applied to the transition from the classical to the Romantic. The Methodist tradition drew its sustenance from Enlightenment sources, but the new movement was shaped by Romantic sensibilities.

More specifically, how did the new school break the mould of the Arminian Enlightenment? In the first place, whereas Methodists had traditionally taught that the crisis of sanctification comes at the end of a long quest, the new view was that it is just the beginning of the quest. After justification, according to Wesley, a protracted period of self-discipline is necessary before death to sin comes.[162] In the era of Mrs Palmer, however, there was a reworking of the tradition. Sanctification, Catherine Booth came to believe, is not a matter of waiting for 'a great and mighty work' but an act of 'simple reception'.[163] God will give the needed faith whenever we want it; consequently holiness is available without waiting for it. Similarly, at Oxford and Brighton it was taught that sanctification is not a terminus but a departure. He proclaimed a crisis experience, declared Pearsall Smith, 'not as a finality, but as the only true *commencement* of a life of progress'.[164] The contrast between the older and the newer views reflects their cultural settings. The traditional Wesleyan position adopted the typical Enlightenment idea that there is a goal for humanity. We must struggle upwards towards holiness. The newer position assumed, with the Romantic age, that the crucial experience of life is possible here and now, with no delay. In the second place, whereas Wesley had expected very few to reach the goal,[165] the holiness school of the late nineteenth century believed the experience should be general among believers. It soon became fashionable to reject the phrase 'the higher Christian life' on the ground that the experience should be normal for the Christian. Webb–Peploe, who early in 1874 was content to use the term, repudiated it twenty years later for this very reason.[166] Holiness was being democratised. If (as Romanticism dictated) the experience of restful faith is immediately available to all, then it becomes 'the normal Christian life' from which anything inferior is an unnecessary declension.

In the third place, there was a shift from the established Methodist conviction that sin can be totally removed from the believer's heart to the view that in a holy life its operation is merely suspended. Although Wesley, in the empirical spirit of the eighteenth century, was not troubled about whether sin was described as suspended or destroyed so long as its absence was truly experienced, one of his conferences pronounced in favour of the eradication of sin at entire sanctification.[167] Methodists were properly called perfectionists, believing that perfection is possible before death. The chief holiness teachers, however, were eager to repudiate perfectionist views.[168] As Keswick teaching crystallised, it was most insistent that sin is never eradicated from human life on earth. Sinful tendencies always remain, even when they are repressed by the power of Christ.[169] Keswick was sensitive to the risk that eradicationism might lead to professions of sinlessness that would discredit the whole movement. It had to be on its guard because many Methodists, the Salvation Army and a number of fringe sectaries continued to uphold the belief that (as they put it) salvation is from *all* sin. In 1895 one of the sectarian leaders, Reader Harris of the Pentecostal League, rather melodramatically offered £100 if any Keswick speaker could supply scripture proof of 'the necessity of sin in the Spirit-filled believer'. Sin, replied R. C. Morgan in *The Christian*, is 'a *fact* in the Spirit-filled man . . . [but] *sinning* is not a *necessity* in a Spirit-filled man'.[170] Eradicationism was put to flight. The triumph of the idea of suspension, however, was not simply the result of guarding the flank against extreme teaching. It was also inherent in the logic of the mainstream holiness movement, for the notion that sin can be 'kept under' or 'repressed' (rather than excised or discarded) was bound up with a dynamic psychology, implying constant process in the human mind. Such a view fitted naturally into a Romantic estimate of the importance of the interior life, the growing, organic world within.[171] The favourite image of Keswick teachers to express the idea was significantly the organic one of the branch abiding in the vine of Christ.[172] Thus the Methodist inheritance was remoulded – and the process was one whereby Enlightenment assumptions gave way to those of the Romantic age.

AFFINITIES OF HOLINESS

Music bears its testimony to the same transformation. The holiness move-ment was bound up with a significant shift in musical taste. The primary symptom was simply that music was given unprecedented prominence. The Salvation Army had its marching bands and 'Hallelujah lasses' with tambourines.[173] Holiness Methodists stirred to mission work entered villages led by a singing band with 'an English concertina'.[174] There was large-scale hymn singing at the Brighton conference and it became a valued feature of the Keswick conventions.[175] The holiness movement, furthermore, became closely identified with the techniques of Sankey, Moody's singing companion. The revivalism that preceded the holiness era in the 1860s had already brought forth 'Richard Weaver's artless but powerful rendering of Revival melodies' and the similar style of Philip Phillips, the 'Singing Pilgrim',[176] yet it was Sankey who took the religious world by storm with his *Sacred Songs and Solos*. He filled a vacuum for popular participation in church music recently created by the abolition of traditional bands and folk choirs, a process just about complete by the 1870s.[177] The enthusiastic welcome for his style was a popular revolt against the respectability of the elaborate hymns and tunes preferred by organists. 'People want to sing, not what they *think*', argued R. W. Dale, 'but what they *feel*'.[178] Sankey catered for their taste. His style was valued by Moody because it was so close to that of the music hall.[179] Sankey's compositions were celebrated for their tunes, not their harmonies, as even their staunchest defenders were bound to admit.[180] But the melodious was what Romantic taste required. It also called for a devotional atmosphere. Consequently the settings for *Hymns of Consecration and Faith*, the Keswick hymn book, were 'generally soft and low'.[181] The new phase of piety adopted a musical idiom suited to the spirit of the age.

Something of the new ethos was a result of the larger part played by women in this stage of popular Protestantism. Keswick was seen as a landmark in the emancipation of women, at least in the religious sphere. Until the creation of the convention, it was claimed in 1907, few women had accepted the commission entrusted by Christ to Mary to deliver his message openly.[182] This was certainly a misrepresentation, both of the extent of female public ministry beforehand and of the degree of freedom given to women at Keswick. The growth of female preaching in the revivalist atmosphere of the 1860s and separate ladies' meeting at Mildmay from 1862 had created precedents.[183] At Keswick ladies were permitted to address female gatherings only, though at several subsidiary conventions the gender bar was abolished.[184] The Salvation Army went further, establishing equality of the sexes among its officers. By 1915 at least half were women.[185] Keswick definitely attracted women. Their proportion of the convention-goers increased over the years, and when a missionary call was first given at Keswick, it was women who were first to respond.[186] To a critic (albeit a friendly Methodist), the piety of the Oxford conference of 1874 'could have been more robust and manly'.[187] Women contributed a significant proportion of the hymnody of the holiness movement. Apart from Frances Havergal (who wrote more hymns in the Keswick collection than any other), there were Miss C. May Grimes, Fanny Crosby, Charlotte Elliott and Jean Sophia Pigott, who actually came in person to the convention.[188] What was the connection between Keswick spirituality and the larger share of female involvement? Romantic sentiment dictated that purity and love should be staple themes of the convention, and according to the stereotypes of the day, these were female qualities. Their prominence may owe a debt to female participation; and in turn the themes must have made an appeal to women. More concretely, the call to total surrender undoubtedly had attractions in an age when female submission was axiomatic. Frances Havergal liked thinking of Christ as 'Master'. 'It is perhaps my favourite title', she wrote, 'because it implies rule and submission; and this is what love craves. Men may feel differently, but a true woman's submission is inseparable from deep love.' A female friend concurred in preferring the title 'Master' and so did Jessie Penn-Lewis, the most accomplished lady speaker associated with Keswick.[189] This form of female piety was almost certainly the root of the growing practice at the end of the century of addressing public prayer to the Lord Jesus rather than to the Father through him.[190] Women were refashioning devotional practice through the holiness movement.

Patterns of behaviour were altered less. Holiness was so much an internal matter of personal consciousness, a trysting of the elevated soul with its God, that the practicalities of everyday living were generally passed over in silence. Dozens of Keswick addresses can be scanned in vain without discovering any detailed guidance. The rationale was that 'the teaching deals with great general principles rather than specific practices'.[191] When holiness teachers did descend from the highest planes, they would normally dwell on the need to abandon 'all doubtful things'.[192] This grey area contained every practice over which a question mark lingered in the mind. Its definition must have led to bouts of anguish for sensitive consciences. A barrier was effectively erected against playing cards for money, patronising the theatre, opera or ballroom and attending horse races (except to distribute tracts).[193]

It was very rare for anyone in the circle of readers of *The Christian* to raise
a voice in favour of any of these activities, but in 1885 there was an isolated
letter, emanating (significantly) from Grosvenor Mansions, Westminster,
contending that at *some* theatres there was legitimate entertainment without
any suggestion of evil.[194] In general, however, traditional Evangelical
prohibitions were reinforced. Was it right, a perplexed enquirer asked
H. F. Bowker at the 1880 Keswick, to play croquet, bagatelle, cards and so
on to kill time? 'Shall I sit with Christ to judge the world', came the stern
reply, 'and see anyone whom I have helped to kill time?' His partner on the
platform, Pastor Stockmeyer, felt it necessary to add that an exception must
be made for play with children.[195] Recreation was just about legitimate,
but not in a state of heedlessness. 'Natural necessity', declared Page in
The King's Highway, 'and the example of St John, who recreated himself
with sporting with a tame partridge, teach us that it is lawful to relax
and unbend our bow, but not to suffer it to be unready or unstrung.'[196]
For all its emphasis on the inner life, holiness teaching did not blunt the
Evangelical imperative to be prepared for action.

The chief innovation was the strengthening of temperance opinion. The
coming of the American influences in 1873–5 coincided with an upsurge
in temperance enthusiasm in the churches, at least in Nonconformity and
Scotland, following the licensing legislation of Gladstone's government
in 1872.[197] Pearsall Smith was very hot on this question. Should every
Christian, he was asked at the Brighton conference, abandon alcohol? 'A
thousand times, yes', he answered.[198] Moody also cast the mantle of his
prestige over total abstinence.[199] A. T. Pierson, another American, was
equally insistent that 'the wine-cup' bears the stamp of this world.[200]
American revivalist opinion was more advanced on this question than
British and through the holiness incursion of the 1870s reinforced incipient
tendencies towards rejection of alcohol and, indeed, prohibitionism. The
most borderline issue was smoking. There was relatively little thought
in the nineteenth century of injury to health, or else the fringe of the
holiness movement that took up faith healing might have created a stir
over tobacco.[201] Pierson claimed 'that those who accept Keswick teaching
practically abandon tobacco, from an inward sense of its being promotive
of carnal self-indulgence', but in 1892 one Keswick speaker commented
that there had been smokers about, for he had noticed a great deal of
odour that was not of sanctity.[202] Those who liked their pipe could appeal
to the example of Spurgeon, who had declared that he smoked to the glory
of God, and in the 1920s there were still vain attempts by enthusiasts to
exhort convention-goers to perceive an inconsistency between smoking and
holiness.[203] Over tobacco there was more resistance than over alcohol. So
it was chiefly temperance attitudes that were fostered by the movement.[204]
Previous taboos were undoubtedly reinforced, and that strongly, by the
holiness impulse; but on the whole Evangelical attitudes to the world were
not transformed by what was intrinsically an otherworldly movement.

THE BRITISH HOLINESS MOVEMENT

The appeal of the holiness message, notwithstanding the emergence of the Salvation Army and a number of other popular bodies, was overwhelmingly to the upper middle classes. The revivalist world that initially received it had an upper-middle-class, even an aristocratic, tinge. Pennefather, for instance, found on coming to his Barnet congregation 'many true Christians here among the upper classes';[205] gentry patronised full-time evangelists; peers even acted as revivalists themselves. Pearsall Smith's original *entrée* was to West End drawing rooms and country house parties. The sins he condemned were peculiarly suited to his audiences. 'Does the sudden pull of the bell', he asked, 'ever give notice in the kitchen that a good temper has been lost by the head of the household?'[206] In the years around 1870 the middle classes generally enjoyed longer hours of leisure, the fruit of economic prosperity. A whole literature sprang up discussing how it could legitimately be used.[207] Attendance at the conventions, which necessarily implied the possession of a good deal of leisure, provided a congenial answer for the conscientious Christian. It was sometimes claimed that Keswick attracted a wide social cross-section, but the resort was one that deliberately catered for the elite of Lakeland visitors.[208] Those who were of lower social standing were very obvious and called forth comment – like the camp of sixty to seventy who were 'mainly factory-workers, clerks and artizans' at the beginning of the twentieth century and the twenty from the Barnsley collieries in 1912.[209] In 1895 Keswick was criticised for becoming 'a Convention for the rich alone'.[210] The explanation of its social appeal is to be found in the nature of its message. The greater educational opportunities of the upper middle classes meant that they had commonly acquired a taste for Wordsworth, the poetic temper and elevating spiritual influences. The call to holiness, with all its Romantic affinities, was bound to have far more impact on them than on lower social groups. Although Keswick teaching was later to spread to a wider public, its initial constituency was drawn very largely from the well-to-do.

The varying attractions of sanctification by faith to different sectors of society help explain the denominational pattern of support. The new teaching made far more inroads among Evangelical Anglicans, with their higher average social standing, than among Evangelical Nonconformists. From the start the Church of England supplied the bulk of the convention speakers. Resistance at the Islington Clerical Meetings to Keswick teaching on sanctification was steadily eroded. In 1892 its doctrine was still being repudiated at Islington by Canon Hoare, but in that year Ryle, long an unyielding opponent and now Bishop of Liverpool, gave the movement a qualified imprimatur by offering prayer on its platform when Moody was the speaker.[211] By the dawning of the new century Keswick teaching went unchallenged at Islington and so had clearly triumphed in Anglican Evangelicalism.[212] Within the other denominations it did not achieve the same sway. Among Scottish Presbyterians there were house-parties including some fifteen to twenty ministers from each of the three main denominations at Keswick in 1900, but the overall contingent was not large.[213] Congregational and Baptist ministers had managed to muster a meeting of between fifty and sixty during the Brighton conference,[214] but Congregationalism was not to be deeply affected. Pearsall Smith was proud to have influenced a number of Baptists, including some members of Spurgeon's congregation,[215] but the only Baptist speaker to gain prominence on the Keswick platform before 1900 was F. B. Meyer, significantly the most urbane minister of his denomination. John Brash became a Keswick teacher and claimed that lots of Methodists attended, but even he felt rather out of place in so Anglican a gathering.[216] One Methodist minister who received the blessing at Keswick, W. H. Tindall, founded in 1885 a Methodist holiness convention at Southport, and one of its most incisive speakers, Dr E. E. Jenkins, had received entire sanctification at Brighton.[217] But Southport, while becoming a focus for holiness teaching in Methodism, had the effect of diverting members of the denomination away from Keswick. Apart from considerations such as time, Southport tolerated the eradicationism that Keswick ruled out of court.[218] So Anglican dominance in the mainstream of the holiness movement was assured.

Yet, as in America, the movement also created a tendency to separate from existing churches in order to teach holiness without reserve. 'Soon', wrote Page of the Methodist holiness movement in the early 1870s, 'the difficulty was to check the disposition to form separate organizations, and to discourage all movements which tended to the formation of a "Church within a Church" . . . '[219] The crucial decision, never rescinded, not to form a Methodist holiness organisation was taken at a conference at Wakefield in 1874.[220] To a large extent holiness enthusiasm was contained. The original ardour of the Salvation Army for 'the fire of the Holy Ghost' cooled. By the early years of the twentieth century, when General Booth was asked whether the Army taught entire sanctification as earnestly as formerly, he replied, 'When a man talks about full consecration, we say to him, "Go and *do* something"'.[221] The Army had none the less brought the experience of sanctification to the founders of two lesser holiness bodies, the Faith Mission in Scotland and the Star Hall in Manchester. But the Faith Mission was careful not to draw members away from their own churches, preferring to set up undenominational halls that would act as feeders for local congregations.[222] A similar policy was pursued by the Pentecostal League of Reader Harris, formed in 1891 'to spread Scriptural Holiness by unsectarian methods' from a London base, and later by the Overcomer League of Jessie Penn-Lewis. Both had their own magazines, *Tongues of Fire* and *The Overcomer* (founded 1909).[223] Yet the fissiparity of the American holiness movement that created twenty-five denominations by 1907[224] was also a British phenomenon. Already by 1884 there were thirteen independent congregations with their own magazine, *The Holiness Advocate*.[225] The International Holiness Mission

(1906) broke away from the Pentecostal League to set up separate churches; the Calvary Holiness Church separated (1934) from the IHM because it wished to permit faith healing; the Pentecostal Church of Scotland (1906) divided from the Parkhead Congregational Church over entire sanctification; and the Emmanuel Holiness Church (1916) was set up by an individual holiness teacher in Birkenhead.[226] This sectarian fringe was the context in which the Pentecostal movement was to spring to life in the first decade of the twentieth century.[227] Consequently, it was more important than it may appear. In itself, however, this phenomenon was remarkably small-scale. The strongest (apart from the Salvation Army) of the separatist bodies, the IHM, had only twenty-seven churches with about one thousand members when it merged with the Church of the Nazarene, based in America, in 1952.[228] Holiness separatism was weak in Britain both because the Methodists deliberately set their face against it and because of the remarkable hegemony of Keswick.

The holiness movement ushered in a new phase in Evangelical history. There was, it was said, between 1870 and 1876 'a change of religious climate'.[229] The holiness teaching that caught on in these years, though having many and various antecedents, was primarily an expression of the spirit of the age. It was a Romantic impulse, harmonising with the premillennialism and faith mission principle that had similar origins. It challenged the beliefs about sanctification held by both Calvinists and Arminians, creating a common Christianity of experience. The fresh spirituality revitalised congregations and induced many to offer for missionary service. In 1885 some 1,500 to 2,000 people attended the Keswick Convention; by 1907 there were between 5,000 and 6,000.[230] The success of Keswick led to a host of imitations, including Bridge of Allan as the main convention for Scotland and Llandrindod Wells for Wales. The message was spread by a battery of publications including Keswick's own journal, *The Life of Faith*. New Evangelical agencies of the late nineteenth century naturally took their colour from the movement. The Christian Unions at Cambridge and Oxford, the Bible Training Institute, Glasgow, for preparing Christian workers, and many obscure mission halls had intimate links with Keswick.[231] The undenominational tone they shared was to exercise a powerful influence on twentieth-century Evangelicalism. In part, the holiness movement exerted a broadening tendency. By shifting the fulcrum of Christianity from the head to the heart, it blurred ecclesiastical boundaries and softened the doctrinal inheritance. It is consequently not surprising that it was one of the forces behind the ecumenical movement of the twentieth century.[232] Yet at the same time it was a narrowing force. There was created, it was said, 'a new sect of "undenominationalists"'.[233] Keswick in particular fits all the standard criteria of a sect – a voluntary association, exclusiveness, personal perfection as the aim, and so on – and especially of a conversionist sect.[234] In no sense, as in the case of most sects, was it a refuge for the socially deprived, but otherwise the sectarian tendency was marked. It formed, wrote Webb-Peploe to Hopkins, 'a spiritual freemasonry which the outer world cannot apprehend'.[235] Secular society, and even the generality of torpid Christians, formed an alien and often hostile world. The adherents of Keswick were turning in on a shared but private experience. They were accepting that Evangelicalism, which had come so near to dominating the national culture at mid-century, was on the way to becoming an introverted subculture.

[6]

Walking Apart:
Conservative and Liberal
Evangelicals in the
Early Twentieth Century

Can two walk together, except they be agreed? (Amos 3:3)

The unity of Evangelicalism was broken during the 1920s. The movement
had always been marked by variety in doctrine, attitude and social composition, but in the years after the First World War it became so sharply
divided that some members of one party did not recognise the other as
Evangelical – or even, sometimes, as Christian. Polarisation was by no
means total, for co-operation between the two wings, liberal and conservative, continued in a number of organisations. Yet disagreement was sufficiently acute to cause schism in several Evangelical institutions including
the Church Missionary Society. Many deeply regretted the partisanship. J. E.
Watts-Ditchfield, Bishop of Chelmsford, wished to hear less and less of
'Evangelicals with a label', whether conservative or liberal.[1] But it was not
to be. When a similar hope was expressed by a writer to *The Record* in 1934,
another correspondent pointed out the scriptural injunction to withdraw
from those teaching other than the truth. Only lately, he continued in
disgust, an Evangelical in the daily press had urged that the feeding of the
five thousand was merely a sharing of lunches.[2] Conservatives could not
tolerate liberal views of this kind. The split became deep and permanent.

In the United States at the same period there was a comparable division.
The Evangelical world erupted into violent polemic between Fundamentalists and Modernists. Both terms were used in Britain. Charges of
Modernism were levelled in 1913 against George Jackson, a candidate for a
theological chair, by his conservative opponents in Methodism. The word
had already become familiar, not least because the Vatican had suppressed
what was styled Modernism in the previous decade. Modernism, whether
Protestant or Catholic, was an attempt to present Christianity in terms

of modern thought, to translate traditional doctrines into a contemporary idiom. The word 'Fundamentalism' emerged later. It originated in America to describe the position of those who wished to defend the fundamentals of the faith. A series of booklets called *The Fundamentals* had been issued between 1910 and 1915 to affirm basic beliefs. Although a few of the authors were British, the booklets were an American venture that created far more of a stir on the other side of the Atlantic. In 1920 an American Baptist newspaper editor called for a conference of those ready 'to do battle royal for the Fundamentals' and the word Fundamentalism entered standard usage.[3] Four years later, as a Scottish commentator noted, the term was not yet naturalised in Britain. 'Yet', he went on, 'the thing which the uncomely word describes is not unfamiliar to us here. It denotes the position of those who tenaciously cling to traditional views of Bible inspiration, and who by the intensity of their convictions are compelled to oppose to the uttermost the more elastic teachings of many modern Biblical critics.'[4] There was some reluctance to employ the term in Britain, for it was felt to be alien, uncouth and pejorative. Yet some were prepared to wear the label. The journal of the Wesley Bible Union, for instance, changed its title in 1927 to *The Fundamentalist*.[5] There was sympathy for the American Fundamentalist struggle and some exchange of personnel. It is therefore quite mistaken to hold (as it sometimes has been held) that Britain escaped a Fundamentalist controversy. Evangelicalism in Britain as well as in America suffered from fiercely contested debates in the 1920s.

The issues, furthermore, were very similar. The conservatives made the status of the Bible central. Although, as will appear, they differed among themselves in their views of the inspiration and interpretation of scripture, they were united in treating it as uniquely trustworthy and authoritative. Many spoke of the verbal inspiration of the Bible and stressed its literal interpretation. They were concerned to defend certain doctrines, among which they normally placed the imminence of the second coming. Nearly all conservatives also embraced holiness teaching, generally in its Keswick form. Liberals, on the other hand, wished to be able to reinterpret theology in fresh terms. One of them pleaded in 1913 for 'the development of thought and doctrine'.[6] They were often eager to bring greater beauty and dignity into worship. Churchmanship in general, they considered, had been too much neglected in the past. Battle lines between conservatives and liberals stretched across a wide terrain of thought and action. Conservatives often saw the scientific principle of evolution as a threat to the proper interpretation of the Bible, whereas liberals dismissed their reservations as obscurantism. Conservatives blamed modern entertainments, particularly on church premises, for the decline in religious practice, but liberals saw theatricals, sport and the like as wholesome incentives to churchgoing. The 'social gospel' was condemned by conservatives as a diversion from the gospel for individuals at a time when liberals wanted to demonstrate their sense of responsibility for society. Each of these questions also divided American

Evangelicals. Although the balance of contentious issues was rather different – evolution, for example, being more prominent in the United States – the occasions of controversy in themselves were identical.

The rift in the Evangelical ranks appeared because of different responses to the same cultural mood. The liberals were rightly perceived at the time to be innovators. They wished to modify received theology and churchmanship in the light of current thought. Inevitably their ideas were swept along by the Romantic currents that had already been flowing powerfully in the later nineteenth century. Biblical inspiration, for example, was reinterpreted as of a piece with the uplifting power of the arts. It was defined by a Methodist college tutor as 'that which yields insight into beauty, truth, and goodness, and God.' Inspiration was said to make an impact comparable to that of Wordsworth's poetry, Bach's Mass in B Minor or the view of the Langdale Pikes.[7] In similar fashion, age-encrusted doctrine was to be recast in dynamic form, preferably with a scientific gloss. 'The unfolding purpose of redemption', the Dean of Manchester told a liberal Evangelical devotional conference, 'is also the unfolding purpose of creation. It is evolution on the highest and grandest scale.'[8] Leading Methodists, like their liberal Anglican contemporaries, were imbued with a new sacramental spirit as they realised they were the heirs of the treasury of Catholic practice. 'The past', wrote one of them, 'with its conquests, its fragrance, its saints, its immortal splendour, is ours . . .'[9] It was all consonant with the trends towards greater theological breadth and greater liturgical height that had begun to gather force before 1900. By the 1920s a Romantic gale was blowing across the Evangelical landscape.

Conservatives were by no means secure from the winds of change. It was supposed at the time, by friend and foe alike, that conservatives stood for traditional, received views. In *Letters to a Fundamentalist*, published in 1930 by the Student Christian Movement Press, Percy Austin confidently identifies his own Modernist position as 'the newer view-point', and his imaginary Fundamentalist correspondent as an upholder of 'the *traditional* interpretation of Christian truth'. 'In effect', he goes on, 'you say that what has been handed down to us from our forbears *is* truth, and we must cherish it, and pass it on unaltered to those who shall come after us.'[10] This estimate of the debate, however, was a total misperception. So-called 'conservatives' were in fact advancing causes of recent growth. Their views on verbal inspiration and literal biblical interpretation were derived, as Chapter 3 has shown, by the impinging of Romanticism on a section of Evangelical opinion in the early nineteenth century. Occasionally somebody would point out that conservative views of the Bible did not have a long ancestry. When in 1911 the issues surrounding inerrancy were given a protracted airing, one contributor reminded the participants that in 1853 only the Recordites, a minority of Evangelicals in the Church of England, believed in verbal inspiration.[11] Such voices were drowned in the welter of controversy. Conservatives maintaining premillennialism likewise supposed that their tenets were traditional. 'There has been', complained one, 'a removal of the Evangelical centre of vision from the expectation of the personal return of the King . . .'[12] In reality it was the doctrine of the personal return that was the novelty among Evangelicals, going back only to the knot of innovators around Irving. Belief in inerrancy may have been spreading in the 1920s; premillennialism certainly was. Conservative Evangelicals were as much swayed by Romantic attitudes as were their opponents. The only contrast was that the conservatives were affected in different ways.

THE RISE OF BIBLICAL CRITICISM

Among the causes of the divisions of the 1920s, a primary place must be given to the emergence of conflicting estimates of the Bible. The rise of the higher criticism – that is, broad analysis of the development of the text, as opposed to the lower criticism, the close study of details such as particular words – has usually been seen as the new factor in the late nineteenth-century understanding of scripture. In reality, as will appear, the progress of stronger views of inspiration, bolstering conservative opinion, was of equal importance. Yet it is true that the importation of German critical views by the more advanced scholars did much to foster liberal Evangelicalism. In 1861, when *Essays and Reviews* first drew widespread attention in the Church of England to critical methods and conclusions, Evangelicals were numbered among the book's most convinced opponents. Anyone leaning to its approach was by definition Broad Church.[13] The premisses of critics were, after all, rooted in the intellectual milieu of German philosophy. Nations, it was assumed, develop their distinctive values gradually over time. When the principle was applied to the history of Israel, it could only be supposed that the noble monotheism of the Pentateuch arose at a late stage. The compilation of the first five books of the Old Testament was therefore assigned to the seventh century BC at the earliest. Analysis that distinguished different sources in the text underpinned the theory. All this remained bound up, in the British view of the 1860s, with the sceptical tendencies in religion that were summed up as German neology.[14] It was foreign to Evangelicalism.

The contented sense that Britain was a bastion of reverence for the Bible was first undermined in the later 1870s. William Robertson Smith, the brilliant young Professor of Hebrew and Old Testament in the Free Church College at Aberdeen, wrote an article on 'The Bible' for the *Encyclopaedia Britannica* which assumed the validity of the most recent German scholarship. His views attracted much uncomprehending censure. Most serious, in the eyes of the Free Church committee that examined his position, was his attitude to Deuteronomy. Sayings attributed there to Moses were, according to Smith, the inventions of a later age. His sole innovation, Smith submitted in his own defence, was to hold that scripture 'makes use of certain forms of literary presentation which have always been thought legitimate in ordinary composition, but which were not always understood to be used in the Bible'. The investigating sub-committee believed that the resort to a theory of 'dramatic personations, appropriate in poetry and parable' was too improbable in the case of Deuteronomy to be 'a safe position from which to defend the historical truth and inspired authority of the Bible'. The committee concluded that, although there was some cause for grave concern, there were no grounds for a charge of heresy.[15] After three years during which the issue rumbled through the complex Presbyterian legal machinery, the General Assembly in 1880 determined, by 299 votes to 292, that Smith should still be permitted to teach for the Free Church. A further *Encyclopaedia Britannica* article, however, appeared to be a flouting of the church's solemnly expressed concern over critical questions and in 1881 Smith was dismissed by a large majority. Two years later he found asylum as Reader in Arabic at Cambridge.[16]

Smith's purpose was clear. He was intending to remould the study of the Bible according to the Romantic canons generally accepted in Germany. As he testified, he was trying to reintroduce what had been lost in 'the epoch of Rationalism'. He believed that the loss had been the notion of revelation, which was 'never a mechanical, dead, unintelligible thing'. Rather 'the Biblical Literature' was 'an organic part of the history of the church in the ages of revelation'.[17] Religious truth, that is to say, had gradually been perceived through the ongoing experience of the people of God. His Evangelical contemporaries who had been brought up in an intellectual framework deriving from the Enlightenment, Smith's 'epoch of Rationalism', found the theoretical gulf from the young scholar's premises too wide to bridge. Even the most thorough antagonist of Smith's views among English Nonconformists, Alfred Cave, did no justice to his views. The explanation is to be found in the title of one of Cave's later books: *The Inspiration of the Old Testament Inductively Considered* (1888). Cave was tied to Enlightenment categories such as induction that made constructive engagement with Smith impossible.[18] The appeal of the up-to-date approach to Old Testament scholarship was, however, irresistible. Smith himself was so patently free of scepticism and unorthodoxy as to inspire others to tread the same path. Already his teacher, A. B. Davidson, had taken some steps in that direction. Two further cases debated by the Free Church Assembly in 1890 raised questions of biblical criticism as well as of theological orthodoxy, and in both instances charges were dropped after investigation. In 1902 George Adam Smith, whose position on Old Testament criticism was substantially identical to that of Robertson Smith, was likewise effectively acquitted. In a solidly Evangelical denomination biblical criticism had become accepted.[19] In the Church of Scotland its inroads were just as great by the end of the century. John McMurtrie, editor of its magazine *Life and Work* and a noted Evangelical, would point to his extensive collection of German critical literature as 'my wicked library'.[20] At least among the ministers in Scotland, the new approach had come to stay.

The same was true in England. Fears that criticism was close to unbelief were allayed by the magisterial work of the so-called 'Cambridge Trio'. A. J. Hort, J. B. Lightfoot and B. F. Westcott, each in a different way, applied rigorous scholarly standards to the establishment and exegesis of the New Testament text, reaching conclusions that Evangelicals found generally unexceptionable – and even spiritually helpful.[21] The publication of *Lux Mundi* in 1889 announced the conversion of younger Anglo-Catholics to moderate critical opinions.[22] Two years later, S. R. Driver, Regius Professor of Hebrew at Oxford, presented a summary of recent Old Testament studies as entirely compatible with orthodoxy.[23] It was all reassuring to Evangelicals with intellectual aspirations. Congregationalists, with their predisposition to free inquiry, were foremost in the field. In 1893 a collection of essays by Congregationalists called *Faith and Criticism* was published. W. H. Bennett of Hackney and New Colleges unreservedly accepted the late dating of the Pentateuch in his Old Testament essay. If W. F. Adeney of New College was much more conservative in his study of the New Testament, the flair of P. T. Forsyth combined a zealous delineation of the person of Christ as redeemer with clear reservations about the 'old-Protestant theory of a book-revelation'.[24] Despite the best efforts of Alfred Cave, Congregationalists were evidently abandoning resistance to the modern approach. From 1892 summer schools held at their Mansfield College, Oxford, began to disseminate the new learning.[25] By 1895 the higher criticism had likewise been generally, though not universally, accepted by Wesleyan theological tutors, and had attracted a significant recruit in Driver's Primitive Methodist pupil, A. S. Peake.[26] It was surprising how rapidly Methodist ministers accepted critical conclusions. 'The trouble will come', it was rightly prophesied a few years later, 'when preachers are so absolutely honest as to say in the pulpit all they say to one another, and tell out all they believe and disbelieve.'[27] The first of the classic Fundamentalist controversies in Britain was to erupt when a Methodist did speak out.

OPPOSITION TO BIBLICAL CRITICISM

There were earlier signs of the coming storm. Spurgeon's charge that many ministers were on the Down Grade included, as a minor dimension, a protest against novel ideas about the Bible.[28] F. B. Meyer, then a rising Baptist, reviewed *Faith and Criticism* with expressions of dismay about the influence of its teachings on the next generation of Congregational ministers.[29] With certain exceptions, Baptists were certainly less inclined to critical innovations than other Nonconformists. Fringe Evangelical groups were most hostile. The tiny International Christian Mission, a holiness body based exclusively at 83–5 Queen's Road, Brighton, lamented among the signs of the times for 1898 that, 'The Word of God is assailed by professing Christians'.[30] This, more significantly, was the painful charge levelled against R. F. Horton, the cultured and spiritually minded minister of Lyndhurst Road Congregational Church, Hampstead, when he published *Inspiration and the Bible* in 1888. He had imbibed Driver's views at Oxford, where he had become the first Nonconformist to hold a fellowship. For his pains he was denounced by a host of assailants including Spurgeon and Joseph Parker of the City Temple. Even the aunt with whom he lived withdrew from his ministry in protest.[31] Among the Evangelicals of the Church of England there was an ominous calm. The standard case heard on their platforms was that the Christian estimate of scripture should be that of Christ himself.[32] Occasionally an adventurous analysis was put forward. As early as 1878 Edward Batty, of St John's, Fulham, declared at the Islington Clerical Meeting that they ought 'to admit that certain historical parts of the Bible were allegorical or open to different interpretations, and to show that they were fully alive to the importance of the claims of just, honest, reverential, and scholarly criticism'. But the cries of 'No, no' that greeted his suggestion that the authority of a passage in the gospel of John was open to challenge showed where majority feeling lay.[33] There was likely to be heavy weather ahead.

Opposition to the higher criticism first became organised in 1892. A Bible League was created, according to its object, 'to promote the Reverent Study of the Holy Scriptures, and to resist the varied attacks made upon their Inspiration, Infallibility, and Sole Sufficiency as the Word of God.'[34] Its immediate occasion seems to have been the appearance of *The Inspiration and Authority of the Bible* by John Clifford, a Baptist leader strikingly open to modern trends of thought, who, like Horton but more guardedly, was trying to popularise a newer understanding of the Bible.[35] Resistance was initially located on the Baptist fringe, around Spurgeon and the boundary with undenominational revivalism. Successive secretaries were John Tuckwell, a London Baptist minister; A. H. Carter, later Minister of Hounslow Undenominational Church and editor of the League's *Bible Witness*; and (from 1912) Robert Wright Hay, a former BMS missionary, Minister of Talbot Tabernacle, Notting Hill (an 'energetic Gospel centre') and an intimate friend of R. C. Morgan, editor of *The Christian*.[36] It was originally a small-scale affair, holding occasional rallies where Tuckwell might lecture on 'The Bible Right: confirmed by Babylonian archaeology',[37] but it gradually drew in more eminent figures from a wider range of denominations. Dinsdale Young, a well-known Methodist preacher, Dr C. H. Waller, a tutor in the CMS college at Highbury, and, crucially, Prebendary H. E. Fox, clerical secretary of the CMS from 1895 to 1910, were induced to identify with the organisation.[38] It was sufficiently strong by 1914 to hold a summer school at Littlehampton addressed by a dozen speakers.[39] Its essential message is summed up by the title of a publication three years later: *Christ or the Higher Critics*.[40]

The Bible League did much to stiffen opinion. Frequently its influence can be detected behind outbursts of opposition to the higher criticism. At Cambridge, for instance, a Bible League conference immediately preceded a schism in the Evangelical student movement in 1909–10 that anticipated the divisions in the wider ecclesiastical world fifteen or so years later.[41] A Cambridge Inter-Collegiate Christian Union (CICCU) had existed since 1877 for the promotion of evangelism, prayer and missionary commitment. A British College Christian Union had emerged in the 1890s to co-ordinate such bodies in higher education, taking the name of Student Christian Movement (SCM) in 1905. In the next two years the General Secretary of the SCM, Tissington Tatlow, received letters from Cambridge protesting against speakers in whom higher critical opinions blended with broader doctrinal views than were desired.[42] Nothing was done, for the settled policy of the SCM was to accept the new approach to the Bible. A great number of other issues, which were also to arise again on the wider scene in the 1920s, complicated the ensuing discussions within and around the CICCU. At the root of the debate, however, was the status of the Bible. When the CICCU disaffiliated from the SCM in 1910, it declared 'its first and final reference to the authority of Holy Scripture as its inerrant guide in all matters concerned with faith and morals'.[43] There were similar secessions from the other movements for young people. In 1916 the Aldersgate Street Young Men's Christian Association left its parent body and in 1921 a number of groups previously affiliated to the Young Women's Christian Association came together as the Christian Alliance of Women and Girls, standing for 'full allegiance to the Word of God and separation for His work'.[44] Strongly held views about the Bible were beginning to create institutional divisions.

VERBAL INSPIRATION AND INERRANCY

The strong views commonly included a belief in verbal inspiration. Critics might suppose that the Bible is merely the record of revelation, wrote Meyer in 1893, but 'we believe that God revealed Himself in the *words* of Scripture . . .'[45] Meyer stood in the verbal inspirationist tradition that went back to Robert Haldane and Louis Gaussen in the early nineteenth century. The Brethren, a body moulded at that time by the same influences that affected Haldane, formed a continuing citadel of the stronger view of inspiration. In an article published during 1921 in their magazine *The Witness*, its editor, Henry Pickering, enquired, 'Have we an inspired Word of God?' The answer was a ringing affirmative. The very letters, even the Hebrew punctuation marks, were inspired: had not Jesus confirmed that every jot and tittle of the law was eternal?[46] The cause had advanced steadily among the Evangelical clergy in the Church of England. J. C.

Ryle, Bishop of Liverpool from 1880 to 1900, undoubtedly represented the majority of clerical opinion in the party of which he was a trusted leader when he declared his unhesitating belief in verbal inspiration.[47] The same view was widespread in popular Evangelical apologetics. It was usually qualified by the statement that only the original documents were inspired in this way – a convenient proviso that made the hypothesis untestable.[48] The qualification, if sometimes securing greater intellectual respectability, could itself lead on to some strange inferences. It was held by one defender of plenary inspiration that every one of the original inspired words exists somewhere in the world, often in very ancient manuscripts.[49] There can be no doubt that belief in verbal inspiration had become common by the early twentieth century.

Yet it was rare for spokesmen, let alone scholars, in the Evangelical community to claim that the Bible is free from error. A. H. Burton, a non-practising doctor with a private income and a Brethren background, was one of the few to do so. In an article on 'The inerrancy of the Bible' he set out a simple antithesis between those who affirmed it and the higher critics who denied it.[50] An examination of the chief statements about scripture by Evangelicals in the first half of the twentieth century has revealed a remarkable absence of assertions of inerrancy. Only a couple, by D. M. McIntyre, later Principal of the Bible Training Institute, Glasgow, and W. E. Vine, a Brethren leader, were discovered. Even W. H. Griffith Thomas, Principal of Wycliffe Hall, Oxford, from 1905 to 1910, and a well-known Evangelical Anglican champion of a conservative view of scripture in the early twentieth century, though inclining towards inerrancy, avoided any explicit endorsement. Likewise G. T. Manley and T. C. Hammond, the leading exponents of the conservative position after the divergence of the 1920s, did not assert the inerrancy of the Bible. The problem, of course, was that the apparent discrepancies of scripture had been thoroughly canvassed for centuries and it was hard to fly in the face of them. Yet in America at the same time a stern repudiation of the possibility of error in a book given by a God of truth was massively elaborated by B. B. Warfield, so that the sparseness of British statements to the same effect is matter for comment.[51] Why did Evangelical leaders in Britain take this course?

One of the explanations is the restraining influence of Henry Wace. As a former Professor of Ecclesiastical History and then Principal at King's College, London, from 1875 to 1897, Wace was a scholar and ecclesiastical statesman of some weight. As Dean of Canterbury from 1903 until his death in 1924, he played a leading part in Evangelical counsels. At the Islington Clerical Meeting of 1911 he provoked considerable dissent among the more liberally inclined by avowing what he called the traditional theory of scripture. It included the axiom that in history as well as doctrine the Bible is free from error. Yet, for all the apparent conservatism of his position, he admitted there might be trivial mistakes of the text.[52] He held, as he often put it, the 'substantial truth' of scripture – and that fell short

of absolute inerrancy. 'Are there a few inaccuracies of detail?' he asked
at a conference in 1921. 'How could it be otherwise in a short sketch of so
many ages of development?'[53] The *Journal of the Wesley Bible Union* noted with
disappointment his willingness to surrender the detailed accuracy of Genesis.[54] To his friends he would commend Luther's attitude to the Bible, an
eagerness to grasp the leading truths 'without becoming a slave to verbal inspiration'.[55] He had originally been no party man, being drawn into the Evangelical ranks by a shared hostility to ritualism at the turn of the century, and
so he felt no initial sympathy for Ryle's rigidity about the words of scripture.
Rather the foundation of his position was a scholar's disdain for what he saw
as the aberrations of recent German study of the Old Testament. His remedy
for erroneous criticism was better criticism.[56] By involvement with the
Bible League, whose vice-president he became,[57] he made it impossible to
identify the conservative position on the Bible with wilder denunciations of
the higher criticism or rigid statements about inerrancy. Furthermore, his
intellectual premisses reveal a deeper reason why it was uncommon to
deduce inerrancy from the trustworthiness of God. Whether the substantial
truth of the Old Testament, he wrote, 'involved minute exactitude in all
details is a matter partly for common sense, but chiefly for determination
by the facts . . .'[58] Appeal to common sense and the facts was the stock
in trade of a thinker whose mind was shaped by the familiar Anglo-Saxon
empiricism stemming from the Enlightenment. Wace was as wedded to
this tradition as was the Congregationalist Alfred Cave. The resistance to
the higher criticism was not grounded in a doctrine of inerrancy because,
at least among the educated, inerrancy held no more attractions than the
conclusions of the higher critics.

The motive force for the anti-critical movement came primarily, as in
America, from individuals and groups holding the advent hope. This was
no more an absolute rule than it was in America.[59] Nevertheless there was
a tight link between the premillennialist movement and the defence of the
Bible. 'Those who stood by the great truth of the Lord's return', it was
said at an Advent Testimony meeting in 1921, 'were firm on the authority
and infallibility of the Scriptures as the actual Word of God.'[60] The link
was literal interpretation. 'It is a principle of vital importance to the study
of Scripture', declared Fuller Gooch, a leading exponent of prophecy, in
1886, 'that the literal signification of words should be accepted in all cases
except where the obvious nature of the language employed necessitates
a figurative or symbolic sense. Only by a continuous violation of this
principle can the personal reign of Christ during the millennial era be
eliminated from revelation.'[61] Those who were tied to literalism could
hardly avoid believing in verbal inspiration. That is why the two trends
had grown up together during the nineteenth century. In the early twentieth
century, the denominations most affected by Fundamentalism were those
most touched by adventism – the Brethren, Anglican Evangelicals and the
Baptists. Conversely, Congregationalism was almost immune to both.

W. B. Selbie could be heard warning his fellow-Congregationalists in 1922 against the literal interpretation of scripture,[62] but his effort was hardly necessary. The case of Methodism is the exception that proves the rule. As will be seen, it was hardly touched by adventism. Yet the leader of the Fundamentalist party in Wesleyan Methodism, H. C. Morton, was by 1918 preaching the second coming.[63] In Morton's case, Bible defence came before adventism, but the association between the two is once more clear. The primary impetus for militancy on behalf of the Bible came from those who had embraced the advent hope.

THE CHRISTIAN HOPE

Another reason for the Evangelical divisions of the 1920s is therefore the rise of premillennialism. The rival version of the Christian hope, postmillennialism, had gone into serious decline. A few still held in the early years of the twentieth century that Christ would return in person once the preaching of the gospel had established his reign in all lands.[64] But interpretations of postmillennialism had commonly broadened with the years. 'Modern Methodism', it was said just after the opening of the twentieth century, 'has deliberately projected the second Advent into so distant a future that it is scarcely even named.'[65] High hopes for the far-off future merged imperceptibly with the idea of progress. By 1916 a leading Methodist was prepared to state that 'no visible return of Christ to the earth is to be expected'.[66] It was not only Methodists who followed this course. The editor of *Life and Work*, the magazine of the Church of Scotland, reaffirmed a Christian belief in progress despite the horrors of the First World War. Although apocalyptic speculation is fruitless, he claimed, 'there can be but one "evolution of society", one "social development"; it is the coming of the Kingdom of God'.[67] Likewise at Cromer, the devotional conference for liberal Evangelicals of the Church of England, a verse of a popular hymn was changed from:

> Brothers, this Lord Jesus shall return again
> With His Father's glory, with His angel train.

It appeared as:

> Brothers, this Lord Jesus dwells with us again
> In His Father's wisdom, o'er the earth to reign.[68]

Postmillennialism had become little more than an aspiration after the spread of Christian values.

Premillennialism, however, had made steady progress in the later nineteenth century. There was an annual conference for the Study of Prophetic

Truth at Clapham from 1884, and in the same year a session of the devotional Mildmay Conference was given over to the subject for the first time.[69] Crucially, advent teaching had early become intertwined with the Keswick message.[70] Association with the flowing tide of the holiness movement ensured that prophecy swept along increasing numbers. It became popular with the young. The Student Volunteer Movement for Foreign Missions, an international body launched in 1886 with the motto 'The Evangelisation of the world in this generation', gathered strength from the Keswick fringe.[71] Although there was no time for the conversion of the world, its members held, it was necessary to preach the gospel to every nation. That done, Christ would return. Missionary work would bring back the King. The Church Missionary Society was among the bodies feeling the benefit in a fresh wave of recruits.[72] Keswick and the new missionary enthusiasm alike disproportionately affected the Church of England. By 1901 a speaker at the Islington Clerical Meeting felt able to assume that all his hearers believed in the premillennial advent.[73] At least in the Church of England, prophetic teaching had become firmly established by the dawn of the new century.

The form of prophetic teaching making most headway was the futurist version. All the predictions of Daniel and Revelation, its advocates argued, were still to be fulfilled. The dispensationalism of J. N. Darby, the most systematic brand of futurism, captured many minds with its vision of a coming rapture of the church. It was the view generally accepted by Evangelical Churchmen who attended Keswick. 'Every day', remarked an incredulous Methodist, 'they are waiting for the saints to be caught up – the captain from his ship, the engine-driver from his locomotive, the mother from her family, &c.'[74] By 1892, the editor of *The Christian*, who had previously maintained neutrality between different schools, came down on the side of 'dispensational truth'.[75] Probably the greatest factor in favour of dispensationalism was the publication in 1909 of the Scofield Bible with footnotes expounding a Darbyite interpretation. Already four years later it was said to be 'so largely used by students and Christian workers'.[76] It accustomed its readers to seeing the biblical text through dispensationalist eyes. Although the writings of Henry Grattan Guinness, such as *The Approaching End of the Age* (1878), sustained the vitality of the alternative historicist version of premillennial teaching,[77] there can be no doubt that dispensationalism was the predominant form of the advent hope by the First World War.

The apocalyptic atmosphere of wartime encouraged prophetic speculation. At the outbreak of the First World War the only premillennialist organisation in Britain was the Prophecy Investigation Society, which exuded an air of rather musty erudition. About a hundred devotees assembled twice a year for the reading of arcane papers.[78] The war livened it up. 'The Rev. F. L. Denman', it was reported of one meeting, 'directed the attention of the members to the striking way in which several passages in Daniel xi. fit the character and conduct of the Kaiser.'[79] Hostilities in the Middle East created expectations in a wider constituency. The Jews might soon return to the Promised Land, a sure sign of the second coming. With British troops massing in Sinai for an advance on Jerusalem in the autumn of 1917, two ministers suggested to F. B. Meyer that there should be an effort to awaken Christians to the fulfilment of prophecy around them. Meyer secured the endorsement of other ministers known to be premillennialists, approached the Prophecy Investigation Society for its backing and launched the first of what was to be a permanent series of monthly London public meetings on 13 December. While preparations were going ahead, the government issued the Balfour Declaration announcing British support for the return of the Jews to Palestine. Four days after the first public meeting General Allenby received the surrender of Jerusalem.[80] The Advent Testimony and Preparation Movement enjoyed an auspicious beginning.

The message spread by a variety of means. Advent Testimony monthly meetings were widely reported in the Christian press; its magazine, *Advent Witness*, circulated extensively; and several of its members wrote books, of which E. L. Langston's *How God is Working to a Plan* (1933) was one of the most popular. The greatest publicity coup, however, was the conversion to the cause of Christabel Pankhurst, the ex-suffragette, who published a number of premillennialist works beginning with *The Lord Cometh* in 1923. In the autumn of 1926 she undertook a campaign tour for Advent Testimony, bringing, it was said, 'fresh inspiration' to the movement.[81] Douglas Brown, Baptist minister at Balham and a member of the Advent Testimony council, did a great deal to propagate premillennial teaching. In 1921 there broke out in East Anglia, especially among the fishermen, one of the last mainland revivals of the old-fashioned spontaneous type. Brown was the pivotal figure, delivering gospel addresses at Lowestoft and in the vicinity. The ingathering of converts, he reported to an Advent Testimony meeting, was 'largely through the preaching of the truth of the Lord's coming'. On thirty-one consecutive afternoons he spoke for fifty minutes on the second advent.[82] Others similarly discovered that premillennial enthusiasm helped evangelistic endeavour. The Pilgrim Preachers, for instance, a band of travelling young men drawn from the Brethren, proclaimed (according to their leader) '"the coming of the Lord draweth nigh", and that it is a case of *now or never* with the unsaved to decide for Christ'.[83] Association with gospel zeal helped in turn to propagate prophetic views. For the first time in many quarters they were being accepted as the orthodoxy of popular Evangelicalism.

The spread of the futurist version of the advent hope in the 1920s had important implications. By contrast with historicists, who paid a great deal of attention to public affairs, past and present, for the vindication of their views, futurists concentrated on the intricacies of scripture to the virtual exclusion of issues in the world. The sermons of Fuller Gooch on adventist themes were so incomprehensible to newspaper reporters that their accounts became gibberish.[84] There was little point in trying to identify the figures of prophecy since by definition they were future. At its fullest, interest in contemporary events was therefore a matter of looking out for signs of the emergence of a pattern of affairs similar to that predicted for the last days – like the combination of ten powers within the territory of the former Roman Empire to play the part of the toes of the statue in Daniel 2. Futurism encouraged the introversion that was a hallmark of interwar conservative Evangelicalism. There was another significant divergence of futurists from historicists in the identification of Antichrist. Historicists followed Protestant tradition in casting the papacy in that role. The Roman Catholic Church represented the great apostasy from the true faith predicted in scripture.[85] Futurists, on the other hand, believed that the Antichrist was still to come. They were consequently less inclined to militant anti–Catholicism. At the same time, however, they were expecting the Protestant world to lapse into unbelief on a vast scale. Higher criticism seemed a sinister symptom of the anti–Christian teaching subverting Christendom that had to be stoutly resisted. 'A falsely called Christian charity', declared an adventist magazine in 1919, 'has led many to temporize with these deadly doctrines, so that some have become swamped by the rising tide of apostasy.'[86] The fierce, denunciatory tone of Fundamentalism – in so far as it was heard in Britain – was largely spawned by the futurist prophetic school.

Futurism also created a gloomy worldview. Already, before the war, a Methodist had remarked that adventist clergymen were deeply pessimistic. 'Looking for our Lord's speedy coming', he explained, 'they expect things to go from bad to worse, and frankly tell me they have no hope of amelioration.'[87] The war and its aftermath confirmed and extended such attitudes. Premillennialists rejected the vision of 'the rosy Christian idealist – that honest, earnest, believer in the essential goodness of Humanity, who supposes that the Millennium is to be the automatic result of a gradual improvement in men and things'. God had revealed otherwise. 'He tells us plainly, not that the development of the Kingdom will bring the King, but that the King Himself must come to establish the Kingdom; and that He, not man, is to make the Kingdom fit for men to live in.'[88] Effort to reform the world was pointless, even perhaps an impious attempt to frustrate the purposes of God. Sympathy for progressive politics waned. Organised labour seemed a sinister force in both industry and politics. In the wake of the General Strike of 1926 readers of *The Life of Faith* were assured that this 'revolutionary plot . . . being hatched against the British Constitution . . . *was the rising of an Anti-Christ*'. 'I am not discussing politics', insisted the contributor, 'but as one who loves his Lord . . . I believe the time has come for Christians . . . to prepare themselves and their land for that which the Bible prophesies shall come to pass.'[89] Premillennialists, as in this case, normally proclaimed their distance from politics, yet rallied to the defence of the established order. Pessimism readily passed over into conservatism.

HEIGHTENED SPIRITUALITY

A further factor behind the interwar Evangelical schism was the holiness movement that has been discussed in Chapter 5. Its effects were ambiguous. The spirituality of the movement, as the Broadlands conference illustrates, could reinforce the trend towards softening doctrinal definitions. Keswick, as will be seen, was the setting for a tussle between more liberal and more conservative elements.[90] The outcome, however, could be in little doubt, for Keswick teaching was in general strongly associated with a non-critical understanding of the Bible and the advent hope. Its exponents, according to conservative Evangelicals, were beacons in the gathering gloom. 'I travel from Land's End to the Shetland Isles', wrote one in 1925, 'and I find wherever there is a real Keswick school minister there one finds the ungodly being awakened and led to Christ . . .'[91] More critical observers noticed the cultivation of the internal life, the camaraderie with the likeminded symbolised by the use of the adjective 'dear' in reference to Christian colleagues and commented that this ethos encouraged a narrowing of horizons.[92] The Keswick movement was still growing in size and influence in the 1920s, its message of 'fuller consecration' being disseminated by literature, lesser conventions and a variety of organisations. Its essentially Romantic spirituality was in itself too irenical to provoke adherents into militant Fundamentalism, but the Keswick allegiance did a great deal to glue together the conservative coalition.

The Methodist version of the holiness tradition played a similar role within the Wesleyan denomination. Its embodiment was Samuel Chadwick, a gifted devotional writer and from 1913 Principal of Cliff College, a denominational centre in Derbyshire for training lay workers. 'There is no Methodist doctrine of Inspiration, or of the Second Coming', he reminded a holiness meeting at the 1912 conference. 'But there is a distinctively Methodist doctrine of holiness.'[93] Among Wesleyans, therefore, entire sanctification was the potential rallying ground of theological conservatives. It had already been noticed that the holiness people for the most part did not embrace the higher criticism.[94] The leaders of the Fundamentalist faction that emerged in the Jackson affair of 1913, George Armstrong Bennetts and Harold Morton, were both advocates of entire sanctification.[95] So was Dinsdale Young, the most eminent Methodist to be drawn into the faction.[96] Samuel Chadwick, however, stood apart from the Fundamentalist campaign against individuals judged to hold erroneous views. In 1919 he called for an end to the 'wrangling and haggling' of the heresy hunt, condemning the 'heterodoxy of temper' displayed by the militant Wesley Bible Union a year later.[97] He ensured that *Joyful News*, the widely circulating weekly associated with Cliff College, remained aloof from controversy. Dinsdale Young was kept at a distance from the college and the Southport Convention, the main holiness platform.[98] Chadwick and his circle believed in the positive work of preaching the gospel, not in negative campaigns that aroused animosity.[99] The mildness and self-restraint of this approach were the natural fruit of teaching on personal sanctification. The Methodist holiness tradition, with a few exceptions, generated conservative Evangelicalism rather than Fundamentalism.

Other movements of opinion on the fringe of the holiness movement tended to stoke up spiritual fires to a more intense heat. From the early days there was a section, drawing inspiration from the American Dr Cullis, that believed physical healing, as well as victory over sin, to be available through faith in Christ.[100] 'When He has complete control in the fully surrendered life', it was said in 1921, 'He is responsible for directing our bodily lives – and is responsible for our health.'[101] This writer, like several others, did not shrink from the implication that illness is the result of sin. Only in exceptional cases, he contended when challenged by many dismayed correspondents, are the consecrated allowed to be invalids.[102] It was more normal to hold that sickness is not necessarily the result of want of faith, but occasional talk of 'bondage about doctors and nurses' was a sign of the anti-modern disposition of Fundamentalism.[103]

Another intensified version of holiness teaching pointed in the same direction. Some began to talk of a baptism of the Holy Ghost distinct from the experience of entire consecration. One source was the Pentecostal League of Reader Harris. Its leadership was taken over after his death in 1909 by Oswald Chambers, who a few years before had entered 'years of heaven on earth' through the baptism of the Holy Ghost.[104] Another source was the Japan Evangelistic Band, established in 1903, whose founder, A. Paget Wilkes, taught that sanctification is twofold, entailing cleansing from indwelling sin and then 'an incoming and indwelling of the Holy Ghost'.[105] But the chief source was the Welsh Revival of 1904–5. Spreading through much of Wales and affecting churches elsewhere in Britain, ordinary church life was suspended, whole communities anxiously sought salvation and some 100,000 people professed conversion.[106] A young candidate for the Calvinistic Methodist ministry, Evan Roberts, underwent a vivid spiritual experience that made him the central figure of the revival. Twelve years later he expounded his experience in a work written jointly with Jessie Penn-Lewis of the Overcomer League, *War on the Saints*. The remedy for the assault of deceiving spirits on the children of God was to be found in 'the Baptism of the Holy Spirit'.[107] Although such teaching was suspect at Keswick, from which Jessie Penn-Lewis had withdrawn in 1909, it was disseminated by fringe periodicals like *The Overcomer* and minor conventions at Matlock and elsewhere.[108] It helped ensure that a section of Evangelicalism, albeit a small one, remained firmly committed to the conservative side in the years after the First World War.

It was also in this atmosphere that Pentecostalism was born. Talk of the 'baptism of the Holy Ghost' in the holiness movement prepared the way. There were even thoughts of the possibility of the restoration of the gift of tongues, which was understood as the ability to speak other languages and so to evangelise the world.[109] The Welsh revival created fresh longings after the dynamic of the first-century church. The early leaders of two of the Pentecostal denominations, Daniel Powell Williams of the Apostolic Church and George and Stephen Jeffreys of Elim, were converted then together with many of the early rank and file.[110] A report on the Welsh Revival by F. B. Meyer contributed to the beginnings of Pentecostalism in Los Angeles in 1905. Although there were earlier manifestations in the American mid-west, the movement usually traces the origin of its worldwide spread to what followed in Los Angeles. Revival broke out in Azusa Street and speaking in tongues was heard.[111] Belief that a new outpouring of the Holy Spirit had begun soon reached Norway, where ecstatic utterances were witnessed early in 1907 by A. A. Boddy, Vicar of All Saints', Sunderland. At Boddy's request, T. B. Barratt, the Methodist minister who had brought the dramatic manifestations to Norway, now carried them to Sunderland, which became a major centre for their dissemination in the years up to the First World War. There were similar outbreaks elsewhere, and from 1909 Cecil Polhill, one of the 'Cambridge Seven' who had gone out as missionaries to China in 1885, organised regular meetings in Sion College, on the Thames Embankment in London, for 'all seeking Salvation, Sanctification, the Baptism of the Holy Spirit and Divine Healing'.[112] By July 1908 there were already thirty-two known centres in Britain where Pentecostal gifts were exercised.[113] A new dimension was added to the Evangelical world.

The pioneers Boddy and Polhill, as loyal Anglicans, tried to discourage the tendencies to separatism that soon appeared, particularly in Wales. The 'spoken word' movement began to teach that scriptural church government was through an elaborate hierarchy of apostles, prophets and others appointed through ecstatic utterance. Daniel Powell Williams, who received a call to apostleship in 1913, set about consolidating the Pentecostal assemblies that were springing up within this pattern. They became the Apostolic Church.[114] Another growing organisation was the Elim Evangelistic Band, led by the energetic George Jeffreys. First formed in Ulster in 1915, its work spread through Britain in the interwar years until, by 1939, the Elim Foursquare Gospel Alliance, as it had become known, claimed to have established 280 churches. Jeffreys, who was to leave Elim in a dispute in 1939–41, was the driving force. He would hold evangelistic and healing campaigns, usually in significant centres of population, and the converts would be gathered into a new cause.[115] Its connexional structure resembled the polity of Methodism. The Assemblies of God, by contrast, upheld the autonomy of local churches. It was formed in 1924 by small bodies eager to remain independent of the encroachments of the Apostolic Church.[116] It differed also from Elim in asserting that speaking in tongues is always the initial evidence of baptism in the Holy Spirit.[117]

Pentecostalism was united, however, in its advent teaching, which was often more prominent than its advocacy of tongues, and its summons 'back to the Bible'. 'This book, neglected by so many pulpits today', declared a short account of the denomination, 'is the basis of Elim's Fundamentalism.'[118] Yet ordinary conservative Evangelicals, and even other self-professed Fundamentalists, repudiated the whole movement. 'The question', announced *The Life of Faith* in answer to queries in 1922, 'as to the possibility of the periodical appearance of miraculous gifts during the course of this dispensation is one which still gives rise to acute differences of opinion. Fortunately, there is no need for us to come to any definite conclusion on this point in order to see how unscriptural, and, indeed, how utterly subversive of genuine spirituality, are the corybantic exhibitions associated with particular types of present-day "Pentecostalism".'[119] The position of the Pentecostalists in relation to Fundamentalism, it has been suggested, was similar to the position of the Quakers in relation to Puritanism: having similar origins, occupying much common ground and yet totally repudiated by the larger body.[120] Although spurned by others, Pentecostalists brought vigorous reinforcement to the conservative wing of Evangelicalism.

BROADENING THEOLOGY

The slackening doctrinal standards on the liberal wing also help explain the divisions of the 1920s. The principle of free inquiry coupled with a taste for the Romantic had begun to broaden the theology of Nonconformists in the later nineteenth century.[121] By the interwar years a typical publication of Congregationalists was *The Religion of Wordsworth* (1936), by the scholar-minister, A. D. Martin. It taught the religion of gratitude as illustrated by the poet.[122] Among younger Methodists such as Robert Newton Flew there were similar trends of thought. In 1918 Flew criticised the narrowness of the early Methodist preachers, who, he claimed, 'had not seen a vision of God affirming the world as good, as delighting in the colour and gaiety and many-sidedness of human life, ceaselessly operative as in Nature . . .'[123] A comparable widening of horizons is apparent in *Changing Creeds and Social Struggles* (1893) by Charles Aked, a Baptist minister at Liverpool eventually to be translated to the United States. But Aked was unusually broad for a Baptist, and Meyer was in due course to point out to him the limits of orthodoxy.[124]

The drift of opinion led to the New Theology controversy of 1907–10. R. J. Campbell, occupant of Congregationalism's premier pulpit at the City Temple, shocked the religious public with opinions so immersed in philosophical idealism as to verge on pantheism. Deity and humanity, he held in *The New Theology* (1907), are 'fundamentally and essentially one'.[125] The implications, worked out in a supplementary volume on *Christianity and the Social Order*, were no less alarming. 'The churches', he wrote, 'have nothing to do with getting men into heaven.' Their task was rather to hasten the kingdom of God, which was equated with the socialist order being championed by the Independent Labour Party.[126] As his leading opponent, P. T. Forsyth, insisted, Campbell had broken entirely with any theology of the cross. To the Evangelical press, the New Theology seemed so nonsensical – an 'extraordinary farrago' – as to pose little threat.[127] Campbell's supporters rallied in a Liberal Christian League, but by 1915 even ardent opponents could scent out few continuing followers.[128] In that year Campbell renounced his theology and was received into the Church of England.[129] While ministers who had abandoned Evangelical belief persisted in Congregationalism – indeed Bernard Snell of Brixton became Chairman of the Congregational Union in 1917 and T. Rhondda Williams of Brighton followed him in 1929[130] – by and large the Nonconformist denominations remained within the bounds of Evangelicalism.

There were comparable doctrinal developments in the Evangelical party of the Church of England. The time was fast passing, declared C. J. Procter, Vicar of Islington, in 1905, when religious people distrusted the increase of knowledge. 'Theological interpretation', he went on, 'like every other branch of knowledge, is a progressive science . . .'[131] When such sentiments were uttered from the chair of the Islington Clerical Meeting, very much the magisterium of the party, it is not surprising that others went further. In 1912, at the Ridley Hall reunion of old members, the vice-principal of the college, J. R. Darbyshire, delivered what was long remembered as 'that famous address' on 'Gospel and Culture'.[132] Darbyshire, then in his early thirties, voiced opinions in public that were held by many younger Evangelical clergy in private. An adequate philosophical basis for Evangelicalism was called for. The need was pressing because of the gathering strength of the Anglo-Catholic party, confident in its assertion of the authority of the church. Evangelicals sometimes appealed to the principles of the Reformation, 'but it is hard to see exactly to what this talk amounts' and Calvinism was not essential to Evangelicalism in any case. To claim authority for an infallible book was unacceptable, because (here Darbyshire follows the standard Anglo-Catholic case) it leads to individualism: each reader makes his own interpretation the final court of appeal. The proper Evangelical attitude is 'Experimentalism'. Theory is to be tested by religious experience through history. Thus the inspiration of the Bible 'lies in the intensity of the spiritual experiences recorded therein'. Varieties of religious experience (here the speaker echoes William James) must be recognised as valid. At present Evangelicals had fallen into the snare of renouncing the world. 'We must be for ever so presenting the Gospel to the unlearned in terms of a traditional phraseology if we are to be recognized as Evangelical, that we have no time to feed the thoughtful, inspire the ambitious, and shew the glory of consecrating the secular.' The remedy was a rapprochement between gospel and culture. There must be

Evangelical church music and belles lettres.[133] Darbyshire's views were eventually to take him beyond Evangelicalism and to the Archbishopric of Cape Town, but at the time he caught the mood of his hearers. Experience, not dogma, was to be exalted. The ablest young Evangelicals, swayed by the taste of the times, were looking for fresh ground to occupy.

Theological change at a popular level was accelerated by the First World War. The question of prayers for the dead, which had already been agitated in peacetime,[134] suddenly became a matter of pressing pastoral importance. The bereaved yearned to pray for those lost in the carnage. Public prayer for the departed, rare in 1914 in the Church of England, was sanctioned by authority in 1917.[135] Preaching at a united Free Church memorial service in the same year, a Wesleyan minister pronounced the practice legitimate.[136] Hopes about the eternal destiny of those who had died for their country furthered the erosion of the demarcation between heaven and hell. As early as 1914 Dean Wace, with studied ambiguity, wrote in *The Record* that 'we may confidently be assured that those who meet their death on the battlefields of this war in the spirit of faith in Christ, and in simple devotion to duty, will be received by Him in the sense of those gracious words, "Well done, good and faithful servant", and may hope to be admitted in some degree into the joy of their Lord'.[137] Salvation by death in battle was endorsed by many others in much less cautious terms.[138] The idea of a second chance of salvation after death entered Evangelical thinking. J. D. Jones endorsed the doctrine of probation in the after-life at the Congregational Union assembly in 1916 and published a book that teetered on the brink of belief in universal salvation.[139] The availability of salvation for those dying impenitent was rumoured to be preached in a few Wesleyan pulpits.[140] In a more general way, the war dissolved reservations about expressing views previously judged unorthodox. Speaking one's mind seemed to be a duty to the dead. Traditionalists were alarmed by daring opinions spelt out in the pulpit in the wake of the war.[141] In exactly the same way, traditionalists themselves felt bound to battle for the truth, especially against errors supposedly concocted by the theological professors of Germany.[142] Polarisation was encouraged by the war.

Doctrinal debate between the wings of Evangelical opinion centred on two areas, atonement and Christology. The understanding of the atonement handed down from the Evangelical fathers was expounded in a paper by Bishop Moule at the 1904 Islington Clerical Meeting. 'Substitution' and 'vicarious punishment', words expressing the belief that Christ took the place of guilty sinners at his death, were not in the Bible, Moule admitted, yet various passages left him wondering how else to articulate their meaning.[143] It was claimed by conservatives such as Langston in the 1920s that their opponents supposed the death of Christ to be 'not substitutionary, but exemplary'.[144] The more liberal usually preferred to describe the death of Christ as representative: his suffering was in some sense on our behalf. They wished to deny a whole series of notions surrounding substitution. Canon de Candole, a liberal Anglican leader, declared in a sermon in 1921 that God's anger was not appeased by the offering of his Son. The idea was revolting.[145] Likewise Leslie Weatherhead, then a Methodist *enfant terrible*, wished to deny the axiom stated in the Book of Hebrews that 'without the shedding of blood there is no forgiveness of sins'. 'In our modern view', he boldly asserted, 'this is simply not true.'[146] Conservatives insisted that the cross must be seen as a sacrifice in which the justice of God was satisfied; liberals wished to discard legalistic interpretations in which the love of God was obscured. For many of the more conservative including E. A. Knox, who retired as Bishop of Manchester in 1921, and Albert Mitchell, the leading lay liturgiologist among the Evangelicals, the doctrine of the cross was the heart of the debate between the two sides.[147]

Christology was also divisive. Again the more liberal made the running. Some contended that the omniscience of Christ must be given up.[148] That, however, was far from radical since it was a tenet championed by P. T. Forsyth, the foe of R. J. Campbell's New Theology. Others went further and treated Christ as primarily an example. If Christ were presented as the greatest exemplar, declared Canon Storr in 1933, people would be shamed into recognising their shortcomings.[149] Some were prepared to recast the traditional understanding of the person of Christ. Frank Lenwood disturbed Congregationalism with his avowal in *Jesus: Lord or Leader?* (1930) that he could not accept the divinity of Christ.[150] Weatherhead was barely less drastic. 'I think Christ's divinity', he wrote in 1932, 'was not endowed, but achieved by His moral reactions, so that He climbed to an eminence of character which the word human was not big enough to describe.'[151] The virgin birth, to many a buttress of the orthodox doctrine of the incarnation, was specifically assailed. Congregationalism had been troubled by this issue before the war,[152] and in 1935 Donald Soper, a young Methodist famous for his open-air speaking, was accused of denying that Christ was born of a virgin.[153] Evangelical Anglicanism was hardly afflicted with outright rejections, but it was thought worthwhile for *The Record* to carry a sermon devoted to the subject in 1925.[154] To the conservative, such vagaries were not mere theological speculations. They were a betrayal of the Christian faith itself.

The spread of liberal theology among Anglican Evangelicals had a measure of institutional support. A number of Merseyside clergy created in 1906 the Group Brotherhood for private discussion. Other groups were formed in imitation and from 1908 there was an annual conference. At first it was not specifically liberal. Rather its purpose was study and, it was hoped, the publication of books to inculcate Evangelical teaching.[155] Numbers grew following the war and in 1923 it was reconstructed as the Anglican Evangelical Group Movement (AEGM). Although it still deliberately avoided adopting the word 'liberal' in its title for fear of causing offence,[156] the movement was associated with a collection of essays entitled *Liberal Evangelicalism* and issued a set of fifty-three pamphlets to publicise the same position.[157] 'It is the mind of Christ, not the letter of Holy Scripture, which is authoritative', runs the introduction to *Liberal Evangelicalism*. 'The modern Evangelical is dissatisfied with some of the older and cruder penal substitutionary theories of the Atonement.'[158] At this stage Canon Vernon Storr was drawn into the organisation. Storr became its driving force and, from 1930, its president. He had not previously been identified with the Evangelical party, but the combination of intellectual breadth and spiritual experience that became the hallmark of the movement was very much Storr's creation. From 1928 it ran its own equivalent of Keswick, an annual devotional conference at Cromer that from the first year attracted more than a thousand.[159] In the 1930s it also planned its own retreats.[160] The movement was always largely clerical, never seeking to draw in the laity, but it achieved significant membership: some 200 clergy by 1923 and 1,500 by 1935.[161] Although certain members were connected with the Modern Churchmen's Union, an explicitly Modernist body,[162] it adopted a basis of recognisably Evangelical belief. Its members naturally attracted the criticism that they were 'claiming to be Evangelicals while wishing to enthrone Reason in place of Divine Revelation'.[163] It nevertheless did much to provide progressive clergymen with a shield of fellowship to defend them against the darts of enraged parishioners.

A parallel body called the Fellowship of the Kingdom emerged in Methodism. In 1917 a group of younger Wesleyan ministers in London began to meet for discussion and prayer. They discovered a number of like-minded cells, some of which went back as far as 1908. Groups sprang up elsewhere during 1919 and in the following year the first annual conference was held at Swanwick. Although non-Wesleyans were admitted and there were groups for lay preachers, the bulk of support, as in the AEGM, came from ministers.[164] The movement had three watchwords: Quest, Crusade and Fellowship. Quest was a desire for valid spiritual experience. The members felt the Methodist holiness tradition, with its particular jargon and shibboleths, to have 'passed beyond our horizon'.[165] A fresh start had to be made in the discovery of Jesus as a companion in the modern world. Crusade was the novel name for an evangelistic campaign. The organisation specialised in missions conducted by several ministers together. Fellowship was the mutual support of members in the groups meeting fortnightly. No group was permitted to have more than fifteen attenders because intimacy was essential.[166] Inspiration was drawn from W. Russell Maltby, Warden of the Wesley Deaconess Order, and J. A. Findlay, tutor in New Testament at Didsbury College.[167] Canon E. A. Burroughs, a leading figure in the AEGM, also provided some of the early vision through his book, *The Valley of Decision* (1916).[168] Bonds were forged with the AEGM from 1930 onwards.[169] The Fellowship of the Kingdom was the crucible in which was forged what the denominational history calls 'the typical "Jesus religion" school of recent Methodism'.[170] It was one of the chief expressions of liberal Evangelicalism.

RISING CHURCHMANSHIP

The parting of the ways between Evangelicals was hastened by the continued growth among some of High Church sympathies, attention to the eucharist and a desire 'for beauty in worship. Tensions in this area were already apparent at the Islington Clerical Meeting in 1883. P. F. Eliot, later Dean of Windsor, remarked that there was sometimes 'too much coquetting with Dissent'. He would not move an inch from 'Church principles' for the sake of co-operating with Dissent and there must be an end to the Evangelical neglect of sacramental teaching.[171] Others, on the other hand, felt that a common allegiance to the gospel made united work with Nonconformists advisable, a view often subsequently repeated at Islington.[172] The attractions of tradition nevertheless continued to draw erstwhile Evangelicals towards the High Church school. E. H. Pearce, Bishop of Worcester, who after an upbringing at All Souls', Langham Place, had taken that path, declared in 1924 that his generation had inadequately appreciated the 'spiritual procession that paces all down the ages'.[173] The centre of gravity within the Evangelical school undoubtedly shifted upwards. By 1909 it was noticed that a new Evangelical party was forming, which, apart from giving time to study, refused to stress ritual differences and firmly believed in church order.[174] The tendency crystallised in support for the idea of 'Central Churchmanship' propounded by J. Denton Thompson, shortly to be Bishop of Sodor and Man, in a book of that title in 1911. The AEGM entered into part of this heritage. That organisation, according to Storr, saw a larger place for ritual and held a greater sense of churchmanship than its Evangelical predecessors.[175] Loyalty to the forms of the Church of England was increasing.

The most tangible aspect was the trend towards more elaborate church decorations and tolerance of ritual practices once judged to be High Church. By the start of the twentieth century, the use of the surplice for preaching, though still resisted by a handful of diehards, had been accepted even by rigid opponents of ritualism.[176] At this stage to call a clergyman a liberal Evangelical was to refer to his views not on inspiration or theology, but on liturgical arrangements. On entering the church of such a liberal Evangelical in 1904, a correspondent of *The Record* discovered 'cross and flowers on the Table, Eastward Position adopted, Litany Desk and intoned service, black stoles with gold crosses'.[177] All was alien to Evangelical custom, but progressives were wishing to end the assumption that Evangelical theology and Low Church practice necessarily went together. Another correspondent reported that her church had the eastward position, flowers, a cross on the communion table and a surpliced choir, but sound teaching. Since homes were now 'more artistically beautiful' than in the past, why should not churches be so too?[178] Seventeen years further on the same issues were still under debate, but now for liberal Evangelicals it was the norm rather than the exception to wear white stoles at weddings and turn east for the creed.

They might be willing to have candles lit for 8 a.m. celebration, to speak readily of 'altar' and 'eucharist' and to use the word 'Catholic' freely.[179] As Anglo-Catholics were pressing forward with liturgical innovations such as incense and Italianate robes, they dragged progressive Evangelicals – at a very great distance – behind them. In the remoter parishes of Herefordshire it was still customary in the late 1930s to hold services without a surpliced choir, with prayers said rather than intoned and the 'Protestant type' of churchmanship firmly in place.[180] Such practices had by no means been banished from the city churches of conservative clergy either, but they had come to have something of a curiosity appeal.

The fiercest wrangling within Evangelicalism on a point of ritual was about the position adopted by the officiating clergyman at holy communion. The position that was to triumph in the later twentieth century, in which the clergyman faces the congregation from behind the holy table, was rare before the Second World War.[181] In most buildings it was physically impossible since the table stood against the east wall. A High Churchman would use the eastward position in which he stood with his back to the congregation facing the altar. It was intended to symbolise his role as a priest offering sacrifice to God on behalf of the people. Such an understanding was anathema to Evangelicals, for whom the sacrifice of Calvary could in no sense be re-enacted in the communion service. Hence, Evangelicals officiated at the north side of the communion table, the position that had been general before the innovations of the mid-nineteenth-century ritualists. Congregations were able to observe the clergyman's manual acts from the side so as to ensure that there was no sacerdotal mumbo-jumbo. For an Evangelical to employ the eastward position was 'a hoisting of the enemy's colours'.[182] Whenever the liberally inclined expressed a willingness to use the eastward position it caused a furore. To declare the practice allowable, as was done by Guy Rogers in a liberal manifesto of 1917, was to throw down the gauntlet.[183] For the Cromer convention communion services to employ the eastward position, as they did from 1935, was almost an act of secession from the Evangelical body.[184] The controversy was particularly troublesome to the Church Pastoral Aid Society. Conservatives constantly feared that its prohibition of grants to parishes adopting the eastward position would be rescinded. Its chairman and secretary nervously confirmed in 1917 that the society's views had not changed; the conservatives registered their satisfaction that the rule was being maintained in 1935; and debate on the question of a change of policy rumbled on even in the dark days of 1941.[185] The liturgical issue divided Evangelicals on substantially the same lines as the theological issue, though, if anything, liturgical conservatism was more powerful.

Public alarm at the ritual innovations of advanced Anglo-Catholics had led to the appointment of a Royal Commission on Ecclesiastical Discipline which sat from 1904 to 1906. It was Dean Wace who chose the ground on which Evangelicals were to rally in defence of Protestantism. There was no hope of persuading the Royal Commission to recommend the enforcement of the rubrics of the existing Book of Common Prayer. There was doubt about their interpretation. In any case most Evangelicals were less than scrupulous in observing their provisions: few held services on holy days or used the prayer for the church militant on days when there was no holy communion.[186] Wace moreover wished to secure the support of moderates of all schools. He therefore appealed to the practice of the first six centuries of the church, urging that later developments such as the eastward position and the use of incense should be banned from the Church of England.[187] Despite protests from diehards like Samuel Garratt, who regarded certain sixth-century ceremonies with horror,[188] Wace attracted the signatures of most leading Evangelicals and more than 4,000 clergy altogether.[189] The division over the proper extent of opposition to ritual innovation was ominous for Evangelical unity.

A more serious division came later. Among the recommendations of the Royal Commission was the revision of the Book of Common Prayer to accommodate the more general High Church practices. In the decade after the First World War the final stages of the protracted process caused serious strains. Evangelicals were particularly dismayed at provisions for the reservation of the consecrated elements, since Anglo-Catholics would wish to worship them as the body and blood of Christ. They mounted a sustained campaign against the Revised Prayer Book, which will need to be considered again shortly. Most Evangelicals felt the issue intensely: how could loyal sons of the Reformation, asked one conservative, be accessories to 'an Act of National Apostasy'?[190] They demanded that the church, and subsequently Parliament, should reject the innovation. Once the new Prayer Book was officially endorsed by the convocation of the Church of England, however, the Evangelical representatives there accepted that the battle had been lost.[191] There was no question of asking Parliament to overturn the decision of the church. The AEGM concurred, holding a conference on how to come to terms with the new book.[192] The main body of Evangelicals, on the other hand, felt betrayed by the liberal wing.[193] The fact that several of the turncoats, but no continuing opponents of the Revised Prayer Book, were elevated to the episcopal bench in the years up to the Second World War kept the grievance fresh. The question of how far to go in resisting the Anglo-Catholic ascendancy in the Church of England fractured the Evangelical party.

The Free Churches, as Nonconformity now liked to be called, could not remain immune to the rising standard of churchmanship. The example of the Church of England, the attractions posed to educated young people by Anglican ceremony and the persistent Romantic atmosphere of middle-brow culture all dictated change in that direction. The phrase 'Lord's Supper' was discarded in favour of 'Sacrament of Holy Communion', the rationale being that the former pointed merely to the circumstances of its institution but the latter identified its nature.[194] The Fellowship of the Kingdom helped spread an appreciation of eucharistic worship. The Methodist Sacramental Fellowship, launched in 1935, encouraged the same trend.[195] More frequent communion, the use of service books and the observance of the Christian year were making headway among the Presbyterians of Scotland,[196] but some of the most significant liturgical developments there were undertaken by the Congregationalist John Hunter, Minister of Trinity Church, Glasgow. He loved to speak of 'the Holy Catholic Church', administered communion in Anglican style and compiled the often reprinted *Devotional Services for Public Worship*.[197] By 1925 another Congregationalist, W. E. Orchard, was conducting mass with wafers, incense and Catholic punctilio at the King's Weigh House in London.[198] He preached on how to make the most of Lent. 'On Ash Wednesday morning', he recommended, 'say to your wife, "My dear, is there any virtue you would like me to acquire?"'[199] Orchard was one of the Free Churchmen who took the path to Rome.[200] If such aberrations fed the flames of conservative Evangelical anger, they were infrequent. Far more typical of progressive interwar Nonconformity was the worship at Ealing Green Congregational Church under Wilton Rix. The minister wore cassock and gown and, like many of his congregation, preferred kneeling for prayer. Choir stalls for robed singers were introduced, the pulpit was balanced on one side by a lectern on the other, a communion table was central and eventually, in 1936, a cross was added.[201] It was a world apart from the plain unpolished services that were still usual among the more traditional.

The divergence between liberals and conservatives was apparent on a number of points of church order. One was the ministry of women. The spread of female higher education and the successful campaign seeking votes for women meant that demands were heard in the early twentieth century for female ordination. In the mainstream denominations it was permitted by 1930 only among Congregationalists and Baptists, whose decentralised polity would have made prohibition virtually impossible. The Wesleyan Conference determined in 1926 to accept female candidates for the ministry, but deferred action until later – which turned out to be 1973.[202] In the Church of England women could serve as deaconesses and, from the creation of the Church Assembly in 1920, could share in some aspects of the government of the church. Sterner Evangelicals such as Wace had resolutely opposed this development, arguing that the apostle Paul's prohibition of women speaking in church was 'absolutely decisive for Christian men'.[203] Prejudice against female ministry was said to be strongest 'in old-fashioned circles where the literalist doctrine of Scriptural inspiration still holds the field'.[204] On the other side, Hatty Baker, a Congregationalist who had acted as a minister without official recognition, argued that the churches should not bind themselves to Paul's pre-Christian rabbinic thought-world. It was wrong to discriminate against women, relegating them to the teapots, bread and butter; male and female qualities were both needed in the ministry; and 'none but a woman can understand the agony of a woman's heart'.[205]

Guy Rogers, a leader of the AEGM, put forward a comparable, though less distinctly feminist, case in the 1930s.[206] In general the tension was the usual conservative/liberal one, with a large body of uncommitted opinion in the middle. The question rarely pressed. It might be right in pure logic that women should be allowed to enter the ministry of the church, said *The Record* in 1936, but there was no demand for it.[207] The question of female ordination reflected rather than created the tendency to polarisation in the Evangelical world.

SCIENCE AND RELIGION

A factor that played a more active part in encouraging division was debate on the relation of science to religion. The focus was almost exclusively on evolution. Evangelicals had rapidly learned to live with Darwin's discoveries. Theologians took account of it in their schemes; scientists treated it as an assumption in their work. The Wesleyan W. H. Dallinger and the Anglican G. T. Manley both held that recent scientific developments that took evolution for granted tended to undercut the materialist philosophies of Spencer and Haeckel.[208] Evolution was by no means a bogey to the popular Evangelical press.[209] Only isolated individuals occasionally protested that Darwin's unproved views did contradict Christian teaching on the special creation of humanity.[210] In 1924 A. C. Dixon, the Baptist son of a frontier farmer-preacher in the American South who had risen to become one of Spurgeon's successors as the Minister of the Metropolitan Tabernacle, delivered a ninety-minute harangue against evolutionary theory under the auspices of the Bible League. *The Record* expected its readers to think Dixon was flogging a dead horse.[211] In the following year, when the anti-evolution campaign in the United States reached its climax, a spokesman for the Christian Evidence Society commented that, by contrast, there was now less interest in Europe in the relations of science and religion, 'owing to the fact that religious people do not oppose the findings of natural science to-day; and men of science do not attack religion'.[212] In 1926 *The Christian* deplored the foundation of an anti-evolution society in Georgia designed, intriguingly, to banish every teacher in the world who expounded Darwinism.[213] Many Evangelicals had no qualms about evolution.

Certain liberals went further, wishing to remould theology around the new scientific truth. The chief exponent of the need for doctrinal reconstruction in the light of evolution was Canon E. W. Barnes, a mathematician, sometime Fellow of Trinity College, Cambridge, and a Fellow of the Royal Society. He had been brought up to accept evolution as scientific fact, and, lacking ecclesiastical party loyalties, had little regard for Evangelical susceptibilities. Human evolution, he believed, meant steady development. The fall of man, he roundly declared in a sermon at the 1920 British Association meetings, was not a historical event but a parable explaining the origin of sin. Interpretation of biblical passages like the Genesis account of the fall, he explained in a subsequent sermon, must be revised in the light of scientific discoveries.[214] Bramwell Booth, who associated evolution with T. H. Huxley and his hostility to the Salvation Army, denounced Barnes's view unsparingly.[215] W. St Clair Tidsall, a supporter of the Bible League, criticised the sermons in two leading articles in *The Record*, and *The Christian* weighed in with the claim that Barnes 'not only surrenders the Fall but with it the doctrine of the vicarious Atonement'.[216] Here was the nub of the objections. It was feared that if humanity was not understood as fallen, there was no need for redemption. The Evangelical panorama of salvation was at risk. Barnes's critics were not so much defending the text of scripture as perceiving the thin end of a theological wedge. Evolution was not condemned outright. The first of a series of articles dealing with the subject in *The Christian* distinguished sharply between creative evolution, the validity of which was left to Barnes and his fellow-scientists, and moral evolution, the idea that human character makes progress over time.[217] Nevertheless, the 'monkey sermons' had made Barnes a symbolic figure, a champion of modern thought. Progressive Evangelicals eagerly co-opted him into the team that wrote *Liberal Evangelicalism* and had him address the AEGM.[218] Conservatives vigorously denounced his appointment as Bishop of Birmingham in 1924.[219] Barnes provoked a novel degree of polarisation on evolution.

After 1920 the undercurrent of popular hostility to evolution surfaced more frequently. Some conservatives were careful to go no further than a general wariness of evolutionary theory. It was still, according to Samuel Chadwick of the Methodist holiness tradition, no more than a hypothesis.[220] Others were far less reserved. Harold Morton of the Wesley Bible Union obtained an MA from the Intercollegiate University of Britain and America for a thesis published as *The Bankruptcy of Evolution*.[221] The Union's *Journal* was the periodical most committed in the 1920s to the anti-evolution cause, but the new antagonism spread to others. It was the opinion of a leading conservative Evangelical Anglican in 1933 that 'our Lord's personality, by its uniqueness, thrust evolution on to the dust-heap'.[222] Basil Atkinson, a Cambridge librarian and a rather eccentric champion of most conservative Evangelical causes, put forward a more popular apologetic line. 'The polar bear', he observed, 'has small hairs on its feet which prevent it from slipping on the ice. How could they have possibly evolved?'[223] He also insisted that no species had been known to pass over the border into another.[224] The contention that there was a missing link in the evolutionary chain separating humanity from the animal kingdom was frequently heard.[225] A small group including Basil Atkinson set up in 1935 an Evolution Protest Movement. Its figurehead was Sir Ambrose Fleming, Professor of Electrical Engineering at University College, London, and author of a number of anti-evolution books, and it set about corresponding with the Board of Education and the BBC about official endorsements of Darwinism.[226] That it existed is evidence for an element of anti-evolutionary thinking in conservative Evangelicalism; that it remained small is evidence for the weakness of the cause, even among conservatives.

THE USE OF LEISURE

Divergence between liberals and conservatives extended to the question of leisure. Wherever the influence of Keswick was felt, there was a tendency to reduce the circle of permitted activities. 'God was calling them', it was said at the 1930 convention, 'to an utter separation from everything that was questionable.'[227] Novelties such as the wireless were particularly suspect. Undesirable plays and operas were broadcast; there was little distinctive about Sunday programmes; and listening-in wasted time. On the other hand it was a blessing to the bed-ridden. 'Speaking generally', said one mediating contributor to a spirited debate in the weekly associated with Keswick, 'syncopated music, and programmes labelled "variety", are usually items that may well be excluded by the child of God, but much of the music of the old masters broadcast is sweet and ennobling . . . '[228] Cinema created wider differences. A contributor to *The British Weekly* reported in 1921 that news coverage had improved and the long 'film-story' had become customary. There was no hint of criticism, except that American films had virtually displaced domestic products.[229] To others, however, the cinema was simply a more alluring form of the theatre. Conservatives let loose a tirade of invective. There should be a crusade against 'nasty pictures in picturedromes'. The people should not be evangelised by Christian films, because the cinema is 'one of the devil's chief agencies for keeping them away from the Cross'. 'In many districts the cinema is synonymous with sin . . .'[230] Evangelicals divided between those who gave a discriminating welcome to new agencies of popular culture and those who viewed them with horror.

'Many look with dismay', commented a rather smug Brethren observer, 'upon young people flocking to the Theatre, Picture Palaces, and other places of amusement, yet at the same time are associated with the same *in miniature* in Churches and Chapels.'[231] No popular entertainments might sully the purity of a Brethren assembly, but it is true that they were becoming common on other church premises. The attempt to grapple with declining attendances by providing what the people wanted had gathered force with the years.[232] The First World War accelerated the trend. Returning troops demanded the use of premises for the dancing and other entertainments they had grown to expect on active service.[233] Since 'lads and lasses will want to meet each other while the world lasts', according to the magazine of the Church of Scotland, it was good that the church, rather than the streets or the picture houses, should provide their 'opportunities for harmless pleasure'.[234] Regular members of congregations, furthermore, wanted to use church facilities for their recreation. South London churches between the wars provided facilities for tennis, badminton and athletics, discussion, singing and drama, though churches in the Evangelical tradition normally drew the line at the whist drives promoted elsewhere.[235] There was always the evangelistic motive to supply justification. At mission services in the Brighouse United Methodist circuit, 'One pleasing feature has been the number of converts from the football teams associated with the three churches'.[236] Even churches in the Keswick orbit were advised that church sports clubs were appropriate if the aim was right.[237] Church-sponsored recreation was common across a broad Evangelical spectrum.

Yet worries were abroad. In 1912 H. C. Morton, later of the Wesley Bible Union, saw the decline in Methodist membership as a consequence of giving the young people amusements rather than training them in main church activities.[238] By 1935 a triumph had been won by the grumblers at denominational level, for the Methodist Conference passed a resolution against dramatic entertainment on church premises not in accordance with the spiritual life of the church.[239] For the tighter sects dancing was anathema and sport irrelevant.[240] Similar attitudes were promulgated by Advent Testimony. 'Antics of various kinds, such as smoking, drinking, dancing, theatricals, etc.', the vain efforts to fill the churches, were contrasted with the 'faithful preaching of the word', which alone brought people to Christ.[241] Most disturbingly, the worldliness of bazaars, concerts, clubs and billiards was ousting prayer. For about twenty years, it was said in 1932, weekly prayer meetings had become rare in Methodism. In nine months of regular preaching, a missionary deputation speaker had to announce only two week-night prayer meetings.[242] 'Restore the Prayer Meeting!', urged a *Life of Faith* leading article in 1926.[243] One method of recovering a spiritual atmosphere was to exclude the fun of entertainment from the duty of Christian giving. At Toxteth Tabernacle, Liverpool, for example, 'No bazaars, concerts, or other questionable methods of raising funds are countenanced.'[244] The same attitude, assisted by Keswick's influence and favourable treasurer's reports, spread through many Evangelical Anglican congregations during the 1930s.[245] Conservative opinion increasingly understood the world in dualistic terms. Entertainment was of the darkness, not of the light.

Darkest of all, in the eyes of many, was recreation that desecrated the sabbath. The Presbyterian churches appealed in 1919 to the people of Scotland for the observance of the weekly day of rest,[246] and in general sabbatarianism was stronger north of the border. Evangelicals throughout Britain, however, normally remained strict, refusing to take a Sunday newspaper ('the worst of all secularising influences').[247] The churches themselves deplored the decision of the London County Council in 1922 to open public parks for games on Sundays,[248] but it was the Lord's Day

Observance Society that led the battle against infringements of the sabbath. It protested against a Sunday evening radio debate between Bernard Shaw and Miss Madeleine Carroll on 'sex-appeal in cinematograph films' and achieved some minor successes like the suppression of a rodeo at the White City Stadium.[249] Divergence came over Sunday cinema opening. The Lord's Day Observance Society, supported by bodies such as the Evangelical Alliance, resisted a Sunday Entertainments Bill designed to legalise the showing of films.[250] The Council of Christian Churches on Social Questions, however, had declared in favour of localities being able to decide for or against Sunday opening, and the bill passed into law with that provision.[251] The liberal Evangelical Bishop of Croydon, E. S. Woods, gained a certain fame – which was notoriety among Evangelicals – by supporting Sunday opening locally, and was soon chairing a committee that selected films for showing on Sunday evenings.[252] He was almost alone in public advocacy of breaking with this Evangelical shibboleth, but there were other signs of greater flexibility on the question among the more progressive. One Bradford Wesleyan minister held that Christ intended much more latitude than the Old Testament on sabbath observance, and another that there would have to be give and take on its enforcement.[253] If sabbatarianism was still general, it was becoming more diluted in some quarters.

THE SOCIAL GOSPEL

A further cause of division among interwar Evangelicals lay in different attitudes to social reform. Many of the more conservative believed that liberals had turned aside from the true gospel to a 'social gospel'.[254] The impression was given at the time, and has often persisted down to the present, that the social gospel was an alternative to the Evangelical approach, an attempt to change human beings by transforming their environment rather than by touching their hearts. In reality, however, the social gospel was grounded in Evangelicalism. It was an application of the crusading style of reform (discussed in Chapter 4) to society overall. Sin was diagnosed in social structures, which therefore must be remodelled. Occasional social gospellers, such as the Congregationalist Fleming Williams, did profess to have abandoned (as he put it) 'theological metaphysics' for the sake of 'altering the condition of things', but men who thus departed from Evangelical belief were rare.[255] Scott Matheson, the United Presbyterian author of *The Church and Social Problems* (1893), was adamant in his priorities. 'Social reform', he declared, 'ought never to draw the Church aside from her proper work of saving men.'[256] Campbell Morgan, known for his biblical exposition at Westminster Chapel, was quite prepared to devote a sermon on the eve of a London County Council election in 1919 to the need for the regulation of the drainage, atmosphere, smoke and traffic of the capital.[257] For the generation of Scottish and Nonconformist ministers at the height of their powers between the early 1890s and about 1920 a combination of social concern and evangelistic zeal came naturally.

The social gospel was generated primarily by practical experience of Christian work. It was a response to the difficulties of mission, particularly in the cities. Thus Hugh Price Hughes, its leading Methodist exponent, argued that 'evangelistic work has been too exclusively individualistic . . . we must do our utmost to promote the social welfare of the people'.[258] Likewise, Richard Mudie-Smith, a Baptist deacon and social investigator, contended that the gospel must affect the environment. 'If cleaner streets, better housing, sweeter homes do not come within the scope of our aim', he wrote, 'neither will those who are convinced that they have a right to these things come within the shadow of our places of worship.'[259] The social gospel was an evangelistic strategy for reaching the working classes. Intellectual influences naturally played a part in its formation too. The theology of F. D. Maurice stirred some to contemplate the divine pattern for the nation.[260] The teaching of T. H. Green and other idealist philosophers that the state has a duty to promote the moral development of its members had some effect.[261] Social Darwinism and the Romantic critique of industrialism in John Ruskin and William Morris, powerful intellectual currents of the time, swept along many in the Nonconformist ministry.[262] The challenge, real and imaginary, of revolutionary socialism also stirred greater attention to the welfare of the masses. 'There are two alternatives before us to-day', announced Hughes in 1887, '– Christianity or revolution.'[263] John Clifford, the other leading exponent of a Christian message for society, was taking up a phrase from *The Communist Manifesto* when in 1888 he launched the 'social gospel' as a campaigning slogan in an address to the Baptist Union.[264] The movement therefore represented a broadening of the horizons of Nonconformists, but it did not cut them off from their Evangelical roots.

An equivalent tendency existed among Evangelicals in the Church of England, but it remained weak. The participation of Evangelicals in the Christian Social Union, the Anglican body that took up social questions, was largely nominal: a few bishops and other dignitaries acted as presidents and vice-presidents of branches.[265] The predominant attitude, expressed in an editorial in *The Record* in 1904, was that social conditions might be important, but that conversion was the great remedy: 'surroundings will not save a soul'.[266] Few criticisms of the social structure, to which most were firmly wedded, entered their minds. Attitudes nevertheless partially altered during the first decade of the twentieth century, an unavoidable consequence of the greater attention paid by the public at large to social questions. An address on pastoral work by Denton Thompson to the Islington Clerical Meeting in 1898 had been fairly narrow in scope, but on the same subject in 1910 he gave much of his space to social problems.[267]

At Islington in 1913 Guy Rogers, a leading spirit of liberal Evangelicalism, cited Maurice's condemnation of capitalist competition with approval and looked forward to a more even distribution of wealth.[268] Most prominent among Evangelical Anglicans committed to social reform was J. E. Watts-Ditchfield, first Bishop of Chelmsford from 1914. Organised labour and organised Christianity, he contended in 1918, must combine to end preventible poverty, and his political sympathies had long been with Labour.[269] Significantly, however, Watts-Ditchfield's background was in Lancashire Wesleyanism, and he was ordained an Anglican clergyman only when the door to the Methodist ministry was closed.[270] When, in 1908, the Islington Clerical Meeting was devoted to social problems, it is equally significant that some of the speakers had to be drawn from outside the Evangelicals' ranks: George Lansbury, the Labour politician from Poplar, and A. J. Carlyle, Secretary of the Christian Social Union.[271] After Islington, correspondents of *The Record* expressed rank-and-file opinion: 'A Country Incumbent'asked why the clergy should take more interest now, when conditions were better, than they had in social questions twenty years ago; another opposed the stance of the Islington speakers, fearing that the church was being duped by the enemy of God into alliances inimical to Christianity.[272] The social gospel was not for them.

In the interwar years liberal Evangelicals in all denominations commonly believed that concern with social questions was a dimension of Christian mission. In a manifesto of 'Neo-Evangelicalism' in 1921, Frank Mellows, Vicar of Sparkhill, declared that its adherents preached a social as well as an individual gospel, attacking the evils of bad housing, inadequate wages and commercial tyranny as frequently as personal ones.[273] In Congregationalism, the venerable A. E. Garvie, Principal of Hackney and New College, took a leading part in interdenominational discussion of social issues, published a treatise on *The Christian Ideal for Human Society* (1930) and issued the more popular *Can Christ save Society?* (1933).[274] Methodism regularly made official pronouncements on social questions.[275] The Church of Scotland was responsible for an impressive array of institutions for orphans, the destitute and the elderly.[276] Yet even among the more liberal there was a tendency to withdraw somewhat from the vanguard of reform. The Methodist George Jackson believed that Christianity has social implications, but felt that the church should work at a deeper level than creating programmes for change. It should provide 'not so much the machinery of social reform as the spiritual driving power without which the best machinery is no better than so much scrap iron'.[277] Neither the Fellowship of the Kingdom nor the AEGM was forward with schemes of reconstruction. The initiative passed from the Nonconformist Conscience of prewar days to the Anglican heavyweights, Charles Gore, William Temple and R. H. Tawney. The Industrial Christian Fellowship, a drastic remodelling of the Christian Social Union, had the support of a number of Evangelicals including Guy Rogers, but they were overshadowed by others.[278] Evangelicals in general were keeping their distance from the pressing domestic public issues of the day.

The tendency to withdrawal was most marked among Evangelicals of a more conservative stamp. Anglicans of the Keswick school, by and large, needed little convincing that social reform lay beyond their province. The process of change was therefore more evident outside the Church of England. The Salvation Army was exceptional in remaining institutionally committed to a wide variety of social ministries.[279] Other bodies of conservative doctrinal inclinations shifted towards a more conservative stance on social questions. COPEC, the Conference on Politics, Economics and Citizenship promoted by Temple in 1924, attracted the sympathy of some conservative Evangelicals, but no general enthusiasm.[280] Instead they concentrated on questions which, unlike industrial relations or housing, could be analysed in terms of personal responsibility. In addition to the Sunday question, drunkenness and gambling were the great bugbears. The temperance campaign of Nonconformity was sustained after the war even in conservative circles. 'Alcohol', stated *The Journal of the Wesley Bible Union* unequivocally, 'is wholly evil when used as a beverage.'[281] The chief official Baptist social concern was about intemperance.[282] The Brethren were almost solidly teetotal, and some were even prepared to take political action, shunned by others in the sect, for the sake of putting down the drink scourge.[283] Gambling was also loudly condemned. Greyhound racing and football pools were the prime targets of censure.[284] Voices were occasionally raised on behalf of the unemployed,[285] but the trend among conservatives to deal with moral questions rather than broader social problems was a feature of the times. There was in Britain, just as there was in the United States, what has been called 'the great reversal':[286] a repudiation by Evangelicals of their earlier engagement with social issues.

THE GREAT REVERSAL

Why did a great reversal take place? One reason was a disenchantment with politics. Nonconformity had been highly politicised in the later nineteenth century. Its identification with the Liberal Party was never closer than at the 1906 election, when anger at a Conservative Education Act led to an unprecedented degree of electioneering by Nonconformist leaders. Disappointment followed. The Liberals, despite a huge Commons majority, failed to repeal the Education Act. Chapel membership began to fall, and some blamed the loss of spiritual power on over-absorption in public affairs. While Nonconformity 'has been making numerous and ardent politicians', it was complained, 'it has made scarce any saints'.[287] There was, furthermore, a growing trend for the most opulent and the most anti-Catholic among the Nonconformists to go over to the Conservative side.[288] Hence by the time of the 1910 elections many Free Church leaders became wary of close identification with Liberalism. The trend was encouraged by a parallel sense on the other side of the ecclesiastical divide that partisanship decreased the spiritual influence of the clergy.[289] The revulsion from politics was for many a distancing from social reform. 'Our fathers', commented *The Methodist Recorder* in 1912, 'were much more concerned about the glory of God and the dishonour done to him than about any social problems.' They dwelt on people's sins, not their rights. This was the spirit of the New Testament.[290] The recoil from politics was noticed and welcomed north of the border.[291] The process was nearly complete before the First World War, so that the accepted wisdom in the Free Churches in the 1920s was to keep political clamour at arm's length. 'It is not the business of the Christian Church to initiate legislation', stated a pamphlet issued by the Fellowship of the Kingdom, 'but it is the function of those who would follow Jesus to educate public opinion . . .'[292]

The eclipse of the social gospel is also partly explained by the belief that it was socialist. There was in fact no equivalence between the two. Hugh Price Hughes offered a social analysis that, when stripped of its bombastic rhetoric, was quite traditional. At a period when it was beginning to be recognised that poverty was more often the result of low pay and irregular work than of personal irresponsibility, Hughes still attributed it to laziness or vice.[293] Clifford, by contrast, was the leader of a short-lived Christian Socialist League in the mid-1890s[294] and wrote two Fabian tracts, *Socialism and the Teaching of Christ* (1897) and *Socialism and the Churches* (1908). From 1907 the Wesleyan J. E. Rattenbury attracted crowds to the West London Mission to hear denunciations of capitalist wrongs mingled with gospel addresses.[295] Socialism made most headway among the Wesleyans. By 1909 sixty-five of their ministers were members of a socialist Sigma Club led by S. E. Keeble, the author of *Industrial Day-Dreams* (1896).[296] Alarm was sufficient to bring about the creation of a Nonconformist Anti-Socialistic Union in 1909. It received little Free Church support, however, and a year later it had turned into an Anti-Socialist Union of Churches with Anglicans as the main speakers.[297] One of their number, Prebendary Webb-Peploe, represented the strong hostility to socialism that was the normal stance of Anglican Evangelicals.[298] It savoured too much of revolution, atheism and the subversion of the family to appear compatible with Christianity. The turbulence of the war, the Russian Revolution and the aftermaths of both made many Nonconformists more cautious. Clifford's own successor at Westbourne Park Baptist Church, Paddington, preaching in 1921, denounced materialistic demands for a social utopia that entailed the downgrading of religion.[299] Industrial unrest served to illustrate 'the subtle influence of Socialism, syndicalism and Atheism, helped . . . by funds from Moscow and elsewhere . . .'[300] The 'red scare' so widespread in the early 1920s made many feel that tampering with the social order was inopportune.

There were theological worries about the social gospel as well. It could seem over-optimistic about the possibilities of perfecting the human condition. Hughes, in fact, was swayed both by the Wesleyan tradition and by the Brighton holiness convention of 1875 towards the belief that human beings need not sin. Hence it was possible to anticipate a day 'when justice and love and peace will reign with unchallenged supremacy in every land; and when men will literally do the will of God on earth as angels do it in heaven'.[301] Although Clifford was influenced by the socialist contention that human beings are moulded by the conditions of their environment, he was careful to insist that outward changes could not do all for humanity. According to Jesus, he explained, 'the inward is chief'.[302] Critics remained unconvinced by such reservations. It was folly, declared a Wesleyan before the First World War, to expect a better social fabric 'if human nature is to remain what it is'.[303] The social gospel seemed to treat conversion as superfluous. 'It treated man', declared the conservative Evangelical Prebendary A. W. Gough in 1925, 'as one whose life could be made right by the putting right of his circumstances, by the reordering of society, by the pulling down of the existing structure and the setting up of something else.'[304] Conversion, on the other hand, was 'a short cut to social reform'.[305] Once a person was regenerate, relations with others would be changed. Some good might come from COPEC, admitted the editor of *The Life of Faith*, but 'we do not regret being old-fashioned enough to believe that when once the human heart gets right with God, everything else falls into line'.[306] It followed that Christian effort must be directed into evangelism rather than social reform.

The most resounding condemnations of the social gospel came from those with a sharper theological axe to grind. High hopes of reform, it was argued, were bound up with a false eschatology. Social gospellers, in the broadening postmillennialist tradition, expected the kingdom of God to be realised on earth by the steady advance of Christian values. Thus the vision of the perfected City of God in the Book of Revelation, according to Hughes, would be realised at Charing Cross.[307] The key to the teaching of Jesus, according to Clifford, is the kingdom of God, which is to be identified with the divine will for the social order.[308] The growing premillennialist school, however, rejected such ideas out of hand. It looked for a king, not a kingdom. Only with the return of Christ would human affairs be put right. The dominance of premillennialism among Anglican Evangelicals goes a long way towards explaining their immunity to the appeal of the social gospel before the First World War. The spread of popular adventism from the end of the war was heavily responsible for the retreat of non-Anglicans from social involvement. In its initial manifesto, the Advent Testimony Movement asserted that 'all human schemes of reconstruction must be subsidiary to the Second Coming of our Lord, because all nations will then be subject to His rule'.[309] E. L. Langston, a leading Anglican premillennialist, elaborated a critique of COPEC on precisely this basis.[310] Even efforts for international harmony now seemed futile. The Congregational Union autumn assembly of 1923 declared its faith in the League of Nations as the only way of securing peace. 'Students of the Word of God', growled the editor of *The Advent Witness*, 'have come to a different conclusion, for, is it not said that when the league of ten kings (Rev. xvii.12) is formed, their one all-absorbing and united aim will be to *make war with Christ*?'[311] Premillennialists distrusted the League. The advent hope supplanted all other Christian hopes for the future. Wherever it was held it ensured that the ideological gap between liberal and conservative Evangelicals was a yawning gulf.

FUNDAMENTALIST CONTROVERSIES

The strains within Evangelicalism snapped in a series of crises between 1913 and 1928. Although the various mutual suspicions that have been enumerated entered into the debates, the central issue in each case was the infallibility of scripture. Conservatives believed that loyalty to the Bible itself was under threat. The first crisis contained echoes of the New Theology controversy, which had been settled only a couple of years before, but it was different in kind.[312] Whereas R. J. Campbell had put himself outside the Evangelical school, the battle surrounding George Jackson in 1913 was over the future direction of Evangelicalism within the Wesleyan denomination. Were higher critical views acceptable? In 1912 Jackson was designated to occupy a chair at Didsbury College, Manchester, one of the four Wesleyan theological colleges, but in the same year he delivered a lecture that was expanded for publication as *The Preacher and the Modern Mind*. With the needs of educated young people in mind, he held that biblical criticism must be respected. Stiff opposition to the confirmation of his appointment gathered force just before the Wesleyan Conference of 1913. With masterly skill, Jackson convinced conference that his views on the Bible were by no means radical or extreme. A committee report exonerating his book from a charge of doctrinal unsoundness was accepted by 336 votes to 27. He took up office. That, however, did not end the debate. Jackson's opponents joined together as the Wesley Bible Union, issued a monthly journal and entered on a struggle to persuade conference to eliminate alleged heresy from the connexion. Their efforts were fruitless. The chief effect was to ensure that the conservative cause in Methodism was branded as the obsession of a few ill-tempered fanatics. The virulence of the Wesley Bible Union was counter-productive.[313]

Better known is the controversy of 1922 in the Church Missionary Society (CMS), 'the barometer of the Evangelical party'.[314] Some of its missionaries in Bengal expressed publicly their disquiet at the spread of higher critical views as early as 1907.[315] Conflict broke out when, in 1917, a party of the liberally inclined memorialised the CMS committee to tolerate candidates with broader opinions on topics including biblical research. The more conservative were outraged. Prebendary H. E. Fox, a former Secretary of the CMS and the President of the Bible League, took decisive action. At his instigation a counter-memorial was organised and partly through his pressure, a concordat was reached laying down belief in revelation, inspiration and the authority of scripture as essential in candidates.[316] It was Fox who demanded an explanation from a Hong Kong CMS missionary who in 1919 spoke of the Old Testament stories as myths; and it was Fox who called for action in solidarity with the Bible Union of China formed by conservative missionaries. 'Are we to sit still and do nothing?' he asked. 'Is respect for the Society to keep us silent, while its agents are preaching and teaching doctrines altogether inconsistent with those on which it was founded?'[317] Behind the CMS dispute lay the combative vigour of the Bible League.

Affairs came to a head following an address on the Old Testament at a CMS summer school in 1921. The earlier concordat, according to the conservatives, was not being observed. Their campaign was co-ordinated by D. H. C. Bartlett, Vicar of St Luke's, Hampstead, who acted as Secretary of the Fellowship of Evangelical Churchmen (FEC), a body formed in the wake of the 1917–18 debate.[318] At the December general committee meeting of the CMS, the subject of the summer school address was raised by S. H. Gladstone, treasurer of the society and president of the FEC, but inconclusively.[319] At the March general committee, Bartlett proposed a motion endorsing the authority of scripture, but action was deferred until after a private consultative conference of Evangelical leaders at Coleshill in June. The general committee reconvened for a trial of strength in July. Because membership was open to any clerical supporters, there were 614 recorded attenders. An amendment that CMS agents need adhere only to the Nicene Creed and article VI of the Church of England was followed by a compromise amendment suggested by a team of bishops. Although it was carried, Fox, Bartlett, Gladstone and their circle felt it was insufficiently firm on Christ's endorsement of scriptural authority. After consulting members of the FEC, they determined to set up an alternative to the CMS, which was dubbed The Bible Churchmen's Missionary Society (BCMS). A CMS sub-committee, followed by another committee meeting, failed to heal the breach. By March 1923 seventy-eight clergy had resigned their membership of the CMS and thirty remained undecided.[320] By its fourth anniversary in 1926 the BCMS had ninety missionaries and ten paid home staff.[321] The rift had the effect of weakening the conservative influence in the original society, but the BCMS, unlike the Wesley Bible Union, pursued a steady course of constructive work. Several redoubtable champions of a high view of the Bible, including E. L. Langston and G. T. Manley, remained with the CMS. The schism was caused by biblical conservatives, but the split it created was not straightforwardly between conservatives and liberals. The division was within the conservative ranks.

Controversy had already rocked the Keswick Convention, another seasoned Evangelical vessel. Evan Hopkins, the prophet of sound doctrine at

Keswick, died early in 1919.[322] In the same year Bishop Watts-Ditchfield, a believer in the annihilation rather than the punishment of the wicked after death and so suspect in more stringent quarters, was a speaker at Keswick, and Cyril Bardsley and H. L. C. V. de Candole, both broadening Anglicans, had already been on its platform.[323] So it seemed reasonable for R. T. Howard, Principal of St Aidan's College, Birkenhead, and a leading light of the body soon to become the AEGM, to give an address in which he dwelt on the presence of God at all times, in all places and in everything. A member of the audience rose indignantly to question whether so pantheistic a talk was in accordance with the word of God; the Keswick council declined to publish an account of it; and it was soon assailed in a pamphlet as being little different from R. J. Campbell's New Theology.[324] The pamphlet's writer, James Mountain, was a Keswick veteran in his late seventies who had been in the movement from its inception, a Baptist who had been Minister of St John's Free Church, Tunbridge Wells, and a man of strong, if changeable, opinions.[325] Casting himself as a Mr Valiant-for-Truth, he led a band of folk from in and about Tunbridge Wells who were disgusted by the declension of the times. 'Shall the floods of German criticism', he asked, 'overwhelm the ripened fields of Keswick Truth, even as the hordes of German Huns overran the stricken fields of Belgium?'[326] He was particularly persistent in his hounding of Charles Brown and F. C. Spurr, two Baptists who also spoke at the 1920 Keswick, on the grounds that they had previously toyed with higher critical views.[327] It was an acrimonious affair that subsided only when Mountain turned his attention elsewhere.

While the consequences of Mountain's charges rumbled on, the ex-Chairman of the Keswick council and son of the convention's founder, John Battersby Harford, went into print in defence of critical views of the Old Testament entertained by Herbert Ryle, Dean of Westminster. D. F. Douglas-Jones, a retired colonel from Worthing and a Vice-President of the Bible League, was roused to ire, demanding that the other members of the council should dissociate themselves from such opinions.[328] An alarmed council did so, although pressure – from the Liverpool Keswick auxiliary, for instance – that Battersby Harford should resign from the council was ignored.[329] 'In view of the present unsettlement in respect of religious belief', announced the council, 'we are impressed with the necessity of maintaining the Keswick tradition of closest possible loyalty to the Word of God as the fully inspired and authoritative revelation of His Will, in all the ministry of the platform.'[330] There was to be a further crisis in the affairs of Keswick in 1928, when Stuart Holden was eased out of the chair after he and the council had been charged by *The Life of Faith* with going Modernist. That incident, however, was a response to Holden's proposal to sever the semi-official relation between *The Life of Faith* and the convention, and a reaction against his excessive personal dominance of the movement.[331] There was no chance by that stage of Keswick being lost to the conservatives. Indeed there never had been. In 1920–1 what happened was that the boundaries of Keswick were defined so as to exclude a more advanced section of Evangelical opinion than had hitherto been tolerated. Keswick perceptibly narrowed so as to become a rallying ground for conservatives, although conservatives of many shades. The characteristic noise of Keswick was still what was heard by listeners to a broadcast service in 1933: 'the sound of the rustling of the Bible leaves'.[332]

There were other jarrings. A proposal for the merging of Nonconformists into a Free Church Federation in 1919 was what first prompted James Mountain into militancy. It was feared that the Federation would adopt an inadequate creed and would lead on to incorporation with Anglican sacerdotalism.[333] Accordingly Mountain launched a Baptist Bible Union, which was to be his power-base for half a dozen years. In 1922 a body of the same title was to be formed in America that was eventually to emerge as a separate denomination.[334] Mountain's organisation showed similar tendencies. In 1923 it was reconstructed as a Bible Baptist Union to which churches could affiliate. If apostasy spread, it was to be the basis of 'an out-and-out Biblical Church'.[335] The precipitating factor leading to this development was the election of T. R. Glover, a Cambridge scholar and supporter of SCM, to be Vice-President of the Baptist Union in 1923. Glover was best known for his weekly religious column in *The Daily News*, in which, according to a Bible League speaker, he wrote, 'with flippant humour and half-contemptuous comment, on the Holy Scriptures'.[336] The election began a spillage of churches out of the Union that Mountain hoped to mop up. The scheme, however, rapidly fell apart, and in 1925 the organisation, by a fresh mutation, became the undenominational Believers' Bible Union.[337] A parallel attempt to create a Missionary Trust for supporting sound missionaries also collapsed.[338] Better piloted was the plan of E. J. Poole-Connor for a link between various undenominational mission halls and churches leaving their denominations. Begun in 1922, this project became the Fellowship of Independent Evangelical Churches, which was steadily to expand.[339] Disagreements also racked the Churches of Christ, among whom Modernism was scented at the new Overdale College between 1923 and 1927, and the Calvinistic Methodists of Wales, among whom Tom Nefyn Williams criticised received views in 1927 in a way more reminiscent of R. J. Campbell than of recent upsets.[340] The Baptists were again disturbed in 1932 by dispute about a booklet issued by Glover, in which he questioned the substitutionary nature of the atonement.[341] Britain was by no means immune to Fundamentalist controversies.

MODERATION

'There is no doubt', declared *The Life of Faith* in 1925, 'that the divergence between what are known, on the one hand, as the Fundamentalists, and, on the other, as the Modernists, exceeds, in the United States, anything known in this country . . .'[342] Although conservatives and liberals did pull in opposite directions in Britain, acrimony was less widespread and less drastic in its consequences than in America. With the exception of the CMS rift, controversies were contained. One explanation for the relatively moderate tone of debate is the institutional framework within which Evangelicals operated. It is true that the theological colleges tended to fragment the Evangelical school in the Church of England, with Ridley Hall leading the way in a liberal direction and, in 1929, only St John's, Highbury, and the BCMS College in Bristol receiving the approval of *The Fundamentalist*.[343] Yet all types met at the annual Islington Conference, where conservative and liberal speakers were often deliberately balanced. Although certain of the local clerical meetings fell into the hands of one grouping or another, they sometimes provided further common ground. The Evangelical Candidates' Ordination Council, established in 1925 to increase the supply of clergy, reflected every shade of opinion within the party.[344] There was similar diversity at the annual Conference of Evangelical Churchmen begun at Cheltenham in 1916 and moved to Oxford in 1929.[345] Its chairman at Oxford, Christopher Chavasse, used his prestige as first Master of St Peter's Hall, an Evangelical foundation, to keep the party united. Like certain others, he consciously adopted a centrist position. At an interdenominational level the Evangelical Alliance likewise tended to consolidate the tradition. At its conferences in the early 1920s eminent Fundamentalists, centrists and progressives spoke together in defence of the gospel. Among the centrists were J. D. Jones, the statesmanlike figure who helped hold Congregationalism together, and M. E. Aubrey, who, as Secretary of the Baptist Union from 1925, was to oppose tendencies to fissiparity.[346] Spurgeon's College, the one Nonconformist theological institution approved by *The Fundamentalist*, was steered back into Baptist denominational life by its principal, P. W. Evans.[347] The circuit system of Methodism meant that it was rarely possible for a congregation to build up an ethos widely different from the denominational norm. In Scottish Presbyterianism a conservative like Alexander Frazer of Tain frowned on anything other than full involvement in the life of the Kirk.[348] Denominational allegiance was a powerful brake on divergence.

In general, the Protestant cause had a similar effect. Anti-Catholicism still aroused powerful emotions in mainland Britain. The threat to the Protestant community in Ireland in the convulsions over Home Rule and independence between 1911 and 1924 tugged at Evangelical heartstrings. The Protestant Truth Society and its 'Wycliffe Preachers' were delighted to fan the flames of sectarian hatred, not least in Liverpool.[349] There was similar populist activity in Scotland during the interwar years.[350] Yet anti-Catholicism was part of the worldview of the most urbane. C. J. Cadoux, a scholarly Oxford Congregationalist and avowed Evangelical Modernist, could be contemptuous about Rome because of her repression of free enquiry.[351] The sustained struggle against the introduction of the

Revised Prayer Book bound together the popular and the educated strands of Protestant passion, eliciting an enormous volume of support. In 1918 a memorial against changes in the communion service was presented to the Archbishop of Canterbury signed by nine bishops, 3,000 clergy and 100,000 laymen.[352] The Church Association sprang into life, holding rallies and trying to co-ordinate political opposition. The National Church League, the result of a merger of smaller Protestant bodies in 1906, concentrated chiefly on issuing literature. The campaign proved victorious when, in December 1927, the House of Commons refused its sanction for the use of the Prayer Book and repeated its decision in the following year. Another bout of railing against Romish practices followed in 1932–3 with the denunciation of celebrations of the centenary of the Oxford Movement. Evangelical Churchmen in successive dioceses went into opposition to any official countenancing of the events.[353] The effect of all this rousing of the latent spirit of Protestant defence is clear. The attempt to turn the Church of England into 'an annexe of Rome', declared *The Record* in 1924, must lead all Evangelicals, whatever adjective they would insert before Evangelical, to make common cause against medievalising obscurantism.[354] In the following year the same newspaper ended a correspondence on the higher criticism because, it said, Evangelicals must unite against the sacerdotal challenge.[355] Notwithstanding the defection of the AEGM in 1927, the tendency of militant Protestantism was to inhibit divisions on other issues.

Another factor that minimised acrimony and schism was the restraint of the conservative Evangelicals as opposed to the Fundamentalists. Graham Scroggie, Minister of Charlotte Baptist Chapel, Edinburgh, was at pains to differentiate between the two. Apart from Modernists and the worldly, he argued, Christians could be divided into Fundamentalists and another class who, though sympathising with Fundamentalists, would not accept the label or 'contend for truth at the expense of charity'.[356] These, the moderate conservatives in the Evangelical range of opinion, included Scroggie and many others who would not reject biblical criticism out of hand. J. Russell Howden, one of the numerous Anglican clergymen in this category, used to distinguish between the right and the wrong kinds of criticism.[357] Likewise the Wesleyan Samuel Chadwick, guardian of the Methodist holiness tradition, believed that biblical criticism could not be ignored.[358] Several of these men – Stuart Holden, F. B. Meyer, Campbell Morgan and Scroggie himself – visited America and returned deploring the damage done to the gospel by raging Fundamentalism.[359] Scroggie insisted that premillennialism, although a tenet he embraced himself, should never become a condition of fellowship in Britain and thought the Apostles' Creed a sufficient declaration of orthodoxy.[360] Whereas in America the premillennial hope was the rallying cry of the Fundamentalists associated with the Bible Institutes, Principal McIntyre of the only fully fledged Bible Institute in Britain (in Glasgow) was not himself a committed premillennialist and, accordingly, his college lost favour with extremists.[361]

When *The Life of Faith* wished to resist the tide of liberalism, its answer was not vituperation but a weekly Bible School article contributed by McIntyre.[362] Of McIntyre it was later complained, 'We could never get him to denounce any one'.[363]

Most tellingly, the moderate conservatives struck at the power base of the militants, the Bible League. Its ex-secretary and editor, A. H. Carter, came back from the United States in 1923 breathing fire and brimstone, determined to imitate the tactics of American Fundamentalists.[364] The moderates pre-empted a fresh Bible League campaign by backing a new Fraternal Union for Bible Testimony. The committee, it was announced, felt strongly that 'it is futile to engage in mere declamation and denunciation, and that error can only be effectively countered by an intelligent and positive presentation of the Evangelical position'.[365] Annual Albert Hall rallies were supplemented by meetings up and down the country. Their organiser, a young Baptist minister named C. T. Cook, deplored the 'poisonous cloud of suspicion' emitted by irresponsible opponents of liberal theology.[366] The out-flanked Bible League vainly pointed to its thirty years of experience in the field, and Carter, on another visit to the United States, contented himself with lashing the Fraternal Union as open to Modernists.[367] The manoeuvre was decisive for the future course of Evangelicalism in Britain: moderates, not Fundamentalists, henceforward held the initiative on the conservative wing.

THE ANATOMY OF CONSERVATIVE EVANGELICALISM

What was the strength of conservative Evangelicalism? Snippets of local news reveal that enthusiasts could gather audiences in many parts of England. An interdenominational committee in Manchester held a convention on 'The Fundamentals of Bible Truth'; a similar convention was held at Uttoxeter, although all its attenders were contained in a garden; at Kingston upon Thames for sixteen days a local pastor conducted a campaign that began with a parade of scripture text carriers through the market square; Walworth Road Baptist Church in London held daily prayer meetings under the banner of the Sound Gospel Movement; and a Liverpool and Merseyside Fundamentals Fellowship held meetings in the 1930s.[368] Yet many of the attenders of these gatherings probably had only the haziest notions of whether their faith demanded vocal defence. A better gauge of commitment is the support for the various societies. The Advent Testimony Movement published a useful breakdown of its 1,103 members in September 1919, rather under two years from its inception; of these, 395 were male, 708 female. Two were bishops, 132 other clergy and ministers, and eighteen were military and naval officers; 367 lived in Greater London and 234 in the Home Counties, which together account for more than half the members.[369] The south coast resorts, perhaps Britain's Bible belt, contributed a particularly large number of supporters.[370] Membership figures were given for the last time in December 1922 – possibly because afterwards they fell – as 2,316.[371] The impression is of a small band of the well-to-do pursuing a good cause. Another body, the Fellowship of Evangelical Churchmen, had about 700 members in 1922 and 1,400 in 1934. In 1924 about ninety assembled for its annual conference.[372] Its supporters felt themselves to be isolated figures.

Neither Advent Testimony nor the FEC, however, were solidly Fundamentalist bodies, for both attracted numbers of the more moderate conservatives. The three most Fundamentalist organisations, enjoying mutual recognition, were the Bible League, the Wesley Bible Union and the Baptist Bible Union. Membership figures are available for none of them. At its height, in 1923–4, the Bible League was holding 330 meetings a year, but that gives little indication of committed support.[373] The Wesley Bible Union could muster only ten or twelve backers for its heresy hunts in the Wesleyan Conference. Although it reported the addition of 1,600 new members during 1930, its strength before that was not large and many of its supporters were elderly.[374] When the Believers' Bible Union, as the Baptist Bible Union had become, was wound up in 1928, a mere 130 subscribers to its magazine transferred, as recommended, to the Wesley Bible Union.[375] It seems clear that organised Fundamentalism in Britain was a weak force.

Financial stringency was both cause and effect of low membership. The collections at Advent Testimony monthly meetings, it was announced by Meyer in 1921, did not cover the costs. 'As believers in the Second Advent', he commented, 'they could not, of course, get into debt.'[376] Mountain's wife paid off the losses on the Believers' Bible Union *Bible Call* in its latter years, and Prebendary Fox enjoyed private means that may well have been channelled into the Bible League.[377] The Wesley Bible Union received a meagre regular income in 1917–18 and 1918–19: £258 and £382 respectively.[378] For a special venture the Union was able to secure promises of £1,000 and £500 from two members of the committee, one of them probably the wealthy businessman and ex-MP R. W. Perks.[379] This venture, however, was not pursued, and substantial sums were hard for any organisation to come by. Sometimes they came with strings attached. For example, £100 was given to the London City Mission to pay for evangelists on condition that they would proclaim 'Advent Truth and Testimony'.[380] The largest donor to Fundamentalist funds may well have been John Bolton, a Leicester manufacturer of children's wear whose advertisements for 'Chilprufe' studded the Evangelical press. His giving was the mainstay of the Baptist Bible Union and it is significant that he was invited to join the committee of the Wesley Bible Union at a time when it was looking for fresh injections of funds.[381] Noting the large gifts made to Fundamentalism in America, Morton complained in 1926 that the great need in England was money.[382] He was right: the contrast in this area goes a long way towards explaining the different trajectories of the Evangelical communities in the two countries. In Britain the extremists were starved of funds.

The conservatives, whether Fundamentalist or moderate, put their energies into a host of causes. The various faith missions provided an outlet for separatist tendencies without disturbing the peace of the existing denominations. Bodies imitating Hudson Taylor's China Inland Mission (1865) had multiplied. Missionaries were despatched without guaranteed stipends, relying in faith on the generosity of the Christian public. Grattan Guinness's Regions Beyond Missionary Union (1872) was followed by the Egypt General Mission (1897), the Sudan United Mission (1903), the Evangelical Union of South America (1911) and many others.[383] Undenominational missionary colleges sprang up to serve them, such as All Nations and Ridgelands. Other Bible colleges, primarily equipping Christians for service at home, also emerged, often ephemerally. One of the permanent institutions was the Bible College of Wales (1924), 'founded on faith and carried on by faith'.[384] There were also conference centres, like Slavanka, opened in Bournemouth in 1921 in connection with the Russian Missionary Society, which was to be the scene of many gatherings of keen Evangelicals.[385]

Other causes channelled their enthusiasms. There was the British Israel Movement, convinced that the ten lost tribes of Israel were to be identified with the Anglo-Saxon race. The esoteric 'science' of pyramidology was a fascinating occupation for leisure hours. It was supposed that the Great Pyramid of Egypt, built as it was by Hebrew slave labour, incorporated in its dimensions a prediction of the fortunes of the British Empire. An astonishing number of Evangelicals gave credence to this peculiar quasi-religious expression of imperial pride. They included James Mountain, Dinsdale Young and the Elim leader George Jeffreys.[386] Anti-semitism also fed on the Fundamentalist fringe. J. J. R. Armitage, a Liverpool incumbent and a British Israelite, was particularly virulent, supporting the driving of Einstein out of Germany because he was a Jew.[387] In a few isolated cases anti-semitism actually blended with fascism. G. H. Woods, a member of the Wesley Bible Union, was also a Divisional Officer of the British Fascists.[388] In general, however, the efforts of the International Hebrew Christian Alliance and sympathisers with the Jewish people minimised the growth of popular anti-semitism.[389] All these causes had the effect of turning conservative Evangelicals away from assaults on their liberal brethren. The diversity of the Evangelical mosaic inhibited the growth of power blocs.

If the liberals had gained the ascendancy in certain areas in the present, the conservatives adopted a grand strategy designed to give them control of the future. Mission to youth was a priority, often the overriding priority. 'Concentrate on young people', said Bishop Taylor Smith, an indefatigable conservative platform speaker, 'they will bring you in the biggest dividends . . .'[390] There were, of course, many long-standing youth organisations. In several cases, such as Christian Endeavour, they trained young people already associated with the churches.[391] The pressing need was now for pioneering evangelism to the unchurched. One of the chief organisations in the field was the Young Life Campaign begun in 1911 by Frederick and Arthur Wood. It specialised in missions for teenagers in towns where members of several churches co-operated. At Nottingham in 1921 there were reports of hundreds of decisions for Christ, more than four hundred new members and a continuing prayer fellowship with nine subsidiary district circles left behind.[392] The Children's Special Service Mission (1867) dealt with a younger age group, particularly through the seaside missions. Its offshoot the Scripture Union (1897) provided daily Bible reading notes for all ages.[393] Varsities and Public School Camps were another branch, catering for potential leaders. Eric Nash, a pertinacious bachelor clergyman always known as 'Bash', devoted himself to implementing his own prayer, 'Lord, we claim the leading public schools for your kingdom'.[394] Other bodies expanded in the interwar years: the undenominational Crusaders' classes (1906), providing camps and weekly Christian instruction for the children of the middle classes; the Covenanters, a rough equivalent normally aiming for a lower social grade and usually linked with the Brethren (1930); the Campaigners (1922), a conservative Evangelical version of Scouting based loosely on the Scottish clan system; and the Boys' Life Brigade (1899), rather less military in ethos than the Boys' Brigade.[395] There was dissatisfaction with other youth movements. Why, it was asked, should the church introduce 'the co-worship of Mars, Diana and the fairies through the formation of Boys' Brigades, Boy Scouts, Wolf Cubs, Girls Guildries, Girl Guides and Brownies'?[396] Organisations for the young had to be single-eyed. That was true also of the Inter-Varsity Fellowship (IVF), a body linking the university Christian Unions that will need further attention. 'To win a student for Christ', an IVF meeting was told in 1934, 'is to win what might be called "a keyman".'[397] That was the essence of the moderate conservatives' response to the defection from the truth, as they saw it, of the liberals in the interwar period. There was little point in denouncing their opponents. The task was to win the next generation for the truth.

THE INTERWAR DIVERGENCE

The disagreements of the interwar period had their roots in the impact of Romantic thought on Evangelicalism. Conservatives might appeal to the facts of common sense and reject the theories of the liberals as speculative,[398] but in reality their views were just as much affected by Romantic currents as those of their opponents. The liberals, on the other hand, might dismiss the ideas of the conservatives as outmoded notions unworthy of consideration by the educated, but the conservatives held their convictions precisely because they were influenced by movements of opinion within the intelligentsia over the previous century or so. If the broadening theology and heightened churchmanship of the progressives owed a debt to Romantic thought and taste, the crucial beliefs in verbal inspiration, the premillennial advent and holiness by faith held by the so-called traditionalists were of the same intellectual provenance. The divergence, however, was not solely a consequence of changing ideas. It also sprang from contrasting reactions to circumstances. How should the churches respond to the growing availability of leisure activities and social benefits and the resultant decline in churchgoing? The liberal formula was to follow the trends of secular society, to provide entertainments and promote reform, to insist on the relevance of the churches to everyday life. Guy Rogers, speaking in 1933, declared 'the Liberal Evangelical was interested in housing, whether cinemas should be opened on Sundays, . . . the perils facing the League of Nations . . . the establishment of a Christian civilisation'. He rejected 'the narrow views of the Gospel which thought of it simply in terms of individual life'.[399] Conservatives, it was true, took some pride in holding to a narrower view of the gospel, refusing to follow contemporary taste and being prepared to go into the wilderness for the sake of truth. Liberals clung to the integration of Evangelical religion with society that was the legacy of the nineteenth century; conservatives changed their approach because they judged society to have moved too far away from Christian values. In one sense, therefore, the liberals were traditionalists and the conservatives were radicals. In any case, from the blend of intellectual and practical influences there emerged alternative strategies: accommodation to the trends of secular society or resistance to them.[400]

Friction between the two parties, however, was less acute than it might have been. Fundamentalist controversies did exist in Britain, but they were storms in a teacup when compared with the blizzards of invective that swept contemporary America. Centrists helped to hold Evangelicalism together with the arguments of institutional loyalty and Protestant defence. Moderate conservatives, such as Russell Howden, Samuel Chadwick and Graham Scroggie, exerted a restraining influence. Energies were channelled into foreign missions and youth evangelism as well as into more recondite causes. Obsessional theories about conspiracies of Jews, Jesuits or Bolsheviks to corrupt civilisation through the spread of picture palaces, subversive literature and the teaching of evolution are to be found in the magazines of the Fundamentalist bodies,[401] but they were effectively marginalised. Those who believed that charity is Laodicaean lukewarmness were not allowed to dominate. Despite the divergence, crises were relatively few. A basic explanation is to be found in the nature of the fissures that appeared. The cleavage between conservatives and liberals was far from absolute. On different issues it was at different places along the Evangelical spectrum. Few believed in biblical inerrancy or opposed Darwinism outright, but many adhered to holiness teaching and retreated from the political implications of the social gospel. There was therefore a broadening continuum of Evangelical opinion in this period, rather than a simple separation into two camps. The denominations can usefully be located on the continuum. The Brethren, among whom there was no thought of a liberal pressure group and no need for a conservative one, were to be found near the Fundamentalist pole, along with several smaller sects. The Baptists, possessing no liberal group but having a conservative Bible Union, came next. The Church of England's Evangelical party, torn between the AEGM and the FEC but also having much centrist opinion, was in the middle. Methodism had an increasingly powerful progressive body, the Fellowship of the Kingdom, together with a weak Bible Union, and so stood marginally nearer the liberal pole. Congregationalism, with no need of a liberal group and no conservative one until after the Second World War, was closer to that point. The Presbyterians of Scotland and the Calvinistic Methodists of Wales were perhaps near the Church of England and Methodism. In many instances differences of opinion within the denominations had become as important as those between them. By the Second World War, Evangelicalism had become much more fragmented than it had been a century before.

[7]

The Spirit Poured Out: Springs of the Charismatic Movement

And it shall come to pass afterward, that I will pour out my spirit upon all flesh (Joel 2:28)

In 1963 charismatic renewal came to Beckenham. George Forester, Vicar of St Paul's, and a group of parishioners received 'the baptism of the Holy Spirit', started speaking in tongues and began to hold weekly fellowship meetings for the exercise of spiritual gifts. Beckenham was one of the first cases to hit the headlines, but elsewhere in the Church of England others had already entered a similar experience.[1] Scotland was also affected. 'Strange new sect in Scottish kirk', reported the Glasgow *Sunday Mail*; the 'sect' was said to observe 'a form of worship bordering on the supernatural'.[2] An unfamiliar phenomenon was springing up. Speaking in tongues, the practice of glossolalia, had hitherto been confined to the Pentecostal tradition, but now there were outbreaks within the mainstream churches. It was not 'inarticulate gibberish', according to one Methodist recipient, but 'a beautiful flow of words' that expressed a sense of joyful praise.[3] Speaking in tongues was the most obvious feature of a movement that was beginning in many parts of the world during the early 1960s. It first received the label 'charismatic' – that is, 'of the gifts of the Spirit' – in the United States in 1962.[4] During the next quarter century it was to become a powerful force in British Christianity.

Its impact was chiefly felt in existing churches. Although from the start Anglo-Catholics were involved and from 1967 there was a renewal movement in the Roman Catholic Church, many recruits came from Evangelicalism. The first charismatic prayer meetings in the Church of England were held by an Evangelical clergyman in Burslem. The first parish to enjoy corporate renewal was St Mark's, Gillingham, served by a vicar who came from the Evangelical citadel of All Souls', Langham Place. The main propagator of renewal in the 1960s and early 1970s was Michael Harper, a curate at All Souls' when he received the baptism in the Spirit in 1963.[5] Renewal gained early footholds in the Revival Fellowships of the Methodists and the Baptists.[6] Harper and his circle, the leading figures in the early stages of the movement, adopted a strategy of permeating existing denominations and so were scrupulous to avoid appearing to rival old structures. The Fountain Trust, set up with Harper as general secretary in 1964 and *Renewal* as its magazine from the following year, had no membership, held no regular London meetings and encouraged people baptised in the Spirit to return to their own congregations. The Trust was to close down in 1980 precisely because it had achieved great success in implanting vigorous renewal movements in each of the main denominations.[7] The spread of renewal was nevertheless a painful business. Tensions between the renewed and the traditionalists in particular congregations arose frequently, especially over the conduct of worship. At one Methodist church in the North-West, when charismatics raised their arms during a chorus in a characteristic gesture of praise, the preacher stopped the singing to enquire whether they wished to leave the room. Despite subsequent discussions, the charismatics seceded from the congregation.[8] In other instances renewal triumphed and the traditionalists departed. By such adjustments the number of denominational congregations with a charismatic tone steadily increased.

Alongside renewal in the historic denominations there was a dimension of the charismatic movement outside them that is coming to be called Restorationism. Originally known as the 'house churches', because they met for worship in the homes of members, many congregations soon ceased to match their label when they outgrew private houses and so rented or bought more substantial accommodation. Some, like the Methodist group in the North-West, began as breakaway bodies of the charismatics who felt unwelcome in their previous churches. Yet Restorationism antedates renewal. Its origins have been traced to groups of independent Evangelicals, mostly Brethren in background, whose leaders held a series of conferences in Devon from 1958 to consider how to restore the pattern of church life found in the New Testament.[9] They were anti-denominational by conviction. Their ablest spokesman, Arthur Wallis, set out their mature views in *The Radical Christian* (1981), a denunciation of compromise with existing structures. 'The axe', he writes, 'is laid to the root of the tree.'[10] By the mid-1980s there were several categories of Restorationists. The churches led by Bryn Jones and based on Bradford formed probably the largest connexion, publishing *Restoration* magazine, selling Harvestime goods and running Bible Weeks that attracted thousands from 1976. A looser connexion, with Gerald Coates and John Noble as leaders and greater strength in the South-East, organised festivals from 1983.[11] Other connexions, sometimes included in the last category but in fact largely separate, were based on Basingstoke, Aldershot and elsewhere.[12] There were groupings professing distinctive beliefs: churches associated with Wally North held that the new birth differs in time from conversion and is to be identified with baptism in the Spirit and the coming of holiness; churches influenced by South Chard, Somerset, baptised in the name of Jesus only.[13] On the fringe of Restorationism there were other bodies such as the Icthus Fellowship of South London[14] that did not embrace its anti-denominational stance. It was a fluid pattern of rapidly growing congregations.

CHARISMATIC ORIGINS

Charismatics in the Church of England, according to one of their leaders, are best defined as those who have been influenced by classical Pentecostal teaching and practice.[15] The existing Pentecostal churches were undoubtedly a major source of charismatic experience. David du Plessis, a South African Pentecostalist who travelled the world propagating the baptism in the Spirit in the older denominations, made effective ecumenical contacts in Britain from 1959 onwards.[16] Speaking in tongues had spread from British Pentecostalists to isolated individuals in other denominations during the years, and the process seemed to be accelerating in the later 1950s.[17] Several of the early charismatics in the 1960s, including George Forester of Beckenham, received the baptism in the Spirit through the laying on of hands by Pentecostalists.[18] The Full Gospel Business Men's Fellowship International, an American body founded by a Pentecostal layman to organise Christian dinner gatherings, fostered the spread of spiritual gifts by holding a much publicised convention in London in 1965 and by establishing chapters in many parts of the country subsequently. David Wilkerson's *The Cross and the Switchblade* (1963), an account of his ministry as a Pentecostal pastor among New York drug addicts, did much to show the power of the baptism in the Spirit in transforming lives.[19] Restorationism drew some of its inspiration from the Apostolic Church, the Pentecostal body that set out to imitate the full range of church offices mentioned in the New Testament.[20] The charismatic movement owed a substantial debt to classical Pentecostalism.

Nevertheless, a gulf soon opened between the two. The Fountain Trust never invited Pentecostalists to address its meetings for fear of being tainted by their reputation for unwise behaviour.[21] Conversely, Alfred Missen, General Secretary of the Assemblies of God, left a Fountain Trust international conference in 1971 early because he did not feel at one with the participants. Pentecostalists generally were suspicious that the new movement emphasised testimonies at the expense of Bible teaching, compromised with the doctrinal errors of liberals and Roman Catholics and inexplicably failed to swell their own ranks.[22] Charismatics were also virtually unanimous in denying that speaking in tongues is the indispensable first sign of baptism in the Spirit, a position upheld by the Assemblies of God, though not by Elim.[23] There was even disagreement within the new movement about whether the breakthrough to a fresh experience of the Holy Spirit can properly be called 'baptism'. Harper was prepared to drop the term in deference to non-charismatics who argued that all true Christians are baptised in the Spirit.[24] There was a further divergence between charismatics and Pentecostalists about their attitude to receiving the 'baptism'. Traditionally, Pentecostalists had tarried for the experience with careful self-examination for moral shortcomings. It was a sign of their rootedness in the holiness tradition. Charismatics, by contrast, looked for a sudden sense of release rather than for any moral transformation.[25] That was symptomatic of an ethos that stressed immediacy, the human capacity for instant heightened awareness. For all its legacy from Pentecostalism, the charismatic movement had different cultural affinities.

A major influence in the formation of the movement, as part of the Pentecostal evidence has already illustrated, came from the United States. There, an initial centre of charismatic renewal was the Episcopal church of St Mark's, Van Nuys, California, whose rector received the baptism of the Holy Spirit in 1959 through two members of the congregation who had Pentecostal contacts.[26] A journal published by the renewed Episcopalians, *Trinity*, stirred interest in Britain, as did a favourable editorial in *Churchman* for September 1962. Passing visits in the following year by two ministers from California, Frank Maguire, an Episcopalian, and Larry Christenson, a Lutheran, helped establish a charismatic nucleus in London.[27] Subsequently, a steady stream of American literature and personnel did much to expand and consolidate the British movement. The renewal of the congregation at St Margaret's, Aspley, in Nottingham, for instance, was brought about in 1973 through an account of the events at Van Nuys.[28] The teaching of the Restorationists was reinforced between 1975 and 1977 by visits from Ern Baxter, one of the 'Fort Lauderdale Five' who in America asserted the importance of Christians submitting to the authority of apostolic figures.[29] Most significant were the visits in 1984–6 to England and in 1987 to Scotland by John Wimber, the author of *Power Evangelism* (1985). Drawing together denominational charismatics and Restorationists, Wimber proclaimed that signs and wonders were to be expected as agents of church growth.[30] Although a few drew back, his message gave fresh impetus to the charismatic cause in Britain. Repeatedly the new world was called in to bring vision to the old.

The charismatic movement was moulded most powerfully, however, by its context. Young people of the 1960s, in Britain as in America, were turning in large numbers to a counter-culture, the world of hippies and drop-outs, drugs and flower power. 'Make love not war' was the slogan of the day. In most aspects of the counter-culture, such as pop art or rock music, there was a deliberate violation of 'good taste'. Although in the 1970s these tendencies were contained, they were not reversed. Rather what had been fringe concerns became pervasive, the attitudes of the counter-culture rapidly infiltrating the social mainstream. The new stance was in revolt against a technocratic society dominated by scientific rationality. The traditional, the institutional, the bureaucratic were rejected for the sake of individual self-expression and idealised community. Religiosity, particularly with an oriental flavour, played its part in the revolt.[31] The official report on *The Charismatic Movement in the Church of England* (1981) pointed out that the rise of the counter-culture and of the charismatic movement were simultaneous. It diagnosed the movement as 'a form of Christianised existentialism'.[32] Just as the poet Allen Ginsberg explored the Eastern way of allowing his voice to utter sounds beyond his conscious direction, so the hallmark of the charismatic was glossolalia – 'the evangelical answer to mystical ecstasy'.[33] The new ethos formed a hospitable setting for the early days of the charismatic movement. 'The climate of opinion', as Harper put it, 'was against such a movement until the sixties.'[34] In that decade renewal created a Christian version of the counter-culture.

THE RISE OF CULTURAL MODERNISM

The cultural revolution of the 1960s was made possible by the broader circumstances of the times. The growth of international trade in the postwar world had created unprecedented affluence. The young, feeling that prosperity could be taken for granted, set out on a quest for higher values. Thrown together in the expanding institutions of higher education, they looked for something to replace the surrounding materialism. The Vietnam War increasingly symbolised for them the consequences of the capitalism against which they were rebelling. A sudden upsurge of radical attitudes was to be expected. Much of the vocabulary of revolt was supplied by the popular Marxism of the day. The opinions of the youthful *avant-garde*, however, drew their primary inspiration from deeper cultural currents. In the 1960s the ideas generated by an innovatory elite around the turn of the century began to impinge on a mass public. Before that decade twentieth-century novelties had been confined in most spheres to narrow groups of cognoscenti; now there was a rush by the rebels to embrace them as an alternative to the blended legacy of the Enlightenment and Romanticism that dominated public taste. The religious dimension of the counter-culture shared this genealogy. The charismatic movement was a product of the diffusion of cultural Modernism.

It is unfortunate that the same word 'Modernism' is applied to two different movements of opinion in the early twentieth century, one theological, the other cultural. Theological Modernism, the position of Bishop Barnes, was a desire to bring Christian doctrine up to date, an extension of theological liberalism. Modernism as a cultural phenomenon was something much broader, the result of a shift of sensibility as major as the transition from the Enlightenment to Romanticism a century before.[35] 'On or about December 1910 human nature changed', wrote Virginia Woolf, herself one of the leading exponents of the new mood. The date, though provocatively precise, refers to the opening of the first exhibition in London of Post-Impressionist art, one of the chief symptoms of the transition. 'All human relations shifted', Virginia Woolf went on, '– those between masters and servants, husbands and wives, parents and children. And when human relations change there is at the same time a change in religion, conduct, politics, and literature.'[36] The consequences for religion have been examined far less than the consequences for literature, but it is possible to set out some of the leading characteristics of the Modernist turn of mind. The movement was centrally concerned with self-expression. In German-speaking lands the desire to express whatever was in the artist's mind led the onset of Modernism to be dubbed 'Expressionism', whether in the form of Kafka's fiction or the architecture of the Bauhaus. Expressionism believed in giving vent to the undifferentiated mixture of thought and feeling that is the normal content of the human mind. It entailed delving beneath the surface of conscious reflection to explore the depths of the subconscious. Intense introspection was followed by frank revelation, not least of sexual feelings. The artistic movement clearly had affinities with the depth psychology of Freud and Jung that was emerging in precisely the same years.

Modernism, furthermore, delighted in the discovery by Nietzsche, perhaps the strongest single influence over the whole movement, of the arbitrariness of language. There is no fixed correspondence, it was beginning to be believed, between words and things signified. Only convention, for instance, dictates that verbs should not be used as nouns. All meaning was called into question and so the normal stood revealed as absurd. It was natural, therefore, for a theatre of the absurd to develop. Likewise it was thought unnecessary for there to be any correspondence between art and the external world. The Bloomsbury Group, the pace-setters of Modernism in Britain, embraced a non-representational theory of art – which is why they rejoiced over the French Post-Impressionists. Boundaries between areas of experience were characteristically dissolved, as in the novels of Virginia Woolf. And there was a revolutionary temper about Modernism. It believed in defying the customary, in shocking accepted taste, in destruction as well as in construction. Its culmination on the Continent was the Dada movement around the end of the First World War that carried anarchy into art, which was to be a form of absolute negation. This strain in Modernism could thrive in times of crisis, almost relishing the economic or military downfall of existing civilisation. Close human relations alone, many supposed, could be salvaged from the chaos. So multi-faceted a phenomenon resists definition, but certain common themes have been summarised: 'a loss of faith in objective reality and in the "word", established language; a fascination with the unconscious; a concern with the pressures of industrial environment and accelerating change; a desire to discover significant artistic structure in increasing chaos'.[37] From this matrix came the innovatory attitudes that were to sway youthful minds in the sixties.

THE OXFORD GROUP

Already in the interwar period the influence of cultural Modernism on Evangelical religion can be detected. There came to prominence in those years a body known as the Oxford Group. Teams of 'life-changers', often consisting chiefly of Oxford undergraduates, descended on a town or village urging their hearers to 'surrender' to God. Interested individuals were drawn into groups where there was frank admission of failures to attain the four ethical absolutes of the movement: absolute honesty, purity, unselfishness and love. Or else they were invited to 'house-parties' where more public 'sharing' of sins pointed them to the change that was possible in their lives also. Adherents were encouraged to spend 'quiet times' in which divine 'guidance' was to be expected in the form of 'luminous thoughts' that should be jotted down in a notebook.[38] The animating force was Dr Frank Buchman, a Lutheran minister from Pennsylvania, 'tall, upright, stoutish, clean-shaven, spectacled, with that mien of scrupulous, shampooed, and almost medical cleanness, or freshness, which is so characteristic of the hygienic American'.[39] It was he who directed the whole operation from small beginnings at Cambridge in 1920–1 until it made a remarkable impact on Britain in the years of deepest economic depression in the early 1930s.

The key to understanding the Oxford Group is to see that it was an exercise in maximum acculturation. Buchman had previously been a college evangelist in America. As the scope of his work widened to embrace the Far East and then Britain, he displayed a refined sensitivity to cultural variations. He was careful, for instance, to use 'lift' instead of 'elevator' when in Britain.[40] He recommended the young men of his international teams to observe the customs and social code of the lands they visited.[41] Even theological terminology was discarded because it formed a possible obstacle to evangelism. Life-changing alone is important, according to a book revised by Buchman. People needed to pass through the experience, 'whatever their various theological inheritance'.[42] Although this undoctrinal approach attracted suspicion from the Evangelical world,[43] for a while it held great appeal for Oxford undergraduates. In the early 1930s lunch-time meetings drew about a hundred and fifty daily. There were scholars as well as sportsmen. Three college chaplains gave their support.[44] Outside the university the main impact was on 'the well-to-do, the cultured, the leisured, and the intelligent'.[45] Indeed the Group earned censure as 'the Salvation Army of the upper classes'.[46] Buchman consciously aimed for leaders of opinion whose change of course would guarantee media attention and so fan the flame of the movement. He formulated a distinctive message that would attract the elite. Consequently Buchmanism was in the vanguard of the evolution of taste. It appealed to those who prided themselves on being up-to-date, to 'us moderns'.[47] The Oxford Group blended Evangelicalism with the first ripples of twentieth-century high culture. Symptoms of Modernism can be recognised in many features of the movement.

SELF-EXPRESSION

A vein of joyful spontaneity ran through the whole Oxford Group. There was no observance of the 'proper thing'. Speakers would lean against the arm of a chair or sit on a table.[48] Meetings were scenes of 'laughter and commonplace speech'.[49] 'It's such fun', was a pet phrase.[50] The 'sharing' that was a feature of the movement meant testimony or confession in public or in private. Public sharing could appear ridiculous. At a house party a woman confessed to having allowed herself to think, 'Fancy Mavis coming to communion in an orange blouse!'[51] Yet to a general practitioner who identified himself with the Group, the mischief of repression could be undone by 'free and unreserved self expression.'[52] The sharing of personal sin was treated as 'the price of release'.[53] As critics were quick to point out, personal sin was often sexual sin, especially among young men of undergraduate age.[54] The medical practitioner reported that in an Oxford house-party sex matters had frequently been discussed, always helpfully.[55] One of Buchman's American aides coined a phrase that was daring for its day: 'God-control is the best birth-control'.[56] Defenders of the Group might contend that there was no preoccupation with sex and Beverley Nichols might be disappointed at the reserve shown about the subject,[57] but the eagerness with which prudery was cast to the winds was shocking in interwar Britain. In its unstuffiness and frankness, the Oxford Group was an innovative agent of self-expression.

All this was clearly bound up with psychological interests. It might not be fair, remarked two commentators, to describe Buchman as a 'Freudian Psychologist', but they were inclined to think the judgement not far wide of the truth.[58] Groupers believed they were engaged in a form of therapy. One of the Oxford chaplains who identified with the movement eulogised 'the pastoral side of the work, the process of deep cure, by which a sex complex is cured, or an inferiority complex released into the perfection of love which knows no fear'.[59] The practice of mutual confession was in fact an anticipation of the technique of group therapy that developed in the wake of the Second World War.[60] Groupers on the fringe of Buchmanism began to speak of 'Divine Healing', pointing out the falsity of the antithesis between soul and body.[61] Confession and reparation in at least one case led to the disappearance of a nervous ailment.[62] The magazine *Groups* secured for its readers the services of a consulting psychologist.[63] And there was praise for the skills of Jesus in this field. 'It is evident', wrote L. Wyatt Lang, 'from the meaning underlying His parables that He had made careful research into psychological processes, and was a very excellent psychologist.'[64] The two churchmen of the day who led the way in a rapprochement between psychology and religion, L. W. Grensted and Leslie Weatherhead, were both enthusiasts for the Group.[65] It was bound up with the rising tide of depth psychology that was a feature of the interwar period.

The Groupist quest for divine guidance was condemned in some quarters as another symptom of the supplanting of true religion by psychological dabbling. Adherents might penetrate only 'to the mysterious depths of the subconscious mind by relaxing the watchfulness of reason'.[66] Here was the essential stricture: irrationality. God does guide, argued Bishop Knox, but there is a need to test for false guidance by using our minds.[67] The Group on the other hand advocated the suspension of rational processes during the quiet time to ensure 'our absolute negation' to everything but the will of God.[68] It was a sign of the Group's participation in the general trend in European thought to downgrade reason, to diminish the claims of critical reflection.[69] Truth was perceived in moments of disclosure as self-validating as those in Proust. 'The age of miracles is still with us', announces the authoritative statement of Oxford Group methods in the section on 'Guidance'.[70] Hensley Henson, Bishop of Durham, made the same point in censuring the Group. 'It seeks the proofs of divine action', he wrote, 'in what is abnormal, amazing, even miraculous.'[71] Reason could be transcended by direct contact with God. The appeal of the idea in the early 1930s was an indication of a spreading attitude in twentieth-century civilisation.

COMMUNITY AND LIFESTYLE

'The first thing that struck me', wrote the Bishop of Calcutta about his initial experience of a house-party, 'was the wonderful spirit of fellowship which characterised the Group . . .'[72] It was the camaraderie which, as Grensted observed, made the movement particularly beneficial to solitary clergy and which, as others observed, attracted lonely students including isolated Rhodes scholars from the dominions.[73] A distinctive patois bound the Group together. To detractors it was all too closely related to current American slang.[74] Others noted Buchman's tendency to coin maxims like 'revival which continues in survival' and 'sin blinds, sin binds', reminiscent of American advertising technique but also of the habit common among Modernist artists of putting their programmes into slogans.[75] Buchmanite usage in everyday language is best caught by the fictional account of the movement in John Moore's *Brensham Village*, where the new Grouper rector uses expressions like 'scrumptious', 'ripping', and 'awfully jolly'. In this context first names were *de rigueur*. 'The Groupers', comments Moore, '. . . would have addressed the Holy Apostles themselves by their Christian names, or rather they would have abbreviated them and called Saint Peter Pete.'[76] So much help could be drawn from their tight-knit house groups that there were frequent complaints that Groupers neglected to attend regular church activities.[77] Commentators were right to discern in Group solidarity a reaction against individualism, although they were divided into those who praised (like Grensted) and those who deplored (like Henson).[78] J. H. Oldham, Secretary of the International Missionary Council, saw the Groupers as achieving 'life in community'. 'May it not be', he asked, 'that they are rediscovering the truth that the meaning of life is found in relations between persons?'[79] It was only with the Bloomsbury Group that this view became a commonplace in England. For Buchman's movement to represent the same principle was to align itself with a fundamental assumption of progressive thought in its day.

There was a certain holy worldliness about members of the Oxford Group. It is false, argued an editorial in *Groups*, to contrast the sacred and the secular. Religion is not 'a separate compartment of life', distinct from ordinary experience. On the contrary, Christianity is 'a way of living life', so that God approves of 'washing steps or keeping ledgers' as much as religious work.[80] 'Absolute Honesty in business', explained a Group manual, 'means our being level, our playing the game of business as cleanly as we would play any other game.'[81] Religion was to be embodied in every human activity, injecting a strong dose of happiness. Leisure was there to be enjoyed. There were grumbles about immodesty when a girl Grouper took a sun-bathe, and a rector reported sternly that the pleasure-loving Groupers desecrated the Lord's Day by country rambles and seaside trips at the weekend.[82] Smoking, like drinking, bridge and make-up, was rare in the Group. At a house-party of some five hundred, only three or four smoked.[83] Yet Groupers insisted that such matters of personal behaviour were left to the individual conscience, or, as they preferred to say, to guidance. The absence of rigid codes of prohibition is best illustrated by the Group's favourable attitude to that old Evangelical bugbear, the theatre. A girl of about twenty with a Fundamentalist mother who disapproved of theatres entered the movement. Far from abandoning theatre-going, the girl learned from the Group merely how to agree to differ with her mother.[84] By the 1936 national assembly, the Group was itself mounting a sketch, a minor anticipation of the movement's postwar purchase of the Westminster Theatre in order to put on uplifting productions.[85] Art could be God-controlled. In any and every sphere the changed life should reveal itself. By contrast with the conservative Evangelicals of their day, the Groupers did not believe in withdrawal. Far from shrinking from the world, they were out to conquer it.

ORGANISATION AND AUTHORITY

Groupism was a nebulous phenomenon. Membership was undefined by card or ceremony. A puzzled judge investigating whether the Group was a legal entity that could receive legacies enquired whether anything happened when a person joined. 'No', replied the ingenious counsel for Buchman, 'I think it is as invisible as joining the Church of England.'[86] The judge went on to hold that the Oxford Group was so lacking in organisation that in law it did not exist.[87] The same unstructured style was reflected in the Group's worship, or lack of it. A Methodist was struck by the absence of hymns at a London rally.[88] When Buchman conducted a Sunday morning meeting during a house-party to replace a church service, it would consist of only a quiet time and a Bible reading, with possibly a short prayer and a verse of a hymn.[89] An anti-ecclesiastical note crept into the movement's thinking. By contrast with the Group, the church seemed 'stale'.[90] Dwelling on this aspect of the movement, Hensley Henson insisted that, since the Group provided for all the spiritual needs of its members, other systems were superfluous and would naturally be abandoned. A sectarian logic was at work.[91] Buchman's aim, however, was permeation, not replacement. Groupers avoided holding meetings in church hours, encouraged participation in the sacraments of members' own churches and contended that they were not intending to supplant existing denominations.[92] 'Our only organisation', declared Buchman, 'is the Church.'[93] But that stance, while somewhat reassuring to existing churches, was itself anti-institutional. Ecclesiastical structures were matters of profound indifference. Planned activity for any purpose other than life-changing, whether registering members, observing worship or launching a church, was superfluous. The anti-organisational temper so marked among the Bohemian creators of Modernist art reappeared in the Oxford Group. It discarded the prayer and praise, kneeling and standing, of normal religious meetings, according to an apologist, 'in line with the present age'.[94]

So protean was the movement that it had to be held together by firm discipline. Henson was disgusted with 'the oracular despotism of "Frank"'.[95] Although Buchman often effaced himself at public meetings, he kept the whole Group on a tight rein. 'When guided', and the qualification is important, 'he would leave the leadership to another.'[96] In order to counter the charge that guidance was arbitrary, but also in order to control the movement, Buchman taught that guidance must be 'checked' with others – perhaps with a local group, but if necessary with the 'Inner Group'. How this mechanism operated is clear from occasions when it broke down. Methodist Groupers who undertook campaigns on their own initiative received correspondence from the leadership containing the repeated phrase 'You have not checked your guidance with us'. Dismayed by this 'new infallibility', they dropped the word 'Oxford' and developed their work as simple 'Groupers'.[97] Parallels began to be drawn between the Oxford Group and the Continental dictatorships.[98] Some substance was lent to the charge by the presence of two Nazi Groupers at the 1933 Oxford house-party, a visit by Buchman to the Berlin Olympics in 1936 and the change of direction in the movement from the mid-30s.[99] Buchman started to pay more attention to Continental Europe and national flags were carried at Groupist rallies.[100] The atmosphere became highly militaristic. 'After a silent period of communion', during the 1936 national assembly at Castle Bromwich, 'bugles were sounded and drums beaten as 1,000 young men marched to the front followed by a contingent of girls.'[101] Something verging on a personality cult was grafted on to the movement, with Buchman being installed in 'the world centre' at 45 Berkely Square, London, and international broadcasts by the leader.[102] The ethos had been transformed even before, in May 1938, Buchman announced the slogan that was to supersede 'Oxford Group' as the movement's title: 'Moral Re-Armament'.[103] In the postwar world, up to and beyond Buchman's death in 1961, it was to continue in its much more politicised form, but in Britain it would never repeat its impact of the early 1930s. For a while this strange chameleon-like body had matched its environment with remarkable success. It had led the way in absorbing elements of Modernist culture into the Evangelical bloodstream.

THE CHARISMATIC STYLE

The next radically new variant of Evangelical religion to strike Britain appeared in the 1960s in the form of charismatic renewal. It showed no particular awareness of a lineage deriving from the Oxford Group, but affinities were nevertheless substantial. The charismatic stress on the role of the Holy Spirit, for example, had been anticipated by the Group. At a house-party in 1934, an observer commented, 'the work of the Third Person of the Trinity received particular emphasis'.[104] 'One feels', declared a Groupist clergyman, 'the breath of the Spirit sweeping through the meetings, cleansing, convicting, empowering . . .'[105] The movement seemed in 1931 a channel for 'a fresh baptism of the Spirit'.[106] Nor did resemblances end there, for, as will appear, most of the chief characteristics of the Group that reflected the Modernist idiom were to resurface in the renewal movement. It was not a matter of continuity of personnel. Although Cuthbert Bardsley, a full-time Grouper in the 1930s, gave encouragement to charismatic activities as Bishop of Coventry in the 1970s, he was exceptional in spanning the chronological gulf between the popularity of the two movements.[107] Because both appealed particularly to the young, there was a gap of more than a generation between their chief constituencies. There seems to have been no direct transmission of influence from the one to the other. The explanation for the similarity is rather that each movement was closely adapted to its milieu. Although the cultural setting of the 1960s differed sharply from that of the 1930s, the relevant change during the intervening years was that an *avant-garde* outlook confined before the war to a small number had created by the 1960s an extensive counter-culture. The ideas of the few had reached a mass audience, even if in the 1960s it was a youthful minority. The attitudes that clustered round Expressionism early in the century had by the sixties become an 'Expressive Revolution'.[108] The Oxford Group was an accommodation of Evangelicalism to the first, the charismatic movement a comparable accommodation to the second.

The new style was obvious in worship. 'One of the clearest marks of a true outpouring of the Spirit', according to Harper, 'is the free and spontaneous worship which those affected offer to God, sometimes for hours on end.'[109] Vibrant music, usually played on guitars, repeated choruses, openness to interruption by worshippers praying, prophesying, speaking in tongues or interpreting, and sheer length were typical of the charismatic idiom. Loud celebration was normally varied by 'periods of deep, soaring silence' or 'quiet verses of commitment'.[110] There was a wealth of new songs, many of the earlier ones being collected in *Sound of Living Waters* (1974) and *Fresh Sounds* (1976). Perhaps the most characteristic feature was the use of the body in worship. 'The hands', it was said, 'as well as the lips can be so expressive – as they are raised or clapped . . .'[111] The lifting of hands in adoration became the party badge of those affected by renewal, but hands could also be laid on other worshippers in prayer, arms could be linked for corporate singing, hugs could show affection and feet could tap. The London leaders of emergent Restorationism were asked to leave their regular meeting place because of noise and threatened damage to the floorboards through exuberant leaping and dancing.[112] Headlines were attracted when, at the final eucharist of a pre-Lambeth charismatic conference in 1978, '25 Anglican bishops led a dance round the communion table half-way up the steps at the east end of the choir in Canterbury Cathedral'.[113] The Oxford Group had delighted in spontaneity, but, in a liturgically unbending era, had never ventured to carry it over into public worship. In the more flexible 1960s and 1970s, the charismatic movement dissolved the familiar contours of church services wherever it appeared. For charismatics worship was expressive, not functional.[114] They wished to lay bare what they felt for God, and so recovered what had long been deficient in the Evangelical tradition, the priority of praise. It was a Christian version of 'doing your own thing', a principle near the heart of the expressive revolution.

The practice of healing, which charismatics saw as a gift of the Spirit, reveals further affinities with contemporary secular culture. Interest in divine healing, already fairly widespread, was the avenue for several pioneers into the charismatic movement.[115] Renewal meetings, like one at St Paul's, Hainault, in 1974, would sometimes concentrate on therapy. A reporter described the queue stretching forward to where three clergy offered prayer. 'A number prayed for keel over backwards. Well-positioned experienced stewards ease them gently to the floor, where some lie prostrate for five or ten minutes.'[116] Although physical healing was often sought and sometimes evidently received, 'inner healing' was often the focus of attention. This could sometimes mean deliverance from demonic

influence, and certain renewed churches specialised in exorcism.[117] More
often it meant prayer counselling of individuals or else mutual confession
reminiscent of the Oxford Group.[118] At Canford Magna Parish Church a
team of thirty was set aside as counsellors; the Crusade for World Revival
(1964) launched *The Christian Counsellor's Journal*; and institutions sprang
up such as Briercliffe House, Lancashire, 'a home which seeks to minister
the wholeness of the Lord Jesus Christ to those who are in need of prayer,
Christian love, healing of mind, body or spirit'.[119] There was much
preoccupation with 'release from tension and inhibitions', the 'shadow side
of one's personality' and the 'collective unconscious of the human racial
mind'.[120] Taking people deeper and deeper into 'psychological healing',
admitted Harper, sometimes diverted the movement from evangelism.[121] It is
clear that renewal was permeated by the assumptions of depth psychology,
especially of the Jungian variety. It was part of a spreading tendency in later
twentieth-century Britain.

INSIGHT AND EXPERIENCE

Insight was often exalted by charismatics against reason. The finest education, according to Harper, must yield to 'the utterance of wisdom or
knowledge' that brings spiritual perception, 'a flash of inspiration'.[122] Just
like Groupers, members of the new movement believed in direct messages
from God. A Solihull house church was customarily exhorted to 'listen to
what God is saying'.[123] A charismatic, it has been observed, will 'often
confidently assert that "God told me"'.[124] Prophecy, according to the
charismatic understanding, is a result of listening for the voice of God.[125]
The transcendence of the rational, so scandalous to church leaders in the
1930s, was once more condemned by opponents . Does 'the true and living
God ever deal with his people in ways that deliberately bypass their minds?',
demanded a stern Reformed critic of the movement.[126] Charismatics were
in no doubt that he does. There had long been, according to a leading
Baptist adherent, an 'unbalanced emphasis on the intellect and the ability of
human reason'.[127] The rationalist bias, Harper asserted, could be traced back
to Aquinas, and through him to Aristotle. Aquinas spent his life showing
that man has no direct contact with immaterial reality. It was reassuring,
however, that 'Aquinas did have an overwhelming experience of God just
before his death, which upset most of his theories'.[128] The Eastern church
had avoided this bane of Western Christendom. 'The former has allowed
much more scope for the Holy Spirit and His more direct ways of inspiration',
wrote Harper, 'whereas the latter has emphasised reason and logic.'[129] Light
could come from the East. The exaltation of the non-rational was of a piece
with the desire for intensified perception that emerged in the sixties.
    Experience was likewise elevated above theology in the charismatic scale
of values. When asked at an Evangelical theological college what renewal

was about, Harper replied, 'It's about an experience of God'.[130] 'Theology of itself', he once wrote, 'does not provide strength. Bad theology can be more harmful than no theology at all.'[131] One charismatic who did ably undertake the theological enterprise was the Scot Thomas Smail, Harper's successor as Director of the Fountain Trust in 1975 and author of *Reflected Glory* (1975). Yet Smail illustrates the point. After four years in office he resigned to become a lecturer in doctrine[132] and eventually, disenchanted with the froth of the movement, he was to move outside renewal circles entirely. 'The stress on experience', Harper admitted, 'will not please some. It may be thought too subjective'.[133] That was the main burden of conservative Evangelical criticism, resulting in sharp polarisation during the 1960s.[134] Some kept up the barrage in the 1980s. Unconcern with theology, it was suggested, led to toleration of error: 'modernists and Roman Catholics are drawn in and do not cease to be modernists and Roman Catholics'.[135] Doctrinal diversity, as in the Oxford Group, had the function of ensuring that the movement was inclusive. Renewal could justly claim to be a unifying force among the churches. But avoidance of theological rigidity was more than a chosen policy. It was of the essence of the movement. Renewal, according to Harper in 1971, 'has no great theologians. Its teaching is varied and unsystematic'.[136] Dialogue with traditional Evangelicals later made Anglican charismatics wary of exalting the emotions at the expense of the intellect, but Restorationists continued to expect doctrine to be in perpetual flux as God revealed fresh themes.[137] Like the experience-oriented generation of the sixties as a whole, there was a tendency for charismatics to erect ideological fluidity into a virtue.

COMMUNITY AND CREATIVITY

Community became a watchword of the movement. Experience of the Spirit brought people together. Harper had previously seen the church as 'a collection of individuals . . . A religious club, if you like', but he came to recognise it as 'a living thing, an organism'.[138] David Watson, a powerful evangelist whose church at St Michael-le-Belfrey, York, became the showpiece of Anglican renewal, set out an influential communitarian vision in *I Believe in the Church* (1978). A high level of commitment to other church members was expected. It was common for adherents of renewed congregations to move house in order to be nearer the place of worship and each other.[139] Dinners, parties, picnics, away-days, weekends and church holidays fostered solidarity.[140] House groups for mutual care and evangelism became characteristic, forming another parallel with the Oxford Group.[141] And holism found expression in the creation of communities. Families would band together, as in the Post Green Community begun in 1975 in the home of Sir Thomas and Lady Lees at Lytchett Minster in Dorset.[142] A south coast Baptist church established Hunter's Moon, a home where six ladies of all ages could live communally; and the Sisters of the Jesus Way, a Methodist group, held their property in common.[143] Part of the motive for the communitarian approach was a desire to resist the pressures of a secularising society, and in particular to buttress Christian family life.[144] But it also reflected the paramountcy of personal relationships that the movement shared with Bloomsbury and the radicals of the 1960s. 'Every-where', according to a minister of an Exeter house church, 'everything is based on relationships.'[145] Charismatics were aiming for the characteristic goal of the sixties counter-culture: 'purified community'.[146]

The new movement, rejoicing in its spiritual freedom, broke with many a shibboleth. Harper rejected the rigidity of what he called 'the evangelical code of behaviour'.[147] Wallis denounced sabbatarianism.[148] Members of a house church scandalised the Christian people of Aberdare by buying ice cream on Sunday, reading the Sunday newspaper and drinking wine at dinner.[149] Gerald Coates paraded his love of the cinema, the theatre and pop music, openly discussed masturbation and wore a canary yellow suit. His meetings at Cobham were dismissed as 'just religious show biz'.[150] The whole movement released a surge of creativity that included making banners, designing graphics, writing songs, playing instruments, moulding pottery and performing sacred dance.[151] Craft and coffee shops became a charismatic cottage industry.[152] Technical skills found an outlet in operating grand public address systems and the humble overhead projectors that permitted congregations to worship unencumbered with hymn books.[153] Drama, far from being condemned, was harnessed to Christian purposes, with acted presentations in worship, mime in the streets and evangelistic puppet shows. David Watson's congregation generated a full-time theatre company, Riding Lights.[154] There was an extraordinarily unEvangelical delight in symbol – 'a love of oil, candles, crosses etc.'.[155] The resulting artistic efflorescence was very reasonably labelled 'inchoate sacramentality'.[156] 'Verbal communication', a charismatic folk arts hand-book declared, is 'clumsy and wearying'.[157] Although the disintegration of the Protestant tradition embodied in such a comment was real enough, the primary influence at work was not Catholicism. Rather the uninhibited exuberance, the penchant for the arts and the downgrading of the verbal all bear the stamp of Modernism.

STRUCTURE AND AUTHORITY

There was an anti-structural bias among charismatics. 'They reject alto-gether', declared Harper, 'the concept of the Church as an institution.'[158] New Testament structure, Wallis believed, was not about organisation but about people. Denominations are contrary to the divine will and worst of all is the 'religious hotchpotch' of the World Council of Churches.[159] 'Denominationalism', Coates roundly announced, 'is sin!'[160] Even churches in historic denominations found that ties with unrenewed congregations slackened.[161] Within the charismatic world informality reigned. As among Groupers, first names were standard: Lady Lees and her husband Sir Thomas, a member of the General Synod, became 'Faith and Tom'.[162] What was sometimes styled 'holy mirth' punctuated their meetings. God was saying, explained Wallis, 'Let laughter return'.[163] 'Let's chat a prophecy', was the approach of another Restorationist leader.[164] Early Fountain Trust conferences were largely unstructured. 'We have always found', wrote Harper, 'that when we have *not* organised, the Holy Spirit has worked more freely.' Shortly after his initial experience of the Spirit, Harper dropped the careful planning of sermons and a giant file of matters pending disappeared into the waste-paper basket.[165] People had to be flexible in the King's Church, Aldershot, 'since constant change is here to stay in our church'.[166] The ultimate rationale was that 'God is never stationary'.[167] Like so many radicals of the period, charismatics believed in dispensing with landmarks.

The fluidity of charismatic proceedings made it essential for leaders to impose discipline. A person who supposed himself to be prophesying but was in fact venting his own feelings would be instructed to sit down.[168] As leadership became more demanding, ministry teams emerged. Elders were commonly appointed in renewed Anglican, Methodist and Baptist congregations to provide kindly but firm pastoral guidance.[169] Harvestime churches regularly possessed a collective leadership.[170] Division arose within charismatic circles, however, over the role of apostles, that is, travelling teachers with 'translocal' responsibilities. Although contemporary figures might in certain respects exercise apostolic functions, stated the leading Evangelical Anglican charismatics, 'the apostles have no successors'.[171] The Restorationists around Bryn Jones, on the other hand, came to believe in the mid-1970s that today's apostles possess an authority to which elders of local churches should submit. From American teachers they learned that there is a 'structure of authority directly from the throne of God', passing down through apostles to elders and ultimately to ordinary believers.[172] Ron Trudinger of Basingstoke expressed a full-blooded version of this theory in *Built to Last* (1982). Denominational charismatics and many in the less tightly organised house churches were alarmed by the abrogation of Christian freedom entailed by the new 'shepherding principles', and cases of the abuse of power soon came to light.[173] A branch of Restorationism was becoming as authoritarian as the Oxford Group. Both, while denying legitimacy to existing Christian institutions in the growing spirit of the twentieth century, erected rigid structures of authority of their own.

SUPPORT FOR THE CHARISMATIC MOVEMENT

The social composition of the whole charismatic movement also resembled that of Buchmanism. Charismatics were overwhelmingly young and drawn from the middle classes. St Margaret's at Aspley in Nottingham, for example, which before renewal had few worshippers in the 18–50 age range, afterwards reflected far more closely the age structure of its parish because it drew in younger adults.[174] Restorationists were predominantly young, the first large wave of recruits to the house churches in the early 1970s having been mostly in their early twenties – the teenagers of the 1960s.[175] St Michael-le-Belfrey in York, it was reported, had a high turnover in its congregation because it 'tends to attract those who are in professions which move them on every few years'.[176] Likewise the arrival of a charismatic vicar in a rural parish in the Home Counties filled the church with commuters.[177] Restorationism also attracted small businessmen, civil servants, doctors, nurses, solicitors and accountants in abundance. Elders were commonly graduates, and Bryn Jones's church at Bradford included four holders of PhDs.[178] The contrast with Pentecostalism is total. In the 1950s Elim contained virtually no professionals, in fact few but working-class adherents.[179] 'While the sociological roots of the healthy movements of the Spirit in the past have been among the masses', admitted a leading Baptist charismatic, 'this is not so today . . . it appears we are largely a middle-class movement . . .'[180] The appeal was predominantly to the educated young – to those most affected by the new cultural currents flowing from the 1960s onwards.

The pattern of geographical spread was closely related to the social composition of the movement. Where young professionals were most numerous, on the outer rim of London and in the adjacent Home Counties, charismatics were thickest on the ground. Renewed congregations were also common on the edge of other cities. In the early stages up to 1965, the movement was strong relative to population in South-West England and there were smatterings in the Midlands, Yorkshire and Scotland, but the North-East, the North-West and Wales were hardly affected.[181] The North of England was still regarded as bleak territory twenty years later.[182] Most denominations were significantly affected by the new religious climate. By 1965 more than a hundred ministers were claimed to have received the baptism in the Spirit.[183] In 1979 it was estimated that 10 per cent of Anglican clergy, and a rather smaller proportion of the laity, had entered the experience.[184] Promise for the future was guaranteed by the multiplication of diocesan renewal conferences from 1982 and the increase of charismatic ordinands – composing some 80 per cent of those in training at St John's College, Nottingham, by 1978.[185] Richard Hare, the Bishop Suffragan of Pontefract, an adherent from 1973, was for a long time the only episcopal charismatic, but in 1986 Michael Whinney, Bishop of Southwell, became an adviser to the Anglican Renewal Movement, and in the following year George Carey, already a charismatic, was consecrated Bishop of Bath and Wells.[186] The Methodist renewal magazine *Dunamis* published 6,000 copies by 1976, and 250 of the recipients were ministers.[187] The United Reformed Church, created by a Congregational–Presbyterian merger in 1972, had its

Group for Evangelism and Renewal, and the Baptists, whose charismatic congregations expanded markedly, were the most drastically affected of the Free Churches.[188] Alongside the historic denominations there was the rapid growth of the Restorationists, who by 1985 were guessed to number about 30,000.[189] The charismatic movement was poised to become the prevailing form of Protestantism in twenty-first-century Britain.

CHARISMATICS AND EVANGELICALS

Was the movement a prolongation of the Evangelical tradition? Its impact on Catholics, in the Roman as well as the Anglican communion, might suggest otherwise. At Canford Magna Parish Church the charismatic element, it was said, 'tends to cover over the more normal divisions of Catholic and Evangelical'.[190] When John Stott publicly disavowed the movement at Islington in 1964, charismatics were effectively distanced from the main body of Evangelicals.[191] Renewal could be condemned outright, especially for divisiveness. '. . . I have marked evidence', wrote a Cheltenham vicar, 'that Satan is active in and through it.'[192] In 1977 Stott was still doubting whether prophecy among charismatics was a genuine gift from God.[193] In that year, however, the publication of a report of discussions between charismatics and non-charismatics called 'Gospel and Spirit' reflected a rapprochement in the Church of England. 'We share the same evangelical faith', they declared; and they recognised that the worship and spirituality of Evangelicals and charismatics so overlapped already 'as to be almost indistinguishable'.[194] From 1979 Spring Harvest, an annual week-long training conference in evangelism, brought together keen charismatics and non-charismatics in a way reminiscent of Keswick in an earlier generation.[195] A study of Restorationism has located it firmly in the Evangelical Protestant tradition.[196] Furthermore, as a Scottish Roman Catholic bishop remarked, the effect of renewal on a Catholic was usually to give him 'something of the evangelical emphasis on Jesus as his personal Saviour'.[197] If the charismatic movement brought Christians of different backgrounds together, it did so on a basis that was discernibly Evangelical in appearance.

Conversion received fresh emphasis among most charismatics. 'The experience of the new birth', insisted Wallis, 'is more fundamental, more radical than that of receiving the Spirit.'[198] A Methodist office-holder explained that he was not born again until his contact with the charismatic movement.[199] Although in charismatic hymnody there was some shift away from concepts like 'sin' and 'salvation' to less abstract terms like 'healing' and 'life', an analysis has concluded that there was continuity in essentials between Evangelical and charismatic vocabulary.[200] There was a consequent accent on activism, especially in evangelism and counselling. 'Before this blessing', recalled a leader at a Bethnal Green mission, 'the young people would not go into the open air, but now, praise God, there is hunger for precious souls.'[201] There was, admitted Harper, a risk of downgrading the Word of God in the excitement of seeing 'spectacular manifestations'.[202] In all branches of the movement, however, a constant appeal to scripture prevented any retreat from biblicism. Harper also feared the removal of the death of Christ from its central position in the thought and experience of the believer.[203] It was in this area that some movement from the earlier Evangelical consensus was discernible, with the new life of the Christian frequently attributed to the resurrection as well as, or even instead of, the cross. The new emphasis on the resurrection, however, was just as evident in the non–charismatic as in the charismatic hymnody of the 1970s.[204] George Carey, writing on the atonement in 1986, reminded charismatics that even spiritual gifts are 'as much the gifts of Calvary as they are of Pentecost'.[205] Although crucicentrism was a little sapped, the substance of Evangelicalism found expression in the charismatic movement. It was altered, not superseded.

The charismatic upsurge represented another mutation in the Protestant tradition comparable to that which created Evangelicalism in the eighteenth century and that which modified it in the nineteenth. Once more a fresh cultural current impinged on popular religion. This time the spread of Modernism was behind the growth of renewal and Restorationism. Charismatics themselves sometimes noticed the affinity. 'When human words seem inadequate', wrote two Methodist adherents, 'the Holy Spirit inspires other, seemingly unintelligible words (rather like abstract art, some may say!) . . .'[206] The movement was rooted ultimately in the changed mood of the early twentieth century that gave rise to non-representational art, stream–of–consciousness literature and a preoccupation with the non–rational in all its forms. Many of the movement's features had been anticipated by the Oxford Group in the 1930s, when Buchman trimmed his sails to catch the new winds of secular influence. He remoulded Evangelicalism to suit the preferences of an elite already affected by the twentieth century's revolution in taste. By the 1960s the assumptions of a mass audience in and about the youth culture were shaped by Modernist canons. A religious movement sha ing its ethos was likely to grow, and, as the counter–culture was assimilated to the mainstream culture during the 1970s, to become a major force in popular Christianity. That is what happened to renewal. Charismatics succeeded where the Groupers failed because their time had come. Both represented an adaptation of Evangelical religion to the trends of the twentieth century.

[8]

Into a Broad Place:
Evangelical Resurgence in the
Later Twentieth Century

. . . out of the strait into a broad place, where there is no straitness. (Job 36:16)

In 1967 a National Evangelical Anglican Congress was held at the University of Keele. It was the chief landmark in a postwar Evangelical renaissance that was gathering momentum well before the charismatic movement reinforced the process. Numbers, morale and impact all greatly increased. The place of Keele in the development of Evangelicalism in the Church of England has been compared to that of the Second Vatican Council in the Roman Catholic Church shortly before.[1] Repercussions were felt among all the Evangelicals of Britain, in the Anglican communion worldwide and in the whole of international Protestantism. There was at the time a sense of making history. 'The atmosphere', it was reported, 'was as exhilarating as on Derby Day.' Youth and ability were to the fore among 'the bright, thrusting, unsquashable men and women . . . who gave this congress an unmistakable glitter.'[2] At a time when the Church of England was in institutional flux, with canon law, liturgy and church government all in the melting pot, Evangelicals determined to be involved in its remodelling. The fourth of the six sections of the resulting Keele statement was devoted to 'The Church and its Structures'. No longer would other traditions be able to determine the terms of debate within the church. There was also a declaration that Evangelical Anglicans would participate in the church unity movement. 'We desire', announced the statement, 'to enter this ecumenical dialogue fully.' As subsequent letters to the press made plain, Evangelicals accepted that there was something for them to learn through ecumenism. It was an admission that they did not possess a monopoly of truth.[3] Perhaps most important, the statement endorsed social involvement. 'Evangelism and compassionate service', it said, 'belong together in the mission of God.' There was a commitment to give serious attention to the problems of society.[4] No longer would Evangelicals be able to regard their task as withdrawal from the world in the company, if possible, of other souls to be snatched from it. A decade later the significance of Keele was summed up as a symptom of a 'release from the ghetto'.[5]

It was no more than a symptom, for the trends consolidated at Keele had already been emerging beforehand. Ten years earlier, at the Islington Clerical Conference of 1957, Maurice Wood as chairman pointed out that Evangelicals were producing more ordination candidates than any other party: 'the future is ours', he concluded.[6] An Eclectic Society of younger Evangelical clergy existed from 1955 as a ginger group with growing influence.[7] There was a small number of Evangelical laymen who were prepared to give time to the Church Assembly.[8] One of their chief concerns was with church relations in the light of ecumenical progress. Social involvement was less prominent before Keele, but the Independent Evangelical Frederick Catherwood had already published *The Christian in Industrial Society* (1964). There was a steady widening of horizons that was sustained and accelerated after Keele. The process was unnecessary among liberal Evangelicals, who in general had long been committed to participation in the institutional life of their denominations, to advocacy of church unity and to concern with social issues. Rather, it was a broadening of the conservative Evangelical tradition. The postwar Evangelical renaissance was in fact a movement among those of firmly orthodox belief. Keele represents the triumph of the conservatives in the Evangelical party of the Church of England. Its chairman, John Stott, the Rector of All Souls', Langham Place, in central London, could draw attention afterwards to the fact that all its speakers were conservatives.[9] Although the most striking resurgence of the traditionalists was in the Church of England, there were similar developments in other existing denominations and in new church groupings. Those with attitudes to the Bible that had come to be labelled conservative in the interwar period gained greater prominence. They were responsible for something approaching an Evangelical Revival.

It seemed called for in the later twentieth century. However difficult it may be to conceptualise, secularisation was a stark reality. Church membership had been falling since the 1920s, and, although the process was arrested in the wake of the Second World War, there was a catastrophic collapse in the 1960s.[10] Adult church attendance dropped to a mere 11 per cent of the English population by 1979, to 13 per cent of the Welsh population by 1982 and to 17 per cent of the Scottish population by 1984.[11] Religion was increasingly marginal in people's lives. In 1966 two-thirds of marriages in England and Wales still took place in church; by 1980, the figure was fewer than a half.[12] The 1944 Education Act decreed that religious instruction and a daily act of worship should be compulsory in state schools.[13] By the 1970s both provisions were widely ignored with impunity. The television and the motor car dealt a drastic blow to Sunday School attendance in the 1950s.[14] Christian practice was ceasing to be buttressed by custom. Religious change was followed by moral change. In the 1960s traditional moral values based on the Christian ethic disintegrated. The pill heralded the permissive society in the field of sexual morality. The statute book was liberalised. Homosexual practice and abortion ceased to be crimes in 1967 and divorce by consent was permitted from 1969.[15] Even if church leaders often saw reason to condone or applaud such developments in the name of a more humane society, it was hard to disguise the shrinking of Christianity and its influence. A demanding task faced the churches: the turning of the religious tide.

THE RANGE OF EVANGELICAL OPINION

Four schools of thought coexisted in British Evangelicalism at the time of the Second World War. Although they shaded into each other, the bodies of opinion are clearly distinguishable. The liberal school, eager to welcome fresh light from modern thought and other Christian traditions, was powerful in the Church of England and Methodism, finding expression in the Anglican Evangelical Group Movement (AEGM) and the Fellowship of the Kingdom.[16] It was stronger in Congregationalism, weaker in the Church of Scotland and so weak as to be virtually absent from the Baptists. A second, centrist school tried to minimise the divide that had opened in the 1920s between liberals and conservatives. Typically, like Max Warren, General Secretary of the Church Missionary Society from 1942 to 1963, the centrists wished to hyphenate no word like liberal or conservative with Evangelical.[17] In the Church of England it was also the position of men such as Bryan Green, who was prepared to ignore differences of opinion with other Christians in his zeal for evangelism, and Bishop Christopher Chavasse, who wished to hold Evangelicals together for the defence of Protestantism.[18] This was the prevailing stance in the Church of Scotland and Methodism, while the influential 'Genevan school' of Congregationalists led by Nathaniel Micklem, orthodox, scholarly and liturgically minded, falls into the same category.[19] Ernest Payne, subsequently General Secretary of the Baptist Union, was one of a smaller number of Baptists who held similar views.[20] The liberals and the centrists together supplied the leadership in all the denominations except the smallest.

The third body of opinion inherited its moderate conservatism from the interwar debates. In the Church of England the bastion of conservatism, whether moderate or otherwise, was the Fellowship of Evangelical Churchmen, but, since the Anglican school was defined partly in terms of its liturgical practice, the Church Pastoral Aid Society, which still made grants only to parishes adhering to the north side position, must also be reckoned a conservative institution.[21] The Revival Fellowships of the Free Churches were soon to rally similar opinion: the Baptist body, formed in the 1930s, gathered strength and began annual conferences in 1954; the much smaller Congregational and Methodist equivalents began in 1947 and 1952 respectively.[22] 'Definite' Evangelicals, as the moderate conservatives sometimes preferred to call themselves, also existed outside such organisations. Equally these bodies included some who should be located in the fourth category, the Fundamentalists. The Advent Testimony Movement was one of several interdenominational organisations that contained a significant number of this persuasion, but articulate Fundamentalism remained weak in Britain. Conservatives like Stott were eager to repudiate the label when it became a matter of public debate in the mid-1950s.[23] They themselves, however, were by no means influential. The conservatives as a whole formed the obscurer section of a community that had been marginalised by the Catholic drift of religious life and the secular drift of national life during the earlier twentieth century. Despite numbering extremely powerful preachers such as the Methodist W. E. Sangster in their ranks, in the years around 1940 the conservative Evangelicals were probably at their nadir.[24] The remarkable resurgence symbolised by Keele demands explanation.

LIBERALS AND CENTRISTS

One factor is that the liberal impulse represented by the AEGM steadily lost its vigour. After the war it was regretfully recalled that Vernon Storr, 'our master', had died in 1940,[25] and no comparable figure took his place. The Cromer Convention, suspended in wartime, was revived in 1947 and 1948, only to fall victim to the rising costs of the period.[26] Steadily 'a less evangelical liberalism gained control'.[27] The movement became largely cerebral, issuing study outlines for group meetings and holding conferences. Numbers fell away, though there were still some 1,000 clerical members in 1950 and annual conferences were still being organised in the 1960s. The Methodist Fellowship of the Kingdom remained stronger, with about 1,800 members in 1950, and maintained more of a devotional temper.[28] The Union of Modern Free Churchmen, on the other hand, a preponderantly Congregational body, struck out on more advanced lines of thought and kept up something of its impetus into the 1960s.[29] The decay of organised liberalism was most marked in the Anglican body. It was partly a consequence of success. AEGM members were elevated to ecclesiastical office – in the single year 1946 the movement provided three diocesan bishops, one dean and at least three archdeacons – and so had less time or enthusiasm for sectional organisations. But it was also because its message was hardly electrifying: R. R. Williams, later Bishop of Leicester, declared in 1947 that its first purpose was to be a support of 'sober, central, Anglican churchmanship'.[30] In the 1950s one of its few advantages was that the editor of *The Church of England Newspaper and the Record*, formed by a merger of its two constituents in 1949, was a steady supporter – as well as being, from 1954, secretary of the Modern Churchmen's Union.[31] With his termination of office in 1959, the transfer of ownership to new hands in the following year and the appointment of a conservative as editor, liberalism lost one of its chief remaining props.[32] During the 1960s liberal Evangelicalism finally dissolved into the broad middle way of the Church of England.

Centrist Evangelicals possessed great dynamic in the later 1940s. Max Warren masterminded a series of schemes for putting Evangelicalism more obviously on the ecclesiastical map. In 1942 he launched the Evangelical Fellowship for Theological Literature (EFTL), a body designed to foster serious scholarship by younger members of the party in the Church of England. Numbering about 200 at its peak, it was by no means simply a liberal body, for its ranks in 1950 included conservatives such as T. C. Hammond and J. W. Wenham. From its membership were drawn the contributors to a series called the St Paul's Library, the first publication being *The Ministry of the Word* by Donald Coggan, subsequently Archbishop of Canterbury. Many EFTL members rose to the episcopal bench or theological chairs.[33] Warren was likewise behind a conference whose papers were published under the title *Evangelicals Affirm* (1948), urging the central importance of evangelism on the bishops of the Lambeth Conference, and a team statement of the Evangelical Anglican position, *The Fulness of Christ* (1950).[34] Warren's aim of welding together Evangelicals of all shades enjoyed some success. In 1951, for instance, it was agreed that the AEGM proctors in the Church Assembly should join the other group of Evangelicals for united action.[35] As time went by, however, there was a tendency for EFTL members to loosen their Evangelical moorings and sail off in a liberal direction.[36] A similar process took place in the interdenominational Student Christian Movement (SCM), which in the 1950s successfully continued its interwar role of drawing together speakers and students holding many types of theological opinion. In 1957 it had more than 7,000 members. In the 1960s, however, it became increasingly identified with radical stances and support melted away.[37] Centrism was probably most successful in Scotland, where D. P. Thomson and Tom Allan were leaders of an effective movement of co-ordinated lay evangelism, which began in 1947 and was known in the later 1950s as the 'Tell Scotland' campaign. Although the Church of Scotland took the lead, most of the other Protestant denominations participated. In the practical work of evangelism theological differences were ignored. Thomson, for instance, delighted in drawing personnel from both the SCM and the Inter-Varsity Fellowship.[38] Confidence in evangelistic campaigns, however, waned among the less conservative in the Scottish churches during the 1960s. In Britain as a whole, as the distance between the poles of theological opinion widened, the scope for centrist enterprise declined.

A CLIMATE OF SERIOUSNESS

Circumstances favoured conservative Evangelical growth much more than in the interwar period. The war itself was strangely beneficial. It is true, of course, that the churches suffered losses of manpower, premises and, in many cases, surrounding homes. On the other hand, the war generated an idealism of hope for the future, blended with a dedication to turning the dream into reality. The Dunkirk spirit had a spiritual dimension.[39] 'The amazing heroism', wrote a contributor to *The Advent Witness*, 'which has been displayed daily at sea, on land and in the air by those in the war makes us wonder whether we sacrifice enough for Christ in *our* war.'[40] In the ideological conflict of wartime and the ensuing Cold War, conservatives knew where they stood. If sin was the enemy within, according to Alan Redpath, Minister of Duke Street Baptist Church, Richmond, in 1953, 'Communism was the enemy without'.[41] Conviction ran deep and evangelism was in the air. In 1945 the Church of England published *Towards the Conversion of England*, the report to the Church Assembly of a commission on evangelism chaired by Bishop Chavasse. Although little official action followed, there was at least a London diocesan mission in 1949.[42] Maurice Wood believed there had been a swing from the prewar emphasis on pastoral work to a postwar stress on evangelism.[43] During his chairmanship of the Islington Conference, from 1952 to 1961, the theme was usually some aspect of gospel work, and conservatives came increasingly to the fore. In 1953, when John Stott addressed Islington for the first time, his subject was training the laity for house-to-house visitation.[44] In Scotland the same atmosphere was the backdrop to the Tom Allan campaigns, and evangelism received a fresh fillip from the most recent spontaneous revival movement in British history, the Hebrides Revivals of 1950 and 1952.[45] The Methodists organised a series of significantly named 'Christian Commando Campaigns' in the late 1940s; the Baptists sponsored an evangelistic 'Baptist Advance' in 1949–51; and the Congregationalists co-ordinated a Forward Movement in 1950–3.[46] At the Albert Hall the evangelist Tom Rees preached to packed audiences on undenominational lines, reaching his fiftieth rally there in 1955.[47] The legacy of war was a willingness to consider ultimate values in the population at large and a preparedness to respond on the part of the churches.

The prevailing theological tone of the 1940s and 1950s was also more sympathetic to conservative Evangelical preoccupations. A disappointed Congregationalist noted in 1942 the fashion of pronouncing Christian humanism and liberalism dead.[48] The biblical theology associated with C. H. Dodd, an attempt to think back into the minds of the biblical writers, was uncongenial to liberals.[49] So was the neo-orthodox systematic theology of Karl Barth. Conservatives could share in its repudiation of liberal nostrums, but that does not mean they endorsed its whole position. On the contrary, as J. Stafford Wright, Principal of Tyndale Hall, Bristol, explained in 1957, neo-orthodoxy seemed to them merely a 'newer liberalism'. Although rightly teaching an existential encounter with Christ, it was wrong in failing to base itself on the New Testament records as written down.[50] The divergence was so sharp as to occasion a schism in the Edinburgh

University Christian Union, which came under the influence of the Barthian theology of Professor T. F. Torrance and so was disaffiliated in 1953 by the Inter-Varsity Fellowship.[51] Neo-orthodoxy nevertheless provided a context in which conservative Evangelical opinions were not dismissed out of hand.

The radical theology that came into vogue in the 1960s also served, paradoxically, to strengthen the conservative position. Conservative Evangelicals were more prepared than most to denounce what they saw as departures from orthodoxy. *Honest to God* (1963), by J. A. T. Robinson, Bishop of Woolwich, was mildly deprecated by the Archbishop of Canterbury, but roundly dismissed by the conservative J. I. Packer as 'a plateful of mashed-up Tillich, fried in Bultmann and garnished with Bonhoeffer'.[52] An address to the Baptist Union assembly in 1971 by Michael Taylor, Principal of the Northern Baptist College, in which he questioned the divinity of Christ, led to an upsurge of conservative opinion that carried in the following year's assembly a fuller statement of belief than the Union had ever previously professed.[53] The views of Don Cupitt, Dean of Emmanuel College, Cambridge, especially in *The Myth of God Incarnate* (1975), and of David Jenkins, Bishop of Durham from 1984, were controverted equally firmly by Evangelicals with traditional beliefs. Conservatives gained credit for standing up for received Christian convictions.

THE ECUMENICAL MOVEMENT

One of the chief developments in the world church after the Second World War was the accelerating momentum of the unity movement. Its effects on Evangelicals were ambiguous, but they could not avoid it. The standard Evangelical view had been that external uniformity was unimportant and so there were risks of being too involved in the quest for reunion.[54] Students of prophecy were positively hostile. When the World Council of Churches (WCC) was set up in 1948, its purpose was to include all shades of thought, according to an editorial in *The Advent Witness*, and it would even welcome Roman Catholics and Greek Orthodox. Hence it was 'but a shadow of mystery Babylon, that great apostate body typified by the great whore of Revelation 17'.[55] Such attitudes were common on the Baptist fringe, racking the denomination in Scotland during the 1950s and leading the more conservative in England and Wales to demand the withdrawal of the Baptist Union from the WCC during the 1960s.[56] Principled opposition to ecumenical involvement led, as we shall see, to a schism in conservative Evangelical ranks in the late 1960s.[57] By 1974 disquiet had spread more widely at the interpretation by the WCC of the gospel in socio-political terms, particularly through the fund to combat racism,[58] and subsequently the Salvation Army actually ceased to be a full member. But the most outspoken opposition to the ecumenical trend was aroused by the scheme for Anglican–Methodist reunion put forward in 1963. It was to be expected that some Methodists would be unhappy, especially with the proposal that their ministers should submit to what could be interpreted as episcopal reordination. The validity of their earlier ministry was being slighted. Equally intransigent, however, was the bulk of the conservative Evangelicals in the Church of England, who objected not only to apparent reordination, but also to their exclusion from the commission that had drawn up the proposals. In alliance with Anglo-Catholics they ensured that the scheme was inadequately supported in 1969, 1971 and 1972, and so lapsed.[59] Conservative Evangelicals gained a reputation for opposing the ecumenical movement.

Those in the Church of England nevertheless insisted that they were far from being outright opponents of church unity. They wished to reunite with the Free Churches, but only on acceptable terms such as those that had created the Church of South India in 1947.[60] From 1955 many conservative Evangelicals joined the Weeks of Prayer for Christian Unity that sprang up around the country and usually participated in the local Councils of Churches that sponsored them. Growing contact with other Christians did a great deal to moderate their traditional anti-Catholicism. The changes of the Second Vatican Council made Rome less fearsome, and charismatic fellowship began to break down the Protestant–Catholic divide. Keele welcomed the possibility of dialogue with Roman Catholics on the basis of scripture; a decade later David Watson, to the scandal of some, was describing the Reformation as a tragedy.[61] Among Evangelical Anglicans, it was said in 1977, 'old-fashioned Protestants have died out'.[62] That was an exaggeration, for, especially in the Church Society that resulted from the merger of the Church Association and National Church League in 1950, there remained a phalanx for whom the defence of Reformation principles was the overriding priority. As high-level consultations between Anglicans and Roman Catholics steadily demarcated increasing common ground between the churches, Church Society threatened in 1986 that there would be a secession from the Church of England if it continued moving towards Rome.[63] Majority opinion had nevertheless shifted a long way. In 1970 leading Evangelicals and Anglo-Catholics were able to present a joint scheme for reunion in England.[64] The popular Protestantism that had made possible the defeat of the Revised Prayer Book in 1927–8 was in sharp decline.

Hence the traditional defiance of Anglo-Catholic liturgical practices faded away. During the 1950s there remained parishes such as St Mary-le-Port, Bristol, where the black gown was still worn for preaching, the sternly Calvinist *Hymns of Grace and Glory* were sung and collections went to the Irish Church Missions, the Trinitarian Bible Society and the Sovereign Grace Union. In 1952–3 there was a *cause célèbre* when the Bishop of London refused to ordain two Evangelicals who felt bound in conscience not to wear the white stole at the service.[65] North side celebration of communion was a conservative party badge; matins and evensong, which was often the better attended, were the main Sunday services; and there was strong attachment to the text of the 1662 Prayer Book interpreted in a Protestant sense. The 1961 Islington Conference was warned by its chairman of the perils of parish communion, which had already become normal outside conservative Evangelical circles.[66] During the 1960s, however, the new wave of Evangelical clergy was spilling out beyond the party's previous parishes, and some of them began to tolerate customary practices. At youth services there were concessions to modern language. And a number of junior clergy, with Colin Buchanan at their head, were beginning to contribute to the issues of liturgical revision in the church. In 1965 Series II was published as a modern alternative to the Prayer Book, and soon the more progressive Evangelical parishes were experimenting with it.[67] Even before the publication of *The Alternative Service Book* in 1980, most Evangelicals had ceased to use the 1662 order except for an early morning communion service. Keele went so far as to declare – though this was its most controversial pronouncement – that Evangelicals would 'work towards weekly communion as the central corporate service of the church'.[68] So drastic a reversal of policy represented a major rapprochement with the Anglo-Catholics. It issued in co-operation rather than conflict over liturgical matters in the General Synod during the 1970s.[69] More charitable church relations, both between and within denominations, were an important dimension of the increasing confidence of mainstream Evangelicalism during the period.

CONSERVATIVE EVANGELICAL STRENGTHS

Keswick remained a potent source of inspiration for conservative Evangelicals. At first after the Second World War its style did not change. 'It has been truly said', wrote a commentator in 1949, 'that the Keswick Convention is not a preaching festival. Its main purpose is to show from the scriptures how Christians may experience the *full* salvation which may be theirs in Christ.'[70] The message, however, was challenged from within conservative Evangelical circles during the 1950s. Leaders of the Rwanda Revival, a vigorous phase of African Christianity that attracted much attention, testified that there was no once-for-all experience of sanctification such as Keswick proclaimed.[71] In the manner of an angry young man of the time, J. I. Packer, from a Reformed standpoint, argued in 1955 that 'Keswick teaching is Pelagian through and through'.[72] Probably in response, 'a new breadth of vision' was evident at Keswick by 1960, with attention to the sins of the church, the role of the unconscious and the need for discipline as well as rest in the spiritual life.[73] By 1972 John Stott was delivering Bible 'studies' rather than the less expository Bible 'readings' that were traditional.[74] Keswick was becoming a preaching festival. The charismatic movement supplied an alternative mode of spirituality in keeping with the times. *The Life of Faith*, the newspaper associated with the convention, lost readers steadily until, in 1980, it was transformed into a magazine for Christian families without the note of victory by faith.[75] A devotional temper expressed in diffuse Romantic terms no longer appealed to the young. Keswick in its new form still helped to glue together Evangelicals from different denominations, but its most influential days as the power-house of the movement were over.

The conservative Evangelical tradition benefited from a range of other organisations. Youth work was maintained, not least because the interwar strategy of sowing seed for the future was showing its value by yielding a rich crop of leaders. In particular, the 'Bash Camps' for public schoolboys produced, among others, Michael Green, an able writer and evangelist, Dick Lucas, a powerful London preacher, and John Stott.[76] Scripture Union expanded its range of literature and activities, and an Inter-School Christian Fellowship was launched in 1947 to co-ordinate Evangelical groups in the education system.[77] To the interdenominational Crusaders, there was added, from 1953, a similar national youth organisation catering for Anglicans, the Pathfinder Movement.[78] From 1956 there was an annual 'Christian Holiday Crusade' at Butlin's Camp in Filey, beamed particularly at young people.[79] A resoundingly successful venture was the publication, in 1966, of *Youth Praise*, a collection of modern choruses designed to appeal to the burgeoning 'pop culture'. The undenominational missionary societies such as the Overseas Missionary Fellowship – the former China Inland Mission – did much to channel youthful enthusiasms into dedicated service. By their networks of officials, missionaries, literature and meetings they reinforced the zeal of conservative Christians. To their number was added, from 1962, Operation Mobilisation, an international body with roots in Spain designed to train and deploy young people in short-term evangelistic ventures.[80] For mission at home the Evangelical Alliance began to adopt a more active role. It produced an innovative glossy magazine, *Crusade*, from 1955; it issued a thorough study of evangelistic strategy, *On the Other Side* (1968); and it sponsored a short-lived annual assembly for Evangelicals of all denominations in 1965 and 1966.[81] All these activities expressed the evangelistic vitality of conservative Evangelicalism. They help explain both its effective recruitment and its acquisition of an increasingly up-to-date image.

Probably the most important factor in both these respects, however, was the impact of Billy Graham. In 1954–5, 1966–7 and 1984–5 the American evangelist held mass crusades in Britain. From the beginning huge numbers thronged in – 80,500 of them in the first week at Harringay in 1954.[82] Although there were widespread initial reservations, even among conservative Evangelicals, about importing an American with his razzamatazz, vast choirs and banks of technical equipment, Graham was brilliantly disarming. On arrival at Southampton in 1954, holding up a Morocco-bound Bible, he said, 'I am here to preach nothing but what is in this book, and to apply it to our everyday lives. I am not going to talk about your national problems or transgressions, as we have 10 times more in the United States.'[83] There were indeed criticisms, especially on his visits in the 1960s, that Graham failed to address public questions, including the Vietnam War.[84] There was also censure, normally rejected by actual attenders, on the ground that he was using techniques of mass suggestion.[85] Supposed converts, it was alleged, soon gave up church attendance. Ten months after the Harringay crusade, however, 64 per cent of the previous non-churchgoers who had come forward as 'enquirers' were still attending.[86] It was also asserted that 'the working classes . . . responded very little'.[87] An analysis of 1,317 enquirers in 1966, however, showed that 360 were unskilled or semi-skilled industrial workers. If skilled working people and members of working-class households are added, it is plain that Billy Graham was reaching extensively beyond the middle classes.[88] The crusades had enormous knock-on effects. 'Church life has been quickened', reported a Berkshire rector in 1955, 'several converts are worshipping keenly and winning others, finance has increased, study groups are thriving, and my own vision widened.'[89] Graham's imitators in mass evangelism – Eric Hutchings, Dick Saunders and Luis Palau among them – offered him the sincerest form of flattery. By declining to support him, many liberals eliminated themselves from the mainstream of Evangelical life in Britain. To those who supported him, a category extending beyond the conservative Evangelicals but having them as its core, he administered a powerful tonic.

THE REALM OF SCHOLARSHIP

More significant even than the Billy Graham crusades as an explanation for the advance of conservative Evangelicalism in the postwar period was the Inter-Varsity Fellowship (IVF). It had emerged during the 1920s and had been formally established in 1928 as a body linking the university students who followed the Cambridge Inter-Collegiate Christian Union in separation from the Student Christian Movement. Its basis of faith was resolutely conservative but by no means extreme: the first clause, for example, affirmed not the inerrancy of the Bible but the 'infallibility of Holy Scripture, as originally given'.[90] Students of diverse backgrounds, though few in most universities before the Second World War, were welded into tight-knit Christian Unions dedicated to zealous propagation of the faith under the watchful eyes of IVF travelling secretaries. The organising genius at the hub of the IVF for forty years from 1924 was Douglas Johnson, a London medical student of retiring disposition and studious habits who was particularly devoted to the weighty Reformed theologians of America. With the postwar expansion of higher education, the bodies affiliated to the IVF grew in numbers, scale and confidence. The collapse of the SCM gave them a clear field in the 1970s, by which time the title of the umbrella organisation was changed to 'Universities and Colleges Christian Fellowship' to mark its expanding role outside the university sector. Christian Union members naturally rose to positions of leadership in the various denominations. Thus, as Bishop of Barking, Hugh Gough, who had been a travelling secretary in 1927, gave crucial episcopal support to Billy Graham's first visit; J. Ithel Jones, IVF representative for Wales from 1933, became Principal of the South Wales Baptist College twenty-five years later; and Howard Belben, a CICCU member in the early 1930s, went on to be Principal of the Methodist Cliff College.[91] The Graduates' Fellowship (GF), consisting of ex-CU members, helped sustain their conservative theological convictions and encouraged them to express the faith in their professional lives. The proliferating branch organisations included the particularly large Christian Medical Fellowship (1949) and Research Scientists' Christian Fellowship (1944), whose members, swayed by the distinguished Brethren surgeon A. Rendle Short, took the lead in repudiating interwar conservative suspicions of evolution.[92] As early as 1948 a GF member, D. R. Denman, la.er Professor of Land Economy at Cambridge, was eager to study the problems raised by the social sciences for 'the Christian mind'.[93] The IVF was broadening the horizons of those with conservative theological views.

The work of the IVF was particularly noteworthy in biblical and related studies. So sparse did contemporary scholarship on acceptable lines seem in this field that, in 1943, the publishing arm of IVF was reissuing a work by the deceased D. M. McIntyre.[94] Already, in 1938, the IVF had formed a Biblical Research Committee designed to remove 'the reproach of obscurantism and anti-intellectual prejudice' from Evangelical Christianity. From 1942 there were academic Tyndale Lectures at the IVF's annual conference for theological students, in 1945 Tyndale House in Cambridge was opened as a centre for biblical studies and from the same year there was a Tyndale Fellowship for Biblical Research.[95] Thirty years later, between twenty-five and thirty of its members held teaching posts in British universities. The Old Testament specialist in the early years was W. J. Martin, Rankin Lecturer in Semitic Studies at Liverpool; his New Testament equivalent was F. F. Bruce, from 1959 to be Rylands Professor of Biblical Criticism and Exegesis at Manchester. Both were Brethren.[96] 'There is nothing', Bruce assured younger scholars in 1948, 'in the pursuit of source-criticism in the Biblical field which is necessarily incompatible with the outlook of the I.V.F. . . .'[97] Another enterprise, spearheaded by Douglas Johnson of the IVF, was the London Bible College, an interdenominational body for training graduates in Christian work that commenced classes in 1943. Like IVF and Tyndale House, the college owed much of its financial support to John Laing, an enormously successful Brethren building contractor.[98] The result of all these activities revolving in the orbit of the IVF was a resurgence, on a conservative basis, of Evangelical scholarship.

The transmission of scholarship to the public was another of Johnson's aims. 'A vital and up-to-date new Evangelical literature', he wrote in 1948, 'which will present truly biblical theology in the finest and simplest possible English style, is an essential need for this generation of Christian workers.'[99] The IVF undertook to fill the gap. It published, in addition to a growing list of other titles, a set of Bible study notes edited by G. T. Manley, entitled *Search the Scriptures* (1934–7); a digest of systematic theology, Archdeacon T. C. Hammond's *In Understanding be Men* (1936); the *New Bible Handbook* (1947), *New Bible Commentary* (1953) and *New Bible Dictionary* (1962); and a series of Tyndale commentaries on individual books of the Bible (from 1956).[100] When the Keele Congress Report recommended study material, more titles (30) were listed from IVF than from any other publisher. Second came Hodder and Stoughton (27), whose publications, though not as exclusively conservative as those of IVF, included many of that stamp. The Church Pastoral Aid Society issued 21, the Church Book Room Press 12 and the Marcham Manor Press, a recent firm concentrating on asserting the Evangelical position in Anglican debates, nine.[101] The Christian Brethren Research Fellowship, a group in which F. F. Bruce was prominent, published from 1963 a series of booklets that did much to stir hitherto rather introspective assemblies into facing similar issues to those raised at Keele.[102] *The Evangelical Quarterly*, founded in 1929 for the 'defence of the historic Christian faith', and the *Journal* of the Victoria Institute, a body concentrating on apologetic questions, especially in the area of science, were other vehicles for the dissemination of the conservative position. Both were edited for a while by F. F. Bruce.[103] There was a direct effect on the pulpit. The systematic exposition of the meaning of scripture came into fashion.[104] It was partly in imitation of the pulpit giants, particularly John Stott and Martyn Lloyd-Jones. But it was also because the intellectual tools were now available. Although the weightiest theological publishing in Britain remained in the hands of the SCM Press, it became increasingly difficult to dismiss conservative Evangelicals as disinclined to thought.

REFORMED AND SECTARIAN WINGS

The IVF graduates' magazine announced in 1950 that there was to be a conference at Westminster Chapel on 'the distinctive theological contribution of the English Puritans'. It was the beginning of a revival of interest in the Reformed theological tradition, especially in the seventeenth century. The prime movers were two Oxford students, one of them J. I. Packer. The Minister of Westminster Chapel, Martyn Lloyd-Jones, became the enthusiastic chairman of an annual Puritan Conference.[105] A Welshman who left medicine to enter the ministry, Lloyd-Jones awed packed congregations with his blend of logic, fire and close attention to the text of scripture. He functioned (in his own words) as 'the theologian of the IVF'.[106] For Lloyd-Jones the preoccupation with the Puritans was no reversion to the Baroque, but an engagement with their thought to discover what was applicable today. He was not a seventeenth-century man, as he put it, but an eighteenth-century man who believed in 'using the seventeenth-century men as the eighteenth-century men used them'.[107] Neo-Puritanism became a potent force. In 1963, at its height, the Puritan Conference attracted some 350 people, the majority young.[108] To students at the time Reformed doctrine seemed 'very novel, intoxicating to some, unnerving to many'.[109] It was disseminated by the Evangelical Library, an institution built on a collection of Puritan divinity made by Geoffrey Williams, a Strict Baptist bibliophile.[110] *The Banner of Truth*, a monthly magazine, was launched in 1955 and a publishing house under the same name two years later.[111] By 1960 there was a warning from the Islington platform that ultra-Calvinist views were straining the unity of Anglican Evangelicals.[112] With the encouragement of Lloyd-Jones, the Evangelical Movement of Wales crystallised in 1955 around a magazine and annual conference to rally individuals disquieted by the theological laxity within their denominations. Though not unanimously Calvinist, that was its predominant tone.[113] In Scotland another mixed Evangelical circle with Reformed leadership gathered about the figure of William Still, Minister since 1945 of Gilcomston South Parish Church, Aberdeen, and another prominent personality in the IVF. Resolutely attached to the Church of Scotland, they assembled annually at Crieff from 1971. Ten years later 170 attended.[114] In its various forms the Reformed revival was a sign of the theological appetite in sections of the conservative Evangelical world. It simultaneously bolstered the strength of the growing conservative movement and injected a divisive element into its ranks.

Sectarian expressions of Evangelicalism continued to grow in the postwar era, though in most cases at a rather slower rate than before the war. By 1979 there were nearly 550 Assemblies of God and 350 Elim churches in England alone.[115] The Apostolic Church, the third force in British Pentecostalism, enjoyed its greatest support in Wales and Scotland, where its congregations were more numerous than those of the Assemblies or Elim.[116] Ordinary Evangelicals had normally repudiated the Pentecostalists. 'The usual line of attack is to use threadbare illustrations of "unfortunate incidents" . . .'[117] It was generally held that the supernatural gifts championed by the Pentecostalists had ceased with the passing of the early church, so that alleged modern instances were counterfeit. The rise of the charismatic movement made it difficult – though not impossible for the hard-liners – to sustain that line of argument. Upward social mobility among the Pentecostalists also made their acceptance into the Evangelical fold smoother during the 1960s and 1970s. A fresh Pentecostal sector, however, had risen through immigration from the West Indies. Few black newcomers found their way into existing congregations, even Pentecostal churches. Instead, they established their own sects: the New Testament Church of God (with 23 congregations in 1962), the Church of God of Prophecy (16), the Church of God in Christ (7) and several smaller groupings.[118] As in many other spheres, there was little integration into Evangelical church life. The one existing body to recruit heavily among West Indians, the Seventh-Day Adventists, was generally accepted in conservative circles, even if some suspected that it should be classified with the heretical cults.[119] Likewise the Church of the Nazarene, an American denomination which the main holiness churches had joined, shared in local inter-church activities.[120] The sect which gave most to pan-Evangelical work, however, was the Brethren. Although its narrowest segment, the Exclusives, gained notoriety in a succession of scandals,[121] the mainstream of the Open Brethren emerged increasingly as a denomination willing to change with the times. 'Assemblies' transformed themselves into 'Evangelical Churches'. The traditional resistance to full-time ministry crumbled, so that by 1980 34 per cent of 246 churches surveyed thought it a good idea.[122] Eminent Brethren, as we have seen, served and financed the IVF and its satellites. Conservative Evangelicalism derived a great deal of vitality from its sectarian dimension.

INTO THE WORLD

A consequence of the rise of the conservative Evangelicals was a change in their habits. Their introverted attitudes in the 1940s cultivated a distinctive style: 'unworldly, diligent in attendance at weekly prayer meetings, meticulous about quiet times, suspicious of the arts, missionary-minded, hostile to new liturgical ideas.'[123] The decline of the Keswick imperative gradually opened them to change. In 1947 J. W. Wenham, who was to go on to teach at Tyndale Hall, Bristol, urged in an IVF newsletter that ministers should drop their blanket prohibitions on the cinema, the theatre and tobacco. They were erecting false barriers that hampered the gospel. A wider onslaught on Evangelical taboos was launched for similar reasons in a Scripture Union book, *Culture, Class and Christian Beliefs*, by John Benington in 1973. Such criticisms slowly sapped inhibitions, but far more came about through the social change of the 1960s. Permissiveness was echoed, albeit dimly, among Evangelicals. At Keele half the congress erupted into laughter about some indiscreet remarks on contraception; ten years later, young Christian nurses were sometimes prepared to justify abortion on demand and a few Evangelicals were arguing that homosexual acts within a stable relationship are 'not a contravention of the biblical teaching'.[124] The youth culture was married to the gospel. The Salvation Army's Joystrings, a group of guitar-playing girls, led the way in 1964.[125] Cliff Richard, a converted pop singer who contrived to remain at the top of his career for decades, provided continuing inspiration.[126] From 1974 there was an annual Christian rock festival, Greenbelt. *Buzz* magazine, begun in 1964, attained a circulation of more than 30,000 in 1981 by catering for the gospel pop teenage market.[127] By 1976 Gavin Reid, evangelistic secretary of the CPAS, was opening a musical event for youth fellowships with the remark, 'Let's have a feeling of wrapped-around-ness.'[128] In the same year, during an Evangelical teaching conference session on a simpler life-style, a 'young man with a wispy moustache and tie-dyed jeans spoke poignantly of collecting waste-paper in Australia'.[129] The gulf that had once yawned between the church and the world had virtually disappeared.

Until well into the 1960s, social involvement remained under the cloud of suspicion it had attracted in the 1920s. It was typical that after an innovatory paper on the social implications of the gospel at the National Assembly of Evangelicals in 1966, 'some members were suspicious of a return to "the social gospel" and called for a more direct "witness"'.[130] Yet there were persistent traditions of social commitment. The Salvation Army, without compromising its beliefs, resolutely served the needs of the body as well as those of the soul.[131] Organisations with unimpeachable conservative Evangelical credentials such as the London City Mission maintained a philanthropic role.[132] Archdeacon Hammond, the IVF's early theologian, also wrote on social ethics.[133] George Duncan of St Thomas's, Edinburgh, declared in 1948 that some Evangelicals might 'find a greater place than they do for matters of social reform, such as housing, etc. Even a casual glance at the Old Testament prophets shows how clearly God was and is concerned in these matters.'[134] The greatest ideological obstacle to the more forthright expression of such views was adventism. The premillennial teaching so widespread in conservative Evangelical circles directly inhibited social action. His expectation of the second event, wrote W. G. Channon, a rising young Baptist minister, in 1949, made him realise that it was not the business of the church to Christianise society. Rather, the church was to evangelise until, when God had called out his people, Christ would return.[135] In succeeding decades, however, premillennialism went into decline. A milestone was the publication in 1971 by Iain Murray of *The Puritan Hope*, a reassertion on historical grounds of the postmillennial position. The premillennial message was already disappearing from the Keswick platform, and by the 1970s it was ceasing to be a feature even of the Brethren. Many conservative Evangelicals, while adhering to the belief in a personal second coming guarded by the IVF basis of faith, moved more or less unconsciously to an amillennial view. With the fading of the gloomy opinion that the world was under imminent sentence of death, effort to improve it seemed more worthwhile. A pent-up potential for social involvement was released.

The times seemed to call for action. The permissive society challenged Evangelical Christians at a traditionally sensitive point, their defence of sexual morality. Many rallied to the support of Mary Whitehouse, whose National Viewers' and Listeners' Association was established in 1965 to stem the tide of sex and violence that seemed to be overwhelming the media.[136] Eddy Stride, Rector of Spitalfields and a former shop steward, who had long been censuring the complacency of the 'middle-class, inward-looking Church', participated in several public protests against pornography in 1970.[137] Several eminent Evangelicals were recruited to Lord Longford's investigation of pornography in the following year,[138] a year that witnessed an upsurge of symbolic action against 'moral pollution'. Dubbed 'Festival of Light' by the recently converted broadcaster, Malcolm Muggeridge, an embryonic organisation held local rallies throughout the country to illuminate warning beacons. The culmination was a rally in Trafalgar Square on 25 September, followed by a march to Hyde Park. Although not wholly Evangelical in support, its orientation is clear from the evidence that 84 per cent of attenders at a follow-up rally five years later saw evangelism as a better remedy than legislation for Britain's moral decline.[139] The organisation became permanent as the Nationwide Festival of Light, which subsequently branched into CARE Trust (for research) and CARE Campaigns (for pressure group activity). A similar semi-spontaneous movement arose in 1985–6 to oppose what seemed another symptom of permissiveness, the deregulation of Sunday shop opening hours. Support extended well beyond Evangelical ranks and, remarkably, intended government legislation was defeated by a revolt of backbench Conservative MPs.[140] The widest enthusiasm for public campaigns, as in the nineteenth century, appeared when the target, in Evangelical eyes, was sin. Much of the renewed impetus for socio-political action sprang from an eagerness to take up broadly moral issues.

Sheer need did, however, play its part in prompting action. The dimensions of poverty in the Third World led, in 1968, to the creation of The Evangelical Alliance Relief (TEAR) Fund, which rapidly tapped funds from congregations that previously might have hesitated to give to Christian Aid. A symptom of changing attitudes was the supersession, around 1970, of the traditional vast arrays of produce at harvest festivals by token displays accompanied by collections for TEAR Fund. The Fund gave rise in 1974 to Tearcraft, an enterprise marketing goods from less developed countries, and that in turn to Traidcraft, an independent company with similar aims. Extremely influential in this field was R. J. Sider's *Rich Christians in an Age of Hunger* (1977), a biblical case for aid to the Third World originally aimed at an American audience. The multiple deprivation of the inner cities at home acted as a significant, if lesser, stimulus. David Sheppard, Warden of the Mayflower Centre in the East End of London and subsequently Bishop of Liverpool, set up a range of social programmes that he at first conceived as evangelistic bridges.[141] Subsequently his work *Built as a City* (1974) espoused and inspired more adventurous strategies of mission. The Frontier Youth Trust and later the Evangelical Coalition for Urban Mission pioneered fresh ventures. At the Nottingham National Evangelical Anglican Congress of 1977 a section not in the draft was added to the published statement on 'The gospel in urban areas'.[142] Inner-city issues were sufficiently salient to force themselves on the attention of at least a section of the Evangelical public.

Overseas influences helped to foster the new social awareness. Participation in ecumenical life made Evangelicals take up a stance on social questions, even if at first it was largely a repudiation of the policies publicised by the World Council of Churches. The 1968 Uppsala assembly of the WCC, by defining the mission of the church in partly socio-political terms, compelled self-scrutiny by those propounding an alternative view.[143] Dutch Reformed social thought stemming from Abraham Kuyper and Hermann Dooyeweerd was a more constructive factor. Its advocates in Britain were few, but in the late 1960s included Alan Storkey, a pioneer of Evangelical social analysis and subsequently the author of *A Christian Social Perspective* (1979). Influences from America were more widespread but more diffuse, tending to reinforce rather than initiate trends in British opinion. An exception must be made for writings from the Mennonite tradition. In particular, J. H. Yoder's work *The Politics of Jesus* (1972) fostered a new sympathy for a theologically grounded pacifism among British Evangelicals. The writings of Jim Wallis of the Sojourners' Community were also popular. From 1974, furthermore, there was international sanction for Evangelical social commitment. At Lausanne a congress on world evangelisation expressed repentance for previous Evangelical neglect in this field. The statement was partly a British achievement, a result of a strong rebuke by John Stott. Yet a Radical Discipleship group wished to go further in stating the social implications of the gospel. Led by Samuel Escobar, a South American who had grafted elements of liberation theology on to Evangelicalism, it called for a dedication to freedom, justice and human fulfilment.[144] The relationship between evangelism and social activity was more closely defined by a conference at Grand Rapids in 1982. 'They are like the two blades of a pair of scissors', its report declared, 'or the two wings of a bird.'[145] The British experience was part of a worldwide trend that steadily gathered momentum.

The increased emphasis on social responsibility also possessed its own national dynamic. The mushrooming of sociology in postwar British universities was bound to have consequences in a movement so strongly moulded by graduates. When IVF threw its weight behind social involvement, the trend was unstoppable. In this process the appearance of *Whose World?* (1970), a summons to formulate a Christian mind on all aspects of human affairs, was crucial. Its author, though cautiously employing a pseudonym, was Oliver Barclay, the IVF General Secretary. The Shaftesbury Project, designed to promote thought and action in every sphere of involvement, was developed by Alan Storkey on the fringe of the IVF from 1969 onwards. Its third director, John Gladwin, moved directly to become Secretary of the Board for Social Responsibility of the Church of England in 1982.[146] More systematic training in relating the faith to the forces at work in the modern world was provided by the London Institute for Contemporary Christianity, a brainchild created by John Stott after his retirement from All Souls' in 1975. Unfettered discussion of such questions was found from 1977 in the pages of *Third Way*, a fortnightly (then monthly) magazine that reached a circulation of more than 3,000 ten years later. Its readership breakdown in 1986 is illuminating: 52 per cent read *The Guardian* and 32 per cent *The Times*. By contrast, at the National Evangelical Anglican Congress in 1977, 60 per cent took *The Daily Telegraph*.[147] Evangelicals now included a liberally minded wing bearing no resemblance to the interwar stereotype of their forefathers. In expanding they had broadened.

GROWING PAINS

The diversity of the Evangelical movement created tensions. Several surrounded the figure of Martyn Lloyd-Jones, an Independent by temperament and conviction.[148] He was regularly prepared to pursue a distinctive line of policy, standing aside, for example, from Billy Graham's crusades as a cheapening of the gospel.[149] Partly through the Westminster Fellowship, an interdenominational ministers' fraternal that met in his chapel from the end of the war, Lloyd-Jones came to enjoy widespread and deeply felt respect.[150] The tercentenary in 1962 of the Great Ejection of Nonconformist ministers from the Church of England turned his mind to the issue of what unity Evangelicals should prize. In 1963 he spoke to the Puritan Conference about John Owen on schism.[151] On 18 October 1966 an incident took place that was to dramatise a fracture in the Evangelical world. Lloyd-Jones was invited to speak at the opening public meeting of the National Assembly of Evangelicals on the issue of unity. To the horror of members of his audience who valued their existing denominational allegiances, he urged that, although separation from liberals was no schism, separation from fellow Evangelicals was. Immediately afterwards John Stott rose from the chair to voice his belief that scripture was against the speaker – an act, though not an opinion, he subsequently regretted.[152] Lloyd-Jones's call for Evangelicals to leave their present churches was dismissed by nearly all those in the Church of England as being (in the phrase of their newspaper) 'nothing short of hare-brained',[153] and in other 'mixed denominations' he was little heeded. The appeal nevertheless reinforced the existing aversion of the Baptist Revival Fellowship to the ecumenical movement as an engine for compromising the truth and, during the next few years, just as Lloyd-Jones took Westminster Chapel out of the Congregational Union, so a number of Baptists withdrew from their Union. The Fellowship of Independent Evangelical Churches was immeasurably strengthened by Lloyd-Jones's support; the Evangelical Movement of Wales in 1967 permitted churches disenchanted with their previous denominations to affiliate direct;[154] and *The Evangelical Times* was launched in the same year as the monthly organ of principled separatism. A British Evangelical Council, formed in 1953 and also backed by Lloyd-Jones, acted as an umbrella organisation for the anti-ecumenical bodies. Enjoying the membership of the Free Church of Scotland, by 1981 it could claim to represent more than 2,000 congregations.[155] Predominantly but by no means exclusively Reformed in theological tone, it represented a significant force in the Evangelical World.

Some of the strains engendered by charismatic renewal have already been considered. Its separatist wing, the Restorationists, formed a rapidly expanding Christian presence in the 1980s.[156] But the assimilation of the renewal movement by existing churches was perhaps the more remarkable development. At Keele in 1967 there was no united opinion about whether charismatic manifestations were of the same sort as the New Testament 'gifts of the Spirit'.[157] By contrast, ten years later at the Nottingham Evangelical Anglican Congress, hands were raised in worship and charismatic leaders including Michael Harper and David Watson delivered addresses. Only a few jarring notes were heard. Gerald Bray, librarian of Tyndale House and subsequently editor of *Churchman*, for example, voiced continuing doctrinal misgivings about the movement. In general, however, as Harper remarked, 'the charismatic divide was given the last rites'. So deeply enmeshed in Evangelical Anglican life had the movement become between 1967 and 1977 that one commentator spoke, with perhaps a little exaggeration, of 'a dominating position for charismatics'.[158] Among Baptists, the Mainstream organisation formed in 1979 drew together traditional Evangelicals and charismatics in regular conferences.[159] One of its founders, Paul Beasley-Murray, went on to become Principal of Spurgeon's, the denomination's largest college, in 1986. Although there were many instances of local tension, overall the Baptists were adapting to the new influences. The British Evangelical Council could not manage the same feat. Sympathy for renewal was anathema to hard-line Reformed views, and, after strenuous efforts at containment, the issue eventually exploded with the seizure of *The Evangelical Times* by the anti-charismatics in 1986.[160] The new style represented by the charismatic movement proved acceptable to a majority of Evangelicals in the older denominations, but not to most of those who frowned on ecumenical involvement. Were the cultural forms of the twentieth century to be accepted or rejected? There were the makings of polarisation around this fundamental question.

There were signs of divergence around another issue, the interpretation of the Bible. If one consideration had been paramount among interwar conservative Evangelicals, it was the appeal to the text of scripture. In the postwar era, however, the proliferation of Bible versions meant that variations in the text were in widespread circulation. Although more than half the attenders at a Keswick youth meeting in 1970 still read the Authorised Version,[161] by that date the Revised Standard Version was in general use. The New English Bible attracted only a small following among Evangelicals, but the Good News Bible and then the New International Version achieved high popularity.[162] Discrepancies made it harder to settle issues by quoting biblical texts. Consequently, criteria were needed for establishing what the Bible meant. As was pointed out in 1974 by Tony Thiselton, subsequently Principal of St John's College, Durham, this was the question of hermeneutics. It was particularly acute when trying to tease out biblical teaching on ethics for application to the social problems of the day.[163] It was also a difficulty for Evangelicals as they took opposite sides on the question of whether women should be ordained in the Church of England.[164] Opponents pointed to the letter of scripture about women not having authority over men and keeping silence in church; supporters suggested that the statement about the barrier between male and female having been abolished in Christ took precedence. Hermeneutics was a pressing matter. The word was bandied about, with much ribald comment, at Nottingham in 1977.[165] Some were alarmed that the authority of scripture was being undermined. Dick Lucas, Rector of St Helen's, Bishopsgate, warned the 1979 Islington Conference that the new hermeneutic might prepare the way for a fresh bout of liberal scholarship.[166] The threatening storm burst in 1982 over two articles in *Churchman* by James Dunn, soon to be Professor of Divinity at Durham, propounding a view of the Bible that was too liberal for some of the journal's sponsors.[167] In the succeeding dispute, the editor was dismissed, a new editorial board formed and the dispossessed party founded a fresh journal, *Anvil*, in 1984. Thiselton, significantly, was on the Anvil Trust. In 1986 J. I. Packer was still having to give a steadying address to the Anglican Evangelical Assembly on hermeneutics.[168] The Bible was no longer treated as a simple unifying force in the Evangelical world. It had become a bone of contention.

Evangelicals in the Church of England faced another issue around 1980, but it was less a controversy and more a mood of self-doubt. It was labelled 'the Evangelical Anglican identity problem'. By the later 1970s traditional landmarks had been removed. An attempt by some older Evangelicals at Nottingham to insert a reference to the Thirty-Nine Articles and the Book of Common Prayer in the Congress statement came to naught.[169] Basics had already been brought into question. We need to ask, according to a leading article in *The Church of England Newspaper* on David Sheppard's *Built as a City*, 'whether the traditional evangelical understanding of the Gospel is in fact as biblical as it is often assumed to be'.[170] At Nottingham the statement admitted that 'we give different emphasis to the various biblical expressions of atonement': substitution was no longer central for all.[171] The party, as J. I. Packer commented in a booklet on the identity problem, was less cohesive at Nottingham than at Keele.[172] Although the number of self-professed Evangelicals in the General Synod increased from 1970 to 1980, their solidarity weakened.[173] '*The* great question-mark', according to Colin Buchanan, 'which had to be hung against the proposal that "we" should hold another Congress in 1977 was whether there existed any identifiable "we" to do it'.[174] John Stott's answer to such queries was unequivocal. They were committed to Bible and gospel, and so could not drop the title 'Evangelical'.[175] Yet debate continued for the next couple of years.[176] Institutional measures were taken to consolidate the party. Since 1960 a Church of England Evangelical Council had brought together representative leaders, and from 1980 there were broader consultations.[177] Since 1983 there has been an Anglican Evangelical Assembly with a combination of elected and nominated members, which at last supplanted Islington as the party's main forum.[178] The possibility of merging imperceptibly into the mainstream of church life seemed to have been averted.

LOOKING TO THE FUTURE

The heirs of the interwar conservative Evangelical tradition remained a distinctive movement, cutting across denominational allegiances, after the time of Keele. Though more fragmented, they were still conscious of an underlying unity. It is possible to locate their loyalties more precisely. Their greatest strength lay in the Anglican and Baptist denominations. At the first National Assembly of Evangelicals in 1965, Anglicans were reported to be easily the largest single group amongst them, with Baptists second.[179] At the same event the following year, about a quarter were Anglican and a quarter Baptist.[180] In 1985–6 readers of *Third Way* were 49 per cent Anglican and 22 per cent Baptist.[181] Attenders at the 1976 Festival of Light rally were 42 per cent Anglican and 22 per cent Baptist. Pentecostal churches and charismatic house fellowships contributed 9 per cent, Evangelical or Free Evangelical churches 6 per cent, Methodists 5 per cent and Brethren 3 per cent to this gathering.[182] All these figures are affected by – among other factors – their exaggerated reflection of the denominational balance in South-East England. A northern catchment area might have strengthened the Methodist presence: there had been since 1970 an organisation called Conservative Evangelicals in Methodism,[183] and many Methodists outside it remained Evangelicals. In Wales Anglicans would have been far less numerous, and in Scotland Presbyterians would have been significantly represented. The future of the Evangelical movement nevertheless lay disproportionately in the hands of two denominations. In 1986, for the first time, more than half the Anglican ordinands in residential colleges were said to be Evangelical.[184] Alone among the Free Churches, the Baptists reported growth in 1987.[185] The continuing expansion of the Restorationists would in due course affect the balance, the Church of Scotland possessed an increasing Evangelical sector, and the conservative bodies of the British Evangelical Council had emerged with a rugged tenacity. The kaleidoscope of Evangelicalism would turn again to create a new pattern. But growth was intended and expected. The movement was likely to occupy a more salient position within British Christianity in the twenty-first century than in the twentieth.

[9]

Time and Chance:
Evangelicalism and Change

. . . time and chance happeneth to them all. (Eccles. 9:11)

Evangelical religion in Britain has changed immensely during the two and
a half centuries of its existence. Its outward expressions, such as its social
composition and political attitudes, have frequently been transformed.
Its inward principles, embracing teaching about Christian theology and
behaviour, have altered hardly less. Nothing could be further from the
truth than the common image of Evangelicalism being ever the same. Yet
Evangelicals themselves have often fostered the image. They have claimed
that their brand of Christianity, the form once delivered to the saints,
has possessed an essentially changeless content so long as it has remained
loyal to its source. In a Commons debate of 1850 a Unitarian referred
to discoveries in theology since the reign of Elizabeth I. 'Discoveries
in theology!' snorted Sir Robert Inglis, an Evangelical defender of the
Church of England: ' . . . all the truths of religion are to be found in the
blessed Bible; and all "discoveries" which do not derive from that book
their origin and foundation, their justification and their explanation, are
worth neither teaching nor hearing.'[1] Such a claim to stability is a common
feature of conservative Protestantism.[2] It is no wonder that outsiders, taking
Evangelicals at their word, have often treated them as perversely impervious
to change and so perennially old-fashioned. The germ of truth in that
claim is that Evangelical religion has been consistently marked by four
characteristics. Conversionism, activism, biblicism and crucicentrism have
been transmitted down the generations. They have formed a permanent
deposit of faith. Each of the characteristics, however, has found expression
in many different ways, and one of them, activism, was a novelty that set
Evangelicals apart from earlier Protestantism. Other features of Evangelical
doctrine and piety, opinion and practice, have varied from time to time.
Views on eschatology and spirituality have been particularly subject to
change. So the movement did not manage a total escape to a world of
eternal truths. It was bound up in the flux of events.

The reality was sometimes noticed by evangelicals themselves. The great nineteenth-century Congregationalist R. W. Dale was acutely aware of the changing theological fashions within the movement.[3] Occasionally it was recognised that change was not merely a matter of theology. 'To say that the Church has remained unaffected by influences permeating our national life', declared the Secretary of the National Sunday School Union in 1900 when analysing the altered tone of teaching during the previous half-century, 'would be to assert that we are independent of our social environment'.[4] But it was not until the Lausanne Congress of 1974 that it was commonly admitted by Evangelicals that the shape of their religion is influenced by the environment. Evidence from the mission field that the embodiment of the faith is deeply affected by its cultural setting seemed incontrovertible.[5] What this study has explored is the same interaction between Christianity and its setting in Britain.

Changing socio-economic and political conditions affected Evangelicalism and its potential recruits in ways that drastically moulded its size, self-image, strategy and teaching. When personally controlled firms became large-scale conglomerates, for example, it was no longer expected that employees would follow the religious preferences – often Evangelical – of their employers. New wealth permitted the state to provide educational and philanthropic facilities that had previously been supplied by the churches, and so to weaken the bonds between working-class people and evangelistic agencies. Such forces decreased church attendance around the end of the nineteenth century, sapped Christian confidence and so encouraged attempts to remodel Evangelicalism with a view to improving its impact. Again, political crises over Ireland, conjuring up the spectre of papist oppression, often stirred up the powerful spirit of anti-Catholicism. The First World War provoked heart-searching questions about doctrines surrounding the fate of the dead. Events in the public realm necessarily impinged on religious groups. Yet socio-economic and political developments fashioned Evangelical responses from the raw material of their existing attitudes. With other opinions they would have reacted differently. The cultural context, not economics or politics, does most to explain the shape of Evangelical religion. Conditions and crises in economic and political life might generate new phases of behaviour and even new expressions of belief, but rarely did they determine fundamental trends in Evangelical life. That role was normally reserved for the dominant ideas of the age.

The most influential bodies of thought were not distinctly religious. It is frequently assumed, especially by church historians, that theologians were the crucial innovators. Authors like F. D. Maurice are treated as the trend-setters for subsequent generations. Theologians, however, have usually been followers of trends set in other fields. Maurice, for instance, was deeply swayed by the organic view of society that was the hallmark of Romantic theorists.[6] Lay opinion was more affected by the general cultural

atmosphere than by Maurice's expression of it. The basic trends in Evangelicalism were shaped by the shifts in cultural mood that eventually altered the
orientation of the whole population. Changes in the intellectual climate have
a significant impact on any social movement setting great store by ideas,
whether political, educational or religious. Churches, which usually carry
heavy doctrinal baggage, are particularly susceptible. Hence Christian beliefs
and practices have reflected developments in high culture. The novelties
of the philosophers and creative artists have been transmitted, often after
some delay, to the Evangelical world. The crucial determinants of change
in Evangelical religion have been the successive cultural waves that have
broken over Western civilisation since the late seventeenth century. Popular
Protestantism has been remoulded in turn by the Enlightenment of Locke,
the Romanticism of Coleridge and the Modernism associated with, among
others, the Bloomsbury Group. That is not to suggest that the currents of
high cultural ideas have flowed clear and crystal between Evangelical shores.
On the contrary, the streams have been muddied by other influences and
at some stages have even run underground. The doctrines derived most
clearly from shifts in taste in the intellectual *avant-garde* have subsequently
been modified within Evangelicalism. Thus the holiness teaching of the
later nineteenth century, very much a symptom of the Romantic inclinations
of the period, was adapted to fit the Calvinist theological inheritance of its
Anglican proponents. The resulting Keswick school was far from being
simply a product of the contemporary intellectual climate. Yet what was
distinctive about it did derive primarily from the spirit of the age, and can
be understood only in that light.

The process of change can best be seen as a pattern of diffusion. Ideas
originating in high culture have spread to leaders of Evangelical opinion and
through them to the Evangelical constituency. By this means the novelties
of one age have become the commonplaces of the next. Alongside the
secular press, popular Protestantism has been among the chief agencies for
the transmission of innovating ideas from the tiny cultural elite that forms
them to the mass of the population that embraces them, often unaware of
their origins. The diffusion has had two main dimensions, the social and
the spatial. Ideas, that is to say, have spread downwards from the elite to
the masses and outwards from the centre to the periphery. Groups higher
in the social scale, usually enjoying higher standards of education, tend to
absorb fresh attitudes earlier than lower groups.[7] They are the ones who
usually read books and magazines first. But then the newer views seep
down to lower social groups. Wilberforce, writing in 1797, recognised
that 'the free and unrestrained intercourse, subsisting amongst the several
ranks and classes of society, so much favours the general diffusion of the
sentiments of the higher orders'.[8] The variation according to position on
the social scale helps explain why, within Evangelicalism, Anglicans, with
their strong support among the gentry and professionals, were normally
more forward than Nonconformists in embracing new cultural attitudes.

Thus it was Anglicans, together with the socially superior Brethren and Catholic Apostolic Church, who disproportionately favoured the novel premillennialism of the nineteenth century. But the relation between elite and masses in the churches has never been founded on class distinctions alone. The ministry constituted a body of professional opinion-formers. Consequently, ideas would often reach a congregation first through the minister. Lower-class congregations could sometimes be charged with fresh enthusiasms before neighbours of more exalted social standing. Yet the general principle remains valid. Cultural diffusion within Evangelicalism was normally a matter of the percolation of ideas down the social scale.

The second dimension was spatial, the spread of new ideas outwards from cultural centres. Personal contacts, and especially addresses at conferences, were at least as important as literature in the dissemination of Evangelical novelties. Hence some areas would adopt new attitudes long before others. New teaching would normally be welcomed in London long before it was appreciated in the South-West or the North of England, let alone the remoter parts of Wales and Scotland. Although the difference between the regions was partly a matter of ingrained local preferences, which have survived the industrial and communications revolutions to a far greater extent than is normally recognised,[9] the spatial variation was far more the result of differing degrees of proximity to the sources of fresh waves of opinion, and especially to London. Most trends of thought seized the capital and its environs first – whether Hugh Price Hughes's social gospel or charismatic renewal. Metropolitan views took time to spread elsewhere. There was no direct correlation, however, between distance from London and the rapidity with which new opinion was taken up. The great cities functioned as subsidiary cultural centres, radiating outwards to their own hinterlands influences received from London, supplemented by occasional indigenous developments. Manchester, Bristol, Edinburgh and similar places ensured that trends spread in their own vicinities before they had affected areas nearer London that lacked a major urban focus – Suffolk, for example. There were also local centres of influence, often some sort of Evangelical training college (such as the Methodist Cliff College in Derbyshire), that spread particular messages in their own neighbourhoods. The general effect of spatial diffusion was to put more urbanised areas ahead of more rural parts, but that pattern was far from absolute since local centres or even individual enthusiasts could propagate new ideas in unexpected spots.[10] National variations were overridden in a pattern that straddled the boundaries between England, Wales and Scotland, so that developments usually affected Swansea before Herefordshire and Glasgow before Westmorland. It was in the periphery of Britain that the old ways lingered longest.[11] Traditional revivals in the twentieth century, for instance, have taken place chiefly in Wales, Cornwall, East Anglia, the Moray Firth coast of Scotland and the Hebrides. Spatial diffusion explains a great deal about the state of Evangelicalism.

The deepest divisions in the Evangelical world generally arose from the impact of the cultural waves. Denominational splits form an excellent index to the advance of fresh ideas. Repeatedly, new wine broke old bottles. Methodism, representing undiluted Enlightenment Protestantism, generated a momentum that carried it, despite John Wesley's wishes, beyond the bounds of the Church of England. The severance between New Lights and Old Lights in Scottish Presbyterian Dissent showed the impossibility of those who thought like Jonathan Edwards of remaining in fellowship with those adhering to the thought-world of the Westminster Confession. The same pre-Evangelical Calvinism was the ground from which certain Baptists in the South-East of England and Presbyterians in the North-West of Scotland refused to be dislodged. Hence there arose the Strict Baptists and the Free Presbyterians. The initial onset of Romanticism gave rise in the 1830s to two premillennialist bodies, the Catholic Apostolic Church and the Brethren. Its subsequent impact in the form of holiness teaching led to the foundation of bodies such as the Salvation Army and the Pentecostalists. Premillennialism, its associated attitude to the Bible and the holiness movement together created the matrix of interwar conservative Evangelicalism with all its tendencies to fission. And charismatic renewal, so largely an expression of cultural Modernism, could not be confined within existing structures, but also erected its own. That is not to say that every denominational split in the period can be traced back to a clash of cultural styles: on the contrary, several Methodist secessions and the Disruption of the Church of Scotland were the result of conflicts about control of institutions. Differences stemming from shifts of cultural mood can nevertheless be detected within and between congregations of the same denomination throughout the period. Deep-seated theological debates such as the Robertson Smith affair or the Down Grade Controversy were usually about whether truth was being compromised by the intellectual trends of the times. The assimilation of new ideas was naturally unsettling.

Because Evangelicalism has changed so much over time, any attempt to equate it with 'Fundamentalism' is doomed to failure. It is often assumed that the equation can be made; and a substantial treatise published by James Barr in 1977 identified the Fundamentalism of its title at least with the conservative variety of Evangelicalism in the postwar period.[12] Evangelicals, including conservatives, have generally repudiated the term in Britain.[13] If the word is used in a precise theological sense, then it defines a deductive approach to biblical inspiration, the belief that since the Bible is the word of God and God cannot err, the Bible is inerrant. That has been a current in Evangelicalism since the 1820s, but it never became unanimous and was weak in the early twentieth century, even among conservatives. Its greater popularity in the postwar period has been associated primarily with the esteem of the Reformed wing of Evangelicalism for B. B. Warfield and it has been treated with reserve by others.[14] If 'Fundamentalism' is taken in a social sense to describe a group so fanatically committed to its religion that it lashes out against opponents in mindless denunciation, there were only two stages when this unsavoury attitude disfigured Evangelicalism. Between about 1840 and 1890 many Anglican Evangelicals became obsessive in the desire to eliminate Romanising doctrines and ritual from their church; and in the aftermath of the First World War an extreme section of Evangelical opinion, though not the conservative leadership, attempted to take up the fight of their American cousins against 'Modernist' theological tendencies. In Britain such Fundamentalism – Evangelicalism with an inferiority complex – was at most times relatively weak. Only if Fundamentalism is defined in a third way, as the championing of fundamental Christian orthodoxies, can the term be applied to the Evangelical movement as a whole with any degree of plausibility. Even then, some of the more liberal thinkers within the movement would have been unhappy in that role. It is best to admit that Fundamentalism in any sense has been merely one feature among many, at some times and in some places, of Evangelical religion.

Lord Salisbury, the Conservative Prime Minister at the end of the nineteenth century, entertained a distaste for Evangelicalism. He wrote of its 'reign of rant' and 'nasal accents of devout ejaculation', and again of its 'incubus of narrow-mindedness . . . brooding over English society'.[15] The narrowness of Evangelical life has been a frequent reproach. It is true that its tendency to erect barriers against worldliness often did make it a restricted sphere. Its large claims and internal idiosyncrasies made it an easy target for cheap satire. Yet it has shaped the thought-world of a large proportion of the population. It has exerted an immense influence both on individuals and on the course of social and political development, particularly in the later nineteenth century. And it has shown a receptivity that goes some way towards modifying the charge of narrowness. Evangelical religion has been in contact with shifts in the mood of the intellectual elite. Like so many other aspects of British life, from political rhetoric to wallpaper design, it was affected by alterations in taste. In mediating high cultural changes to a mass public it brought its adherents into the mainstream of Western civilisation. Certainly Evangelicalism created its own backwaters, but overall it was no stagnant pool. The process of diffusion meant that the world of popular Protestantism was in flux. There was enormous variation in Evangelicalism over time; and at any particular moment there was an intricate pattern of beliefs, attitudes and customs. So there was an element of breadth – a broad range of opinion – that could be obscure to the eye of the contemporary observer and has all too frequently been overlooked by the historian. Moulded and remoulded by its environment, Evangelical religion has been a vital force in modern Britain.

Notes

ABBREVIATIONS USED IN THE NOTES

AFR	*Anglicans for Renewal*
AW	*The Advent Witness*
BC	*The Bible Call*
BW	*The British Weekly*
C	*The Christian*
CEN	*Church of England Newspaper*
CG	*Christian Graduate*
CO	*The Christian Observer*
CW	*The Christian World*
F	*The Fundamentalist*
JEH	*The Journal of Ecclesiastical History*
JWBU	*The Journal of the Wesley Bible Union* (which took the title *The Fundamentalist* in 1927)
KH	*The King's Highway*
LCMM	*The London City Mission Magazine*
LE	*The Liberal Evangelical*
LF	*The Life of Faith*
LW	*Life and Work*
MBAPPU	*The Monthly Bulletin of the Advent Preparation Prayer Union*
MR	*The Methodist Recorder*
MT	*The Methodist Times*
R	*The Record*
T	*The Times*
W	*The Witness*
WV	*Wesley's Veterans*, ed. J. Telford (London, n.d.)

CHAPTER 1: PREACHING THE GOSPEL

1 R. T. Jones, *The Great Reformation* (Leicester, 1985) G. Rupp, *Religion in England, 1688–1791* (Oxford, 1986), pp. 121, 125.
2 G. R. Balleine, *A History of the Evangelical Party in the Church of England* (London, 1951 edn), p. 40 n. Other general studies of Anglican Evangelicalism are: G. W. E. Russell, *A Short History of the Evangelical*

Movement (London, 1915); L. Elliott-Binns, *The Evangelical Movement in the English Church* (London, 1928); and D. N. Samuel (ed.) *The Evangelical Succession in the Church of England* (Cambridge, 1979). On the broader movement there is E. J. Poole-Connor, *Evangelicalism in England* (Worthing, 1966 edn).

3 Watts, preface to J. Jennings, *Two Discourses* (1723), quoted by G. F. Nuttall, 'Continental Pietism and the Evangelical Movement in Britain', in J. van den Berg and J. P. van Dooren (eds), *Pietismus und Reveil* (Leiden, 1978), p. 226.

4 The term is studiously avoided in Sir H.M. Wellwood, *Account of the Life and Writings of John Erskine, D.D.* (Edinburgh, 1818).

5 J. Milner, 'On Evangelical religion', *The Works of Joseph Milner*, ed. I. Milner, Vol. 8 (London, 1810), p. 199.

6 For example, T. Haweis to S. Walker, 16 July 1759, in G. C. B. Davies, *The Early Cornish Evangelicals, 1735–60: A Study of Walker of Truro and Others* (London, 1951), p. 174; cf. J. D. Walsh, 'The Yorkshire Evangelicals in the eighteenth century: with especial reference to Methodism', PhD thesis, University of Cambridge, 1956, appendix D.

7 The alternative usage of applying 'Evangelical' to the Anglican party and 'evangelical' to others of like mind outside the Church of England can be misleading. It has been adopted by E. Jay (*The Religion of the Heart: Anglican Evangelicalism and the Nineteenth-Century Novel* (Oxford, 1979), ch. 1, sect. 1, esp. p. 17) in order to deny the 'common spiritual parentage' of Anglicans and non-Anglicans in the movement. In reality, for all their divergences, their common inheritance was far more significant than this usage suggests.

8 E. Hodder, *The Life and Work of the Seventh Earl of Shaftesbury, K.G.* (London, 1888), p. 738.

9 H. Venn (ed.), *The Life and a Selection from the Letters of the late Rev. Henry Venn, M.A.* (London, 1835), pp. vii f.

10 J. C. Ryle, *Knots Untied* (London, 1896 edn), p. 9.

11 D. Voll, *Catholic Evangelicalism: The Acceptance of Evangelical Traditions by the Oxford Movement during the Second Half of the Nineteenth Century* (London, 1963).

12 G. W. E. Russell, 'Recollections of the Evangelicals', *The Household of Faith* (London, 1902), pp. 240 f., 245.

13 Wesley, 'The new birth', *The Works of John Wesley*, Vol. 2, ed. A. C. Outler (Nashville, Tenn., 1985), p. 187.

14 *Life of Ann Okely*, quoted by J. Walsh, 'The Cambridge Methodists', in P. Brooks (ed.), *Christian Spirituality: Essays in Honour of Gordon Rupp* (London, 1975), p. 258.

15 Milner, 'On Evangelical religion', pp. 201–5.

16 *R*, 2 May 1850.

17 R. W. Dale, *The Old Evangelicalism and the New* (London, 1889), p. 13.

18 Ryle, *Knots Untied*, pp. 4–9.

19 Garbett (ed.), *Evangelical Principles* (London, 1875), p. xiv.

20 *C*, 5 October 1888, p. 5.

21 Warren, *What is an Evangelical? An Enquiry* (London, [1944]), pp. 18–39.

22 J. R. W. Stott, *What is an Evangelical?* (London, 1977), pp. 5–14.

23 Packer, *The Evangelical Anglican Identity Problem*, Latimer House Studies, 1 (Oxford, 1978), pp. 20 ff.

24 C. W. McCree, *George Wilson McCree* (London, 1893), p. 20.

25 *WV*, Vol. 1, pp. 74 f.

26 *C*, 15 July 1875, p. 19.

27 N. G. Dunning, *Samuel Chadwick* (London, 1933), p. 54.

28 M. C. Bickersteth, *A Sketch of the Life and Episcopate of the Right Reverend Robert Bickersteth, D.D., Bishop of Ripon, 1857–1887* (London, 1887), pp. 27 f.

29 Edwards, 'The distinguishing marks of a work of the true Spirit', *Select Works*, Vol. 1 (London, 1965), p. 106. Walsh, 'Yorkshire Evangelicals', p. 290. J. Lackington, *Memoirs of the Forty-Five First Years of the Life of James Lackington* (London, 1795), p. 161.

30 T.D.B. in *CO*, January 1852, p. 3.

31 W. Hanna, *Memoirs of the Life and Writings of Thomas Chalmers, D.D., LL.D.*, Vol. 1 (Edinburgh, 1851), ch. 8.

32 Haslam, *From Death into Life* (London, n.d.), p. 48.

33 Venn, *The Complete Duty of Man*, 3rd edn (London, 1779), p. xi.

34 Russell, 'Recollections of the Evangelicals', p. 238.

35 Dale, *Old Evangelicalism and the New*, pp. 51–7.

3 ϳ *Evangel*, Summer 1987.

37 *The Journal of the Rev. John Wesley, A.M.*, ed. N. Curnock, Vol. 2 (London, 1911), pp. 333 f. (25 January 1740).

38 R. A. Knox, *Enthusiasm* (Oxford, 1950), ch. 21.

39 Warren, *What is an Evangelical?*, p. 26.

40 G. W. E. Russell, *Mr Gladstone's Religious Development* (London, 1899), p. 7.

41 C. D. Field, 'Methodism in Metropolitan London, 1850–1920: a social and sociological study', DPhil thesis, University of Oxford, 1975, p. 232.

42 *On the Other Side: The Report of the Evangelical Alliance's Commission on Evangelism* (London, 1968), p. 184.

43 A. T. Pierson, *Forward Movements of the Last Half Century* (New York, 1900), p. 207.

44 G. W. E. Russell, *Sir Wilfrid Lawson* (London, 1909), pp. 3 f. J. Burgess, *The Lake Counties and Christianity: The Religious History of Cumbria, 1780–1920* (Carlisle, 1984), pp. 88–95.

45 Edwards, 'A narrative of surprising conversions', *Select Works*, Vol. 1, p. 40.

46 Simeon, 'On the new birth', in A. Pollard (ed.), *Let Wisdom Judge: University Addresses and Sermon Outlines by Charles Simeon* (London, 1959), p. 51.

47 G. Redford and J. A. James (eds), *The Autobiography of William Jay*, 2nd edn (London, 1855), p. 22.

48 For example, *WV*, Vol. 4, p. 19 (J. Pawson).

49 *Revival*, 21 January 1860, p. 21.

50 R. Carwardine, *Transatlantic Revivalism: Popular Evangelicalism in Britain and America, 1790–1865* (Westport, Conn., 1978), p. 125.

51 M. Raleigh (ed.), *Alexander Raleigh: Records of his Life* (Edinburgh, 1881), p. 15.

52 J. Cox, *The English Churches in a Secular Society: Lambeth, 1870–1930* (New York, 1982), pp. 248 f.

53 J. Milner, 'The nature of the Spirit's influence on the understanding', *Works*, ed. I. Milner, Vol. 8.

54 Carwardine, *Transatlantic Revivalism*, pp. xiv, 63, 99.

55 Horton, *An Autobiography* (London, 1917), p. 37.

56 O. Chadwick, *The Victorian Church*, Vol. 1, 2nd edn (London, 1970), pp. 250–62.

57 D. M. Thompson, 'Baptism, Church and Society in Britain since 1800', Hulsean Lectures, University of Cambridge, 1984, pp. 12–17.

58 G. Bugg, *Spiritual Regeneration Not Necessarily Connected with Baptism* (Kettering, 1816). [C. Marsh], *The Life of the Rev. William Marsh, D.D.* (London, 1867), p. 131.

59 Sumner, *Apostolical Preaching Considered, in an Examination of St Paul's Epistles* (London, 1815), p. 137 n.

60 Walker, *The Gospel Commission* (Edinburgh, 1826).

61 W. Y. Fullerton, *C. H. Spurgeon* (London, 1920), pp. 305 ff.

62 *Auricular Confession and Priestly Absolution: Lord Ebury's Prayer-Book Amendment Bill* (London, 1880), p. 2.

63 *CEN*, 5 February 1965, p. 7.

64 Edwards, 'Narrative', p. 47.

65 J. Bull, *Memorials of the Rev. William Bull* (London, 1864), p. 248.

66 T. Waugh, *Twenty-Three Years a Missioner* (London, n.d.), p. 62.

67 *WV*, Vol. 1, pp. 99, 233; Vol. 2, p. 91.

68 J. Lawson, 'The people called Methodists: 2: "Our discipline"', in R. Davies and G. Rupp (eds), *A History of the Methodist Church in Great Britain*, Vol. 1 (London, 1965), pp. 189, 198.

69 Lackington, *Memoirs*, pp. 128 f.

70 S. Mechie, *The Church and Scottish Social Development, 1780–1870* (London, 1960), pp. 52 ff.

71 Dale, 'The Evangelical Revival', *The Evangelical Revival and other Sermons* (London, 1880), p. 35.

72 A. Russell, *The Clerical Profession* (London, 1980), chs 3 and 4.

73 C. Bridges, *The Christian Ministry*, 3rd edn (London, 1830), p. 477.

74 *CO*, March 1850, p. 213.

75 G. H. Sumner, *Life of Charles Richard Sumner, D.D.* (London, 1876), p. 212. Bickersteth, *Bickersteth*, p. 153.

76 'English Evangelical clergy', *Macmillan's Magazine*, 1860, pp. 119 f., quoted by W. D. Balda, '"Spheres of Influence": Simeon's Trust and its implications for Evangelical patronage', PhD thesis, University of Cambridge, 1981, pp. 196, f., 199.

77 R. P. Heitzenrater, *The Elusive Mr. Wesley: 1: John Wesley his Own Biographer* (Nashville, Tenn., 1984), p. 21.

78 H. Moore, *The Life of Mrs Mary Fletcher*, 11th edn (London, 1844), p. 150.

79 J. B. B. Clarke (ed.), *An Account of the Infancy, Religious and Literary Life of Adam Clarke, LL.D., F.A.S., &c., &c., &c.*, Vol. 1 (London, 1833), p. 191.

80 Field, 'Methodism in Metropolitan London', p. 46.

81 [Chalmers,] *Observations on a Passage in Mr Playfair's Letter* (Cupar, Fife, 1805), p. 10. I. H. Murray, 'Thomas Chalmers and the revival of the church', *Banner of Truth*, March 1980, p. 16.

82 *Evangelical Magazine*, 1803, p. 203, quoted by G. F. Nuttall, *The Significance of Trevecca College, 1768–91* (London, 1969), p. 7.

83   W. Selwyn, in H. Scholefield, *Memoir of the late Rev. James Scholefield, M.A.* (London, 1855), p. 335.

84   S. Neill, *A History of Christian Missions*, 2nd edn (Harmondsworth, Middlesex, 1986), pp. 213–16.

85   J. C. Pollock, *The Cambridge Seven* (London, 1955).

86   G. B. A. M. Finlayson, *The Seventh Earl of Shaftesbury, 1801–1885* (London, 1981), p. 322.

87   More, *An Estimate of the Religion of the Fashionable World* (London, 1808 edn), p. 146.

88   Heitzenrater, *Wesley*, Vol. 1, p. 149.

89   J. Dale, 'The theological and literary qualities of the poetry of Charles Wesley in relation to the standards of his age', PhD thesis, University of Cambridge, 1961, p. 145.

90   *WV*, Vol. 3, p. 57 (John Nelson).

91   ibid., Vol. 2, pp. 183 f. (George Shadford).

92   W. and T. Ludlam, *Essays Scriptural, Moral and Logical*, Vol.2 (London, 1817), p. 99, quoted by Walsh, 'Yorkshire Evangelicals', p. 14; cf. G. Reedy, *The Bible and Reason: Anglicans and Scripture in Late Seventeenth-Century England* (Philadelphia, 1985), ch. 5, pt III.

93   K. Moody-Stuart, *Brownlow North: The Story of his Life and Work* (Kilmarnock, [1904]), p. 185.

94   J. Macpherson, *Henry Moorhouse: The English Evangelist* (London, n.d.), p. 94.

95   H. E. Hopkins, *Charles Simeon of Cambridge* (London, 1977), p. 161.

96   For example, N. Anderson, *An Adopted Son* (Leicester, 1985), p. 289.

97   *BW*, 5 March 1896, p. 325; 26 March 1896, p. 379.

98   Venn, *Complete Duty*, p. 51. 'The fifteen articles of the Countess of Huntingdon's Connexion', in E. Welch (ed.), *Two Calvinistic Methodist Chapels, 1743–1811* (London, 1975), p. 88.

99   Bickersteth, *A Scripture Help Designed to Assist in Reading the Bible Profitably*, 17th edn (London, 1838), p. 2.

100   W. J. C. Ervine, 'Doctrine and diplomacy: some aspects of the life and thought of the Anglican Evangelical clergy, 1797–1837', PhD thesis, University of Cambridge, 1979, ch. 3; cf. below, pp. 86–91.

101   On Anglicans, cf. J. L. Altholz, 'The mind of Victorian orthodoxy: Anglican responses to "Essays and Reviews", 1860–1864', *Church History*, vol. 51, no. 2 (1982).

102   Spurgeon, *The Greatest Fight in the World* (London, 1896), p. 27, quoted by P. S. Kruppa, *Charles Haddon Spurgeon: A Preacher's Progress* (New York, 1982), p. 374.

103   Barrett, 'The secularisation of the pulpit', in *Congregational Year Book*, 1895, p. 27.

104   Gladstone, 'The Evangelical movement: its parentage, progress, and issue', *Gleanings from Past Years*, Vol. 7 (London, 1879), p. 207.

105   Wesley to Mary Bishop, 7 February 1778, *The Letters of the Rev. John Wesley, A.M.*, ed. J. Telford, Vol. 6 (London, 1931), pp. 297 f.

106   *WV*, Vol. 1, p. 118 (Christopher Hopper).

107   W. H. Goold (ed.), *The Works of the Rev. John Maclaurin*, Vol. 1 (Edinburgh, 1860), pp. 63–102.

108   Bridges, *Christian Ministry*, p. 320.

109 *R*, 12 January 1934, p. 15 (Stephen Neill). *CEN*, 5 March 1954, p. 8 (Bishop Joost de Blank).

110 Dale, *The Atonement* (London, 1875). Denney, *The Death of Christ* (London, 1902). Stott, *The Cross of Christ* (Leicester, 1986). Forsyth, *The Cruciality of the Cross* (London, 1909); *Positive Preaching and the Modern Mind* (London, 1907); *The Work of Christ* (London, 1910).

111 A. J. Davidson (ed.), *The Autobiography and Diary of Samuel Davidson, D.D., LL.D.* (Edinburgh, 1899), p. 64.

112 Maltby, *Christ and his Cross* (London, 1935); cf. W. Strawson, 'Methodist theology, 1850–1950', in R. Davies *et al.* (eds), *A History of the Methodist Church in Great Britain*, Vol. 3 (London, 1983), pp. 217 f.

113 Raleigh (ed.), *Raleigh*, p. 281.

114 Arnott, *The Brethren* (London, 1970 edn), p. 17.

115 Gore, *The Incarnation of the Son of God* (London, 1891); cf. A. M. Ramsey, *From Gore to Temple: The Development of Anglican Theology between 'Lux Mundi' and the Second World War, 1889–1939* (London, 1960).

116 'Annual address to the Methodist Societies', *Minutes of Several Conversations . . . of the People called Methodists* (London, 1892), pp. 374 f.

117 Baldwin Brown, *The Divine Life in Man* (London, [1860]). See also C. Binfield, '"No quest, no conquest." Baldwin Brown and Silvester Horne', *So Down to Prayers: Studies in English Nonconformity, 1780–1920* (London, 1977), p. 195. Scott Lidgett, *The Spiritual Principle of the Atonement* (London, 1897); cf. Scott Lidgett, *My Guided Life* (London, 1936), pp. 149–58.

118 *R*, 13 January 1939, p. 26.

119 *CEN*, 7 April 1967, p. 3.

120 Scott, *The Force of Truth* (Edinburgh, 1984 edn), p. 65.

121 Law, *A Serious Call to a Devout and Holy Life*, 20th edn (Romsey, 1816), p. 266.

122 Hall, 'On the substitution of the innocent for the guilty', in O. Gregory (ed.), *The Works of Robert Hall, A.M.*, Vol. 5 (London, 1839), pp. 73–103.

123 Fremantle, 'Atonement', in Garbett (ed.), *Evangelical Principles*, pp. 86–92.

124 E. Steane, *The Doctrine of Christ developed by the Apostles* (Edinburgh, 1872), p. viii. Pope, *The Person of Christ* (London, 1875), p. 51.

125 Shaw, 'What is my religious faith?', *Sixteen Self Sketches* (London, 1949), p. 79.

126 I. E. Page (ed.), *John Brash: Memorials and Correspondence* (London, 1912), p. 95. Strawson, 'Methodist theology', pp. 202, 215 ff.

127 D. Johnson, *Contending for the Faith: A History of the Evangelical Movement in the Universities and Colleges* (Leicester, 1979), p. 359.

128 Venn, *Complete Duty*, p. xiii.

129 M. N. Garrard, *Mrs Penn-Lewis: A Memoir* (London, 1930), pp. 26, 168, 197.

130 H. A. Thomas (ed.), *Memorials of the Rev. David Thomas, B.A.* (London, 1876), p. 37.

131 Rattenbury, 'Socialism and the old theology', *Six Sermons on Social Subjects* (London, [1908]), pp. 82 f.

132 M. R. Pease, *Richard Heath, 1831–1912* (n.p., [1922]), pp. 48 ff.

133 J. H. Pratt (ed.), *The Thought of the Evangelical Leaders: Notes of the Discussions of The Eclectic Society, London, during the Years 1798–1814* (Edinburgh, 1978), pp. 165 ff., 505 ff. For the background, see A. P. F. Sell, *The Great Debate: Calvinism, Arminianism and Salvation* (Worthing, 1982).

134 Wilberforce to Robert Southey, 5 December [?], 2519/63, National Library of Scotland, quoted by P. F. Dixon, 'The politics of emancipation: the movement for the abolition of slavery in the British West Indies, 1807–33', DPhil thesis, University of Oxford, 1971, p. 86.

135 J. Bossy, *The English Catholic Community, 1570–1850* (London, 1975), pp. 184 ff.

136 N. Sykes, *Church and State in the Eighteenth Century* (Cambridge, 1954). G. F. A. Best, *Temporal Pillars: Queen Anne's Bounty, the Ecclesiastical Commissioners, and the Church of England* (Cambridge, 1964). J. C. D. Clark, *English Society, 1688–1832* (Cambridge, 1985).

137 M. R. Watts, *The Dissenters: From the Reformation to the French Revolution* (Oxford, 1978).

138 A. L. Drummond and J. Bulloch, *The Scottish Church, 1688–1843* (Edinburgh, 1973). C. G. Brown, *The Social History of Religion in Scotland since 1730* (London, 1987).

CHAPTER 2: KNOWLEDGE OF THE LORD

1 H. J. Hughes, *Life of Howell Harris, the Welsh Reformer* (London, 1892), p. 10; cf. G. F. Nuttall, *Howel Harris, 1714–1773: The Last Enthusiast* (Cardiff, 1965).

2 G. E. Jones, *Modern Wales: A Concise History, c. 1485–1979* (Cambridge, 1984), p. 130. There is now D. L. Morgan, *The Great Awakening in Wales* (London, 1988).

3 A. Dallimore, *George Whitefield: The Life and Times of the Great Evangelist of the Eighteenth-Century Revival*, Vol. 1 (London, 1970), chs 3–7.

4 L. Tyerman, *The Life and Times of the Rev. John Wesley, M.A.*, Vol. 1 (London, 1871), pp. 179 f., 233. Tyerman's is still the most authoritative biography. S. Ayling, *John Wesley* (London, 1979) is the most recent reliable study.

5 Dallimore, *Whitefield*, Vol. 2 (Edinburgh, 1980), chs 5, 8. A. Fawcett, *The Cambuslang Revival: The Scottish Evangelical Revival of the Eighteenth Century* (London, 1971).

6 Edwards, 'A narrative of surprising conversions' [1737], *Select Works*, Vol. 1 (London, 1965). *The Journal of the Rev. John Wesley, A.M.*, ed. N. Curnock, Vol. 1 (London, 1909), pp. 83 f. (9 October 1738). G. D. Henderson, 'Jonathan Edwards and Scotland', *The Burning Bush: Studies in Scottish Church History* (Edinburgh, 1957), pp. 151–5. See also I. H. Murray, *Jonathan Edwards: A New Biography* (Edinburgh, 1987).

7 Dallimore, *Whitefield*, Vol. 1, p. 14.

8 Doddridge to Daniel Wadsworth, 6 March 1741, in G. F. Nuttall, *Calendar of the Correspondence of Philip Doddridge, D.D. (1702–1751)*, Historical Manuscripts Commission JP 26 (London, 1979), p. 130.

9 R. Brown, *The English Baptists of the Eighteenth Century* (London, 1986), p. 77.

10 D. W. Lovegrove, 'The practice of itinerant evangelism in English Calvinistic Dissent, 1780–1830', PhD thesis, University of Cambridge, 1980, p. 54.

11 R. Currie et al., *Churches and Churchgoers: Patterns of Church Growth in the British Isles since 1700* (Oxford, 1977), pp. 147, 151.

12   Lovegrove, 'Itinerant evangelism', pp. 247 f., 252.

13   Currie *et al.*, *Churches and Churchgoers*, pp. 139 f.

14   ibid., pp. 21 ff. A. D. Gilbert, *Religion and Society in Industrial England: Church, Chapel and Social Change, 1740–1914* (London, 1976), pp. 28 f.

15   C. G. Brown, *The Social History of Religion in Scotland since 1730* (London, 1987), p. 61. Baptists and Congregationalists, wrongly classified by Brown as Presbyterian Dissenters, are excluded from this proportion.

16   H. Venn, *The Complete Duty of Man*, 3rd edn (London, 1779), p. iii.

17   Wesley to Ann Bolton, 15 April 1771, *The Letters of the Rev. John Wesley, A.M.*, ed. J. Telford, Vol. 5 (London, 1931), p. 238.

18   Venn, *Complete Duty*, pp. vii ff.

19   A. Booth, *The Reign of Grace from its Rise to its Consummation* [1768], 8th edn (London, 1807), p. 17.

20   J. Lackington, *Memoirs of the Forty-Five First Years of the Life of James Lackington* (London, 1795), p. 48. Lackington's *Memoirs* are particularly revealing because their author had been zealous but had lapsed. He subsequently returned to the Methodist fold, as recounted in *The Confessions of J. Lackington* (London, 1804).

21   Lackington, *Memoirs*, p. 61.

22   [J. Bean], *Zeal without Innovation: Or the Present State of Religion and Morals Considered* (London, 1808), p. 87.

23   Wesley to Dr George Horne, 19 March 1762, *Letters*, ed. Telford, Vol. 4, p. 175.

24   Milner, 'On Evangelical religion' [1789], *The Works of Joseph Milner*, ed. I. Milner, Vol. 8 (London, 1810), pp. 203 f.

25   *The Journal of the Rev. John Wesley, A.M.*, ed. N. Curnock, Vol. 5 (London, [1913?]), p. 244 (1 December 1767).

26   Dallimore, *Whitefield*, Vol. 2, pp. 544 f.

27   S. L. Ollard, *The Six Students of St Edmund Hall Expelled from the University of Oxford in 1768* (London, 1911).

28   For example, F. K. Brown, *Fathers of the Victorians: The Age of Wilberforce* (Cambridge, 1961), p. 310.

29   R. Sher and A. Murdoch, 'Patronage and party in the Church of Scotland, 1750–1800', in N. Macdougall (ed.), *Church, Politics and Society: Scotland, 1408–1929* (Edinburgh, 1983), pp. 203–7.

30   G. Eliot, 'Janet's repentance', *Scenes of Clerical Life* [1858], ed. T. A. Noble (Oxford, 1985), p. 194.

31   ibid., p. 252.

32   Tyerman, *Wesley*, Vol. 1, pp. 406–15.

33   *WV*, Vol. 1, p. 121; Vol. 2, p. 12; Vol. 3, p. 86.

34   J. Walsh, 'Methodism and the mob in the eighteenth century', *Popular Belief and Practice*, Studies in Church History, vol. 8, ed. G. J. Cuming and Derek Baker (Cambridge, 1972). Lovegrove, 'Itinerant evangelism', ch. 5.

35   F. Baker, 'The people called Methodists: 3: Polity', in R. Davies and G. Rupp (eds), *A History of the Methodist Church in Great Britain*, Vol. 1 (London, 1965), pp. 222 f.

36   J. Kent, 'Wesleyan membership in Bristol, 1783', in *An Ecclesiastical Miscellany*, Bristol and Gloucestershire Archaeological Society Records Section, vol. 11, ed. D. Walker *et al.* (Bristol, 1976), p. 106.

37   Lackington, *Memoirs*, p. 70.

38   Baker, 'Polity', pp. 224 f.

39 *WV*, Vol. 1, pp. 25 f.
40 Lackington, *Confessions*, pp. 190 ff.; *Memoirs*, pp. 129, 149.
41 Edwards, 'Narrative', p. 50.
42 Brown, *Baptists*, pp. 87 ff.
43 G. C. B. Davies, *The Early Cornish Evangelicals, 1735–60: A Study of Walker of Truro and Others* (London, 1951), pp. 66–70, ch. 4.
44 W. H. Goold (ed.), *The Works of the Rev. John Maclaurin* (Edinburgh, 1860), p. xvii.
45 Kent, 'Wesleyan membership', pp. 107–11.
46 T. C. Smout, 'Born again at Cambuslang: new evidence on popular religion and literacy in eighteenth-century Scotland', *Past & Present*, no 97 (1982), p. 117. Gilbert, *Religion and Society*, p. 67.
47 Brown, *Religion in Scotland*, p. 150. The proportion should perhaps be higher, because textile trades are excluded. Artisan prominence here and elsewhere is clear despite such problems of definition. See also below, p. 111.
48 C. D. Field, 'The social structure of English Methodism: eighteenth–twentieth centuries', *British Journal of Sociology*, vol. 28, no. 2 (1977), p. 202.
49 ibid.
50 H. More, *Thoughts on the Importance of the Manners of the Great* (London, 1788). W. Wilberforce, *A Practical View of the Prevailing Religious System of Professed Christians in the Higher and Middle Classes in this Country Contrasted with Real Christianity* (London, 1797).
51 Lackington, *Memoirs*, p. 72.
52 G. Malmgreen, 'Domestic discords: women and the family in East Cheshire Methodism, 1750–1830', in J. Obelkevich *et al.* (ed.), *Disciplines of Faith: Studies in Religion, Politics and Patriarchy* (London, 1987), p. 60.
53 Smout, 'Born again', p. 116. Kent, 'Wesleyan membership', p. 107.
54 D. M. Valenze, *Prophetic Sons and Daughters: Female Preaching and Popular Religion in Industrial England* (Princeton, NJ, 1985).
55 W. F. Swift, 'The women itinerant preachers of early Methodism', *Proceedings of the Wesley Historical Society*, vol. 28, no. 5 (1952), and vol. 29, no. 4 (1953).
56 M. G. Jones, *Hannah More* (Cambridge, 1952).
57 Eliot, 'Janet's repentance', pp. 205 f.
58 A. Everitt, *The Pattern of Rural Dissent: The Nineteenth Century* (Leicester, 1972), ch. 2.
59 J. Macinnes, *The Evangelical Movement in the Highlands of Scotland, 1688 to 1800* (Aberdeen, 1951).
60 Everitt, *Rural Dissent*, pp. 20 ff.
61 For example, *WV*, Vol. 1, p. 184.
62 On regional distribution, see p. 109.
63 See pp. 42, 45–6, 48–50, 60, 153–5, 171–4.
64 J. D. Walsh, 'The Yorkshire Evangelicals in the eighteenth century: with especial reference to Methodism', PhD thesis, University of Cambridge, 1956, pp. 33 ff., 314.
65 Brown, *Baptists*, pp. 68 ff.
66 'A collection of hymns for the use of the people called Methodists', *The Works of John Wesley*, Vol. 7, ed. F. Hildebrandt *et al.* (Oxford, 1983), pp. 81, 123, 338.

67   *Arminian Magazine*, vol. 1, no. 1 (1778), pp. 9–17.
68   G. F. Nuttall, 'The influence of Arminianism in England', in G. O. McCulloh (ed.), *Man's Faith and Freedom: The Theological Influence of Jacobus Arminius* (New York, 1962), pp. 60 f.
69   Wesley to Newton, 14 May 1765, *Letters*, ed. Telford, Vol. 4, p. 298.
70   Nuttall, 'Influence', pp. 56 f.
71   Wesley on T. Vivian to Wesley, 10 October 1748, in Davies, *Cornish Evangelicals*, p. 85.
72   R. Davies, 'The people called Methodists: 1: "Our doctrines"', in Davies and Rupp (eds), *Methodist Church*, Vol. 1, pp. 167 f.
73   For example, Tyerman, *Wesley*, Vol. 1, p. 551. *WV*, Vol. 7, pp. 24 ff., 39, 66.
74   Davies, '"Our doctrines"', pp. 176–9.
75   F. Baker, *John Wesley and the Church of England* (London, 1970), esp. chs 10, 17.
76   Lackington, *Memoirs*, p. 179.
77   Hempton, *Methodism and Politics*, ch. 3.
78   W. R. Ward, *Religion and Society in England, 1790–1850* (London, 1972), chs 4, 6. W. R. Ward (ed.), *The Early Correspondence of Jabez Bunting, 1820–1829*, Camden Fourth Series, vol. 11 (London, 1972). W. R. Ward, *Early Victorian Methodism: The Correspondence of Jabez Bunting, 1830–1858* (Oxford, 1976).
79   Baker, 'Polity', p. 232.
80   Valenze, *Prophetic Sons and Daughters*, p. 20. See also J. C. Bowmer, *Pastor and People: A Study of Church and Ministry in Wesleyan Methodism from the Death of John Wesley (1791) to the Death of Jabez Bunting (1858)* (London, 1975).
81   E. Welch (ed.), *Two Calvinistic Methodist Chapels, 1743–1811* (London, 1975), pp. xiii f.
82   C. E. Watson, 'Whitefield and Congregationalism', *Transactions of the Congregational Historical Society*, vol. 8, no. 4 (1922), p. 175.
83   Welch (ed.), *Calvinistic Methodist Chapels*, pp. xi f., xvi. G. F. Nuttall, *The Significance of Trevecca College, 1768–91* (London, 1969), pp. 4 ff.
84   J. Walsh, 'Methodism at the end of the eighteenth century', in Davies and Rupp (eds), *Methodist Church*, Vol. 1, p. 292.
85   ibid. Welch (ed.), *Calvinistic Methodist Chapels*, p. xvii.
86   Dallimore, *Whitefield*, Vol. 2, pp. 157 f.
87   Welch (ed.), *Calvinistic Methodist Chapels*, pp. x f., xiv, 22, 45.
88   ibid., p. 18.
89   C. E. Watson, 'Whitefield and Congregationalism', p. 242.
90   Welch (ed.), *Calvinistic Methodist Chapels*, p. xi.
91   T. Beynon (ed.), *Howell Harris, Reformer and Soldier (1714–1773)* (Caernarvon, 1958), e.g. p. 168 (19 April 1763).
92   T. Scott, *The Force of Truth* [1779] (Edinburgh, 1984), pp. 27, 33, 44–8, 51, 52, 61, 66.
93   ibid., pp. 75, 100, 102 f.
94   Davies, *Cornish Evangelicals*, pp. 31 f.
95   Walsh, 'Yorkshire Evangelicals', pp. 117 ff.
96   T. Haweis, *The Life of William Romaine, M.A.* (London, 1797), p. 27.
97   Tyerman, *Wesley*, Vol. 3, p. 49.

98   Walker to Thomas Adam, 11 October 1759, in Davies, *Cornish Evangelicals*, p. 176.
99   Berridge to [Mrs Blackwell], n.d., in C. Smyth, *Simeon and Church Order* (Cambridge, 1940), p. 169.
100 F. Baker, *William Grimshaw, 1708–1763* (London, 1963), esp. ch. 17.
101 A. S. Wood, *Thomas Haweis, 1734–1820* (London, 1957), pp. 149 ff.
102 J. Venn, in H. Venn (ed.), *The Life and a Selection from the Letters of the Rev. Henry Venn, M.A.* (London, 1834), p. 171.
103 A. W. Brown, *Recollections of the Conversation Parties of the Rev. Charles Simeon, M.A.* (London, 1863), p. 107. See also Smyth, *Simeon and Church Order*, ch. 6.
104 Wood, *Haweis*, p. 115.
105 Smith, *Simeon and Church Order*, pp. 240–3. Davies, *Cornish Evangelicals*, pp. 212 f.
106 W. D. Balda, '"Spheres of influence": Simeon's Trust and its implications for Evangelical patronage', PhD thesis, University of Cambridge, 1981, esp. ch. 3.
107 M. R. Watts, *The Dissenters: From the Reformation to the French Revolution* (Oxford, 1978), pp. 436 ff.
108 G. F. Nuttall, 'Methodism and the older Dissent: some perspectives', *Journal of the United Reformed Church Historical Society*, vol. 2, no. 8 (1981), pp. 272 f.
109 Letter of 22 February 1765, National Library of Wales MS 5453C, in R. T. Jones, *Congregationalism in England, 1662–1962* (London, 1962), p. 161.
110 Davies, *Cornish Evangelicals*, pp. 75, 171 ff. 198.
111 Nuttall, *Correspondence of Philip Doddridge*, p. xxxv.
112 Nuttall, 'Methodism and the older Dissent', pp. 271 f.
113 Preface to *The Experience of Mr. R. Cruttenden* (London, 1744), p. vii.
114 K. R. Manley, 'The making of an Evangelical Baptist leader', *Baptist Quarterly*, vol. 26, no. 6 (1976), p. 259.
115 Brown, *Baptists*, pp. 79, 81.
116 Watts, *Dissenters*, pp. 451 f.
117 Brown, *Baptists*, pp. 67–70, 109–12.
118 J. Gillies, 'Memoir', in Goold (ed.), *Works of Maclaurin*, pp. xv ff.
119 Sir H. W. Moncrieff Wellwood, *Account of the Life and Writings of John Erskine, D.D.* (Edinburgh, 1818), pp. 144, 113, 134, 225.
120 J. Erskine, 'Memoir', in *Extracts from an Exhortation to the Inhabitants of the South Parish of Glasgow by the late Rev. Dr John Gillies* (Glasgow, 1819), pp. 9, 17, 14.
121 Sher and Murdoch, 'Patronage and party'.
122 G. Struthers, *The History of the Rise, Progress and Principles of the Relief Church* (Glasgow, 1843), p. 254.
123 Dallimore, *Whitefield*, Vol. 2, pp. 86–90.
124 Brown, *Religion in Scotland*, p. 31.
125 Especially in G. F. Nuttall, *Richard Baxter and Philip Doddridge: A Study in a Tradition*, Friends of Dr Williams's Library Fifth Lecture (London, 1951), p. 19. See also Nuttall, *Richard Baxter* (London, 1965); Nuttall (ed.), *Philip Doddridge, 1702–51: His Contribution to English Religion* (London, 1951); Nuttall, *Correspondence of Philip Doddridge*.

126 Whitefield to Doddridge, 21 December 1748, in J. Gillies (ed.), *The Works of the Reverend George Whitefield, M.A.*, Vol. 2 (London, 1771), p. 216.

127 Nuttall, 'George Whitefield's "Curate": Gloucestershire Dissent and the revival', *JEH*, vol. 27, no. 4 (1976).

128 Nuttall, 'Methodism and the older Dissent', p. 261.

129 Nuttall, 'Questions and answers: an eighteenth-century correspondence', *Baptist Quarterly*, vol. 27, no. 2 (1977). Manley, 'An Evangelical Baptist leader', pp. 260–9.

130 R. Wodrow, *Analecta*, Vol. 3 (Edinburgh, 1843), pp. 342, 379. Wodrow to Mrs Wodrow, 12 May 1727, *The Correspondence*, ed. T. M'Crie, Vol. 3 (Edinburgh, 1843), pp. 302 f.

131 G. H. Jenkins, *Literature, Religion and Society in Wales, 1660–1730* (Cardiff, 1978), esp. pp. 306–9. Jones, *Modern Wales*, pp. 128 ff.

132 J. A. Newton, *Susanna Wesley and the Puritan Tradition in Methodism* (London, 1968), pp. 138 f.

133 F. Baker, 'Wesley's Puritan ancestry', *London Quarterly and Holborn Review*, vol. 187, no. 3 (1962). R. C. Monk, *John Wesley: His Puritan Heritage* (London, 1966), pp. 245 f.

134 Monk, *Wesley*, pp. 36–41.

135 Lackington, *Memoirs*, pp. 94 f.

136 *WV*, Vol. 1, pp. 16, 212; Vol. 2, p. 22; Vol. 4, pp. 9, 242; Vol. 7, pp. 14, 17. See also I. Rivers, '"Strangers and pilgrims": sources and patterns of Methodist narrative', in J. C. Hilson et al. (ed.), *Augustan Worlds* (Leicester, 1978), p. 195.

137 *WV*, Vol. 2, p. 54.

138 Professor J. H. Liden of Uppsala in his journal, 2 November 1769, quoted by R. P. Heitzenrater, *The Elusive Mr Wesley: 2: John Wesley as seen by Contemporaries and Biographers* (Nashville, Tenn., 1984), p. 89.

139 J. A. Newton, *Methodism and the Puritans*, Friends of Dr Williams's Library Eighteenth Lecture (London, 1964), pp. 9–17.

140 Baker, *Wesley and the Church of England*, p. 52. Monk, *Wesley*, pp. 216, 182–5. P. Collinson, 'The English conventicle', in *Voluntary Religion*, Studies in Church History, vol. 23, ed. W. J. Sheils and D. Wood (Oxford, 1986). J. Lawson, 'The people called Methodists: 2: "Our discipline"', in Davies and Rupp (eds), *Methodist Church*, Vol. 1.

141 G. Rupp. *Religion in England (1688–1791)* (Oxford, 1986), pp. 111, 326.

142 C. J. Abbey, *The English Church and its Bishops, 1700–1800*, Vol. 1 (London, 1887), pp. 151 ff.

143 J. Walsh, 'Origins of the Evangelical Revival', in G. V. Bennett and J. D. Walsh (eds), *Essays in Modern English Church History in Memory of Norman Sykes* (London, 1966), p. 156. Walsh, 'Yorkshire Evangelicals', p. 53 n.

144 ibid. Brown, *Simeon*, p. 70.

145 Hervey, Letter of 12 January 1748, *The Works of the late Reverend James Hervey, A.M.*, Vol. 6 (London, 1807), p. 11.

146 [Bean], *Zeal without Innovation*, ch. 3, sect. V.

147 *WV*, Vol. 4, p. 38.

148 E. Duffy, 'Primitive Christianity revived: religious renewal in Augustan England', in *Renaissance and Renewal in Christian History*, Studies in Church History, vol. 14, ed. D. Baker (Oxford, 1977), p. 291. See

also J. S. Simon, *John Wesley and the Religious Societies* (London, 1921), ch. 1.
149 M. Schmidt, *John Wesley: A Theological Biography*, Vol. 1 (London 1962), p. 99.
150 R. P. Heitzenrater (ed.), *Diary of an Oxford Methodist: Benjamin Ingham, 1733–1734* (Durham, NC, 1985), pp. 8 f., 37 f.
151 R. P. Heitzenrater, *The Elusive Mr Wesley: 1: John Wesley his own Biographer* (Nashville, Tenn., 1984), p. 58.
152 Lawson, "'Our discipline'", pp. 190–6.
153 ibid., p. 194 n. Lackington, *Memoirs*, p. 67.
154 Walsh, 'Origins', pp. 146 ff. See also H. D. Rack, 'Religious societies and the origins of Methodism', *JEH*, vol. 38, no. 4 (1987), which points out the inconsistent relationship between Methodism and the older societies.
155 Wesley, 'A plain account of Christian perfection', in F. Whaling (ed.), *John and Charles Wesley*, The Classics of Western Spirituality (London, 1981), p. 299.
156 H. T. Hughes, 'Jeremy Taylor and John Wesley', *London Quarterly and Holborn Review*, vol. 174, no. 4 (1949), pp. 303 f. Schmidt, *Wesley*, Vol. 1, pp. 73–81.
157 Wesley, 'Christian perfection', p. 299; cf. Schmidt, *Wesley*, Vol. 1, pp. 82–5.
158 Wesley, 'Christian perfection', p. 299; cf. J. G. Green, *John Wesley and William Law* (London, 1945); E. W. Baker, *A Herald of the Evangelical Revival* (London, 1948).
159 Schmidt, *Wesley*, Vol. 1, pp. 48–57.
160 R. P. Heitzenrater, 'John Wesley and the Oxford Methodists, 1725–35', PhD thesis, Duke University, NC, 1972, pp. 513 f. See also J. Hoyles, *The Waning of the Renaissance, 1640–1740: Studies in the Thought and Poetry of Henry More, John Norris and Isaac Watts* (The Hague, 1971), pt 2.
161 Schmidt, *Wesley*, Vol. 1, pp. 213–17. J. Orcibal, 'The theological originality of John Wesley and continental spirituality', in Davies and Rupp (eds), *Methodist Church*, Vol. 1, p. 90.
162 ibid., pp. 90 f.
163 J. Walsh, 'The Cambridge Methodists', in Peter Brooks (ed.), *Christian Spirituality: Essays in Honour of Gordon Rupp* (London, 1975), pp. 278–82.
164 A. C. Outler (ed.), *John Wesley* (New York, 1964), pp. 9 f. Baker, *Wesley and the Church of England*, pp. 32–50.
165 G. Rupp, 'Introductory essay', in Davies and Rupp (eds), *Methodist Church*, Vol. 1, p. xxxiv.
166 W. R. Ward, 'Power and piety: the origins of the religious revival in the early eighteenth century', *Bulletin of the John Rylands University Library of Manchester*, vol. 63, no. 1 (1980), pp. 237–48.
167 P. C. Erb (ed.), *Pietists: Selected Writings*, The Classics of Western Spirituality (London, 1983), pp. 1–96.
168 Ward, 'Power and piety', pp. 232–7.
169 Nuttall, 'Continental pietism and the Evangelical Movement in Britain', in J. van den Berg and J. P. van Dooren (eds), *Pietismus und Reveil* (Leiden, 1978), pp. 209–19; cf. W. M. Williams, *The Friends of Griffith Jones*, Y Cymmrodor, vol. 46 (London, 1939).
170 W. G. Addison, *The Renewed Church of the United Brethren, 1722–1930* (London, 1932).
171 Erb (ed.), *Pietists*, pp. 291–330.

172   C. W. Towlson, *Moravian and Methodist* (London, 1957), chs 3–6.
173   *WV*, Vol. 3, p. 31.
174   R. T. Jenkins, *The Moravian Brethren in North Wales*, Y Cymmrodor, vol. 45 (London, 1938), p. 9.
175   Walsh, 'Cambridge Methodists', pp. 263 f.
176   Towlson, *Moravian and Methodist*, ch. 7.
177   Nuttall, *Baxter and Doddridge*, p. 19; 'Influence of Arminianism', p. 60.
178   C. Hill, 'Puritans and "the dark corners of the land"', in *Change and Continuity in Seventeenth-Century England* (London, 1974). G. F. Nuttall, 'Northamptonshire and *The Modern Question*: a turning-point in eighteenth-century Dissent', *Journal of Theological Studies*, n.s., vol. 16, no. 1 (1965), pp. 104 f. B. R. White, *The English Baptists of the Seventeenth Century* (London, 1983), p. 74.
179   S. Neill, *A History of Christian Missions*, 2nd edn (Harmondsworth, Middlesex, 1986), pp. 187–92.
180   W. T. Whitley, *Calvinism and Evangelism in England especially in Baptist Circles* (London, [1933]), p. 4.
181   E. Benz, 'The Pietist and Puritan sources of early Protestant world mission (Cotton Mather and A. H. Francke)', *Church History*, vol. 20, no. 2 (1951), p. 43.
182   Edwards, 'God's sovereignty in the salvation of men'. *Select Works*, Vol. 1, p. 233.
183   Edwards, 'The distinguishing marks of a work of the true Spirit', *Select Works*, Vol. 1, p. 98.
184   Booth, *Reign of Grace*, pp. 59 ff.
185   Carey, *Enquiry* (London, 1961), sect. 1.
186   Edwards, *An Account of the Life of the late Rev. Mr. David Brainerd . . .* (Boston, Mass., 1749). R. T. Handy, *A History of the Churches in the United States and Canada* (Oxford, 1976), pp. 89, 92.
187   E. D. Potts, *British Baptist Missionaries in India, 1793–1837: The History of Serampore and its Missions* (Cambridge, 1967), p. 13.
188   James Hutton to Zinzendorf, 14 March 1740, in Heitzenrater, *Wesley*, Vol. 2, pp. 69 f.
189   *WV*, vol. 4, p. 228.
190   Walker to Thomas Adam, 2 October 1755, in Davies, *Cornish Evangelicals*, p. 134.
191   Lovegrove, 'Itinerant evangelism'.
192   D. E. Meek, 'Evangelical missionaries in the early nineteenth-century Highlands', *Scottish Studies*, 28 (1987), esp. p. 20.
193   Walsh, 'Methodism at the end of the eighteenth century', pp. 299 f.
194   R. H. Martin, *Evangelicals United: Ecumenical Stirrings in Pre-Victorian Britain, 1795–1830* (Metuchen, NJ, 1983), pt 2. A. L. Drummond and J. Bulloch, *The Scottish Church, 1688–1843* (Edinburgh, 1973), pp. 151 f. E. Stock, *The History of the Church Missionary Society*, Vol. 1 (London, 1899), pt. 2.
195   Although this view is at variance with that expressed by C. W. Towlson (*Moravian and Methodist*, p. 175), it is partly indicated by his ch. 3. See below, pp. 45, 49–50.
196   Rupp, *Religion in England*, p. 422.
197   R. T. Kendall, *Calvin and English Calvinism to 1649* (Oxford, 1979), pt 2.

198 M. M. Knappen (ed.), *Two Elizabethan Puritan Diaries* (Chicago, 1933), pp. 14 f.

199 Kendall, *Calvin and English Calvinism*, ch. 3. M. C. Bell, *Calvin and Scottish Theology: The Doctrine of Assurance* (Edinburgh, 1985), pp. 45 ff.

200 S. Petto, *The Voyce of the Spirit*, 1654, epistle dedicatory, quoted by G. F. Nuttall, *The Holy Spirit in Puritan Faith and Experience* (Oxford, 1946), p. 58.

201 Guthrie, *The Christian's Great Interest* (London, 1901), pp. 195 f.

202 Perkins, 'A treatise tending unto a declaration whether a man be in the estate of damnation or in the estate of grace' [1589], *The Works of . . . W. Perkins*, Vol. 1 (Cambridge, 1608), p. 367.

203 For example, Bell, *Calvin and Scottish Theology*, p. 81.

204 *The Confession of Faith* (Edinburgh, 1810), ch. 18/3, p. 106.

205 Brooks, *Precious Remedies* (Evesham, 1792), pp. 189, 211 f., 213–22.

206 Baker, *Grimshaw*, p. 43.

207 O. C. Watkins, *The Puritan Experience* (London, 1972), p. 11. Baxter nevertheless treats the evidence of works as inconclusive. N. H. Keeble, *Richard Baxter: Puritan Man of Letters* (Oxford, 1982), pp. 134 ff.

208 For example, Bell, *Calvin and Scottish Theology*, p. 82.

209 Weber, *The Protestant Ethic and the Spirit of Capitalism* (London, 1930), ch. 4A.

210 P. G. Lake, *Moderate Puritans and the Elizabethan Church* (Cambridge, 1982), p. 159.

211 Willison, 'A sacramental directory' [1716] in W. M. Hetherington (ed.), *The Practical Works of the Rev. John Willison* (Glasgow, [1844]), pp. 166 f. Willison was later to support the revival. Henderson, 'Edwards and Scotland', p. 154.

212 Hughes, *Harris*, p. 12.

213 'Collection of hymns', ed. Hildebrandt *et al.*, p. 517.

214 *Journal of John Wesley*, Vol. 2, pp. 13 (12 July 1738), 37 (August 1738). Schmidt, *Wesley*, Vol. 1, pp. 286–96, discusses the Moravian testimonies without pointing out that Wesley's concern was with the relation of justification to assurance, not with justification only. See also A. S. Yates, *The Doctrine of Assurance with Special Reference to John Wesley* (London, 1952), ch. 4.

215 Wesley to Rev. Arthur Bedford, 28 September 1738, *Works of John Wesley*, Vol. 25, ed. F. Baker (Oxford, 1980), pp. 562 ff.

216 Yates's suggestion (*Doctrine of Assurance*, p. 72) that there is gradual development away from regarding assurance as essential to salvation is belied by his own evidence, not least the letter to Bedford (cf. n. 215).

217 Yates, *Doctrine of Assurance*, pp. 63 ff.

218 R. Southey, *The Life of Wesley* (London, 1820), Vol. 1, p. 295.

219 Brown, *Simeon*, p. 320. W. Myles, *The Life and Writings of the late Reverend William Grimshaw*, 2nd edn (London, 1813), pp. 109 f.

220 Davies, *Cornish Evangelicals*, pp. 153 f.

221 Venn, *Complete Duty*, p. 126.

222 [Bean], *Zeal without Innovation*, p. 158.

223 Milner, *The Essentials of Christianity Theoretically and Practically Considered* (London, 1855), p. 189.

224 Edwards, 'Narrative', p. 42.

225 Booth, *Reign of Grace*, pp. 55 f., 239 f.

226 *WV*, Vol. 2, p. 145; Vol. 3, p. 125.

227 *WV*, Vol. 6, p. 22.

228 *WV*, Vol. 3, p. 173; vol. 6, p. 41. Edwards, 'Distinguishing marks', *Select Works*, Vol. 1.

229 Venn, *Complete Duty*, p. 127.

230 *WV*, Vol. 3, pp. 97 f.

231 T. Jackson (ed.), *The Lives of Early Methodist Preachers*, 5th edn, Vol. 2 (London, n.d.), p. 283.

232 Whitefield, *Journals*, p. 57.

233 *WV*, Vol. 1, p. 33.

234 For example, 'The contrite heart', no. IX of the Olney hymns. M. F. Marshall and J. Todd, *English Congregational Hymns in the Eighteenth Century* (Lexington, Ky, 1982), p. 131.

235 Edwards, 'Narrative', p. 3.

236 ibid., pp. 8, 17.

237 ibid., pp. 38 ff.

238 ibid., p. 39.

239 Edwards, *Religious Affections* [1746] (*Works*, Vol. 2), ed. J. E. Smith (New Haven, Conn., 1959), p. 205.

240 R. I. Aaron, *John Locke*, 3rd edn (Oxford, 1971).

241 Hutcheson, *Illustrations on the Moral Sense* [1728], ed. B. Peach (Cambridge, Mass., 1971).

242 Especially by Perry Miller in *Jonathan Edwards* (n.p., 1949).

243 N. Fiering, *Jonathan Edwards's Moral Thought in its British Context* (Chapel Hill, NC, 1981), pp. 35–40.

244 Edwards, *Freedom of the Will* [1754] (*Works*, Vol. 1), ed. P. Ramsey (New Haven, Conn., 1957), ch. 4.

245 ibid., p. 43.

246 Edwards, *Religious Affections*, p. 205.

247 Hughes, 'Taylor and Wesley', pp. 298 f.

248 Wesley to Samuel Wesley, 10 December 1734, *Works of John Wesley*, Vol. 25, p. 407.

249 Hoyles, *Waning of the Renaissance*, pp. 101, 105.

250 Heitzenrater, 'Wesley and the Oxford Methodists', p. 511. V. H. H. Green, *Young Mr Wesley: A Study of John Wesley and Oxford* (London, 1961), pp. 116 n., 315.

251 R. E. Brantley, *Locke, Wesley, and the Method of English Romanticism* (Gainesville, Fla, 1984), pp. 68, 113, 83 f.

252 E. H. Sugden (ed.), *Wesley's Standard Sermons*, Vol. 2 (London, 1921), pp. 216 f.

253 A. R. Winnett, *Peter Browne: Provost, Bishop, Metaphysician* (London, 1974), pp. 108 f. See also Brantley, *Locke, Wesley*, ch. 1; J. C. Hindley, 'The philosophy of enthusiasm', *London Quarterly and Holborn Review*, vol. 182, no. 2 (1957).

254 *Journal of John Wesley*, Vol. 1, p. 424 (29 January 1738).

255 ibid., Vol. 1, p. 151 (8 February 1736).

256 Hindley, 'Philosophy of enthusiasm', p. 106.

257 1744 Methodist Conference minutes, quoted by Simon, *Wesley and the Methodist Societies*, p. 207.

258 Wesley, 'An earnest appeal to men of reason and religion' [1743], *Works of John Wesley*, Vol. 11, ed. G. R. Cragg (Oxford, 1975), pp. 46, 56.

259 Wesley, 'On conscience', *Works* (London, 1872), Vol. 7, pp. 188 f.

260 Hindley, 'Philosophy of enthusiasm', *London Quarterly and Holborn Review*, vol. 182, no. 3 (1957), pp. 204–7.

261 *WV*, Vol. 3, p. 65.

262 ibid., Vol. 1, p. 177.

263 P. Gay, *The Enlightenment: An Interpretation* (London, 1967), is a classic statement of this view. Donald Davie is an honourable exception in contending for the alignment of Methodism and the orthodox Old Dissent with the Enlightenment: see especially his *Dissentient Voice* (Notre Dame, Ind., 1982), chs 1 and 2.

264 Toland, *Christianity not Mysterious* (London, 1695); cf. R. E. Sullivan, *John Toland and the Deist Controversy* (Cambridge, Mass., 1982).

265 R. N. Stromberg, *Religious Liberalism in Eighteenth-Century England* (London, 1954), p. 43.

266 ibid., pp. 44 ff.; cf. J. P. Ferguson, *An Eighteenth Century Heretic: Dr Samuel Clarke* (Kineton, Warwickshire, 1976).

267 Drummond and Bulloch, *Scottish Church*, pp. 31–4.

268 R. B. Sher, *Church and University in the Scottish Enlightenment: The Moderate Literati of Edinburgh* (Edinburgh, 1985).

269 Watts, *Dissenters*, pp. 464–78.

270 L. Stephen, *History of English Thought in the Eighteenth Century*, 2nd edn (London, 1881), Vol. 2, ch. 12, pts 5 and 6.

271 Booth, *Reign of Grace*, p. 9.

272 Wellwood, *Erskine*, pp. 55, 59.

273 *WV*, Vol. 2, p. 116.

274 *WV*, Vol. 2, p. 247.

275 *WV*, Vol. 2, p. 168. Lackington, *Memoirs*, p. 50.

276 Lockington, *Memoirs*, p. 51.

277 *Works of John Wesley*, Vol. 1, ed. A. C. Outler (Abingdon, Tenn., 1984), p. 104.

278 Lackington, *Memoirs*, p. 179.

279 Wesley, *Primitive Physic* [1747], ed. A. W. Hill (London, 1960), p. 94.

280 *Journal of John Wesley*, Vol. 7, p. 13 (26 August 1784).

281 Wesley to Dr Thomas Rutherforth, 28 March 1768, *Letters*, ed. Telford, Vol. 5, p. 364.

282 Schmidt, *Wesley*, Vol. 1, p. 272.

283 F. Dreyer, 'Faith and experience in the thought of John Wesley', *American Historical Review*, vol. 88, no. 1 (1983). Brantley, *Locke, Wesley*, esp. chs 1 and 2.

284 B. Semmel, *The Methodist Revolution* (London, 1974), pp. 87–96.

285 Wesley to Maxfield in T. Coke and H. Moore, *The Life of the Rev. John Wesley, A.M.* (London, 1792), p. 337.

286 *WV*, Vol. 1, pp. 123, 210; Vol. 3, p. 69; Vol. 4, p. 239.

287 Milner, 'The treatment which Methodism, so called, has received from the critical and monthly reviewers', *Works*, Vol. 8, p. 214. Davies, *Cornish Evangelicals*, p. 140.

288 Nuttall, 'Methodism and the older Dissent', p. 271. Booth, *Reign of Grace*, p. 271.
289 S. Mews, 'Reason and emotion in working-class religion, 1794–1824', *Schism, Heresy and Religious Protest*, Studies in Church History, vol. 9, ed. D. Baker (Cambridge, 1972).
290 H. McLachlan, *The Methodist Unitarian Movement* (Manchester, 1919).
291 Walsh, 'Origins', pp. 148–53. Dr Walsh tells me that he has altered his view to that expressed in the text.
292 E. Halévy, *The Birth of Methodism in England*, ed. B. Semmel (Chicago, 1971).
293 K. MacLean, *John Locke and English Literature of the Eighteenth Century* (New Haven, Conn., 1936), pp. 2 f, 11.
294 J. C. D. Clark, *English Society, 1688–1832* (Cambridge, 1985), esp. ch. 2, pt 1.
295 Edwards, *The Great Awakening* (*Works*, Vol. 4), ed. C. C. Goen (New Haven, Conn., 1972), p. 38. Davies, *Cornish Evangelicals*, p. 32.
296 Watts, *Philosophical Essays* (1733), Essay 6 introductory paragraph, and preface, quoted by MacLean, *Locke and Literature*, pp. 1, 15.
297 ibid., pp. 15, 23, 124.
298 Watts, *Logick* (London, 1725), p. 505, quoted by W. S. Howell, *Eighteenth-Century British Logic and Rhetoric* (Princeton, NJ, 1971), p. 336.
299 Hoyles, *Waning of the Renaissance*, p. 176.
300 ibid., p. 162, and pt 3 generally.
301 Doddridge, *A Course of Lectures on the Principal Subjects in Pneumatology, Ethics and Divinity* (London, 1763).
302 M. Deacon, *Philip Doddridge of Northampton* (Northampton, 1980), p. 99.
303 Doddridge to John Nettleton, [February] 1721, in Nuttall, *Correspondence of Philip Doddridge*, p. 2.
304 Wellwood, *Erskine*, p. 20. V. L. Collins, *President Witherspoon: A Biography* (Princeton, NJ, 1925), Vol. 1, p. 16.
305 Handy, *United States and Canada*, p. 83.
306 Dallimore, *Whitefield*, Vol. 2, pp. 88 ff.
307 D. Scott, *Annals and Statistics of the Original Secession Church* (Edinburgh, [1886]), p. 16.
308 *Narrative and Testimony* (1804) of the Anti-Burghers quoted by J. M'Kerrow, *History of the Secession Church* (Glasgow, 1841), p. 443.
309 J. McL. Campbell, *Reminiscences and Reflections*, ed. D. Campbell (London, 1873), chs 2–4.
310 J. Kennedy, *The Days of the Fathers in Ross-shire* (Inverness, 1897), p. 114.
311 ibid., p. 116.
312 W. Wilson, *The History and Antiquities of Dissenting Churches and Meeting Houses in London, Westminster and Southwark*, Vol. 4 (London, 1814), p. 550.
313 Lovegrove, 'Itinerant evangelism', p. 184.
314 T. M. Bassett, *The Welsh Baptists* (Swansea, 1977), pp. 95 ff.
315 Brown, *Baptists*, pp. 129 f.
316 Handy, *United States and Canada*, p. 179.
317 Whitley, *Calvinism and Evangelism*, p. 38.
318 Warburton, *Mercies*, 2nd pt, 4th edn (London, 1859), p. 41.
319 R. C. Chambers and R. W. Olver, *The Strict Baptist Chapels of England*, 5 vols (London, 1952–68).

320 T. Scott in J. H. Pratt (ed.), *The Thought of the Evangelical Leaders: Notes of the Discussions of The Eclectic Society, London, during the years 1798–1814* (Edinburgh, 1978), p. 231. Milner, 'Scriptural proof of the influence of the Holy Spirit on the understanding', *Works*, Vol. 8, p. 258.

321 Scott, *Force of Truth*, p. 26. Venn, *Complete Duty*, pp. 48, 152.

322 Miller, *Edwards*, p. 45.

323 *Arminian Magazine*, May 1786, p. 253.

324 Venn, *Complete Duty*, p. 48.

325 L. P. Fox, 'The work of the Rev. Thomas Tregenna Biddulph, with special reference to his influence on the Evangelical movement in the west of England', PhD thesis, University of Cambridge, 1953, pp. 67–73. Haweis, *Romaine*, pp. 18, 27, 46, 61, 54. Davies, *Cornish Evangelicals*, p. 207.

326 Milner, 'The trial of prophets', *Works*, Vol. 8, p. 285.

327 W. J. Turrell, *John Wesley, Physician and Electrotherapist* (Oxford, 1938), pp. 18–24.

328 Wesley, *Primitive Physic*, p. 25.

329 'Collection of hymns', ed. Hildebrandt *et al.*, p. 74.

330 Edwards, *Religious Affections*, p. 452.

331 'Account of the life of the Rev. John Witherspoon, D.D., LL.D.', *The Works of John Witherspoon, D.D.* (Edinburgh, 1804), Vol. 1, p. xvii.

332 Venn, *Complete Duty*, p. 2.

333 Conder to Rev. H. March, 2 July 1824, in E. R. Conder, *Josiah Conder: A Memoir* (London, 1857), pp. 246 f.

334 Pratt (ed.), *Evangelical Leaders*, p. 231.

335 Brown, *Simeon*, p. 269.

336 Fox, 'Biddulph', p. 66.

337 Wesley, Preface to Bishop Hall, 'Meditations and vows, divine and moral', in J. Wesley (ed.), *A Christian Library*, Vol. 4 (London, 1819), p. 106.

338 *WV*, Vol. 5, p. 249.

339 Walsh, 'Methodism at the end of the eighteenth century', p. 287.

340 D. Newsome, *The Parting of Friends: A Study of the Wilberforces and Henry Manning* (London, 1966), p. 51.

341 Pratt (ed.), *Evangelical Leaders*, pp. 230 ff; cf. M. L. Clarke, *Paley: The Evidence for the Man* (London, 1974); D. L. LeMahieu, *The Mind of William Paley* (Lincoln, Neb., 1976).

342 Lackington, *Confessions*, p. 35.

343 D. F. Rice, 'Natural theology and the Scottish philosophy in the thought of Thomas Chalmers', *Scottish Journal of Theology*, vol. 24, no. 1 (1971).

344 S. A. Grave, *The Scottish Philosophy of Common Sense* (Oxford, 1960).

345 J. Walker, *The Theology and Theologians of Scotland, chiefly of the Seventeenth and Eighteenth Centuries* (Edinburgh, 1872), p. 73.

346 Collins, *Witherspoon*, Vol. 1, p. 41.

347 Witherspoon, 'Lectures on moral philosophy', *Works*, Vol. 7 (Edinburgh, 1805), p. 47.

348 ibid., pp. 25, 46.

349 The legacy in American Evangelical thought is well documented: T. D. Bozeman, *Protestants in an Age of Science: The Baconian Ideal and Antebellum Religious Thought* (Chapel Hill, NC, 1977); G. M. Marsden, *Fundamentalism and American Culture: The Shaping of Twentieth-Century Evangelicalism,*

1870–1925 (New York, 1980), pp. 14–17. On Britain, cf. R. Anstey, *The Atlantic Slave Trade and British Abolition, 1760–1810* (London, 1975), pp. 177 f.

350 A. C. Chitnis, *The Scottish Enlightenment and Early Victorian English Society* (London, 1986).

351 D. W. Bebbington, *Patterns in History* (Leicester, 1979), ch. 4.

352 Semmel, *Methodist Revolution*, takes up this theme.

353 J. Bellamy, 'The millennium', *Sermons*, ed. J. Sutcliff (Northampton, 1783), p. 51, cited by W. R. Ward, 'The Baptists and the transformation of the church, 1780–1830', *Baptist Quarterly*, vol. 25, no. 4 (1973), p. 171.

354 Schmidt, *Wesley*, Vol. 1, p. 101 n.

355 *WV*, Vol. 1, p. 76.

356 Goold (ed.), *Works of Maclaurin*, Vol. 2. Venn, *Complete Duty*, p. 423. Wilberforce, *Practical View*, p. 402.

357 Lackington, *Memoirs*, p. 70.

358 Wesley, 'A plain account of Christian perfection', in Outler (ed.), *John and Charles Wesley*, p. 359. See also pp. 153–5, 171–4.

359 Newton, *Wesley and the Puritans*, p. 11.

360 Davies, *Cornish Evangelicals*, p. 158; cf. Booth, *Reign of Grace*, pp. 213 f.

361 Fox, 'Biddulph', p. 54.

362 Marshall and Todd, *Congregational Hymns*, pp. 102–13. Pratt (ed.), *Evangelical Leaders*, p. 77.

363 *WV*, Vol. 5, pp. 217 f.

364 Anstey, *Atlantic Slave Trade*, pp. 193–8.

365 Pratt (ed.), *Evangelical Leaders*, p. 77.

366 *WV*, Vol. 1, pp. 113, 96; Vol. 4, pp. 203 ff.

367 Pratt (ed.), *Evangelical Leaders*, pp. 236 f.

368 ibid., p. 468.

369 Wilberforce, *Practical View*, p. 48.

370 Anstey, *Atlantic Slave Trade*, pp. 128–39, 159. B. Hilton, 'The role of providence in Evangelical social thought', in D. Beales and G. Best (eds) *History, Society and the Churches* (Cambridge, 1985), esp. pp. 223 f.

371 E. L. Tuveson, *Millennium and Utopia* (Berkeley, Calif., 1949).

372 I. H. Murray, *The Puritan Hope* (Edinburgh, 1971).

373 Wellwood, *Erskine*, pp. 125 f.

374 Edwards, 'Some thoughts concerning the present revival of religion in New England' [1743], *Great Awakening*, p. 354; cf. E. L. Tuveson, *Redeemer Nation: The Idea of America's Millennial Role* (Chicago, 1968).

375 Edwards, 'An humble attempt to promote explicit agreement and visible union of God's people in extraordinary prayer', *Apocalyptic Writings (Works, Vol. 5)*, ed. S. S. Steen (New Haven, Conn., 1977).

376 ibid., p. 88.

377 Doddridge, *Lectures*, p. 584. Wellwood, *Erskine*, pp. 126 f., 501. J. Conder, *An Analytical and Comparative View of All Religions* (London, 1838), pp. 584–92.

378 Carey, *Enquiry*, p. 12. Carey's endorsement of Edwards is mistaken for disagreement by the editor (pp. xii f.).

379 W. H. Oliver, *Prophets and Millennialists: The Uses of Biblical Prophecy in England from the 1790s to the 1840s* (Auckland, 1978), pp. 86 f.

380 Pratt (ed.), *Evangelical Leaders*, pp. 256 ff.
381 Stirling General Associate (Anti-Burgher) Presbytery Minutes, 9 January 1781, Central Regional Archives, CH 3/286/1, quoted by Brown, *Religion in Scotland*, p. 35.
382 Chalmers, *The Christian and Civic Economy of Large Towns*, Vol. 1 (Glasgow, 1821), p. 168.
383 [Bean], *Zeal without Innovation*, ch. 3, sect. I. See also p. 78.
384 Edwards, *Freedom of the Will*, p. 131.
385 A. G. Fuller, 'Memoirs of the Rev. Andrew Fuller', in *The Complete Works of the Rev. Andrew Fuller*, Vol. 1 (London, 1831), p. cxv. Fuller disclaimed 'moderate Calvinism', which he identified with Richard Baxter's position. He called his own system 'strict Calvinism'.
386 Wellwood, *Erskine*, p. 380.
387 [Bean], *Zeal without Innovation*, p. 56.
388 J. Scott, *The Life of the Rev. Thomas Scott*, 6th edn (London, 1824), p. 446.
389 The classic exposition of moderate Calvinism remains Walsh, 'Yorkshire Evangelicals', ch. 1; cf. Davies, *Cornish Evangelicals*, pp. 154 ff.
390 [Bean], *Zeal without Innovation*, p. 53.
391 R. I. and S. Wilberforce, *The Life of William Wilberforce*, 2nd edn, Vol. 2 (London, 1839), p. 136.
392 Venn, *Complete Duty*, p. xiii.
393 ibid., ch. 10.
394 Wellwood, *Erskine*, p. 381.
395 Scott, *Scott*, p. 664.
396 Edwards, *Freedom of the Will*, esp. pp. 35–40, 360.
397 Scott, *Force of Truth*, p. 78.
398 Scott, *Scott*, p. 664.
399 For example, Fuller in 1783, quoted by Whitley, *Calvinism and Evangelism*, p. 33.
400 Pratt (ed.), *Evangelical Leaders*, p. 223.
401 Nuttall, 'Northamptonshire and *The Modern Question*'.
402 J. Gadsby, *A Memoir of William Gadsby* (Manchester, 1842), p. 50.
403 Pratt (ed.), *Evangelical Leaders*, pp. 222 ff.
404 E. F. Clipsham, 'Andrew Fuller and Fullerism: a study in Evangelical Calvinism', *Baptist Quarterly*, vol. 20, no. 3 (1963), pp. 110–13.
405 W. T. Owen, *Edward Williams, D.D., 1750–1813: His Life, Thought and Influence* (Cardiff, 1963), p. 97 n. J. Milner, *The History of the Church of Christ*, 2nd edn, Vol. 2 (London, 1810), p. 386 n. Henderson, 'Jonathan Edwards and Scotland', p. 159.
406 Tyerman, *Wesley*, Vol. 2, p. 339.
407 G. Lawton, *John Wesley's English: A Study of his Literary Style* (London, 1962), p. 291.
408 Simeon to G. A. Underwood, 2 October 1817, Cheltenham File, Simeon Trust MSS, quoted by Balda, '"Spheres of influence"', pp. 76 f.
409 Davies, *Cornish Evangelicals*, ch. 5.
410 Chadwick, *Victorian Church*, Vol. 1, pp. 449 f.
411 S. J. Brown, *Thomas Chalmers and the Godly Commonwealth in Scotland* (Oxford, 1982), pp. 132 f.
412 Lovegrove, 'Itinerant evangelism', ch. 2.

413 J. Walford, *Memoirs of the Life and Labours of the Late Venerable Hugh Bourne* (London, 1855), Vol. 1, p. 173. See also p. 26.

414 For example, Jabez Bunting as cited by J. H. S. Kent, 'The doctrine of the ministry', *The Age of Disunity* (London, 1966), p. 85.

415 *The Works of the Rev. John Wesley, A.M.*, 3rd edn, Vol. 7 (London, 1829), p. 207.

416 Baker, *Wesley and the Church of England*, ch. 15.

417 Walsh, 'Methodism at the end of the eighteenth century', p. 288.

418 *WV*, Vol. 1, p. 150.

419 Brown, *Baptists*, p. 105.

420 W. R. Ward, 'Baptists and the transformation of the church'.

421 Sher, *Church and University*, pp. 50–6.

422 Davies, *Cornish Evangelicals*, p. 71.

423 D. M. Thompson, *Denominationalism and Dissent, 1795–1835: A Question of Identity*, Friends of Dr Williams's Library 39th Lecture (London, 1985), esp. p. 13.

424 Dallimore, *Whitefield*, Vol. 2, p. 92.

425 Martin, *Evangelicals United*, pts II and III.

426 D. M. Rosman, *Evangelicals and Culture* (London, 1984), ch. 8. T. W. Herbert, *John Wesley as Editor and Author* (Princeton, NJ, 1940), pp. 88–97.

427 C. Binfield, *So Down to Prayers: Studies in English nonconformity, 1780–1920* (London, 1977), ch. 3.

428 J. Erskine, 'Memoir', in *Extracts from an Exhortation to the Inhabitants of the South Parish of Glasgow by the late Rev. Dr John Gillies* (Glasgow, 1819), p. 6.

429 ibid., p. 7. Herbert, *Wesley*, p. 47.

430 Hall, 'Review of Foster's Essays', *The Miscellaneous Works and Remains of the Rev. Robert Hall* (London, 1846), p. 446.

431 Wesley to Samuel Furly, 15 July 1764, *Letters*, ed. Telford, Vol. 4, p. 256.

432 ibid., p. 290.

433 Sher, *Church and University*, pp. 57 f.

434 J. Dale, 'The theological and literary qualities of the poetry of Charles Wesley in relation to the standards of his age', PhD thesis, University of Cambridge, 1961, ch. 7.

435 *Arminian Magazine*, March 1785, p. 151.

436 Jones, *Congregationalism*, p. 166.

437 Marshall and Todd, *Congregational Hymns*, pp. 53 f., 71. Hoyles, *Waning*, p. 228.

438 Binfield, *So Down to Prayers*, p. 45. In *A Gathered Church: The Literature of the English Dissenting Interest, 1700–1930* (London, 1978), Donald Davie points out the classicism of Watts's Calvinism (pp. 25–8, 35), but mistakenly denies it to Charles Wesley or the early Evangelicals of the Church of England (chs 3 and 4); cf. Rosman, *Evangelicals and Culture*.

439 Marshall and Todd, *Congregational Hymns*, pp. 156 ff.

440 Dale, 'Poetry of Charles Wesley', ch. 5.

441 ibid., pp. 104, 108, 127, 146.

442 'Invitation to sinners', in G. Osborn (ed.), *The Poetical Works of John and Charles Wesley* (London, 1868), Vol. 4, p. 371. This paragraph is based on Dale, 'Poetry of Charles Wesley', ch. 6.

443 'Collection of hymns', ed. Hildebrandt *et al.*, p. 74.

444 Wesley to Richard Boardman (?), 12 January 1776, *Letters*, ed. Telford, Vol. 6, p. 201.
445 *Arminian Magazine*, 1781, p. iv.
446 For example, *WV*, vol. 4, p. 228. T. Jackson, *Recollections of My Own Life and Times* (London, 1873), p. 216.
447 E. Martin, 'Sale of Wesley's publications', *Proceedings of the Wesley Historical Society*, vol. 1 (1897), p. 90.
448 Jackson, *Recollections*, pp. 25 f.
449 Herbert, *Wesley*, p. 1.
450 Lackington, *Memoirs*, p. 73.
451 H. F. Mathews, *Methodism and the Education of the People, 1791–1851* (London, 1949), pp. 31 f., 184.
452 ibid., p. 182.
453 Lackington, *Confessions*, p. 184.
454 Nuttall, *Trevecca College*.
455 P. B. Cliff, *The Rise and Development of the Sunday School Movement in England, 1780–1980* (Nutfield, Surrey, 1986), p. 25.
456 Martin, *Evangelicals United*, ch. 8.
457 Mathews, *Methodism and Education*, p. 172.
458 V. Kiernan, 'Evangelicalism and the French Revolution', *Past & Present*, no. 1 (1952).
459 Brown, *Fathers of the Victorians*, esp. foreword.
460 J. Pollock, *Wilberforce* (London, 1977), ch. 7. R. J. Hind, 'William Wilberforce and the perceptions of the British people', *Historical Research*, vol. 60, no. 143 (1987). For Evangelical attacks on popular culture, see p. 132.
461 Jones, *More*, pp. 134 ff, 104–7.
462 L. and J. C. F. Stone, *An Open Elite? England, 1540–1880* (Oxford, 1984), p. 327.
463 Wellwood, *Erskine*, p. 72. A. Russell, *The Clerical Profession* (London, 1980), p. 114.
464 R. F. Wearmouth, *Methodism and the Common People of the Eighteenth Century* (London, 1945), pp. 202–11.
465 F. K. Prochaska, *Women and Philanthropy in Nineteenth-Century England* (Oxford, 1980), pp. 8 f.
466 Heitzenrater, *Wesley*, Vol. 1, p. 135.
467 Welch (ed.), *Calvinistic Methodist Chapels*, pp. xiv f.
468 *George Whitefield's Journals* (n.p., 1960), p. 395.
469 See pp. 121 ff.
470 W. Myles, *A Chronological History of the People called Methodists*, 3rd edn (London, 1803), p. 183.
471 D. G. Mathews, *Religion in the Old South* (Chicago, 1977), ch. 4.
472 Anstey, *Atlantic Slave Trade*, chs 4–8.
473 S. Drescher, *Econocide: Economic Development and the Abolition of the British Slave Trade* (Pittsburgh, 1977).
474 Anstey, *Atlantic Slave Trade*, ch. 9.
475 S. Drescher, 'Public opinion and the destruction of British colonial slavery', in James Walvin (ed.), *Slavery and British Society, 1776–1846* (London, 1982), pp. 37–40.

476   M. Craton, *Testing the Chains: Resistance to Slavery in the British West Indies* (Ithaca, NY, 1982).
477   Pollock, *Wilberforce*. Anstey, *Atlantic Slave Trade*, chs 10, 11, 14. C. D. Rice, 'The missionary context of the British anti-slavery movement', in Walvin (ed.), *Slavery and British Society*. R. Anstey, 'Religion and British slave emancipation', in D. Eltis and J. Walvin (eds), *The Abolition of the Atlantic Slave Trade* (Madison, Wis., 1981).
478   S. Drescher, 'Two variants of anti-slavery: religious organization and social mobilization in Britain and France, 1780–1870', in C. Bolt and S. Drescher (eds), *Anti-Slavery, Religion and Reform: Essays in Memory of Roger Anstey* (Folkestone, 1980), p. 48.
479   S. Drescher, *Capitalism and Antislavery: British Mobilization in Comparative Perspective* (London, 1986), ch. 6, esp. p. 131. G. Stephen, *Anti-Slavery Recollections in a Series of Letters addressed to Mrs Beecher Stowe* [1854] (London, 1971), p. 248.
480   J. Owen, *Memoir of the Rev. T. Jones, late of Creaton* (London, 1851), p. 160.
481   Witherspoon, *The Charge of Sedition and Faction against Good Men, especially Faithful Ministers, considered and accounted for* (Glasgow, 1758), p. 31.
482   R. Hall, 'An apology for the freedom of the press' [1793], in O. Gregory (ed.), *The Works of Robert Hall, A.M.* (London, 1839), Vol. 4, pp. 45–144. *The Trial of Wm. Winterbotham . . . for Seditious Words* (London, 1794).
483   Lovegrove, 'Itinerant evangelism', p. 224.
484   Gregory (ed.), *Works of Hall*, Vol. 4, p. 146.
485   A. Fuller, 'Thoughts on civil polity' [1808], *Complete Works*, Vol. 5 (London, 1832), p. 532.
486   Hempton, *Methodism and Politics*, pp. 47 f.
487   Kent, 'Wesleyan membership', pp. 111 f.
488   Newton to Mrs P—, August. 1775, in *The Works of the Rev. John Newton* (Edinburgh, 1837), p. 250.
489   Lawson, '"Our discipline"', p. 195.
490   Hempton, *Methodism and Politics*, ch. 2. Walsh, 'Methodism at the end of the eighteenth century', pp. 304 ff.
491   Wilberforce, *Practical View*, p. 403.
492   I. Bradley, 'The politics of godliness: Evangelicals in parliament, 1784–1832', DPhil thesis, University of Oxford, 1974.
493   Walsh, 'Methodism at the end of the eighteenth century', p. 303.
494   Evans, *A Letter to the Rev. Mr John Wesley occasioned by his Calm Address* (Bristol, 1775), p. 11, quoted by E. A. Payne, 'Nonconformists and the American Revolution', *Journal of the United Reformed Church History Society*, vol. 1, no. 8 (1976), p. 220.
495   John Rippon cited in ibid., p. 210.
496   Sher, *Church and University*, pp. 267 ff.
497   Handy, *United States and Canada*, p. 140.
498   For example, Hall, 'On toleration', in Gregory (ed.), *Works of Hall*, Vol. 6, pp. 370–96.
499   Scott, *Force of Truth*, p. 44 n.
500   Clarke, 'The origin and end of civil government', *The Miscellaneous Works of Adam Clarke, LL.D., F.A.S.*, Vol. 7 (London, 1836), p. 249.

501 Hempton, *Methodism and Politics*, pp. 30–43. Semmel, *Methodist Revolution*, pp. 88 ff.
502 Sher, *Church and University*, pp. 281–6.
503 Shaftesbury, *Characteristicks of Men, Manners, Opinions, Times in Three Volumes*, 6th edn (London, 1737), Vol. 3, p. 400, cited by J. Hook, *The Baroque Age in England* (London, 1976), p. 48. See also J. Steegman, *The Rule of Taste from George I to George IV* (London, 1968).
504 M'Kerrow, *Secession Church*, pp. 845–9.
505 Edwards, 'Narrative', p. 57.

CHAPTER 3: A TROUBLING OF THE WATER

1 D. M. Rosman, *Evangelicals and Culture* (London, 1984), pp. 35 f.
2 F. K. Brown, *Fathers of the Victorians: The Age of Wilberforce* (Cambridge, 1961), pp. 518 ff.
3 I. Bradley, *The Call to Seriousness: The Evangelical Impact on the Victorians* (London, 1976), pp. 194 f.
4 A. R. Vidler, *The Church in an Age of Revolution* (Harmondsworth, Middlesex, 1961), p. 49.
5 M. Hennell, *Sons of the Prophets: Evangelical Leaders of the Victorian Church* (London, 1979), pp. 9–15. Rosman, *Evangelicals and Culture*, pp. 24–37. See also E. R. Sandeen, *The Roots of Fundamentalism: British and American Millenarianism, 1800–1930* (Chicago, 1970), ch. 1; H. Willmer, 'Evangelicalism, 1785 to 1835', Hulsean Prize Essay, University of Cambridge, 1962; I. S. Rennie, 'Evangelicalism and English public life, 1823–1850', PhD thesis, University of Toronto, 1962.
6 R. Currie et al., *Churches and Churchgoers: Patterns of Church Growth in the British Isles since 1700* (Oxford, 1977), pp. 21–5.
7 E. R. Norman, *Church and Society in England, 1770–1970* (Oxford, 1976), pp. 52–5.
8 S. J. Brown, *Thomas Chalmers and the Godly Commonwealth in Scotland* (Oxford, 1982), ch. 3. R. A. Cage and E. O. A. Checkland, 'Thomas Chalmers and urban poverty: the St John's Parish experiment in Glasgow, 1819–1837', *Philosophical Journal*, vol. 13, no. 1 (1976).
9 J. H. Stewart, *Thoughts on the Importance of Special Prayer for the General Outpouring of the Holy Spirit* (London, 1821), p. 9; cf. D. D. Stewart, *Memoir of the Life of the Rev. James Haldane Stewart, M.A.*, 2nd edn (London, 1857), pp. 91–102.
10 R. Carwardine, *Transatlantic Revivalism: Popular Evangelicalism in Britain and America, 1790–1865* (Westport, Conn., 1978), p. 63.
11 E. Irving, *For Missionaries after the Apostolical School: A Series of Orations* (London, 1825), p. 18.
12 W. T. Gidney, *The History of the London Society for Promoting Christianity among the Jews from 1809 to 1908* (London, 1908), p. 70.
13 A. L. Drummond, 'Robert Haldane at Geneva, 1816–17', *Records of Scottish Church History Society*, vol. 9, no. 2 (1946). T. Stunt, 'Geneva and British Evangelicals in the early nineteenth century', *JEH*, vol. 32, no. 1 (1981), esp. p. 40.

14 A. Haldane, *The Lives of Robert Haldane of Airthrey, and his Brother, James Alexander Haldane*, 5th edn (Edinburgh, 1855), pp. 429 f., 454.

15 *Dialogues on Prophecy*, vol. 1 (London, 1827), p. 212.

16 J. Williams, 'Memoirs of the Rev. Robert Hawker, D.D.', in *The Works of the Rev. Robert Hawker, D.D.*, Vol. 1 (London, 1831).

17 *The Sinner Saved: or Memoirs of the Life of William Huntington* (London, [1813]).

18 W. Carus, *Memoirs of the Life of the Rev. Charles Simeon, M.A.*, 2nd edn (London, 1857), p. 417.

19 J. J. Evans, *Memoir and Remains of the Rev. James Harington Evans, M.A.*, 2nd edn (London, 1855), pp. 31–37, 30.

20 Carus, *Simeon*, pp. 566 f.

21 Evans, *Evans*, p. 27.

22 H. H. Rowdon, *The Origins of the Brethren, 1825–1850* (London, 1967), pp. 61 ff., 67 f. See also T. C. F. Stunt, 'John Henry Newman and the Evangelicals', *JEH*, vol. 21, no. 1 (1970).

23 E. Irving, *The Last Days: A Discourse on the Evil Character of these our Times, proving them to be the "Perilous Times" of the "Last Days"*, 2nd edn (London, 1850), pp. 451–6.

24 H. L. Alexander, *Life of Joseph Addison Alexander*, Vol. 1 (1870), p. 290, quoted by P. E. Shaw, *The Catholic Apostolic Church sometimes called Irvingite* (Morningside Heights, NY, 1946), p. 50.

25 A. L. Drummond, *Edward Irving and his Circle* (London, n.d.) is still the most useful general analysis of Irving.

26 Irving, *For the Oracles of God: Four Orations. For Judgment to Come: An Argument in Nine Parts* (London, 1823), p. 104.

27 Carlyle, *Reminiscences* [1887], ed. C. E. Norton (London, 1972), p. 195.

28 M. O. W. Oliphant, *The Life of Edward Irving*, 4th edn (London, n.d.), p. 96.

29 Carlyle, *Reminiscences*, p. 240. Irving, *Judgment to Come*, p. 307.

30 Irving, *Babylon and Infidelity Foredoomed of God*, Vol. 1 (Glasgow, 1826), pp. 308 f.

31 S. T. Coleridge to Daniel Stuart, [8?] July 1825, in E. L. Griggs (ed.), *Collected Letters of Samuel Taylor Coleridge*, Vol. 5 (Oxford, 1971), p. 474.

32 Irving, *Babylon and Infidelity*, p. 309; *Judgment to Come*, p. 138.

33 Coleridge to Edward Coleridge, 23 July 1823, in Griggs (ed.), *Letters of Coleridge*, Vol. 5, p. 286.

34 Irving, *Missionaries*, pp. vii f.

35 W. Hanna, *Memoirs of the Life and Writings of Thomas Chalmers, D.D., LL.D.*, Vol. 3 (Edinburgh, 1851), p. 160.

36 For example, Irving, *Missionaries*, p. xiv. R. J. White (ed.), *The Political Thought of Samuel Taylor Coleridge* (London, 1938).

37 Irving, *Missionaries*, pp. vii, 84, 85.

38 M. H. Abrams, *Natural Supernaturalism: Tradition and Revolution in Romantic Literature* (London, 1971), p. 32.

39 C. R. Sanders, *Coleridge and the Broad Church Movement* (Durham, NC, 1942). M. H. Bright, 'English literary Romanticism and the Oxford Movement', *Journal of the History of Ideas*, vol. 40, no. 3 (1979).

40 G. S. R. Kitson Clark, 'The Romantic element: 1830 to 1850', in J. H. Plumb (ed.), *Studies in Social History: A Tribute to G. M. Trevelyan* (London, 1955), pp. 230, 214–17.
41 See pp. 62 f.
42 *Morning Watch*, March 1830, p. 34. See also S. C. Orchard, 'English Evangelical eschatology, 1790–1850', PhD thesis, University of Cambridge, 1969; W. H. Oliver, *Prophets and Millennialists: The Uses of Biblical Prophecy in England from the 1790s to the 1840s* (Auckland, NZ, 1978); D. Hempton, 'Evangelicals and eschatology', *JEH*, vol. 31, no. 2 (1980); D. W. Bebbington, 'The advent hope in British Evangelicalism since 1800', *Scottish Journal of Religious Studies* (forthcoming).
43 Rather confusingly, Harrison calls the premillennialists 'millenarian' and the postmillennialists 'millennialist'. J. F. C. Harrison, *The Second Coming: Popular Millenarianism, 1780–1850* (London, 1979), pp. 5, 208.
44 Cuninghame, *A Dissertation on the Seals and Trumpets of the Apocalypse* (London, 1813). T. R. Birks, *A Memoir of the Rev. Edward Bickersteth*, Vol. 2 (London, 1856 edn), p. 45.
45 Frere, *A Combined View of the Prophecies of Daniel, Esdras, and St. John*, 2nd edn (London, 1815), pp. iv f, 210–16, esp. p. 212.
46 Irving, *Babylon and Infidelity*, Vol. 1, pp. v–viii; Vol. 2, pp. 23 n., 243.
47 J. J. Ben-Ezra, *The Coming of Messiah in Glory and Majesty*, trans. Irving (London, 1827), p. xlix.
48 R. H. Martin, *Evangelicals United: Ecumenical Stirrings in Pre-Victorian Britain, 1795–1830* (Metuchen, NJ, 1983), chs 8 and 9. M. Vrete, 'The restoration of the Jews in English Protestant thought, 1790–1840', *Middle Eastern Studies*, vol. 8, no. 1 (1972).
49 Sandeen, *Roots of Fundamentalism*, p. 12.
50 *Dialogues*, vol. 1, p. 208.
51 Carlyle, *Reminiscences*, p. 287.
52 E. Miller, *The History and Doctrines of Irvingism, or the So-Called Catholic and Apostolic Church*, Vol. 1 (London, 1878), pp. 35–46.
53 *Dialogues*, vol. 3, p. 2.
54 R. Wallis (ed.), *Millenialism and Charisma* (Belfast, 1982), p. 1.
55 Ben-Ezra, *Coming of Messiah*, pp. vi, xlix.
56 J. H. Pratt (ed.), *The Thought of the Evangelical Leaders: Notes of the Discussions of The Eclectic Society, London, during the Years 1798–1814* [1856] (Edinburgh, 1978), p. 256. Simeon to Miss E. Elliott, 19 February 1830, in Carus, *Simeon*, pp. 658 f.
57 H. McNeile, *A Sermon preached at the Parish Church of St Paul, Covent Garden, on Thursday Evening, May 5, 1826, before the London Society for Promoting Christianity amongst the Jews* (London, n.d.), pp. 8, 23, 25; G. T. Noel, *A Brief Enquiry into the Prospects of the Church of Christ, in Connexion with the Second Advent of Our Lord Jesus Christ* (London, 1828), pp. 28, 37.
58 J. H. Stewart, *A Practical View of the Redeemer's Advent, in a Series of Discourses*, 2nd edn (London, 1826), p. ix.
59 Harris, *The Great Commission* (London, 1842), p. 122.
60 D. Brown, *Christ's Second Coming: Will it be Premillennial?* (Edinburgh, 1846), pp. 13 ff.
61 ibid., 3rd edn (Edinburgh, 1853), pp. 10, 8.

62   E. Hodder, *The Life and Work of the Seventh Earl of Shaftesbury, K.G.* (London, 1888 edn), pp. 385, 524, 735.
63   Brown, *Christ's Second Coming*, 3rd edn, p. 10.
64   Blaikie, *Brown*, pp. 333, 44.
65   Brown, *Christ's Second Coming*, 3rd edn, p. 455.
66   T. R. Birks, *First Elements of Sacred Prophecy* (London, 1843), p. 3.
67   Elliott, *Horae Apocalypticae: Or, a Commentary on the Apocalypse . . .* [1844], 2nd edn, Vol. 1 (London, 1846), preceding p. 117.
68   S. Garratt, *Signs of the Times*, 2nd edn (London, 1869), pp. ix ff.
69   Cumming, *Apocalyptic Sketches* (London, 1848), p. 3; cf. R. Buick Knox, 'Dr John Cumming and Crown Court Church, London', *Records of Scottish Church History Society*, vol. 22, no. 1 (1984).
70   Stewart, *Stewart*, p. 307. R. Braithwaite, *The Life and Letters of Rev. William Pennefather, B.A.* (London, 1878), p. 253.
71   The first was *The Second Coming, the Judgement, and the Kingdom of Christ* (London, 1843). An annual volume was published up to 1858.
72   Waldegrave, *New Testament Millennarianism [sic]* (London, 1855).
73   *British and Foreign Evangelical Review*, vol. 4, no. 14 (1855), p. 698.
74   Maitland, *An Enquiry into the Grounds on which the Prophetic Period of Daniel and St. John has been supposed to consist of 1260 years* (London, 1826).
75   *Dialogues*, vol. 1, p. 366. Birks, *Sacred Prophecy*, p. 2.
76   Miller, *Irvingism*, Vol. 2, pp. 266 f.
77   Rowdon, *Origins of the Brethren*, ch. 1 and ch. 9, sect. 2. Sandeen, *Roots of Fundamentalism*, ch. 3. See also W. G. Turner, *John Nelson Darby* (London, 1926).
78   J. Sargent, *Memoir of the Rev. Henry Martyn, B.D.*, 8th edn (London, 1825), p. 426.
79   A. W. Brown, *Recollections of the Conversation Parties of the Rev. Charles Simeon* (London, 1863), p. 100.
80   Wilson, *Lectures on the Evidences of Christianity*, Vol. 1 (London, 1828), p. 455.
81   Horne, *An Introduction to the Critical Study and Knowledge of the Holy Scriptures*, Vol. 1 (London, 1818), pp. 435 f.
82   Rosman, *Evangelicals and Culture*, p. 40. T. R. Preston, 'Biblical criticism, literature and the eighteenth-century reader', in I. Rivers (ed.), *Books and their Readers in Eighteenth-Century England* (Leicester, 1982), pp. 105 f.
83   R. Hawker, *The Evidences of a Plenary Inspiration* (Plymouth, [c.1794]), pp. 21 f., 31, 50 ff.
84   Pratt (ed.), *Evangelical Leaders*, pp. 152 f., 2.
85   Haldane, *Haldanes*, ch. 18, esp. p. 412.
86   Haldane, *The Evidence and Authority of Divine Revelation* (Edinburgh, 1816), pp. 134 f.
87   Martin, *Evangelicals United*, pp. 123–31. Rennie, 'Evangelicalism and public life', pp. 42–9.
88   Haldane, *Haldanes*, p. 505.
89   Haldane, *Haldanes*, pp. 511–15. J. Medway, *Memoirs of the Life and Writings of John Pye Smith, D.D., LL.D., F.R.S., F.G.S.* (London, 1853), ch. 17.
90   H[enry] D[rummond], *A Defence of the Students of Prophecy* (London, 1828), p. 23.
91   Way, *The Latter Rain*, 2nd edn (London, 1821), p. v.

92   *CO*, 1843, p. 806.
93   'Modern millenarianism', *Eclectic Review*, March 1829, p. 214.
94   Bonar, *Prophetical Landmarks* (London, 1847), p. 274.
95   Rowdon, *Origins of the Brethren*, p. 52.
96   Sandeen, *Roots of Fundamentalism*, pp. 107 ff.
97   Haldane, *Haldanes*, p. 515.
98   Gaussen, *Theopneustia: The Plenary Inspiration of the Holy Scriptures* (London, 1841), pp. 27 f.
99   For example, J. Conder, *An Analytical and Comparative View of All Religions* (London, 1838), p. 514.
100 Gaussen, *Theopneustia*, ch. 3, p. 37.
101 W. J. Abraham, *The Divine Inspiration of Holy Scripture* (Oxford, 1981), p. 33.
102 Gaussen, *Theopneustia*, p. 25.
103 Haldane, *Divine Revelation*, p. 138.
104 Gaussen, *Theopneustia*, pp. ii, 27.
105 *CO*, September 1854, p. 625, Medway, *Pye Smith*, p. 285.
106 Abraham, *Divine Inspiration*, pp. 16 f.
107 Medway, *Pye Smith*, pp. 307 f. Harris in *New College, London: The Introductory Lectures Delivered at the Opening of the College* (London, 1851), p. 33. T. R. Birks, *Modern Rationalism and the Inspiration of the Scriptures* (London, 1853), pp. 101–12.
108 Haldane, *Haldanes*, p. 516.
109 A. C. Cheyne, *The Transforming of the Kirk: Victorian Scotland's Religious Revolution* (Edinburgh, 1983), pp. 7 f. Professor Cheyne, however, characterises these opinions as symptomatic of 'Scotland's religious conservatism', not recognising their novelty.
110 *R*, 24 October 1850.
111 *CO*, April 1861, p. 256.
112 *Dialogues*, vol. 1, p. 368.
113 Drummond, *Irving*, pp. 138 f., 153, 167 f. See also G. Strachan, *The Pentecostal Theology of Edward Irving* (London, 1973).
114 Miller, *Irvingism*, Vol. 1, pp. 64, 346; cf. Shaw, *Catholic Apostolic Church*.
115 See pp. 58 f.
116 Noel, *Prospects of the Church*, pp. 155 f.
117 *Dialogues*, vol. 1, pp. 346, 40.
118 Harris, *Great Commission*, pp. 11, 124.
119 See 142, 143 f.
120 W. Hanna (ed.), *Letters of Thomas Erskine of Linlathen from 1800 till 1840* (Edinburgh, 1877), pp. 66.
121 Erskine, *The Unconditional Freeness of the Gospel*, 4th edn (Edinburgh, 1831), p. 88, quoted in Hanna (ed.), *Erskine*, p. 376. See also D. Finlayson, 'Aspects of the life and influence of Thomas Erskine of Linlathen, 1788–1870', *Records of Scottish Church History Society*, vol. 20, no. 1 (1978).
122 [Drummond], *Defence*, p. 39. Hanna (ed.), *Erskine*, p. 127.
123 D. Campbell, *Memorials of John McLeod Campbell, D.D.*, Vol. 1 (London, 1877), pp. 51–4; cf. G. M. Tuttle, *So Rich a Soil: John McLeod Campbell on Christian Atonement* (Edinburgh, 1986).
124 Irving, *Last Days*, p. 451.

125 J. P. Newell, 'A nestor of Nonconformist heretics: A. J. Scott (1805–1866)', *Journal of the United Reformed Church History Society*, vol. 3, no. 1 (1983). Hanna (ed.), *Erskine*, pp. 127 ff. F. Maurice, *The Life of Frederick Denison Maurice*, 2nd edn, Vol. 2 (London, 1884), pp. 406 ff.

126 Irving, *Sermons, Lectures, and Occasional Discourses* (London, 1828), p. v.

127 Irving, *The Orthodox and Catholic Doctrine of Our Lord's Human Nature* (London, 1830), p. vii.

128 D. Newsome, *Two Classes of Men: Platonism and English Romantic Thought* (London, 1973), ch. 5.

129 F. Irving, *Missionaries*, pp. 28, 18.

130 F. R. Coad, *A History of the Brethren Movement* (Exeter, 1968), ch. 1.

131 *Autobiography of George Müller*, ed. G. F. Bergin (London, 1905), pp. 223, 16. See also p. 39.

132 H. and G. Taylor, *Hudson Taylor*, 2 vols (London, 1911 and 1918). See also B. Stanley, 'Home support for overseas missions in early Victorian England, c. 1838–1873', PhD thesis, University of Cambridge, 1979, chs 7 and 8.

133 J. Hudson Taylor, *A Retrospect*, 2nd edn (London, 1898), p. 41.

134 *Dialogues*, vol. 3, p. vii; vol. 2, p. 4.

135 Irving, *Last Days*, p. 447.

136 Thelwall, *Sermons, chiefly on Subjects connected with the Present State and Circumstances of the Church and the World* (London, 1833).

137 *A Memoir of the Rev. Henry Budd* (London, 1855), p. 449.

138 Irving, *Last Days*, p. xxxviii.

139 *Budd*, p. 449.

140 *Dialogues*, vol. 3, p. 472. H. Budd, *Infant-Baptism the Means of National Reformation according to the Doctrines and Discipline of the Established Church* (London, 1827), p. 235.

141 Irving, *Babylon and Infidelity*, Vol. 2, p. 264.

142 *Dialogues*, vol. 1, p. 349.

143 Drummond, *Defence*, p. 58.

144 R. L. Lively, 'The Catholic Apostolic Church and the Church of Jesus Christ of Latter-Day Saints: a comparative study of two minority millenarian groups in nineteenth-century England', DPhil thesis, University of Oxford, 1978, p. 108.

145 Drummond, *Defence*, pp. 57 f.

146 Griggs (ed.), *Letters of Coleridge*, Vol. 6, p. 976 n.

147 Irving, *Last Days*, pp. 121, 124–30.

148 T. Hill (ed.), *Letters and Memoir of the late Walter Augustus Shirley* (London, 1849), p. 177.

149 Coad, *Brethren Movement*, pp. 29 f.

150 Irving, *Last Days*, pp. 122 f.

151 Irving, *Homilies on the Sacraments: Vol. 1: On Baptism* (London, 1828), p. 434.

152 Oliphant, *Irving*, p. 216.

153 Irving, *Last Days*, p. 121.

154 Budd, *Infant-Baptism*, p. vii.

155 Hill (ed.), *Shirley*, p. 130. *Dialogues*, vol. 3, p. 472. F. D. Maurice, *The Kingdom of Christ*, Vol. 1 (London, 1838), pp. 104 ff.

156 Newsome, *Two Classes of Men*, p. 30.

157 *Dialogues*, vol. 2, pp. 4 f.

158 Irving, *Missionaries*, p. 83.
159 *Dialogues*, vol. 2, p. 242.
160 Irving, *Last Days*, p. 132.
161 *Dialogues*, vol. 3, p. 472.
162 Drummond, *Defence*, pp. 61–4.
163 *Dialogues*, vol. 1, pp. 373 f.
164 S. W. Gilley, 'Newman and prophecy, Evangelical and Catholic', *Journal of the United Reformed Church History Society*, vol. 3, no. 5 (1985). Stunt, 'Newman and the Evangelicals', p. 71. See also D. Newsome, 'Justification and sanctification: Newman and the Evangelicals', *Journal of Theological Studies*, vol. 15, pt 1 (1964); and 'The Evangelical Sources of Newman's Power', in J. Coulson and A. M. Allchin (eds), *The Rediscovery of Newman* (London, 1967).
165 H. Tristram (ed.), *John Henry Newman: Autobiographical Writings* (New York, 1957), pp. 202–6, 208.
166 E. A. Knox, *The Tractarian Movement, 1833–1845* (London, 1933), pp. 124 ff.
167 D. Newsome, *The Parting of Friends: A Study of the Wilberforces and Henry Manning* (London, 1966).
168 P. Toon, *Evangelical Theology, 1833–1856: A Response to Tractarianism* (London, 1979), ch. 1.
169 *Budd*, p. 602.
170 See pp. 147 ff.
171 Bickersteth, *Christian Hearer*, 2nd edn (London, 1826), pp. 128–42.
172 J. E. Gordon, *Original Reflections and Conversational Remarks chiefly on Theological Subjects* (London, 1854), p. 315.
173 G. F. A. Best, 'Evangelicals and the Established Church in the early nineteenth century', *Journal of Theological Studies*, vol. 10, pt 1 (1959).
174 Lord Henley, *A Plan of Church Reform* (London, 1832).
175 *Dialogues*, vol. 2, p. 252.
176 O. Chadwick, *The Victorian Church*, Vol. 1, 2nd edn (London, 1970), pp. 36 f.
177 [R. B. Seeley], *Essays on the Church* (London, 1834).
178 Rennie, 'Evangelicalism and public life', pp. 300–3.
179 Chalmers, *Lectures on the Establishment and Extension of National Churches* (London, 1838).
180 D. W. Bebbington in *Baptist Quarterly*, vol. 27, no. 8 (1978), pp. 376 ff. R. W. Davis, 'The Strategy of "Dissent" in the repeal campaign, 1820–1828', *Journal of Modern History*, vol. 36, no. 4 (1966).
181 Chadwick, *Victorian Church*, Vol. 1, pp. 60 ff.
182 H. S. Skeats and C. S. Miall, *History of the Free Churches of England, 1688–1891* (London, 1891), pp. 479 f.
183 D. M. Lewis, *Lighten their Darkness: The Evangelical Mission to Working-Class London, 1828-1860* (Westport, Conn., 1986), ch. 3. J. Wolffe, 'The Evangelical Alliance in the 1840s: an attempt to institutionalise Christian Unity', in *Voluntary Religion*, Studies in Church History, vol. 23, ed. W. J. Sheils and D. Wood (Oxford, 1986).
184 *CO*, 1843, pp. iii f. See also pp. 136 f.
185 J. H. Newman, *Apologia pro Vita Sua, being a History of his Religious Opinions* [1864] (London, 1946 edn), p. 197.

186   Irving, *Babylon and Infidelity*, p. 400.
187   *Random Recollections of Exeter Hall in 1834–1837* (London, 1838), p. 135.
188   J. C. Colquhoun, *William Wilberforce: His Friends and His Times* (London, 1867), p. 7.
189   *Dialogues*, vol. 2, p. 251.
190   B. Hilton, 'The role of providence in Evangelical social thought', in D. Beales and G. Best (eds), *History, Society and the Churches* (Cambridge, 1985), pp. 225–8.
191   Dialogues, vol. 2, p. 258.
192   Rennie, 'Evangelicals and public life', p. 158. *Random Recollections*, p. 144.
193   *Dialogues*, vol. 1, pp. 5 f.
194   ibid., vol. 1, p. 211; vol. 3, p. 423.
195   I. McCalman, 'Unrespectable radicalism: infidels and pornography in early nineteenth-century Britain', *Past & Present*, 104 (1984), pp. 84 ff.
196   *Dialogues*, vol. 1, p. 39.
197   Drummond, *Defence*, p. 110.
198   R. W. Davis, *Dissent in Politics, 1780–1830: The Political Life of William Smith, M.P.* (London, 1971), esp. ch. 11.
199   Irving, *Sermons, Lectures . . .*, p. ix.
200   Martin, *Evangelicals United*, pp. 131–40.
201   K. R. M. Short, 'London's General Body of Protestant Ministers: its disruption in 1836', *JEH*, vol. 24, no. 4 (1973).
202   E. Norman, *The English Catholic Church in the Nineteenth Century* (Oxford, 1984), ch. 1.
203   D. Bowen, *The Protestant Crusade in Ireland, 1800–70* (Dublin, 1978), esp. pp. 89, 99.
204   D. Hempton, *Methodism and Politics in British Society, 1750–1850* (London, 1984), ch. 5.
205   G. I. T. Machin, *The Catholic Question in English Politics, 1820 to 1830* (Oxford, 1964).
206   Davis, 'Strategy of "Dissent"'.
207   G. F. A. Best, 'The Protestant constitution and its supporters', *Transactions of the Royal Historical Society*, 5th series, vol. 8 (1958), p. 108. Marsh, *Marsh*, pp. 126 ff.
208   Irving, *Babylon and Infidelity*, pp. x f.; *Last Days*, pp. 489–508.
209   *Protestant Churchman*, October 1871, p. 493. I am grateful for this reference to Dr J. R. Wolffe.
210   L. H. Lees, *Exiles of Erin: Irish Immigrants in Victorian London* (Manchester, 1979), p. 15.
211   S. Gilley, 'English attitudes to the Irish in England, 1780–1900', in C. Holmes (ed.), *Immigrants and Minorities in British Society* (London, 1978).
212   G. F. A. Best, 'Popular Protestantism in Victorian Britain', in R. Robson (ed.), *Ideas and Institutions of Victorian Britain* (London, 1967). E. R. Norman, *Anti-Catholicism in Victorian England* (London, 1967). W. L. Arnstein, *Protestant versus Catholic in Mid-Victorian England: Mr Newdegate and the Nuns* (Columbia, Mo., 1982). J. R. Wolffe, 'Anti-Catholicism in mid-nineteenth-century Britain', DPhil thesis, University of Oxford, 1985.
213   Elliott, *Horae Apocalypticae*, Vol. 4, p. 279.
214   *Witness*, 9 January 1850.

215 G. I. T. Machin, *Politics and the Churches in Great Britain, 1832 to 1868* (Oxford, 1977), pp. 94–9.

216 McNeile, *Nationalism in Religion: A Speech delivered at the Annual Meeting of the Protestant Association, held in the Exeter Hall, on Wednesday, May 8, 1839* (n.p., n.d.), pp. 2, 4.

217 Norman, *Anti-Catholicism*, ch. 2. Machin, *Politics and the Churches*, ch. 5, pt 5.

218 W. Ralls, 'The Papal Aggression of 1850: a study in Victorian anti-Catholicism', *Church History*, vol. 43, no. 2 (1974). Norman, *Anti-Catholicism*, ch. 3.

219 Ben-Ezra, *Coming of Messiah*, pp. viii f.

220 Rowdon, *Origins of the Brethren*, p. 17.

221 *CO*, January 1844, p. 128.

222 Brooks, *Advent and Kingdom*, p. 340.

223 Waldegrave, *New Testament Millenarianism*, p. 424.

224 Harris, *Great Commission*, ch. 3.

225 *CO*, January 1844, p. 128.

226 G. F. Berwick, 'Life of Francis Close', vol. 8 (1938), p. 25, quoted by Hennell, *Sons of the Prophets*, p. 107.

227 P. Fairbairn, *The Interpretation of Prophecy* [1864] (London, 1964 edn), p. vii.

228 Lively, 'Catholic Apostolic Church', p. 258. Although the sample includes some twentieth-century members, they are relatively few.

229 Rowdon, *Origins of the Brethren*, pp. 302 ff.

CHAPTER 4: THE GROWTH OF THE WORD

1 T. Hardy, *Jude the Obscure* [1896] (London, 1978), p. 93.

2 I. Bradley, *The Call to Seriousness: The Evangelical Impact on the Victorians* (London, 1976), p. 38.

3 O. Anderson, 'The reactions of Church and Dissent towards the Crimean War', *JEH*, vol. 16, no. 4 (1965), p. 215.

4 J. Wigley, *The Rise and Fall of the Victorian Sunday* (Manchester, 1980), pt 3.

5 G. M. Young, *Victorian England: Portrait of an Age* [1936], 2nd edn (London, 1953), p. 5.

6 J. S. Mill, 'Essay on Liberty' [1859], *On Liberty and Considerations on Representative Government*, ed. R. B. McCallum (Oxford, 1946), p. 61.

7 ibid., chs 3 and 4, esp. pp. 62, 78.

8 W. E. Gladstone, 'The Evangelical movement: its parentage, progress and issue', *British Quarterly Review*, July 1879, p. 6.

9 Paper by J. Coates at the Elland Society, 14 April 1803, cited by J. D. Walsh, 'The Yorkshire Evangelicals in the eighteenth century: with especial reference to Methodism', PhD thesis, University of Cambridge, 1956, p. 327.

10 J. Jerram (ed.), *The Memoirs and a Selection from the Letters of the Late Rev. Charles Jerram, M.A.* (London, 1855), p. 295.

11 W. J. Conybeare, 'Church parties', *Edinburgh Review*, no. 200 (1853), p. 338. The figure is doubted by O. Chadwick (*The Victorian Church*, Vol. 1, 2nd edn (London, 1970), p. 446), but on inadequate grounds.

12   A. Haig, *The Victorian Clergy* (London, 1984), p. 2.
13   R. Brent, *Liberal Anglican Politics: Whiggery, Religion and Reform, 1830–1841* (Oxford, 1987), p. 119.
14   T. Hill (ed.), *Letters and Memoir of the late Walter Augustus Shirley, D.D.* (London, 1849). *R*, 16 March 1848.
15   B. E. Hardman, 'The Evangelical party in the Church of England, 1855–1865', PhD thesis, University of Cambridge, 1964, ch. 2.
16   W. S. F. Pickering, 'The 1851 religious census: a useless experiment?', *British Journal of Sociology*, vol. 18, no. 4 (1967), pp. 393 f.
17   K. S. Inglis, 'Patterns of religious worship in 1851', *JEH*, vol. 11, no. 1 (1960), pp. 80 ff.
18   *Prospects for the Eighties* (London, 1980), p. 23.
19   R. Currie *et al.*, *Churches and Churchgoers: Patterns of Church Growth in the British Isles since 1700* (Oxford, 1977), p. 22. R. B. Walker, 'Religious changes in Cheshire, 1750–1850', *JEH*, vol. 17, no. 1 (1966), pp. 80 ff.
20   A. D. Gilbert, *Religion and Society in Industrial England: Church, Chapel and Social Change, 1740–1914* (London, 1976), p. 32.
21   Currie *et al.*, *Churches and Churchgoers*, pp. 147 f.
22   C. G. Brown, *The Social History of Religion in Scotland since 1730* (London, 1987), p. 61.
23   W. D. Balda, '"Spheres of influence": Simeon's Trust and its implications for Evangelical patronage', PhD thesis, University of Cambridge, 1981, p. 187.
24   B. I. Coleman, *The Church of England in the Mid-Nineteenth Century: A Social Geography* (London, 1980), pp. 8–25. See also A. Everitt, *The Pattern of Rural Dissent: The Nineteenth Century* (Leicester, 1973); and pp. 26 f.
25   H. McLeod, 'Class, community and region; the religious geography of nineteenth-century England' in *A Sociological Yearbook of Religion in Britain*, vol. 6, ed. M. Hill (London, 1973).
26   Coleman, *Church of England*, pp. 40 f.
27   B. Stanley, 'Home support for overseas missions in early Victorian England, *c.*1838–1873' PhD thesis, University of Cambridge, 1979, p. 201.
28   For example, R. M. Goodridge, 'Nineteenth-century urbanization and religion: Bristol and Marseilles, 1830–1880', in *A Sociological Yearbook of Religion in Britain*, vol. 2, ed. D. Martin (London, 1969), pp. 126 f.
29   H. McLeod, *Religion and the Working Class in Nineteenth-Century Britain* (London, 1984), p. 13.
30   H. McLeod, *Class and Religion in the Late Victorian City* (London, 1974), pp. 299 f.
31   C. Booth, *Life and Labour of the People in London: Third Series: Religious Influences*, Vol. 7 (London, 1902), p. 396.
32   J. Cox, *The English Churches in a Secular Society: Lambeth, 1870–1930* (New York, 1982), p. 32.
33   Booth, *Life and Labour*, Vol. 7, p. 112.
34   G. Crossick, 'The emergence of the lower middle class in Britain: a discussion', in G. Crossick (ed.), *The Lower Middle Class in Britain, 1870–1914* (London, 1977), p. 19.
35   McLeod, *Class and Religion*, p. 33.
36   C. D. Field, 'The social structure of English Methodism: eighteenth–twentieth centuries', *British Journal of Sociology*, vol. 28, no. 2 (1977), p. 209.

37 E. R. Wickham, *Church and People in an Industrial City* (London, 1957), p. 107.
38 Gilbert, *Religion and Society*, p. 63.
39 P. Hillis, 'Presbyterianism and social class in mid-nineteenth-century Glasgow: a study of nine churches', *JEH*, vol. 32, no. 1 (1981), pp. 55, 63.
40 Stanley, 'Home support', p. 198.
41 J. Obelkevich, *Religion and Rural Society: South Lindsey, 1825–1875* (Oxford, 1976), p. 239.
42 Gilbert, *Religion and Society*, p. 63.
43 Field, 'English Methodism', p. 216.
44 S. Yeo, *Religion and Voluntary Organisations in Crisis* (London, 1976), pp. 118 ff. Hillis, 'Presbyterianism and social class', pp. 57, 62.
45 C. Kemble, *Suggestive Hints on Parochial Machinery* (London, 1859), p. 29. On pew rents, cf. C. G. Brown, 'The costs of pew-renting: church management, church-going and social class in nineteenth-century Glasgow', *JEH*, vol. 38, no. 3 (1987).
46 R. F. Horton, in G. Haw (ed.), *Christianity and the Working Classes* (London, 1906), p. 87.
47 A. A. MacLaren, *Religion and Social Class: The Disruption Years in Aberdeen* (London, 1974), pp. 128–31.
48 B. and F. Bowers, 'Bloomsbury Chapel and mercantile morality: the case of Sir Morton Peto', *Baptist Quarterly*, vol. 30, no. 5 (1984), pp. 210–20.
49 The decline of church discipline can be traced in C. Binfield, *Pastors and People: The Biography of a Baptist Church: Queen's Road, Coventry* (Coventry, 1984), pp. 35, 74, 93, 105, 156.
50 For example, *Labour Leader*, 19 May 1894, p. 2.
51 M. C. Bickersteth, *A Sketch of the Life and Episcopate of the Right Reverend Robert Bickersteth, D.D., Bishop of Ripon, 1857–1884* (London, 1887), p. 70.
52 Haw (ed.), *Christianity and the Working Classes*, p. 16.
53 Horton in ibid., p. 87.
54 A. E. Dingle, 'Drink and working-class living standards in Britain, 1870–1914', *Economic History Review*, 2nd series, vol. 25, no. 4 (1972), pp. 608–12.
55 W. R. Lambert, *Drink and Sobriety in Victorian Wales, c.1820–c.1895* (Cardiff, 1983), p. 32.
56 P. Bailey, *Leisure and Class in Victorian England* (London, 1978), p. 137. T. Mason, *Association Football and English Society, 1863–1915* (Brighton, 1980), p. 26.
57 E. Royle, *Victorian Infidels: The Origins of the British Secularist Movement, 1791–1866* (Manchester, 1974), p. 237.
58 Cox, *English Churches*, pp. 102 f. On rural folk religion: Obelkevich, *Religion and Rural Society*, ch. 6; D. Clark, *Between Pulpit and Pew: Folk Religion in a North Yorkshire Fishing Village* (Cambridge, 1982).
59 H. Pelling, 'Popular attitudes to religion', *Popular Politics and Society in Late Victorian Britain* (London, 1968), p. 19.
60 R. Carwardine, 'The Welsh Evangelical community and "Finney's Revival"'. *JEH*, vol. 29, no. 4 (1978), p. 467.
61 Currie *et al.*, *Churches and Churchgoers*, p. 106.
62 R. B. Walker, 'The growth of Wesleyan Methodism in Victorian England and Wales', *JEH*, vol. 24, no. 3 (1973), p. 270.

63 E. P. Thompson, *The Making of the English Working Class* (Harmondsworth, 1968 edn), pp. 427–30, 919–23.

64 E. J. Hobsbawm and G. Rudé, *Captain Swing* (Harmondsworth, 1973 edn), pp. 248–51.

65 P. Stigant, 'Wesleyan Methodism and working-class radicalism in the North, 1792–1821', *Northern History*, vol. 6 (1971). J. Rule, 'Methodism and Chartism among the Cornish miners', *Bulletin of the Society for the Study of Labour History*, vol. 22 (1971).

66 Currie *et al.. Churches and Churchgoers*, pp. 107–13.

67 S. E. Koss, '1906: revival and revivalism', in A. J. A. Mason (ed.), *Edwardian Radicalism, 1900–1914* (London, 1974).

68 Gilbert, *Religion and Society*, p. 195; cf. Currie *et al.*, *Churches and Churchgoers*, p. 111.

69 J. Kendall, *Rambles of an Evangelist*, pp. 42 f., quoted by Carwardine, 'Welsh Evangelical community', p. 470.

70 Walker, 'Growth of Wesleyan Methodism', pp. 268, 271.

71 See J. S. Werner, *The Primitive Methodist Connexion: Its Background and Early History* (Madison, Wis., 1984), pp. 44 171–4.

72 W. Leach to J. Bunting, 22 October 1832, in W. R. Ward (ed.), *Early Victorian Methodism: The Correspondence of Jabez Bunting, 1830–1858* (Oxford, 1976), pp. 20 f.

73 Werner, *Primitive Methodist Connexion*, chs 2 and 3.

74 J. Kent, *Holding the Fort: Studies in Victorian Revivalism* (London, 1978), pp. 49 f.

75 Carwardine, 'Welsh Evangelical community'.

76 R. Carwardine, *Transatlantic Revivalism: Popular Evangelicalism in Britain and America, 1790–1865* (Westport, Conn., 1978), pp. 97–133.

77 A. Bennett, *Anna of the Five Towns* [1902] (Harmondsworth, 1963), ch. 5.

78 *Elgin Courier*, quoted by *Revival*, 31 March 1860, p. 103.

79 J. E. Orr, *The Second Evangelical Awakening in Britain* (London, 1949).

80 *Revival*, 21 January 1860, p. 22.

81 ibid., 25 February 1860, p. 61.

82 ibid., 18 February 1860, p. 53; 28 January 1860, p. 30.

83 ibid., 25 February 1860, p. 61; 31 March 1860, p. 102.

84 *Revival*, 28 April 1860, p. 133. Carwardine, *Transatlantic Revival*, p. 133.

85 Hardman, 'Evangelical party', pp. 319 ff.

86 *Revival* for the first half of 1860.

87 O. Anderson, 'Women preachers in mid-Victorian Britain: some reflexions on feminism, popular religion and social change', *Historical Journal*, vol. 12, no. 3 (1969).

88 F. R. Coad, *A History of the Brethren Movement* (Exeter, 1968), pp. 167–74.

89 See pp. 162 ff.

90 H. James, *The Country Clergyman and his Work* (London, 1890), pp. 154 f.

91 Kemble, *Parochial Machinery*, p. 23.

92 C. Bridges, *The Christian Ministry*, 3rd edn (London, 1830), p. 471.

93 F. K. Prochaska, *Women and Philanthropy in Nineteenth-Century England* (Oxford, 1980), p. 99; cf. H. D. Rack, 'Domestic visitation: a chapter in early nineteenth-century evangelism', *JEH*, vol. 24, no. 4 (1973).

94 The scheme was in large measure evangelistic, even though it is often discussed as an exercise in poor relief. R. A. Cage and E. O. A. Checkland, 'Thomas Chalmers and urban poverty: the St John's parish experiment in Glasgow, 1819-1837', *Philosophical Journal*, vol. 13, no. 1 (1976).

95 Lord Henley, *A Plan of Church Reform*, 2nd edn (London, 1832), p. 14 n.

96 James, *Country Clergyman*, p. 148.

97 F. K. Prochaska, 'Body and Soul: Bible nurses and the poor in Victorian London', *Historical Research*, Vol. 60, no. 143 (1987).

98 L. E. Shelford, *A Memorial of the Rev. William Cadman, M.A.* (London, 1899), p. 44.

99 G. H. Sumner, *Life of Charles Richard Sumner, D.D.* (London, 1876), p. 248.

100 Hardman, 'Evangelical party', pp. 268 f.

101 E. Hodder, *Life of Samuel Morley* (London, 1888 edn), pp. 94–100. R. Carwardine, 'The evangelist system: Charles Roe, Thomas Pulford and the Baptist Home Missionary Society', *Baptist Quarterly*, vol. 28, no. 5 (1980).

102 S. J. Price, *A Popular History of the Baptist Building Fund* (London, 1927).

103 W. Hanna, *Memoirs of the Life and Writings of Thomas Chalmers, D.D., LL.D.*, Vol. 4 (Edinburgh, 1852), ch. 19.

104 A. Peel, *These Hundred Years: A History of the Congregational Union of England and Wales, 1831–1931* (London, 1931), pp. 302–16. E. A. Payne, *The Baptist Union: A Short History* (London, 1958), pp. 104 f.

105 James, *Country Clergyman*, p. 156.

106 *Occasional Paper* (Church Pastoral-Aid Society), no. 53 (1858), p. 6.

107 W. Cuff, *Fifty Years' Ministry, 1865–1915* (London, 1915), pp. 40 f., 45 f.

108 *Occasional Paper* (CPAS), no. 53 (1858), p. 8.

109 D. M. Lewis, *Lighten their Darkness: The Evangelical Mission to Working-Class London, 1828-1860* (Westport, Conn., 1986), ch. 5.

110 J. M. Weylland, *These Fifty Years: Being the Jubilee Volume of the London City Mission* (London, 1884), esp. p. 334. C. Binfield, *George Williams and the Y.M.C.A.* (London, 1973), pp. 151–5, chs 6, 13, 14.

111 J. Wood, *The Story of the Evangelization Society* (London, n.d.). H. D. Brown, *By Voice and Book: The Story of the Christian Colportage Association* (London, n.d.). L. A. G. Strong, *Flying Angel: The Story of the Missions to Seamen* (London, 1956).

112 Hodder, *Morley*, p. 218.

113 *C*, 8 January 1880, p. 13.

114 Address of 1858 in *Speeches of the Earl of Shaftesbury, K.G.* [1868] (Shannon, 1971), p. 308, quoted by G. B. A. M. Finlayson, *The Seventh Earl of Shaftesbury, 1801–1885* (London, 1981), p. 410.

115 For example, G. Kitson Clark, *Churchmen and the Condition of England, 1832–1885* (London, 1973), pp. 71–4.

116 See pp. 213–17.

117 K. Heasman, *Evangelicals in Action: An Appraisal of their Social Work in the Victorian Era* (London, 1962), p. 14.

118 J. Rose, *Elizabeth Fry* (London, 1980).

119 G. Wagner, *Barnardo* (London, 1979).

120 E. R. Norman, *Church and Society in England, 1770–1970* (Oxford, 1976), esp. pp. 62–7. C. M. Elliott, 'The Political Economy of English Dissent, 1780–1840', in R. M. Hartwell (ed.), *The Industrial Revolution* (Oxford, 1970).

121   Cage and Checkland, 'Chalmers and urban poverty', pp. 37 ff.
122   J. B. Sumner, *Christian Charity* (London, 1841), pp. vii f., xii.
123   B. W. Noel, *The State of the Metropolis Considered* (London, 1835), p. 21.
124   J. Clifford, *Jesus Christ and Modern Social Life* (London, [1872]), p. 35.
125   Bridges, *Christian Ministry*, p. 472.
126   Bickersteth, *Bickersteth*, pp. 68 f.
127   J. Stoughton, *Congregationalism in the Court Suburb* (London, 1883), pp. 60 f.
128   Kemble, *Parochial Machinery*, pp. 24–7.
129   Yeo, *Religion and Voluntary Organisations*, p. 58.
130   Bradley, *Call to Seriousness*, p. 122.
131   *Nottingham Athenaeum*, vol. 1 (1860), pp. 16–20, 43 ff., 64 ff.
132   J. Venn, 'Charity Schools', *CO*, September. 1804, p. 542, quoted by M.
       Hennell, *John Venn and the Clapham Sect* (London, 1958), p. 137.
133   T. W. Laqueur, 'The cultural origins of popular literacy in England, 1500–
       1850', *Oxford Review of Education*, vol. 2, no. 3 (1976), p. 255. R. Houston,
       'The literacy myth?: illiteracy in Scotland, 1630–1760', *Past & Present*, no.
       96 (1982), pp. 98 f.
134   T. C. Smout, 'Born again at Cambuslang: new evidence on popular religion
       and literacy in eighteenth-century Scotland', *Past & Present*, no. 97 (1982),
       p. 122.
135   R. S. Schofield, 'Dimensions of illiteracy, 1750–1850', *Explorations in Economic
       History*, vol. 10, no. 4 (1973).
136   W. W. Champneys, *Parish Work: A Brief Manual for the Younger Clergy*
       (London, 1866), pp. 19 f.
137   T. W. Laqueur, *Religion and Respectability: Sunday Schools and Working Class
       Culture, 1780–1850* (New Haven, Conn., 1976). P. B. Cliff, *The Rise and
       Development of the Sunday School Movement in England, 1780–1980* (Nutfield,
       Redhill, Surrey, 1986).
138   Kemble, *Parochial Machinery*, p. 21 n.
139   Laqueur, *Religion and Respectability*, p. 89.
140   Cox, *English Churches*, p. 80 n.
141   H. C. Colman, *Jeremiah James Colman* (London, 1905), p. 126.
142   Bickersteth, *Bickersteth*, p. 231.
143   Finlayson, *Shaftesbury*, pp. 251 f.
144   H. J. Burgess, *Enterprise in Education: The Story of the Work of the Established
       Church in the Education of the People prior to 1870* (London, 1958), pp.
       224, 142 ff., 160.
145   M. Sturt, *The Education of the People: A History of Primary Education in England
       and Wales in the Nineteenth Century* (London, 1967), pp. 21–7. Stoughton,
       Congregationalism, p. 63.
146   Burgess, *Enterprise in Education*, p. 224. The Wesleyan figure is for 1847:
       D. Hempton, *Methodism and Politics in British Society, 1750–1850* (London,
       1984), p. 171.
147   J. M. Goldstrom, *The Social Content of Education, 1808–1870: A Study of
       the Working-Class School Reader in England and Ireland* (Shannon, Ireland,
       1972), p. 19. Cox, *English Churches*, pp. 96 f. See also W. M. Humes
       and H. M. Paterson (eds), *Scottish Culture and Scottish Education, 1800–1980*
       (Edinburgh, 1983).
148   James, *Country Clergyman*, p. 118.

149 For example, O. Chadwick, *Victorian Miniature* (London, 1960).

150 Obelkevich, *Religion and Rural Society*, p. 35.

151 D. W. Bebbington, *The Nonconformist Conscience: Chapel and Politics, 1870–1914* (London, 1982), p. 31. *Witness*, 30 May 1854.

152 F. M. L. Thompson, 'Landowners and the rural community', in G. E. Mingay (ed.), *The Victorian Countryside*, Vol. 2 (London, 1981), p. 469.

153 P. Joyce, *Work, Society and Politics: The Culture of the Factory in Later Victorian England* (Hassocks, Sussex, 1980).

154 A. Howe, *The Cotton Masters, 1830–1860* (Oxford, 1984), pp. 61 f.

155 T. R. Blumer: G. E. Milburn, *Piety, Profit and Paternalism: Methodists in Business in the North-East of England, c.1760–1920* (Bunbury, Cheshire, 1983), p. 22.

156 R. Balgarnie, *Sir Titus Salt, Baronet* (London, 1877), pp. 142 f. Viscount Leverhulme, *Viscount Leverhulme* (London, 1927), pp. 95 f.

157 T. H. W. Idris: *Baptist Times*, 12 January 1906, p. 22.

158 J. B. Johnson: R. Moore, *Pit-Men, Preachers and Politics: The Effects of Methodism in a Durham Mining Community* (London, 1974), p. 83.

159 G. Stephen, *Anti-Slavery Recollections in a Series of Letters addressed to Mrs Beecher Stowe* [1854] (London, 1971), p. 161.

160 C. Binfield, '"Self-harnessed to the Car of Progress." Baines of Leeds and East Parade: a church and a dynasty', *So Down to Prayers: Studies in English Nonconformity, 1780–1920* (London, 1977), p. 79.

161 G. and W. Grossmith, *The Diary of a Nobody* [1892], (Harmondsworth, Middlesex, 1965 edn), p. 24.

162 B. Harrison and P. Hollis, 'Chartism, Liberalism and the life of Robert Lowery', *English Historical Review*, vol. 82, no. 3 (1967).

163 G. Crossick, *An Artisan Elite in Victorian Society: Kentish London, 1840–1880* (London, 1978), p. 142.

164 Moore, *Pit-Men*, pp. 142 ff.

165 Booth, *Life and Labour*, Vol. 7, p. 399.

166 Binney, *Is it Possible to make the Best of Both Worlds?*, 9th edn (London, 1855), pp. 94 f.

167 Coleman, *Church of England*, p. 7; cf. O. Anderson, 'The incidence of civil marriage in Victorian England and Wales', *Past & Present*, no. 69 (1975). In Scotland, however, marriage was a civil contract, and so ecclesiastical involvement was purely voluntary.

168 Cox, *English Churches*, pp. 97–100.

169 Gilbert, *Religion and Society*, pp. 89 f. Obelkevich, *Religion and Rural Society*, chs 4 and 5.

170 Moore, *Pit-Men*, pp. 124–32. Werner, *Primitive Methodist Connexion*, pp. 157–61.

171 C. Binfield, *So Down to Prayers*, pp. 26 f.

172 J. Lea, 'The growth of the Baptist denomination in mid-Victorian Lancashire and Cheshire', *Transactions of the Historic Society of Lancashire and Cheshire*, vol. 124 (1972), p. 143.

173 James, *Country Clergyman*, pp. 163 ff.

174 A. L. Drummond and J. Bulloch, *The Church in Late Victorian Scotland, 1874–1900* (Edinburgh, 1978), pp. 168 ff.

175 J. Burgess, *The Lake Counties and Christianity: The Religious History of Cumbria, 1780–1920* (Carlisle, 1984), p. 96.

176   Chadwick, *Victorian Church*, Vol. 2, p. 223.
177   Cox, *English Churches*, pp. 26 f., 282 f., 290 ff.
178   B. Harrison, *Separate Spheres: The Opposition to Women's Suffrage in Britain* (London, 1978). B. Heeney, 'The beginnings of church feminism: women and the councils of the Church of England, 1897–1919', *JEH*, vol. 33, no. 1 (1982), esp. p. 108 (Dean Wace).
179   Anderson, 'Women preachers', p. 468 n. Heeney, 'Church feminism', p. 90 n.
180   A. T. Pierson, *Forward Movements of the Last Half Century* (New York, 1900), ch. 13.
181   Z. Fairfield, *Some Aspects of the Woman's Movement* (London, 1915), appendix. See pp. 174 f.
182   Anderson, 'Women preachers'. Prochaska, *Women and Philanthropy*.
183   R. A. Knox, *A Spiritual Aeneid* (London, 1918), pp. 5 f.
184   H. Thornton, *Family Prayers* (London, 1834).
185   S. Butler, *The Way of All Flesh* (London, 1903). E. Gosse, *Father and Son* (London, 1907).
186   L. Hoare, *Hints for the Improvement of Early Education and Nursery Discipline* (London, 1819); *Friendly Advice on the Management and Education of Children* (London, 1824). J. H. Townsend (ed.), *Edward Hoare, M.A.*, 2nd edn ₋ondon, 1896), p. 7. See also Rosman, *Evangelicals and Culture*, ch. 4.
187   Shaftesbury's diary, 5 September 1840, quoted by Finlayson, *Shaftesbury*, p. 131.
188   *R*, 18 January 1855, p. 2, citing the *Leader*, as quoted by Hardman, 'Evangelical party', p. 133.
189   On Dickens: V. Cunningham, *Everywhere Spoken Against: Dissent in the Victorian Novel* (Oxford, 1975), ch. 8. On Eliot: E. Jay, *The Religion of the Heart: Anglican Evangelicalism and the Nineteenth-Century Novel* (Oxford, 1979), ch. 4.
190   G. Best, 'Evangelicalism and the Victorians', in A. Symondson (ed.), *The Victorian Crisis of Faith* (London, 1970), p. 48 f.
191   *The World of Cant* (London, 1880), p. 143; cf. A. Mursell, *Memories of My Life* (London, 1913), pp. 185 ff.
192   W. Wilberforce, *A Practical View of the Prevailing Religious Systems of Professed Christians in the Higher and Middle Classes in this Country Contrasted with Real Christianity*, 4th edn (London, 1797), p. 453.
193   M. Hennell, 'Evangelicalism and worldliness, 1770–1870', in G. J. Cuming and D. Baker (eds), *Popular Belief and Practice*, Studies in Church History, vol. 8 (Cambridge, 1972), p. 230.
194   J. H. Pratt (ed.), *The Thought of the Evangelical Leaders: Notes of the Discussions of The Eclectic Society, London, during the Years 1798–1814* (Edinburgh, 1978), pp. 157–62; cf. Rosman, *Evangelicals and Culture*, pp. 75–8.
195   A.W., 'The Theatre; and can it be improved?', *CO*, May 1851, p. 300.
196   J. Kay, *A Defence of the Legitimate Drama* (Edinburgh, 1883), p. 18.
197   G. S. Barrett, 'The secularisation of the church', in *Congregational Yearbook*, 1895, p. 47.
198   Rosman, *Evangelicals and Culture*, ch. 6, esp. p. 137.
199   M. Raleigh (ed.), *Alexander Raleigh: Records of his Life* (Edinburgh, 1881), p. 22.
200   P. Horn, *Education in Rural England, 1800–1914* (Dublin, 1978), p. 193.

201 C. Binfield, "'Old fashioned Dissenting narrowness": Crabb Robinson and the Patissons', *So Down to Prayers*, ch. 3. T. S. James, 'Home life', in R. W. Dale, *Life and Letters of John Angell James* (London, 1862 edn), p. 382, quoted by Cunningham, *Everywhere Spoken Against*, p. 48.

202 Rosman, *Evangelicals and Culture*, ch. 8, sect. C; cf. Jay, *Religion of the Heart*, pp. 195–202.

203 Cunningham, *Everywhere Spoken Against*, p. 59. J. Briggs and I. Sellers (eds), *Victorian Nonconformity* (London, 1973), pp. 117 f.

204 Cunningham, *Everywhere Spoken Against*, p. 62.

205 *CO*, September 1845, p. 522.

206 Hardman, 'Evangelical party', p. 377.

207 *T*, 27 December 1860, p. 8, cited by Hardman, 'Evangelical party', p. 79.

208 Bradley, *Call to Seriousness*, p. 28. G. Unwin and J. Telford, *Mark Guy Pearse: Preacher, Author, Artist* (London, 1930), p. 29.

209 J. B. B. Clarke (ed.), *An Account of the Infancy, Religious and Literary Life of Adam Clarke, LL.D., F.A.S.*, Vol. 2 (London, 1833), p. 38.

210 H. A. Thomas (ed.), *Memorials of the Rev. David Thomas, B.A.* (London, 1876), p. 4.

211 A. Delves, 'Popular recreation and social conflict in Derby, 1800–1850', in E. and S. Yeo (eds), *Popular Culture and Class Conflict* (Brighton, 1981). Hennell, *Sons of the Prophets*, p. 106. P. Bailey, *Leisure and Class in Victorian England: Rational Recreation and the Contest for Control, 1830–1885* (London, 1978), pp. 18 f.

212 G. Eliot, *Middlemarch* [1871–72] (Harmondsworth, Middlesex, 1965), p. 191.

213 S. K. Phillips, 'Primitive Methodist confrontation with popular sports: case study of early nineteenth century Staffordshire', in R. Cashman and M. McKernan (eds), *Sport: Money, Morality and the Media* (Sydney, NSW, n.d.).

214 B. Harrison, 'Animals and the state in nineteenth-century England', *Peaceable Kingdom: Stability and Change in Modern Britain* (Oxford, 1982), pp. 115 f., 118. A. Lloyd, *The Great Prize Fight* (New York, 1977), esp. ch. 16.

215 See p. 113 f.

216 Colman, *Colman*, p. 354.

217 See pp. 71 f.

218 Stephen, *Anti-Slavery Recollections*, p. 248.

219 For example, F. J. Klingberg, *The Anti-Slavery Movement in England* (New Haven, Conn., 1926).

220 G. A. Catherall, *William Knibb: Freedom Fighter* (n.p., 1972), p. 66; cf. K. R. M. Short, 'Jamaican Christian missions and the Great Slave Rebellion of 1831–2', *JEH*, vol. 27, no. 1 (1976).

221 J. C. Gill, *The Ten Hours Parson: Christian Social Action in the 1830s* (London, 1959).

222 For example, D. Bowen, *The Protestant Crusade in Ireland, 1800–70* (Dublin, 1978), p. 221 (A.R.C. Dallas).

223 G. I. T. Machin, *Politics and the Churches in Great Britain, 1832–1868* (Oxford, 1977), pp. 169–77.

224 K. Ingham, 'The English Evangelicals and the Pilgrim Tax in India, 1800–1862', *JEH*, vol. 3, no. 2 (1952).

225 S. E. Maltby, *Manchester and the Movement for National Elementary Education, 1800–1870* (Manchester, 1918), p. 67.
226 Binfield, *Pastors and People*, ch. 7. Bebbington, *Nonconformist Conscience*, ch. 7.
227 P. McHugh, *Prostitution and Victorian Social Reform* (London, 1980), ch. 7.
228 G. Battiscombe, *Shaftesbury: A Biography of the Seventh Earl* (London, 1974), p. 147.
229 A. Mearns, *The Bitter Cry of Outcast London* [1883] (Leicester, 1970), pp. 16 f.
230 *Occasional Paper* (CPAS), no. 133 (1884), p. 5.
231 A. E. Dingle, *The Campaign for Prohibition in Victorian England: The United Kingdom Alliance, 1872–1895* (London, 1980). L. L. Shiman, *The Crusade against Drink in Victorian England* (London, 1986).
232 Sargent, *Martyn*, p. 67.
233 Wigley, *Victorian Sunday*, pp. 53–7, 64–7. Finlayson, *Shaftesbury*, pp. 313–16.
234 J. G. Bowran, *The Life of Arthur Thomas Guttery, D.D.* (London, n.d.), p. 63.
235 T. W. Moody, 'The Irish university question of the nineteenth century', *History*, vol. 43, no. 2 (1958).
236 P. Wright, *Knibb 'the Notorious': Slaves' Missionary, 1803–1845* (London, 1973), p. 126.
237 Bebbington, *Nonconformist Conscience*, pp. 52 f.
238 B. Harrison, *Drink and the Victorians: The Temperance Question in England, 1815–1872* (London, 1971), pp. 269, 273.
239 D. B. Davis, 'The emergence of immediatism in British and American antislavery thought', *Mississippi Valley Historical Review*, vol. 49, no. 2 (1962).
240 A. Miall, *Life of Edward Miall* (London, 1884), pp. 29 ff.
241 M. J. D. Roberts, 'Pressure-group politics and the Church of England: the Church Defence Institution, 1859–1896', *JEH*, vol. 35, no. 4 (1984).
242 W. H. Mackintosh, *Disestablishment and Liberation: The Movement for the Separation of the Anglican Church from State Control* (London, 1972). D. M. Thompson, 'The Liberation Society, 1844–1868', in P. Hollis (ed.), *Pressure from Without in Early Victorian England* (London, 1974).
243 Hardman, 'Evangelical party', ch. 7. P. M. H. Bell, *Disestablishment in Ireland and Wales* (London, 1969), pp. 96–109.
244 D. W. Bebbington, 'Nonconformity and electoral sociology, 1867–1918', *Historical Journal*, vol. 27, no. 3 (1984). K. O. Morgan, *Wales in British Politics, 1868–1922* (London, 1963).
245 J. G. Kellas, 'The Liberal Party and the Scottish church disestablishment crisis', *English Historical Review*, vol. 79, no. 1 (1974).
246 I. G. C. Hutchison, *A Political History of Scotland, 1832–1924: Parties, Elections and Issues* (Edinburgh, 1986), pp. 84, 116 f.
247 D. E. H. Mole, 'The Church of England and society in Birmingham c.1830–1866', PhD thesis, University of Cambridge, 1961, p. 266. Bickersteth, *Bickersteth*, pp. 32, 189.
248 Bebbington, 'Nonconformity and electoral sociology'.
249 J. H. Newman, *Apologia pro Vita Sua* [1864] (London, 1946), p. 193.
250 J. Foster, 'On some of the causes . . .', *Essays in a Series of Letters to a Friend* (London, 1805); cf. Rosman, *Evangelicals and Culture*, pp. 203 f.
251 H. Crooke, *The Spirit No Respecter of Persons in His Gifts and Graces* (London, 1755), p. 15, quoted by Walsh, 'Yorkshire Evangelicals', p. 147 n.

252 Finlayson, *Shaftesbury*, p. 336.

253 J. G. Breay, 'The pastor's obligations to the church of God', *The Faithful Pastor Delineated* (London, 1844), quoted by Mole, 'Church and society in Birmingham', p. 75.

254 E. Stock, *The History of the Church Missionary Society*, Vol. 2 (London, 1899), pp. 63, 550.

255 W. B. Brash, *The Story of Our Colleges, 1835–1935* (London, 1935), p. 72.

256 A. de Q. Robin, *Charles Perry, Bishop of Melbourne* (Nedlands, Western Australia, 1967), p. 15. Hardman, 'Evangelical party', pp. 396, 409.

257 See above, p. 123.

258 W. Robertson Nicoll, *My Father: An Aberdeenshire Minister, 1812–1891* (London, 1908), pp. 62, 72.

259 N. G. Brett-James, *The History of Mill Hill School, 1807–1923* (Reigate, [1925]), p. 219.

260 A. S. Wilkins, *Our National Universities* (London, 1871), p. 342 n.

261 They are unsympathetically portrayed by Butler, *Way of All Flesh*, pp. 231–4.

262 J. D. Walsh, 'The Magdalene Evangelicals', *Church Quarterly Review*, no. 159 (1958). J. A. Venn, *A Statistical Chart to Illustrate the Entries at the Various Colleges in the University of Cambridge, 1544–1907: Descriptive Text* (Cambridge, 1908), p. 10.

263 D. Rosman, 'Evangelicals and culture in England, 1790–1833', PhD thesis, University of Keele, 1979, p. 365.

264 Hardman, 'Evangelical party', pp. 402, 409.

265 A. C. Downer, *A Century of Evangelical Religion in Oxford* (London, 1938), pp. 70 f., 66 f.

266 J. B. McCaul, *A Memorial Sketch of the Rev. Alexander McCaul, D.D.* (London, 1863), p. 15. Stoughton, *Congregationalism*, p. 65.

267 J. S. Black and G. Chrystal, *The Life of William Robertson Smith*, (London, 1912). See pp. 184 f.

268 Mole, 'Church and society in Birmingham', p. 89.

269 Pfleiderer, *The Development of Theology in Germany since Kant and its Progress in Great Britain since 1825* (London, 1890), ch. 2 (Samuel Davidson and Robertson Smith qualify as biblical critics). B. M. G. Reardon, *Religious Thought in the Victorian Age* (London, 1980), ch. 12, pp. 456 f.

270 R. A. Soloway, *Prelates and People: Ecclesiastical Social Thought in England, 1783–1852* (London, 1969), pp. 107–16.

271 S. Waldegrave, *New Testament Millennarianism* (London, 1855).

272 C. H. Davis to editor, *R*, 4 January 1861, p. 4.

273 Horne, *An Introduction to the Critical Study and Knowledge of the Holy Scriptures*, 4 Vols (London, 1818); ct. p. 87. McCaul, *The Old Paths* (London, 1837). L. Sergeant, 'Christopher Benson', *DNB*.

274 T. Cooper, 'Joseph Baylee', *DNB*. G. Goodwin, 'John Buxton Marsden'. *DNB*.

275 G. B. Smith, 'Thomas Rawson Birks', *DNB*.

276 *Obituary: The Very Rev. William Goode, D.D., Dean of Ripon* (London, 1883), reprinted from *Clerical Journal*, p. 4; cf. P. Toon, *Evangelical Theology, 1833–1856: A Response to Tractarianism* (London, 1979), pp. 117 ff.

277 F. Boase, *Modern English Biography*, Vol. 6 (Truro, 1921), col. 64.

278   Garbett, *The Bible and its Critics* (London, 1861); *The Dogmatic Faith* (London, 1867); cf. R. W. Macan, *Religious Changes in Oxford during the Last Fifty Years* (London, 1918), p. 12.

279   D. S. Margoliouth, 'Robert Payne Smith', *DNB*.

280   W. G. D. Fletcher, 'Nathaniel Dimock', *DNB, 1901–1911*.

281   P. Fairbairn, *The Interpretation of Prophecy* (London, 1964), pp. xvii–xxii. W. G. Blaikie, 'Patrick Fairbairn', *DNB*.

282   A. P. F. Sell, *Defending and Declaring the Faith: Some Scottish Examples, 1860–1920* (Exeter, 1987), chs 7 and 9.

283   R. S. Franks, 'The theology of A. M. Fairbairn', *Transactions of the Congregational Historical Society*, vol. 13, no. 3 (1939).

284   A. W. W. Dale, *The Life of R. W. Dale of Birmingham* (London, 1898), pp. 324 f., 710–17.

285   The ablest analysis of Forsyth remains W. L. Bradley, *P. T. Forsyth: The Man and his Work* (London, 1952).

286   Finlayson, *Shaftesbury*, p. 349.

287   A. Haig, *The Victorian Clergy* (London, 1984), p. 49.

288   L. Stephen, *Life of Henry Fawcett* (London, 1885), p. 94.

289   G. S. Spinks, *Religion in Britain since 1900* (London, 1952), p. 10 n; cf. Chadwick, *Victorian Church*, Vol. 2, ch. 8.

290   J. W. Burrow, *Evolution and Society* (Cambridge, 1966), esp. ch. 6.

291   Lecky, *A History of the Rise and Influence of Rationalism in Europe* (London, 1865). Chadwick, *Victorian Church*, Vol. 2, pp. 114 f., 11–23.

292   N. Barlow (ed.), *The Autobiography of Charles Darwin, 1809–1882* (London, 1958), p. 87.

293   Birks, *Supernatural Revelation* (London, 1879), p. 136. See also J. R. Moore, *The Post-Darwinian Controversies* (Cambridge, 1979).

294   J. Kent, *From Darwin to Blatchford: The Role of Darwinism in Christian Apologetic, 1875–1910* (London, 1966), pp. 20–8.

295   P. Mathias, *The First Industrial Nation: An Economic History of Britain, 1700–1914* (London, 1969), p. 378.

296   Cox, *English Churches*, ch. 6.

297   Yeo, *Religion and Voluntary Organisations*, esp. pp. 105 ff. Joyce, *Work, Society and Politics*, pp. 339 f.

298   S. Meacham, *A Life Apart: The English Working Class, 1890–1914* (London, 1977).

299   K. Hardie, 'Socialism' in *Labour Leader*, February 1894, p. 5.

300   J. H. Harley in *Labour Leader*, 8 February 1907, p. 595.

301   McLeod, *Class and Religion*, p. 25.

302   *R*, 2 January 1863, p. 2.

303   Birks, *Supernatural Revelation*, p. vi.

304   *R*, 2 January 1867; cf. R. Ferguson and A. M. Brown, *Life and Labours of John Campbell, D.D.* (London, 1867).

305   A. P. F. Sell, 'Henry Rogers and *The Eclipse of Faith*', *Journal of the United Reformed Church History Society*, vol. 2, no. 5 (1980).

306   Justus to editor, *CO*, September 1847, p. 519.

307   'Theological liberalism', *British Quarterly Review*, April 1861, p. 488.

308   J. Angus, *Theology an Inductive and a Progressive Science* (London, n.d.), pp. 20 f.

309   N. Goodman, *The Established Church a Hindrance to Progressive Thought* (Manchester, 1873).

310   Raleigh (ed.), *Raleigh*, p. 282.

311   Finlayson, *Shaftesbury*, p. 575.

312   D. A. Johnson, 'The end of the "evidences": a study in Nonconformist theological transition', *Journal of the United Reformed Church History Society*, vol. 2, no. 3 (1979).

313   Thomas, *Thomas*, p. 49.

314   C. S. Horne, *A Popular History of the Free Churches* (London, 1903), p. 421.

315   H. C. G. Moule, 'The Evangelical School III' in *R*, 18 January 1901, p. 79. J. Scott Lidgett, *My Guided Life* (London, 1936), p. 73. I. E. Page (ed.), *John Brash: Memorials and Correspondence* (London, 1912), p. 48. Bradley, *Forsyth*, pp. 94–7.

316   M. D. Johnson, 'Thomas Gasquoine and the origins of the Leicester conference', *Journal of the United Reformed Church History Society*, vol. 2, no. 10 (1982).

317   Binfield, '"No quest, no conquest." Baldwin Brown and Silvester Horne', *So Down to Prayers*, pp. 189–99.

318   Raleigh (ed.), *Raleigh*, p. 283.

319   T. Waugh, *Twenty-Three Years a Missioner* (London, n.d.), p. 33. Birks, *The Victory of Divine Goodness*, 2nd edn (London, 1870), pp. 42–8. E. R. Garratt, *Life and Personal Recollections of Samuel Garratt* (London, 1908), p. 79. See G. Rowell, *Hell and the Victorians* (Oxford, 1974), pp. 123–9.

320   R. T. Jones, *Congregationalism in England, 1662–1962* (London, 1962), p. 265.

321   R. W. Dale, *The Old Evangelicalism and the New* (London, 1889), pp. 38 ff.

322   Booth, *Life and Labour*, Vol. 7, p. 119.

323   *Sword and the Trowel*, July 1876, p. 306.

324   *Baptist*, 4 November 1881, quoted by P. S. Kruppa, *Charles Haddon Spurgeon: A Preacher's Progress* (New York, 1982), p. 416.

325   Payne, *Baptist Union*, ch. 7, supplemented by E. A. Payne, 'The Down Grade controversy: a postscript', *Baptist Quarterly*, vol. 28, no. 4 (1979) and by Kruppa, *Spurgeon*, ch. 8.

326   Spurgeon, *An All-Round Ministry* (London, 1900), p. 17, quoted by Kruppa, *Spurgeon*, p. 374.

327   Kruppa, *Spurgeon*, p. 424.

328   Payne, 'Down Grade controversy', p. 149.

329   A. Bentley, 'The transformation of the Evangelical party in the Church of England in the later nineteenth century', PhD thesis, University of Durham, 1971, p. 202.

330   N. Yates, *The Oxford Movement and Anglican Ritualism* (London, 1983), pp. 25 ff.

331   R. Braithwaite, *The Life and Letters of Rev. William Pennefather, B.A.* (London, 1878), p. 454.

332   Finlayson, *Shaftesbury*, p. 519.

333   O. Chadwick, *The Victorian Church*, 2nd edn, Vol. 1 (London, 1970), pp. 495–501.

334   J. Bentley, *Ritualism and Politics in Victorian Britain* (Oxford, 1978).

335   One of the knuckle–dusters is displayed at Clevedon Court, Somerset.

336 P. Toon and M. Smout, *John Charles Ryle: Evangelical Bishop* (Cambridge, 1976), p. 67.

337 Garratt, *What Shall We Do? Or, True Evangelical Policy* (London, 1881), pp. 15, 24.

338 S. Butler, *The Way of All Flesh* [1903] (Harmondsworth, Middlesex, 1966), pp. 402–5. The changes, however, are antedated by Butler (Jay, *Religion of the Heart*, p. 268).

339 *R*, 19 January 1883, p. 59 (Talbot Greaves).

340 J. Bateman, *The Life of the Right Rev. Daniel Wilson, D.D.*, Vol. 1 (London, 1860), p. 182.

341 Bickersteth, *Bickersteth*, pp. 28 f.

342 Shelford, *Cadman*, p. 61.

343 D. Voll, *Catholic Evangelicalism* (London, 1963), esp. pt 2, ch. 2. Kent, *Holding the Fort*, ch. 7.

344 Garbett, *Is Union Desirable?* (London, 1871).

345 Garbett, *Religious Thought in the Nineteenth Century* (Southport, [1877]), p. 4.

346 J. Morley, *Death, Heaven and the Victorians* (London, 1971), p. 30. J. F. White, *The Cambridge Movement: The Ecclesiologists and the Gothic Revival* (Cambridge, 1962), p. 188.

347 J. Bateman, *The Church Association: Its Policy and Prospects considered in a Letter to the Chairman*, 2nd edn (London, 1880), p. 86.

348 Waldegrave to the Rev. Henry Ware, 7 July 1868, Waldegrave MS Letter Book 4, quoted by Burgess, *Lake Counties and Christianity*, p. 57.

349 Shelford, *Cadman*, p. 62.

350 D. M. Murray, 'From Disruption to Union', in D. B. Forrester and D. M. Murray (eds), *Studies in the History of Worship in Scotland* (Edinburgh, 1984).

351 W. H. Harwood, *Henry Allon, D.D.* (London, 1894), p. 35. M. J. Street, *F. B. Meyer: His Life and Work* (London, 1902), pp. 83, 92. *CW*, 12 July 1906, p. 3 (Bernard Snell).

352 Binfield, 'Dissenting Gothic', *So Down to Prayers*.

353 Spurgeon, *Lectures to My Students*, Vol. 2 (London, 1887), p. 77.

354 Ward, *Religion and Society*, pp. 144–7.

355 J. Inglis, 'The Scottish churches and the organ in the nineteenth century', PhD thesis, University of Glasgow, 1987.

356 Chadwick, *Victorian Church*, Vol. 1, pp. 218 ff.

357 Waldegrave to the Rev. G. H. Ainger, Waldegrave MS Letter Book 2, quoted by Burgess, *Lake Counties and Christianity*, p. 56.

358 Garratt, *Garratt*, p. 252.

359 *R*, 10 June 1887, p. 561.

360 *R*, 18 September 1876.

361 N. G. Annan, *Leslie Stephen* (London 1951), ch. 3.

362 Strachey to Woolf, October 1904, quoted by M. Holroyd, *Lytton Strachey: A Critical Biography*, Vol. 1 (London, 1967), p. 198.

363 Holroyd, *Strachey*, Vol. 1, p. 267.

CHAPTER 5: HOLINESS UNTO THE LORD

1 I. E. Page, *A Long Pilgrimage with Some Guides and Fellow Travellers* (London, 1914), p. 162. On the holiness tradition, see R. Brown, 'Evangelical

ideas of perfection: a comparative study of the spirituality of men and movements in nineteenth-century England', PhD thesis, University of Cambridge, 1965.

2   D. B. Hankin, in *Account of the Union Meeting for the Promotion of Scriptural Holiness, held at Oxford, August 29 to September 7, 1874* (London, n.d.), p. 84.

3   M. E. Dieter, *The Holiness Revival of the Nineteenth Century* (Metuchen, NJ, 1980), p. 178. See p. 94 f.

4   *C*, 15 July 1875, p. 17; 12 August 1886, p. 6. *LF*, September 1880, p. 163. See pp. 81–6.

5   Mr Grane from Shanklin. *Meeting . . . at Oxford*, p. 210.

6   P. Brown, 'The holy man in late antiquity', *Society and the Holy in Late Antiquity* (London, 1982), p. 121.

7   *Meeting . . . at Oxford*, p. iv.

8   Wesley, 'A plain account of Christian perfection', in *John and Charles Wesley*, ed. F. Whaling, The Classics of Western Spirituality (London, 1981), p. 334.

9   ibid., p. 329.

10 ibid., pp. 335, 326. The standard monograph in this field is H. Lindström, *Wesley and Sanctification* (Stockholm, 1946).

11 Alexander, *Christian Holiness Illustrated and Enforced in Three Discourses* (Ewood Hall, near Halifax, 1800), p. 14.

12 Arthur, *The Tongue of Fire*, 10th edn (London, 1857), p. 48.

13 *KH*, January 1873, pp. 5 f. (W. Waters); September 1874, p. 295 (C. W. L. Christian); December 1872, p. 413 (W. G. Pascoe).

14 *KH*, January 1872, p. 34; September 1874, p. 295.

15 *KH*, January 1872, p. 5; June 1872, p. 203; April 1874, p. 112.

16 Page, *Long Pilgrimage*, p. 140.

17 J. A. Beet, *Holiness as Understood by the Writers of the Bible* (London, 1880), p. 53. Pope, *A Compendium of Christian Theology*, Vol. 3 (2nd edn, London, 1880), pp. 44–61. Pope, however, held (unlike Wesley) that genuine holiness must be unconscious: cf. W. Strawson, 'Methodist theology, 1850–1950', in R. Davies *et al.* (eds), *A History of the Methodist Church in Great Britain* Vol. 3 (London, 1983), pp. 225 f.

18 Page, *Long Pilgrimage*, p. 145.

19 I. E. Page (ed.), *John Brash: Memorials and Correspondence* (London, 1912), p. 36. F. H. Cumbers (ed.), *Richmond College, 1843–1943* (London, 1944), pp. 101 f.

20 H. T. Smart, *The Life of Thomas Cook* (London, 1913), p. 34. *KH*, October 1873, p. 347.

21 *KH*, October 1872, p. 338. T. H. Bainbridge, *Reminiscences*, ed. G. France (London, 1913), p. 87.

22 *KH*, October 1872, p. 338; December 1872, p. 414. Page, *Long Pilgrimage*, pp. 160, 196. Page, *Brash*, pp. 2 f., 26. R. M. Pope, *The Life of Henry J. Pope* (London, 1913), p. 88.

23 Bainbridge, *Reminiscences*, pp. 55 f. *KH*, October 1873, p. 346. Page (ed.), *Brash*, pp. 144, 147.

24 *KH*, June 1872, p. 186.

25 Page, *Brash*, p. 214.

26 *KH*, March 1873, p. 99.

27   *KH*, April 1874, p. 144.
28   Crewdson, *A Beacon to the Society of Friends* (London, 1835), p. 77.
29   E. Isichei, *Victorian Quakers* (London, 1970), pp. 7, 9.
30   D. E. Swift, *Joseph John Gurney: Banker, Reformer and Quaker* (Middletown, Conn., 1962), p. 175.
31   Isichei, *Victorian Quakers*, p. 12.
32   George Fox to Lady Claypole, *Journal of George Fox* (London, 1908), Vol. 1, p. 432, quoted by G. F. Nuttall, 'George Fox and his Journal', *The Puritan Spirit* (London, 1967), p. 185.
33   Robert Barclay, *An Apology for the True Christian Divinity*, 14th edn (Glasgow, 1886), p. 171.
34   *Book of Christian Discipline of the Religious Society of Friends in Great Britain* (London, 1883), pp. 98 (baptism with the Holy Ghost), 101 (rest). *Journal of the Life, Travels and Gospel Labours of William Williams* (Dublin, 1839), p. 13 (full surrender), quoted by H. H. Brinton, 'Stages in spiritual development as exemplified in Quaker journals', in H. H. Brinton (ed.), *Children of Light: In Honor of Rufus M. Jones* (New York, 1938), p. 395.
35   H. Pearsall Smith, *The Unselfishness of God and How I Discovered It* (London, 1903), ch. 29.
36   *Book of Christian Discipline*, p. 99.
37   Isichei, *Victorian Quakers*, p. 17. H. Pearsall Smith, *Unselfishness*, pp. 232 f. M. N. Garrard, *Mrs. Penn-Lewis: A Memoir* (London, 1930), pp. 34, 177.
38   H. Pearsall Smith, *Unselfishness*, pp. 119, 225. R. A. Parker, *A Family of Friends: The Story of the Transatlantic Smiths* (London, 1959), pp. 36 f.
39   *Meeting . . . at Oxford*, pp. 59, 202, 228, 38.
40   *Record of the Convention for the Promotion of Scriptural Holiness held at Brighton, May 29th to June 7th, 1875* (Brighton, n.d.), p. 335.
41   *Memoir of T. D. Harford-Battersby* (London, 1890), pp. 110 f. J. E. Cumming, 'The founder and some of the leaders', in C. F. Harford (ed.), *The Keswick Convention: Its Message, its Method and its Men* (London, 1907), pp. 60–3.
42   F. R. Coad, *A History of the Brethren Movement* (Exeter, 1968), pp. 262 f.
43   C. H. Mackintosh, *The Assembly of God*, pp. 35 f., quoted by W. Reid, *Plymouth Brethrenism Unveiled and Refuted* (Edinburgh, 1875), pp. 105 f.
44   C. H. Mackintosh, *Sanctification: what is it?*, 2nd edn, pp. 10, 19, quoted by Reid, *Plymouth Brethrenism*, pp. 272 f., 290.
45   George Goodman in *W*, October 1919, p. 160.
46   *C*, 17 September 1874, p. 11.
47   J. E. Orr, *The Second Evangelical Awakening in Britain* (London, 1949), p. 220. H. Pickering (ed.), *Chief Men among the Brethren*, 2nd edn (London, 1931), pp. 102 ff. Orr calls him 'Hambledon'.
48   *R*, 18 February 1874.
49   R. Pearsall Smith to editor, *R*, 24 April 1874.
50   H. Pearsall Smith, *Unselfishness*, pp. 190, 234 f.
51   Coad, *Brethren Movement*, pp. 168 f.
52   C. H. Mackintosh, *The Three Appearings*, p. 31, quoted by Reid, *Plymouth Brethrenism*, p. 290.
53   *Revival*, 4 November 1869, p. 3.
54   R. Braithwaite, *The Life and Letters of Rev. William Pennefather, B.A.* (London, 1878), pp. 290, 336, 305, 297.

55 ibid., pp. 325, 12, 316, 360 f.
56 *Harford-Battersby*, pp. 152 f. J. S. Reynolds, *Canon Christopher of St. Aldate's' Oxford* (Abingdon, 1967), p. 180. See p. 6.
57 Braithwaite, *Pennefather*, pp. 303, 379, 261.
58 *Revival*, 5 November 1868, p. 620.
59 Braithwaite, *Pennefather*, p. 271.
60 *C*, 5 February 1874, pp. 3 f.; 1 July 1875, p. 1.
61 *Some Records of the Life of Stevenson Arthur Blackwood, K.C.B.*, compiled by a friend and edited by his widow (London, 1896), p. 347.
62 A. Smellie, *Evan Henry Hopkins: A Memoir* (London, 1920), pp. 53 f. *Revival*, 4 November 1869, p. 6. Mrs Boardman, *Life and Labours of the Rev. W. E. Boardman* (London, 1886), pp. 156 ff. *Stevenson Blackwood*, p. 133. *C*, 17 September 1874, p. 10. Reynolds, *Christopher*, pp. 131 f. *Harford-Battersby*, p. 156. Braithwaite, *Pennefather*, pp. 431, 291. *R*, 24 May 1875.
63 *Revival*, 4 November 1869, p. 3.
64 H. Bonar, *Life of the Rev. John Milne of Perth*, 5th edn (London, 1868), pp. 337–40.
65 *C*, 15 October 1874, p. 8.
66 Boardman, *Boardman*, p. 161. *C*, 30 April 1874, p. 13; 21 October 1875, p. 14; 23 April 1874, p. 18; 7 May 1874, p. 8; 4 November 1875, p. 17.
67 O. Anderson, 'Women preachers in mid-Victorian Britain: some reflexions on feminism, popular religion and social change', *Historical Journal*, vol. 12, no. 3 (1969), esp. pp. 470–4. See also pp. 116 f.
68 J. Radcliffe, *Recollections of Reginald Radcliffe* (London, n.d.), p. 107.
69 H.W.S., *The Way to be Holy* (London, 1867), consists of articles reprinted from *The Revival*.
70 Dieter, *Holiness Revival*, p. 109, n. 51. 'D. Morgan Esq.', an English publisher, must in fact be R. C. Morgan.
71 *Revival*, 11 November 1869, p. 1; 4 November 1869, p. 15; 30 December 1869, p. 13; 20 January 1870, p. 13.
72 G. E. Morgan, *A Veteran in Revival: R. C. Morgan: His Life and Times* (London, 1909), pp. 126 f. D. W. Whittle and W. Guest (eds), *P. P. Bliss, Joint Author of "Sacred Songs and Solos": His Life and his Work* (London, 1877), p. 55.
73 Braithwaite, *Braithwaite*, pp. 280 f.
74 Radcliffe, *Radcliffe*, p. 118.
75 ibid.
76 Morgan, *Morgan*, p. 85.
77 *Meeting . . . at Oxford*, p. 58.
78 *Revival*, 14 January 1860, p. 22. Radcliffe, *Radcliffe*, p. 118 (Baptist Noel).
79 *Revival*, 28 January 1860, pp. 26, 27.
80 J. F. Findlay, *Dwight L. Moody: American Evangelist, 1837–1899* (Chicago, 1969), pp. 127 ff., 130 f., 149–55, 165 f.
81 J. Kent, *Holding the Fort: Studies in Victorian Revivalism* (London, 1978), p. 136.
82 W. H. Daniels, *D. L. Moody and his Work* (London, 1875), p. 249. Kent, *Holding the Fort*, pp. 143 f., 146. J. C. Ryle to editor, *R*, 28 May 1875. Dean Close to editor, *R*, 21 June 1875.
83 Daniels, *Moody*, pp. 425, 431, 432. On Moody's preaching, cf. Kent, *Holding the Fort*, pp. 169–204.

84   Kent, *Holding the Fort*, ch. 6. See also p. 174.
85   *KH*, June 1874, p. 213.
86   *C*, 22 January 1874, p. 5.
87   Findlay, *Moody*, p. 132.
88   Kent, *Holding the Fort*, p. 186.
89   *C*, 7 May 1874, p. 6. *R*, 24 May 1875. *C*, 19 May 1875, p. 9.
90   Findlay, *Moody*, pp. 342 n.6, 407 n.37, 408, 412 n.46. *C*, 4 August 1892, p. 23.
91   W. B. Sloan, *These Sixty Years: The Story of the Keswick Convention* (London, n.d.), p. 19.
92   Ryle to editor, *R*, 28 May 1875. Close to editor, *R*, 21 June 1875.
93   Page, *Brash*, p. 146.
94   Dieter, *Holiness Revival*, ch. 2. T. L. Smith, *Revivalism and Social Reform* (New York, 1965 edn).
95   Dieter, *Holiness Revival*, pp. 22 f. Page, *Long Pilgrimage*, p. 193. *KH*, September 1874, p. 295.
96   *Convention . . . at Brighton*, p. 217. Boardman, *Boardman*, pp. 253 f. J. B. Figgis, *Keswick from Within* (London, 1914), p. 17.
97   *Revival*, 4 November 1869, pp. 1 f. Boardman, *Boardman*, pp. 155–76. *Meeting at Oxford*, p. 73. *Convention . . . at Brighton*, pp. 383 f.
98   Dieter, *Holiness Revival*, pp. 27–32. Kent, *Holding the Fort*, ch. 8, pt 2.
99   Kent, *Holding the Fort*, pp. 342–7. *Meeting . . . at Oxford*, p. 52 ('the altar Christ').
100 Kent, *Holding the Fort*, ch. 8, pt 3.
101 Dieter, *Holiness Revival*, pp. 96–106. V. Synan, *The Holiness-Pentecostal Movement in the United States* (Grand Rapids, Mich., 1971).
102 *KH*, March 1872, pp. 74 f.; November 1872, pp. 364–72.
103 W. G. Pascoe quoted by Dieter, *Holiness Revival*, p. 167.
104 H. Pearsall Smith, *Unselfishness*, pp. 239–88.
105 For example, Anderson, 'Women preachers', p. 477.
106 Smiles, *Self-Help*, new edn (London, 1860), pp. 253, 293.
107 *Revival*, 9 January 1868, p. 17.
108 *Meeting . . . at Oxford*, p. 45.
109 *R*, 22 January 1875.
110 Smiles, *Self-Help*, p. 52.
111 T. R. Tholfsen, *Working Class Radicalism in Mid-Victorian England* (London, 1976), pp. 26–34, 61–5, 72 ff.
112 See p. 169.
113 J. W. Burrow, *Evolution and Society* (London, 1966), chs 5 and 6. A. W. Coats, 'The historist reaction in English political economy, 1870–90', *Economica*, new series, vol. 21, no. 4 (1954). A. Porter, 'Cambridge, Keswick and late nineteenth-century attitudes to Africa', *Journal of Imperial and Commonwealth History*, vol. 5, no. 1 (1976), p. 16.
114 M. J. Wiener, *English Culture and the Decline of the Industrial Spirit, 1850–1980* (Cambridge, 1981), ch. 3.
115 Arnold, *Culture and Anarchy*, ed. J. D. Wilson (Cambridge, 1971), p. 49.
116 Smith, *Revivalism and Social Reform*, pp. 113, 142.
117 *R*, 24 May 1875. C. Jerdan, 'Recent holiness teaching', *United Presbyterian Magazine*, vol. 9 (1892), p. 50. G. Jackson, 'Some Evangelical short-comings', *A Parson's Log* (London, 1927), p. 143.

118 Fox to Dr Elder Cumming, in S. M. Nugent, *Charles Armstrong Fox: Memorials* (London, n.d.), p. 210.

119 C. Binfield, "'Old-fashioned Dissenting narrowness"': Crabb Robinson and the Pattissons', *So Down to Prayers: Studies in English Nonconformity, 1780–1920* (London, 1977), p. 46.

120 J. Westbury-Jones, *Figgis of Brighton: A Memoir of a Modern Saint* (London, 1917), p. 213.

121 *C*, 25 July 1895, p. 14.

122 Wiener, *Decline of the Industrial Spirit*, pp. 46–65.

123 *Meeting . . . at Oxford*, p. 134.

124 E. H. Hopkins, *The Law of Liberty in the Spiritual Life* (London, 1884), p. 15.

125 *Meeting . . . at Oxford*, pp. 78 f.

126 Pearsall Smith to editor, *R*, 24 April 1874.

127 *Revival*, 10 December 1868, p. 683.

128 *R*, 18 January 1889, p. 56.

129 F. Meinecke, *Historism: The Rise of a New Historical Outlook* [1923], trans. J. E. Anderson (London, 1973). D. W. Bebbington, *Patterns in History* (Leicester, 1979), ch. 5.

130 *Meeting . . . at Oxford*, p. 42.

131 More, *Practical Piety* (London, 1830), pp. 2 f.

132 Bonar to G. T. Fox, quoted by Fox to editor, *R*, 18 June 1875.

133 Jerdan, 'Holiness teaching', p. 49.

134 D. D. Sceats, 'Perfectionism and the Keswick Convention, 1875–1900', MA thesis, University of Bristol, 1970, esp. p. 72.

135 Smart, *Cook*, p. 175.

136 Wesley, 'Christian perfection', p. 314.

137 For example, *Meeting . . . at Oxford*, p. 228.

138 *R*, 18 January 1882; cf. *R*, 22 January 1875, 21 January 1876.

139 Ryle to editor, *R*, 28 May 1875. Ryle, *A Letter on Mr Pearsall Smith's Brighton Convention by the Rev. John C. Ryle* (Stradbroke, Suffolk, 1875). Ryle, *Holiness* (London, 1877, and still in print); cf. Kent, *Holding the Fort*, pp. 351–4.

140 For example, Jerdan, 'Holiness teaching', p. 52.

141 J. C. Pollock, *The Keswick Story* (London, 1964), pp. 35 f.

142 J. B. Harford and F. C. Macdonald, *Handley Carr Glyn Moule, Bishop of Durham* (London, 1922), pp. 118 f. R. Matthews, *English Messiahs: Studies of Six English Religious Pretenders, 1656–1927* (London, 1936), ch. 5.

143 W. H. Aldis and W. M. Smith (introd.), *The Message of Keswick and its Meaning* (London, 1957), pp. 67, 70, 100.

144 *R*, 21 January 1878.

145 *Meeting . . . at Oxford*, p. 59.

146 Ryle, *Letter on . . . Brighton Convention*, p. 1.

147 A. T. Pierson, *Forward Movements of the Last Half Century* (New York, 1900), p. 21.

148 E. V. Jackson, *The Life that is Life Indeed: Reminiscences of the Broadlands Conference* (London, 1910), p. 19.

149 Smellie, *Hopkins*, p. 63.

150 *C*, 1 April 1886, p. 19.

151 H. Pearsall Smith, *Unselfishness*, pp. 205–25. Boardman, *Boardman*, p. 29. Page, *Brash*, pp. 10, 48. H. D. Rawnsley, *Literary Associations of the English Lakes*, Vol. 1 (Glasgow, 1894), pp. 135 f.

152 Battersby to editor, *R*, 14 June 1875.

153 *R*, 24 May 1875.

154 Bonar to G. T. Fox, quoted by Fox to editor, *R*, 18 June 1875.

155 *R*, 24 May 1875.

156 See p. 219.

157 See p. 28.

158 Page, *Brash*, pp. 35, 110.

159 Harford–Battersby to editor, *R*, 14 June 1875.

160 'The Brighton Convention and its opponents', *London Quarterly Review*, October 1875, p. 98.

161 Page, *Brash*, pp. 37 f.

162 Wesley, 'Christian perfection', pp. 335 f.

163 F. de L. Booth-Tucker, *The Life of Catherine Booth the Mother of the Salvation Army*, 3rd edn (London, 1924), Vol. 1, p. 208.

164 *Meeting . . . at Oxford*, p. 54.

165 Wesley, 'Christian perfection', p. 323.

166 *C*, 22 January 1874, p. 14. H. W. Webb-Peploe, *The Life of Privilege, Possession, Peace and Power* (London, 1896), pp. 28 f.

167 Wesley, 'Christian perfection', pp. 374, 320.

168 Pearsall Smith to editor, *R*, 24 April 1874.

169 *C*, 15 July 1880, p. 12; 29 July 1880, p. 12; 12 August 1880, p. 10. Smellie, *Hopkins*, p. 81.

170 *C*, 14 November 1895, p. 9; 21 November 1895, p. 21.

171 N. Frye, 'The drunken boat: the revolutionary element in Romanticism', in N. Frye (ed.), *Romanticism Reconsidered* (New York, 1963), pp. 8 ff.

172 Aldis and Smith (introd.), *Message of Keswick*, p. 43.

173 R. Sandall, *The History of the Salvation Army*, Vol. 2 (London, 1950), chs 18–21.

174 E. A. Wood, *Memorials of James Wood, LL.D., J.P., of Grove House, Southport* (London, 1902), p. 257.

175 *Convention . . . at Brighton*, pp. 10, 18 f. F. S. Webster, 'Keswick hymns', in Harford (ed.), *Keswick Convention*.

176 Morgan, *Veteran in Revival*, p. 174 n.

177 V. Gammon, '"Babylonian performances": the rise and suppression of popular church music, 1660–1870', in E. Yeo and S. Yeo (eds), *Popular Culture and Class Conflict* (Brighton, 1981), esp. p. 78.

178 R. W. Dale in G. Jackson, *Collier of Manchester: A Friend's Tribute* (London, 1923), p. 152 n.

179 Morgan, *Veteran in Revival*, pp. 172 f; cf. Kent, *Holding the Fort*, ch. 6.

180 J. M. Crane (ed.), *The Autobiography of Maria Vernon Graham Havergal* (London, 1888), p. 190.

181 Smellie, *Hopkins*, p. 178.

182 S. M. Nugent, 'Women at Keswick', in Harford (ed.), *Keswick Convention*, p. 195.

183 Anderson, 'Women preachers'. Braithwaite, *Pennefather*, p. 362.

184 Garrard, *Mrs Penn-Lewis*, pp. 194 f.

185 Z. Fairfield, *Some Aspects of the Woman's Movement* (London, 1915), p. 229.
186 Nugent, 'Women at Keswick', pp. 199 f.
187 *KH*, November 1874, p. 380.
188 H. Lockyer, *Keswick: The Place and the Power* (Stirling, [1936]), pp. 33 f.
189 M. V. G. Havergal, *Memorials of Frances Ridley Havergal* (London, 1880), pp. 138, 350. Garrard, *Penn-Lewis*, p. 29.
190 E.T.A. to editor, *C*, 18 July 1895, p. 16.
191 A. T. Pierson, 'The message: its practical application', in Harford (ed.), *Keswick Convention*, p. 93.
192 For example, H. F. Bowker in *C*, 4 November 1875, p. 9. I. E. Page in *KH*, June 1872, p. 196.
193 Pierson, *Forward Movements*, p. 34. T. Waugh, *Twenty-Three Years a Missioner* (London, n.d.), p. 142.
194 Charles Hollis to editor, *C*, 19 March 1885, p. 22.
195 *C*, 12 August 1880, p. 10.
196 *KH*, June 1872, p. 197.
197 D. W. Bebbington, *The Nonconformist Conscience: Chapel and Politics, 1870-1914* (London, 1982), pp. 47 f.
198 *Convention . . . at Brighton*, p. 289.
199 For example, *C*, 9 September 1875, p. 9.
200 Pierson, 'The message', p. 93.
201 Boardman, *Boardman*, ch. 16.
202 Pierson, 'The message', p. 94. *C*, 11 August 1892, p. 19.
203 P. S. Kruppa, *Charles Haddon Spurgeon: A Preacher's Progress* (New York, 1982), pp. 219 f. *LF*, 11 August 1926, p. 899.
204 Kent, *Holding the Fort*, p. 317, reaches the same conclusion.
205 Braithwaite, *Pennefather*, p. 303.
206 *Meeting . . . at Oxford*, p. 181.
207 P. Bailey, '"A mingled mass of perfectly legitimate pleasures": the Victorian middle class and the problem of leisure', *Victorian Studies*, vol. 21, no. 1 (1977).
208 J. D. Marshall and J. K. Walton, *The Lake Counties from 1830 to the Mid-Twentieth Century* (Manchester, 1981), pp. 188 ff.
209 J. S. Holden, 'Young men at Keswick', in Harford (ed.), *Keswick Convention*, p. 209. J. B. Figgis, *Keswick from Within* (London, 1914), p. 163.
210 Pollock, *Keswick Story*, p. 111.
211 *R*, 18 January 1892, p. 71. *C*, 4 August 1892, p. 23.
212 *R*, 18 January 1901, pp. 88 f.; 17 January 1902, pp. 67 f.
213 *C*, 2 August 1900, p. 11. Smellie, *Hopkins*, p. 124.
214 *Convention . . . at Brighton*, p. 456.
215 *C*, 24 September 1874, p. 12.
216 Page (ed.), *Brash*, pp. 106, 109, 185.
217 Page (ed.), *Brash*, p. 214. Page, *Long Pilgrimage*, p. 249.
218 *To the Uttermost: Commemorating the Diamond Jubilee of the Southport Methodist Holiness Convention, 1885–1945* (London, 1945), esp. pp. 63, 75.
219 Page (ed.), *Brash*, p. 146.
220 *KH*, November 1874, p. 391.
221 Page, *Long Pilgrimage*, p. 46.

222	Govan, *Spirit of Revival*, pp. 22, 24, 31, 33, 40. J. Rendel Harris (ed.), *The Life of Francis William Crossley* (London, 1900), ch. 5.
223	Ford, *Steps of John Wesley*, pp. 90 ff. Garrard, *Penn-Lewis*, p. 235.
224	R. M. Anderson, *Vision of the Disinherited: The Making of American Pentecostalism* (New York, 1979), p. 37.
225	Ford, *Steps of John Wesley*, p. 29.
226	An illuminating analysis of the first three is the substance of Ford, *Steps of John Wesley*. The fourth is discussed in T. R. Warburton, 'Organisation and change in a British Holiness Movement', in B. R. Wilson (ed.), *Patterns of Sectarianism* (London, 1967).
227	See pp. 196.
228	Ford, *Steps of John Wesley*, p. 130 n.
229	T. H. Darlow, in W. Y. Fullerton, *F. B. Meyer: A Biography* (London, n.d.), p. 36.
230	*R*, 2 August 1907, p. 679.
231	On CICCU: J. C. Pollock, *A Cambridge Movement* (London, 1953). On the creation of BTI: *C*, 16 June 1892, p. 8.
232	This is evident in C. H. Hopkins, *John R. Mott, 1865–1955: A Biography* (Grand Rapids, Mich., 1979).
233	Morgan, *Veteran in Revival*, p. 190.
234	Wilson (ed.), *Patterns of Sectarianism*, pp. 23 f., 27.
235	Smellie, *Hopkins*, p. 83.

CHAPTER 6: WALKING APART

1	Letter of December 1923 in E. N. Gowing, *John Edwin Watts-Ditchfield: First Bishop of Chelmsford* (London, 1926), p. 229.
2	H. A. H. Lea to editor, *R*, 12 January 1934, p. 18.
3	G. M. Marsden, *Fundamentalism and American Culture: The Shaping of Twentieth-Century Evangelicalism, 1870–1925* (New York, 1980), pp. 118–23, 159.
4	*LW*, June 1924, p. 122 (J. N. Ogilvie).
5	*JWBU*, August 1927.
6	*BW*, 29 May 1913, p. 226 (P. Watchurst).
7	J. A. Chapman, *The Bible and its Inspiration* (n.p., n.d. [c.1930]), pp. 14, 5.
8	*R*, 7 July 1933, p. 397.
9	K. H. Boynes, *Our Catholic Heritage* (n.p., n.d. [c.1927]), p. 8.
10	P. Austin, *Letters to a Fundamentalist* (London, 1930), pp. 26 f.
11	W. A. Challacombe to editor, *R*, 10 March 1911, p. 236. See pp. 90 f.
12	H. Cockayne to editor, *R*, 30 March 1922, p. 213.
13	I. Ellis, *Seven against Christ: A Study of 'Essays and Reviews'* (Leiden, 1980), p. 115.
14	J. Rogerson, *Old Testament Criticism in the Nineteenth Century* (London, 1984).
15	*Free Church of Scotland Special Report of the College Committee on Professor Smith's Article Bible* (Edinburgh, 1877), pp. 20, 16, 8 f.
16	J. S. Black and G. W. Chrystal, *The Life of William Robertson Smith* (London, 1912).
17	*Special Report*, p. 22.

18 W. B. Glover, *Evangelical Nonconformists and Higher Criticism in the Nineteenth Century* (London, 1954), pp. 128 f., 186–93.
19 R. A. Riesen, *Criticism and Faith in Late Victorian Scotland: A. B. Davidson, William Robertson Smith and George Adam Smith* (Lanham, Md, 1985).
20 *LW*, May 1912, p. 134.
21 S. Neill, *The Interpretation of the New Testament, 1861–1961* (Oxford, 1964), pp. 33–97.
22 A. M. Ramsey, *From Gore to Temple* (London, 1960), pp. 5–8.
23 Driver, *An Introduction to the Literature of the Old Testament* (Edinburgh, 1891).
24 Forsyth, 'Revelation and the Person of Christ', in *Faith and Criticism* (2nd edn, London, 1893), p. 109.
25 R. T. Jones, *Congregationalism in England, 1662–1962* (London, 1962), p. 258.
26 Glover, *Nonconformists and Higher Criticism*, pp. 205–11. J. T. Wilkinson, *Arthur Samuel Peake: A Biography* (London, 1971), pp. 24 f.
27 I. E. Page (ed.), *John Brash: Memorials and Correspondence* (London, 1912), p. 74.
28 See pp. 145 f.
29 *C*, 1 June 1893, p. 11. The author is identified at 8 June 1893, p. 19.
30 *Newness of Life*, January 1898, p. 1.
31 R. F. Horton, *An Autobiography* (London, 1917), pp. 84–98.
32 For example, H. Wace in *R*, 16 January 1903, p. 63.
33 *R*, 18 January 1878.
34 *R*, 25 June 1909, p. 673.
35 *C*, 12 May 1892, p. 7; 14 July 1892, p. 8.
36 *Baptist Handbook*, 1918, p. 133. *LF*, 7 March 1923, p. 269. G. E. Morgan, *A Veteran in Revival: R. C. Morgan: His Life and Times* (London, 1909), pp. 157 f.
37 *C*, 13 February 1896, p. 26.
38 *R*, 25 June 1909, p. 673. *C*, 4 January 1906, p. 12. *JWBU*, March 1915, p. 61.
39 *JWBU*, March 1915, pp. 60–3.
40 A. G. Wilkinson, *Christ or the Higher Critics* (London, 1917).
41 *JWBU*, April 1915, p. 79.
42 D. Johnson, *Contending for the Faith: A History of the Evangelical Movement in the Universities and Colleges* (Leicester, 1979), p. 70.
43 J. C. Pollock, *Cambridge Movement* (London, 1953), p. 178.
44 *JWBU*, May 1921, pp. 115 f. *LF*, 18 June 1924, p. 714.
45 *C*, 1 June 1893, p. 11.
46 *W*, September 1921, pp. 99 f.
47 *Expository Thoughts on St John's Gospel*, Vol. 1, p. vii, quoted by M. L. Loane, *John Charles Ryle, 1816–1900* (London, 1983), p. 60.
48 For example, H. D. Brown, *The Bible: The Word of God* (London, n.d.), p. 44.
49 *BC*, December 1922, p. 95 (W. R. Rowlatt-Jones).
50 *AW*, April 1921, pp. 187 f; cf. F. W. Pitt, *Windows on the World: A Record of the Life of Alfred H. Burton, B.A., M.D.* (London, n.d.), pp. 16 f. 27, 35.
51 D. F. Wright, 'Soundings in the doctrine of scripture in British Evangelicalism in the first half of the twentieth century', *Tyndale Bulletin*, vol. 31 (1980), pp. 100 ff.
52 *R*, 13 January 1911, p. 50.

53 Wace, 'Science and the Bible', in H. Wace *et al.*, *Creative Christianity* (London, 1921), p. 17.
54 *JWBU*, March 1922, p. 56.
55 *R*, 10 January 1924, p. 19.
56 Wace, *The Bible and Modern Investigation* (London, 1903). *R*, 14 October 1920, p. 790.
57 *LF*, 12 December 1923, p. 1535.
58 *R*, 5 October 1922, p. 650. For the contrast with a deductive approach to inspiration, see pp. 89 f.
59 Marsden, *Fundamentalism and American Culture.*
60 *R*, 27 April 1922, p. 279 (W. Young).
61 *C*, 11 March 1886, p. 24. See also pp. 88 f.
62 *AW*, October 1922, p. 113.
63 E. Morton and D. Dewar, *A Voice Crying in the Wilderness: A Memoir of Harold Christopherson Morton* (London, 1937), pp. 34 f.
64 For example, Lover of Keswick to editor, *LF*, 25 August 1926, p. 960.
65 Page (ed.), *Brash*, p. 176.
66 F. Ballard, *Christian Reality in Modern Light* (London, 1916), p. 383.
67 *LW*, November 1918, p. 164; May 1919, p. 69.
68 *R*, 3 July 1931, p. 441.
69 *C*, 22 June 1893, p. 20; 10 July 1884, p. 16.
70 See p. 152.
71 A. T. Pierson, *Forward Movements of the Last Half Century* (New York, 1900), p. 159 n.
72 A. Porter, 'Evangelical enthusiasm, missionary motivation and West Africa in the late nineteenth century: the career of G. W. Brooke', *Journal of Imperial and Commonwealth History*, vol. 6, no. 1 (1977), pp. 38 ff.
73 *R*, 18 January 1901, p. 99 (Prebendary Webb-Peploe).
74 Page (ed.), *Brash*, p. 186. For dispensationalism, see p. 86.
75 *C*, 21 July 1892, p. 8.
76 *C*, 26 June 1913, p. 14.
77 For historicism, see pp. 85.
78 Garratt to C. R. M'Clenaghan, 8 March 1906, in E. R. Garratt, *Life and Personal Recollections of Samuel Garratt* (London 1908), p. 165.
79 *R*, 29 November 1917, p. 805.
80 *MBAPPU*, June 1919, pp. 1 f.; *AW*, December 1923, pp. 134 f.; May–June 1947, pp. 232 f.
81 *LF*, 8 September 1926, p. 1021. *R*, 11 November 1926, p. 786.
82 *C*, 28 April 1921, p. 11.
83 E. Luff to editor, *C*, 14 July 1921, p. 27; cf. J. W. Newton, *The Story of the Pilgrim Preachers* (London, n.d.).
84 J. Cox, *The English Churches in a Secular Society: Lambeth, 1870–1930* (New York, 1982), p. 257.
85 *C*, 11 March 1886, p. 18 (Grattan Guinness).
86 *MBAPPU*, August 1919, p. 19 (A. H. Burton).
87 Page (ed.), *Brash*, p. 68.
88 *C*, 13 February 1919, p. 22 (G. E. Morgan).
89 *LF*, 26 May 1926, p. 547 (G. H. Lancaster).
90 See p. 171 and pp. 218 ff.

91 A. Close to editor, *LF*, 13 May 1925, p. 535.
92 G. Jackson, 'Some Evangelical shortcomings', *A Parson's Log* (London, 1927), p. 143.
93 *MR*, 1 August 1912, p. 22.
94 Page (ed.), *Brash*, p. 74.
95 *JWBU*, July 1915, p. 148; March 1917, pp. 53–60.
96 *R*, 13 July 1922, p. 482.
97 *JWBU*, August 1919, p. 177; February 1920, p. 25.
98 H. Murray, *Dinsdale Young: The Preacher* (London, 1938), pp. 108 f.
99 J. I. Brice, *The Crowd for Christ* (London, 1934), esp. pp. 150 f.
100 Mrs Boardman, *Life and Labours of the Rev. W. E. Boardman* (London, 1886), ch. 16. Pierson, *Forward Movements*, ch. 30.
101 *LF*, 22 June 1921, p. 689.
102 *LF*, 29 July 1921, p. 849.
103 *LF*, 7 December 1921, p. 1409. Victory to editor, *LF*, 31 August 1921, p. 1006.
104 *Oswald Chambers: His Life and Work* (London, 1959 edn), p. 48. For the Pentecostal League, see pp. 173 f., 178.
105 E. W. Gosden, *Thank You, Lord! The Eightieth Anniversary of the Japan Evangelistic Band, 1903–1983* (London, 1982), p. 82.
106 E. Evans, *The Welsh Revival of 1904* (London, 1969), p. 146.
107 *War on the Saints* (Leicester, 2nd edn, 1916), pp. 284–95.
108 M. N. Garrard, *Mrs Penn-Lewis: A Memoir* (London, 1930), ch. 10.
109 *LF*, December 1881, p. 236.
110 Evans, *Welsh Revival*, pp. 192 ff.
111 R. M. Anderson, *Vision of the Disinherited: The Making of American Pentecostalism* (New York, 1979), ch. 4.
112 D. Gee, *Wind and Flame* (n.p., 1967), chs 3–5. See also P. Lavin, *Alexander Boddy, Pastor and Prophet* (London, 1986).
113 A. F. Missen, *The Sound of a Going* (Nottingham, 1973), pp. 7 f.
114 Anderson, *Vision*, pp. 159 f. Evans, *Welsh Revival*, p. 194.
115 B. R. Wilson, *Sects and Society* (London, 1961), ch. 2; cf. E. C. W. Boulton, *George Jeffreys: A Ministry of the Miraculous* (London, 1928) and D. W. Cartwright, *The Great Evangelists: The Lives of George and Stephen Jeffreys* (Basingstoke, 1986).
116 Gee, *Wind and Flame*, pp. 126–30.
117 Wilson, *Sects and Society*, p. 22 n.
118 *Labourers with God: Being a Brief Account of the Activities of the Elim Movement* (London, [*c.*1943]), p. 30.
119 *LF*, 14 June 1922, p. 732.
120 Anderson, *Vision*, p. 6.
121 See pp. 143 f.
122 G. F. Nuttall, 'A. D. Martin', *The Puritan Spirit* (London, 1967), p. 328.
123 G. S. Wakefield, *Robert Newton Flew, 1886–1962* (London, 1971), p. 44.
124 I. Sellers, *Salute to Pembroke* (n.p., 1960), ch. 4. *CW*, 14 June 1906, p. 4.
125 Campbell, *The New Theology* (London, 1907), p. 74; cf. K. Robbins, 'The spiritual pilgrimage of the Rev. R. J. Campbell', *JEH*, vol. 30, no. 2 (1979).
126 Campbell, *Christianity and the Social Order* (London, 1907), pp. vii, 182.
127 *C*, 27 September 1906, p. 10.

128 *JWBU*, July 1915, p. 157.
129 R. J. Campbell, *A Spiritual Pilgrimage* (London, 1916), chs 10, 11.
130 Cox, *English Churches*, pp. 245 f. T. Rhondda Williams, *How I found my Faith* (London, 1938).
131 *R*, 13 January 1905, p. 38.
132 L. Elliott Binns to editor, *R*, 21 April 1921, p. 253.
133 *Ridley Hall, Cambridge: Annual Letter and Report of Triennial Reunion, 1912* (n.p., n.d.), pp. 22–33.
134 *MR*, 29 February 1912, p. 5 (Dinsdale Young). *C*, 14 August 1913, p. 8.
135 A. Wilkinson, *The Church of England and the First World War* (London, 1978), pp. 176 ff.
136 *JWBU*, April 1917, pp. 80 f. (W. T. Kitching).
137 *R*, 11 December 1914, p. 1125.
138 *JWBU*, November 1915, p. 246.
139 *W*, March 1920, p. 233. *If a Man die* (London, 1917).
140 *JWBU*, March 1915, p. 56.
141 For example, S. E. Burrows to editor, *C*, 29 January 1920, p. 18.
142 For example, *LCMM*, February 1919, p. 13 (Sir C. E. Tritton).
143 *R*, 15 January 1904, p. 97.
144 *R*, 18 September 1924, p. 591.
145 D. H. C. Bartlett to editor, *R*, 17 August 1922, p. 549.
146 K. Weatherhead, *Leslie Weatherhead: A Personal Portrait* (London, 1975), p. 61.
147 G. W. Bromiley, *Daniel Henry Charles Bartlett, M.A., D.D.: A Memoir* (Burnham-on-Sea, Somerset, 1959), p. 30. A. Mitchell to editor, *R*, 28 January 1922, p. 632.
148 G. Jackson, *The Preacher and the Modern Mind* (London, 1912), p. 166.
149 *R*, 26 May 1933, p. 311.
150 Jones, *Congregationalism*, p. 447.
151 Weatherhead, *Jesus and Ourselves* (London, 1930), p. 261.
152 *C*, 25 October 1906, p. 11; 29 November 1906, p. 9.
153 *JWBU*, May 1935, p. 94; September 1935, p. 200.
154 *R*, 24 December 1925, p. 918 (T. J. Pulvertaft).
155 *R*, 3 March 1933, p. 117 (E. A. Knox).
156 G. Rogers, *A Rebel at Heart: The Autobiography of a Nonconforming Clergyman* (London, 1950), p. 170.
157 G. H. Harris, *Vernon Faithfull Storr: A Memoir* (London, 1943), pp. 50 ff.
158 *Liberal Evangelicalism: An Interpretation* (London, [1923]), pp. vi f.
159 Harris, *Storr*, pp. 54 f.
160 *R*, 21 April 1933, p. 215.
161 Harris, *Storr*, pp. 50, 53.
162 Rogers, *Rebel*, p. 172.
163 *LF*, 20 January 1926, p. 61.
164 K. H. Boynes, *The Fellowship of the Kingdom* (London, [1922]).
165 J. A. Chapman, *Our Methodist Heritage* (London, [1919?]), p. 4.
166 H. G. Tunnicliff, *The Group* (London, [1920?]), p. 5.
167 J. M. Turner, 'Methodism in England, 1900–1932', in R. Davies *et al. A History of the Methodist Church in Great Britain*, Vol. 3 (London, 1983), pp. 319 f.
168 Chapman, *Methodist Heritage*, p. 2. Boynes, *Our Catholic Heritage*, p. 4.

169 Harris, *Storr*, p. 56.
170 W. Strawson, 'Methodist theology, 1850–1950', in Davies *et al.* (eds), *Methodist Church*, vol. 3, p. 206.
171 *R*, 19 January 1883, p. 56.
172 For example, *R*, 15 January 1904, pp. 100 ff. (W. H. Griffith Thomas).
173 *R*, 27 November 1924, p. 763.
174 *R*, 17 December 1909, p. 1278.
175 *R*, 21 January 1926, p. 55.
176 F. Courtenay Burroughs to editor, *R*, 9 September 1904, p. 898.
177 C. H. Tomkins to editor, *R*, 19 August 1904, p. 839.
178 Mary E. Burstow to editor, *R*, 26 August 1904, p. 858.
179 *R*, 3 March 1921, p. 149.
180 *R*, 8 October 1937, p. 627.
181 *R*, 10 March 1933, p. 127.
182 A. Mitchell to editor, *R*, 30 September 1904, p. 967.
183 *R*, 12 July 1917, p. 489.
184 *R*, 5 July 1935, p. 418.
185 T. A. Ballard and T. C. Chapman to editor, *R*, 27 September 1917, p. 649. *R*, 27 September 1935, p. 578. *R*, 27 June 1941, p. 235. *R*, 4 July 1941, p. 242.
186 *R*, 18 January 1907, p. 61.
187 *R*, 15 January 1904, pp. 99 f.
188 Garratt to editor, *R*, 11 November 1904, p. 1142; 9 December 1904, p. 1246; cf. Garratt, *Garratt*, ch. 9.
189 *R*, 3 February 1905, p. 99.
190 G. Denyer to editor, *R*, 1 December 1927, p. 854.
191 *R*, 23 June 1927, p. 466.
192 *R*, 21 July 1927, p. 542.
193 *R*, 1 December 1927, p. 852.
194 Boynes, *Our Catholic Heritage*, p. 11.
195 G. S. Wakefield, *Methodist Devotion: The Spiritual Life in the Methodist Tradition* (London, 1966), pp. 103 f.
196 D. Murray, 'Disruption to Union', in D. B. Forrester and D. M. Murray *Studies in the History of Worship in Scotland* (Edinburgh, 1984), pp. 90–3.
197 L. S. Hunter, *John Hunter, D.D.: A Life* (London, 1922), ch. 10.
198 *LF*, 27 May 1925, p. 600.
199 *BW*, 19 February 1920, p. 456.
200 Orchard, *From Faith to Faith* (London, 1933).
201 C. Binfield, 'Freedom through discipline: the concept of little church', in *Monks, Hermits and the Ascetic Tradition*, Studies in Church History, vol. 23, ed. W. J. Sheils (Oxford, 1985), pp. 441 f.
202 *LF*, 28 July 1926, p. 838. G. T. Brake, *Policy and Politics in British Methodism, 1932–1982* (London, 1984), pp. 314–28.
203 B. Heeney, 'The beginnings of church feminism: women and the councils of the Church of England, 1897–1919', *JEH*, vol. 33, no. 1 (1982), pp. 105, 108.
204 C. M. Coltman, 'Post-Reformation: the Free Churches', in A. Maud Royden, *The Church and Woman* (London, 1925), p. 116.

205 Baker, *Women in the Ministry* (London, 1911), pp. 13, 48 f., 55, 43.
206 *R*, 10 February 1933, p. 80; 13 April 1933, p. 208.
207 *R*, 18 September 1936, p. 569.
208 Strawson, 'Methodist theology', pp. 185 f. *R*, 13 January 1905, p. 38.
209 *C*, 17 September 1885, p. 8. *LF*, December 1887, p. 260.
210 H. H. Evans to editor, *C*, 23 September 1887, p. 16; 2 May 1895, p. 22.
211 *R*, 23 October 1924, p. 689. For Dixon, cf. *C*, 9 February 1893, p. 17.
212 C. L. Drawbridge to editor, *R*, 30 July 1915, p. 540.
213 *C*, 11 February 1926, p. 4.
214 *Church Family Newspaper*, 10 September 1920, pp. 8, 10.
215 J. Barnes, *Ahead of his Age: Bishop Barnes of Birmingham* (London, 1979), pp. 125–32. B. Booth, *These Fifty Years* (London, 1929), ch. 21.
216 *R*, 2 September 1920, p. 692; 9 September 1920, p. 708. *C*, 9 September 1920, p. 3.
217 *C*, 23 September 1920, pp. 1 f.
218 Barnes, 'The future of the Evangelical movement', in *Liberal Evangelicalism*. Barnes, *Barnes*, p. 175.
219 *LF*, 8 October 1924, p. 1192.
220 *F*, November 1927, p. 200.
221 *JWBU*, November 1923, p. 248. Morton and Dewar, *A Voice crying*, pt IV.
222 *R*, 29 September 1933, p. 549 (H. E. Boultbee).
223 B. Atkinson, *Is the Bible True?* (London, 1933), p. 49.
224 *R*, 24 June 1926, p. 427.
225 *R*, 9 October 1924, p. 658 (H. C. Morton). *LCMM*, October 1927, p. 156.
226 *F*, January 1935, p. 9; May 1941, p. 97; March/April 1943, pp. 24–9. *C*, 21 February 1935, p. 8.
227 *R*, 18 July 1930, p. 474 (H. Earnshaw Smith).
228 J. Forbes Moncreiff to editor, *LF*, 14 July 1926, p. 748. Sister L. Holt to editor, *LF*, 25 August 1926, p. 954. Winifred M. Gould to editor, *LF*, 1 September 1926, p. 983.
229 *BW*, 18 August 1921, p. 357.
230 *JWBU*, January 1918, p. 20. J. Lingard to editor, *LF*, 9 April 1924, p. 408. *LCMM*, July 1924, p. 102.
231 *W*, August 1919, p. 128 (D. Hewines).
232 See pp. 113, 127 f.
233 *C*, 5 February 1920, pp. 3 f.
234 *LW*, March 1922, p. 52.
235 Cox, *English Churches*, p. 219.
236 *BW*, 11 March 1920, p. 535.
237 *LF*, 16 May 1923, p. 556.
238 Morton to editor, *MR*, 21 March 1912, p. 6.
239 R. E. Jones to editor, *MR*, 8 August 1935, p. 18.
240 Wilson, *Sects and Society*, pp. 82, 84 (Elim).
241 *AW*, May 1922, p. 51 (A. H. Burton).
242 R. H. A. Morton to editor, *MR*, 10 November 1932, p. 20.
243 *LF*, 6 October 1926, pp. 1131 f.
244 *BC*, January 1925, p. 16.
245 R. E. A. Lloyd to editor, *R*, 12 June 1936, p. 375, and succeeding correspondence. *R*, 18 November 1938, p. 739.

246   *LW*, June 1919, p. 88.

247   H to editor, *LF*, 16 July 1924, p. 815.

248   *BW*, 13 July 1922, p. 309.

249   *R*, 25 January 1935, p. 57; 11 January 1935, p. 26.

250   *R*, 7 April 1932, p. 9; 6 March 1931, p. 143.

251   *R*, 20 February 1931, p. 117. J. Wigley, *The Rise and Fall of the Victorian Sunday* (Manchester, 1980), p. 193.

252   *C*, 3 November 1932, p. 5. *R*, 17 November 1933, p. 651.

253   *BW*, 27 November 1919, p. 206.

254   For example, Dean Wace in *R*, 17 March 1921, pp. 182 f.

255   *CW*, 6 June 1889, p. 65.

256   A. Scott Matheson, *The Church and Social Problems* (London, 1893), p. v.

257   *BW*, 6 March 1919, p. 401.

258   *MT*, 1 January 1885, p. 1.

259   Mudie-Smith (ed.), *The Religious Life of London* (London, 1904), p. 13.

260   Grant, *Free Churchmanship*, pp. 173 ff.

261   For example, D. P. Hughes, *The Life of Hugh Price Hughes* (London, 1905), p. 134.

262   K. S. Inglis, 'English Nonconformity and social reform, 1880–1900', *Past & Present*, no. 13 (1958). J. H. S. Kent, 'Hugh Price Hughes and the Nonconformist conscience', in G. V. Bennett and J. D. Walsh (eds), *Essays in Modern English Church History in Memory of Norman Sykes* (London, 1966). D. W. Bebbington, 'The city, the countryside and the social gospel in late Victorian Nonconformity', in *The Church in Town and Countryside*, Studies in Church History, vol. 16, ed. D. Baker (Oxford, 1979).

263   Hughes, *Social Christianity: Sermons delivered in St James's Hall, London*, 3rd edn (London, 1890), p. 15.

264   *CW*, 4 October 1888, pp. 758 f; cf. K. Marx and F. Engels, *The Communist Manifesto* (Harmondsworth, Middlesex, 1967), p. 116. See also D. Thompson, 'John Clifford's social gospel', *Baptist Quarterly*, vol. 21, no. 5 (1986).

265   *R*, 6 December 1907, p. 1066.

266   *R*, 1 January 1904, p. 8.

267   *R*, 21 January 1910, p. 72.

268   *R*, 17 January 1913, pp. 67 f.

269   *R*, 17 January 1918, pp. 37 f. Watts-Ditchfield, 'The Church and the Labour Movement', *Churchman*, January 1908.

270   Gowing, *Watts-Ditchfield*, pp. 10 f.

271   *R*, 17 January 1908, pp. 63, 67.

272   A country incumbent to editor, *R*, 31 January 1908, p. 106. F. D. Stammers to editor, *R*, 7 February 1908, p. 125.

273   *R*, 3 March 1921, p. 149.

274   A. E. Garvie, *Memories and Meanings of my Life* (London, 1938), pp. 241 ff.

275   Brake, *Policy and Politics*, chs 10 and 11.

276   *LW*, April 1934, pp. 161–4.

277   Jackson, 'The church and the social gospel', *Reasonable Religion* (London 1922), p. 139.

278   G. Studdert-Kennedy, *Dog-Collar Democracy: The Industrial Christian Fellowship* (London, 1982), esp. p. 40.

279 F. Coutts, *The History of the Salvation Army*, Vol. 6, *The Better Fight*, (London, 1973).
280 *JWBU*, May 1924, pp. 106 f. *LF*, 16 April 1924, p. 415.
281 *JWBU*, July 1917, p. 161.
282 D. W. Bebbington, 'Baptists and politics since 1914', in K. W. Clements (ed.), *Baptists in the Twentieth Century* (London, 1983), p. 86.
283 *W*, September 1920, pp. 323 ff.
284 Bebbington, 'Baptists and politics', p. 87.
285 ibid., p. 85. *C*, 3 March 1932, p. 5.
286 D. Moberg, *The Great Reversal: Evangelism versus Social Concern* (Philadelphia, 1972).
287 A Nonconformist Minister, *Nonconformity and Politics* (London, 1909), p. 130, quoted by D. W. Bebbington, *The Nonconformist Conscience: Chapel and Politics, 1870–1914* (London, 1982), p. 158.
288 D. W. Bebbington, 'Nonconformity and electoral sociology, 1867–1918', *Historical Journal*, vol. 27, no. 3 (1984).
289 *R*, 3 December 1909, p. 1224; 18 August 1911, p. 750.
290 *MR*, 4 January 1912, p. 3.
291 *LW*, July 1912, p. 197.
292 A. G. James, *The Spirit of the Crusade* (London, 1927), p. 16.
293 H. P. Hughes, 'The problem of London pauperism', *The Philanthropy of God* (London, 1892), p. 195.
294 *Labour Leader*, 9 February 1895, p. 2; cf. P. d'A. Jones, *The Christian Socialist Revival, 1877–1914: Religion, Class and Social Conscience in Late-Victorian England* (Princeton, NJ, 1968).
295 Rattenbury, *Six Sermons on Social Subjects* (London, [1908]).
296 M. Edwards, *S. E. Keeble: Pioneer and Prophet* (London, 1949), pp. 67 f.
297 *CW*, 8 April 1909, p. 13; 28 April 1910, p. 4.
298 *R*, 6 December 1907, p. 1066; 3 January 1908, p. 11.
299 *BW*, 7 April 1921, p. 9 (S. W. Hughes).
300 G. P. Thomas to editor, *BW*, 28 April 1921, p. 66.
301 Hughes, 'The Christian hope', *Ethical Christianity* (London, 1892), p. 76; cf. J. G. Mantle *Hugh Price Hughes* (London, 1901), pp. 49 f.
302 Clifford, *God's Greater Britain* (London, 1899), p. 164.
303 Page (ed.), *Brash*, p. 66.
304 *R*, 26 March 1925, p. 214.
305 *R*, 3 September 1925, p. 609 (London City Mission advertisement).
306 *LF*, 16 April 1924, p. 445.
307 *CW*, 14 May 1891, p. 395.
308 Thompson, 'John Clifford's social gospel', p. 214.
309 *R*, 8 November 1917, p. 750.
310 *R*, 18 September 1924, p. 591.
311 *AW*, November 1923, p. 123.
312 *MT*, 19 June 1913, p. 3.
313 D. W. Bebbington, 'The persecution of George Jackson: a British Fundamentalist controversy', in *Persecution and Toleration*, Studies in Church History, vol. 21, ed. W. J. Sheils (Oxford, 1984).
314 H. Cockayne to editor, *R*, 30 March 1922, p. 213.
315 *R*, 18 January 1907, p. 70.

316 Bromiley, *Bartlett*, p. 22. W. S. Hooton and J. S. Wright, *The First Twenty-Five Years of the Bible Churchmen's Missionary Society (1922–47)* (London, 1947), pp. 5 f.
317 D. H. C. Bartlett to editor, *R*, 6 April 1922, p. 224. Fox to editor, *C*, 28 July 1921, p. 22. Fox to Bartlett, April 1921, in Bromiley, *Bartlett*, pp. 26 f.
318 Bromiley, *Bartlett*, pp. 24–7.
319 *R*, 15 December 1921, p. 829.
320 G. Hewitt, *The Problems of Success: A History of the Church Missionary Society, 1910–1942*, Vol. 1 (London, 1972), pp. 467–71. Bromiley, *Bartlett*, pp. 27–36.
321 *R*, 11 November 1926, p. 786.
322 *R*, 31 July 1919, p. 646.
323 *W*, March 1920, p. 234. J. B. Figgis, *Keswick from Within* (London, 1914), p. 160.
324 *Church Family Newspaper*, 30 July 1920, p. 10. *JWBU*, October 1920, p. 223. J. Mountain, *The Keswick Convention and the Dangers which threaten it* (n.p., 1920), p. 8.
325 *C*, 6 July 1933, p. 12.
326 Mountain, *Keswick Convention*, p. 14.
327 Mountain, *What Keswick needs* (n.p., 1921). Mountain, *The Bible Vindicated* (n.p., 1921). Mountain, *Rev. F. C. Spurr and Keswick* (n.p., 1921). Mountain, *Rev. F. C. Spurr and his Bible* (n.p., 1922). Charles Brown to editor, *BW*, 14 July 1921, p. 276.
328 Battersby Harford to editor, *R*, 6 January 1921, p. 4. Douglas-Jones to editor, *R*, 13 January 1921, p. 32.
329 *C*, 17 February 1921, pp. 1 f. *JWBU*, July 1921, p. 159.
330 *R*, 28 April 1921, p. 282.
331 J. C. Pollock, *The Keswick Story* (London, 1964), pp. 154 ff.
332 *R*, 21 July 1933, p. 425.
333 *BC*, July–September 1919, p. 1; October–December 1919, p. 4.
334 Marsden, *Fundamentalism and American Culture*, p. 172.
335 *BC*, October 1923, p. 152.
336 *R*, 14 June 1923, p. 387; cf. H. G. Wood, *T. R. Glover: A Biography* (Cambridge, 1953), p. 155.
337 *BC*, July 1925, pp. 100 f.; November 1925, p. 147.
338 *BC*, January 1923, p. 8; February 1925, p. 30.
339 D. G. Fountain, *E. J. Poole-Connor (1872–1962): Contender for the Faith* (Worthing, 1966), pp. 122–8.
340 D. M. Thompson, *Let Sects and Parties Fall: A Short History of the Association of Churches of Christ in Great Britain and Ireland* (Birmingham, 1980), pp. 131 ff. K. O. Morgan, *Rebirth of a Nation: Wales, 1880–1980* (Oxford, 1981), pp. 199 f.
341 Wood, *Glover*, pp. 159–63.
342 *LF*, 20 May 1925, p. 573.
343 *F*, April 1929, p. 84.
344 *R*, 30 December 1925, p. 1607.
345 *R*, 20 September 1917, p. 637; 12 April 1929, p. 237.
346 H. Wace *et al.*, *Creative Christianity* (London, 1921); cf. *R*, 7 June 1923, p. 367; 14 June 1923, p. 391.

347   E. A. Payne, *The Baptist Union: A Short History* (London, 1958), p. 211.
348   J. T. Carson, *Frazer of Tain* (Glasgow, 1966), p. 49.
349   *R*, 30 October 1924, p. 708.
350   S. Bruce, *No Pope of Rome* (Edinburgh, 1985).
351   Cadoux, *Catholicism and Christianity* (London, 1928), p. 55; cf. E. Kaye, 'C. J. Cadoux and Mansfield College, Oxford', *Journal of the United Reformed Church History Society*, vol. 3, no. 8 (1986).
352   G. K. A. Bell, *Randall Davidson, Archbishop of Canterbury*, 3rd edn (London, 1952), p. 1326.
353   *R*, 24 March 1932, p. 184 (Exeter); 6 May 1932, p. 285 (Salisbury); 24 February 1933, p. 103 (London).
354   *R*, 31 July 1924, pp. 504 f.
355   *R*, 19 February 1925, p. 117.
356   *F*, October 1931, p. 226.
357   *LCMM*, February 1927, pp. 29–32.
358   N. G. Dunning, *Samuel Chadwick* (London, 1933), p. 193.
359   *LF*, 17 September 1924, p. 1116 (Holden); 20 October 1926, p. 1189 (Meyer); 30 July 1924, p. 895 (Scroggie). J. Morgan, *This was his Faith: The Expository Letters of G. Campbell Morgan* (n.p., [1954]), p. 245.
360   *LF*, 30 July 1924, pp. 895 f.
361   *C*, 1 November 1934, p. 43. *LF*, 16 June 1926, p. 647 (A. H. Carter).
362   *LF*, 16 January 1924, p. 61.
363   F. F. Bruce, *In Retrospect: Remembrance of Things Past* (London, 1980), p. 300.
364   Carter, *Modernism: The Peril of Great Britain and America* (Hounslow, [1923]); cf. *LF*, 5 December 1923, p. 1447.
365   *LF*, 20 January 1924, p. 122.
366   Cook to editor, *LF*, 3 February 1926, p. 120.
367   *LF*, 12 December 1923, p. 1535; 16 June 1926, p. 647.
368   *JWBU*, December 1920, p. 270; October 1923, p. 220. *LF*, 4 November 1925, p. 1270. *R*, 3 November 1927, p. 777; 24 December 1931, p. 833; 29 July 1932, p. 879.
369   *MBAPPU*, September 1919, p. 32.
370   *MBAPPU*, March 1920, p. 80; April 1920, p. 88; May 1920, p. 96.
371   *AW*, 1923, Financial Statement as at 18 December 1922.
372   D. H. C. Bartlett to editor, *R*, 17 August 1922, p. 549; 3 August 1934, p. 464; 16 October 1924, p. 666.
373   *R*, 12 June 1924, p. 395. Runs of the League's publications, the *Bible Witness* and the *Bible League Quarterly*, have not been discovered.
374   *F*, February 1931, p. 36; February 1928, p. 43.
375   *F*, December 1929, p. 268.
376   *C*, 27 October 1921, p. 21.
377   *BC*, July–September 1928, p. 34. *R*, 20 May 1926, p. 321.
378   *JWBU*, May 1920, p. 98. The first figure is presented as though it were also for 1918–19, but that must be a misprint.
379   Insertion in copy of *JWBU*, December 1920, at John Rylands University Library of Manchester; cf. D. Crane, *The Life-Story of Sir Robert W. Perks Baronet, M.P.* (London, 1909).
380   *LCMM*, August 1925, p. 113.
381   *BC*, April 1925, p. 65. *JWBU*, February 1926, p. 34.

382 *JWBU*, April 1926, p. 82.

383 E. Pritchard, *For Such a Time* (Eastbourne, 1973). G. Swan, *Lacked Ye Anything?* (London, 1913). J. L. Maxwell, *Half a Century of Grace: A Jubilee History of the Sudan United Mission* (London, n.d.). R. and E. Dewhurst, *God Gave the Increase* (London, 1979).

384 *LF*, 5 August 1925, p. 913; cf. N. Grubb, *Rees Howells, Intercessor* (London, 1952).

385 *BC*, November–December 1921, p. 15.

386 *BC*, October 1926, p. 103. Murray, *Young*, pp. 105–8. Wilson, *Sects and Society*, pp. 46 f., 51 f. See also J. Wilson, 'British Israelism: the ideological restraints on sect organisation', in B. R. Wilson (ed.), *Patterns of Sectarianism* (London, 1967).

387 *R*, 5 May 1933, p. 257. Armitage to editor, *R*, 2 June 1933, p. 321.

388 Woods to editor, *F*, September 1933, pp. 211 f.

389 S. Schor and A. P. Gold Levin to editor, *LF*, 30 June 1926, p. 691; 7 July 1926, p. 715. *C*, 7 December 1933, p. 64.

390 A. L. Glegg, *Four Score . . . and More* (London, 1962), p. 60.

391 W. K. Chaplin and M. J. Street, *Fifty Years of Christian Endeavour* (London, 1931).

392 *C*, 27 October 1921, p. 14; cf. F. P. and M. S. Wood, *Youth Advancing* (London, 1961).

393 J. C. Pollock, *The Good Seed: The Story of the Children's Special Service Mission and the Scripture Union* (London, 1959).

394 J. Eddison (ed.), *'Bash': A Study in Spiritual Power* (Basingstoke, 1983), esp. p. 18.

395 R. Manwaring, *From Controversy to Co-Existence: Evangelicals in the Church of England, 1914–1980* (Cambridge, 1985), pp. 57, 59 f. 'Covenanters' Golden Jubilee: a special supplement', *Harvester*, February 1980. J. Kerr, *A Midnight Vision: The Story of Colin Kerr and the Campaigners* (Worthing, 1981). J. Springhall *et al.*, *Sure and Stedfast: A History of the Boys' Brigade, 1883 to 1983* (London, 1983), pp. 70 f.

396 S. to editor, *LF*, 21 March 1923, p. 322.

397 *R*, 12 October 1934, p. 604 (W. H. Aldis).

398 For example, *JWBU*, October 1933, p. 224. *R*, 11 December 1924, p. 824 (Dinsdale Young and Russell Howden).

399 *R*, 27 January 1933, p. 57.

400 A. D. Gilbert, *The Making of Post-Christian Britain* (London, 1980), pt 3.

401 For example, *AW*, July 1922, p. 75. *JWBU*, January 1926, p. 11.

CHAPTER 7: THE SPIRIT POURED OUT

1 *CEN*, 15 November 1963, p. 1; C. H. May to editor, 22 November 1963, p. 6.

2 Quoted by P. Hocken, *Streams of Renewal: The Origins and Early Development of the Charismatic Movement in Great Britain* (Exeter, 1986), p. 96.

3 K. McDougall quoted by E. England, *The Spirit of Renewal* (Eastbourne, 1982), p. 17.

4 Hocken, *Streams of Renewal*, p. 184.

5   ibid., chs 10, 11, 14. M. Harper, *None Can Guess* (London, 1971).
6   Hocken, *Streams of Renewal*, chs 12, 21.
7   Harper, *None Can Guess*, p. 64. England, *Spirit of Renewal*, pp. 153 f.
8   W. Davies, *Rocking the Boat: The Challenge of the House Church* (Basingstoke, 1986), pp. 25 f.
9   Hocken, *Streams of Renewal*, sect. 1.
10 Wallis, *The Radical Christian* (Eastbourne, 1981), p. 10.
11 A. Walker, *Restoring the Kingdom* (London, 1985). Walker has popularised the use of the term 'Restorationism' for all the connexions together, but it should be noted that others would wish to confine the term to Bryn Jones's movement.
12 R. Trudinger, *Built to Last* (Eastbourne, 1982), ch. 2. P. Greenslade, 'The King's Church, Aldershot', in R. Forster (ed.), *Ten New Churches* (Bromley, 1986).
13 J. V. Thurman, *New Wineskins: A Study of the House Church Movement* (Frankfurt am Main, 1982), chs 2, 4. Walker, *Restoring the Kingdom*, pp. 25–9.
14 R. Forster, 'Icthus Christian Fellowship, Forest Hill, London', in Forster (ed.), *Ten New Churches*.
15 J. Gunstone, *Pentecostal Anglicans* (London, 1982), p. 46.
16 Hocken, *Streams of Renewal*, ch. 1, pp. 63–5, 68 f., 72, 128 ff.
17 J. Ford, *In the Steps of John Wesley: The Church of the Nazarene in Britain* (Kansas City, Mo., 1968), pp. 168–72. Hocken, *Streams of Renewal*, p. 64.
18 Hocken, *Streams of Renewal*, p. 76.
19 W. J. Hollenweger, *The Pentecostals* (London, 1971), p. 6. Hocken, *Streams of Renewal*, pp. 147 ff.
20 Walker, *Restoring the Kingdom*, p. 242. See p. 197.
21 Hocken, *Streams of Renewal*, pp. 144 f.
22 J. Ward, 'Pentecostal theology and the charismatic movement', in D. Martin and P. Mullen (eds), *Strange Gifts? A Guide to Charismatic Renewal* (Oxford, 1984).
23 For example, M. Harper, *Walk in the Spirit* (London, 1968), pp. 20 f.
24 Harper, *None Can Guess*, p. 9.
25 Hocken, *Streams of Renewal*, pp. 146 f.
26 D. J. Bennett, *Nine O'Clock in the Morning* (Plainfield, NJ, 1970).
27 Hocken, *Streams of Renewal*, ch. 17.
28 *The Charismatic Movement in the Church of England* (London, 1981), p. 12.
29 Walker, *Restoring the Kingdom*, pp. 77–85.
30 *AFR*, Spring 1985, pp. 3, 6, 7; Winter 1985, pp. 2 f.; Summer/Autumn 1986, pp. 3 f.
31 T. Roszak, *The Making of a Counter Culture* (London, 1970), esp. ch. 4. B. Martin, *A Sociology of Contemporary Cultural Change* (Oxford, 1981).
32 *Charismatic Movement in the Church of England*, pp. 41 f.
33 Martin, *Contemporary Cultural Change*, p. 225.
34 M. Harper, *As at the Beginning* (London, 1965), p. 84.
35 M. Bradbury and J. McFarlane (eds), *Modernism, 1890–1930* (Harmondsworth, Middlesex, 1976).
36 V. Woolf, 'Mr Bennett and Mrs Brown' [1924], *Collected Essays*, Vol. 1 (London, 1966), p. 321.

37   M. Bradbury and J. McFarlane, 'Movements, magazines and manifestos', in Bradbury and McFarlane (eds), *Modernism*, p. 202.

38   'The Layman with a Notebook', *What is the Oxford Group?* (London, 1933). Apart from works cited below, cf. A. W. Eister, *Drawing-Room Conversion* (Durham, NC, 1950) and D. W. Bebbington, 'The Oxford Group Movement between the wars', in *Voluntary Religion,* Studies in Church History, vol. 23, ed. W. J. Sheils and D. Wood (Oxford, 1986).

39   H. Begbie, *Life Changers* (London, 1923), p. 34.

40   T. Driberg, *The Mystery of Moral Re-Armament* (London, 1964), p. 16.

41   A. J. Russell, *For Sinners Only* (London, 1932), p. 160.

42   Begbie, *Life Changers*, 4th edn (London, 1929), p. 21.

43   *R*, 30 September 1932, p. 581; 18 November 1932, p. 689; 30 December 1932, p. 790.

44   G. Lean, *Frank Buchman: A Life* (London, 1985), pp. 132, 156.

45   M. Linton Smith and F. Underhill, *The Group Movement* (London, 1934), p. 36.

46   *R*, 27 January 1933, p. 55.

47   'Layman', *Oxford Group*, p. 50.

48   *R*, 7 October 1932, p. 601.

49   L. W. Grensted, 'Conclusion', in R. H. S. Crossman (ed.), *Oxford and the Groups* (Oxford, 1934), p. 198.

50   *R*, 14 October 1932, p. 617.

51   M. Harrison, *Saints Run Mad* (London, 1934), pp. 93, 81.

52   L. W. H. Bertie, 'Some aspects of the Oxford Group as seen by a medical practitioner', in F. A. M. Spencer (ed.), *The Meaning of the Groups* (London, 1934), p. 39.

53   *R*, 4 December 1931, p. 769.

54   Smith and Underhill, *Group Movement*, p. 42.

55   Bertie, 'Aspects', p. 43.

56   Russell, *Sinners*, p. 279.

57   S. A. King, *The Challenge of the Oxford Groups* (London, 1933), p. 61. B. Nichols, *All I Could Never Be* (London, 1949), pp. 249 f.

58   Smith and Underhill, *Group Movement*, pp. 23 f.

59   G. Allen, 'The Groups in Oxford', in Crossman (ed.), *Oxford*, p. 33.

60   R. Thomson, *The Pelican History of Psychology* (Harmondsworth, Middlesex, 1968), pp. 421 f.

61   *Groups*, May 1934, pp. 641–4.

62   F. C. Raynor, *The Finger of God* (London, 1934), p. 96.

63   *Groups*, June 1934, p. 2.

64   ibid., August 1934, p. 109.

65   Grensted, 'Conclusion'. *BW*, 27 July 1933, p. 340.

66   C. M. Chavasse in *R*, 18 November 1932, p. 689.

67   *R*, 27 October 1933, p. 610.

68   'Layman', *Oxford Group*, p. 70.

69   M. D. Biddiss, *The Age of the Masses: Ideas and Society in Europe since 1870* (Hassocks, Sussex, 1977), pp. 83–91.

70   'Layman', *Oxford Group*, p. 69.

71   H. H. Henson, *The Oxford Groups* (London, 1933), p. 70.

72   Quoted by Smith and Underhill, *Group Movement*, p. 34.

73 Russell, *Sinners*, p. 291. I. Thomas, *The Buchman Group* (London, [1933]), p. 3.
74 W. F. Brown to editor, *MR*, 3 November 1932, p. 20.
75 W. H. Clark, *The Oxford Group: Its History and Significance* (New York, 1951), p. 110.
76 Moore, *Brensham Village* [1946] (London, 1966 edn), pp. 162, 171.
77 H. R. Hammond to editor, *MR*, 28 January 1932, p. 17. *R*, 17 June 1932, p. 388.
78 Grensted, 'Conclusion', p. 199. Henson, *Oxford Groups*, p. 48.
79 Oldham to editor, *T*, 6 October 1933, p. 13.
80 *Groups*, April 1934, pp. 545 f.
81 'Layman', *Oxford Group*, p. 81.
82 *R*, 14 October 1932, p. 617. 'Observer' to editor, *R*, 16 December 1932, p. 766.
83 Harrison, *Saints Run Mad*, p. 99.
84 *R*, 14 October 1932, p. 617.
85 *T*, 27 July 1936, p. 9. Driberg, *Mystery*, p. 143.
86 *T*, 9 March 1939, p. 4.
87 *T*, 10 March 1939, p. 4.
88 *MR*, 17 October 1933, p. 4.
89 Harrison, *Saints Run Mad*, pp. 107 f.
90 Allen, *He that Cometh*, p. 212.
91 Henson, *Oxford Groups*, p. 48.
92 J. W. C. Wand, 'The Groups and the churches', in Crossman (ed.), *Oxford*, p. 168.
93 E. Brunner, *The Church and the Oxford Group* (London, 1937), p. 93.
94 Sir Francis Fremantle, MP, to editor, *T*, 9 December 1933, p. 8.
95 Bishop of Durham to editor, *T*, 19 September 1933, p. 8.
96 Russell, *Sinners*, p. 44.
97 Raynor, *Finger of God*, pp. 108–11, 170 f.
98 Henson, *Oxford Groups*, p. 48. L. P. Jacks, 'Group unity and the sense of sin', in Crossman (ed.), *Oxford*, pp. 117 f.
99 *BW*, 13 July 1933, p. 295. Driberg, *Mystery*, ch. 4.
100 F. N. D. Buchman, *Remaking the World* (London, 1958 edn), pp. 14 f. *T*, 15 July 1935, p. 12.
101 *T*, 27 July 1936, p. 9.
102 *T*, 8 August 1938, p. 8; 27 July 1936, p. 9.
103 Buchman, *Remaking*, pp. 45–8.
104 *R*, 3 August 1934, p. 465.
105 *R*, 29 April 1932, p. 261.
106 *R*, 20 November 1931, p. 729.
107 M. Harper, *A New Way of Living* (London, 1973), pp. 7 f.
108 Talcott Parsons quoted by Martin, *Cultural Change*, p. 15.
109 Harper, *Walk*, p. 43.
110 D. Bridge and D. Phypers, *More than Tongues Can Tell* (London, 1982), pp. 61, 74 f.
111 England, *Spirit of Renewal*, p. 111.
112 Walker, *Restoring the Kingdom*, p. 52.
113 *Renewal*, February/March 1979, p. 11.
114 P. Beall, *The Folk Arts in God's Family* (London, 1984), p. 33.
115 Hocken, *Streams of Renewal*, chs 4, 9, pp. 158 f.
116 *CEN*, 28 June 1974, p. 7.

117 *Charismatic Movement in the Church of England*, p. 16. Walker, *Restoring the Kingdom*, pp. 123 f., 191.

118 R. Peart and W. R. Davies, *What about the Charismatic Movement?* (London, 1980), p. 39.

119 I. Savile, 'Canford Magna Parish Church', in E. Gibbs (ed.), *Ten Growing Churches* (n.p., 1984), p. 181. S. Bruce, *Firm in the Faith* (Aldershot, 1984), p. 143. *AFR*, Autumn 1981, p. [7].

120 Harper, *Beginning*, p. 10. M. Israel, 'The Spirit of truth', in Martin and Mullen (eds), *Strange Gifts?*, pp. 131, 133.

121 England, *Spirit of Renewal*, p. 159.

122 Harper, *Beginning*, p. 105.

123 Thurman, *New Wineskins*, p. 43.

124 A. Mather, 'Talking points: the charismatic movement', *Themelios*, vol. 9, no. 3 (1984), p. 21.

125 Hocken, *Streams of Renewal*, p. 172.

126 V. Budgen, *The Charismatics and the Word of God* (Welwyn, 1985), p. 60.

127 J. Graham, *The Giant Awakes* (London, 1982), p. 112.

128 Harper, *None Can Guess*, p. 150.

129 Harper, *Beginning*, p. 110.

130 *Charismatic Movement in the Church of England*, p. 20.

131 Harper, *Beginning*, p. 94.

132 *Renewal*, February/March 1979, p. 5.

133 Harper, *None Can Guess*, p. 8.

134 'Gospel and Spirit: a joint statement', *Churchman*, vol. 91, no. 2 (1977), p. 103.

135 Budgen, *Charismatics and the Word of God*, pp. 206 f.

136 Harper, *None Can Guess*, p. 8.

137 'Gospel and Spirit', p. 106. Walker, *Restoring the Kingdom*, pp. 154 f.

138 Harper, *None Can Guess*, p. 142.

139 A. Kane, *Let There be Life* (Basingstoke, 1983), p. 88. Savile, 'Canford Magna', p. 180. Thurman, *New Wineskins*, pp. 43, 95.

140 *AFR*, Winter 1985, p. 26.

141 Gunstone, *Pentecostal Anglicans*, ch. 9. R. Trudinger, *Cells for Life* (Basingstoke, 1979).

142 F. Lees, *Love Is Our Home* (London, 1978).

143 Kane, *Let There be Life*, p. 67. Peart and Davies, *Charismatic Movement*, pp. 38 f.

144 Watson, *I Believe in the Church* (London, 1982 edn), pp. 85 ff.

145 J. Hardwidge, 'The Isca Christian Fellowship', in Forster (ed.), *Ten New Churches*, p. 125.

146 Martin, *Cultural Change*, p. 17.

147 Harper, *None Can Guess*, p. 13.

148 Wallis, *Radical Christian*, p. 165.

149 Thurman, *New Wineskins*, p. 61.

150 Walker, *Restoring the Kingdom*, pp. 88 f., 105.

151 P. Beall, *The Folk Arts in God's Family* (London, 1984). A. Long, *Praise Him in the Dance* (London, 1976).

152 For example, Hardwidge, 'Isca Christian Fellowship', p. 128.

153 G. Kendrick (ed.), *Ten Worshipping Churches* (n.p., 1986), pp. 11 f., 76.

154 *Charismatic Movement in the Church of England*, p. 25.

155 *Renewal*, April/May 1979, p. 28.
156 *Charismatic Movement in the Church of England*, p. 37.
157 Beall, *Folk Arts*, p. 55.
158 Harper, *None Can Guess*, p. 143.
159 Wallis, *Radical Christian*, pp. 88, 23.
160 A. Munden, 'Encountering the House Church Movement', *Anvil*, vol. 1, no. 3 (1984), p. 202.
161 Kane, *Let There be Life*, p. 160.
162 *Renewal*, April/May 1979, p. 12.
163 Wallis, *Radical Christian*, p. 171.
164 Walker, *Restoring the Kingdom*, p. 74.
165 Harper, *None Can Guess*, pp. 75, 26 f., 36.
166 Greenslade, 'King's Church', p. 147.
167 Wallis, *Radical Christian*, p. 184.
168 Harper, *None Can Guess*, p. 82.
169 *Charismatic Movement in the Church of England*, p. 37. Peart and Davies, *Charismatic Movement*, p. 13. Kane, *Let There be Life*, p. 127.
170 Thurman, *New Wineskins*, p. 71.
171 'Gospel and Spirit', p. 110.
172 Ern Baxter, quoted by Walker, *Restoring the Kingdom*, p. 145.
173 Walker, *Restoring the Kingdom*, ch. 13.
174 *Charismatic Movement in the Church of England*, p. 14.
175 Walker, *Restoring the Kingdom*, p. 188. D. Halls, 'Community Church in Tottenham, Waltham Forest and Ilford', in Gibbs (ed.), *Ten Growing Churches*, p. 114.
176 *Charismatic Movement in the Church of England*, p. 26.
177 P. Mullen, 'Confusion worse confounded', in Martin and Mullen (eds), *Strange Gifts?*, p. 105.
178 Walker, *Restoring the Kingdom*, p. 188.
179 B. R. Wilson, *Sects and Society* (London, 1961), pp. 106 f.
180 D. McBain, quoted by England, *Spirit of Renewal*, p. 128.
181 Hocken, *Streams of Renewal*, p. 112.
182 *AFR*, Summer/Autumn 1986, p. 4.
183 Harper, *Beginning*, p. 88.
184 Gunstone, *Pentecostal Anglicans*, p. 31.
185 *AFR*, Autumn 1982, p. [7]. England, *Spirit of Renewal*, p. 148.
186 *Charismatic Movement in the Church of England*, p. 9. *AFR*, Spring 1986, p. 3; Spring 1985, p. 8.
187 Peart and Davies, *Charismatic Movement*, p. 1.
188 Gunstone, *Pentecostal Anglicans*, p. 25. P. Beasley-Murray and A. Wilkinson, *Turning the Tide* (London, 1981), p. 37.
189 Walker, *Restoring the Kingdom*, p. 102.
190 Savile, 'Canford Magna', p. 185.
191 *CEN*, 10 January 1964, p. 1.
192 *CEN*, 14 June 1968, p. 1.
193 *CEN*, 22 April 1977, p. 7.
194 'Gospel and Spirit', pp. 102, 105.
195 C. Calver, *He Brings us Together* (London, 1987), pp. 66 f.
196 Walker, *Restoring the Kingdom*, p. 121.

197 England, *Spirit of Renewal*, p. 98.
198 Wallis, *Radical Christian*, p. 53.
199 Peart and Davies, *Charismatic Movement*, p. 36.
200 B. Hopkinson, 'Changes in the emphases of Evangelical belief, 1970–1980: evidence from new hymnody', *Churchman*, vol. 95, no. 2 (1981), pp. 130, 134.
201 R. Shaw, quoted by Hocken, *Streams of Renewal*, p. 156.
202 Harper, *Beginning*, p. 119.
203 ibid., p. 125.
204 Hopkinson, 'Evangelical belief', pp. 131, 134.
205 Carey, *The Gates of Glory* (London, 1986), p. 205.
206 Peart and Davies, *Charismatic Movement*, pp. 9 f.

CHAPTER 8: INTO A BROAD PLACE

1 Canon D. M. Paton in P. Crowe (ed.), *Keele '67: The National Evangelical Anglican Congress Statement* (London, 1967), p. 16.
2 J. C. King, in *CEN*, 14 April 1967, p. 6.
3 Sect. 83 in Crowe (ed.), *Keele '67*, p. 37. Letters to editor, *CEN*, 19 May 1967, p. 6.
4 Sects 20 and 37 in Crowe (ed.), *Keele '67*, pp. 23, 26.
5 C. Buchanan in *CEN*, 11 March 1977, p. 6.
6 *CEN*, 11 January 1957, p. 3.
7 M. Saward, *Evangelicals on the Move*, The Anglican Church Today (London, 1987), pp. 32 f.
8 G. E. Duffield, 'Evangelical involvement: the doctrine of the church', in J. C. King, *Evangelicals Today* (Guildford, 1973).
9 Stott, 'World-wide Evangelical Anglicanism', in ibid., p. 181.
10 R. Currie *et al.*, *Churches and Churchgoers* (Oxford, 1977), p. 30.
11 *Prospects for the Eighties* (London, 1980), p. 5. P. Brierley and B. Evans, *Prospects for Wales* (London, 1983), p. 5. P. Brierley and F. Macdonald, *Prospects for Scotland* (Bromley, 1985), p. 5.
12 *Social Trends*, 1982 edn (London, 1981), p. 193.
13 P. A. Welsby, *A History of the Church of England, 1945–1980* (Oxford, 1984), pp. 19 f.
14 P. B. Cliff, *The Rise and Development of the Sunday School Movement in England, 1780–1980* (Nutfield, Redhill, Surrey, 1986), pp. 318 f.
15 A. Marwick, *British Society since 1945* (Harmondsworth, Middlesex, 1982), ch. 9.
16 See pp. 201 f.
17 F. W. Dillistone, *Into all the World: A Biography of Max Warren* (London, 1980), pp. 60, 154.
18 ibid., pp. 50 f. S. Gummer, *The Chavasse Twins* (London, 1963).
19 R. T. Jones, *Congregationalism in England, 1662–1962* (London, 1962), pp. 450 f., 453–7.
20 W. M. S. West, *To Be a Pilgrim: A Memoir of Ernest A. Payne* (Guildford, 1983).
21 See p. 204.
22 D. M. Thompson, 'The older Free Churches', in R. Davies (ed.), *The Testing of the Churches, 1932–1982* (London, 1982), p. 93. G. W. Kirby to

editor, *CG*, September 1948, p. 11. S. Bruce, *Firm in the Faith* (Aldershot, 1984), p. 45.
23 Stott, in *Fundamentalism: A Religious Problem: Letters to the Editor of The Times and a Leading Article* (London, 1955), pp. 15 f.
24 P. Sangster, *Doctor Sangster* (London, 1962). For general trends, see A. Hastings, *A History of English Christianity, 1920–1985* (London, 1986).
25 Bishop J. W. Hunkin, in *LE*, May 1947, p. 9.
26 *LE*, September 1947, p. 33; September 1948, p. 153.
27 *CEN*, 31 July 1953, p. 6.
28 *LE*, November 1950, pp. 335, 351. *CEN*, 17 April 1964, p. 1.
29 *Modern Free Churchman.*
30 *LE*, May 1947, pp. 11, 13.
31 C. O. Rhodes in *LE*, February 1950, p. 289. *CEN*, 28 May 1954, p. 7.
32 *CEN*, 29 January 1960, p. 3.
33 L. Hickin, 'The revival of Evangelical scholarship', *Churchman*, vol. 92, no. 2 (1978). M. Warren, *Crowded Canvas* (London, 1974), pp. 223 f. *Evangelical Fellowship for Theological Literature: Annual Register*, no. 7 (1950).
34 *Evangelicals Affirm* (London, 1948), p. xi. *LE*, May 1948, p. 114. Warren, *Crowded Canvas*, pp. 167, 224.
35 *LE*, December 1951, p. 403.
36 R. Nixon in *Churchman*, vol. 92, no. 2 (1978), pp. 99 f.
37 Bruce, *Firm in the Faith*, pp. 75 ff.
38 J. Highet, *The Scottish Churches* (London, 1960), ch. 3. D. P. Thomson, *Personal Encounters* (Crieff, Perthshire, 1967), p. 70.
39 K. Robbins, 'Britain, 1940 and "Christian Civilization"', in D. Beales and G. Best (eds), *History, Society and the Churches: Essays in Honour of Owen Chadwick* (Cambridge, 1985).
40 A. W. Smith in *AW*, July–August 1945, p. 51.
41 *CEN*, 19 January 1951, p. 3.
42 Welsby, *Church of England*, pp. 45–8. Gummer, *Chavasse Twins*, ch. 12.
43 *CEN*, 11 January 1952, p. 3.
44 *CEN*, 16 January 1953, p. 3.
45 A. A. Woolsey, *Channel of Revival: A Biography of Duncan Campbell* (Edinburgh, 1974), chs 13–16.
46 G. T. Brake, *Policy and Politics in British Methodism, 1932–1982* (London, 1984), pp. 390 f. Thompson, 'Older Free Churches', p. 93.
47 J. E. Tuck (ed.), *This is My Story* (London, 1955), ch. 1.
48 Jones, *Congregationalism*, p. 450.
49 R. R. Williams in *LE*, May 1947, p. 12.
50 *CEN*, 21 June 1957, p. 7.
51 *CEN*, 27 November 1953, p. 3; 1 January 1954, p. 6; J. W. Roxburgh to editor, 8 January 1954, p. 10; R. A. Finlayson to editor, 22 January 1954, p. 10.
52 *CEN*, 3 May 1963, p. 10.
53 *Baptist Union Directory*, 1973–4, pp. 40 f.
54 Dr C. W. Hale Amos to editor, *R*, 20 August 1937, p. 536.
55 *AW*, September–October 1949, p. 459.
56 I. L. S. Balfour, 'The twentieth century (since 1914)', in D. W. Bebbington (ed.), *The Baptists in Scotland: A History* (Glasgow, 1988), pp. 75 f. *Baptists and Unity* (London, 1967), pp. 36 f.

57   See p. 267f.

58   *CEN*, 16 November 1974, p. 2.

59   R. Davies, 'Since 1932', in R. Davies *et al.* (eds), *A History of the Methodist Church in Great Britain*, Vol. 3 (London, 1983), pp. 374–9.

60   J. I. Packer (ed.), *All in Each Place: Towards Reunion in England* (Appleford, Abingdon, Berks., 1965), esp. pp. 9 f., 15 f. *CEN*, 7 February 1969, pp. 8 f.

61   Sect. 96 in Crowe (ed.), *Keele '67*, p. 39. *CEN*, 22 April 1977, p. 8.

62   J. King in *CEN*, 11 February 1977, p. 6.

63   *CEN*, 7 March 1986, p. 1.

64   C. O. Buchanan *et al.*, *Growing into Union* (London, 1970).

65   *English Churchman*, 9 January. 1953, pp. 14, 15 f., 17, 18; 6 February. 1953, p. 62.

66   *CEN*, 13 January 1961, p. 3.

67   C. Buchanan, 'Liturgy', in King (ed.), *Evangelicals Today*.

68   Sect. 76 in Crowe (ed.), *Keele '67*, p. 35. H. J. Burgess to editor, *CEN*, 21 April 1967, p. 6. P. Crowe to editor, *CEN*, 5 May 1967, p. 7.

69   N. Anderson, *An Adopted Son: The Story of my Life* (Leicester, 1985), pp. 239 ff.

70   *CEN*, 22 July 1949, p. 3.

71   Anderson, *Adopted Son*, p. 142.

72   Packer, '"Keswick" and the Reformed doctrine of sanctification', *Evangelical Quarterly*, vol. 27, no. 3 (1955), p. 158.

73   D. Winter in *CEN*, 29 July 1960, p. 2.

74   *CEN*, 14 July 1972, p. 6.

75   Bruce, *Firm in the Faith*, p. 50.

76   J. Eddison (ed.), *'Bash': A Study in Spiritual Power* (Basingstoke, 1983).

77   J. C. Pollock, *The Good Seed: The Story of the Children's Special Service Mission and the Scripture Union* (London, 1959), pp. 187–92.

78   R. Manwaring, *From Controversy to Co-Existence: Evangelicals in the Church of England, 1914–1980* (Cambridge, 1985), pp. 108 f.

79   A. L. Glegg, *Four Score . . . and More* (London, 1962), pp. 60–3.

80   *Operation Mobilisation: The History* (n.p., n.d.).

81   *CEN*, 8 October 1965, pp. 1, 16; 28 October 1966, pp. 3, 14.

82   *CEN*, 12 March 1954, p. 5; cf. F. Colquhoun, *Harringay Story* (London, 1955); J. Pollock, *Billy Graham: The Authorised Biography* (London, 1966); P. Back, *Mission England – What Really Happened?* (Bromley, 1986).

83   *CEN*, 26 February 1954, p. 5.

84   *CEN*, 28 May 1954, p. 6; 8 July 1966, p. 1.

85   *CEN*, 4 June 1954, p. 2. W. Sargant, *Battle for the Mind* (London, 1957), esp. ch. 6. But cf. Bruce, *Firm in the Faith*, pp. 104–12.

86   W. G. McLoughlin, *Modern Revivalism: Charles Grandison Finney to Billy Graham* (New York, 1959), p. 517. But cf. Highet, *Scottish Churches*, ch. 3.

87   *CEN*, 27 May 1955, p. 2.

88   *CEN*, 30 December 1966, p. 1.

89   G. Carr to editor, *CEN*, 27 May 1955, p. 14.

90   D. Johnson, *Contending for the Faith: A History of the Evangelical Movement in the Universities and Colleges* (Leicester, 1979), p. 359. For CICCU, see p. 188.

91 F. D. Coggan (ed.), *Christ and the Colleges: A History of the Inter-Varsity Fellowship of Evangelical Unions* (London, 1934), pp. 212, 214. F. F. Bruce, *In Retrospect: Remembrance of Things Past* (London, 1980), p. 68.

92 See also correspondence following review of *Is Evolution a Myth?* in *C*, 11 November 1949, p. 12, esp. Bible student to editor, 3 February 1950, p. 10.

93 *CG*, June 1948, p. 32.

94 Bruce, *In Retrospect*, p. 128.

95 F. F. Bruce, 'The Tyndale Fellowship for Biblical Research', *Evangelical Quarterly*, vol. 19, no. 1 (1947), p. 52.

96 Bruce, *In Retrospect*, pp. 127, 110 f.

97 *CG*, March 1948, p. 16.

98 H. H. Rowdon, *London Bible College: The First Twenty-Five Years* (Worthing, 1968). R. Coad, *Laing: The Biography of Sir John W. Laing, C.B.E. (1879–1978)* (London, 1979), pp. 189–92.

99 *CG*, March 1948, p. 8. 'A London graduate' is almost certainly Johnson.

100 D. Williams, *IVP: The First Fifty Years* (Leicester, 1986), p. 7.

101 Crowe (ed.), *Keele '67*, pp. 48–60.

102 *C.B.R.F.* (The Journal of the Christian Brethren Research Fellowship).

103 Bruce, *In Retrospect*, pp. 184–8, 182.

104 J. I. Packer, 'Expository preaching', in *CEN*, 15 January 1960, p. 3.

105 'Introduction', in D. M. Lloyd-Jones, *The Puritans: Their Origins and Successors* (Edinburgh, 1987).

106 E. Davies, 'God's gift to a nation', in C. Catherwood (ed.), *Martyn Lloyd-Jones: Chosen by God* (Crowborough, East Sussex, 1986), p. 185. See also I. H. Murray, *David Martyn Lloyd-Jones: The First Forty Years, 1899–1939* (Edinburgh, 1982) and J. Peters, *Martyn Lloyd-Jones: Preacher* (Exeter, 1986).

107 D. M. Lloyd-Jones, *Preaching and Preachers* (London, 1971), p. 120.

108 *CEN*, 4 January 1963, p. 3.

109 R. Horn, 'His place in Evangelicalism', in Catherwood (ed.), *Lloyd-Jones*, p. 16.

110 *Evangelical Library Bulletin*.

111 'Introduction', in Lloyd-Jones, *Puritans*, p. ix.

112 Maurice Wood in *CEN*, 15 January 1960, p. 3.

113 J. E. Davies, *Striving Together: A Statement of the Principles that Have Governed the Aims and Policies of the Evangelical Movement of Wales* (Bryntirion, Bridgend, 1984), pp. 5, 45.

114 S. B. Ferguson, 'William Still: a biographical introduction', in N. M. de S. Cameron and S. B. Ferguson (eds), *Pulpit & People: Essays in Honour of William Still on his Seventy-Fifth Birthday* (Edinburgh, 1986). Bruce, *Firm in the Faith*, p. 45.

115 *Prospects for the Eighties*, p. 41.

116 W. J. Hollenweger, *The Pentecostals* (London, 1972), p. 191.

117 Tychicus to editor, *LF*, October 1963, quoted by D. Gee, *Wind and Flame* (Croydon, 1967), p. 299.

118 M. J. C. Calley, *God's People: West Indian Pentecostal Sects in England* (London, 1965), pp. 118, 128, 39.

119 G. E. Vandeman to editor, *CEN*, 12 February 1954, p. 10.

120 J. Ford, *In the Steps of John Wesley: The Church of the Nazarene in Britain* (Kansas City, Mo., 1968), p. 274.

121 B. R. Wilson, 'The Exclusive Brethren: a case study in the evolution of a sectarian ideology', in B. R. Wilson (ed.), *Patterns of Sectarianism* (London, 1967).
122 Bruce, *In Retrospect*, p. 289. G. Brown and B. Mills, *'The Brethren': A Factual Survey* (Exeter, 1980), p. 46.
123 J. King in *CEN*, 11 February 1977, p. 6.
124 *CEN*, 14 April 1967, p. 6; 27 January 1978, p. 4. *Third Way*, 29 December 1977, pp. 7 ff.
125 F. Coutts, *The History of the Salvation Army*, Vol. 7, *The Weapons of Goodwill* (London, 1986), pp. 168 ff.
126 D. B. Winter, *New Singer, New Song* (London, 1967).
127 Bruce, *Firm in the Faith*, pp. 129–35, spec. p. 133; p. 50.
128 *CEN*, 20 February 1976, p. 3.
129 *CEN*, 6 February 1976, p. 4.
130 *CEN*, 28 October 1966, p. 14.
131 Coutts, *Salvation Army*, Vol. 7, esp. pp. 18, 180, 326 f.
132 *LCMM*, July 1929, p. 109.
133 T. C. Hammond, *Perfect Freedom* (London, 1938); cf. D. J. Tidball, *Contemporary Evangelical Social Thinking – A Review* (Nottingham, 1977), pp. 5 f.
134 *CG*, June 1948, p. 4.
135 Channon, 'Why I believe Christ is coming', *AW*, May–June 1949, p. 422.
136 M. Whitehouse, *Who Does She Think She Is?* (London, 1971). M. Caulfield, *Mary Whitehouse* (London, 1975).
137 *CEN*, 15 January 1965, p. 16. J. Capon, . . . *and There Was Light: The Story of the Nationwide Festival of Light* (London, 1972), p. 10.
138 *Pornography: The Longford Report* (London, 1972).
139 R. Wallis and R. Bland, *Five Years On: Report of a Survey of Participants in the Nationwide Festival of Light Rally in Trafalgar Square, London, on 25 September 1976* (n.p., n.d.), p. 45.
140 *T*, 16 April 1986, p. 1.
141 *CEN*, 13 January 1960, p. 3.
142 *CEN*, 22 April 1977, p. 10.
143 Tidball, *Social Thinking*, pp. 9 f.
144 *CEN*, 26 July 1974, p. 3; 2 August 1974, pp. 1 f. See also C. R. Padilla (ed.), *The New Face of Evangelicalism* (London, 1976).
145 *Evangelicalism and Social Responsibility: An Evangelical Commitment* (Exeter, 1982), p. 23.
146 *Third Way*, December 1982/January 1983, p. 5.
147 *Third Way*, January 1987, p. 19. *CEN*, 22 April 1977, p. 8.
148 Packer, 'A kind of Puritan', p. 44.
149 Horn, 'His place in Evangelicalism', p. 21.
150 L. Samuel, 'A man under the Word', in Catherwood (ed.), *Lloyd-Jones*, pp. 199 ff.
151 Lloyd-Jones, *Puritans*, pp. 73–100.
152 Horn, 'His place in Evangelicalism', pp. 22 ff. Stott, 'An appreciation', in Catherwood (ed.), *Lloyd-Jones*, p. 207.
153 *CEN*, 28 October 1966, p. 5.
154 Davies, *Striving Together*, pp. 5–8.
155 *British Evangelical Council Newsletter*, Summer 1981.

156 See pp. 230 f.
157 Sect. 14 in Crowe (ed.), *Keele '67*, p. 22.
158 J. Capon, *Evangelicals Tomorrow* (Glasgow, 1977), ch. 4. J. King in *CEN*, 11 February 1977, p. 6.
159 H. L. McBeth, *The Baptist Heritage* (Nashville, Tenn., 1987), p. 525.
160 R. J. Sheehan (ed.), *The Baptism of the Spirit and Charismatic Gifts* (St Albans, [1979]), esp. pp. 2 f. *Evangelical Times*, March 1978, p. 7; May 1985, p. 9; December 1985, p. 3; May 1986, pp. 12 ff.; June 1986, p. 3.
161 *CEN*, 24 July 1970, p. 3.
162 J. Drane, 'Bible use in Scottish churches', in Brierley and Macdonald, *Prospects for Scotland*, pp. 26–9.
163 *CEN*, 11 January 1974, p. 8.
164 *CEN*, 23 November 1966, p. 1; 27 January 1978, p. 4.
165 Capon, *Evangelicals Tomorrow*, ch. 3; cf. T. Thiselton, 'Understanding God's word today', in J. Stott (ed.), *Obeying Christ in a Changing World: 1: The Lord Christ* (London, 1977).
166 *CEN*, 26 January 1979, p. 3.
167 J. Dunn, 'The authority of scripture according to scripture', *Churchman*, vol. 96, no. 2, and vol. 96, no. 3 (1982).
168 *CEN*, 10 January 1986, p. 1.
169 Capon, *Evangelicals Tomorrow*, pp. 32, 34.
170 *CEN*, 25 January 1974, p. 5.
171 Capon, *Evangelicals Tomorrow*, p. 49.
172 J. I. Packer, *The Evangelical Anglican Identity Problem* (Oxford, 1978) p. 30.
173 K. N. Medhurst and G. Moyser, *Church and Politics in a Secular Age* (Oxford, 1988), ch. 11, sect. 6.
174 *CEN*, 11 March 1977, p. 6.
175 J. R. W. Stott, *What Is an Evangelical?* (London, 1977).
176 *CEN*, 27 January 1978, p. 1; 26 January 1979, p. 3; 2 February 1979, p. 2.
177 Stott, 'World-wide Evangelical Anglicanism', p. 180. *CEN*, 9 January 1980, p. 3.
178 Saward, *Evangelicals on the Move*, p. 45.
179 *CEN*, 8 October 1965, p. 16; cf. A. D. Gilbert, *The Making of Post-Christian Britain: A History of the Secularization of Modern Society* (London, 1980), ch. 6.
180 *CEN*, 28 October 1966, p. 3.
181 *Third Way*, January 1987, p. 19.
182 Wallis and Bland, *Five Years On*, p. 30.
183 Brake, *Policy and Politics*, p. 369.
184 Saward, *Evangelicals on the Move*, p. 34.
185 *Baptist Times*, 31 December 1987, p. 7.

CHAPTER 9: TIME AND CHANCE

1 *Hansard*, 3rd series, vol. 110 (1850), col. 713.
2 S. Bruce, *Firm in the Faith* (Aldershot, 1984), p. 79.
3 Dale, *The Old Evangelicalism and the New* (London, 1889).

4 W. M. Groser quoted by P. B. Cliff, *The Rise and Development of the Sunday School Movement in England, 1780–1980* (Nutfield, Redhill, Surrey, 1986), p. 197.

5 J. Stott, in J. Stott and R. T. Coote (eds), *Down to Earth: Studies in Christianity and Culture* (London, 1981), p. vii.

6 B. M. G. Reardon, *Religious Thought in the Victorian Age* (London, 1981), chs 5 and 6.

7 For example, T. Cauter and J. S. Downham, *The Communication of Ideas: A Study of Contemporary Influences on Urban Life* (London, 1954). The process has been described as 'stratified diffusion': J. Cox, *The English Churches in a Secular Society: Lambeth, 1870–1930* (New York, 1982), p. 8.

8 W. Wilberforce, *A Practical View of the Prevailing Religious System of Professed Christians in the Higher and Middle Classes in this Country Contrasted with Real Christianity*, 4th edn (London, 1797), pp. 9 f.

9 D. E. Allen, *British Tastes: An Enquiry into the Likes and Dislikes of the Regional Consumer* (London, 1968). A. P. Cohen (ed.), *Belonging: Identity and Social Organisation in British Rural Cultures*, Anthropological Studies of Britain, 1 (Manchester, 1982).

10 The pattern is comparable to that described in the classic study of the spread of telephones in Sweden by T. Hägerstrand, *Innovation Diffusion as a Spatial Process* (Chicago, 1967 edn), esp. pp. 7 f.

11 For an earlier case-study, cf. G. Donaldson, 'Scotland's conservative north in the sixteenth and seventeenth centuries', *Scottish Church History* (Edinburgh, 1985), pp. 201 f.

12 Barr, *Fundamentalism* (London, 1977), pp. 2–6, 61 f.

13 M. Saward, *Evangelicals on the Move*, The Anglican Church Today (London, 1987), p. 83. N. M. de S. Cameron to editor, *LW*, January 1987, p. 38.

14 J. I. Packer, *'Fundamentalism' and the Word of God* (London, 1958). I. H. Marshall, *Biblical Inspiration* (London, 1982), ch. 3.

15 M. Cowling, *Religion and Public Doctrine in Modern England*, Vol. 1 (Cambridge, 1980), pp. 375 f.

Index